Gender Differences in Aspirations and Attainment
A Life Course Perspective

Edited by
INGRID SCHOON
Institute of Education
University of London

JACQUELYNNE S. ECCLES
University of Michigan

CAMBRIDGE
UNIVERSITY PRESS

University Printing House, Cambridge CB2 8BS, United Kingdom

Cambridge University Press is part of the University of Cambridge.

It furthers the University's mission by disseminating knowledge in the pursuit of education, learning and research at the highest international levels of excellence.

www.cambridge.org
Information on this title: www.cambridge.org/9781107645196

© Cambridge University Press 2014

This publication is in copyright. Subject to statutory exception and to the provisions of relevant collective licensing agreements, no reproduction of any part may take place without the written permission of Cambridge University Press.

First published 2014

Printed in the United Kingdom by Clays, St Ives plc

A catalogue record for this publication is available from the British Library

Library of Congress Cataloguing in Publication data
Gender differences in aspirations and attainment : a life course perspective / edited by Ingrid Schoon, Jacquelynne S. Eccles.
    pages   cm
Includes bibliographical references and index.
ISBN 978-1-107-02172-3 (hardback)
1. Student aspirations–Sex differences.   2. Educational attainment–Sex differences.
3. Level of aspiration–Sex differences.   4. Achievement motivation–Sex differences.
5. Career development–Sex differences.   I. Schoon, Ingrid.   II. Eccles, Jacquelynne S.
LB1027.8.G46 2014
370.15′1–dc23
2014020403

ISBN 978-1-107-02172-3 Hardback
ISBN 978-1-107-64519-6 Paperback

Cambridge University Press has no responsibility for the persistence or accuracy of URLs for external or third-party internet websites referred to in this publication, and does not guarantee that any content on such websites is, or will remain, accurate or appropriate.

Gender Differences in Aspirations and Attainment

What is the role of parents, peers and teachers in shaping school experiences and informing the career choice of males and females? Does the school context matter, and to what extent do educational experiences influence young people's self-concept, values and their outlook to the future? Do teenage aspirations influence later outcomes regarding educational attainment and the assumption of work and family related roles? These questions and more are addressed in the chapters of this book, following lives over time and in context. The book is both innovative and timely, moving the discussion of gender inequalities forward, providing a dynamic and contextualized account of the way gendered lives evolve. Chapters address the role of institutional structures and the wider socio-historical context in helping young men and women to realize their ambitions. A unique feature is the longitudinal perspective, examining the role of multiple interlinked influences on individual life planning and attainment.

INGRID SCHOON is Professor of Human Development and Social Policy in the Institute of Education, University of London.

JACQUELYNNE S. ECCLES is McKeachie/Pintrich Distinguished University Professor in the School of Education, University of Michigan.

Contents

List of figures	*page* ix
List of tables	xiii
Notes on contributors	xvii
List of abbreviations (selected)	xxviii

Part I Introduction   1

    Introduction: conceptualizing gender differences in aspirations and attainment – a life course perspective   3
    INGRID SCHOON AND
    JACQUELYNNE S. ECCLES

Part II The early school years   27

1   Peer influences on gender differences in educational aspiration and attainment   29
    RICHARD A. FABES, SARAH HAYFORD, ERIN PAHLKE, CARLOS SANTOS, KRISTINA ZOSULS, CAROL LYNN MARTIN AND LAURA D. HANISH

2   Beginning school transition and academic achievement in mid-elementary school: does gender matter?   53
    IRENE KRIESI AND MARLIS BUCHMANN

3   Gender differences in teachers' perceptions and children's ability self-concepts   79
    KATJA UPADYAYA AND
    JACQUELYNNE S. ECCLES

4   Emerging gender differences in times of multiple transitions   101
    JENNIFER E. SYMONDS, MAURICE GALTON AND LINDA HARGREAVES

Part III Career planning during adolescence   123

5 What should I do with my life? Motivational, personal, and contextual factors in mastering the transition of graduating from high school   125
DAVID WEISS, BETTINA S. WIESE AND ALEXANDRA M. FREUND

6 Gendered happiness gap? Adolescents' academic wellbeing pathways   146
KATARIINA SALMELA-ARO

7 Uncertainty in educational and career aspirations: gender differences in young people   161
LESLIE MORRISON GUTMAN, RICARDO SABATES AND INGRID SCHOON

8 The challenges facing young women in apprenticeships   182
ALISON FULLER AND LORNA UNWIN

Part IV Choosing a science career   201

9 Do teenagers want to become scientists? A comparison of gender differences in attitudes toward science, career expectations, and academic skill across 29 countries   203
JOHN JERRIM AND INGRID SCHOON

10 Predicting career aspirations and university majors from academic ability and self-concept: a longitudinal applications of the internal–external frame of reference model   224
PHILIP PARKER, GABRIEL NAGY, ULRICH TRAUTWEIN AND OLIVER LÜDTKE

11 Does priority matter? Gendered patterns of subjective task values across school subject domains   247
ANGELA CHOW AND KATARIINA SALMELA-ARO

12 Gender differences in personal aptitudes and motivational beliefs for achievement in and commitment to math and science fields   266
MING-TE WANG AND SARAH KENNY

13	What happens to high-achieving females after high school? Gender and persistence on the postsecondary STEM pipeline LARA PEREZ-FELKNER, SARAH-KATHRYN MCDONALD AND BARBARA SCHNEIDER	285
14	Young people, gender, and science: does an early interest lead to a job in SET? A longitudinal view from the BHPS youth data ANNA BAGNOLI, DIETER DEMEY AND JACQUELINE SCOTT	321
15	Motivational affordances in school versus work contexts advantage different individuals: a possible explanation for domain-differential gender gaps JUTTA HECKHAUSEN	346

Part V   Longer-term consequences of early experiences   363

16	The life course consequences of single-sex and co-educational schooling ALICE SULLIVAN AND HEATHER JOSHI	365
17	Pathways to educational attainment in middle adulthood: the role of gender and parental educational expectations in adolescence MIIA BASK, LAURA FERRER-WREDER, KATARIINA SALMELA-ARO AND LARS R. BERGMAN	389
18	How gender influences objective career success and subjective career satisfaction: the impact of self-concept and of parenthood ANDREA E. ABELE	412

Part VI   The role of context   427

19	Gender differences in attainment across generations from a historical perspective ANNE MCMUNN, ELIZABETH WEBB, MEL BARTLEY, DAVID BLANE AND GOPAL NETUVELI	429
20	Gender inequality by choice? The effects of aspirations on gender inequality in wages SILKE AISENBREY AND HANNAH BRÜCKNER	456

21 Comparing young people's beliefs and perceptions
   of gender equality across 28 different countries   475
   BRYONY HOSKINS AND
   JAN GERMEN JANMAAT

Index   495

Figures

1.1A	Percentage of block play: by sex, peer context, and semester	*page* 39
1.1B	Percentage of language play: by sex, peer context, and semester	40
2.1	Conceptual model of the interrelationship between social background, children's competencies, their transition quality, and academic achievement	62
2.2	Path effects on girls' and boys' transition quality and academic achievement	65
3.1	A basic model of the study	84
3.2	The standardized estimates for the models of teachers' ability and effort perceptions and children's self-concept of math ability at Wave 3 and Wave 4	90
3.3	The standardized estimates for the models of teachers' ability and effort perceptions and children's self-concept of reading ability at Wave 3 and Wave 4	91
4.1	Model of working groups	112
5.1	Psychological factors relevant to mastering the transition from high school to college or an apprenticeship	127
5.2	Discrepancies between actual and ideal parental workforce participation during the preschool years (based on data from Wiese & Freund, 2011)	137
5.3	Female adolescents' preferred future workforce participation for themselves and their future partners when they have preschool children (based on data from Wiese & Freund, 2011)	138

5.4	Male adolescents' preferred future workforce participation for themselves and their future partners when they have preschool children (based on data from Wiese & Freund, 2011)	138
8.1	Key stakeholder priorities	193
9.1	Difference between boys' and girls' average scores on the PISA 2006 science test	207
9.2	Difference between boys' and girls' average scores on the PISA 2006 reading test	209
9.3	A comparison of the importance and value boys and girls place upon science	210
9.4	A comparison of how important boys and girls think different academic subjects are	211
9.5	Estimated odds ratio of whether boys are more likely than girls to expect to become a science professional	214
10.1	Internal/external model	228
10.2	Extended *I/E* model	229
10.3	I/E factor profiles for career aspiration groups	234
10.4	I/E factor profiles for university major groups	235
10.5	Profile of standardized multinomial regression weights for career aspiration groups	241
10.6	Profile of standardized multinomial regression weights for university major groups	241
11.1	Subjective task-value scores of the three groups across the subject domains	255
12.1	Predicting STEM vs. non-STEM college major from math and verbal scores	275
14.1	Aspiration for SET, breakdown by SET groups and gender (N = 6,703)	329
14.2	Trends in aspiration for SET over time, by gender, for strict and wide definitions (N = 6,703)	331
14.3	Aspiration for SET, by gender and age (11–15) (wide SET definition) (N = 3,201)	332

14.4	Change in aspiration for SET across 3-year intervals, by gender for strict and wide definitions (N = 1,511)	333
15.1	Hypothetical life-span trajectories for primary control potential and primary and secondary control striving (from Heckhausen, 1999)	349
15.2	Age-graded sequencing of opportunities to realize various developmental goals (from Heckhausen, 2000)	349
15.3	Striving for gains and avoiding losses in developmental goals across age groups (from Heckhausen, 1997)	350
15.4	Action-phase model of developmental regulation (from Heckhausen, 1999)	355
16.1	Pupils' responses to "I do not like school," at age 16 (1974)	371
16.2	Percentage liking school at age 16 by type of school	371
16.3	Self-concept in math, English, and science	373
16.4	Five or more O-level passes	375
16.5	O-level subject passes	376
16.6	A-level subject passes	377
16.7	Sex composition of highest qualification age 33	378
16.8	Divorce or separation by age 42, by gender and school sector	380
16.9	Social class of cohort member at current or most recent job by age 42 by gender	382
16.10	Occupational segregation (Hakim's classification) at current or most recent job by age 42	383
16.11	Hourly wages (£) of those employed at 42	384
18.1	Average work hours of women and men with and without children across waves 2 to 5	418
18.2	Path models on the influences of the self-concept, parenthood, and average work hours on objective career success at wave 5 for men and women	418

18.3	Path models on the influences of the self-concept, parenthood, and average work hours on career satisfaction at wave 5 for men and women	420
19.1	Gender differences in having a university degree or some higher education by decade of birth	431
19.2	Gender differences in lifetime number of cohabiting partnerships or marriages (as of 2006) by decade of birth	435
19.3	Number of children by gender and decade of birth	436
19.4	Absolute gender gap in proportion in professional or managerial occupation by severe financial hardship	443
19.5	Absolute gender gap in proportion in professional or managerial occupation by father's occupation at age 14: % male excess	443
19.6	Gender differences in mean quality of life score and mean life satisfaction score by age	445
19.7	Gender difference in likelihood of having depressive symptoms by age	445
19.8	Gender differences in the prevalence of limiting long-standing illnesses and difficulties with activities of daily living by age	448
20.1	Estimated aspired and achieved wages	465
20.2	Estimated aspired and achieved gender wage gap	465
21.1	The construction of the four measurement categories that combine responses to the two variables on beliefs in and perceptions of gender equality	482

Tables

2.1	Correlations, means and standard deviations for all covariates	*page* 66
2.2	Direct, indirect, and total effects (standardized) of parental highest education and an emotionally supportive parenting style on boys' and girls' academic achievement	68
2.3	Covariate means by highest parental education and sex	69
3.1	Means and standard deviations	87
3.2	Pearson correlation coefficients between teachers' ability and effort perceptions, children's ability self-concepts and performance in math and reading, and gender and cohort status separately at Wave 3 and at Wave 4 (below diagonal related to math and above diagonal related to reading)	89
3.3	Goodness-of-fit summary for the tested within-level path models of teachers' perceptions and children's ability self-concepts in math and reading	96
4.1	Summary of in-depth studies used for this chapter	105
4.2	Trends in gender differences	117
5.1	Examples of specific SOC-related strategies in the context of the transition from high school to college or an apprenticeship	130
7.1	Descriptive statistics for all variables in analysis	168
7.2	Predicting uncertain educational aspirations (odds ratios contrasting uncertainty relative to aspiring to stay in education in LSYPE and BCS70)	173

7.3	Predicting career aspirations (odds ratio for uncertainty relative to aspiring for a professional or managerial job in LSYPE and BCS70)	174
7.4	Odds ratio (standard error) for association of uncertainty in aspirations and NEET status in LSYPE and BCS70	175
8.1	Starts in the 10 most populated apprenticeship sectors by gender (England 2008/2009–2010/2011)	187
8.2	Percentage of female apprentices in five sectors	188
8.3	Modern Apprenticeship Scotland: 16–19, top 11 frameworks and gender – in training, 2008–2009	189
8.4	Modern Apprenticeship Scotland: aged 20+, top 11 frameworks and gender – in training, 2008–2009	189
8.5	Sector subject area by MA/FMA and gender in Wales (2007–2008)	190
9.1	Expectations of entering a health or physical science occupation versus a non-science profession (odds ratios)	216
10.1	Gender differences in self-concept and achievement	232
10.2	Time 1 career aspirations and Time 2 university majors	234
10.3	Multinomial logit odds ratios for career aspirations	237
10.4	Loglikelihood difference test of constrained multinomial logit models versus free model	239
11.1	Correlations among measures	252
11.2	Fit indices for latent profile analysis models	254
11.3	Mean differences in subject task values and grade point average across the three groups	255
11.4	Gender distribution and grade point average of girls and boys from the three subjective task-value groups	256
11.5	Regression analysis predicting educational aspirations for physical and IT-related science fields	257
12.1	Descriptive characteristics of the study sample	274

12.2	Logistic regression analysis predicting individual STEM versus non-STEM college major from aptitude, motivational beliefs, course enrollment, and family socioeconomic status at 12th grade	277
13.1	Descriptive characteristics of sample population by STEM pipeline course taking	295
13.2	Descriptive characteristics of sample population by STEM pipeline course taking and gender	301
13.3	Odds of declaring a STEM major 2 years after high school by STEM pipeline and gender	308
14.1	Sample size for each wave, Youth Study, British Household Panel Survey 1994–2005	327
14.2	Most frequent SET occupations by gender, based on first mentions of those aspiring to SET careers (N = 1,721)	330
14.3	Cross-tabulation of SET aspirations and SET occupations (N = 1,832)	333
16.1	Attendance at a single-sex school, contrasted with attendance at a mixed school, binary logistic regression	370
16.2	Economic activity at 42, by gender	381
17.1	Correlations (Pearson's r) between the main study variables	400
17.2	Association between gender and parental expectations (N = 894)	401
17.3	Parental educational expectations in Grades 6 and 9. Relation to gender and adolescent/family characteristics (N = 789/701)	402
17.4	Multiple regression analyses separated by gender for adolescent/family characteristics predicting parental educational expectations in Grade 6	402
17.5	Middle adult educational attainment in relation to gender and adolescent/family characteristics (N = 559)	403
17.6	Multiple regression analyses separated by gender for adolescent/family characteristics, parental educational expectations predicting middle adult educational attainment	404

18.1	Descriptive statistics: gender differences (N = 1,015)	417
18.2	Objective career success at wave 5 regressed on parenthood and workload	419
19.1	Gender differences in socioeconomic attainment by decade of birth	433
19.2	Odds ratios for having access to higher education by indicators of family formation in men and women	437
19.3	Regression coefficients for number of years in paid work by indicators of family formation among men and women	439
19.4	Odds ratios of being in a managerial or professional occupation by indicators of family formation among men and women	440
19.5	Gender differences in having been in a managerial or professional occupation	442
19.6	Wellbeing by indicators of family formation among men and women	446
19.7	Limiting long-standing illness by indicators of family formation among men and women	449
19.8	Physical functioning by indicators of family formation among men and women	451
20.1	Concepts and indicators	461
20.2	Cohorts 1960–1964: means and percentages, standard deviation in parenthesis	467
20.3	Coefficients from regression of wages (logged)	469
20.4	Decomposition of the gender wage gap	471
21.1	Descriptive statistics for participation	485
21.2	Size of the four gender-attitude groups	485
21.3	Four gender-attitude groups by country and gender	486
21.4	Levels of prosperity and gender equality across 25 countries	487
21.5	Correlations between GEM, GDP, and attitudes on gender equality	488
21.6	Determinants of participation	490

Contributors

ANDREA E. ABELE is a Professor of Social Psychology at the University of Erlangen-Nürnberg, Germany. Her research interests include career psychology and gender research.

SILKE AISENBREY is an Associate Professor of Sociology at Yeshiva University in New York. She conducted research as a postdoctoral associate at the Center for Research on Inequality and the Life Course (CIQLE) at Yale University and obtained her PhD at the Ludwig-Maximilian University of Munich. Her research interests lie in the areas of social inequality, welfare states, the life course, gender inequality, and sociology of education. She works mainly with quantitative methods, with a particular interest in longitudinal data analysis.

ANNA BAGNOLI is a Fellow of Wolfson College, Cambridge, where she currently works as a Tutor. She is Associate Researcher at the Department of Sociology of the University of Cambridge, where she contributes to the teaching of qualitative research methods. Her PhD, which she carried out at the Centre for Family Research (University of Cambridge, 2001), investigated the identities of young people in England and Italy, with the involvement of a sample of young first generation migrants between the two countries. The chapter she co-authored for this book presents the results of a project investigating girls' and boys' interest in SET careers through secondary analysis of British Household Panel Survey data, for which Dr. Bagnoli and Prof. Scott were awarded a small grant by the Nuffield Foundation.

MEL BARTLEY is Professor Emerita of Medical Sociology in the Department of Epidemiology and Public Health at UCL. She was Coordinator of the ESRC Research Priority Network on Human Capability and Resilience from 2003 to 2006 and Director of the ESRC International Centre for Lifecourse Studies in Society and Health (ICLS) from 2008 to 2012.

MIIA BASK is a Postdoctoral Fellow at the University of Bergen in the Department of Sociology. Her research interests are social inequality and stratification from a longitudinal perspective, mathematical sociology, and social capital and social networks. Her previous publications include studies in social exclusion especially among immigrants and different family constellations. She was a Fellow of the Jacobs Foundation postdoctoral PATHWAYS to Adulthood program and is currently a Visiting Scholar at the Institute for Research in the Social Sciences at Stanford University.

LARS R. BERGMAN is Professor Emeritus in Research Methodology at the Department of Psychology, Stockholm University. His research interests include statistical methods and measurement in longitudinal research, especially concerning the person-oriented approach. His research also includes the study of adaptation in a life-span perspective.

DAVID BLANE is Professor Emeritus of Imperial College London (Department of Primary Care and Public Health) and Professorial Research Associate of University College London (Department of Epidemiology and Public Health). He was formerly (2008–2012) Deputy Director of the ESRC International Centre for Life Course Studies in Society and Health.

HANNAH BRÜCKNER taught at the Ludwig-Maximilian University of Munich and at Yale University before signing on as Professor of Social Research and Public Policy at New York University–Abu Dhabi. She works on a wide range of topics related to the life course, inequality, health, gender, and sexuality. She has published numerous chapters and articles about gender inequality in the labor force, the integration of women in academic workplaces, and adolescent health and sexual behavior. Current research projects focus on timing and sequencing of family formation and career development, as well as gender construction on Wikipedia.

MARLIS BUCHMANN is Professor of Sociology and Director of the Jacobs Center for Productive Youth Development at the University of Zurich. Her research interests include social inequality and the life course, with a special emphasis on childhood and the life stage youth, school-to-work transition and the transition to adulthood, socialization, and competence development.

ANGELA CHOW is a Banting postdoctoral fellow in the Department of Psychology, University of Alberta. Her research focuses on task values and work values, and how these values in adolescence shape developmental pathways to young adulthood and midlife, with particular emphasis on outcomes related to education, career, and wellbeing. Previously she was a Fellow of the Jacobs Foundation postdoctoral PATHWAYS to Adulthood program.

DIETER DEMEY is a Senior Research Assistant at the Economic and Social Research Council (ESRC) Centre for Population Change at the University of Southampton, UK. He works within the thematic area of "household dynamics and living arrangements across the life course," with a focus on living arrangements in mid-life. He conducted his PhD research at the University of Cambridge from 2006 to 2011, investigating the impact of education on the transition to parenthood by analyzing Belgian and British panel data.

JACQUELYNNE ECCLES is the McKeachie/Pintrich Distinguished University Professor of Psychology and Education and Director of the Achievement Research Program at the University of Michigan, editor of *Developmental Psychology*, past president of the Society of Research on Adolescence (SRA), and currently president elect of the Developmental Psychology of the American Psychological Association (APA). She also is a founding member of the Jacobs Foundation postdoctoral Fellowship program PATHWAYS to Adulthood. She has spent the last 35 years studying both group and individual differences in life choices and motivation, identity formation, gender-role socialization, and both family and classroom influences on social development. Her work has been honored by several awards including life-time achievement awards from the Society for Research on Adolescents, the American Psychological Association, the American Psychological Science Society, the Society for the Study of Human Development, and the Self Society, as well as from the Educational and Developmental Psychology divisions of the APA. She has received honorary degrees from the Catholic University of Louvain, Belgium, and the University of Laval in Quebec City, Canada. She is a member of the National Academy of Education, a World Scholar and Fellow at the Institute of Education at the University of London, and Visiting Professor at the University of Tübingen, Germany.

RICHARD A. FABES is the John O. Whiteman Dean's Distinguished Professor of Child Development in the T. Denny Sanford School of Social and Family Dynamics at Arizona State University. He is also one of the Executive Directors of the Lives of Girls and Boys Enterprise, which is a an interdisciplinary set of initiatives that are designed to promote innovative research and its application to the real-life issues and challenges facing girls and boys as they develop. He is also one of the Principal Directors of the Sanford Harmony Program, which is designed to enhance male–female communication and relationships. He has published over 150 peer-reviewed articles, chapters, and books. His most recent projects involve a longitudinal study of gender-related attitudes and beliefs across elementary school, several large-scale studies of teachers' roles in gender socialization, and exploring the dynamics of gender development, as well as a major project on the importance of kindergarten in children's social and academic development.

LAURA FERRER-WREDER, PHD, is an Associate Professor of Psychology at Stockholm University in the Department of Psychology. Her research involves better understanding human development and culture through programs of applied and basic research. Her applied intervention research, for example, has dealt with the design of positive youth development and prevention interventions. She has been an investigator on over 13 intervention efficacy and effectiveness trials. She is presently an associate editor for the journal *Child & Youth Care Forum* and assistant editor of the *Journal of Adolescence*. Dr. Ferrer-Wreder has published widely, including an authored book entitled *Successful Prevention and Youth Development Programs: Across Borders*.

ALEXANDRA M. FREUND is a Professor of Psychology at the University of Zürich, Department of Psychology. She studied psychology at the University of Heidelberg and the Free University of Berlin, where she also received her PhD. She was a postdoctoral fellow at Stanford University and returned to the Max Planck Institute for Human Development in Berlin as a research scientist. After that, she was an Assistant Professor and later an Associate Professor at Northwestern University before she took over the chair for "Applied Psychology: Life-Management" at the University of Zurich. Elected one of the founding members of the Young Academy of Sciences, Professor Freund is also an associate editor of the APA journal *Psychology and Aging* and serves on several editorial boards. Her main research interests focus on the processes of developmental regulation and motivation across the life-span.

ALISON FULLER is Chair in Vocational Education and Work at the Institute of Education, University of London. Previously she was Professor of Education and Work and Director of Research in Southampton Education School, University of Southampton. Alison is currently undertaking research for the Nuffield Foundation on Adult Apprenticeships (with Lorna Unwin, Pauline Leonard, and Gayna Davey) and is a project leader in the ESRC LLAKES Centre focusing on employee-driven innovation, learning, and work organization in the healthcare sector (with Susan Halford and Kate Lyle). She has published widely, including her most recent book *Contemporary Apprenticeship: International Perspectives on an Evolving Model of Learning* (co-authored with Lorna Unwin and published in 2012).

MAURICE GALTON is currently Associate Director of Research in the Faculty of Education at the University of Cambridge and a former Dean of Education at the University of Leicester in the UK. He is best known for his observational studies of primary (elementary) classrooms and is currently involved in looking at the impact on pupils' wellbeing during transition to the secondary (junior high) phase.

LESLIE MORRISON GUTMAN is Research Director at the Department of Quantitative Social Science at the Institute of Education, University of London. Her main research interests include risk and resilience, the formation of educational and career aspirations, and the relationship between wellbeing and educational outcomes from childhood to adolescence. She led an ESRC study examining the linkages among uncertain aspirations, parental expectations, school engagement, self-perception of ability, and later educational outcomes. She is also co-director of an evaluation of a school for vulnerable children. Previously, she was Research Director of the Centre for Research on the Wider Benefits of Learning at the IoE, where she led a number of research projects including risk and protective factors in children's wellbeing, pupil and school effects on children's achievement, the relationship between aspirations and attainment, parenting capabilities, and children's friendships. She was a National Academy of Education/Spencer Foundation Post-Doctoral Fellow and recipient of the Sims Medal for her doctoral thesis examining resilience in children living in poverty, undertaken at the University of Michigan. She has published widely in peer-reviewed journals and books.

LAURA D. HANISH, PHD, is a Professor of Child Development in the T. Denny Sanford School of Social and Family Dynamics at Arizona State University. Key themes in her research include gender, peer relationships, and school-related contexts and outcomes. She is an Enterprise Leader for the Lives of Girls and Boys Enterprise, which is an interdisciplinary set of research and translational initiatives regarding girls' and boys' interactions, relationships, and school success.

LINDA HARGREAVES is Reader in Classroom Learning and Pedagogy at the Faculty of Education, University of Cambridge, UK, where she teaches master's and doctoral students in primary education, and psychology and education. Her research interests center on classroom processes – teacher and pupil interaction, typically involving systematic observation in classrooms – and how these vary across schools (primary/secondary; rural/urban) and different classroom organizations. Major projects include the Teacher Status Project, the Cambridge Primary Review (Director Robin Alexander) and, currently, an ESRC-funded UK–Hong Kong bilateral, "Social Pedagogic Contexts in the Teaching of Mathematics" (SPeCTRM) codirected with Peter Kutnick (The University of Hong Kong), and "Children's Personal Epistemologies: capitalizing on children's and families' beliefs about knowledge for effective teaching and learning," with Dr. Rocio Garcia-Carrion (EC Marie Curie Research Fellow) and Ruth Kershner.

SARAH HAYFORD is a social demographer in the T. Denny Sanford School of Social and Family Dynamics at Arizona State University. Her areas of study include childbearing, family, and social change in the United States and in sub-Saharan Africa. Recent work examines gender differences in adolescent goals for work and family, changes in the timing of first births within marriage, and the childbearing plans of HIV-positive women.

JUTTA HECKHAUSEN grew up in Germany and received her PhD from the University of Strathclyde in Glasgow, Scotland. She joined the Max-Planck-Institute for Human Development in Berlin in 1984 and then became a postdoctoral fellow, junior and senior scientist. In 1995/1996 she was a fellow at the Center for Social and Behavioral Science at Stanford and in 1999 she received the Max Planck Research Award. In 2000, she was offered a professorship and joined the Department of Psychology and Social Behavior at the University of California Irvine. She served as Chair of the Academic Senate at UC Irvine in 2008–2009. Her work is widely published, including articles in *Developmental Psychology*, *Psychology and Aging*, *Journal of Personality and Social Psychology*, and *Psychological Review*. Her most recent book is *Motivation and Action*, published by Cambridge University Press.

BRYONY HOSKINS is Senior Lecturer in Education at the University of Southampton. She is an internationally renowned expert on Active Citizenship and has published widely in this field. Recent EU-funded research projects include the 'Effects of Austerity on Active Citizenship in Europe'. In addition to her research, she leads various modules on globalization, comparative education, and statistics.

JAN GERMEN JANMAAT is Reader of Comparative Social Science at the Centre on Learning and Life Chances in Knowledge Economies and Societies (LLAKES), Institute of Education, London (UK). He teaches on the MA in Comparative Education and has published widely on the relation between education, civic values, and social cohesion. His latest book is *Regimes of Social Cohesion: Societies and the Crisis of Globalization* (co-authored with Andy Green).

JOHN JERRIM is a Lecturer in Economics and Social Statistics at the Institute of Education, University of London. Jerrim's research interests include the economics of education, access to higher education, intergenerational mobility, cross-national comparisons, and educational inequalities. He has worked extensively with the OECD Programme for International Student Assessment (PISA) data, with this research being reported widely in the British media. Jerrim was the recipient of an ESRC Research Scholarship (2006–2010), and was awarded the prize as the "most promising PhD student in the quantitative social sciences" at the University of Southampton. He was a Fellow of the Jacobs Foundation postdoctoral PATHWAYS to Adulthood program, and in October 2011 he was awarded a prestigious ESRC postdoctoral fellowship to continue his research into the educational and labor market expectations of adolescents and young adults. Since then he has won the inaugural ESRC Early Career Outstanding Impact award and has just received an ESRC grant to study cross-national comparisons of educational attainment and social mobility.

HEATHER JOSHI is Professor Emerita at the Institute of Education, University of London, having been the Director of the Centre for Longitudinal Studies and of the Millennium Cohort Study in particular. She was also president of the European Society for Population Economics, of the British Society for Population Studies and the founder president of the Society for Lifecourse and Longitudinal Studies. She was a co-investigator on the project about single-sex schooling summarized here, which was led by the late Diana Leonard.

SARAH KENNY was a research assistant at the University of Michigan, focusing primarily on gender differences in STEM. She is currently an MA student at the London School of Economics, and plans to pursue a doctorate focusing on children and young people's experiences of digital media at home and school.

IRENE KRIESI is a sociologist who currently heads a research section at the Swiss Federal Institute of Vocational Education and Training. Her research, on topics such as social and gender inequality, the transition from childhood and youth to adulthood, education and labor market careers, has been widely published.

OLIVER LÜDTKE is a Professor of Psychological Research Methods at the Humboldt University of Berlin. He received his PhD in Psychology from the Free University of Berlin and worked as a research scientist at the Center for Educational Research at the Max-Planck-Institute for Human Development. His main research interests include the application of multilevel modeling in psychological and educational research, international student achievement studies, and personality development in adolescence.

CAROL LYNN MARTIN is a Professor of Child Development in the T. Denny Sanford School of Social and Family Dynamics at Arizona State University. She is also a director of the Lives of Girls and Boys Enterprise, which promotes innovative research and its application to the real life issues and challenges facing girls and boys. Her research interests include gender development and peer relationships.

SARAH-KATHRYN MCDONALD, Principal Research Scientist in the Academic Research Centers at NORC at the University of Chicago, has more than 25 years' experience serving as a policy analyst, social scientist, evaluation researcher, public affairs advisor, and senior manager with governmental, for profit, and not-for-profit organizations in the US and Europe. Since 2002 she has collaborated with faculty, clients, and staff at NORC on a range of impact evaluations and educational research projects. Other organizations with which she has worked include the US Bureau of the Census; Nuffield College, University of Oxford; Birkbeck College, University of London; and the University of Chicago Consortium on Chicago School Research.

ANNE MCMUNN is a Senior Lecturer in Quantitative Social Science and Population Health, and Graduate Tutor in the Department of Epidemiology and Public Health at University College London. She is also a member of the ESRC International Centre for Life Course Studies in Society and Health.

GABRIEL NAGY is Professor for Quantitative Methods in Educational Research at the Leibniz Institute for Science and Mathematics Education (IPN), Kiel. He received his PhD in psychology at the Free University of Berlin. His research interests include educational and work-related transitions, cognitive and motivational development, latent variable models for interest and ability profiles, and statistical methods for longitudinal and multilevel data.

GOPALAKRISHNAN NETUVELI is a Professor of Public Health at the Institute of Health and Human Development, University of East London. He is also a Visiting Professor at the School of Public Health, Imperial College London and Honorary Professor at the Department of Public Health and Epidemiology, University College London. He is affiliated with the ESRC International Centre for Life Course Studies in Society and Health.

ERIN PAHLKE is an Assistant Professor of Psychology at Whitman College, Washington State.

PHILIP PARKER is a research fellow at the Centre for Positive Psychology and Education (CPPE). His research focuses on social inequality, development, personality, and wellbeing issues related to adolescents' transition from school to work or further education, and uses large longitudinal databases from Australia, the US, UK, Germany and Finland. He received a first-class honors degree in psychology from the SELF research center at the University of Western Sydney and won the Australian Psychological Society Science Prize. His PhD, at the University of Sydney, was on the role of motivational constructs and processes in the development of teacher burnout and subjective wellbeing. He has published in a number of international journals in education, psychology, and sociology, as well as a number of books, chapters and peer-reviewed papers. He was previously a Jacob's Foundation-funded postdoctoral research fellow in the PATHWAYS to Adulthood program.

LARA PEREZ-FELKNER is an Assistant Professor of Higher Education in the College of Education and Department of Sociology at Florida State University. Her research examines how young people's social contexts influence their college and career outcomes. She focuses on the mechanisms that shape entry into and persistence in fields in which they have traditionally been underrepresented. In particular, she investigates racial-ethnic, gender, and socioeconomic disparities in postsecondary educational attainment and entry to scientific career fields. She was a recent Visiting Scholar at the Center for Khmer Studies for cross-national extensions of this work and a Fellow of the Jacobs Foundation postdoctoral PATHWAYS to Adulthood program.

RICARDO SABATES is Senior Lecturer in International Education and Development at the University of Sussex. Much of his work concerns the relationship between education and wider social outcomes such as health and crime. Special interests include the application of quantitative research methods to investigate the strength in the relationship between education and outcomes in the UK and international contexts and the role of education in reducing social inequalities.

KATARIINA SALMELA-ARO is Professor of Psychology at the University of Jyväskylä, and Visiting Professor at the Institute of Education, University of London. She was Research Director of the Helsinki Collegium for Advanced Studies at the University of Helsinki, and Professor in the Finnish Center of Excellence on Learning and Motivation Research. Professor Salmela-Aro is Director of several ongoing longitudinal studies, such as FinEdu and Secretary General of the International Society for the Study of Behavioral Development (ISSBD). She is also a founding member of the PATHWAYS to Adulthood postdoctoral fellowship program. Her main topics are motivation and academic wellbeing using longitudinal studies.

CARLOS SANTOS was trained as a developmental scientist and is currently an Assistant Professor in the Counseling and Counseling Psychology program at

Arizona State University. His research explores how social identities and categories (e.g., being a boy or a girl and Latina/o or white) intersect, and how experiences (e.g., discrimination) and attitudes (e.g., stereotypes) associated with these categories influence youths' identity, relationships, and health.

INGRID SCHOON is Professor of Human Development and Social Policy at the Institute of Education, University of London and is Director of the international postdoctoral Jacobs Foundation Fellowship PATHWAYS to Adulthood. Her research interests are focused on issues of human development across the life course, in particular the transition from dependent childhood to independent adulthood, the intergenerational transmission of (dis)advantage, and the realization of individual potential in a changing socio-historical context. Her work is published widely in peer-reviewed journals. She also has written a monograph on *Risk and Resilience* and co-edited a book with Rainer K. Silbereisen on *Transitions from School to Work*, both published by Cambridge University Press.

BARBARA SCHNEIDER is the John A. Hannah Chair and University Distinguished Professor in the College of Education and Department of Sociology at Michigan State University. Her research and teaching focus on understanding how the social contexts of schools and families influence the academic and social well-being of adolescents as they move into adulthood, with a particular emphasis on improving educational opportunities for students with limited economic and social resources. She is the co-author of 15 books, author of numerous journal articles, and previously editor of *Educational Evaluation and Policy Analysis* and *Sociology of Education*. Schneider was a Fulbright New Centuries Scholar, member of the Sociological Research Association, and Senior Fellow at NORC at the University of Chicago. She is a founding member of the Jacobs Foundation postdoctoral Fellowship program PATHWAYS to Adulthood, and was recently elected President of the American Educational Research Association (AERA).

JACQUELINE SCOTT is Professor of Empirical Sociology in the Faculty of Human, Social and Political Sciences at the University of Cambridge. From 2004 to 2010 she directed the Economic and Social Research Council's (ESRC) Research Priorities Network on Gender Inequalities in Production and Reproduction, where she coordinated projects across eight institutions investigating the changing roles and lifestyles of men and women. The Network investigated why gender inequality is so prevalent within our society and sought to identify ways that greater equality might be achieved. She is the editor of several books about gender inequalities and sociology of family and has published many articles on attitudinal change. She is a member of the Scientific Advisory Board of the European Social Survey and the ESRC National Centre for Research Methods.

ALICE SULLIVAN is a Reader in Sociology at the Institute of Education, University of London. As Director of the 1970 British Cohort Study she leads the team responsible for developing the content, design, and analysis of the 1970 British Cohort Study. Her research interests are focused on social and educational inequalities, including inequalities of social class, gender, and ethnicity. Her published work includes research on social class and gender differences in cognition and educational attainment, Bourdieu and cultural capital, school sector differences, and education policy.

JENNIFER SYMONDS' research interests are in the development of children's psychological and emotional wellbeing at school transition. Recently, she has directed the Changing Key study of musical identity at school transition for the Paul Hamlyn Foundation, investigated adolescents' school engagement as a research fellow on the Learning Futures project for the University of Bristol, and researched adolescent mental health on both the Nuffield Foundation's Changing Adolescence program and as a research fellow on the international PATHWAYS to Adulthood program at the University of Helsinki. Currently she is writing a psychology book for teachers: *Understanding Transition: What Happens to Children and How to Help Them.*

ULRICH TRAUTWEIN is a Professor for Educational Science at the University of Tübingen. His main research interests include educational transitions, the effects of different learning environments on self-concept, interest, and personality development, and the role of self-related cognitions in students' homework behavior. He has published more than 100 scholarly articles in peer-reviewed journals. Trautwein directs two longitudinal large-scale school achievement studies and several large-scale intervention projects. He is also the director of the graduate program Learning, Educational Achievement, and Life Course Development (LEAD), funded by the excellence initiative of the German Federal and State Governments, and is a member of the Jacobs Foundation post-doctoral Fellowship program PATHWAYS to Adulthood.

LORNA UNWIN is Chair in Vocational Education at the Institute of Education, University of London. She has held academic posts at the Open University and University of Sheffield, and was Director of the Centre for Labour Market Studies at the University of Leicester. Her latest books include *Contemporary Apprenticeship: International Perspectives on an Evolving Model of Learning* (co-authored with Alison Fuller and published in 2012). She is editor of the *Journal of Vocational Education and Training*.

KATJA UPADYAYA, PHD, is a research investigator at the Institute of Social Research, University of Michigan. Her research interests include teacher–student and parent–child interaction, causal attributions and beliefs, study and work engagement, academic motivation and performance, gender differences, STEM, and school and work transitions. From 2008 to 2010 she was a Fellow of the Jacobs Foundation post-doctoral PATHWAYS to Adulthood program.

MING-TE WANG is an Assistant Professor of Applied Developmental Psychology and Research Scientist in the Learning Research & Development Center at the

University of Pittsburgh. He received his doctoral degree in Human Development and Psychology from Harvard University, and he was a Fellow of the Jacobs Foundation postdoctoral PATHWAYS to Adulthood program at the University of Michigan. His research focuses on the impact of school climate and family socialization on adolescents' motivational beliefs and the effects of multiple ecological systems on the behavioral, social, and emotional development of youth from diverse socioeconomic and cultural backgrounds. His work emphasizes the interplay of developmental processes across both academic and social domains in adolescence, and situates these processes within family, school, and community contexts.

ELIZABETH WEBB is a Research Associate in the Department of Epidemiology and Public Health at University College London, and a member of the ESRC International Centre for Lifecourse Studies in Society and Health (ICLS).

DAVID WEISS studied psychology at the University of Kiel and the Australian National University. He completed his PhD at the University of Erlangen-Nuremberg, for which he received the Karl-Giehrl Award for the most outstanding dissertation of the year. In 2009, he joined the Department of Psychology at the University of Zurich as a postdoctoral researcher. For his research on age identity, he received the Vontobel Award for Research on Age(ing) in 2011. His main research interests relate to self, identity, and stereotypes from a life-span perspective.

BETTINA S. WIESE is a Professor of Personnel and Organizational Psychology and currently the Managing Director of the Department of Psychology at the RWTH Aachen University, Germany. She received her PhD in psychology from the Free University of Berlin. Her main research interests include the influence of personal goals and self-regulatory strategies on career development and the interplay of work and family during transitions (e.g., return to work after maternity leave).

KRISTINA ZOSULS earned her PhD in Social Psychology, and is currently an associate faculty member at the T. Denny Sanford School of Social and Family Dynamics at Arizona State University.

Abbreviations (selected)

ACT	American College Testing
AGFI	Adjusted Goodness of Fit Index
AIC	Akaike's Information Criterion
A-level	Advanced level (UK)
ANOVA	Analysis of Variance
ARS	Academic Rating Scale (US)
BCS70	British Cohort Study (1970)
BHPS	British Household Panel Survey
BIC	Bayesian Information Criterion
BYS	British Youth Survey
CAB	Childhood and Beyond (Study) (US)
CAPI	Computer Assisted Personal Interview
CATI	Computer Assisted Telephone Interview
CCCI	Civic Competence Composite Indicator
CES-D	Center for Epidemiologic Studies–Depression Scale
CFI	Comparative Fit Index
CIVED	Civic Education Study
COCON	Swiss Survey of Children and Youth
CRELL	Centre for Research on Lifelong Learning
DAA	Differential Ability Analysis
DfE	Department for Education (UK)
DTI	Department of Trade and Industry
ELS	Education Longitudinal Study (US)
ELSA	English Longitudinal Study of Ageing
EOC	Equal Opportunities Commission (UK)
EU	European Union
GCSE	General Certificate of Secondary Education (UK)
GDI	Gender Development Index
GEM	Gender Empowerment Measure
GFI	General Formal Investigation (UK)
GPA	Grade Point Average
HGLM	Hierarchical Generalized Linear Model
HLM	Hierarchical Linear Model
ICC	Intra-Class Correlations

IDA	Individual Development and Adaptation Study (Sweden)
IER	Institute of Employment Rights
ILO	International Labour Organization
IPUMS	Integrated Public Use Microdata Series
IRT	Item Response Theory
ISCO	International Standard Classification of Occupations
IT	Information Technology
LPA	Latent Profile Analysis
LSYPE	Longitudinal Study of Young People in England
MA	Modern Apprenticeship (UK)
MLA	Multilevel Analysis
MRA	Multiple Regression Analysis
MSALT	Michigan Study of Adolescent Life Transitions (US)
NCDS	National Child Development Study (UK)
NCES	US National Center for Educational Statistics
NEET	Not in Education, Employment, or Training
NLS	National Longitudinal Survey (US)
NLSY	National Longitudinal Survey of Youth (US)
NS-SEC	National Statistics Socio-economic Classification (UK)
OECD	Organisation for Economic Co-operation and Development
O-level	Ordinary level (UK)
OLS	Ordinary Least Squares
ORACLE	Observational Research and Classroom Learning Evaluation (UK)
PAQ	Personal Attributes Questionnaire
PISA	Programme for International Student Assessment
PME	Physical Sciences, Mathematics, and Engineering
RMSEA	Root Mean Square Error of Approximation
SAMSAD	Secondary and Middle School Adolescent Development (Study) (UK)
SAT	Scholastic Assessment Test (US)
SDQ	Self-Description Questionnaire
SEM	Structural Equation Modeling
SES	Socioeconomic Status
SET	Science, Engineering, and Technology
SFR	Statistical First Release
SOC	Selection, Optimization, and Compensation Model
SRMR	Standardized Root Mean Square Residual
STEM	Science, Technology, Engineering, and Math
STVs	Subjective Task Values

TIMSS	Third International Mathematics and Science Study
TLI	Tucker-Lewis Index
TOEFL	Test of English as a Foreign Language
TOSCA	Transformation of the Secondary School System and Academic Careers (Germany)
UKRC	UK Resource Centre for Women in Science, Engineering and Technology
UNESCO	United Nations Educational, Scientific and Cultural Organization
VET	Vocational Education and Training (UK)

PART I
Introduction

Introduction: conceptualizing gender differences in aspirations and attainment – a life course perspective

Ingrid Schoon and Jacquelynne S. Eccles

This book introduces a life course perspective to the study of gender differences in aspirations and attainment, addressing the interplay of individual and structural factors in shaping the lives of men and women and how this interplay develops over time and in context. It examines and describes how aspirations, self-concepts, and attainments form and develop during childhood, adolescence, young adulthood, and later in adult life, and brings together evidence from across disciplines to gain a better understanding of the multiple influences on individual lives.

Gender differences in educational attainment and future outlook have been a topic of public debate since the late 1980s. Initially the focus was on the under-representation of females in the sciences. More recently focus has shifted to a concern about the academic underachievement of males – following evidence suggesting that boys were failing to improve their educational performance at the same rate as girls, and that girls were overtaking boys in their academic motivation and the level of qualifications obtained (Arnot, 2002; DiPrete & Buchmann, 2013). Beginning in elementary school, girls outperform boys and this gap continues throughout secondary school and higher education. The academic success and achievements of girls have been hailed as a story of the extraordinary success of post-war egalitarian movements. However, the shift in the gender balance, with girls catching up with or overtaking boys in their academic motivation and academic attainments, has also brought about something of a moral panic, leading to calls for support for underachieving boys to retrieve their educational advantage (Epstein, Elwood, Hey, & Maw, 1998; Younger & Warrington, 2006). The threat of boys' disengagement from the educational system is of particular concern in the current era of growing knowledge economies requiring a highly skilled labor force. However, it has also been argued that recent gains of women in the educational system reflect a "stalled gender revolution" (Carlson, 2011; England, 2010), affecting some groups and some areas of life more than others.

Huge strides have been made over the past half-century in terms of opportunities for women. The proportion of women in further education has grown persistently; women are now more strongly attached to the labor market than ever before, even after childbirth, and are increasingly represented in professional and managerial jobs. In the United States (US) and the United Kingdom (UK), for example, more and more women are taking on the role of main breadwinner in the family, representing a massive upheaval in general gender roles (Rosin, 2012).

Yet, there are persisting gender differences in the household division of labor with women taking on the lion's share of care responsibilities, as well as continuing gender segregation in the labor market. Key legal and economic rights – like equal pay – are yet to become reality. In the UK and the US, for example, women are outnumbered four to one in Parliament and Congress (Inter-Parliamentary Union, 2013), women working full-time are paid on average 15–19% less than men, and two thirds of low-paid workers are women (US Bureau of Labor Statistics, 2012). Furthermore, according to the UK Equal Opportunities Commission (EOC), 41% of pay gap differences are due to career choice.

Explaining gender differences in aspirations and attainment

The size of the gender gap differs considerably by country, by socio-economic background, as well as by race and ethnicity, reflecting complex interactions between individual characteristics and context. Explanations of the persistent gender differences in aspirations and attainment refer to differences in gender socialization and the choices men and women make, gender essentialism, as well as outright gender discrimination. In this book we argue that both structure and agency play a role, and that differences in early experiences can accumulate over time and have long-term implications. In order to gain a better understanding of persisting gender inequalities in attainment, it is vital to learn more about the interlinkages between structural constraints and individual values, attitudes, and capabilities, and to examine experiences of attainment, career choices, and career development in context and over time.

Gender socialization

As women have been catching up in education and labor force participation, one explanation for the persisting gender earnings gap is that women have different expectations than men regarding their labor market achievements and that they choose different career paths due to differences in self-perceptions, goals, and values linked to gender identity. For example, according to the expectancy-value perspective (Eccles, 1987, 2009), identity can be conceptualized in terms of two basic sets of self-perceptions: (a) perceptions related to one's skills, characteristics, and competencies, and (b) perceptions related to personal values and goals and the subjective importance of these various personal characteristics. Previous research suggests that girls tend to underestimate their abilities, especially in math and science; these differences in estimates of one's relative competencies across different subject areas, in turn, can serve as a critical filter regulating access to high-status and high-income occupations because they lead females and males to pursue different courses and occupations (Correll, 2004; Eccles, Wigfield, & Schiefele, 1998; Entwisle & Baker, 1983). Females also express less interest in mathematics and the physical sciences than males and more interest in literature and reading than males – and vice versa (Eccles, 2009). It is important to note that these gender differentiated self-perceptions and values exist despite the fact that females do just as well as males, on average, in science- and math-related courses (see, for example, Chow & Salmela-Aro; Jerrim & Schoon; Parker, Nagy, Trautwein, & Lüdtke; Wang & Kenny, this volume). However, as a consequence of these differentiated beliefs, both men's and women's career aspirations and choices are restricted to occupations that are congruent with these gender-stereotyped self-perceptions and values (Francis & Skelton, 2005; Watt & Eccles, 2008). Alas, the careers that females are more likely to select often provide lower salaries than the occupations that males are more likely to select (Marini & Fan, 1997; Scott, Crompton & Lyonette, 2010; see also Aisenbrey & Brückner, this volume). Gender differences in occupational choice and attainment can thus be understood as an example of social reproduction processes due to gendered perceptions of both one's own capabilities and interests resulting from the fact that males and females have been socialized to have different but equally important goals for their lives (Maccoby & Martin, 1983). Early socialization influences include the cultural milieu, comprising cultural stereotypes and family demographics, as well as the socializer's beliefs and behaviors (Eccles, 1987, 2009).

Gender essentialism

In contrast to theories grounded in social reproduction models of gendered patterns of educational and occupational choice, scholars focused on gender essentialism argue that women and men are *innately* and fundamentally different in interests and skills (Charles, 2011; Charles & Bradley, 2009; Ridgeway, 2009). According to this view, evolution has primed women to have different lifestyle preferences than men that cut across social class, education, and ability differences. Preferences for a "home-centered," "work-centered," or "adaptive" lifestyle can shift over the life course in their salience and emphasis for work versus family orientation (Hakim, 2000). Yet, evolution is assumed to have prepared women to make different occupational choices than men – prioritizing family over careers, preferring work that involves people not things – and it is suggested that these fundamental gender differences start in the very structure of the human brain (Baron-Cohen, 2003; Brizendine, 2006; Burman, Bitan, & Booth, 2008; Buss, 1991; Gurian Institute, Bering, & Goldberg, 2009; Pinker, 2008). This view, however, takes attention away from continuing gender inequalities due to structural discrimination (Fine, 2010).

Gender discrimination

Despite the fact that many barriers have been removed, gender discrimination still exists, even in highly developed countries. In particular, there is persistent evidence about continuing discrimination against women in the labor market (Brückner, 2004; England, 2010; Scott et al., 2010). Even when women succeed in entering top managerial positions or male-dominated occupations, they are often paid less than men, despite having the same or higher-level qualifications and experience. Gender segregation in the workplace persists in terms of there being typical male and female jobs, and a structural devaluation of women's work creating economic penalties for working in the feminized sector (Crompton, 2006; England, 2010; Hegewisch, Williams, & Zhang, 2012; Lewis & Smee, 2009). Particular occupational fields, such as the teaching occupations, have become "feminized," which generally means they are lower status and less well paid, but offer more opportunities for combining work and family/care-related responsibilities. From a structural point of view, gender segregation in the labor market is seen as a by-product of gender discrimination and the gendered nature of the occupational system, which creates constraints for young women and allocates them to subordinate positions in the labor market (Krüger, 2003), often not in the positions, occupations, or fields to which they aspired (Aisenbrey & Brückner, 2006).

Cumulation of experiences

Life chances and opportunities remain circumscribed by gender, ethnicity, social origin, institutional structures, and the social and economic resources inherent in the connections young people have to their families and the wider social context. Furthermore, the notion of time is important, in particular regarding the timing of effects and the cumulation of experiences over time. It has been argued that the persisting and repeated experience of discrimination, of gendered expectations and stereotypes can affect minds, self- and social perceptions, choices and behavior, and in turn become again part of the gendered social world (Correll, 2001; Fine, 2010; Steele, 1997). While the impact of existing gender stereotypes and gender beliefs on an outcome in any one situation may be small, individual lives are lived through multiple, repeating, social relational contexts, and small biasing effects tend to accumulate over the life course, resulting in substantially different pathways and social outcomes for men and women who are otherwise similar in background or ability (Ridgeway & Correll, 2004). In this book we thus adopt a life course perspective to assess influences in early childhood, adolescence, young adulthood, and later life and how these influences change and accumulate over time.

A developmental-contextual approach for the study of motivation and behavior

The chapters included in this book examine the antecedents, correlates, and longer-term outcomes of career aspirations and choices. The main theme running through the book concerns the processes of selection and exclusion that reflect and create gender inequalities in aspirations and attainment. A useful integrative framework for studying gendered pathways and decision making draws on assumptions developed within an ecological life course perspective of human development (Bronfenbrenner, 1979; Elder, 1998; Schoon, 2006) and Eccles' socio-cultural expectancy-value model of motivated behavioral choices (Eccles (Parsons) et al., 1983; Eccles, 1987, 2008). Both approaches are explicit developmental models, taking into account the interplay between structure and agency over time, and conceptualizing the multiple and interlinked influences shaping individual lives. However, while life course theory focuses more on the role of the socio-historical context and institutional structures, the model of motivated behavioral choices focuses more on the role of individual agency and the fit between characteristics of the individual and those of their social environment. Combining both approaches gives a better understanding of the dynamic interplay between agency and structure over time and in context.

Context and timing

According to life course theory, human development is understood to take place in a changing socio-historical context, where the context not merely provides the setting in which individual lives are lived, but through its interactions with the individual constitutes a formative process that makes people who they are (Elder, Johnson & Crosnoe, 2004). Key principles of the life course are (a) that development is a lifelong process; (b) that the antecedents and consequences of behavior can vary according to their timing in a life course; (c) that individuals construct their own life course through the choices and actions they take and within the opportunities and constraints they encounter; and (d) that lives are lived interdependently, and individual experiences are connected to the lives of significant others (Elder, 1998, 1999). A distinctive feature of this ecology is the social inequality associated with class, race, and gender. These are expressed across individual lives and generations in the cumulative dynamics of advantage and disadvantage built up through childhood, adolescence, and the adult years.

The life course perspective views the socio-cultural environment as a crucial influence on human development. Developmental processes occur in a multilevel context and are shaped by social institutions and through interactions with significant others, such as parents, teachers, and peers (Elder, 1998). Individual lives are guided through age-related legal norms as well as population-based norms and informal expectations regarding the timing and sequencing of social roles, or "scripts of life" (Buchmann, 1989; see also Heckhausen, this volume). Age-related norms and expectations can vary by gender, ethnicity, and social class – and are also highly responsive to social change (Elder et al., 2004). For example, changing labor markets requiring a highly skilled labor force led to the widening of educational opportunities in the 1960s, which in turn was associated with increased and extended education participation among previously disadvantaged groups, including women (see McMunn, Webb, Bartley, Blane, & Netuveli, this volume).

Within the life course framework, pathways through life are understood as developmental processes extending over time, and being shaped by complex interdependent relationships, including links to the wider social context, to one's family of origin, to biographical experiences, and individual agency processes. The individual actively steers the developmental process, bringing to each new situation his or her attitudes, expectations, and feelings, which in turn are influenced by his or her history of earlier interactions with the social context in which they grew up.

Interdependent lives and co-regulation

The principle of linked lives in life course theory highlights the role of significant others in regulating and shaping the timing of life trajectories through a network of informal controls (Elder, 1998). This network of shared social relationships can be understood as a developmental context that extends from the family to friends, teachers, neighbors, peers, and work colleagues. In both life course theory and the model of motivated behavior, the expectations, actions, and beliefs of significant others, or key socializers (Eccles, 2009), are understood to direct and channel behavior in certain directions, to transmit values and beliefs, and to influence aspirations and engagement for certain activities. These influences can stretch across generations, including the reproduction of education, occupation, health, and health behaviors.

Significant others can influence perceptions of self-concepts or choice options through the information and experiences they provide (e.g., by encouraging, ignoring, or discouraging various options linked to college education), or they can act as role models that shape views of how best to integrate work and family obligations. The direction of these influences can, however, also be reciprocal, in that the expectations, beliefs, and behaviors of the developing person can affect the expectations, beliefs, and behaviors of those with whom they are interacting. For example, if a young person is doing well at school it is more likely that parents express high educational aspirations for their child than is the case with low academic achievements.

Motivated choices and behavior

In accordance with life course theory the socio-cultural expectancy-value model of motivated behavior emphasizes that individual lives are shaped through ongoing interactions with the environment (Eccles (Parsons) et al., 1983; Eccles, 2008, 2009), and offers a more in-depth understanding of individual choice and agency processes. Individuals continually make choices, both consciously and non-consciously, regarding how they will spend their time and their energy. Many significant gender differences in behavior (e.g., educational and vocational aspirations and choices, and decisions about how to integrate work and family obligations) involve an element of choice, even if these choices are heavily influenced by socialization pressures and cultural norms.

Conceptualizing gendered behavior patterns in terms of choices highlights the importance of understanding what becomes part of an individual's perception of the range of possible choices. Although individuals choose from among several options, they do not consider the full range of objectively available options in making their selections. Many options are never considered because the individual is unaware of their existence. Other options are not seriously considered because the individual has inaccurate information regarding either the option itself or the individual's possibility of achieving the option. Still others may not be seriously considered because they do not fit in well with the individual's various social schema, including those linked to gender. Thus, it is likely that gender roles influence educational and vocational choices, in part, through their impact on individuals' perceptions of the field of viable options, as well as through their impact on individuals' own expectations and subjective task values, and the opportunities provided to each individual to develop their skills and interests. Consistent with a life course perspective, beliefs and opportunities are formed over one's lifetime and each opportunity and choice contributes to the pathway along which each person travels.

In Eccles' model of motivated behavior, an individual's expectations for success and the importance or value the individual attaches to the various options are assumed to be the most proximal psychological influences on the choices people make. These two sets of beliefs (expectations for success and importance of the option or task value), in turn, are assumed to be shaped by cultural norms, social roles, and social experiences, as well as personal experiences and one's interpretations and memories of these experiences, and one's aptitudes, talents, personality, and temperamental characteristics. Understanding the processes shaping individuals' perceptions of their field of viable options is essential to our understanding of the dynamics leading women and men to make different life-defining choices. Furthermore, the model assumes that choices are made within life contexts that present each individual with a wide variety of choices. The choice is often between two or more positive options or between two or more options that have both positive and negative components and consequences. Furthermore, each choice has both long-range and immediate consequences. For example, majoring in engineering or science rather than education might make it more difficult to return to the same level of employment or the same position after a career break due to childbirth.

Eccles' socio-cultural expectancy-value model of motivated behavior is a developmental model, taking into account change across time and across situations (Eccles, 2009). Constructs and processes like self-schema and short- and long-term goals and identity formation change over time in part in response to: (a) the acquisition of new experiences and new information; (b) social and biological clocks that influence the salience of different demands and choices at different ages and in different social niches; (c) entry and exit from different social contexts that influence the salience of different aspects of the social-embedded self as one moves from context to context; and (d) the accumulation of the consequences of prior choices. Because these constructs influence both expectancies and the importance of a task at hand, individuals' behavioral choices will change over time and across situations.

Person × context interactions

According to the person–environment-fit theory (Eccles & Midgley, 1989), behavior, motivation, and associated health and wellbeing are influenced by the fit between the characteristics individuals bring to their social environments and the characteristics of these social environments. Individuals are not likely to do very well, or be very motivated, if they are in social environments that do not meet their psychological needs. For example, if the academic and social environments in the typical junior high or middle school do not fit with the psychological needs of adolescents, then person–environment-fit theory predicts a decline in motivation, interest, performance, and behavior as adolescents move into and through this environment (e.g., see Symonds, Galton, & Hargreaves, this volume). What is critical to note about this argument is not that any transition is bad at this age. Instead it is the specific nature of the transition that matters – and how it matches the developmental status of the individual. The stage-environment-fit theory draws specifically on Elder's (1998) notions of the developmental timing of experiences, arguing that particular types of structural changes, as for example those typical during the shift from elementary school to middle/junior high school, can be inappropriate for early adolescents, and if so, should be changed. The person–environment-fit theory applies to all life stages and transition points, not just the transition from primary to secondary school (e.g., see Salmela-Aro; Heckhausen, this volume). What is crucial is the need to match changing developmental demands to the capacities and resources individuals bring to the situation to facilitate a smooth transition.

Understanding the persisting gender differences in aspirations and attainment requires a broad view of the options and roles available to both men and women, and how these are perceived and evaluated at different life stages. The combination of ecological life course approaches and the socio-cultural expectancy-value model of motivated behavior and person–environment-fit theory provides a conceptual framework that enables us to gain a better understanding of the reciprocal interactions between structure and agency, the dynamic interactions between a changing individual and a changing socio-historical context in shaping aspirations and attainment of men and women. Individual decision making and choice have to be understood against the backdrop of socio-cultural constraints and opportunities, as well as opportunities and challenges arising from the developmental tasks at a particular stage in life and their integration in one's own life and identity.

Outline of the chapters

Assuming that both structure and agency play a role in shaping gendered pathways through life, the chapters in this book examine the role of structural and individual factors in shaping gender differences in career aspirations and attainment within a life course perspective. Because we are most interested in what happens in school and the labor market, we start with experiences in preschool and extend well into adulthood. We selected authors who could address such questions as: What is the role of parents, peers, and teachers in shaping school experiences and informing the career choices of young people? Does the school context matter, and to what extent do education experiences influence young people's self-concept and their outlook to the future? Do teenage aspirations influence later outcomes regarding education attainment and the assumption of work- and family-related roles? What is the role of institutional structures and the wider socio-historical context in helping young people to realize their ambitions? We also stressed the importance of longitudinal studies to answer these questions. Although each chapter alone does not address all of these questions, as a set they contribute to a better understanding of the different influences on career orientations and outcomes across the life course. The book brings together contributions from different Western countries, drawing on evidence from different disciplines including psychology, sociology, economics, epidemiology, and social policy. Thus the chapters in this book present evidence from across different disciplines and from different countries that are characterized by different education systems and policies aimed at reducing gender inequalities in education and employment opportunities.

The following chapters are arranged into five parts: Parts II to V are organized around different life stages, and the final part examines the role of changing societal conditions. Starting with evidence regarding gender differences in academic attainment during childhood and contextual factors that reinforce or reduce these differences, we examine how both individual and contextual influences shape career orientations and attainment among men and women across much of the life-span. First, in Part II, we describe experiences in preschool and during the transition from primary to secondary education, highlighting in particular the role of significant others, such as parents, teachers, and peers, in shaping school adjustment and attainment. In Part III, career planning and individual decision making during adolescence are examined, focusing on motivational, personal, and contextual factors shaping the experiences and decisions of young people. Next, because so much recent research has focused on occupations in science and technology, Part IV is dedicated to the analysis of factors and processes involved in choosing a science career, investigating antecedents and predictors of decisions related to subject choice and career development. Then, the longer-term consequences of early experiences and decisions are examined, looking at the role of school experiences, parental support, and self-concepts as predictors of later career attainment. Last, the specific role of contextual factors in shaping attainment and perceptions of gender equality are discussed in Part VI. Together the contributions build up a picture of the processes and mechanisms underlying gendered career decisions and attainment across the life course.

The early years

The first section of the book focuses on experiences during preschool and the transition from primary to secondary school. Chapter 1, by Richard Fabes and colleagues, examines the role of early peer interactions in contributing to gender differences in educational attainment and aspirations in preschool. Based on a longitudinal observation study, they observe gender differences in classroom behaviors and children's feelings about own- and other-sex children and thoughts about interacting with other-sex peers. The authors challenge a static binary view of socialization, which de-emphasizes individual differences, and introduce the notion of a gradient view, taking into account the time spent with same-sex peers. The authors argue that there are variations in opportunities for peer interaction and exposure to the influence of and interactions with male or female peers, making it necessary to distinguish between peer selection and influence effects. Same-sex peer play leads to engagement in activities that are consistent with stereotypical gender roles, while other-sex peer play reduces engagement in these activities. The study shows that the longer the exposure to same-sex peers, the more the child will show the influence of these experiences. The findings highlight the important role of early peer interactions, which can set the stage for gender differences in educational aspirations and achievement later in life.

Irene Kriesi and Marlis Buchmann, in Chapter 2, address whether the adjustment to everyday life in primary school affects children's future academic attainment. The authors conceptualize the beginning school transition as a status passage in the institutionalized life course, which in turn is shaped by family background, individual competences, and perceived quality of the school transition. They argue that the fit between a child's social self-concepts and the expected competences and behaviors at school entry affect the quality of the beginning school transition, which in turn influences subsequent academic attainment in elementary school. Based on evidence from a longitudinal study, following about 100 Swiss school children between the ages of 6 and 9 years, they find that girls are better prepared than boys for adopting the student role. Girls enter school with more school-relevant knowledge, are more conscientious, and have higher cognitive competencies and a more positive social self-concept. Furthermore, social class-specific perceptions of gender differences affect gender-specific parental expectations and child-rearing practices as well as teachers' ability perceptions and grading, suggesting that gendered and social variations in socialization influences are intertwined. Furthermore, compared to girls, boys' academic achievement depends more strongly on a warm and supportive relationship with parents. The study thus provides novel evidence to indicate that gender-specific socialization practices vary by social background and are less pronounced if parents are highly educated. Moreover, the study shows that teachers rate the academic achievement of children from lower social backgrounds to be lower than that of more privileged pupils. Experiences in the beginning of school transition are crucial in shaping later academic adjustment and may have long-term consequences for gender differences in academic achievement.

The reciprocal associations between teacher perceptions of children's ability and effort and children's ability self-concept of academic attainment during primary school are examined in more detail in the contribution by Katja Upadyaya and Jacquelynne Eccles. Using evidence from the Childhood and Beyond (CAB) study, following three cohorts of children and their teachers from second to sixth grade, they showed that teachers tended to perceive boys as possessing greater ability in math than girls, and girls as having more ability and showing more effort in reading than boys. Although the study found gender differences in teachers' perceptions of ability and effort, teacher expectations are also based on actual academic attainment. The study shows reciprocal effects in that children's performance in math and reading predicted teachers' ability and effort perceptions: when children did well in math or reading, teachers perceived them as having strong abilities and putting forth significant effort in math and reading. Furthermore, the results suggest the existence of expectancy effects in that teachers' perceptions of ability and effort positively predicted children's ability self-concepts in math and reading. Gender differences in boys' and girls' ability self-concepts emerge, even when their actual performance is the same. The study thus suggests that both gender-stereotypical teacher perceptions and actual attainment play a role in shaping individual self-concepts during primary school, illustrating the role of multiple socialization influences during the primary school years.

Chapter 4, by Jennifer Symonds, Maurice Galton, and Linda Hargreaves, examines gender differences in school engagement, aspirations, and attainment in the transition from primary to secondary school, taking into account the co-occurring events of pubertal transition, changing self-concepts, and changing social expectations from peers and families. The authors synthesize findings from a number of in-depth ethnographic studies and quantitative longitudinal research on school transitions conducted in the US and the UK, spanning a 35-year period. The reported evidence suggests that there has been little change in how boys and girls adapt to the experience of puberty and school transition, discussing adjustment across key domains of social and academic identities, aspirations, and achievement. School transitions appear to be particularly challenging regarding boys' academic achievement and girls' self-perceptions. The contribution of gender differences in adaptation was moderated by societal expectations and the provision of activities and structures that promote gender integration and equality. The findings highlight the importance of a socio-cultural approach and attention to person–environment interactions for a better understanding of the emergence of gender differences in aspirations and attainment.

Career planning during adolescence

In Part III, issues related to career planning during adolescence are examined. The chapters address issues related to career aspirations and educational choices in general. How do young people see their future, and what are the constraints and opportunities they are facing? How far in the education system do they expect to go, and what are their experiences following specific decisions, such as choosing vocational versus academic pathways?

David Weiss, Bettina Wiese, and Alexandra Freund investigate the motivational, personal, and contextual factors shaping decisions regarding the transition from high school to college and how young people successfully adapt to the many demands of this transition. In Chapter 5 they introduce the model of selection, optimization, and compensation (SOC) to investigate the importance of self-regulatory processes involved in the selection, pursuit, and maintenance of goals, controlling for the role of gender-related attitudes, personality characteristics, and parental influences. Reviewing evidence from a number of recent empirical studies, they argue that traditional gender-related attitudes can help to buffer the insecurities adolescents face during the transition period. Regarding contextual factors, they show that the influence of parental work participation in different phases of the family life cycle in adolescence can influence the planning of future career- and family-related life goals. The reported evidence highlights the importance of considering multiple influences, involving societal norms and status differences as well as motives and personality differences, when explaining individual developmental trajectories.

Katariina Salmela-Aro examines changes in girls' and boys' life satisfaction and school burnout during the transition to post-comprehensive education. The study draws on longitudinal data collected among Finnish adolescents, showing that the level of life satisfaction was higher and school burnout lower among boys than girls, although the gender gap in life satisfaction reduced during secondary education. While life satisfaction increased among girls in both the vocational and academic tracks, school burnout increased among both girls and boys on the academic track; this shift was most marked among boys. Moreover, school burnout decreased among girls on a vocational track. The findings highlight the role of the changing social context in shaping individual adjustment, as hypothesized in Eccles and Midgley's (1989) theory of stage-environment-fit. The transition to the academic track is very demanding in the Finnish school context, and may lead to a poor fit between the demands of the academic environment and young people's level of competence, at least for some of the students, in particular for girls on the academic track. However, despite increased levels of burnout, young men and women on the academic track show higher levels of life satisfaction than those on the vocational track, suggesting that higher education creates challenges but also offers advantages.

Given the increasing uncertainties regarding educational and occupational opportunities in a changing global context, in Chapter 7 Leslie Morrison Gutman, Ricardo Sabates, and Ingrid Schoon examine gender differences in uncertainty and ask whether certainty in decision making during secondary school offers advantages to being certain regarding one's career choice. Comparing the educational and occupational aspirations of young people growing up in Great Britain during the 1980s and a current cohort born around 1990, they examine the antecedents, correlates, and outcomes associated with uncertain aspirations. Their findings suggest that young people from lower socioeconomic backgrounds and those who had lower prior achievement are more likely to express uncertainty in their career aspirations. There are, furthermore, gender differences in career aspirations in that females are generally more ambitious than males and males express greater uncertainty regarding their aspirations than females. While in the earlier-born cohort uncertainty was associated with problems in establishing oneself in the labor market, in the later-born cohort this association was not apparent. The results show that females may be advantaged when it comes to occupational certainty. The findings also illustrate the role of the wider social context in shaping opportunities for career development, and that in the current socioeconomic climate young people might benefit from an extended period of moratorium in their career choice.

Alison Fuller and Lorna Unwin examine gender stereotypes in vocational training, illustrating the continued segregation of government-funded vocational training programs in the UK. In Chapter 8 they relate their findings to evidence from an EU-funded EQUAL program supporting innovative, transnational projects aimed at tackling discrimination and inequality in the labor market. They argue that young people need to be exposed to gender awareness activities as early as possible in their school careers and show that young people receive very little practical information and guidance about the consequences of pursuing particular occupational pathways. To reduce gender inequalities and to help young people change their attitudes and choices requires a multi-faceted approach, engaging young people in formal opportunities to debate gender and other socio-cultural stereotyping as related to the labor market.

Choosing a science career

The chapters in Part IV focus on the factors and processes associated with choosing a science-related occupation. The chapters address issues of variations in academic ability and aptitude for science-related topics, focusing on how aptitude for science combines with skills in other domains and to what extent young people value science-related fields, as well as the realities of combining career orientation and other life tasks, such as family formation.

In Chapter 9 John Jerrim and Ingrid Schoon analyze gender differences in the academic attainment and occupational aspirations of 15-year-olds as they approach the end of their compulsory schooling. Using data collected for the 2006 Programme for International Student Assessment (PISA) study, they compare gender differences in the performance on standardized tests assessing ability in reading and science; the importance placed on reading, math, and science; as well as the proportion of boys and girls aspiring to a science-related career across 29 developed countries. The findings suggest that although females generally do achieve higher reading scores than males, there are no consistent gender differences in attainment on science tests. Furthermore, girls attach as much importance to science and math as boys. Nonetheless, there are stark gender differences in 15-year-olds' desire to enter a science, technology, engineering, or math (STEM) related occupation. In all 29 countries, boys are more likely than girls to expect entry into a physical science or mathematical career. This pattern is reversed for life sciences and health occupations, as boys are less likely to expect entry into these occupations than girls. There is, however, considerable cross-national variation of the gender effect sizes. The findings are discussed in terms of the intertwining of gender and other societal systems of difference and inequality.

Philip Parker, Gabriel Nagy, Ulrich Trautwein, and Oliver Lüdtke explore gender differences in academic achievement, ability self-concepts, and interest in studying STEM-related fields using data collected for the German longitudinal study Transformation of the Secondary School System and Academic Careers (TOSCA). They apply Marsh's internal/external frame of reference model (Marsh, 1986) to predict career aspirations in a group of German students and explore the validity of the model in predicting choices of university majors 2 years later. Their findings show that individuals tend to compare their performance across multiple domains (i.e., math and English), and that academic self-concept is an important mediator of achievement in predicting career choice. High levels of math achievement and self-concept combined with low levels of English achievement and self-concept predicted career aspirations in the physical sciences, mathematics, engineering, and technology (PME) over other professional fields at school and choice of PME university majors 2 years later. The authors highlight in particular the importance of stereotypical self-evaluations formed in school as a potential barrier to females entering PME fields and to males entering language- and arts-related occupations.

Taking into account how students prioritize their interests across multiple study subjects, in Chapter 11 Angela Chow and Katariina Salmela-Aro investigate how gender differences in intraindividual hierarchies of task values are related to educational attainment and aspirations. According to Eccles' expectancy-value theory, subjective task values of an activity comprise four major components (i.e., importance, enjoyment, utility, and perceived cost or effort) that influence occupational aspirations. Taking a person-centered approach, the study uses latent profile analysis to identify profiles in subjective task values across multiple domains including languages, math and sciences, social studies, and practical subjects (such as music and physical education) within a sample of about 600 Finnish ninth-graders. The identified four groups are characterized by more or less equal preferences for all subjects, preferences for the arts and PE, preferences for math and science, and avoidance of math and science. As one might expect, boys were more likely to rank math and science highly while girls tended to give low ranks for both of these subjects. The task-value patterns across subject levels were associated with gender differences in educational aspiration toward science, engineering, and computer majors. Those young people who valued math and science highly were also more likely to aspire to study these subjects in postsecondary education than those who valued the arts and PE. Males were more likely than females to be in the former group, even after controlling for academic achievement, suggesting that gender differences in aspirations are related more to the task-value profile characteristics than to previous academic achievement. This study highlights the importance of examining intraindividual hierarchies of task-value patterns across subjects to gain a better understanding of gendered differences in aspirations.

Ming-Te Wang and Sarah Kenny (Chapter 12) review the literature on gender differences in personal aptitudes and motivational beliefs and discuss key theoretical concepts used to explain gender differences in choosing a STEM-related career. They furthermore report on their empirical study into how individuals choose between different college majors, taking into account variations in lifestyle values. Their findings suggest that it is not lack of ability that limits female 12th-graders' pursuit of a STEM career, but rather the abundance of other viable choices. Using a person-centered approach, they show that young people with high math and moderate verbal skills are drawn to fields that require strong quantitative skills, while those who show high math and high verbal skills are less likely to choose a STEM college major, presumably because they have a wider range of career options from which to choose. Moreover, examining combinations of academic self-concepts and motivational beliefs, they find that men and women who had already taken a number of math courses, who expect to do well in math and place a low value on working with people are more likely to select college majors in STEM-related fields than those who expected to do less well in math, and valued working with people. For women, choice of STEM-related subjects was also less likely if they placed a high value on putting family needs before work. Wang and Kenny argue that for a better understanding of subject choice one has to consider the combination of ability, self-concept profiles, values, and life goals. To encourage more women into STEM fields it is necessary to emphasize the people-oriented aspects of STEM-related careers and to accommodate the needs and goals of women.

Lara Perez-Felkner, Sarah-Kathryn McDonald, and Barbara Schneider examine gender differences in the secondary school experience, and explore to what extent these are associated with students' postsecondary school attendance and entrance to STEM fields in tertiary education. Using the US Education

Longitudinal Study of 2002 (ELS), in Chapter 13 they show that girls are more academically prepared in math and science, have higher overall expectations about education, and enroll in postsecondary education at higher rates than boys. However, culturally influenced perceptions of weaker female ability on STEM tasks and knowledge appear to steer women to leave STEM fields at the postsecondary level, despite their stronger effort and preparedness in secondary school. Completing more math and science pipeline courses is associated with increased odds of persisting in a STEM major, yet even though boys are "less prepared" in terms of working hard and taking courses, they are still staying in STEM at higher rates than girls. This suggests that preparation during secondary school may not be the crux of the problem; instead interest and subjective experiences around math and science appear to be turning off girls from fields such as physics and computer science.

In Chapter 14 Anna Bagnoli, Dieter Demey, and Jacqueline Scott examine gender-specific trends in science-related aspirations over time (between 1994 and 2005) and assess the predictive power of teenage job aspirations for later entry into science-related occupations. The authors provide evidence from the British Youth Survey, which is part of the British Household Panel Survey (BHPS), comprising quantitative survey data as well as analysis of an open-ended question regarding the career aspirations of young people (between the ages of 13 and 16) related to science, engineering, and technology (SET). The findings suggest that aspirations for SET have generally increased over time since 1994, when the youth survey started, especially among boys. Furthermore, aspirations to become a scientist expressed during adolescence are associated with entry into a SET occupation by age 28, especially among boys. Regarding SET occupations, there are gender differences in choice, with boys aspiring to work in all SET sectors, and girls mainly aspiring to health-related occupations (if they aspire to SET occupations). The fields of chemistry and biology attract similar numbers of boys and girls. The authors also found that adolescents' job aspirations are reasonably stable over time. For those who do change aspirations, change is gender stereotypic, with boys changing *toward* SET and girls changing *away from* SET jobs. The findings point toward an early divergence in the interests for boys and girls, beginning at about age 13 and increasing with age. Analysis of open-ended questions revealed that young adolescents, particularly young females, are already quite aware of the gendered division of paid and unpaid labor and gender inequalities in family-related responsibilities. Boys see careers in science as a positive advantage for their future status as family breadwinners; in contrast, girls see SET careers are something to embark on before starting a family of one's own and as problematic thereafter.

Jutta Heckhausen introduces her motivational theory of life-span development as a conceptual framework for examining the role of individual differences in motivation that mediate differences in effective agency in different life course contexts, including school, work, and family commitments. Reviewing previous research, in Chapter 15 she argues that the school context is more structured and facilitates explicit goal setting and feedback as well as social comparison. The world of work and career is less well structured, and individual differences in motivation and self-regulation have greater consequences on development than experiences in the highly structured school context. Heckhausen argues that due to four gender-related variations in motivational self-regulation (i.e., flexibility of achievement goals, the breadth or selectivity of the achievement motive on certain domains of competence, explicit versus implicit achievement motives, and the capacity for goal engagement and disengagement in response to opportunities in a specific developmental context), females fare better in a more structured context such as the school, while males have an advantage in the less structured domain of work and career.

Longer-term consequences of early experiences

Part V addresses the longer-term consequences of earlier experiences in the family and school system. In particular the role of single-sex schooling, parental support for education and gender self-concepts, differentiating between communal and agency-related orientation as predictors of later outcomes and attainment across multiple domains are assessed.

Alice Sullivan and Heather Joshi (Chapter 16) examine whether attending single-sex versus co-educational secondary schools is associated with longer-term social, psychological, and economic outcomes for men and women. Based on evidence from a nationally representative longitudinal study of men and women born in Great Britain in 1958, they link school experiences to outcomes in middle adulthood (age 42). They found that, after controlling for prior attainment and family background, single-sex schooling had a positive impact on academic outcomes for women but no impact at all for men. Furthermore, single-sex schooling was related to females' getting qualifications in math and sciences and males getting qualifications in English and modern languages. Also, women who attended girls' schools were more confident than co-educated women regarding their abilities in math and sciences, while males at boys' schools were relatively more confident than co-educated males in their abilities in English. The findings support the assumption that single-sex schooling moderates the effect of gender-stereotyping in terms of self-concept and choice of field of study. The experience of single-sex schooling was, however, not associated with attitudes toward the division of labor in the home and had no significant effect on occupational segregation at age 42. Women earned generally less money than men. However, women who attended single-sex schools earned higher wages than women who attended co-educational schools. The authors conclude that single-sex schooling had less impact on many outcomes associated with persistent gender segregation than might have been expected by the proponents of single-sex schooling. However, one also has to take into consideration that among the 1958 age cohort, single-sex schools were attended by relatively privileged pupils within the private sector.

In Chapter 17 Miia Bask, Laura Ferrer-Wreder, Katariina Salmela-Aro, and Lars Bergman examine the role of own and parental education expectations for their children on later academic attainment and highest qualifications achieved. In particular, they examine whether expectations for the future mediate the influence of parental social background and prior academic attainment on later outcomes. The chapter presents original empirical evidence from a Swedish longitudinal study that spans from childhood (age 13) to middle adulthood (mid-40s). Testing assumptions from the Eccles' expectancy-value model of motivation, particularly the family socialization aspect of the model, they show that family social background is an important predicator of several outcomes. In particular, parents with higher socioeconomic status have higher educational expectations for their children, which in turn is associated with later academic attainment. Furthermore, gender preferences in parental aspirations did not emerge until mid-adolescence (Grade 9) when parents developed higher educational expectations for their sons than daughters. Consistent with the expectancy-value model, for both genders, family social background and parental educational expectations in middle adolescence predicted middle adult educational attainment. The importance of grades differed by gender in that mathematics grades were statistically significant predictors of middle adult educational attainment for males but not females; in contrast, females' grades in Swedish predicted their middle adult educational attainment. The findings are consistent with the assumption that parental socialization contributes to differential parent-supported experiences for boys and girls, and leads to gender-stereotypical tracking of males and females into academic subjects and later occupations.

Andrea Abele, in Chapter 18, examines the predictors of career success among men and women in middle adulthood. Career success is defined in terms of positive psychological or work-related outcomes and achievements. In a longitudinal study of over 1,000 German professionals with university degrees, who were followed over a 10-year period between the ages of 27 and 37, she tests hypotheses derived from a dual-impact model of gender- and career-related processes. The model differentiates between outside social expectations and individual self-concepts shaping career success. The outside perspective refers to gender as a social category and to the expectations directed at people belonging to the category of "man" or "woman," while the inside perspective refers to self-concepts regarding "masculinity" and "femininity," or agency versus a more communal orientation. The findings suggest that career interruptions and/or workload reductions due to childcare responsibilities are one of the main reasons for women's lower objective career success than men's. In contrast, parenthood had a slightly positive effect on men's objective career success that was independent of workload. Abele argues that there are still clear expectations directed at mothers and fathers of infant children such that mothers should invest more time in childcare and be more willing to reduce their occupational workload than fathers, whereas fathers should be reliable and responsible breadwinners. These expectations are independent of field of employment. Furthermore, women do not want to copy traditional "male" careers with a clear and unambiguous focus on the work domain at the expense of the private life. Moreover, mothers' career satisfaction partly stems from the fact that they were able to combine work and family. Abele argues that resolving the persisting dilemma regarding combining work and family responsibilities would imply creating flexible part-time work arrangements that would also allow for career advancement.

The role of context

The final part of the book focuses on the role of the wider social context in shaping opportunities and constraints for career development and civic participation. In particular evidence regarding historical trends in gendered attainment across multiple life domains is presented, issues of gender segregation in the labor market and training provision are discussed, and young people's beliefs in and perceptions of gender inequality are examined.

Anne McMunn, Elizabeth Webb, Mel Bartley, David Blane, and Gopal Netuveli examine the extent to which gender differences in attainment across multiple life domains including paid work, socioeconomic position, family formation, health, and subjective wellbeing have decreased since the beginning of the twentieth century. They use evidence from the English Longitudinal Study of Ageing (ELSA). ELSA includes different age cohorts of over 11,000 men and women living in England who were born across the first half of the twentieth century, with the youngest cohort born in the 1950s. The findings suggest that women were much less likely than men to have attended higher education or to have worked in a professional or managerial occupation. There was no evidence of a decrease in these gender differences with each subsequent birth cohort. In fact, gender differences in accessing higher education were greater for those born in the 1950s than for men and women born earlier in the century. The likelihood of having attended higher education or entering a professional or managerial career decreased dramatically by the number of children women had, while men who had two children were significantly more likely to have attended higher education than childless men. The findings suggest that gender inequalities in the domains of education, occupation, and family were deeply entrenched among men and women born during the first half of the twentieth century, and that the advances in gender equality were not so much a gentle shift over the course of the century, but the result of relatively swift and dramatic social change following the second wave of feminism of the 1970s.

Silke Aisenbrey and Hannah Brückner examine whether gendered career choices are the driving force for the wage gap. In Chapter 20, they start out with a longitudinal analysis, showing the development of the gender wage gap across different age cohorts of women born between 1940 and 1964. They then argue that for the youngest cohort, born in 1964, gender differences in education, aspirations and expectations, family obligations, and work-life characteristics do not completely account for the gender wage gap. Instead they find evidence for structural inequalities, generated by the different evaluation of women and men in the labor market. They argue that in order to reduce gender inequalities in attainment one should not expect women to become like men, but that society should aspire to treat men and women more equally.

Using data from the 1999 Civic Education Study (CIVED), in Chapter 21 Bryony Hoskins and Jan Germen Janmaat compare young people's beliefs about and perceptions of gender equality across 28 Organisation for Economic Co-operation and Development (OECD) countries and their attitudes toward civic and political participation. They show that the majority of young people believed in gender equality and did not perceive any form of gender discrimination in their country. They then examine variations in beliefs about and perceptions of gender equality by the country's GDP and its Gender Empowerment Measure, which assesses the degree to which women have been able to use their opportunities and rights, such as the percentage of women in parliament, percentage of senior female officials and managers in a country, and wage differentials. As expected, the belief in gender equality follows patterns of economic growth, confirming theories of gender equality and modernization (Inglehart & Norris, 2003). However, perceptions of gender inequality are not necessarily associated with the economic and social circumstances within a given country, as illustrated by the case of Sweden where awareness of gender inequalities was high despite high levels of economic growth and gender equality. Attitudes toward political participation, in turn, were associated with the combination of beliefs about and perceptions of gender equality. The findings suggest that willingness to engage in actions to create social change requires both the belief in gender equality and the perception of existing inequalities. The authors argue that in order to instigate change it is important to raise awareness regarding existing inequalities, even in highly developed countries.

Summary and conclusion

The chapters in this book, as predicted by Eccles et al.'s expectancy-value theory of achievement-related choices (EVT), show that educational and occupational aspirations and choices are shaped by both gender-stereotypical beliefs and structural constraints. Gender differences become apparent in early childhood, as for example in classroom behavior and the competences manifest at school entry. Furthermore, these gender beliefs appear to become more stereotypical over the life course (as, for example, self-concepts of ability, and preference for SET occupations during secondary school), and are shaped by multiple influences, ranging from early socialization experiences in the family, the school, and peer groups, to gender segregation in the labor force and the provision of training opportunities. As predicted by the life-course developmental theory, gender identity is re-created through everyday social relations with significant others as well as interactions with the wider social context, which accumulate over time.

Following initial experiences in early childhood, self-perceptions and beliefs are created and maintained by multiple, complementary processes acting simultaneously and over time. Small biasing effects can accumulate across different situations and over the life course, resulting in distinct and different behavioral paths and outcomes for men and women who might share similar characteristics regarding capability and social background. These cumulative experiences are internalized and can become self-fulfilling prophecies. For example, gendered beliefs can bias an individual's perception of his/her own competence, independent of his/her underlying capabilities, which in turn can affect engagement and performance. Furthermore, individual agency, i.e., the formulation of ambitions and plans for the future, is intrinsically intertwined with socially structured and gendered processes shaping the formation of individual preferences and values. Processes of individual choice have to be understood against the background of gendered and socially produced perceptions of capabilities and opportunities, and are embedded within socio-cultural constraints and persisting social inequalities. Gender differences in aspirations and attainment are always inextricably bound with other societal systems of differences and inequality, such as class and ethnicity (Arnot, 2002; Eccles, 2008; Ridgeway & Correll, 2004; Schoon, 2010).

Adopting a developmental-contextual life course perspective to the study of motivated choice and behavior provides a deeper understanding of the dynamic and interlinked nature of influences shaping gendered lives, taking into account the multiple spheres of influence and variation in transition experiences within subgroups of the population. The life course perspective shifts our attention from the static to the dynamic, examining the antecedents and the cumulation of experiences over the life course. Furthermore, it conceptualizes social structure as a constitutive force in development (Elder, 1998). Social, economic, demographic, political, and technological forces generate constraints, risks, and uncertainties but also opportunities within which individuals make choices and experience the consequences of these choices. The life course is to a considerable degree a personal construction – but it also entails selective processes and a sifting and sorting of persons into and out of various contexts, where individual lives are continually produced, sustained, and changed by the social context they encounter. A person's position in society continues to be assigned to a considerable extent by his or her family's social position, by ethnic background and gender, and is reinforced through interactions in school, at work, and the wider socio-historical context. To address persisting gender inequalities in aspirations and attainment it is necessary to understand the multiple and interlinked processes involved. To eliminate gender inequality it is not sufficient to address or to eliminate any single factor or process, such as individual aspirations or preferences. An integrative effort is needed, one that develops a more equal evaluation of achievements and symmetrical division of paid and unpaid labor (which includes the provision of family care). It is also necessary to consider the need for instigating change through institutional reform, raising awareness of persistent inequalities, and the advancement of equality-promoting policies across institutions.

References

Aisenbrey, S., & Brückner, H. (2006). *Occupational aspirations, gender segregation, and the gender gap in wages.* New Haven, CT: Yale University, Center for Research on Inequality and the Life Course (Circle). Retrieved from www.yale.edu/ciqle/CIQLEPAPERS/OccupationalAspirations.pdf.

Arnot, M. (2002). *Reproducing gender: Essays on educational theory and feminist politics.* London: Routledge Falmer.

Baron-Cohen, S. (2003). *The essential differences: Men, women and the extreme male brain.* London: Allen Lane.

Brizendine, L. (2006). *The female brain.* New York: Morgan Road/Broadway Books.

Bronfenbrenner, U. (1979). *The ecology of human development: Experiments by nature and design.* Cambridge, MA: Harvard University Press.

Brückner, H. (2004). *Gender inequality in the life course: Social change and stability in West Germany, 1975–1995.* New York: AldineTransaction.

Buchmann, M. C. (1989). *The script of life in modern society: Entry into adulthood in a changing world.* Chicago University Press.

Burman, D. D., Bitan, T., & Booth, J. R. (2008). Sex differences in neural processing of language among children. *Neuropsychologia*, 46(5), 1349–1362. doi: 10.1016/j.neuropsychologia.2007.12.021.

Buss, D. M. (1991). Evolutionary personality psychology. *Annual Review of Psychology*, 42, 459–491.

Carlson, J. (2011). Subjects of stalled revolution: A theoretical consideration of contemporary American femininity. *Feminist Theory*, 12(1), 75–91. doi: 10.1177/1464700110390605.

Charles, M. (2011). A world of difference: International trends in women's economic status. *Annual Review of Sociology* (Vol. 37, pp. 355–371). Palo Alto: Annual Reviews.

Charles, M., & Bradley, K. (2009). Indulging our gendered selves: Sex segregation by field of study in 44 countries. *American Journal of Sociology*, 114, 924–976.

Correll, S. J. (2001). Gender and the career choice process: The role of biased self-assessments. *American Journal of Sociology*, 106(6), 1691–1730.

  (2004). Constraints into preferences: Gender, status, and emerging career aspirations. *American Sociological Review*, 69(1), 93–113.

Crompton, R. (2006). *Employment and the family: The reconfiguration of work and family life in contemporary societies.* Cambridge University Press.

DiPrete, T. A., & Buchmann, C. (2013). *The rise of women: The growing gender gap in education and what it means for American schools.* New York: Russell Sage Foundation.

Eccles, J. S. (1987). Gender roles and women's achievement-related decisions. *Psychology of Women Quarterly*, 11, 135–172. doi: 10.1111/j.1471-6402.1987.tb00781.x.

  (2008). Agency and structure in human development. *Research in Human Development*, 5(4), 231–243. doi: 10.1080/15427600802493973.

  (2009). Who am I and what am I going to do with my life? Personal and collective identities as motivators of action. *Educational Psychologist*, 44(2), 78–89.

Eccles, J. S., & Midgley, C. (1989). Stage/environment fit: Developmentally appropriate classrooms for early adolescents. In R. Ames & C. Ames (Eds.), *Research on motivation in education* (Vol. 3, pp. 139–181). New York: Academic Press.

Eccles, J. S., Wigfield, A., & Schiefele, U. (1998). Motivation to succeed. In W. Damon & N. Eisenberg (Eds.), *Handbook of child psychology* (5th ed., Vol. 3, pp. 1017–1095). New York: Wiley.

Eccles (Parsons), J., Adler, T. F., Futterman, R., Goff, S. B., Kaczala, C., Meece, J. L., & Midgley, C. (1983). Expectancies, values and academic behaviors. In J. T. Spence (Ed.), *Achievement and achievement motives: Psychological and sociological approaches* (pp. 75–146). San Francisco, CA: W. H. Freeman.

Elder, G. H. (1998). The life course as developmental theory. *Child Development*, 69(1), 1–12. doi: 10.2307/1132065.

(1999). *Children of the Great Depression: Social change in life experience* (25th anniversary print). Boulder, CO: Westview Press.

Elder, G. H., Johnson, K. M., & Crosnoe, R. (2004). The emergence and development of life course theory. In J. T. Mortimer & M. J. Shanahan (Eds.), *Handbook of the life course* (pp. 3–19). New York: Springer.

England, P. (2010). The gender revolution: Uneven and stalled. *Gender and Society*, 24(2), 149–166. doi: 10.1177/0891243210361475.

Entwisle, D. R., & Baker, D. P. (1983). Gender and young children's expectations for performance in arithmetic. *Developmental Psychology*, 19, 200–209.

Epstein, D., Elwood, J., Hey, V., & Maw, J. (1998). *Failing boys?* Buckingham: Open University Press.

Fine, C. (2010). *Delusions of gender: The real science behind sex differences*. London: Icon Books.

Francis, B., & Skelton, C. (2005). *Reassessing gender and achievement: Questioning contemporary key debates*. London: Routledge.

Gurian Institute, Bering, S., & Goldberg, A. (2009). *It is a baby girl! The unique wonder and special nature of your daughter from pregnancy to two years*. San Francisco, CA: Jossey-Bass.

Hakim, C. (2000). *Work-lifestyle choices in the 21st century*. Oxford University Press.

Hegewisch, A., Williams, C., & Zhang, A. (2012). *The gender wage gap: 2011*. Washington, DC: Institute for Women's Policy Research.

Inglehart, R., & Norris, P. (2003). *The rising tide: Gender equality and cultural change around the world*. Cambridge University Press.

Inter-Parliamentary Union (2013). *Women in Parliament in 2012: The year in perspective*. Retrieved from www.ipu.org/pdf/publications/WIP2012e.pdf.

Jacobs, J. A. (1989). *Revolving doors: Sex segregation and women's careers*. Stanford University Press.

Krüger, H. (2003). The life course regime: Ambiguities between interrelatedness and individualization. In W. R. Heinz & V. R. Marshall (Eds.), *Social dynamics of the life course: Transition, institutions, and interrelations* (pp. 33–56). Hawthorne, NY: Aldine de Gruyter.

Lewis, R., & Smee, S. (2009). *Closing the gap: Does transparency hold the key to unlocking pay equality? A Fawcett Society thinkpiece for the Gender Equality Forum*. London: Fawcett Society.

Maccoby, E., & Martin, J. (1983). Socialization in the context of the family: Parent–child interaction. In P. H. Mussen & E. M. Hetherington (Ed.), *Handbook of child psychology: Vol. 4. Socialization, personality, and social development* (pp. 1–101). New York: Wiley.

Marini, M. M., & Fan, P.-L. (1997). The gender gap in earnings at career entry. *American Sociological Review*, 62, 588–604.

Marsh, H. (1986). Verbal and math self-concepts: An internal/external frame of reference model. *American Educational Research Journal*, 23, 129.

Pinker, S. (2008). *The sexual paradox: Men, women, and the real gender gap.* New York: Scribner.

Ridgeway, C. L. (2009). Framed before we know it: How gender shapes social relations. *Gender & Society*, 23(2), 145–160. doi: 10.1177/0891243208330313.

Ridgeway, C. L., & Correll, S. J. (2004). Unpacking the gender system: A theoretical perspective on gender beliefs and social relations. *Gender & Society*, 18(4), 510–531.

Rosin, H. (2012). *The end of men: And the rise of women.* London: Viking.

Schoon, I. (2006). *Risk and resilience: Adaptations in changing times.* Cambridge University Press.

(2010). Becoming adult: The persisting importance of class and gender. In J. Scott, R. Crompton, & C. Lyonette (Eds.), *Gender inequalities in the 21st century: New barriers and continuing constraints* (pp. 19–39). Cheltenham, UK: Edward Elgar.

Scott, J., Crompton, R., & Lyonette, C. (Eds.). (2010). *Gender inequalities in the 21st century.* Cheltenham, UK: Edward Elgar.

Steele, C. M. (1997). A threat in the air: How stereotypes shape intellectual identity and performance. *American Psychologist*, 52(6), 613–629.

US Bureau of Labor Statistics (2012). *Highlights of women's earnings in 2011: October 2012, Report 1038.* Retrieved from www.bls.gov/cps/cpswom2011.pdf.

Warrington, M. and Younger, M., with Bearne, E. (2006) *Raising Boys' Achievements in Primary Schools: towards an holistic approach.* Maidenhead, UK: Open University Press.

Watt, H. M. G., & Eccles, J. S. (Eds.). (2008). *Gender and occupational outcomes: Longitudinal assessments of individual, social, and cultural influences.* Washington, DC: American Psychological Association.

PART II

The early school years

1 Peer influences on gender differences in educational aspiration and attainment

Richard A. Fabes, Sarah Hayford, Erin Pahlke, Carlos Santos, Kristina Zosuls, Carol Lynn Martin and Laura D. Hanish

Abstract

A considerable amount of research has documented that the career and academic aspirations and choices of children and adolescents are gender-typed. In general, boys and girls have different career aspirations and career choices, although girls are more flexible in their choices. The purpose of our chapter is to highlight a relatively under-represented source of influence on the development of gendered career aspirations and attainment: the role of peers and peer-related processes. In this chapter, we begin with an overview of key gender gaps in educational-related behaviors, attitudes, and goals. We then discuss some of the literature and guiding theory on peer influences that contribute to educational aspirations and achievement and how this body of research has often overlooked gender differences. We also present new evidence from preschool and elementary school children that identifies some of the gender-based influences peers have on educational and occupational achievement, interests, and attainment. We argue that the gender-segregated nature of children's peer interactions that develops across childhood and adolescence sets the stage for many of the gender differences in attitudes, beliefs, motivations, and behaviors that contribute to gender differences in aspirations and choices.

Introduction

A girl sits at a computer in a preschool classroom wearing a Batman cape when a young boy, Kye, tells her to "Take that off." The girl asks why and Kye tells her that she cannot be Batman because she is "a girl." She tells Kye that she likes Batman and Kye says that she can't because she has "to do girl things." When asked "What are girl things?" Kye responds that "Girls look after babies." He then runs off, arms spread out like Batman flying around the room. (Adapted from Freeburn & Giugni, 2008.)

Support was provided in part by grants from the National Institute of Child Health and Human Development (1 R01 HD45816-01A1), the National Science Foundation (0338864), and the T. Denny Sanford Foundation to Richard A. Fabes, Carol Lynn Martin, and Laura D. Hanish. Support for Erin Pahlke was provided, in part, by a grant from the National Science Foundation (DRL-1138114). Support was also provided by the School of Social and Family Dynamics as part of the Lives of Girls and Boys Enterprise (http://livesofgirlsandboys.org).

In this story, Kye's comments provide vivid evidence that even young children hold strong gender stereotypes about the appropriate aspirations and roles for boys and girls and men and women. His statement that girls have to do "girl things" reflects his belief that there are limits on what girls can aspire to be and what they can do when they grow up. Although this is an amusing anecdotal story, Kye's comments and reactions to the girl wearing a Batman cape also represent serious social pressures and consequences that affect the aspirations and achievement patterns of girls and boys.

A considerable amount of research has documented that the career and academic aspirations and choices of children and adolescents are gender-typed (e.g., Ceci & Williams, 2010; Correll, 2004; Sandberg, Ehrhardt, Ince, & Meyer-Bahlburg, 1991). In general, boys and girls have different career aspirations and career choices, although girls are more flexible in their choices; that is, they are more likely than boys to choose occupations held predominantly by members of the other gender. Moreover, this tendency for cross-gender occupational aspirations and choices among girls appears to increase with age (Eccles, 2011; Sandberg et al., 1991). Other research has shown that gender differences in aspirations and choices are prevalent in most if not all countries (Anker, 1998). As such, these differences are powerful and pervasive.

Many factors have been identified that contribute to gender differences in career aspirations and achievement (see, for example, Ceci & Williams, 2010) and the diverse nature of the chapters in this volume attests to this. The purpose of our chapter is to highlight a relatively under-represented source of influence on the development of gendered career aspirations and attainment: the role of peers and peer-related processes. Kye's reactions to the girl wearing the Batman cape reflect the types of peer responses that shape and mold children's behaviors, motivations, and desires and represent important and powerful sources of socialization. Moreover, the story of Kye reflects the fact that these peer influences begin early in children's development (Fabes, Hanish, & Martin, 2003, 2004; Martin et al., 2013).

In this chapter, we begin with a brief overview of key gender gaps in educational-related behaviors, attitudes, and goals. We then discuss some of the literature and guiding theory on peer influences that contribute to educational aspirations and achievement and how this body of research has often overlooked gender differences. In addition, we present new evidence from preschool and elementary school children that identifies some of the gender-based influences peers have on educational and occupational achievement, interests, and attainment. The first section presents data from preschool children to illuminate patterns of gendered play and their consequences. The second section examines gendered expectations for peer interactions among elementary school students. We argue that the gender-segregated nature of children's peer interactions that develops across childhood and adolescence sets the stage for many of the gender differences in attitudes, beliefs, motivations, and behaviors that contribute to gender differences in aspirations and choices. We end with a discussion of some of the remaining issues in this area.

Gender gaps in academic-related outcomes and processes

Despite efforts over the last several decades to reduce gender achievement gaps, differences in boys' and girls' academic outcomes remain. Beginning in elementary school and continuing through adulthood, females outperform males on literacy achievement tests, and the size of the gap increases with age (e.g., Buchmann, DiPrete, & McDaniel, 2008). Moreover, females are now also increasingly more likely than males to go to college and earn degrees (Freeman, 2005). Gaps in the *types* of degrees males and females pursue in college also remain. For instance, males continue to surpass females in their pursuit of degrees and careers in science, technology, engineering, and math (STEM) fields (Freeman, 2005).

Although the underlying causes of the gender achievement gaps that persist remain unclear, researchers have identified a number of factors that relate to future educational achievement and attainment. These behaviors, attitudes, and goals indicate areas in which boys' and girls' experiences in the school system differ and, as a result, may provide important glimpses into potential explanations for the gender differences that emerge in educational achievement, attainment, and aspirations. In this section, we identify three of these potentially relevant influences on gender differences: behaviors in the classroom, attitudes toward school, and academic goals for the future.

Behavior in classrooms

From the moment they enter school, gaps appear between boys' and girls' behavior in the classroom. In kindergarten, twice as many boys as girls struggle to pay attention (Zill & West, 2001), and throughout childhood and adolescence boys consistently engage in more disruptive classroom behaviors (Downey & Vogt Yuan, 2005; Schaefer, 2004). Further, girls are often rated by teachers as exhibiting more self-control than boys in the classroom (e.g., Ready, LoGerfo, Burkham, & Lee, 2005). Given these gender differences, it is not surprising that starting in prekindergarten and continuing throughout their educational careers, boys are about 4 times more likely than girls to be referred to school administrators, suspended, or expelled (Gilliam, 2005; Skiba, Michael, Nardo, & Peterson, 2000). Poor classroom behavior predicts poor academic achievement (Georges, Brooks-Gunn, & Malone, 2012) and the gender differences in classroom behavior have potentially important implications for understanding the gap in males' and females' educational outcomes (Pahlke, Cooper, & Fabes, 2013).

These gender differences in classroom behavior are often attributed to boys and girls maturing at different rates. In support of this hypothesis, a meta-analysis of temperament in childhood and preadolescence reported a large difference between boys' and girls' effortful control (Cohen's d = −1.01;

Else-Quest, Hyde, Goldsmith, & Van Hulle, 2006). The authors concluded that girls have a stronger ability than boys to regulate their attention and inhibit their impulses – skills that certainly serve girls well in the classroom. Although boys and girls differ in levels of effortful control, boys and girls do not differ substantially in their ability to resist temptation or in their susceptibility to distraction (Else-Quest et al., 2006; Silverman, 2003). Boys may, on the group level, have a slightly harder time regulating their behavior in the classroom, but developmental differences cannot explain all of the differences between boys' and girls' classroom behavior. Unfortunately, however, researchers have largely ignored the role of other factors – such as peer influences – in explaining gender differences in classroom behaviors. For example, Fabes and colleagues (Fabes, Martin, Hanish, Anders, & Madden-Derdich, 2003) found that boys who had a tendency to be dysregulated were more likely to show decreased levels of social and academic competence over time if they played more with other boys. In contrast, girls who were dysregulated had improved social and academic outcomes over time if they played more with other girls. Thus, the peer group seems to play an important regulatory role that contributes to differential social and academic outcomes for boys and girls.

Academic attitudes and goals

In addition to behaving more poorly in the classroom, boys also tend to have more negative attitudes about school than girls throughout their educational careers. In a study of students between the ages of 8 and 18, Sullivan, Riccio, and Reynolds (2008) found small but consistent differences in boys' and girls' negative attitudes about school. As early as kindergarten, gender differences appear in attitudes toward teachers; for example, boys are more likely than girls to think their teachers do not like or care about them (Valeski & Stipek, 2001). As with behavior in classrooms, attitudes toward school and teachers have important implications for future gender gaps in academic outcomes. Negative attitudes toward school and teachers are associated with lower achievement and lower expectations of future success (Baker, 1999; Brier, 1995). Moreover, there appears to be a negative feedback loop in place, as negative achievement leads students to have more negative attitudes about school (Valeski & Stipek, 2001). Slight gender differences in attitudes toward school at the beginning of formal schooling may, over time, result in large gender gaps in achievement and attitudes.

Students' academic goals may also be an important factor in gender gaps in achievement and attainment (see Chow & Salmela-Aro; Parker, Nagy, Trautwein, & Lüdtke; Wang & Kenny; Weiss, Wiese, & Freund, this volume). Although a few decades ago males consistently aspired to and expected to attain higher levels of educational achievement than females (e.g., Marini & Greenberger, 1978), within the last 20 years this gender difference appears to have been largely eliminated (Watt et al., 2012). This change likely both predicts and reflects current gender gaps. A child with the goal of attending college is more likely to make it into a college classroom than a child who does not share this goal. Girls' higher educational aspirations thus likely result in higher educational attainment for girls relative to boys.

Academic goals related to occupational interests are likely also important factors in gender achievement gaps. Starting at a young age, boys are more likely than girls to aspire to jobs stereotyped as masculine by our culture – such as jobs in the STEM fields (Liben & Bigler, 2002; see also Bagnoli, Demey, & Scott; Chow & Salmela-Aro; Parker et al.; Perez-Felkner, McDonald, & Schneider; Wang & Kenny, this volume). Further, girls who are interested in male-dominated career fields in early adolescence often move away from these preferences – and toward female-dominated career fields – by adulthood (Frome, Alfeld, Eccles, & Barber, 2006). Importantly, boys' interest and self-concepts in math are higher than girls' even when controlling for prior math achievement (Simpkins, Davis-Kean, & Eccles, 2006; Updegraff, Eccles, Barber, & O'Brien, 1996; see also Parker et al.; Chow & Salmela-Aro; Perez-Felkner et al.; Wang & Kenny, this volume), suggesting that gender gaps in STEM fields may persist despite the closing gender gap in performance in STEM-related domains.

Prior research investigating the role of gender in children's educational interests and performance has typically focused on the role of gender stereotypes on children's cognitions and behaviors (Ambady, Shih, Kim, & Pittinsky, 2001), and on teachers' and parents' practices with girls and boys (Eccles, Jacobs, & Harold, 1990; see also Kriesi & Buchmann; Upadyaya & Eccles, this volume). Researchers have also identified ways in which girls and boys might approach schoolwork differently (Kenney-Benson, Pomerantz, Ryan, & Patrick, 2006). However, as previously noted, existing research addressing the nature and origins of gender disparities in engagement and interest has not paid sufficient attention to the role of peers in shaping children's beliefs and attitudes related to schooling, learning, and occupational aspirations (Martin & Dinella, 2002). We now turn our attention to this important but relatively overlooked source of influence.

Peer influences on academic-related outcomes and processes

Research on the importance of peer influence on children's development dates back to the early twentieth century (see Ide, Parkerson, Haertel, & Walberg, 1981 for a brief summary of these early studies) and continues to be an important topic (Brechwald & Prinstein, 2011). Studies have consistently shown that peers shape children's expectations and aspirations for further education (Buchmann & Dalton, 2002; Cheng & Starks, 2002), motivation (Ryan, 2001), choice of courses (Crosnoe, Riegle-Crumb, Frank, Field, & Muller, 2008), grades (Cook, Deng, & Morgano, 2007; Ryan, 2001), and scores on achievement tests (Cook et al., 2007) in middle school (Ryan, 2001) and high school (Crosnoe et al., 2008; Schiller, 1999). However, boys and girls do not interact with the same peers: gender differences in peer relationships have been widely reported in the empirical literature (see Ruble, Martin, & Berenbaum, 2006). Few studies, however, have made the link between these literatures – examining how gender differences in peer relationships influence the academic aspirations and attainment of boys and girls.

Reviews of the literature on peer influences on education (Ryan, 2000; Wentzel, 2009) have identified several mechanisms through which peers influence behavior that include: providing information and help, modeling, and enforcing social norms regarding the desirability of educational success. Peer influence may also explain group differences in educational outcomes if there are group-specific norms about education that are enforced by peers (Horvat & Lewis, 2003).

The apparent influence of peers on educational outcomes may also be due to selection effects – for example, students with similar educational goals are likely to seek each other out as friends, which would lead to peer groups with shared aspirations even in the absence of a causal relationship (Kindermann & Skinner, 2009; see also Salmela-Aro, this volume). However, studies of college students show that randomly assigned first-year roommates influence academic performance (Sacerdote, 2001; Zimmerman, 2003). To our knowledge, there are no experimental analyses of peer influence during primary or secondary school, likely because peer networks cannot be randomly assigned. However, studies using methodological (e.g., examining influence during the transition to a new school) and statistical (e.g., controlling for confounding factors, analyzing change scores rather than levels) approaches to minimize selection bias have also found associations between peer characteristics and academic outcomes (Cook et al., 2007; Schiller, 1999).

To date, most research on the influence of peers has focused on the study of older children and adolescents and infrequently on younger children. Peer influences have been studied less often among younger children because peers are generally considered to be less important for them than for older children and teens. Peer influences on educational outcomes and aspirations for younger children have also likely been less studied in part because standardized outcomes are more difficult to define and measure at younger ages. Furthermore, there may have been the assumption that peer influence on school behaviors and achievement was not strong during early childhood (relative to influences during adolescence or adulthood).

However, evidence suggests that peers do have an influence on young children's early school behaviors and adjustment (Fabes, Martin, Hanish, Anders, et al., 2003; Henry & Rickman, 2007). For example, peers influence educational outcomes among preschool children by shaping the development of skills that are important for school readiness (e.g., concentration, effortful control, emotion regulation; see Fabes, Shepard, Guthrie, & Martin, 1997). Other research suggests that having familiar peers at the start of kindergarten promotes the development of positive attitudes toward school in the early years (Ladd, 1990; Ladd & Price, 1987).

Given these findings for young children, the field may benefit from examining the peer-related antecedents to children's educational aspirations and achievement. Importantly, there is now a growing consensus among educators, policymakers, parents, and researchers that what happens to children prior to their entry into the formal learning environments of elementary school has significant effects on their school-related adjustment, aspirations, and achievement (Burchinal et al., 2008; Fabes, Martin, Hanish, Anders, et al., 2003). For example, problems that arise early in children's academic careers predict school dropout (Ensminger & Slusarcick, 1992), later achievement (Grimm, Steele, Mashburn, Burchinal, & Pianta, 2010), delinquency (Tremblay et al., 1992), and mental health difficulties (Caspi, Elder, & Bem, 1987). In contrast, early school success forecasts later positive academic achievement, retention, and attainment (Entwisle, Alexander, & Olson, 1997; Hamre & Pianta, 2001). Thus, young children's early school experiences lay the foundation for their later learning and educational aspirations (Schweinhart & Weikart, 1997). We contend that young children's peer interactions provide a crucial foundation for the development of early school-related attitudes, skills, behaviors, and motivations. Moreover, these foundations vary for boys and girls and contribute to gender differences in educational aspirations and achievement (Fabes et al., 2004). We now turn our attention to these early foundations, beginning with our first empirical section.

Evidence of early peer influences on educational aspirations and achievement

From the earliest years when boys and girls first come together, they have different interactions and relationships with their peers, and they respond differently to those experiences (Fabes et al., 2004). For instance, girls (compared to boys) tend to exhibit interactional styles that are characterized by more cooperative and prosocial behaviors, more verbal interactions, and a greater relationship focus. In contrast, for boys, interactional styles tend to be characterized by more intense positive (exuberance and joy) and negative (anger and frustration) affect and behavior, competition, disruptive and off-task behavior, instrumental problem-solving, and a dominance orientation (Rose & Rudolph, 2006). In our previous research, we have found that interacting with same-sex peers tends to amplify these behaviors and characteristics. For example, Martin and Fabes (2001) found that the more time spent playing with same-sex peers, the more gender-typed children's behavior became over the course of several months (beyond their initial tendencies to engage in gender-typed behavior).

The experiences that boys and girls have in their segregated peer groups contribute to many aspects of their development in both positive and negative ways, and this contribution is likely to be above and beyond the individual differences that lead children to initially select themselves into same-sex peer groups (Martin & Fabes, 2001). Experiences gained within boys' and girls' groups foster different behavioral norms and interaction styles, and, over time, these interactions may promote the development of different school-related skills, attitudes, motives, interests, and aspirations (Berenbaum, Martin, Hanish, Briggs, & Fabes, 2008).

Although there is much speculation about the importance of the different peer subcultures of girls and boys (Leaper, 1994; Maccoby, 1998), direct evidence linking early same-sex peer experiences and behavioral outcomes has been limited. The research that is needed to answer questions about long-term effects on behavior is difficult to conduct, largely due to the need for direct observations of children's behavior and to the difficulties of analyzing complex relationship data. Nonetheless, there is compelling evidence that peer interactions at preschool influence children's behavior in several domains (Martin & Fabes, 2001). These findings have led us to re-conceptualize the prevailing view of peer socialization effects.

Binary and gradient views of peer socialization

The leading conceptual view concerning how playing with girls or playing with boys influences children's development has been a *binary view* of socialization (Maccoby, 1998). According to this view, the socialization experiences children have with same-sex peers are thought to be relatively uniform across all members of the group. Because most children spend relatively more time with same-sex peers than with other-sex peers, they are thought to be exposed to sufficient levels of the peer subculture to experience the influence of those peers. This view can be interpreted as de-emphasizing individual differences and emphasizing the binary nature of the groups – i.e., differences between the sexes. The implication of this view is that there is a low threshold for socialization effects and that a relatively small amount of exposure to one's same-sex peer group is needed to learn the norms and styles of one's own-sex group.

Our data suggest that the binary view needs to be expanded. Rather than finding only binary effects, we have found that individual differences in degree of exposure to same-sex peers made a difference in children's outcomes. Based on this work, we proposed a *gradient view* in which same-sex peer effects are "dosage dependent" – the more exposure a child has to same-sex peers, the more the child will show the influence of these experiences (Martin & Fabes, 2001). For example, we found that boys who played more extensively with boys during the fall term of preschool were observed in the spring term showing higher levels of activity, rough-and-tumble play, playing apart from adults, and gender-typed play (e.g., activities). In contrast, girls who played more with other girls during the fall term of preschool were observed in the spring term showing higher levels of playing near adults and gender-typed play. Thus, in addition to binary effects, gradient effects – i.e., individual differences in same-sex peer exposure – need to be considered.

The binary and gradient views suggest different outcomes of same-sex peer experiences on school-related behavior and success. A strict binary view would suggest that peer socialization should uniformly move children toward the type of behavior, interaction style, or activity consistent with their own gender group. For instance, boys would be expected to become more "rough and tumble," more active, less compliant, less attentive, less regulated, less adult-oriented, and to show more externalizing behaviors and conduct problems. In contrast, girls would be expected to become less rough and tumble, less active, more compliant, more attentive, more well-regulated, more adult-oriented, and show few externalizing behavior problems (Fabes, Hanish, & Martin, 2007; Martin & Fabes, 2001).

Most importantly, guided by the gradient perspective, we expect that the degree to which children play in same-sex peer groups will affect educational outcomes, and this influence will be different for boys and girls. This influence is expected to operate through individual differences in the opportunities children have to be exposed to the skills, influence, and interaction styles of boys' and girls' groups. In particular, children who spend more of their time with peers who are able to focus and shift attention when appropriate and regulate behavior are likely to learn these skills as compared to children who spend more time with dysregulated peers. It is expected that children will learn these behaviors through modeling and vicarious reinforcement/punishment. In addition, they will learn from their peers the rules regulating when certain forms of behavior are expected in school and play situations. Boys (particularly those who play frequently with other boys) would be expected to have more opportunities for exposure to a relatively unregulated style of play and interaction, whereas girls (particularly those who play more frequently with other girls) would be expected to have relatively more opportunities for exposure to regulated and adult-oriented styles of play. Over time, girls' experiences might promote further development of regulated play and prosocial interactional and influence styles compared to boys' experiences (Fabes, Hanish, Martin, Reesing, & Moss, 2012), which would eventually contribute to gender differences in educational outcomes.

In addition to influencing styles of play, peer experiences are likely to influence children's choices of activities. Preschool children are embedded in learning environments with a large number of activity choices. Different play activities in the preschool environment foster the development of different skills and interests. For example, playing with blocks provides opportunities for children to learn about sizes, shapes, numbers, order, area, length, patterns, and weight. Children must make choices about which activities to engage in, and their activity choices may channel their skill and interest development by providing greater opportunities to practice some skills and fewer opportunities to practice other skills (Hanley, Cammilleri, Tiger, & Ingvarsson, 2007). Boys, for instance, have been found to spend more time in math/science activities when playing with other boys than they do when they play alone or when girls play either with peers or alone (Fabes et al., 2007). Because different types of activities place different types of cognitive and learning demands on children (Kontos & Keyes, 1999), an examination of the relations of children's peer contexts and activity engagement to school motivation and adjustment seems critical to understanding the influence of early peer relationships. Moreover, differences in early activity interests and preferences may well set the stage for later differences in educational aspirations and achievement.

Study I: Time use in preschoolers' activity play

To explore the degree to which playing with same-sex peers might influence activity choices of young children, we present data from a short-term longitudinal study in which we observed children over the course of the fall and spring. As part of a larger study, 34 male and 25 female preschoolers (mean age = 48.6 months; range = 37 to 64 months) from two university-affiliated full-day preschools and a community Head Start (federally funded preschool program for low-income families) classroom in a large metropolitan area in the southwestern United States were observed during the course of their daily interactions at school. Using a randomized list of the children, observers conducted brief (10 seconds) observations of each child and noted whether the child was playing alone or with other children (observations of teacher–child interactions were not included in these analyses). When a child was observed playing with peers, the observer recorded the identity of each of the peers (up to a maximum of five). In addition, the observer noted the activity in which the child was engaged (e.g., swinging, block play, dress-up). When the observer finished the list of children, he/she started over. Children were observed principally during free-play time when they were free to choose playmates and activities. A total of 32,356 observations were collected (13,822 observations during the fall semester and 18,534 observations during the spring semester).

We focus our analyses on two types of activities. The first is on block play – stereotypically a masculine activity that is thought to contribute to greater spatial competencies and interests. The second is on language play – which includes talking, reading, singing, and spelling – and reflects play that contributes to greater verbal skills and interests, which is generally stereotyped as a feminine activity. We present the data separately for boys and girls, broken down by type of peer context: playing alone, same-sex dyadic play, other-sex dyadic play, same-sex group play, other-sex group play, and mixed-sex group play (playing with both a same- and other-sex peer). To examine changes over the course of the year, the data are separated for the fall and spring semesters. Finally, because there are different numbers of observations for boys and girls, we present the non-aggregated percentages of play within each of the peer contexts.

As can be seen in Figure 1.1A, across all observations over both semesters, boys engaged in more block play than girls, $t = 13.09$, $p < .001$. What is more interesting, however, is the variability from fall to spring across the various peer

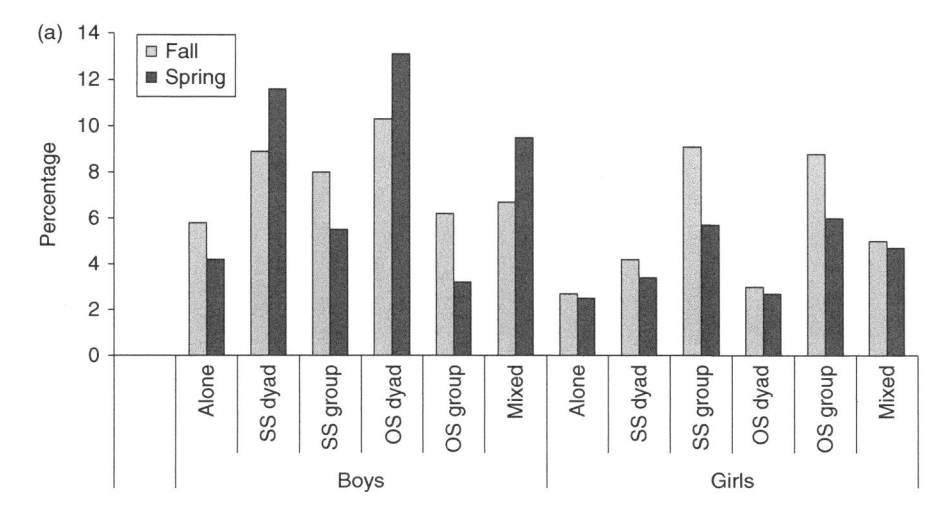

Figure 1.1A *Percentage of block play: by sex, peer context, and semester*

contexts for boys and girls. For boys, the percentage of time spent playing with blocks while playing alone did not change much from fall to spring. Thus, their solitary interest in block play was relatively constant across the year. However, this was not the case for play with peers. For same-sex dyadic and group play, rates of block play among boys increased from fall to spring. In contrast, rates of block play decreased from fall to spring when playing with girls (e.g., other-sex dyadic and group play). In mixed-sex play, when boys were playing with *both* a male and female peer, rates also increased. Thus, the presence of a boy in their peer play increased rates of block play over time whereas the presence of only girls in the peer interactions was related to decreased rates of block play.

For girls, a different pattern emerged. Rates of block play were highest in the fall when they were playing with boys but these rates dropped from fall to spring. Rates were relatively low when playing alone or when playing only with other girls. For girls, rates were relatively unchanged across most of the peer contexts and the effect of peers appears to be that playing with boys was related to a drop in block play over time – which also paralleled the pattern observed for boys when playing with only girls. Such findings suggest that when boys and girls play within peer contexts that involve only members of the other sex, play may become more gender-scripted when they are engaged in activities that are gender-typed for the other sex. Activity play that is gender-typed may make it more difficult to maintain play with other-sex peers. As a result, other-sex play may increasingly move to gender-neutral activities if boys and girls are going to remain together in their play. Thus, block play involving other-sex peers may be reduced over time and children must find other activities to sustain play involving only peers of the other sex (see Figure 1.1A).

For language play (Figure 1.1B), across all observations and contexts, girls evidenced relatively higher rates of language play than did boys, $t = -4.20$, p

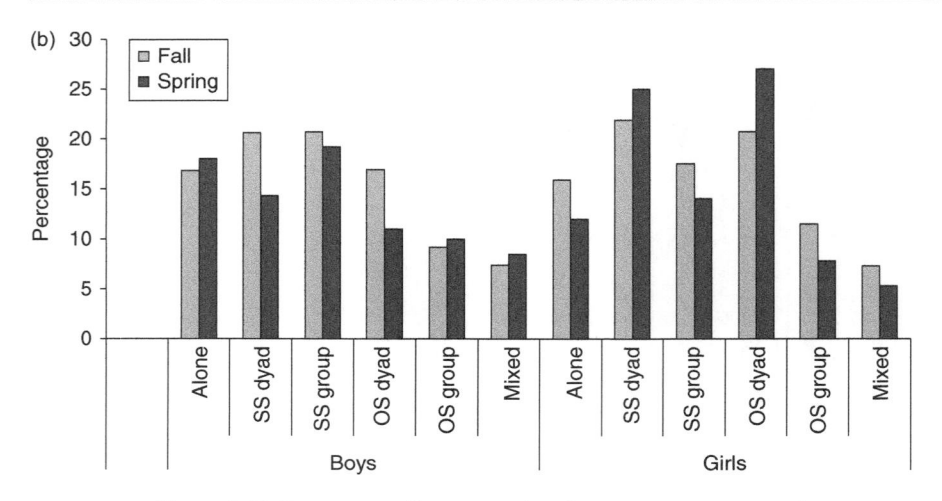

Figure 1.1B *Percentage of language play: by sex, peer context, and semester*

< .001. However, in comparison to the patterns found for block play, we see almost the opposite patterns emerging across peer contexts and semesters. For boys, language play was relatively consistent across peer contexts except when playing with girls (other-sex play) and then was reduced from fall to spring. For girls, language play dropped over time in all peer contexts except for play with other girls, where it increased from fall to spring (see Figure 1.1B).

These findings highlight *binary* effects – within the context of same-sex play, activity engagement appears to lead to overall gender-related differences in the skills and interests boys and girls exhibit. However, other data support a *gradient* effect. Proportion of time spent in same-sex play in the fall was positively correlated with later block play in the spring for boys but not for girls. Importantly, we controlled for level of block play in the fall in these correlations, partial rs = .42 and .13, ps < .01 and n.s., respectively, for boys and girls. In contrast, for language play, greater same-sex play in the fall was positively related to language play in the spring for girls but inversely related for boys, partial rs = .44 and −.39, ps < .01, respectively. Thus, for both sexes, more time spent playing with same-sex peers was related to later gender-typed patterns of activity play beyond their initial levels in the fall that may have led them to select peers who have similar interests. As such, individual differences in same-sex play have a "dosage effect" that reflects a gradient type of influence.

Taken together, these data suggest that same-sex peer play contexts likely contribute to boys' and girls' heightened interest and engagement in activities that are stereotypically consistent with their gender roles. Moreover, rates of engagement while playing alone did not change much from fall to spring, reflecting the fact that there was not a uniform change in interest and engagement in these activities. Rather, the variability observed was in the rates observed across peer contexts and these changes were uniformly in directions that were consistent with gender roles (higher rates in block play for boys and higher rates in language play for girls when involved with same- rather than other-sex peers). Given that spatial abilities foster math skills and verbal abilities foster literacy skills, it appears that the context of peer play may set the stage for gender differences in abilities and interests to emerge.

Attitudes about peers and their relation to educational aspirations and achievement

Although research such as that just reviewed demonstrates the effects of children's preferences for interacting with same-sex children, relatively less is known about the quality of children's thoughts and feelings about same-sex compared to other-sex peers that underlie those preferences (Martin & Ruble, 2010). Gender researchers and casual observers alike often interpret children's gender segregation and occasional negative evaluative comments (such as Kye's comments in the story at the beginning of this chapter) as indications that girl–boy relationships are characterized by animosity; however, existing research provides little support for this view (Kowalski, 2007; Zosuls et al., 2011). This is not to say that children's evaluations of other-sex peers are free of intergroup bias. Children report feeling more positively about their own sex as early as in preschool (Yee & Brown, 1994) and these biases appear to be present throughout the elementary school years (Heyman, 2001; Verkuyten & Thijs, 2001). Nonetheless, important questions remain about the nature of these biases and their consequences for children's peer interactions.

Researchers interested in the role of gender in children's academic achievement and aspirations have typically addressed issues related to gender stereotypes concerning competence in different domains (e.g., boys as superior in science and math) and gender differences in academic-related self-beliefs and academic behaviors (Eccles, Wigfield, Harold, & Blumenfeld, 1993; Kenney-Benson et al., 2006; see also Kriesi & Buchmann; Chow & Salmela-Aro; Parker et al.; Perez-Felkner et al.; Upadyaya & Eccles; Wang & Kenny, this volume). Although these areas are of clear relevance, we suggest that children's interpersonal experiences and attitudes related to same- and other-sex peers might also play an important role in children's academic lives.

Children's propensity to interact more with same-sex peers might affect their school adjustment in positive and negative ways depending on the quality of children's interactions with their peers and their feelings about same- and other-sex children. If children feel uncomfortable with or dislike other-sex children, or fear being teased for interacting with other-sex children, such feelings might negatively impact children's school experiences. For example, discomfort and anxiety associated with interacting with the other sex could limit interactions and engagement in group classroom projects and exercises. In contrast, generally positive feelings about both same- and other-sex peers might serve as protective factors and even promote more positive feelings about school. Thus, gaining a better understanding of how children feel about same- and other-sex peers and how such feelings relate more broadly to children's feelings about school might hold implications for educational outcomes including aspirations and achievement.

Study II: Children's feelings about same- and other-sex children

In a study involving 98 (63 girls, 35 boys) fifth-grade students from schools in the Phoenix, Arizona metropolitan area in the United States, we investigated children's feelings about same- and other-sex children using a new measure we developed that separately assessed positive and negative affective attitudes (Zosuls et al., 2011). Affective attitudes were measured using two scales that separately assess positive (seven items) and negative (seven items) feelings (e.g., happy, angry). For each item, children were asked, "How many boys/girls make you feel ..." and responded on a scale from 0 (*none*) to 3 (*all*). Results from repeated *measures* ANOVAs on each scale were consistent with the idea that children's gender-related intergroup biases are characterized more by in-group favoritism than out-group derogation. Girls and boys showed a positive in-group bias, expressing significantly more positive attitudes about their own group ($F(1, 96) = 60.07$, $p < .001$, $\eta^2 = .39$). In contrast, neither girls nor boys expressed significantly more negative feelings about the other gender ($F(1, 96) = .15$, n.s.), and expressed low levels of negativity toward either gender. Interestingly, only positive affective attitudes were correlated with a more global measure of children's gender-related attitudes toward same- ($r = .41$) and other-sex ($r = .31$) peers used in previous research (Yee & Brown, 1994). This two-item measure asked children to respond to the questions "How do you feel about girls?" and "How do you feel about boys?" on a 7-point scale from 1 (*don't like at all*) to 7 (*like a lot*) with corresponding smiley faces that ranged from a big frown, to a straight neutral mouth, to a big smile. Consistent with intergroup theory perspectives (e.g., Brewer, 2001), our results indicated that children's positive affective attitudes were distinct from their negative affective attitudes. Furthermore, although we can infer some general ideas about children's gender-related intergroup attitudes from their behavioral avoidance of other-sex peers, direct assessment of children's attitudes revealed the rather surprising finding that children expressed little negativity toward other-sex peers. Given these findings, why do children avoid other-sex peers if they do not dislike them? Other aspects of our research program have been addressing the role of children's beliefs and expectancies about interacting with other-sex peers as barriers to cross-sex interactions.

Study III: Children's beliefs and expectations about interacting with same- and other-sex peers

Aside from a lack of research on children's gender-related attitudes, little is known about children's cognitions related to interacting with same- and other-sex peers in various contexts, including school. In the same study of fifth graders, we also explored children's beliefs and expectancies about interacting with same- and other-sex peers. In one set of questions, we presented children with scenarios in which a male or female student working on a project (i.e., putting together a puzzle, presenting a poster) is approached by another student of unspecified gender and asked what they thought the girl or boy would say. Children were presented with response options that were masculine (i.e., independent, self-promoting), feminine (i.e., help-seeking, self-effacing), or neutral statements. Results indicated that both boys and girls expected children to act in gender stereotype-consistent ways and girls were especially likely to expect stereotype-consistent behaviors. For example, the majority of girls expected that a boy would say to another child, "Look at my awesome poster!" whereas girls would say, "Do you think my poster looks ok? I'm not sure it's good." In contrast, although boys' responses were also generally stereotype-consistent, they tended to expect boys to respond in masculine and feminine ways with approximately the same frequency. These results suggest that children, especially girls, approach interpersonal situations with gender-stereotyped expectations about others' behaviors. The stereotypes assessed in this measure are highly relevant to academic contexts and the findings indicate that children, especially girls, expect boys to be assertive and confident and girls to be tentative and self-effacing in their approach to their own work. These expectations likely reinforce classroom dynamics in which boys are more dominant.

Study IV: Perceived costs of interacting with same- and other-sex peers

In addition to gender-stereotyped expectations about interacting with their peers, children might also hold different values and perceived costs related to interacting with same- and same-sex peers. To explore this facet of children's gender-related intergroup relations, our study of fifth graders also assessed children's outcome expectancies related to interacting with same- and other-sex peers. In this measure, we used vignettes of various situations involving interactions with same- and other-sex peers, and asked children about their expectations of inclusion (e.g., being included by a group of girls in a game) and values/enjoyment (e.g., how much they would want to play with a group of same-/other-sex peers), and their expectations of psychological and social costs (e.g., being teased) for interacting with same- and other-sex peers. As expected, children had higher expectations for inclusion and values/enjoyment related to interacting with same-sex peers and perceived greater costs involved with interacting with other-sex peers (Zosuls et al., 2011). Furthermore, regression analyses exploring the relation between children's affective attitudes and outcome expectancies revealed that more positive and less negative feelings about the other sex are related to higher expectancies and values and lower perceived costs related to interacting with the other sex (Zosuls et al., 2011). Thus, children who feel more positively about the other sex also come to the peer context with more positive expectations and thoughts about interacting with other-sex peers. In contrast, children who feel more negatively about the other sex perceive more costs associated with interacting with other-sex peers. Existing research indicates that even infrequently occurring events, such as peers' evaluative comments, can be psychologically impactful and lead to negative attitudes about the other sex (Altermatt, Pomerantz, Ruble, Frey, & Greulich, 2002). Thus, over time, such attitudes are likely to impact their evaluations of interacting with the other sex and their perceptions of educational tasks and opportunities in which they likely will encounter members of the other sex (such as girls who want to take advanced science courses). As such, children's perceptions of the costs associated with engaging in tasks that involve the other sex might adversely lead to negative evaluations about such tasks and their beliefs about their own abilities to succeed in such tasks.

Given these findings, we also expected children who have more positive feelings and expectations related to interacting with both same- and other-sex peers to also feel more positively about their school experiences and like school better. Indeed, our analyses suggest that children who feel more positively about interacting with same- and other-sex peers also report greater school liking ($rs = .23$ and .24, respectively). Furthermore, children who had higher expectancies related to being included by and having fun with the other sex also reported greater school liking ($r = .28$). Although these findings are correlational, they imply that children's gender-related attitudes have implications that extend beyond preferences for friendships and playmates, and may be important to children's more general liking and engagement in school. Clearly more research in this area is needed and our ongoing program of research is investigating these questions.

Conclusions

The body of research reviewed and presented in this chapter underscores the important role that peers can have in influencing educational aspirations and achievement. The data presented in this chapter highlight that peer influences on activity choices and interactions appear early in development and may set the stage for later school experiences and academic trajectories. Our chapter supports the conclusion that peer relationships and interactions differ for boys and girls and that these gender differences may produce differential educational outcomes for boys and girls. As Fabes et al. (2004) argued, peer relationships are frequently organized by gender and these gender-organized relationships have important short- and long-term outcomes for boys and girls in and out of school. Thus, more research is warranted on the role of peers and gender-related school experiences and educational outcomes.

The chapter also identified limitations in the extant literature on peer influences on gender differences in educational aspirations and attainment. When gender is considered in peer relationships research, it is most often considered as a static category. However, as we have discussed in this chapter, gradient approaches are important to consider as variations in girls' and boys' experiences with and attitudes about same- and other-sex peers play an important role in children's peer relationships and stereotyping. Little research, however, has linked gender attitudes toward peers and stereotyping with academic outcomes. The data on gendered attitudes about peers presented in this chapter offer evidence of the effects of gender attitudes and stereotyping in influencing children's behaviors and feelings about school. Additional studies focusing on the specific mechanisms and antecedents of gender attitudes toward peers are needed, as are longitudinal studies investigating the ways in which children's attitudes toward and experiences with same- and other-sex peers influence academic experiences and outcomes.

Another limitation to consider is related to the measurement of educational achievement. Although standardized test scores remain the gold standard in research on education, the intense focus on standardized scores ignores other important educational outcomes – such as school liking, absence from school, and academic engagement – that may affect children's educational performance and adjustment. Moreover, despite their limitations (i.e., lack of standardization), student grades are nonetheless another important educational outcome that need to be considered (and appear to reflect larger gender gaps; see Buchmann et al., 2008).

Additionally, researchers need to carefully consider their data-collection techniques. For example, Fabes and colleagues (Fabes, Martin, & Hanish, 2003) have employed intensive observational methods of preschoolers' peer interactions. Intensive observations offer a dynamic understanding of the complexities involved in children's peer interactions – complexities of dynamics that are difficult to examine using self-report measures taken at one moment in time (DiDonato et al., 2012). A more detailed understanding of children's interpersonal exchanges with same- and other-sex peers can help identify specific behaviors and patterns of interaction that are especially influential or problematic. Thus, such approaches may offer important insights for future interventions as they highlight the gendered-peer processes associated with important educational outcomes.

To understand peers' potential in influencing gender differences in educational achievement and aspiration, researchers need to distinguish between peer selection and influence effects (Crosnoe et al., 2008). Nonetheless, this potential confound is often overlooked in gender differences research on educational outcomes. For example, in research on same-sex schooling and educational outcomes, girls in all-girl schools have sometimes been perceived to hold less gender-stereotyped aspirations than those in mixed-sex schools (e.g., Thompson, 2003; see also Sullivan & Joshi, this volume). However, caution is warranted in attributing these outcomes to the single-sex classroom environment because it may be that girls who are open to non-gender-stereotypic courses and occupations select themselves (or their parents select them) into all-girl schools. Thus, there may be a selection bias such that girls who have non-gender-stereotypic interests are more likely to enroll in single-sex schools. As such, the outcomes are a reflection of these selection processes rather than the influence of the same-sex peer environment. Thus, peer effects may play a role in enhancing qualities of the students that led them to be selected into the classrooms in the first place, but to know this we must control for initial selection effects (Martin et al., 2013). Moreover, there is other evidence that single-sex school environments increase gender-stereotypic behavior and attitudes (Fabes, Martin, Hanish, Galligan, & Pahlke, 2013; Fabes, Pahlke, Martin, & Hanish, 2013; Halpern et al., 2011) because of the increased contact with same-sex peers and the heightened salience of gender within gender-segregated school contexts.

In conclusion, as educators and researchers consider ways to minimize gender gaps in boys' and girls' educational aspirations and achievement, they should consider the ways in which peers may contribute to these gaps. Starting at a young age, boys' and girls' peer groups are segregated, and they have markedly different experiences within these groups. Further, the new data presented in this chapter suggest that peers have the potential to play an important role in shaping boys' and girls' educational outcomes, and that this potential appears early in development. Consideration of the influence of gender-related peer processes on educational achievement and aspirations should also help improve the effectiveness of interventions designed to close gender gaps (Fabes, Hanish, & Martin, 2010).

References

Altermatt, E. R., Pomerantz, E. M., Ruble, D. N., Frey, K. S., & Greulich, F. K. (2002). Predicting changes in children's self-perceptions of academic competence: A naturalistic examination of evaluative discourse among classmates. *Developmental Psychology*, 38, 903–917. doi: 10.1037/0012-1649.38.6.903.

Ambady, N., Shih, M., Kim, A., & Pittinsky, T. L. (2001). Stereotype susceptibility in children: Effects of identity activation on quantitative performance. *Psychological Science*, 12, 385–390. doi: 10.1111/1467-9280.00371.

Anker, R. (1998). *Gender and jobs: Sex segregation of occupations around the world.* Geneva: International Labour Office.

Baker, J. (1999). Teacher–student interaction in at-risk classrooms: Differential behavior, relationship quality, and student satisfaction with school. *The Elementary School Journal*, 100, 57–70. doi: 10.1086/461943.

Berenbaum, S., Martin, C. L., Hanish, L. D., Briggs, P. T., & Fabes, R. A. (2008). Sex differences in children's play. In K. Berkley, J. Herman, & E. Young (Eds.), *Sex differences in the brain: From genes to behavior* (pp. 275–290). New York: Oxford University Press.

Brechwald, W. A., & Prinstein, M. J. (2011). Beyond homophily: A decade of advances in understanding peer influence processes. *Journal of Research on Adolescence*, 21, 166–179. doi: 10.1111/j.1532-7795.2010.00721.x.

Brewer, M. B. (2001). Ingroup identification and intergroup conflict: When does ingroup love become outgroup hate? In R. Ashmore & L. Jussim (Eds.), *Social identity, intergroup conflict, and conflict reduction* (pp. 17–41). New York: Oxford University Press.

Brier, N. (1995). Predicting anti-social behavior in youngsters displaying poor academic achievement: A review of risk factors. *Journal of Developmental and Behavioral Pediatrics*, 16, 271–276. doi: 10.1097/00004703-199508000-00010.

Buchmann, C., & Dalton, B. (2002). Interpersonal influences and educational aspirations in 12 countries: The importance of institutional context. *Sociology of Education*, 75, 99–122. doi: 10.2307/3090287.

Buchmann, C., DiPrete, T. A., & McDaniel, A. (2008). Gender inequalities in education. *Annual Review of Sociology*, 34, 319–337. doi: 10.1146/annurev.soc.34.040507.134719.

Burchinal, M., Howes, C., Pianta, R., Bryant, D., Early, D., Clifford, R., & Barbarin, O. (2008). Predicting child outcomes at the end of kindergarten from the quality of pre-kindergarten teacher–child interactions and instruction. *Applied Developmental Sciences*, 12, 140–153. doi: 10.1080/10888690802199418.

Caspi, A., Elder, G. H., & Bem, D. J. (1987). Moving against the world: Life-course patterns of explosive children. *Developmental Psychology*, 23, 308–313. doi: 10.1037/0012-1649.23.2.308.

Ceci, S. J., & Williams, W. M. (2010). *The mathematics of sex: How biology and society conspire to limit talented women and girls*. Oxford University Press.

Cheng, S., & Starks, B. (2002). Racial differences in the effects of significant others on students' educational expectations. *Sociology of Education*, 75, 306–327. doi: 10.2307/3090281.

Cook, T. D., Deng, Y., & Morgano, E. (2007). Friendship influences during early adolescence: The special role of friends' grade point average. *Journal of Research on Adolescence*, 17, 325–356. doi: 10.1111/j.1532-7795.2007.00525.x.

Correll, S. J. (2004). Constraints into preferences: Gender, status, and emerging career aspirations. *American Sociological Review*, 69, 93–113. doi: 10.1177/000312240406900106.

Crosnoe, R., Riegle-Crumb, C., Frank, K., Field, S., & Muller, C. (2008). Peer group contexts of girls' and boys' academic experiences. *Child Development*, 79, 139–155. doi: 10.1111/j.1467-8624.2007.01116.x.

DiDonato, M. D., Martin, C. L., Hessler, E. E., Amazeen, P. G., Hanish, L. D., & Fabes, R. A. (2012). Gender consistency and flexibility: Using dynamics to understand the relationship between gender and adjustment. *Nonlinear Dynamics Psychology and Life Sciences*, 16, 159–184.

Downey, D. B., & Vogt Yuan, A. S. (2005). Sex differences in school performance during high school: Puzzling patterns and possible explanations. *The Sociological Quarterly*, 46, 299–321. doi: 10.1111/j.1533-8525.2005.00014.x.

Eccles, J. S. (2011). Gendered educational and occupational choices: Applying the Eccles et al. model of achievement-related choices. *International Journal of Behavioral Development*, 35, 195–201. doi: 10.1177/0165025411398185.

Eccles, J. S., Jacobs, J. E., & Harold, R. D. (1990). Gender-role stereotypes, expectancy effects, and parents' role in the socialization of gender differences in self-perceptions and skill acquisition. *Journal of Social Issues*, 46, 182–201. doi: 10.1111/j.1540-4560.1990.tb01929.x.

Eccles, J. S., Wigfield, A., Harold, R., & Blumenfeld, P. (1993). Age and gender differences in children's achievement self-perceptions during the elementary school years. *Child Development*, 65, 830–847. doi: 10.2307/1131221.

Else-Quest, N. M., Hyde, J. S., Goldsmith, H. H., & Van Hulle, C. A. (2006). Gender differences in temperament: A meta-analysis. *Psychological Bulletin*, 132, 33–72. doi: 10.1037/0033-2909.132.1.33.

Ensminger, M. E., & Slusarcick, A. L. (1992). Paths to high school graduation and dropout: A longitudinal study of a first-grade cohort. *Sociology of Education*, 85, 95–113. doi: 10.2307/2112677.

Entwisle, D. R., Alexander, K. L., & Olson, L. S. (1997). *Children, schools, and inequality*. New York: Westview Press.

Fabes, R. A., Hanish, L. D., & Martin, C. L. (2003). Children at play: The role of peers in understanding the effects of childcare. *Child Development*, 74, 1039–1043. doi: 10.1111/1467-8624.00586.

(2004). The next 50 years: Considering gender as a context for understanding young children's peer relationships. *Merrill-Palmer Quarterly*, 50, 260–273. doi: 10.1353/mpq.2004.0017.

(2007). Peer interactions and the gendered social ecology of preparing young children for school. *Early Childhood Services*, 1, 144–156.

(2010). *Interventions to improve relationships between girls and boys*. Paper presented at the biennial Gender Development Research Conference, San Francisco.

Fabes, R. A., Hanish, L. D., Martin, C. L., Reesing, A., & Moss, A. (2012). The effects of young children's affiliations with prosocial peers on subsequent emotionality in social interactions. *British Journal of Developmental Psychology*, 30, 569–585. doi: 10.1111/j.2044-835X.2011.02073.x.

Fabes, R. A., Martin, C. L., & Hanish, L. D. (2003). Qualities of young children's same-, other-, and mixed-sex play. *Child Development*, 74, 921–932.

Fabes, R. A., Martin, C. L., Hanish, L. D., Anders, M. C., & Madden-Derdich, D. A. (2003). Early school competence: The roles of sex-segregated play and effortful control. *Developmental Psychology*, 39, 848–859.

Fabes, R. A., Martin, C. L., Hanish, L. D., Galligan, K., & Pahlke, E. (2013). Gender segregated schooling: A problem disguised as a solution. *Educational Policy*, 26. doi: 10.1177/0895904813492382.

Fabes, R. A., Pahlke, E., Martin, C. L., & Hanish, L. D. (2013). Gender-segregated schooling and gender stereotyping. *Educational Studies*, 39, 315–319. doi: 10.1080/03055698.2012.760442.

Fabes, R. A., Shepard, S. A., Guthrie, I. K., & Martin, C. L. (1997). Roles of temperamental arousal and gender-segregated play in young children's social adjustment. *Developmental Psychology*, 33, 693–702.

Freeburn, T., & Giugni, M. (2008). Girls can't be Batman! *Every Child*, 14, 32–33.

Freeman, C. E. (2005). *Trends in educational equity of girls and women: 2004* (NCES 2005–016). Washington, DC: US Government Printing Office.

Frome, P. M., Alfeld, C. J., Eccles, J. S., & Barber, B. L. (2006). Why don't they want a male dominated job? An investigation of young women who changed their occupational aspirations. *Educational Research and Evaluation*, 12, 359–372. doi: 10.1080/13803610600765786.

Georges, A., Brooks-Gunn, J., & Malone, L. M. (2012). Links between young children's behavior and achievement. *American Behavioral Scientist*, 56, 961–990. doi: 10.1177/0002764211409196.

Gilliam, W. S. (2005). *Prekindergarteners left behind: Expulsion rates in state prekindergarten systems*. Retrieved from www.plan4preschool.org/documents/pk-expulsion.pdf.

Grimm, K. J., Steele, J. S., Mashburn, A. J., Burchinal, M. M., & Pianta, R. C. (2010). Early behavioral associations of achievement trajectories. *Developmental Psychology*, 46, 976–983.

Halpern, D. F., Eliot, L., Bigler, R. S., Fabes, R. A., Hanish, L. D., Hyde, J., et al. (2011). The pseudoscience of single-sex schooling. *Science*, 333, 1706–1707. doi: 10.1126/science.1205031.

Hamre, B. K., & Pianta, R. C. (2001). Early teacher–child relationships and the trajectory of children's school outcomes through eighth grade. *Child Development*, 72, 625–638. doi: 10.1111/1467-8624.00301.

Hanley, G., Cammilleri, A., Tiger, J., & Ingvarsson, E. (2007). A method for describing preschoolers' activity preferences. *Journal of Applied Behavior Analysis*, 40, 603–618. doi: 10.1901/jaba.2007.603-618.

Henry, G. T., & Rickman, D. K. (2007). Do peers influence children's skill development in preschool? *Economics of Education Review*, 26, 100–112. doi: 10.1016/j.econedurev.2005.09.006.

Heyman, G. D. (2001). Children's interpretation of ambiguous behavior: Evidence for a "boys are bad" bias. *Social Development*, 10, 230–247. doi: 10.1111/1467-9507.00161.

Horvat, E. M. N., & Lewis, K. S. (2003). Reassessing the "burden of 'acting white'": The importance of peer groups in managing academic success. *Sociology of Education*, 76, 265–280. doi: 10.2307/1519866.

Ide, J. K., Parkerson, J. A., Haertel, G. D., & Walberg, H. J. (1981). Peer group influence on educational outcomes: A quantitative synthesis. *Journal of Educational Psychology*, 73, 472–484. doi: 10.1037/0022-0663.73.4.472.

Kenney-Benson, G. A., Pomerantz, E. M., Ryan, A. M., & Patrick, H. (2006). Sex differences in math performance: The role of children's approach to schoolwork. *Developmental Psychology*, 42, 11–26. doi: 10.1037/0012-1649.42.1.11.

Kindermann, T. A., & Skinner, E. A. (2009). How do naturally existing peer groups shape children's academic development during sixth grade? *European Journal of Psychological Science*, 3, 31–43.

Kontos, S., & Keyes, L. (1999). An ecobehavioral analysis of early childhood classrooms. *Early Childhood Research Quarterly*, 14, 35–50. doi: 10.1016/S0885-2006(99)80003-9.

Kowalski, K. (2007). The development of social identity and intergroup attitudes in young children. In O. N. Saracho & B. Spodek (Eds.), *Contemporary perspectives on social learning in early childhood education* (pp. 51–84). Charlotte, NC: Information Age Publishing.

Ladd, G. W. (1990). Having friends, keeping friends, making friends, and being liked by peers in the classroom: Predictors of children's early school adjustment? *Child Development*, 61, 1081–1100. doi: 10.2307/1130877.

Ladd, G. W., & Price, J. M. (1987). Predicting children's social and school adjustment following the transition from preschool to kindergarten. *Child Development*, 58, 1168–1189. doi: 10.2307/1130613.

Leaper, C. (1994). Exploring the consequences of gender segregation on social relationships. In C. Leaper (Ed.), *Childhood gender segregation: Causes and consequences* (pp. 67–86). San Francisco, CA: Jossey-Bass.

Liben, L. S., & Bigler, R. S. (2002). The developmental course of gender differentiation: Conceptualizing, measuring and evaluating constructs and pathways. *Monographs of the Society for Research in Child Development*, 67(2, Serial No. 269), 1–147. doi: 10.1111/1540-5834.t01-1-00190.

Maccoby, E. E. (1998). *The two sexes: Growing up apart, coming together*. Cambridge, MA: Belknap Press.

Marini, M. M., & Greenberger, E. (1978). Sex differences in educational aspirations and expectations. *American Educational Research Journal*, 15, 67–79. doi: 10.2307/1162688.

Martin, C. L., & Dinella, L. (2002). Children's gender cognitions, the social environment, and sex differences in the cognitive domain. In A. McGillicuddy-De Lisi & R. De Lisi (Eds.), *Biology, society, and behavior: The development of sex differences in cognition* (pp. 207–239). Westport, CT: Ablex.

Martin, C. L. & Fabes, R. A. (2001). The stability and consequences of young children's same-sex peer interactions. *Developmental Psychology*, 37, 431–446. doi: 10.1037/0012-1649.37.3.431.

Martin, C. L., Kornienko, O., Schaefer, D. R., Hanish, L. D., Fabes, R. A., & Goble, P. (2013). The role of sex of peers and gender-typed activities in young children's peer affiliative networks: A longitudinal analysis of selection and influence. *Child Development*, 84, 921–937. doi: 10.1111.cdev.

Martin, C. L., & Ruble, D. N. (2010). Patterns of gender development. *Annual Review of Psychology*, 61, 353–381. doi: 10.1146/annurev.psych.093008.100511.

Pahlke, E., Cooper, C. E., & Fabes, R. A. (2013). Classroom sex composition and first-grade school outcomes: The role of classroom behavior. *Social Science Research*, 42, 1650–1658. doi: 10.1016/.ssresearch.2013.07.009.

Ready, D. D., LoGerfo, L. F., Burkham, D. T., & Lee, V. E. (2005). Explaining girls' advantage in kindergarten literacy learning: Do classroom behaviors make a difference? *The Elementary School Journal*, 106, 21–38. doi: 10.1086/496905.

Rose, A. J., & Rudolph, K. D. (2006). A review of sex differences in peer relationship processes: Potential trade-offs for the emotional and behavioral development of girls and boys. *Psychological Bulletin*, 132, 98–131. doi: 10.1037/0033-2909.132.1.98.

Ruble, D. N., Martin, C. L., & Berenbaum, S. (2006). Gender development. In W. Damon (Ed.), *Handbook of child psychology* (Vol. 3, pp. 858–932). New York: Wiley.

Ryan, A. M. (2000). Peer groups as a context for the socialization of adolescents' motivation, engagement, and achievement in school. *Educational Psychologist*, 35, 101–111. doi: 10.1207/S15326985EP3502_4.

———. (2001). The peer group as a context for the development of young adolescent motivation and achievement. *Child Development*, 72, 1135–1150. doi: 10.1111/1467-8624.00338.

Sacerdote, B. (2001). Peer effects with random assignment: Results for Dartmouth roommates. *Quarterly Journal of Economics*, 116, 681–704. doi: 10.1162/00335530151144131.

Sandberg, D. E., Ehrhardt, A. A., Ince, S. E., & Meyer-Bahlburg, H. F. L. (1991). Gender differences in children's and adolescents' career aspirations. *Journal of Adolescent Research*, 6, 371–386. doi: 10.1177/074355489163007.

Schaefer, B. (2004). A demographic survey of learning behaviors among American students. *School Psychology Review*, 33, 481–497.

Schiller, K. S. (1999). Effects of feeder patterns on students' transition to high school. *Sociology of Education*, 72, 216–233. doi: 10.2307/2673154.

Schweinhart, L. J., & Weikart, D. (1997). The high/scope preschool curriculum comparison study through age 23. *Early Childhood Research Quarterly*, 12, 117–143. doi: 10.1016/S0885-2006(97)90009-0.

Silverman, I. W. (2003). Gender differences in delay of gratification: A meta-analysis. *Sex Roles*, 49, 451–463. doi: 10.1023/A:1025872421115.

Simpkins, S. D., Davis-Kean, P. E., & Eccles, J. S. (2006). Math and science motivation: A longitudinal examination of the links between choices and beliefs. *Developmental Psychology*, 42, 70–83. doi: 10.1037/0012-1649.42.1.70.

Skiba, R. J., Michael, R. S., Nardo, A. C., & Peterson, R. (2000). *The color of discipline: Sources of racial and gender disproportionality in school punishment.* Bloomington: Indiana Educational Policy Center.

Sullivan, J., Riccio, C., & Reynolds, C. (2008). Variations in students' school- and teacher-related attitudes across gender, ethnicity, and age. *Journal of Instructional Psychology*, 35, 296–305.

Thompson, J. S. (2003). The effect of single-sex secondary schooling on women's choice of college major. *Sociological Perspectives*, 46, 257–278. doi: 10.1525/sop.2003.46.2.257.

Tremblay, R. E., Masse, B., Perron, D., LeBlanc, M., Schwartzman, A. E., & Ledingham, J. E. (1992). Early disruptive behavior, poor school achievement, delinquent behavior, and delinquent personality: Longitudinal analyses. *Journal of Consulting and Clinical Psychology*, 60, 64–72. doi: 10.1037/0022-006X.60.1.64.

Updegraff, K. A., Eccles, J. S., Barber, B. L., & O'Brien, K. M. (1996). Course enrollment as self-regulatory behavior: Who takes optional high school math courses? *Learning and Individual Differences*, 8, 239–259. doi: 10.1016/S1041-6080(96)90016-3.

Valeski, T. N., & Stipek, D. J. (2001). Young children's feelings about school. *Child Development*, 72, 1198–1213. doi: 10.1111/1467-8624.00342.

Verkuyten, M., & Thijs, J. (2001). Ethnic and gender bias among Dutch and Turkish children in late childhood: The role of social context. *Infant and Child Development*, 10, 203–217. doi: 10.1002/icd.279.

Watt, H. M. G., Shapka, J. D., Morris, Z. A., Durik, A. M., Keating, D. P., & Eccles, J. S. (2012). Gender motivational processes affecting high school mathematics participation, educational aspirations, and career plans: A comparison of samples from Australia, Canada, and the United States. *Developmental Psychology*, 48, 1594–1611. doi: 10.1037/a0027838.

Wentzel, K. R. (2009). Peer relationships and motivation at school. In K. Rubin, W. Bukowski, & B. Laursen (Eds.), *Handbook on peer relationships* (pp. 531–547). New York: Guilford.

Yee, M., & Brown, R. (1994). The development of gender differentiation in young children. *British Journal of Social Psychology*, 33, 183–196. doi: 10.1111/j.2044-8309.1994.tb01017.x.

Zill, N., & West, J. (2001). *Entering kindergarten: A portrait of American children when they begin school – Findings from the Condition of Education, 2000.* Washington, DC: US Department of Education.

Zimmerman, D. J. (2003). Peer effects in academic outcomes: Evidence from a natural experiment. *Review of Economics and Statistics*, 85, 9–23. doi: 10.1162/003465303762687677.

Zosuls, K. M., Martin, C. L., Ruble, D. N., Miller, C. F., Gaertner, B. M., England, D. E., & Hill, A. P. (2011). "It's not that we hate you": Understanding children's gender attitudes and expectancies about peer relationships. *British Journal of Developmental Psychology*, 29, 288–304. doi: 10.1111/j.2044-835X.2010.02023.x.

2 Beginning school transition and academic achievement in mid-elementary school: does gender matter?

Irene Kriesi and Marlis Buchmann

Abstract
This chapter examines the individual and social antecedents of boys' and girls' coping with the transition to school and its consequences for their academic achievement in mid-elementary school. In particular, this chapter focuses on the interrelationships between children's family background, individual competencies, beginning school transition, and their later academic achievement. The empirical analyses are based on the child cohort of the Swiss Survey of Children and Youth (COCON) and make use of the first three survey waves (2006–2009) when the children were 6, 7, and 9 years old (N = 963). Path models are estimated for boys and girls. The findings show that before entering school, girls score higher on cognitive competencies, school-relevant knowledge, and conscientiousness, and they have a more positive social self-concept. These competencies affect the transition quality to school and explain why girls find it easier to adopt the student role. Competencies at the age of 6 years as well as the transition quality to school affect academic achievement at the age of 9. Gender differences are also found regarding the effects of social background and competencies on the quality of school transition and academic achievement.

Introduction

For many countries, recent research shows increasing gender differences in academic achievement in favor of girls. They earn better grades and are overrepresented in more demanding school tracks (e.g., Bacher, Beham, & Lachmayr, 2008; Buchmann, DiPrete, & McDaniel, 2008; Entwisle, Alexander, & Olson, 2007; Steinmayr & Spinath, 2008). The reasons for girls' higher achievement over recent years compared to that of boys are still largely unclear. While the media depict boys as the new victims of institutional gender discrimination, recent scientific discussions have considered several potential causes such as the feminization of the elementary school context, gender-specific socialization practices, or gender-stereotypical ability attributions of teachers (for an overview, see Kuhn, 2008; Stamm, 2008). While the feminization of the elementary school context has increased in Switzerland over recent decades, gender-specific socialization practices and ability attributions are no new phenomena. Recent studies for Germany and Switzerland fail to support the hypothesis that female teachers lead to a disadvantage for boys (Hadjar & Lupatsch, 2011; Helbig, 2010; Neugebauer, Helbig, & Landmann, 2010). However, the relevance of the latter two factors for girls' advantage in school has most likely increased since higher education has become a widely accepted educational goal for women also. While in the 1980s the proportion of young women in Switzerland earning a university entrance degree amounted to 43%, the respective proportion earning a university degree was only 26%. In 2011, the respective proportions were an astonishing 57.1% and 52.3%.[1]

The majority of sociological studies examining gender differences in academic achievement focused their attention on various stages (or levels) of the educational career, analyzing the effects of social background (e.g., Breen, Luijkx, Müller, & Pollak, 2010; Entwisle et al., 2007; Mensah & Kiernan, 2010), teachers' grading (Farkas, Sheehan, Grobe, & Shuan, 1990), or recommendation practices (e.g., Ditton, 2007). Psychological studies have mostly analyzed non-cognitive skills and personality traits such as the Big Five (De Fruyt, Van Leeuwen, De Bolle, & De Clercq, 2008; Steinmayr & Spinath, 2008), achievement striving and self-control (Duckworth & Seligman, 2006; Hicks, Johnson, Iacono, & McGue, 2008), intrinsic motivation (Freudenthaler, Spinath, & Neubauer, 2008), or aggression (Farkas et al., 1990). To our knowledge, few studies have ever asked whether the beginning school transition, the starting point of the educational career, differs between boys and girls and, if so, how these differences may affect later academic achievement. Our study attempts to partially fill this gap by examining whether the antecedents and outcomes of the transition to primary school differ between boys and girls. If girls and boys do not cope equally well with this transition, in what respect do their school-relevant competencies and resources differ when entering school? Finally, does the role of the quality of transition to school in determining academic achievement in mid-elementary school differ between boys and girls?

This chapter conceptualizes the beginning school transition as a status passage in the institutionalized life course, representing a critically important event for boys' and girls' developmental processes and outcomes (Entwisle, Alexander, & Olson, 2003). Adopting a life course perspective, we will examine the individual and social antecedents of boys' and girls' coping with the transition to school and its consequences for their academic achievement in mid-elementary school. In particular, this contribution focuses on the interrelationships between children's family background, individual competencies, beginning school transition, and later academic achievement. The latter will be equated with school grades, the most important indicator for school success in the Swiss elementary school system. School grades serve as major selection criteria for secondary school tracks and thus greatly determine a child's educational trajectory and educational outcomes (e.g., Neuenschwander & Malti, 2009).

---

[1] Data source, retrieved September 12, 2013, from: www.bfs.admin.ch/bfs/portal/de/index/themen/15/04/00/blank/uebersicht.html.

The empirical analyses are based on the child cohort of the Swiss Survey of Children and Youth (COCON) and make use of the first three survey waves (2006–2009) when the children were 6, 7, and 9 years old (N = 963).

Theoretical considerations

The beginning school transition represents a status passage in the institutionalized life trajectory, which is relevant for children's further development. It denotes the adoption of the student role and the start of the educational career (Entwisle et al., 2003). Such status passages mark the entry into novel spheres of social interactions characterized by their own social rules and demanding adjustment processes on the part of those who make the transition. The mastery of the transition is consequential for future performance in the new social context and affects further development. When boys and girls make the transition to school, they face the task of adopting the institutionalized student role, which implies the development of work and learning habits, achievement motivation, and the establishment of positive social relationships with teachers and peers (Entwisle & Alexander, 1993; Entwisle et al., 2003; Ladd, Herald, & Kochel, 2006).[2] From a sociological perspective, these school-relevant competencies may be conceptualized as part of a child's social and learning habitus. The term *habitus* refers to a person's demeanor, values, dispositions, and competencies acquired in the socialization process (Bourdieu & Passeron, 1964; Büchner & Brake, 2006). School-relevant parts of the habitus include a child's manners and skills of social interaction, learning strategies, and school-relevant knowledge. Borrowing from the Stage-Environment-Fit model developed by Eccles et al. (1993), we assume that the fit between a child's social and learning habitus and the expected competencies and behaviors institutionalized in the student role will affect the quality of the beginning school transition. In turn, the transition experience should play a role for academic achievement in mid-elementary school. Whether children feel at ease in the new school context and are able to concentrate on the curriculum depends on how well they cope with school entry. In addition, teachers' judgment of children is affected by how well children adopt the student role. If the fit between children's social and learning habitus and the expected competencies and behaviors institutionalized in the student role varies between boys and girls, the gender group with the better fit will have an advantage in coping with the beginning school transition and later academic achievement. Hence, potential

---

[2] The vast majority of Swiss children attend kindergarten before they enter school. However, we assume that children's entry to the first grade of elementary school is the first major educational transition in their lives. The reason is that at the time of data collection in 2006 the structure and educational aims of kindergarten and elementary school differed markedly. In contrast to elementary school, kindergarten was mainly characterized by a focus on playful development and on some structured social activities without specific learning goals.

gender differences in coping with the beginning school transition may thus have lasting consequences for future success in school.

Apart from expected gender differences in the fit between a child's habitus and the expectations of the student role, we assume that particular differences prevail between boys and girls in how social background and school-relevant competencies affect their academic achievement in mid-elementary school. The rationale for this assumption is that some parents and teachers hold gender-stereotypical beliefs about boys' and girls' competencies and personality traits. These beliefs can lead to biased perceptions of children's abilities, and may result in gender-specific socialization practices. Gender-stereotypical socialization practices are assumed to be associated with gender differences in competencies, personality traits, and behaviors (see also Wigfield and Eccles' expectancy-value theory of achievement motivation (2002); and Upadyaya & Eccles, this volume). These gendered competencies and behaviors, in turn, are likely to be relevant for the beginning school transition as well as for later academic achievement. Furthermore, some empirical evidence suggests that the prevalence of gender-stereotypical beliefs may vary by socioeconomic background, resulting in an intertwinement of gender and social background differences. In the next sections, we will formulate specific hypotheses about how gender matters for the quality of the transition to school and academic achievement in mid-elementary school.

The role of boys' and girls' competencies for the beginning school transition and later academic achievement

In Western societies, gender is an important social ordering schema. It is based on widely shared hegemonic cultural beliefs about male and female traits, competencies, and behaviors, portraying fundamental and innate gender differences (Charles & Bradley, 2009; Ridgeway & Correll, 2004; Ridgeway, Li, Erickson, Backor, & Tinkler, 2009). The literature also refers to these gender beliefs as gender-stereotypes. They are particularly pronounced in the realm of personality traits, ability, and academic achievement and affect competence evaluations, aspirations, and individual performance. Stereotypically, girls are perceived as, for example, compassionate, docile, diligent, conscientious, even-tempered, and good at languages. Boys are characterized as physically active, boisterous, competitive, lacking discipline, and good at math, science, and sports (e.g., Bem, 1974; Liben & Bigler, 2002).

Given that gender stereotypes manifest themselves in gendered socialization practices and ability perceptions, it is likely that the factual as well as the perceived competence endowment of girls and boys differ when they enter school. As for socialization, Entwisle et al. (2007) report several empirical studies showing that mothers generally talk more with daughters and use more supportive speech than with sons. They also talk more about books, and praise and encourage daughters more often than sons. Such gender differences based on sex-typed competence beliefs are likely to translate into differences in boys' and girls' competencies and personality traits, which disadvantage boys in the school context. We maintain that girls' competencies and personality traits and thus girls' learning habitus are more in line with the competencies and behaviors requested in school than the boys' social and learning habitus. Consequently, girls may find it easier to adopt the new student role, which in turn facilitates later academic achievement. We will substantiate this lead hypothesis by specifying how three classes of competencies that have been recognized in the literature (e.g., Durham Farkas, Hammer, Tomblin, & Catts, 2007; Entwisle & Alexander, 1993; Entwisle et al., 2007; Farkas, 2003) as relevant for successfully coping with the transition to school differ between boys and girls and may give girls a competitive advantage over boys when making the transition to school and regarding their academic achievement. Given that girls already earned higher school grades in the 1950s (Buchmann et al., 2008), it is likely that these gender differences in competencies are not a new phenomenon. However, as long as girls were not encouraged to earn higher educational credentials, their superior school-relevant competencies and the concomitant competitive advantage did not matter.

Key competencies

The first class of competencies refers to curriculum-related cognitive and pre-academic competencies such as basic cognitive ability, writing numbers and letters, and knowing the alphabet, as well as the related self-concepts of abilities. The second class includes productive competencies, such as achievement striving, self-discipline, or conscientiousness. Third, children require social competencies, which enable them to interact successfully with teachers and classmates.

With respect to the first class we argue that children who are already familiar with the basic knowledge taught and rewarded in first grade, such as a good knowledge of letters, numbers, or quantities, and verbal skills, should adopt the student role more easily and perform better. The results of Durham et al. (2007), showing that oral language skills in kindergarten are an important predictor of academic achievement in mid-elementary school, support this assumption. Empirical evidence also suggests that girls' school-relevant knowledge (i.e., knowledge of letters, numbers, or quantities, and verbal skills) at the time of school entry is more developed (Gullo, 1991; Janus & Offord, 2007). Girls should thus have an advantage over boys when entering school.

Productive competencies such as conscientiousness or achievement motivation enable children to master tasks efficiently and to become goal-oriented. Such competencies are crucial expectations institutionalized in the student role. Well-developed productive competencies are thus likely to facilitate a successful beginning school transition. Girls consistently score higher on productive competencies such as conscientiousness, which partly explains their higher academic achievement (e.g., De Fruyt et al., 2008; Duckworth & Seligman, 2006; Entwisle et al., 2007; Freudenthaler et al., 2008; Hicks et al., 2008).

Children who enter school are expected to establish positive relationships with teachers and classmates. The literature shows that a positive social self-concept plays an important role in mastering this social task (Birch & Ladd, 1996; Buhs & Ladd, 2001). Children equipped with a positive social self-concept, who feel accepted among peers and experience positive peer relationships, do better in school academically (Buhs, 2005; Buhs & Ladd, 2001; Urhahne, 2008; Wentzel, 2005). Consequently they are also likely to succeed more easily in adopting the student role. Empirical evidence suggests that girls' social self-concept is more positive than that of boys (Marsh, 1989; Wilgenbusch & Merrell, 1999).

Regarding children's self-concepts of ability, several psychological and sociological approaches argue that academic achievement is likely to depend on competence beliefs (Bandura, Barbaranelli, Caprara, & Pastorelli, 1996; Correll, 2001; Weiner, 1985). The reason is that if individuals perceive themselves as good at a certain academic domain, they show an interest in it, which translates into better academic performance. Previous literature has consistently shown that girls hold higher competence beliefs in female-typed domains such as languages, whereas boys hold higher competence beliefs in male-typed domains such as math or science (e.g., Jacobs, Lanza, Osgood, Eccles, & Wigfield, 2002; Moser, Keller, & Tresch, 2003; Tiedemann, 2000; Wigfield & Eccles, 2002; see also Parker, Nagy, Trautwein, & Lüdtke; Chow & Salmela-Aro, this volume).

Gender-stereotypical competence perceptions

Teachers' ability perceptions and grading practices are shaped by sex-typed ability beliefs (see Upadyaya & Eccles, this volume). We thus assume that this may affect boys' and girls' academic achievement. Ditton (2007), for instance, claims that group-specific perceptions of academic ability affect teachers' grading. For gender, results provided by both Bonesrønning (2008) and Lavy (2004) show that some teachers reward girls with better grades than boys for comparable performance. Based on additional empirical evidence we surmise that teachers' perception and thus grading practices may even be predominantly based on gender-stereotypical competency and behavior perceptions. Farkas et al. (1990) found that only boys were penalized for disruptive behavior in class, a male-typed behavior, by being given lower course grades. According to Freudenthaler et al. (2008), conscientiousness, a female-typed personality trait, affected only girls', and not boys', given grades positively. In a similar vein, Bossert (1981) and Faulstich-Wieland, Weber, and Willems (2004) found that boys are disciplined faster for (male-typed) unruly behavior. Against this background, we hypothesize that competencies, personality traits, or behaviors play a larger role for academic achievement if they are in line with the predominant gender-stereotype.[3]

Social background and gendered socialization practices

We have argued that gendered socialization practices based on parents' sex-typed ability beliefs would lead to girls' superior school-relevant knowledge and productive and social competencies, which in turn facilitate their adjustment to the student role and their academic achievement. We suspect, however, that this hypothesis may not hold for all girls. The reason is that beliefs in innate gender differences regarding abilities and personality traits vary by socioeconomic background (Koppetsch, 2001; Vester & Gardemin, 2001). Koppetsch's qualitative study on gender roles and social milieus conducted in Germany suggests that medium-educated, (lower-) middle-class men and women adhere most strongly to the conception of biologically determined gender differences. In contrast, well-educated, upper-middle-class individuals hold more egalitarian views, perceiving no innate gender differences in abilities. In the low-educated working class, a mix between essentialist and traditionalist views is dominant. Gender differences are primarily seen as a matter of traditions partly rooted in the physical strength of men. It is likely that such class-specific perceptions of gender differences will also affect gender-specific parental expectations and child-rearing practices. In particular, we advance the hypothesis that gender-stereotypical competency expectations and socialization practices will be strongest in (lower-) middle-class families, supporting higher school-relevant knowledge, better-developed conscientiousness, and a more successful adoption of the student role of girls with this type of social background.

Abundant sociological research shows that social background matters for all children's academic achievement. Family background provides cultural (Bourdieu, 1983) and social capital (Coleman, 1988), affecting parents' socialization practices and thus children's successful adoption of the student role and later academic performance.

Family-related cultural capital refers to parents' educational credentials, competencies, values, and attitudes. Parents rich in cultural capital are able to provide socialization environments within the family, and organize leisure activities that further their children's school-relevant knowledge and competencies. Their offspring are thus endowed with the work and learning habitus required by the school system (e.g., Baumert & Schümer, 2001; Baumert, Watermann, & Schümer, 2003; Bradley & Corwyn, 2002; Cheadle, 2008; Covay & Carbonaro, 2010; Davis-Kean, 2005; De Graaf, De Graaf, & Kraaykamp, 2000; Durham et al., 2007; Farkas, 2003; Farkas & Beron, 2004; Lareau, 2003; Lee & Bowen, 2006). In addition, teachers' competence evaluation is biased in favor of children

---

[3] Due to a lack of data on teachers' competence perceptions we will not be able to test directly whether teachers perceive boys' and girls' competencies and personality traits differently.

from high socioeconomic backgrounds (Bodovski & Farkas, 2008; Ditton, 2007). Class-specific parental socialization practices and competence evaluations by teachers are thus likely to result in a cumulative advantage of boys and girls from middle- and upper-class families regarding the adoption of the student role and academic achievement. However, a possible downside of typical middle-class socialization environments is that children's social self-concept might be lower due to their intensive participation in extracurricular activities. This prevents close ties with peers, which are an important prerequisite for establishing a positive social self-concept (Büchner, 1994; Lareau, 2003).[4]

Following Baumert et al. (2003), we distinguish between a structural and a functional form of family-related social capital. Structural social capital refers to the size of a social network and the intensity of the resulting social relationships (e.g., number of adults in the family and their available time for the children). Functional social capital includes the quality of interaction and communication within a social network such as the family. We argue that children find it easier to adopt the student role and to achieve good grades if their family provides a lot of structural and functional social capital. Generally children benefit from adults, usually their parents, investing a substantial amount of time in their supervision and tutoring. This includes, for example, help with homework or attending school meetings. Such parents usually have high educational aspirations for their children and support high achievement motivation in them, thus resulting in higher academic achievement (Stocké, 2010). The quality of interaction and communication within the family is probably the most important functional social capital. Previous research in developmental psychology has demonstrated that an emotionally supportive parenting style makes it easier for children to explore and cope with new social situations (Kracke & Hofer, 2002; Kreppner, 1999), develop school-relevant competencies and a positive social self-concept (Papastefanou & Hofer, 2002), and perform well in school (Conger et al., 2002).

Girls' and boys' transition quality and academic achievement

As mentioned earlier, previous research addressing the question of gender differences in the beginning school transition and their potential effects on later academic achievement is scarce, yielding mostly indirect answers. A study by Entwisle et al. (2007) shows that parents expect daughters to adapt to school better than sons. This may be so because of some girls' superior school-

---

[4] Ties with peers may also be conceptualized as a form of social capital. Given that our focus is on social capital within the family we refrain from further elaborating the role of peers in the beginning school transition and academic achievement.

relevant competencies, mentioned above, facilitating their beginning school transition. In addition, empirical evidence implies that girls may also be better prepared for the adoption of the student role on a behavioral level. Tresch (2005) found for Switzerland that first-grade girls' behavior was rated as more school-adequate than boys. A qualitative analysis of a US preschool with 3- to 5-year-old children, conducted by Martin (1998), documents that girls were actively instructed by teachers to behave unobtrusively, well-adjusted, and in a docile way. Teachers encouraged girls to pursue structured activities, sitting at tables or on chairs. In contrast to girls, boys were allowed to behave loudly and boisterously, spending a lot of time on unstructured physical activities. These findings imply that teachers' gender-specific socialization practices in preschool settings prepare girls better for their future student role with its emphasis on structured activities in the classroom. Girls should thus find it easier to adopt the student role. This advantage is likely to translate into higher academic achievement in mid-elementary school.

Conceptual model

In order to analyze the antecedents of the transition to elementary school and its effect on later academic achievement, we depart from the conceptual model in Figure 2.1. We assume that children's social background, their competencies before school entry, and the quality of the transition to first grade directly affect their competencies and academic achievement at the end of mid-elementary school. Children's social background and competencies are also expected to play an indirect role, mediated by the quality of the transition to school. Regarding gender differences, we expect that girls find it easier to adopt the student role and do well in school academically due to their higher school-relevant competencies at school entry. This should hold particularly for girls from middle-class families, where parents adhere most strongly to gendered child-rearing practices. Based on research showing that teachers' ability perceptions and grading are influenced by gender stereotypes, we further conjecture that children's competencies and behaviors affect academic achievement more strongly if they are consistent with predominant gender-stereotypical expectations.

Data and methods

The analyses are based on the first three waves of data collection for the Swiss Survey of Children and Youth (Buchmann & Fend, 2004), a multicohort study that includes, among others, a representative sample of a cohort of children born between September 1, 1999 and April 30, 2000 and residing in the German- and French-speaking part of Switzerland (N = 1,117 for the third wave;

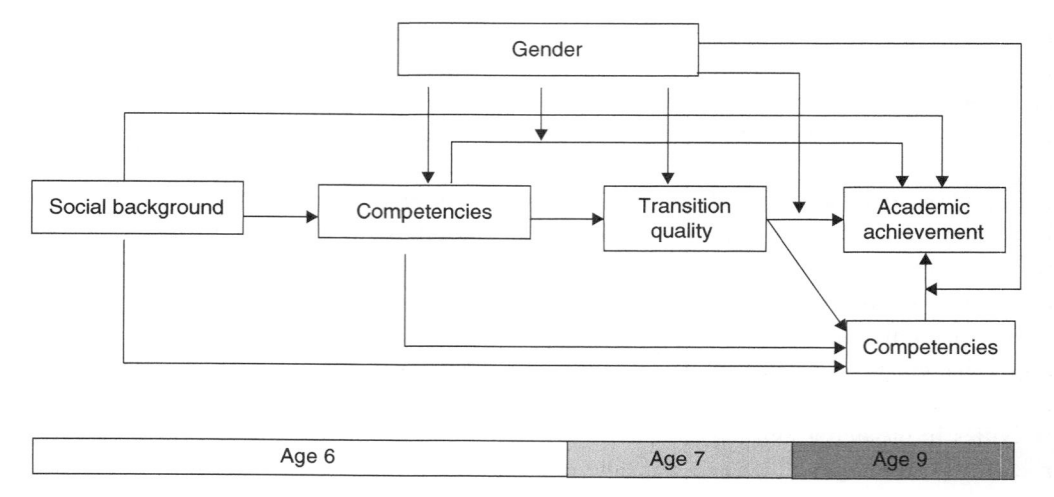

Figure 2.1 *Conceptual model of the interrelationship between social background, children's competencies, their transition quality, and academic achievement*

panel attrition amounts to 12% only). The children were 6, 7, and 9 years old at the time of data collection in 2006, 2007, and 2009.[5] The data was collected by CAPI and CATI interviews as well as written questionnaires. The data used for this chapter was provided by the children themselves and by their primary caregivers. It includes detailed information on the children's social situation and biography; the family context; cognitive, social, and productive competencies; as well as personality characteristics. For the analyses, we selected children who entered school in 2007 (~89%) or 2008 (~8%). Children who entered school before 2007 (3%) were excluded from the analyses due to missing data. The final number of respondents thus amounts to 472 girls and 491 boys.[6] At the time of the third data wave in 2009, the overwhelming majority of the selected children (82.4%) were in third grade. Of the 9-year-olds, 15.9% were in second grade at the time of the third survey wave, either due to a delayed start or due to retention. The remaining few children were in special types of schools without grades, or in fourth grade.

Analytical approach

We employed a path model to estimate both the direct effects of predictors on academic achievement and the indirect ones, i.e., those mediated

---

[5] The samples were drawn by a two-stage method whereby 131 communities (broken down by community type and community size) were selected. Cohort members residing in the selected communities were then randomly sampled on the basis of information provided by the official register of community residents.

[6] The analyses presented here are based on weighted data. The weight corrects for an over-sampling of particular community types, non-response, and a moderate underrepresentation of lower educational strata, nationality, and community type. See Sacchi (2006) for more detailed information.

by other predictors in the model. The path models are based on the maximum-likelihood estimator. All coefficients for kurtosis and skewness are well within accepted limits. Multiple group analysis was employed to examine whether the path coefficients for boys and girls are invariant. Gender differences were assessed by equality constraints on all relevant paths and covariances (nested chi-square difference test) as well as by comparing parameters within and across models (z-test). The results of the two tests were similar. The results shown in Figure 2.1 are based on the model with equality constraints.

The model evaluation is based on several widely used goodness-of-fit measures (see, for example, Byrne, 2001, pp. 79ff.): the root mean square error of approximation (RMSEA) measures the discrepancy per degree of freedom. In a perfectly fitting model the RMSEA value would be 0. By convention, values $<= .06$ indicate a good model fit. The comparative fit index (CFI) and the adjusted goodness-of-fit index (AGFI) have values between 0 and 1. Values close to 1 indicate a very good fit. Chi^2 values are generally documented but should be treated with care. They are very sensitive to sample size and are lacking normal distributions.

Measures

The dependent variable academic achievement is based on the mean of the teacher-rated math and German or French grades in the last school report. The grades range from 1 (very poor) to 6 (excellent).[7] The information was provided by the primary caregiver (mostly the mother, 95%) in the third survey wave. The quality of the transition to school is measured about 6 months after school entry with an index capturing how well a child has adopted the student role. It is composed of three items based on the primary caregivers' assessment of whether the child has quickly learned to do homework, has established a good relationship with the teacher, and is generally coping well with everyday school life ($\alpha = .62$).

The children's competencies include cognitive competencies, social self-concept, conscientiousness, and school-relevant knowledge measured at the age of 6 years, as well as academic self-efficacy, measured at the age of 9 years. The information on school-relevant knowledge and conscientiousness came from the primary caregiver, and the information on the other competencies was collected from the children themselves. The cognitive competencies were assessed with a subscale (six items) of Cattell, Weiss, and Osterland's (1977) "basic intelligence test scale" (Grundintelligenztest), CFT 1. The social self-concept is based on a four-item index, capturing the perceived social acceptance among peers ($\alpha = 0.56$) (Asendorpf & Aken, 1993; Harter & Pike, 1984). Conscientiousness is measured with an index of three items (Asendorpf & van Aken, 2003; Rothbart, Ahadi, & Hershey, 1994).[8] School-relevant knowledge

---

[7] About a third of the children received non-numerical grades. These were coded within the dominant grade schema of 1 to 6 by an elementary school teacher.
[8] $\alpha = 0.6$. Example: "My child is attentive and able to concentrate."

captures knowledge of letters and figures, verbal skills, and an understanding of quantity (three items).[9] Academic self-concept is measured with an index of four items (α = 0.68) based on Asendorpf and Aken (1993).

Family characteristics are measured at the age of 6 and were collected from the primary caregiver: parental highest education is assumed to encompass parents' cultural capital. It differentiates between four educational levels (compulsory school (1), vocational training (2), higher vocational training/vocational college (3), and university training (4)). The socialization context within the family is measured with a supportive parenting index based on three items from the supportive parenting scale of Simons, Lorenz, Conger, and Wu (1992).[10] It measures the emotional support and warmth between parents and children and indicates children's functional social capital. Table 2.1 contains the means, standard deviations, and correlations for all covariates.[11]

Results

Figure 2.2 shows the path coefficients for girls and boys (bold).[12] The model, estimated jointly for boys and girls (see "Data and Methods"), fits well (CFI = 1.0; AGFI = .98; RMSEA = .01). It explains 23% of variance in academic achievement for girls and 25% for boys. The significance levels next to the coefficients indicate whether the path is statistically significant for either girls or boys. Significant gender differences are indicated by path arrows printed in bold. We will first discuss girls' and boys' transition quality and academic achievement and then turn to the description of children's competencies and social background and their role in explaining the beginning school transition quality and academic achievement in mid-elementary school.

Girls' and boys' transition quality and academic achievement

The descriptive findings presented in Table 2.1 show that, at the age of 9, there are no gender differences in academic achievement (grade average of

---

[9] α = 0.51. The items are based on the Academic Rating Scale (ARS) (National Center for Education Statistics, 1994). Examples: "My child shows an understanding of the relationship between quantities – for example, knowing that a group of ten small stones is the same quantity as a group of ten larger blocks"; "My child composes a story with a clear beginning, middle and end."
[10] α = 0.5. Examples: "When your child does something you like or approve of, how often do you let him/her know you are pleased about it?"
[11] To capture possible effects of delayed school entry or retention on the quality of transition and on academic achievement, we tested two control variables that were excluded from the final model due to a lack of statistical significance. The first one distinguished between a minority of children entering school at age 8 instead of 7. The second captured children who were retained after school entry. Similarly, a variable controlling for siblings was excluded due to statistical insignificance.
[12] All theoretically plausible paths were tested when estimating the model. Statistically non-significant paths were then excluded from the final model.

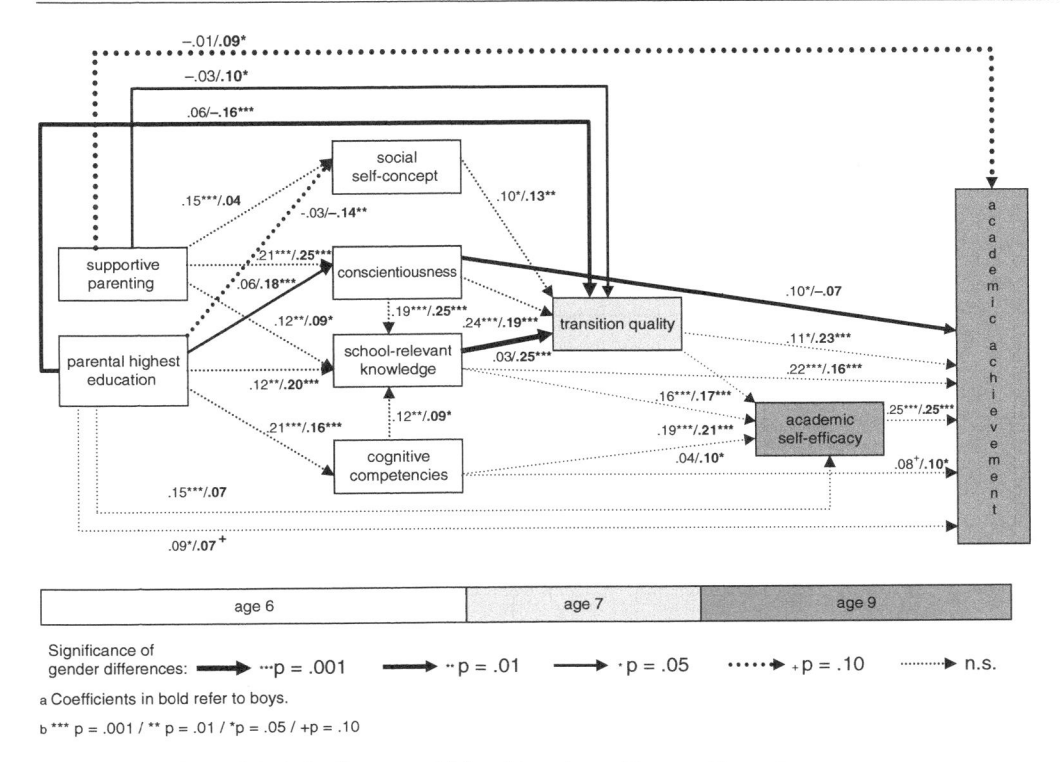

Figure 2.2 *Path effects on girls' and boys' transition quality and academic achievement*

math and German/French based on teachers' rating).[13] However, the transition quality significantly differs between boys and girls. On average, parents report that girls have a higher transition quality, and that they find it easier to adopt the student role when they enter first grade.

As hypothesized, the transition quality plays a significant direct role for later academic achievement (Figure 2.2). The higher the boys' and girls' quality of transition to school, the better their grades in mid-elementary school. We have argued that a more successful transition quality enables these children to better focus on the academic demands of school, which may lead to being more positively perceived by their teachers. Teachers' perception may in turn influence their grading (see also Upadyaya & Eccles, this volume). This latter explanation is indirectly supported by the observed gender difference regarding the relationship between the transition quality and boys' and girls' academic achievement. For boys, the effect is about twice the size of that for girls, statistically significant on the 10% level. Compared to girls, boys' grades at the age of 9 thus depend more on the quality of the beginning school transition. Given that boys

---

[13] A more detailed analysis (not shown) revealed that boys receive slightly better grades in math, girls in German/French. These differences outweighed each other completely when the average of both grades is taken. Models run separately for math and German/French yield more or less comparable results.

Table 2.1. Correlations, means, and standard deviations for all covariates[a]

Boys (N = 491) / Girls (N = 472)	1	2	3	4	5	6	7	8	9	Mean	Standard deviation	Scale
1) grades (academic achievement)		.207***	.210***	.057	.173***	.336***	.216***	−.024	.359***	5.05	0.55	1–6
2) transition quality	.333***		.076*	.042	.048	.089*	.238***	.076*	.189***	5.38	0.74	1–6
3) parental highest education	.116***	−.097*		.032	.213***	.166***	.069	−.026	.204***	2.81	0.86	1–4
4) supportive parenting	.155***	.200***	−.084*		−.016	.161***	.209***	.153***	.019	5.53	0.43	1–6
5) cognitive competencies	.175***	.044	.161***	.002		.162***	.092*	.007	.108*	2.48	1.55	0–6
6) school-relevant knowledge	.322***	.279***	.247***	.129***	.140***		.231***	.024	.233***	4.58	0.96	1.6
7) conscientiousness	.125***	.264***	.160***	.237***	.053	.306***		−.060	.126***	4.79	0.76	1–6
8) social self-concept	.061	.147***	−.147***	.051	−.074	−.026	−.014		.056	3.13	0.54	1–4
9) academic self-efficacy	.368***	.223***	.124***	.075*	.147***	.290***	.170***	.083*		2.94	0.74	1–4
Mean	5.02	5.14	2.79	5.55	2.29	4.32	4.58	3.05	2.95			
Mean difference between boys and girls (t-value and significance)	−0.65 n.s.	−4.64 ***	−0.31 n.s.	0.51 n.s.	−1.97 *	−4.08 ***	−4.07 ***	−2.06 *	0.13 n.s.			
Standard deviation	0.59	0.88	0.88	0.42	1.51	1.03	0.85	0.60	0.70			
Scale	1–6	1–6	1–4	1–6	0–6	1–6	1–6	1–4	1–4			

[a] The significance levels of the mean difference between boys and girls are based on t-tests.

are expected to have more difficulties than girls, it is likely that teachers are more aware of how boys cope with school entry.

The role of boys' and girls' competencies for the beginning school transition and later academic achievement

Table 2.1 reveals that before school entry, at the age of 6, girls have significantly more school-relevant knowledge, are more conscientious, and have higher cognitive competencies and a more positive social self-concept. This supports our assumption that girls' social and learning habitus, which is assumed to be indicated by these competencies, fits the requirements of the institutionalized school context better than that of boys. The multivariate findings confirm this assumption. They show that boys and girls who report a positive social self-concept and who are perceived as conscientious by their parents are also reported to show a higher quality of transition to school. Girls' higher scores on these two competencies may partly explain their more successful adoption of the student role.

Interestingly, school-relevant knowledge at school entry, such as knowledge of letters and figures or verbal abilities, affects the transition quality of boys only. Boys adopt the student role more successfully the more school-relevant knowledge they have. For girls, no such relationship can be observed. This suggests that girls' adoption of the student role depends on a narrower range of competencies than boys'. Girls' school adjustment is only affected by their perceived acceptance among peers and a high level of conscientiousness.

Cognitive competencies do not directly influence the quality of the beginning school transition and the respective path has therefore been excluded from the model. This suggests that the adoption of the student role is not primarily a matter of cognitive intelligence but depends on informal productive and social competencies such as a positive social self-concept, conscientiousness, and, for boys, school-relevant knowledge.

A noteworthy gender difference is observed regarding the direct effects of children's various early competencies on their later academic achievement. While children of both sexes earn better grades the higher their school-relevant knowledge and cognitive competencies before entering school, and the higher their academic self-efficacy in mid-elementary school, conscientiousness only affects girls' grades directly. The more conscientious girls were at school entry, the better their grades at the age of 9. This gender difference, significant at the 5% level, may be explained by gender-specific grading practices of teachers. We have argued that conscientiousness, a female-typed competency, may be perceived more strongly in girls and is thus incorporated in teachers' academic evaluation of girls only.

Table 2.2. *Direct, indirect, and total effects (standardized) of parental highest education and an emotionally supportive parenting style on boys' and girls' academic achievement*

Effects	Boys' academic achievement		Girls' academic achievement	
	Parental highest education	Parenting style (emotionally supportive)	Parental highest education	Parenting style (emotionally supportive)
Direct	.07	.09	.09	−.01
Indirect	.06	.07	.12	.07
Total	.13	.16	.21	.06

Social background and gendered socialization practices

The impact of social background on children's competencies, transition quality, and academic achievement partly varies for boys and girls. We start by discussing the total effects and their decomposition in direct and indirect effects of parental highest education and an emotionally supportive parenting style on academic achievement (see Table 2.2).

All in all, parental highest education, a proxy for parents' cultural capital, plays a larger role for girls' academic achievement than for boys' (total effect .21 for girls, .13 for boys). While the direct effects are more or less comparable (.09 for girls, .07 for boys), the indirect effects, mediated by children's competencies and their transition quality, are stronger for girls (.12) than for boys (.06). Girls' competence level and transition quality thus vary considerably by social background.

Contrary to highest parental education, an emotionally supportive parenting style plays a larger role for boys' academic achievement than for girls' (total effect .06 for girls, .16 for boys). In this case, the indirect effects are equal for both sexes (.07 for boys and girls). The direct effects are clearly more pronounced for boys (−.01 for girls, .09 for boys). The quality of communication and relationships within the family, representing a functional form of social capital, is thus a more important prerequisite for boys' ability to learn and perform. Put differently, and in line with findings from Rutter (1985), girls seem more resilient than boys to a parenting style offering less warmth and emotional support.

In order to better understand the multivariate gender difference in the effect of parental highest education described above, we have additionally compared the means of boys' and girls' competencies, transition quality, and grades broken down by parental education. The rationale for this procedure is our theoretical assumption that gender-stereotypical competency expectations and socialization practices may vary by social background. The results are displayed in Table 2.3.

Rather unexpectedly, parental highest education affects boys' social self-concept negatively, while there is no effect for girls. Boys of university-educated

Table 2.3. *Covariate means by highest parental education and sex*

		Compulsory school		High school/ apprenticeship		College of higher education		University	
		Mean	t-value[a]	Mean	t-value	Mean	t-value	Mean	t-value
Grades (academic achievement)	Girls	4.91	−0.02[n.s.]	4.92	−0.69[n.s.]	5.08	0.89[n.s.]	5.21	1.17[n.s.]
	Boys	4.92		4.96		5.01		5.13	
Transition quality	Girls	5.58	−0.06[n.s.]	5.26	0.36[n.s.]	5.50	5.10[***]	5.41	3.26[**]
	Boys	5.60		5.22		5.00		5.09	
Cognitive competence	Girls	1.39	−1.28[n.s.]	2.12	0.16[n.s.]	2.79	3.12[**]	2.79	0.53[n.s.]
	Boys	1.84		2.10		2.23		2.68	
School-relevant knowledge	Girls	3.89	−0.58[n.s.]	4.45	3.96[**]	4.65	2.57[*]	4.76	0.55[n.s.]
	Boys	4.17		4.06		4.35		4.70	
Conscientiousness	Girls	4.94	0.61[n.s.]	4.72	3.23[***]	4.82	2.73[**]	4.87	0.59[n.s.]
	Boys	4.75		4.44		4.56		4.82	
Social self-concept	Girls	3.13	−0.04[n.s.]	3.17	0.57[n.s.]	3.06	0.19[n.s.]	3.15	3.41[**]
	Boys	3.14		3.14		3.05		2.92	
Academic self-efficacy	Girls	2.71	−0.33[n.s.]	2.82	−0.64[n.s.]	2.91	−0.77[n.s.]	3.20	1.47[n.s.]
	Boys	2.83		2.86		2.98		3.07	
		N_G = 12 N_B = 13		N_G = 192 N_B = 213		N_G = 144 N_B = 131		N_G = 124 N_B = 135	

[a] * p = .05, ** p = .01, *** p = .001, n.s. = not significant.

parents in particular and, to a lesser extent, those with parents with higher vocational credentials feel less accepted by their peers compared to boys with less-educated parents and girls in general. Following Büchner (1994) and Lareau (2003), we expected this negative effect to hold for both boys and girls of highly educated parents, due to their generally highly structured and organized leisure time, restricting peer interactions. An explanation for the gender difference is that upper-class girls may spend a good part of their remaining unstructured leisure time with peers, while boys spend their time alone with computers or video games (see also Andresen, 2008). Descriptive analyses (not shown) confirm that boys with highly educated parents spend less time with peers compared to girls with highly educated parents.

Parental highest education has no effect on girls' level of conscientiousness. For boys, it plays an important role. The more highly educated the parents are, the more conscientious are their sons on average. Furthermore, Table 2.3 shows that the girls' head start in conscientiousness and school-relevant knowledge holds only if their parents have no post-compulsory education or have completed an apprenticeship or higher vocational training. Boys with university-educated parents have a similar level of conscientiousness to girls. This supports our hypothesis that gender-specific socialization practices vary by social background, and are less pronounced if parents are highly educated. Educated parents may be well aware of the productive competencies that are highly valued in school, and their significance for academic success. Given that they recognize the importance attributed to them in the school context, they might also sex-type conscientiousness to a lesser degree as a typical female trait, thus trying to instill it in their daughters and sons.

Figure 2.2 shows a direct influence of parental highest education on boys' transition quality. However, the direction of this effect is rather counterintuitive. The more highly educated the parents are, the lower they estimate the quality of their sons' beginning school transition. For girls, there is no statistically significant effect. Interestingly, the results in Table 2.3 show that boys' lower quality of transition to school compared to that of girls manifests itself only if their parents hold tertiary educational degrees (i.e., higher vocational training, university). These parents may have high expectations for their sons' and daughters' school adjustment and success. While daughters may often be able to meet these expectations, sons may not, due to on average lower competencies. The findings suggest that boys might find it harder to adopt the student role due either to their lower school-relevant knowledge, conscientiousness, or social self-concept at school entry compared to girls of similar social background.

With respect to gender similarities observable in Figure 2.2, highest parental education affects girls' and boys' school-relevant knowledge, cognitive competencies, academic self-efficacy, and grades alike and in positive ways.[14] These

---

[14] Interestingly, the descriptive findings in Table 2.3 show that girls' higher school-relevant knowledge (see means in Table 2.1) is only observable if their parents have vocational training or a degree in higher vocational education. This is in line with the descriptive gender differences in

findings support the well-documented hypothesis that highly educated parents are better able to teach their sons and daughters the competencies required by the institutionalized school context. In addition, the direct (although rather weak) effect of parental highest education on academic achievement at age 9 is in line with Ditton's (2007) claim that teachers systematically underestimate the academic achievement of children from lower social backgrounds.

Emotionally supportive parenting, the family's functional social capital, has a direct positive effect on the quality of the transition to first grade and, to a lesser extent, on academic achievement in mid-elementary school for boys only. Based on the available data it is difficult to explain this statistically significant gender difference. It may be that a supportive parenting style lowers boys' tendency for (in our data unobserved) problematic externalizing behaviors (e.g., Hicks et al., 2008), affecting, in turn, their transition quality and academic achievement positively. Further research is needed to explain these gender differences satisfactorily. For both boys and girls, a supportive parenting style plays an indirect role, mediated by the children's competencies at the age of 6. Girls and boys with more emotionally supportive parents have a higher social self-concept, are more conscientious, and have more school-relevant knowledge. A supportive parenting style thus generally facilitates children's learning and development.

Conclusions

This chapter examined whether boys' and girls' competencies differ when they enter school, and whether such differences affect the quality of the beginning school transition and later academic achievement. The answers to these hitherto little-analyzed questions may help explain why girls increasingly outperform boys in educational achievement. The findings show that our basic conceptual model (see Figure 2.1) holds for boys and girls. Irrespective of gender, children's social background affects their competencies before school entry and their later academic achievement. Children's competencies in turn determine their later academic achievement directly as well as indirectly, mediated by the quality of the transition to school at the age of 7.

Despite these similarities, we found important differences between boys and girls. As hypothesized, girls were generally better prepared than boys for adopting the student role due to their more abundant school-relevant competencies at school entry. Girls' higher competencies may be due to boys' delayed maturation and development (De Fruyt et al., 2008) or gender-specific socialization practices (see also Fabes et al., this volume). Given that the observed gender differences in conscientiousness, school-relevant knowledge, and the social self-concept vary by social background, gender-specific socialization practices are a more likely

---

conscientiousness and further supports the hypothesis that gender differences in school-relevant competencies are a result of gendered socialization practices, which are particularly dominant in vocationally educated middle-class families.

explanation. They point to an intertwinement of gender and social background, which disadvantages boys from vocationally educated middle-class families.

Furthermore, our study has shown that some of the underlying mechanisms explaining the quality of transition to school and later academic achievement vary by gender from school entry onwards. This holds in particular for the differing roles of a supportive parenting style and competencies for boys and girls. The finding that a supportive parenting style has only a direct effect on boys' transition quality and academic achievement is in line with previous empirical evidence suggesting that boys' academic performance depends more strongly on the (emotional) conditions of their family environments (Mensah & Kiernan, 2010). Similarly, Rutter (1985) found that for many psychosocial adversities boys are more vulnerable than girls. However, the mechanisms explaining boys' greater sensitivity in this respect are still largely unclear. The greater importance of conscientiousness for girls and the transition quality for boys supports our assumption that teachers' gender-stereotypical perception of children's abilities and behaviors may affect their grading practices (see also Upadyaya & Eccles, this volume). In the long run this mechanism may disadvantage boys' academic achievement more strongly due to their reported tendency for externalizing behavior (Hicks et al., 2008). Our results thus point to some potential reasons for later gender differences in academic achievement.

Regarding the limitations of our study, our data did not allow for directly testing some of our theoretical assumptions. This pertains in particular to the exact mechanisms through which daughters of vocationally trained middle-class parents gain higher school-relevant competencies. Further research should examine whether these parents do indeed adhere more strongly to the conception of innate gender differences and in what way the ensuing parenting practices differ for boys and girls. We suspect that the stronger adherence may be related to their work experience in the highly sex-segregated occupations that are typically accessible to people with (higher) vocational training. As occupational sex segregation goes hand in hand with the conception of innate gender differences (Charles & Bradley, 2009), the respective work experience may be generalized and transferred to other life domains such as child rearing (Kohn & Schooler, 1983).

Another limitation pertains to the lack of teacher data on competence perception and its relevance for grading. Further research is needed in order to better understand under which circumstances and to what extent teachers draw on gender-stereotypic competency and behavior perception when grading boys' and girls' school performance. This would clarify whether these criteria are indeed responsible for the gender-specific effects of conscientiousness and the transition quality on boys' and girls' grades and whether this mechanism may vary by subject or school level.

Finally, long-term analyses for Switzerland and other countries with highly stratified school systems could establish at which point in the school career girls' higher achievement manifests itself clearly and whether the relevant factors may vary over the educational career.

In sum, our chapter has shed light on the significance of a successful beginning school transition for children's later academic achievement. It has highlighted gender differences in the mechanisms at work, demonstrating that the individual and social antecedents of coping with the transition to school partly vary for boys and girls.

References

Andresen, S. (2008). Kinder und soziale Ungleichheit: Ergebnisse der Kindheitsforschung zu dem Zusammenhang von Klasse und Geschlecht. In B. Rendtorff & A. Prengel (Eds.), *Kinder und ihr Geschlecht* (pp. 35–48). Opladen and Farmington Hills, MI: Barbara Budrich.

Asendorpf, J. B., & Aken, M. (1993). *Pictorial scale of perceived competence and social acceptance: Deutsche Fassung (PSCA-D) und Instruktion Harter-Skala ab 3. Klasse.* Berlin: Humboldt Universität, Institut für Psychologie.

Asendorpf, J. B., & van Aken, M. A. G. (2003). Validity of big five personality judgments in childhood: A 9 year longitudinal study. *European Journal of Personality*, 17, 1–17.

Bacher, J., Beham, M., & Lachmayr, N. (2008). *Geschlechterunterschiede in der Bildungswahl.* Wiesbaden: VS Verlag.

Bandura, A., Barbaranelli, C., Caprara, G. V., & Pastorelli, C. (1996). Multifaceted impact of self-efficacy beliefs on academic functioning. *Child Development*, 67, 1206–1222.

Baumert, J., & Schümer, G. (2001). Familiäre Lebensverhältnisse, Bildungsbeteiligung und Kompetenzerwerb. In J. Baumert, E. Klieme, M. Neubrand, M. Prenzel, U. Schiefele, W. Schneider, et al. (Eds.), *PISA 2000: Basiskompetenzen von Schülerinnen und Schülern im internationalen Vergleich* (pp. 323–407). Opladen: Leske + Budrich.

Baumert, J., Watermann, R., & Schümer, G. (2003). Disparitäten der Bildungsbeteiligung und des Kompetenzerwerbs. *Zeitschrift für Erziehungswissenschaft*, 6, 46–71.

Bem, S. L. (1974). The measurement of psychological androgyny. *Journal of Consulting and Clinical Psychology*, 42, 155–162.

Birch, S. H., & Ladd, G. W. (1996). Interpersonal relationships in the school environment and children's early school adjustment: The role of teachers and peers. In J. Juvonen & K. R. Wentzel (Eds.), *Social motivation: Understanding children's school adjustment* (pp. 199–225). Cambridge University Press.

Bodovski, K., & Farkas, G. (2008). "Concerted cultivation" and unequal achievement in elementary school. *Social Science Research*, 37, 903–919.

Bonesrønning, H. (2008). The effect of grading practices on gender differences in academic performance. *Bulletin of Economic Research*, 60, 245–264.

Bossert, S. T. (1981). Understanding sex differences in children's classroom experiences. *Elementary School Journal*, 81, 255–266.

Bourdieu, P. (1983). Ökonomisches Kapital, kulturelles Kapital, soziales Kapital. In R. Kreckel (Ed.), *Soziale Ungleichheiten* (pp. 183–198). Göttingen: Verlag Otto Schartz & Co.

Bourdieu, P., & Passeron, J.-C. (1964). *Die Illusion der Chancengleichheit: Untersuchungen zur Soziologie des Bildungswesens am Beispiel Frankreichs.* Stuttgart: Klett.

Bradley, R. H., & Corwyn, R. F. (2002). Socioeconomic status and child development. *Annual Review of Psychology*, 53, 371–399.

Breen, R., Luijkx, R., Müller, W., & Pollak, R. (2010). Long-term trends in educational inequality in Europe: Class inequalities and gender differences. *European Sociological Review*, 26, 31–48.

Buchmann, C., DiPrete, T. A., & McDaniel, A. (2008). Gender inequalities in education. *Annual Review of Sociology*, 34, 319–337.

Buchmann, M., & Fend, H. (2004). *Context and competence: Swiss longitudinal survey of children and youth. Research proposal.* Bern: Swiss National Science Foundation.

Büchner, P. (1994). (Schul-) Kindsein heute zwischen Familie, Schule und ausserschulischen Freizeiteinrichtungen: Zum Wandel des heutigen Kinderlebens in der Folge von gesellschaftlichen Modernisierungsprozessen. In P. Büchner, M. Grundmann, J. Huinink, L. Krappmann, B. Nauck, D. Meyer, & S. Rothe (Eds.), *Kindliche Lebenswelten, Bildung und innerfamiliale Beziehungen* (pp. 9–39). Munich: Verlag Deutsches Jugendinstitut.

Büchner, P., & Brake, A. (Eds.). (2006). *Bildungsort Familie: Transmissionen von Bildung und Kultur im Alltag von Mehrgenerationenfamilien.* Wiesbaden: Springer.

Buhs, E. S. (2005). Peer rejection, negative peer treatment, and school adjustment: Self-concept and classroom engagement as mediating processes. *Journal of School Psychology*, 43, 407–424.

Buhs, E. S., & Ladd, G. W. (2001). Peer rejection as an antecedent of young children's school adjustment: An examination of mediating processes. *Developmental Psychology*, 37, 550–560.

Byrne, B. M. (2001). *Structural equation modeling with AMOS: Basic concepts, applications, and programming.* Mahwah, NJ and London: Lawrence Erlbaum Associates.

Cattell, R. B., Weiss, R. H., & Osterland, J. (1977). *Grundintelligenztest Skala 1 (CFT 1).* Göttingen: Hogrefe.

Charles, M., & Bradley, K. (2009). Indulging our gendered selves? Sex segregation by field of study in 44 countries. *American Journal of Sociology*, 114, 924–976.

Cheadle, J. (2008). Educational investment, family context, and children's math and reading growth from kindergarten through the third grade. *Sociology of Education*, 81, 1–31.

Coleman, J. S. (1988). Social capital in the creation of human capital. *American Journal of Sociology*, 94, S95–S120.

Conger, R. D., Ebert Wallace, L., Sun, Y., Simons, R. L., McLoyd, V. C., & Brody, G. H. (2002). Economic pressure in African American families: A replication and extension of the family stress model. *Developmental Psychology*, 38, 179–193.

Correll, S. J. (2001). Gender and the career choice process: The role of biased self-assessments. *American Journal of Sociology*, 106, 1691–1730.

Covay, E., & Carbonaro, W. (2010). After the bell: Participation in extracurricular activities, classroom behavior, and academic achievement. *Sociology of Education*, 83, 20–45.

Davis-Kean, P. E. (2005). The influence of parent education and family income on child achievement: The indirect role of parental expectations and the home environment. *Journal of Family Psychology*, 19, 294–304.

De Fruyt, F., Van Leeuwen, K., De Bolle, M., & De Clercq, B. (2008). Sex differences in school performance as a function of conscientiousness, imagination and the mediating role of problem behaviour. *European Journal of Personality*, 22, 167–184.

De Graaf, N. D., De Graaf, P., & Kraaykamp, G. (2000). Parental cultural capital and educational attainment in the Netherlands: A refinement of the cultural capital perspective. *Sociology of Education*, 73, 92–111.

Ditton, H. (2007). Der Beitrag von Schule und Lehrern zur Reproduktion von Bildungsungleichheit. In R. Becker & W. Lauterbach (Eds.), *Bildung als Privileg: Erklärungen und Befunde zu den Ursachen der Bildungsungleichheit* (pp. 243–271). Wiesbaden: VS Verlag für Sozialwissenschaften.

Duckworth, A. L., & Seligman, M. E. P. (2006). Self-discipline gives girls the edge: Gender in self-discipline, grades, and achievement test scores. *Journal of Educational Psychology*, 98, 198–208.

Durham, R. E., Farkas, G., Hammer, C. S., Tomblin, B. J., & Catts, H. W. (2007). Kindergarten oral language skill: A key variable in the intergenerational transmission of socioeconomic status. *Research in Social Stratification and Mobility*, 25, 294–305.

Eccles, J. S., Midgley, C., Wigfield, A., Buchanan, C. M., Reuman, D., Flanagan, C., & Mac Iver, D. (1993). Development during adolescence: The impact of stage-environment fit on adolescents' experiences in schools and families. *American Psychologist*, 48, 90–101.

Entwisle, D. R., & Alexander, K. L. (1993). Entry into school: The beginning school transition and educational stratification in the United States. *Annual Review of Sociology*, 19, 401–423.

Entwisle, D. R., Alexander, K. L., & Olson, L. S. (2003). The first-grade transition in life course perspective. In J. T. Mortimer & M. J. Shanahan (Eds.), *Handbook of the life course* (pp. 229–250). New York: Kluwer Academic/Plenum Publishers.

(2007) Early schooling: The handicap of being poor and male. *Sociology of Education*, 80, 114–138.

Farkas, G. (2003). Cognitive skills and noncognitive traits and behaviors in stratification processes. *Annual Review of Sociology*, 29, 541–562.

Farkas, G., & Beron, K. (2004). The detailed age trajectory of oral vocabulary knowledge: Differences by class and race. *Social Science Research*, 33, 464–497.

Farkas, G., Sheehan, D., Grobe, R. P., & Shuan, Y. (1990). Cultural resources and school success: Gender, ethnicity, and poverty groups within an urban school district. *American Sociological Review*, 55, 127–142.

Faulstich-Wieland, H., Weber, M., & Willems, K. (2004). *Doing gender im heutigen Schulalltag. Empirische Studien zur sozialen Konstruktion von Geschlecht in schulischen Interaktionen*. Weinheim/Münschen: Juventa.

Freudenthaler, H. H., Spinath, B., & Neubauer, A. C. (2008). Predicting school achievement in boys and girls. *European Journal of Personality*, 22, 231–245.

Gullo, D. F. (1991). The effects of gender, at risk status and number of years of preschool on children's academic readiness. *Early Education and Development*, 2, 32–39.

Hadjar, A., & Lupatsch, J. (2011). Geschlechterunterschiede im Schulerfolg. Spielt die Lehrperson eine Rolle? *Zeitschrift für Soziologie der Erziehung und Sozialisation*, 31(1), 79–94.

Harter, S., & Pike, R. (1984). The pictorial scale of perceived competence and social acceptance for young children. *Child Development*, 55, 1969–1982.

Helbig, M. (2010). Sind Lehrerinnen für den geringeren Schulerfolg von Jungen verantwortlich? *Kölner Zeitschrift für Soziologie und Sozialpsycholgie*, 62, 93–111.

Hicks, B. M., Johnson, W., Iacono, W. G., & McGue, M. (2008). Moderating effects of personality on the genetic and environmental influences of school grades helps to explain sex differences in scholastic achievement. *European Journal of Personality*, 22, 247–268.

Jacobs, J. E., Lanza, S., Osgood, D. W., Eccles, J. S., & Wigfield, A. (2002). Changes in children's self-competence and values: Gender and domain differences across grades one through twelve. *Child Development*, 73, 509–527.

Janus, M., & Offord, D. R. (2007). Development and psychometric properties of the early development instrument (EDI): A measure of children's school readiness. *Canadian Journal of Behavioural Science*, 39, 1–22.

Kohn, M. L., & Schooler, C. (1983). Stratification, occupation, and orientation. In M. L. Kohn & C. Schooler (Eds.), *Work and personality: An inquiry into the impact of social stratification* (pp. 5–33). Norwood, NJ: Ablex Publishing.

Koppetsch, C. (2001). Milieu und Geschlecht: Eine kontextspezifische Perspektive. In A. Weiss, C. Koppetsch, A. Scharenberg, & O. Schmidtke (Eds.), *Klasse und Klassifikation: Die symbolische Dimension sozialer Ungleichheit* (pp. 109–138). Wiesbaden: Westdeutscher Verlag.

Kracke, B., & Hofer, M. (2002). Familie und Arbeit. In M. Hofer, E. Wild, & P. Noack (Eds.), *Lehrbuch Familienbeziehungen: Eltern und Kinder in der Entwicklung* (pp. 94–123). Göttingen: Hogrefe.

Kreppner, K. (1999). Beziehung und Entwicklung in der Familie: Kontinuität und Diskontinuität bei der Konstruktion von Erfahrungswelten. In M. Grundmann (Ed.), *Konstruktivistische Sozialisationsforschung* (pp. 180–207). Frankfurt am Main: Suhrkamp.

Kuhn, H. P. (2008). Geschlechterverhältnisse in der Schule: Sind die Jungen jetzt benachteiligt? Eine Sichtung empirischer Studien. In B. Rendtorff & A. Prengel (Eds.), *Kinder und ihr Geschlecht* (pp. 49–71). Opladen and Farmington Hills, MI: Barbara Budrich.

Ladd, G. W., Herald, S. L., & Kochel, K. P. (2006). School readiness: Are there social prerequisites? *Early Education and Development*, 17, 115–150.

Lareau, A. (2003). *Unequal childhoods: Class, race, and family life*. Berkeley: University of California Press.

Lavy, V. (2004). *Do gender stereotypes reduce girls' human capital outcomes? Evidence from a natural experiment* (NBER Working Paper 10678). Cambridge, MA: National Bureau of Economic Research.

Lee, J. S., & Bowen, N. K. (2006). Parent involvement, cultural capital, and the achievement gap among elementary school children. *American Educational Research Journal*, 43, 193–218.

Liben, L. S., & Bigler, R. S. (2002). The developmental course of gender differentiation: Conceptualizing, measuring, and evaluating constructs and pathways. *Monographs of the Society for Research in Child Development*, 67.

Marsh, H. W. (1989). Age and sex effects in multiple dimensions of self-concept: Preadolescence to early-adulthood. *Journal of Educational Psychology*, 81, 417–430.

Martin, K. A. (1998). Becoming a gendered body: Practices of preschools. *American Sociological Review*, 63, 494–511.

Mensah, F. K., & Kiernan, K. E. (2010). Gender differences in educational attainment: Influences of the family environment. *British Educational Research Journal*, 36, 239–260.

Moser, U., Keller, F., & Tresch, S. (2003). *Schullaufbahn und Leistung: Bildungsverlauf und Lernerfolg von Zürcher Schülerinnen und Schülern am Ende der 3. Volksschulklasse*. Bern: hep.

National Center for Education Statistics. (1994). *School and staffing survey 1993–1994: Principal's survey*. Washington, DC: US Department of Education.

Neuenschwander, M. P., & Malti, T. (2009). Selektionsprozesse beim Übergang in die Sekundarstufe I und II. *Zeitschrift für Erziehungswissenschaft*, 12, 1–17.

Neugebauer, M., Helbig, M., & Landmann, A. (2010). Can the teacher's gender explain the "boy crisis" in educational attainment? *Working Paper – Mannheimer Zentrum für empirische Sozialforschung*, 133.

Papastefanou, C., & Hofer, M. (2002). Familienbildung und elterliche Kompetenzen. In M. Hofer, E. Wild, & P. Noack (Eds.), *Lehrbuch Familienbeziehungen: Eltern und Kinder in der Entwicklung* (pp. 168–191). Göttingen: Hogrefe.

Ridgeway, C. L., & Correll, S. J. (2004). Unpacking the gender system: A theoretical perspective on gender beliefs and social relations. *Gender & Society*, 18, 510–531.

Ridgeway, C. L., Li, Y. E., Erickson, K. G., Backor, K., & Tinkler, J. E. (2009). How easily does a social difference become a status distinction? Gender matters. *American Sociological Review*, 74, 44–62.

Rothbart, M., Ahadi, S., & Hershey, K. (1994). Temperament and social behavior in childhood. *Merill Palmer Quarterly*, 40, 21–39.

Rutter, M. (1985). Resilience in the face of adversity: Protective factors and resistance to psychiatric disorder. *British Journal of Psychiatry*, 147, 598–611.

Sacchi, S. (2006). *Dokumentation der Stichprobengewichtung zur Erstbefragung der drei COCON-Kohorten*. Zürich: Cue Sozialforschung.

Simons, R. L., Lorenz, F. O., Conger, R. D., & Wu, C. I. (1992). Support from spouse as a mediator and moderator of the disruptive influence of economic strain on parenting. *Child Development*, 63, 1282–1301.

Stamm, M. (2008). Underachievement von Jungen: Perspektiven eines internationalen Diskurses. *Zeitschrift für Erziehungswissenschaft*, 11, 106–124.

Steinmayr, R., & Spinath, B. (2008). Sex differences in school achievement: What are the roles of personality and achievement motivation? *European Journal of Personality*, 22, 185–209.

Stocké, V. (2010). Schulbezogenes Sozialkapital und Schulerfolg der Kinder: Kompetenzvorsprung oder statistische Diskriminierung durch Lehrkräfte? In B. Becker & D. Reimer (Eds.), *Vom Kindergarten bis zur Hochschule: Die Generierung von ethnischen und sozialen Disparitäten in der Bildungsbiographie*. Wiesbaden: VS Verlag.

Tiedemann, J. (2000). Parents' gender stereotypes and teachers' beliefs as predictors of children's concept of their mathematical ability in elementary school. *Journal of Educational Psychology*, 92, 144–151.

Tresch, S. (2005). Soziale Kompetenzen bei Schuleintritt. In U. Moser, M. Stamm, & J. Hollenweger (Eds.), *Für die Schule bereit? Lesen, Wortschatz, Mathematik und soziale Kompetenzen beim Schuleintritt* (pp. 99–112). Oberentfelden: Sauerländer.

Urhahne, D. (2008). Sieben Arten der Lernmotivation: Ein Überblick über zentrale Forschungskonzepte. *Psychologische Rundschau*, 59, 150–166.

Vester, M., & Gardemin, D. (2001). Milieu, Klasse und Geschlecht: Das Feld der Geschlechterungleichheit und die "protestantische Arbeitsethik." In B. Heintz (Ed.), *Geschlechtersoziologie: Sonderheft der Kölner Zeitschrift für Soziologie und Sozialpsycholgie* (pp. 454–486). Wiesbaden: Westdeutscher Verlag.

Weiner, B. (1985). An attributional theory of achievement motivation and emotion. *Psychological Review*, 92(4), 79–94.

Wentzel, K. R. (2005). Peer relationships, motivation, and academic performance at school. In A. J. Elliot & C. S. Dweck (Eds.), *Handbook of competence and motivation* (pp. 279–296). New York: Guilford.

Wigfield, A., & Eccles, J. S. (2002). The development of competence beliefs, expectancies for success, and achievement values from childhood through adolescence. In A. Wigfield & J. S. Eccles (Eds.), *Development of achievement motivation* (pp. 91–120). San Diego, CA: Academic Press.

Wilgenbusch, T., & Merrell, K. W. (1999). Gender differences in self-concept among children and adolescents: A meta-analysis of multidimensional studies. *Social Psychology Quarterly*, 14, 101–120.

3 Gender differences in teachers' perceptions and children's ability self-concepts

Katja Upadyaya and Jacquelynne S. Eccles

Abstract

The aim of the present study is to investigate the associations between primary school teachers' perceptions of ability and effort and children's ability self-concepts and performance in math and reading. Moreover, special focus is put on the possible gender differences in teachers' ability and effort perceptions. The study uses data from the Childhood and Beyond (CAB) Study in which three cohorts of elementary school children and their teachers were followed. The sample includes 849 children (240 second-graders, 246 third-graders, and 363 fifth-graders) and their teachers. Information concerning children's ability self-concepts and actual performance in math and reading was gathered during the spring term. Teachers rated the children's ability and effort at the same time. The results show, first, that teachers' perceptions of ability and effort positively predict children's ability self-concepts in math and reading. Moreover, gender differences are found in teachers' perceptions: teachers tend to rate boys as having higher abilities in math than girls, and they tend to rate girls as putting more effort into reading than boys.

Teachers' perceptions, children's ability self-concepts, and gender differences

Teachers begin looking for possible causes for their students' achievement early in their school career (Clark & Artiles, 2000), and the two most common elements to which teachers refer are individual children's academic abilities and effort (Weiner, 1994). Children's performance in different domains often predicts teachers' perceptions concerning their abilities and effort (Carr & Kurtz-Costes, 1994; Natale, Viljaranta, Lerkkanen, Poikkeus, & Nurmi, 2009; Hughes, Gleason, & Zhang, 2005), and there is also evidence linking teacher perceptions to children's subsequent performance and motivation (Upadyaya, Viljaranta, Lerkkanen, Poikkeus, & Nurmi, 2012). However, less is known about the extent to which teachers' ability and effort perceptions predict children's ability self-concepts over the primary school years. Moreover, the associations between teachers' perceptions and children's academic outcomes can be affected by gender stereotypes. Some studies have suggested that gender bias occurs in the ways teachers interpret boys' and girls' academic achievement (Fennema, Peterson,

Carpenter, & Lubinski, 1990; Li, 1999; Tiedemann, 2000a). For example, when explaining children's success in math, teachers easily attribute boys' success to ability, whereas girls' success in math is attributed to effort (Fennema et al., 1990; Tiedemann, 2000a, 2002). However, not all studies have reported such gender differences in teachers' perceptions (Holloway & Hess, 1985; Natale et al., 2009), which highlights the importance of examining them further. Consequently, the present study investigated the impact of teachers' ability and effort perceptions on children's ability self-concepts in math and reading over the primary school years. Moreover, the possible gender differences in teachers' perceptions were examined, controlling for the level of children's performance in math and reading and for children's age (e.g., cohort status).

The two main causes to which teachers usually attribute children's academic successes and failures are an individual child's abilities (e.g., talent or aptitude in different domains) and effort (e.g., how hard the child tries to accomplish tasks) (Weiner, 1994). Teachers may, for example, think that some children succeed at school because of their innate abilities, whereas other children succeed because they are hard working (Graham, 1984, 1990). These perceptions, in turn, impact teachers' behavior and interaction with their students (Li, 1999). For example, teachers' perceptions are typically communicated to children indirectly through teachers' emotional responses and feedback, which can sometimes be very subtle and unconscious (Graham, 1990). However, when communicated to children, teachers' perceptions may further influence children's subsequent academic self-perceptions, motivation, and performance (Clark, 1997; Graham, 1990; Jussim, 1989; Jussim & Eccles, 1992; Li, 1999), all of which are particularly sensitive to environmental changes during the early school career (Jacobs, Lanza, Osgood, Eccles, & Wigfield, 2002). Moreover, teachers may hold different beliefs concerning boys' and girls' academic performance (Fennema et al., 1990; Li, 1999; Tiedemann, 2002), and some studies have suggested that girls are more sensitive to teachers' feedback than boys (Jussim, Eccles, & Madon, 1996; Roberts, 1991). Consequently, the present study set out to investigate how teachers' ability and effort perceptions would predict primary school children's ability self-concepts in math and reading. Moreover, the possible gender differences in teachers' perceptions and children's ability self-concepts are investigated, also controlling for children's performance and cohort status.

Theoretical background

Teachers' perceptions concerning their students' achievement have typically been investigated in the framework of the attributional theory of motivation (Weiner, 1985, 1986) and the expectancy-value model of motivation (Eccles et al., 1983; Wigfield & Eccles, 2000). According to the attributional theory of motivation, children's academic achievement is typically explained by several internal or external causal attributions that children, parents, and teachers deploy (Weiner, 1986, 1994). Internal explanations, such as ability and effort, are especially important in motivating children to do well at school (Weiner, 1994). Thus, a large amount of empirical research has focused on these two perceptions (Cole, 1991; Herbert & Stipek, 2005; Holloway & Hess, 1985; Jussim, 1989; Tiedemann, 2000a, 2002). Teachers' perceptions of children's ability and effort are similar to each other in that they both refer to internal qualities of a child (Weiner, 1986). However, they are different in the sense that ability is usually considered a stable and uncontrollable characteristic, whereas effort is typically assumed to be unstable and a characteristic within the control of a child (Weiner, 1986). For example, it has been assumed that a child cannot control the amount of his/her "innate" ability, but can easily control and change the amount of effort he/she puts into tasks (Weiner, 1994).

According to the expectancy-value model of motivation (Eccles et al., 1983; Wigfield & Eccles, 2000), teachers are significant socializers whose perceptions may impact children's ability self-concepts, interests, and academic motivation (Eccles et al., 1983; Madon et al., 2001; Tiedemann, 2000b; Upadyaya et al., 2012). Previous research has shown that teachers' perceptions concerning individual children's academic achievement are typically communicated to children indirectly through teachers' feedback and emotional responses (Butler, 1994; Clark & Artiles, 2000; Georgiou, Christou, Stavrinides, & Panaoura, 2002; Graham, 1990; Hall, Villeme, & Burley, 1989). For example, teachers may show pity or blame toward children according to their perceptions of the amount of ability and effort the children have (Graham, 1990). Further, especially at the beginning of primary school, children easily assimilate teachers' perceptions of their ability and effort into their own ability self-concepts (Cole, 1991; Rosenholtz & Simpson, 1984; Tiedemann, 2000b). For example, teachers' expectations concerning children's future performance and achievement usually come to be reflected in children's expectations for their own achievement (Herbert & Stipek, 2005; Kuklinski & Weinstein, 2001; Madon et al., 2001; Tiedemann, 2000b). Moreover, teachers' perceptions and expectations concerning individual children impact the ways teachers interact with them, which can further predict children's competence beliefs and future expectations (Eccles-Parsons, Kaczala, & Meece, 1982). For example, when teachers have high expectations for a student, they typically express more praise to him/her and provide the student with more challenging materials, which, in turn, predicts increases in a student's expectations of his/her future competence (Eccles et al., 1983).

Gender differences in teachers' perceptions

Some research has also found differences in teachers' perceptions based on children's gender. These differences are typically related to teachers' perceptions concerning their pupils' achievement in specific domains, such as math and reading, rather than to their perceptions concerning children's overall academic successes. Previous studies indicate that teachers tend to stereotype math as a male domain, which is further reflected in teachers' perceptions and expectations concerning the math achievement of individual students (Li, 1999). For example, boys' success in math is typically attributed to ability, whereas girls' success in math is attributed to effort (Fennema et al., 1990; Jussim, 1989; Tiedemann, 2000a). Moreover, teachers easily overrate boys' math abilities and have higher expectations for their future success (Li, 1999). Teachers also perceive girls as working harder than boys and needing to exert more effort than boys to do well in math (Siegle & Reis, 1998; Tiedemann, 2000a, 2002). However, not all studies have found gender differences in teachers' perceptions concerning children's ability and effort in success situations (Holloway & Hess, 1985; Natale et al., 2009), which shows a need to study the possible gender differences in teachers' perceptions further.

While the consequences of teachers' perceptions on children's academic performance and motivation have been widely discussed, less is known about the origins of the gender differences in teachers' perceptions. It has been suggested that one possible source for teachers' gender-stereotypic beliefs is broader cultural beliefs. According to stereotype, math is "a male domain," whereas languages are more female-dominated (Eccles, Freedman-Doan, Frome, Jacobs, & Yoon, 2000; Li, 1999; Tiedemann, 2002). In addition, most of the studies emphasize that the associations between teachers' perceptions and children's performance and motivation are typically reciprocal (Li, 1999; Tiedemann, 2000b). Thus, teachers are aware of girls' lower self-perceptions related to math, even though their performance might be equal to that of boys (Tiedemann, 2000a). Regardless, gender differences exist both in teachers' and children's perceptions, especially as the children grow older (Tiedemann, 2002).

Gender difference biases may also exist in teachers' feedback and interaction with the students. For example, some teachers give more feedback related to intellectual quality of work to girls than they do to boys (Dweck, Davidson, Nelson, & Enna, 1978). Moreover, some teachers give boys more opportunities to speak in math classes than girls because they are more active and teachers perceive them as performing better in math than girls (Eccles et al., 1983; Tiedemann, 2000a, 2002). Some research has also suggested that girls are more sensitive to teachers' evaluative feedback (Jussim et al., 1996; Roberts, 1991) than boys and thus teachers' perceptions may have a stronger impact on their motivation and self-perceptions.

Teachers' perceptions, children's ability self-concepts, and academic performance

Teachers' ability and effort perceptions are also closely related to children's academic performance and motivation. These associations are usually reciprocal (Li, 1999; Tiedemann, 2000a); children's academic performance and motivation may predict teachers' perceptions and vice versa. Previously, it has been found that when children's academic performance is high, teachers tend to think that children's success is related to their abilities (Carr & Kurtz-Costes, 1994; Holloway & Hess, 1985; Hughes et al., 2005). Moreover, when children show high academic motivation, teachers tend to believe their academic success is due to children's effort, whereas children's high performance and motivation are usually associated with teachers' ability perceptions (Natale et al., 2009; Upadyaya et al., 2012). Further, studies on expectancy effects have shown that teachers' confidence in each student's ability can have a small positive impact on the student's actual performance (Dweck, 1986; Eccles et al., 1983; Jussim et al., 1996) and task motivation (Natale et al., 2009).

Teachers' feedback is usually based on their perceptions of the causes of children's performance (Graham, 1990), and as such may be partly responsible for the changes that occur in children's ability self-concepts over the school years. At the beginning of primary school children usually have very high ability self-concepts, which are also related to high academic learning and achievement (Eccles, Wigfield, & Schiefele, 1997). However, over the school years children's ability self-concepts in different domains decline (Aunola, Leskinen, Onatsu-Arvilommi, & Nurmi, 2002; Bouffard, Marcoux, Vezeau, & Bordeleau, 2003; Jacobs et al., 2002) and stabilize (Wigfield et al., 1997). It is possible that this occurs partly because children's understanding of the evaluative feedback they receive from their teachers increases (Stipek & Mac Iver, 1989; Wigfield & Eccles, 2000), and because, especially during the early elementary school years, children assimilate their teachers' perceptions of their ability and effort into their own ability self-concepts (Tiedemann, 2000b). However, less is known about how teachers' ability and effort perceptions predict children's ability self-concepts over the school years, and about the possible gender biases in teachers' perceptions. Consequently, in the following we examine the impact of teachers' perceptions of children's ability and effort on children's self-concepts in math and reading, taking into account gender, age, and children's actual performance. First, we assess gender differences in teachers' ability and effort perceptions, controlling for students' academic performance. Second, we assess gender differences in children's ability self-concepts and academic performance. Third, we test the pathways linking teachers' ability and effort perceptions and children's academic performance to children's ability self-concepts in math and reading, taking into account gender and age differences. In a final step we test whether these associations hold over two separate waves of the study. A basic model of the study is presented in Figure 3.1.

We hypothesize that teachers would perceive boys as having more abilities than girls and girls as putting more effort in their schoolwork than boys (H1). We expect that this would be true especially in math (H2). In addition, we hypothesize that boys have higher self-concept of math ability than girls, whereas girls have higher self-concept of reading ability than boys (H3). Moreover, we assume that older children have lower ability self-concepts (H4) and higher performance in math and reading than younger children (H5).

[Figure: A basic model of the study showing relationships between Gender, Teachers' perceptions of ability, Teachers' perceptions of effort, Performance in math/reading, Age (e.g., cohort status), and Ability self-concept in math/reading]

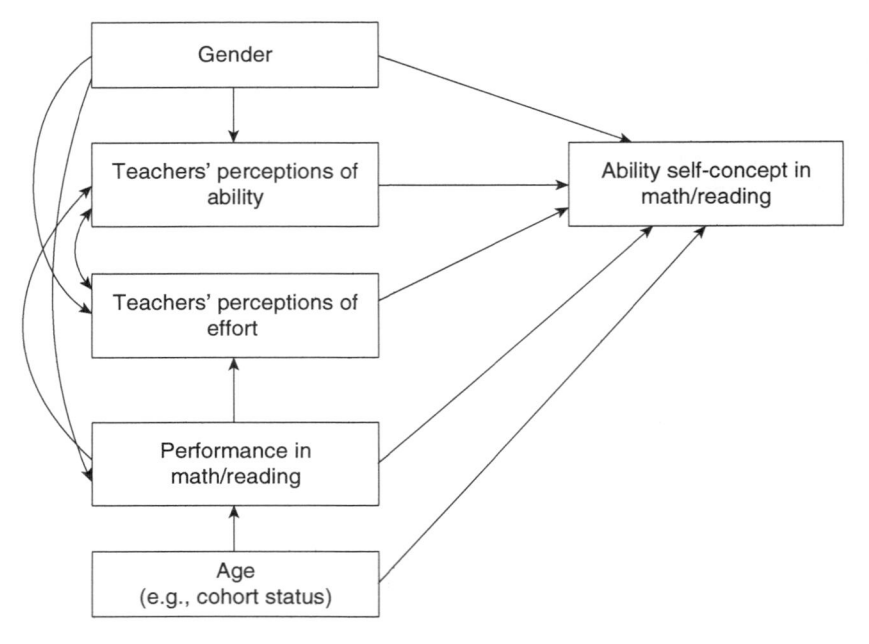

Figure 3.1 *A basic model of the study*

Method

Participants and procedure

We use data from the Childhood and Beyond (CAB) Study in which three cohorts of children and their teachers and parents were followed over many years, beginning in 1986 when the members of the youngest cohort were in kindergarten (see Eccles, Wigfield, Harold, & Blumenfeld, 1993). To best describe the associations between teachers' perceptions and children's ability self-concepts across the primary school years, the present study focused on the third and fourth waves following children from the second to sixth grades (i.e., ages 7–11). This sample consists of three cohorts of 849 children attending school in Southeastern Michigan and their teachers; 240 were second-graders (118 girls, 122 boys), 246 were third-graders (126 girls, 120 boys), and 363 were fifth-graders (189 girls, 174 boys) at Wave 3. The Wave 4 data was collected 1 year after Wave 3. There were 127 teachers who participated in the study; the vast majority were female, white, and had elementary school teaching credentials. The vast majority of the children were from middle-class backgrounds, and 92% of the children were European-American. Children completed a questionnaire concerning their math and reading ability self-concepts, and teachers rated their students' innate ability and effort during the spring term of the study.

Children's measures

Self-concept of ability (SCA) in math and reading

Children completed a questionnaire concerning their SCA in math and reading once during the spring term. Children answered a set of five questions with illustrations concerning their perceptions of their abilities in math and then in reading (i.e., "How good at math are you?" and "How good would you be at learning something new in reading?") (see Eccles et al., 1993 and Jacobs et al., 2002 for a report on these scales). Children answered these questions using a 7-point Likert scale (the anchors were 1 = *not at all good*, and 7 = *very good*). Two sum scores were calculated for children's self-concepts of ability in math and reading as the mean of the five items concerning their self-concept in each skill. The Cronbach's alpha reliabilities for children's ability self-concepts were .79 for math and .84 for reading.

Performance in math and reading

Information concerning children's performance in math and reading was obtained from school reports at the end of the school year. Grades were coded on a scale of 1–16, where 1 represented an F– and 16 an A+. The math grades ranged between 3 and 15 ($M = 11.43$, $SD = 2.17$). Similarly, the grades for reading performance ranged between 6 and 15 ($M = 11.77$, $SD = 2.14$).

Demographics

Children's gender in the present study was coded 1 = female, 2 = male. Age (e.g., cohort status) was coded as follows: 1 = second-graders (7 years old), 2 = third-graders (8 years old), and 3 = fifth-graders (10 years old) at Wave 3.

Teachers' measures

Teachers' ability and effort perceptions

Teachers filled in a questionnaire once during each spring term of the study concerning each of their students' innate ability and effort in math and reading. In the questionnaire, teachers were asked to rate how much they believed each individual child in their class had innate ability in math and reading, and how much effort they put into their tasks (i.e., "Compared to other children, how much innate ability or talent does this child have in each of the following?" with the alternatives of math and reading; and "Compared to other children, how hard does this child try in each activity area listed below?" with the alternatives of math and reading). Teachers answered the questions using a 7-point Likert scale (the anchors were 1 = *very little/not at all hard*, and 7 = *a lot/very hard*). The intra-class correlations (ICC) for teachers' ability and effort perceptions in math and reading ranged from .71 to .76.

Analytic strategy

As the teacher-report data had a hierarchical structure and teachers' perceptions showed high intra-class correlations, the research questions were analyzed using a multilevel modeling technique (Duncan et al., 1997; Muthén, 1997). Multilevel modeling provides a tool that enables the variance in the observed variables to be differentiated into two components: variation due to the similarity among children in the class taught by the same teacher (*between-level variation*) and variation due to differences among individual children (*within-level variation*). Because special focus was put on child-related variables and gender differences in teachers' perceptions, all the models were carried out at the within-level. Two within-level path models were carried out separately for math- and reading-related teachers' perceptions, children's ability self-concepts, and performance. Moreover, because the teachers changed every year, the models were carried out separately for each wave of the study. This also enabled us to control for students' grouping in individual teachers' classrooms at each wave, and to assess whether the same processes between the independent and dependent variables would hold across the waves. Moreover, children's gender and cohort status was controlled for in all the models. All the analyses were performed using the Mplus statistical package (Version 6; Muthén & Muthén, 1998–2000). Using the missing data method, we were able to utilize all observations in the dataset. Because the variables were skewed, the parameters of the models were estimated using the maximum likelihood robust MLR estimator (Muthén & Muthén, 1998–2000), which is robust to the non-normality of observed variables. The goodness of fit for the estimated models was evaluated using five indicators: χ^2 test, Comparative Fit Index (CFI), Tucker-Lewis Index (TLI), Root Mean Square Error of Approximation (RMSEA), and Standardized Root Mean Square Residual (SRMR).

Results

Gender differences in teachers' perceptions of ability and effort

The analyses were begun by investigating the possible gender differences in teachers' ability and effort perceptions. The means and standard deviations of all the variables are presented in Table 3.1. The correlations between teachers' ability and effort perceptions, children's ability self-concepts and performance in math and reading, and gender and cohort status are presented in Table 3.2, separately for Wave 3 and for Wave 4. These initial results suggested

Table 3.1. *Means and standard deviations*

	Boys				Girls			
	Wave 3		Wave 4		Wave 3		Wave 4	
	M	SD	M	SD	M	SD	M	SD
Math self-concept	5.62	1.03	5.56	1.10	5.26	1.00	5.12	1.06
Reading self-concept	5.44	1.20	5.34	1.11	5.70	1.03	5.56	1.07
Math performance	11.34	2.25	11.67	1.85	11.51	2.09	11.66	1.77
Reading performance	11.44	2.06	11.58	1.79	12.08	2.18	12.04	1.76
Perceptions of math ability[t]	5.17	1.39	5.10	1.38	4.87	1.44	4.88	1.31
Perceptions of math effort[t]	5.09	1.67	4.98	1.67	5.28	1.43	5.28	1.39
Perceptions of reading ability[t]	4.96	1.47	4.91	1.45	5.24	1.46	5.09	1.41
Perceptions of reading effort[t]	4.92	1.58	4.66	1.61	5.47	1.33	5.32	1.33

[t] = Teachers' perceptions.

that there were gender differences in teachers' perceptions of ability and effort: teachers perceived boys as having greater abilities in math than girls, and girls as having greater abilities and effort in reading than boys. Further analyses with *t*-tests confirmed these results by showing that there were gender differences at Wave 3 in teachers' math-related ability perceptions $t(873) = -3.11$, $p < .01$, favoring boys ($M = 5.17$, $SD = 1.39$) over girls ($M = 4.87$, $SD = 1.44$), and in teachers' reading-related ability $t(887) = 2.83$, $p < .01$ and effort $t(893) = 5.66$, $p < .01$ perceptions, favoring girls ($M = 5.24$, $SD = 1.46$) and ($M = 5.47$, $SD = 1.33$) over boys ($M = 4.96$, $SD = 1.47$) and ($M = 4.92$, $SD = 1.58$). Similarly, at Wave 4 gender differences emerged in teachers' math-related ability perceptions $t(740) = -2.21$, $p < .05$, favoring boys ($M = 5.10$, $SD = 1.38$) over girls ($M = 4.88$, $SD = 1.31$), in teachers' math-related effort perceptions $t(736) = 2.67$, $p < .01$, favoring girls ($M = 5.28$, $SD = 1.39$) over boys ($M = 4.98$, $SD = 1.67$), and in teachers' reading-related effort perceptions $t(746) = 6.08$, $p < .001$, favoring girls ($M = 5.32$, $SD = 1.33$) over boys ($M = 4.66$, $SD = 1.61$).

Gender differences emerged also in children's ability self-concepts in math at Wave 3 $t(996) = -5.55$, $p < .001$ and at Wave 4 $t(913) = -6.17$, $p < .001$, favoring boys ($M = 5.62$, $SD = 1.03$ at Wave 3 and $M = 5.56$, $SD = 1.09$ at Wave 4) over girls ($M = 5.26$, $SD = 1.00$ at Wave 3 and $M = 5.12$, $SD = 1.06$ at Wave 4). Similarly, gender differences emerged in children's ability self-concepts in reading at Wave 3 $t(994) = 3.79$, $p < .001$ and at Wave 4 $t(914) = 3.10$, $p < .01$, favoring girls ($M = 5.70$, $SD = 1.03$ at Wave 3 and $M = 5.56$, $SD = 1.07$ at Wave 4) over boys ($M = 5.44$, $SD = 1.20$ at Wave 3 and $M = 5.34$, $SD = 1.11$ at Wave 4).

Moreover, the results showed that girls' performance in reading was slightly better than that of boys' at Wave 3 $t(766) = 4.17$, $p < .001$ ($M = 12.08$, $SD = 2.18$ for girls and $M = 11.44$, $SD = 2.06$ for boys) and at Wave 4 $t(765) = 3.66$, $p < .001$ ($M = 12.05$, $SD = 1.76$ for girls and $M = 11.56$, $SD = 1.79$ for boys). No gender differences occurred in children's math performance.

Associations between teachers' ability and effort perceptions, children's ability self-concepts and performance in math and reading, and gender and cohort status

Next, path models (Figure 3.1) were run to test associations between teachers' ability and effort perceptions, children's ability self-concepts and performance in math and reading, and gender and cohort status. Four separate models were carried out for teachers' perceptions and children's outcomes in (a) math and (b) reading and at Wave 3 and Wave 4. The models included paths from children's gender, performance, and cohort status, and teachers' perceptions to children's ability self-concepts, as well as paths from children's gender and performance to teachers' perceptions. Moreover, children's age (e.g., cohort status) was controlled for in children's performance, and due to their high initial correlations, teachers' perceptions of ability and effort were let to correlate with each other. To identify the final models, all the statistically non-significant paths were set to zero.

Teachers' perceptions and children's ability self-concept in math

The final model for teachers' perceptions and children's self-concept of math ability at Wave 3 (Table 3.2, Figure 3.2) fit the data well. The results showed, first, that boys had higher ability self-concept in math than girls. Teachers also perceived boys as having higher ability in math than girls. However, no gender differences emerged in teachers' perceptions of effort. Second, teachers' perceptions of individual children's ability and effort and children's high math performance were positively associated with children's ability self-concept in math. Moreover, children's high performance in math was positively associated with teachers' ability and effort perceptions. Finally, younger children had higher math ability self-concept than children in older cohorts.

The final model for teachers' perceptions and children's self-concept of math ability at Wave 4 (Table 3.2, Figure 3.2) fit the data well. The results showed,

Table 3.2. *Pearson correlation coefficients between teachers' ability and effort perceptions, children's ability self-concepts and performance in math and reading, and gender and cohort status separately at Wave 3 and at Wave 4 (below diagonal related to math and above diagonal related to reading)*

	1	2	3	4	5	6
Wave 3						
1. Ability perception	–	.54***	.26***	.46***	–.10**	.01
2. Effort perception	.58***	–	.13***	.40***	–.19***	.02
3. Ability self-concept	.28***	.21***	–	.16***	–.12***	–.18***
4. Performance	.41***	.37***	.25***	–	–.15***	.26***
5. Gender	.11**	–.06	.17***	–.04	–	–.02
6. Cohort status	–.02	–.02	–.09*	.30***	–.02	–
Wave 4						
1. Ability perception	–	.50***	.31***	.39***	–.06	.00
2. Effort perception	.53***	–	.14***	.29***	–.22***	–.05
3. Ability self-concept	.38***	.27***	–	.13***	–.10**	–.08*
4. Performance	.38***	.32***	.26***	–	–.13***	.21***
5. Gender	.08*	–.10**	.20***	.00	–	–.02
6. Cohort status	.02	–.04	–.10**	.26***	–.02	–

Note: * $p < .05$, ** $p < .01$, *** $p < .00$.

first, that boys had higher ability self-concept in math than girls. Teachers also perceived girls as having higher effort in math than boys. However, no gender differences emerged in teachers' perceptions of ability. Moreover, teachers' perceptions of individual children's ability and effort and children's high math performance were positively associated with children's ability self-concept in math. Further, children's high performance in math was positively associated with teachers' ability and effort perceptions. Finally, younger children had higher math ability self-concept than children in older cohorts.

Teachers' perceptions of children's ability self-concept in reading

The model for teachers' ability and effort perceptions and children's self-concept of reading ability (Table 3.2, Figure 3.3) also fit the data well. The results showed, first, that girls had higher ability self-concept in reading than boys. Teachers also perceived girls as putting in more effort in reading than boys. However, no gender differences emerged in teachers' perceptions of individual

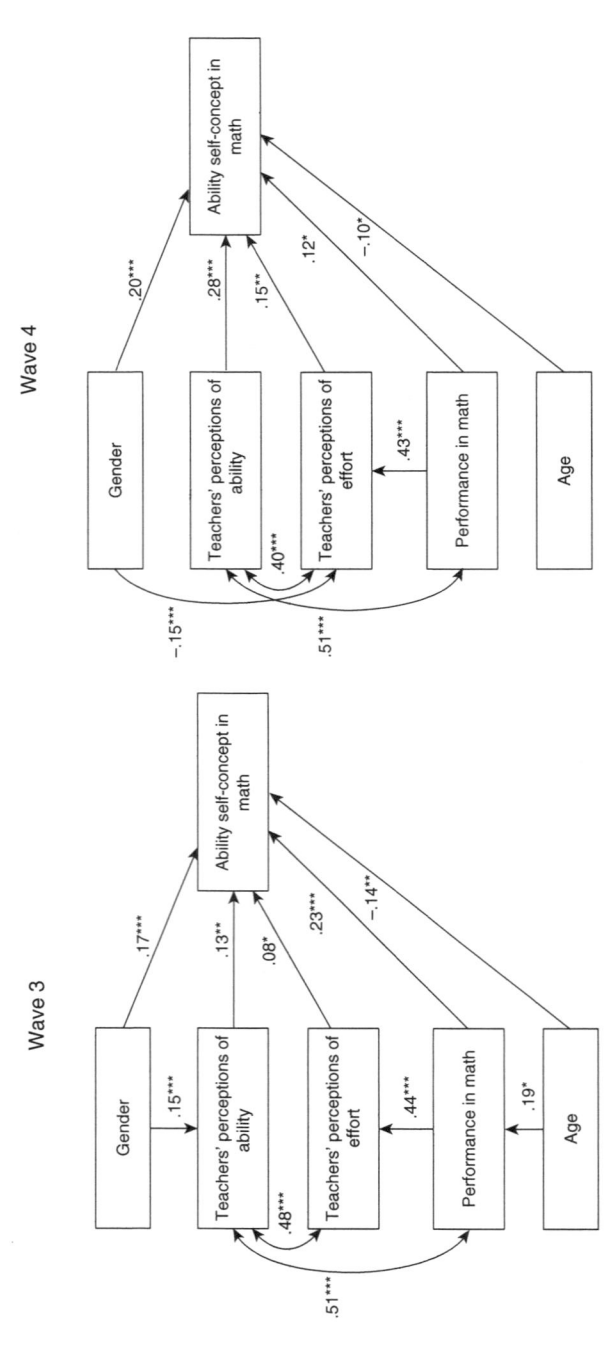

Figure 3.2 *The standardized estimates for the models of teachers' ability and effort perceptions and children's self-concept of math ability at Wave 3 and Wave 4*

Note: * p < .05, ** p < .01, *** p < .001.

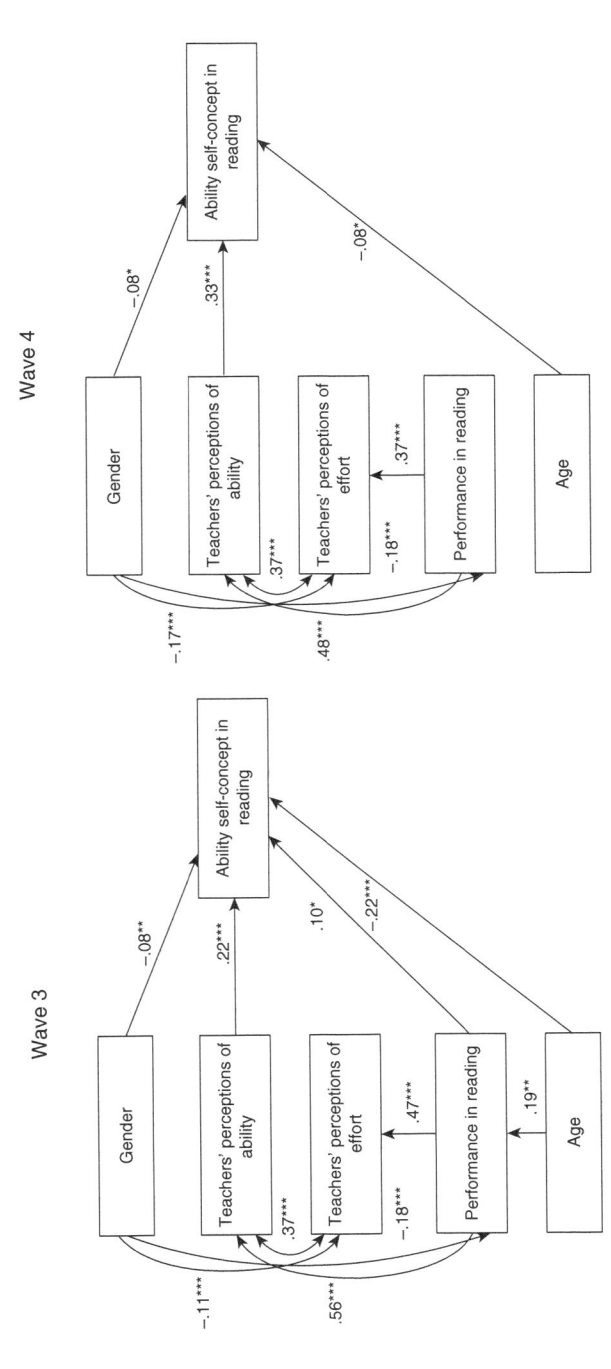

Figure 3.3 *The standardized estimates for the models of teachers' ability and effort perceptions and children's self-concept of reading ability at Wave 3 and Wave 4*

Note: * p < .05, ** p < .01, *** p < .001.

children's abilities in reading. Second, teachers' ability perceptions were positively associated with children's ability self-concept in reading. However, no associations were found between teachers' perceptions of effort and children's ability self-concept in reading. Moreover, children's high performance in reading was positively associated with children's self-concept of reading ability and teachers' perceptions of ability and effort. Further, children in younger cohorts had higher ability self-concept in reading than children in older cohorts. Finally, the modification indices suggested that the fit of the model would be increased by estimating the path from children's gender to their reading performance, showing that girls had slightly higher performance in reading than boys.

The model for teachers' ability and effort perceptions and children's self-concept of reading ability at Wave 4 (Table 3.2, Figure 3.3) also fit the data well. The results showed, first, that girls had higher ability self-concept in reading than boys. Teachers also perceived girls as putting in more effort in reading than boys. However, no gender differences emerged in teachers' perceptions of individual children's abilities in reading. Second, teachers' ability perceptions were positively associated with children's ability self-concept in reading. However, no associations were found between teachers' perceptions of effort and children's ability self-concept in reading. Moreover, children's high performance in reading was positively associated with teachers' perceptions of ability and effort. However, no associations were found between children's reading performance and ability self-concept in reading. Further, children in younger cohorts had higher ability self-concept in reading than children in older cohorts. Finally, the modification indices suggested that the fit of the model would be increased by estimating the path from children's gender to their reading performance, showing that girls had slightly higher performance in reading than boys.

Discussion

The results of the present study indicated that, as expected (H1 and H2), teachers tended to perceive boys as possessing greater ability in math than girls (Wave 3), and girls showing more effort in math than boys (Wave 4). In reading, teachers perceived girls as showing more effort than boys (at Wave 3 and Wave 4). However, gender differences in actual performance occurred only in reading, where girls slightly outperformed boys (at both waves). Girls also showed higher ability self-concept in reading, which may reflect girls valuing reading more highly than boys (Wigfield et al., 1997). In math, both boys and girls performed equally. Despite this, as expected (H3), girls had lower ability self-concept in math than boys (at both waves). These findings are consistent with previous findings illustrating that gender differences may emerge in boys' and girls' ability self-concepts even when their actual performance would be the same (Herbert & Stipek, 2005). It has also been found that teachers are typically aware of girls' lower ability self-concepts in math (Tiedemann, 2000a).

It has been suggested that teachers' and parents' perceptions concerning children's achievement may be partially responsible for the gender differences in children's ability self-concepts (Frome & Eccles, 1998; Herbert & Stipek, 2005; Jacobs & Eccles, 2000). Our results showed that gender differences existed in teachers' perceptions, which might have been reflected in children's ability self-concepts. Teachers' perceptions of children's achievement are usually communicated to children via their emotional responses and interaction with the students, which may further influence children's self-perceptions (Graham, 1990; Jussim & Eccles, 1992; Li, 1999). For example, teachers' feedback for boys more often indicates that they have high abilities, whereas praise for girls reflects other nonintellectual aspects of performance, which may reflect teachers' gender-stereotypic thinking, leading boys to highlight the role of abilities and girls the role of effort in their performance (Dweck et al., 1978). It is also possible that girls have lower self-concept in some academic domains because they are more sensitive than boys to others' evaluative feedback (Jussim et al., 1996; Roberts, 1991).

Similar results have also been found among parents, and it has been shown that, despite their performance level, boys and girls are treated differently by their parents already early in their childhood (Eccles et al., 2000; Frome & Eccles, 1998). Thus, it can be difficult to determine where the gender biases in teachers' and parents' and own perceptions originate (Eccles et al., 2000). One possible source is the broader cultural belief that math is a male domain, which is reflected in teachers' perceptions of and interaction with their students (Li, 1999; Tiedemann, 2002). In addition, media may strengthen these cultural beliefs and perceptions concerning boys' and girls' talents and performance (Eccles et al., 2000). Further, some studies have found that gender differences can be related to children's actual performance level and are especially strong among lower-performing groups (Tiedemann, 2002).

Our results also showed that age-related differences occurred in teachers' math-related perceptions; at the earlier grades (Wave 3) teachers perceived boys as having higher math abilities than girls, whereas later on (Wave 4) these differences disappeared. However, during the later grades (Wave 4) teachers perceived girls as putting in more effort in math than boys. Previously it has been suggested that gender stereotypes become more prominent in adults' perceptions as the children grow older (Rytkönen, Aunola, & Nurmi, 2005; Yee & Eccles, 1988), and our results partly supported this notion as teachers increasingly highlighted the role of effort in girls' outcomes in math where gender-stereotypic thinking is typically more highlighted than in other domains. Similarly, teachers perceived girls as showing more effort in reading than boys over the school years, which may also be due to the accuracy in teachers' perceptions (Jussim & Harber, 2005) as at both waves girls outperformed boys in reading. However, to better understand these processes in different domains, more studies would be needed in the future to examine the development of gender differences in teachers' ability and effort perceptions. Further, the results showed that teachers' ability and effort perceptions were positively associated with children's ability self-concepts in math, whereas in reading only teachers' ability perceptions were positively associated with children's ability self-concepts. These results may reflect expectancy effects that occur in teachers' perceptions: when teachers expect children to show strong abilities and to put great effort into their school work, these expectations usually show in children's academic outcomes (Dweck, 1986; Eccles et al., 1983; Jussim et al., 1996) and motivation (Natale et al, 2009; Upadyaya et al., 2012). In addition, teachers are typically well aware of children's actual skills and perceptions and thus their perceptions may show in children's ability self-concepts simply because they are accurate (Jussim & Harber, 2005). However, no associations were found between teachers' effort perceptions and children's ability self-concept in reading. These domain-specific differences may reflect the fact that success in mathematics is generally thought to be more due to aptitude or abilities than effort (Stipek, 1984), and it might be easily reinforced by both ability and effort perceptions of the teacher. Success in reading, especially during primary school, may require more hard work as beginning readers have to put a lot of effort into their tasks to acquire the needed skills. Therefore, children may feel that as they have to work hard in literacy they might not have the related abilities (Dweck & Leggett, 1988; Eccles et al., 1983). However, when teachers have confidence in children's abilities in reading, children can easily maintain a positive self-concept of reading ability.

Moreover, the results showed that children's performance in math and reading were associated with teachers' ability and effort perceptions: when children did well in math or reading, teachers perceived them as having strong abilities and putting forth significant effort in math and reading. Similarly, in previous studies, it has been found that when children's academic performance is high, teachers tend to think their success is related to their abilities (Carr & Kurtz-Costes, 1994; Hughes et al., 2005; Natale et al., 2009; Upadyaya et al., 2012) and effort (Fennema et al., 1990).

The results also indicated that when children were performing well in math and reading, they had high ability self-concepts in math and reading. These findings are consistent with the results of some previous studies showing that children's ability self-concepts are usually closely linked to their actual performance in the same domain (Aunola et al., 2002; Chapman & Tunmer, 1997; Denissen, Zarrett, & Eccles, 2007; Eccles et al., 1997; Eshel & Kurman, 1991; Helmke & van Aken, 1995; Herbert & Stipek, 2005; Marsh, 1990; Valentine, DuBois, & Cooper, 2004). However, during the later primary school years (Wave 4) no associations were found between children's performance and ability self-concept in reading. It is possible that as children grow older other aspects of their motivation, such as valuing reading (Wigfield et al., 1997), become more important in determining their ability self-concept in reading,

The results showed further that, as expected (H4 and H5), younger children had a higher level of self-concept of math and reading ability than older children, whereas children in older cohorts showed higher math and reading performance than younger children. These results are in line with the previous studies showing that when children enter into primary school they have typically very high self-concept in various domains, which, however, starts decreasing during the school years (Bouffard et al., 2003; Wigfield & Eccles, 2000).

Limitations

There are several limitations that should be taken into consideration when generalizing the findings of the present study. First, this study focused on investigating teachers' perceptions of ability and effort in children's success. Thus, the results of the present study can be generalized only to success situations. Second, it is possible that teachers' perceptions were associated with children's self-concept of ability simply because they were accurate (Jussim & Harber, 2005). Third, other variables that were not studied here may have contributed to the results of the present study. For example, previous studies have shown that the general social classroom climate moderates the ways teachers' expectations and perceptions are communicated to children, and thus they may have a different impact on children's outcomes. In addition, in different classrooms, the level of gender stereotypes may vary (Eccles et al., 1983; Eccles-Parsons et al., 1982). Fourth, most of the participating children came from a middle-class white background; thus the results can be generalized only to this group. Similar work needs to be done on other ethnic/racial and social class groups and other cultures. Fifth, even though the results showed that teachers' perceptions were associated with children's ability self-concepts, it is less clear how teachers' perceptions are communicated to children in their every day interactions. It would be important to investigate these processes in more detail in future studies.

Conclusions and future directions

The present study confirmed the results of some previous studies that have found gender differences in teachers' perceptions of ability and effort. Similarly, teachers tended to highlight boys' abilities in math and girls' effort both in math and reading. Our results added to the previous findings by showing that age-related differences occurred in teachers' perceptions in math: at the earlier primary school grades (Wave 3) teachers perceived boys as having more abilities in math than girls, whereas later on (Wave 4) the role of effort in girls' outcomes was more pronounced. More studies in the future would be needed to examine the development of gender differences in teachers' perceptions concerning children's outcomes in different domains. Moreover, even though gender differences may occur in teachers' perceptions, less is known about the extent to which teachers' perceptions predict the development of gender differences in children's perceptions. Thus, in the future, it would be important to study the extent to which teachers' perceptions impact the development of gender

Table 3.3. *Goodness-of-fit summary for the tested within-level path models of teachers' perceptions and children's ability self-concepts in math and reading*

Model	N	χ^2	df	p	CFI	TLI	RMSEA	SRMR
Wave 3								
Math	1,047	16.54	5	0.01	0.98	0.93	0.05	0.05
Reading	1,047	18.30	7	0.01	0.98	0.95	0.04	0.05
Wave 4								
Math	944	13.93	8	0.08	0.99	0.97	0.03	0.06
Reading	944	12.49	9	0.19	0.99	0.99	0.04	0.06

differences in children's self-perceptions and performance in math, reading, and other academic domains (Li, 1999). Moreover, some studies have indicated stronger gender differences in different subgroups, such as lower-achieving students (Tiedemann, 2002). In the future, it will be important to study these subgroups further in a longitudinal design.

Furthermore, teachers and educators should be aware of the possible gender-stereotypic beliefs in children's and teachers' perceptions. The results of the present study suggest that teachers should balance between feedback of individual children's innate ability and effort in math and reading, and give their students the feeling of both competency and diligence (Craven, Marsh, & Debus, 1991), as well as a mastery orientation and incremental views of abilities (Kamins & Dweck, 1999). Moreover, children interpret teachers' perceptions and feedback according to their understanding of the concepts of ability and effort, which varies by age, gender, skill level, subject area, and cultural background (Graham, 1990; Kärkkäinen & Räty, 2010; Li, 1999; Tiedemann, 2002). For example, older children have a better understanding of the associations between one's ability, effort, and academic outcomes, as well as gender stereotypes in different domains (Dweck & Leggett, 1988; Eccles et al., 1983; Graham, 1990; Nicholls, 1978). Teachers should be aware of the developmental changes that occur in children's understanding of academic abilities and effort (see also Nicholls, 1978) and give children age-appropriate feedback concerning their innate talents and hard work, which would best support children's academic motivation and learning. Moreover, the associations between teachers' perceptions of their students' abilities, effort, and gender may change over time. In future studies, it will be important to study them further.

References

Aunola, K., Leskinen, E., Onatsu-Arvilommi, T., & Nurmi, J.-E. (2002). Three methods for studying developmental change: A case of reading skills and self-concept. *British Journal of Educational Psychology*, 72, 343–364.

Bouffard, T., Marcoux, M.-F., Vezeau, C., & Bordeleau, L. (2003). Changes in self-perceptions of competence and intrinsic motivation among elementary schoolchildren. *British Journal of Educational Psychology*, 73, 171–186.

Butler, R. (1994). Teacher communications and student interpretations: Effects of teacher responses to failing students on attributional inferences in two age groups. *British Journal of Educational Psychology*, 64, 277–294.

Carr, M., & Kurtz-Costes, B. E. (1994). Is being smart everything? The influence of student achievement on teachers' perceptions. *British Journal of Educational Psychology*, 64, 263–276.

Chapman, J. W., & Tunmer, W. E. (1997). A longitudinal study of beginning reading achievement and reading self-concept. *British Journal of Educational Psychology*, 67, 279–291.

Clark, M. D. (1997). Teacher response to learning disability: A test of attributional principles. *Journal of Learning Disabilities*, 30, 69–79.

Clark, M. D., & Artiles, A. J. (2000). A cross-national study of teachers' attributional pattern. *The Journal of Special Education*, 34, 77–89.

Cole, D. A. (1991). Change in self-perceived competence as a function of peer and teacher evaluation. *Developmental Psychology*, 27, 682–688.

Craven, R. G., Marsh, H. W., & Debus, R. L. (1991). Effects of internally focused feedback and attributional feedback on enhancement of academic self-concept. *Journal of Educational Psychology*, 83, 17–27.

Denissen, J. J. A., Zarrett, N. R., & Eccles, J. S. (2007). I like to do it, I'm able, and I know I am: Longitudinal couplings between domain-specific achievement, self-concept, and interest. *Child Development*, 78, 430–447.

Duncan, T. E., Duncan, S. C., Alpert, A., Hops, H., Stoolmiller, M., & Muthén, B. (1997). Latent variable modeling of longitudinal and multilevel substance use data. *Multivariate Behavioral Research*, 32, 275–318.

Dweck, C. S. (1986). Motivational processes affecting learning. *American Psychologist*, 41, 1040–1048.

Dweck, C. S., Davidson, W., Nelson, S., & Enna, B. (1978). Sex differences in learned helplessness, II: The contingencies of evaluative feedback in the classroom and III: An experimental analysis. *Developmental Psychology*, 14, 268–276.

Dweck, C. S., & Leggett, E. L. (1988). A social-cognitive approach to motivation and Personality. *Psychological Review*, 95, 256–273.

Eccles, J. S., Adler, T. F., Futterman, R., Goff, S. B., Kaczala, C. M., Meece, J., & Midgley, C. (1983). Expectancies, values, and academic behaviors. In T. J. Spence (Ed.), *Achievement and academic motives* (pp. 75–146). New York: Freeman.

Eccles, J. S., Freedman-Doan, C., Frome, P., Jacobs, J., & Yoon, K. S. (2000). Gender role socialization in the family: A longitudinal approach. In T. Eckes & H. M. Trautner (Eds.), *The developmental social psychology of gender* (pp. 333–360). Mahwah, NJ: Lawrence Erlbaum.

Eccles, J. S., Wigfield, A., Harold, R. D., & Blumenfeld, P. (1993). Age and gender differences in children's self- and task perceptions during elementary school. *Child Development*, 64, 830–847.

Eccles, J. S., Wigfield, A., & Schiefele, U. (1997). Motivation to succeed. In W. Damon & N. Eisenberg (Eds.), *Handbook of child psychology* (Vol. 3). New York: John Wiley & Sons, Inc.

Eccles-Parsons, J. S., Kaczala, C. M., & Meece, J. L. (1982). Socialization of achievement attitudes and beliefs: Classroom influences. *Child Development*, 53, 322–339.

Eshel, Y., & Kurman, J. (1991). Academic self-concept, accuracy of perceived ability and academic attainment. *British Journal of Educational Psychology*, 61, 187–196.

Fennema, E., Peterson, P. L., Carpenter, T. P., & Lubinski, C. A. (1990). Teachers' attributions and beliefs about girls, boys, and math. *Educational Studies in Math*, 21, 55–69.

Frome, P., & Eccles, J. S. (1998). Parents' influence on children's achievement-related perceptions. *Journal of Personality and Social Psychology*, 74, 435–452.

Georgiou, S., Christou, C., Stavrinides, P., & Panaoura, G. (2002). Teacher attributions of student failure and teacher behavior toward the failing student. *Psychology in the Schools*, 39, 583–595.

Graham, S. (1984). Teachers feelings and student thoughts: An attributional approach to affect in the classroom. *The Elementary School Journal*, 85, 90–104.

——— (1990). Communicating low ability in the classroom: Bad things good teachers sometimes do. In S. Graham & V. S. Folkes (Eds.), *Attribution theory: Applications to achievement, mental health, and interpersonal conflict* (pp. 17–36). Hillsdale, NJ: Lawrence Erlbaum.

Hall, B. W., Villeme, M. G., & Burley, W. W. (1989). Teachers' attributions for students' academic success and failure and the relationship to teaching level and teacher feedback practices. *Contemporary Educational Psychology*, 14, 133–144.

Helmke, A., & van Aken, M. A. G. (1995). The causal ordering of academic achievement and self-concept of ability during elementary school: A longitudinal study. *Journal of Educational Psychology*, 87, 624–637.

Herbert, J., & Stipek, D. (2005). The emerge of gender differences in children's perceptions of their academic competence. *Applied Developmental Psychology*, 26, 276–295.

Holloway, S. D., & Hess, R. D. (1985). Mothers' and teachers' attributions about children's mathematical performance. In I. E. Siegel (Ed.), *Parental belief systems: The psychological consequences for children* (pp. 177–199). Hillsdale, NJ: Lawrence Erlbaum.

Hughes, J. N., Gleason, K. A., & Zhang, D. (2005). Relationship influences on teachers' perceptions of academic competence in academically at-risk minority and majority first grade students. *Journal of School Psychology*, 43, 303–320.

Jacobs, J. E., & Eccles, J. S. (2000). Parents, task values, and real-life achievement-related choices. In C. Sansone & J. M. Harackiewicz (Eds.), *Intrinsic and extrinsic motivation: The search for optimal motivation and performance* (pp. 405–439). San Diego, CA: Academic Press.

Jacobs, J. E., Lanza, S., Osgood, D. W., Eccles, J. S., & Wigfield, A. (2002). Changes in children's self-competence and values: Gender and domain differences across grades one through twelve. *Child Development*, 73, 509–527.

Jussim, L. (1989). Teacher expectations: Self-fulfilling prophecies, perceptual biases, and accuracy. *Journal of Personality and Social Psychology*, 57, 469–480.

Jussim, L., & Eccles, J. S. (1992). Teacher expectations II: Construction and reflection of student achievement. *Journal of Personality and Social Psychology*, 63, 947–961.

Jussim, L., Eccles, J., & Madon, S. (1996). Social perception, social stereotypes, and teacher expectations: Accuracy and the quest for the powerful self-fulfilling prophecy. *Advances in Experimental Social Psychology*, 28, 281–388.

Jussim, L., & Harber, K. D. (2005). Teacher expectations and self-fulfilling prophecies: Knowns and unknowns, resolved and unresolved controversies. *Personality and Social Psychology Review*, 9, 131–155.

Kamins, M. L., & Dweck, C. S. (1999). Person versus process praise and criticism: Implications for contingent self-worth and coping. *Developmental Psychology*, 35, 835–847.

Kärkkäinen, R., & Räty, H. (2010). Parents' and teachers' views of the child's academic potential. *Educational Studies*, 36, 229–232.

Kuklinski, M. R., & Weinstein, R. S. (2001). Classroom and developmental differences in a path model of teacher expectancy effects. *Child Development*, 72, 1554–1578.

Li, Q. (1999). Teachers' beliefs and gender differences in mathematics: A review. *Educational Research*, 41, 63–76.

Madon, S., Smith, A., Jussim, L., Russell, D. W., Eccles, J., Palumbo, P., & Walkiewicz, M. (2001). Am I as you see me or do you see me as I am? Self-fulfilling prophecies and self-verification. *Personality and Social Psychology Bulletin*, 27, 1214–1224.

Marsh, H. W. (1986). Verbal and math self-concepts: An internal/external frame of reference model. *American Educational Research Journal*, 23, 129–149.

(1990). Causal ordering of academic self-concept and academic achievement: A multiwave, longitudinal panel analysis. *Journal of Educational Psychology*, 82, 646–656.

Muthén, B. (1997). Latent variable modelling of longitudinal and multilevel data. In A. Raftery (Ed.), *Sociological methodology* (pp. 453–480). Boston, MA: Blackwell.

Muthén, L., & Muthén, B. O. (1998–2010). *Mplus: User's guide*. Los Angeles, CA: Muthén & Muthén.

Natale, K., Viljaranta, J., Lerkkanen, M.-K., Poikkeus, A.-M., & Nurmi, J.-E. (2009). Cross-lagged associations between kindergarten teachers' causal attributions and children's task motivation and performance in reading. *Educational Psychology*, 29, 603–619.

Nicholls, J. G. (1978). The development of the concepts of effort and ability, perception of academic attainment, and the understanding that difficult tasks require more ability. *Child Development*, 49, 800–814.

Roberts, T.-A. (1991). Gender and the influence of evaluations on self-assessments in achievement settings. *Psychological Bulletin*, 109, 297–308.

Rosenholtz, S. J., & Simpson, C. (1984). The formation of ability conceptions: Developmental trend or social construction? *Review of Educational Research*, 54, 31–63.

Rytkönen, K., Aunola, K., & Nurmi, J.-E. (2005). Parents' causal attributions concerning their children's school achievement: A longitudinal study. *Merrill-Palmer Quarterly*, 51, 494–522.

Siegle, D., & Reis, S. M. (1998). Gender differences in teacher and student perceptions of gifted students' ability and effort. *Gifted Child Quarterly*, 42, 39–47.

Stipek, D. J. (1984). Gender differences in children's attributions for success and failure on math and spelling tests. *Sex Roles*, 11, 969–981.

Stipek, D. J., & Mac Iver, D. (1989). Developmental change in children's assessment of intellectual competence. *Child Development*, 60, 521–538.

Tiedemann, J. (2000a). Gender-related beliefs of teachers in elementary school mathematics. *Educational Studies in Mathematics*, 41, 191–207.

(2000b). Parents' gender stereotypes and teachers' beliefs as predictors of children's concept of their mathematical ability in elementary school. *Journal of Educational Psychology*, 92, 144–151.

(2002). Teachers' gender stereotypes as determinants of teacher perceptions in elementary school mathematics. *Educational Studies in Mathematics*, 50, 49–62.

Upadyaya, K., Viljaranta, J., Lerkkanen, M.-K., Poikkeus, A.-M., & Nurmi, J.-E. (2012). Cross-lagged relations between preschool teachers' causal attributions and children's interest value and performance in math. *Social Psychology of Education: An International Journal*, 15, 181–206.

Valentine, J. C., DuBois, D. L., & Cooper, H. (2004). The relation between self-beliefs and academic achievement: A meta-analytic review. *Educational Psychologist*, 39, 111–133.

Weiner, B. (1985). An attributional theory of achievement motivation and emotion. *Psychological Review*, 92, 548–573.

(1986). *An attributional theory of motivation and emotion*. New York: Springler-Verlag.

(1994). Integrating social and personal theories of achievement striving. *Review of Educational Research*, 64, 557–573.

Wigfield, A., & Eccles, J. E. (2000). Expectancy-value theory of achievement motivation. *Contemporary Educational Psychology*, 25, 68–81.

Wigfield, A., Harold, R. D, Freedman-Doan, C., Eccles, J. S., Suk Yoon, K., Arbreton, A. J. A., & Blumenfield, P. C. (1997). Change in children's competence beliefs and subjective task values across the elementary school years: A 3-year study. *Journal of Educational Psychology*, 89, 451–469.

Yee, D. K., & Eccles, J. S. (1988). Parent perceptions and attributions for children's math achievement. *Sex Roles*, 19, 317–333.

4 Emerging gender differences in times of multiple transitions

Jennifer E. Symonds, Maurice Galton and Linda Hargreaves

Abstract

Gendered identities can develop throughout the life-span in an undulating process spurred by significant physiological, cognitive, and social events. Two important developmental transitions occur in early adolescence: changing schools and puberty. This chapter reviews the development of gender identity and gender differences in school engagement, aspirations, and achievement during these multiple transitions. It synthesizes the findings of in-depth, longitudinal studies of school transition from the early 1970s to the 2000s. Most gender differences documented by this literature occur independently of school transition. These regard children's friendships, dating, emotional health, attitudes to learning, and academic competencies. With school transition comes the tendency for girls to focus more on their physical and emotional selves, and a risk for boys to disengage from education. Gender differences in early adolescents' attitudes toward subjects, learning, and career choice appear to have reduced since the 1970s as wider social stereotypes have changed. However, the majority of gender differences noted are conserved across time, suggesting a great deal of biological and social stability across 40 years.

Introduction

This chapter reviews different in-depth studies examining the development of gender identity and gender differences in school engagement, aspirations, and achievement during adolescence, in particular during the transition to secondary school, which coincides with pubertal changes. It is argued that although gender differences in attitudes toward learning and career and subject choice appear to have reduced since the 1970s, many gender differences persist across time, suggesting considerable biological and social stability. In early adolescence, children have to cope with multiple, gendered changes to their bodies and minds in the course of puberty. In addition, many children move schools in two- or three-tier educational systems. At transition to middle or secondary school, they encounter a larger and older peer group, subject-specialist teachers, a different timetable and curriculum, and more complex buildings and grounds. This chapter is interested in how gender differences perhaps already present in the biological and social worlds of early adolescents interact with school transition, and how the school transition influences the development of gender differences.

Not to be confused with biological sex, gender is perceived as the outcome of biology interlinked with social and personal constructions of sex roles. These forces operate as a feedback loop that through the millennia has shaped much of our genetic and cultural inheritance of what it is to be female or male. Influences on gender flow from many levels: from our mammalian ancestry, from our cultural heritage, intergenerationally, and within the life-span – all experienced by people in the second-by-second real time of living. People can actively shape gender for themselves personally and in society by rejecting or utilising these influences. Gender is therefore accepted as being innate, learned (e.g. Bandura, 1977), and created.

Imagine that gender differences are a ball rolling onwards. Biology pushes the ball (by providing sex hormones and physical development) while people pull it with their will to personally act out and sustain male or female differences in society. Pulling requires both logic and action. For example, as children grow, they develop their conceptual understanding of gender through observation. Gendered events that commonly occur at marked points in the life-span, such as, for females, growing breasts, wearing one's first pair of stiletto heels, and pregnancy, can be understood by children as maturity status markers (Symonds, 2009a) that they strive toward.

Children internalize information about gender by using a system in the mind called the gender schema (Bem, 1981), which gathers, sorts, and stores their observations. The gender schema provides a basis for children's gendered rationales and activities. Although each child's schema is personalized, there are commonalities across children due to their observations of typical gendered activities in society. The gender schema is also intertwined with children's perceptions of themselves and their morals, values, and motives. This multidimensional psychological self, also known as the self-concept (Epstein, 1973; Markus & Wurf, 1987), activates our emotions and is influenced by them: for example, when one feels depressed for not achieving one's goals, or is unmotivated to achieve these due to a bout of depression. In this way, the gender schema can link to people's emotions. For example, a new boy may feel worthless after he is rejected from his year group's sports team because personal sporting abilities are used as a status symbol in the new school to define being a successful male.

At school transition, children encounter new information that can influence their gender schema, hence how they think about gender and themselves. Teachers in the new school may stress a need for children to think about career planning, encouraging them to question which careers are suitable for their aptitudes, attitudes, and gender. Furthermore, children moving from small primary or elementary schools gather first-hand experience of the gendered attitudes and dating behaviors of older children in their new school. New members of their age group may stimulate their perceptions of themselves and their gender, like the girl from a different feeder school who wears dangly earrings. Children may wish to emulate these behaviors, or hold themselves back until they feel ready.

Children's bodies and brains are changing rapidly across school transition, in gender-specific ways. Girls are observed to first develop breast buds and pubic hair on average at 11.06 years old (Coleman & Coleman, 2002), meaning that, at least for girls, school transition often coincides with the onset of puberty. Puberty creates sex differences through three main events. In gonadarche, sex hormones travel from the pituitary through the blood to the testes and the ovaries. Here they stimulate the secretion of testosterone or estrogen, which facilitate sperm and egg production and the development of sexual organs (Sisk & Foster, 2004). Adrenarche is the increase of adrenal androgen at around the age of 6 to 8 years that prompts the development of pubertal hair for both genders and facial hair and deepening of the voice for boys (Fechner, 2003). Third is a growth spurt of similar duration for both sexes. These events can occur simultaneously or differentially (Dahl, 2004), making the exact start of puberty difficult to pinpoint, although we know these events happen sooner on average for girls.

Generally, girls experience gonadal and adrenal development 6 months to 1 year earlier than boys (Fechner, 2003) and begin their growth spurt earlier. However, because girls are shorter at the time of their growth spurt this often results in males being taller in adulthood (Tanner, Whitehouse, Marubini, & Resele, 1976). Girls are also more likely to increase in body mass earlier than boys (around 6 years versus 9.5 years) (Fechner, 2003) and at puberty tend to gain body fat while boys gain muscle (Eccles, 1999). There are also sex differences in the timing of brain development at puberty. Peak cerebral volume is reached at around age 10.5 years for girls and at age 14.5 years for boys (Lenroot et al., 2007). The decrease in gray matter observed in the front temporal lobes, known as synaptic pruning (Giedd et al., 1999), also generally occurs earlier for girls than for boys, by about 2 years (Lenroot et al., 2007).

Puberty and school transition represent two respective changes in status: from sexually inactive child to feminine or masculine adolescent, and from primary or elementary school pupil to middle or secondary school pupil. The blossoming of female sexuality and focus on puberty, and the move to being an older pupil, may encourage people to hold more adult expectations of children in secondary school. Such changes in expectations are the subject of Hill and Lynch's (1983) Gender-Intensification Hypothesis (p. 201), which expects that gender differences will increase during early adolescence due to children being expected to behave as more male or female than before. Transitioning children are at risk for subscribing to these stereotypes, as at this age children believe in gender stereotypes more strongly than when they are older (Simmons & Blyth, 1987) and in comparison to older teenagers (Comber, 2001). Possibly, because of a lack of observational and cognitive experience, early adolescents are less able to evaluate gender as a product of our evolutionary and cultural history, and see it more as a destined difference between the sexes.

Children can reproduce gendered stereotypes by behaving in line with them and by using them to evaluate other people. This may be especially true of boys, who, in comparison to girls, typically have more rigid gendered identities and more strongly avoid acting like the opposite sex (Simmons, Burgeson, Carlton-Ford, & Blyth, 1987; Whitehead, 2006). The surge of gender-specific information and the change in gendered expectations in early adolescence may dispose children of this age toward activities that reinforce their gender identity and away from those that contradict it (Wigfield & Eccles, 1994). This tendency might be particularly strong at school transition where, it is suggested, children tend to rely on fundamentally stable aspects of the self-concept such as biological sex to organize their identity and behaviors (Jackson & Warin, 2000).

In summary, our theoretical toolbox positions gender as a historical and continued interaction between people and their environments, as a psychological schema, and as part of the self-concept. With these tools we craft our expectations that, at transition, gender differences develop according to children's experiences of puberty, changing expectations of gender roles, and observations of gender in their new environment. Following the focus of this book, we are most interested in how gendered experiences at school transition are manifest in children's academic and personal development. In a systematic review of 155 quantitative and qualitative studies on early adolescent psychology at school transition, Gray, Galton, McLaughlin, Clarke, and Symonds (2011) found that roughly 20% reported on gender. Of these studies, most describe whether a measured aspect of children's psychology, such as self-esteem, differs on average by gender as children change schools. Only a handful of the studies on gender use a range of techniques to observe and analyze gender differences across a variety of topics, resulting in a larger set of data on gender per study. We therefore use this small set of in-depth studies as the primary source material for this review, and complement their findings with evidence from the remaining studies on gender as noted by Gray et al. (2011).

The in-depth studies (see Table 4.1) include quantitative research, studies that use a range of quantitative and qualitative techniques and report them separately (multiple methods), and ethnographies. They are set in either the United Kingdom (UK) or the United States (US), where the majority of school transition research has been carried out. The children from these studies transferred to junior high schools in the US and to middle or secondary schools in the UK when they were aged 11 to 13. In each country, the schools were state-funded and mixed in gender. In comparison to elementary and primary schools, secondary, middle, and junior high schools offer subject-specialist teaching, a larger pupil body, and more extensive buildings and grounds. Therefore the environmental changes experienced by the children in these studies were more or less the same. It is also important to note that SAMSAD and the Milwaukee study document the experiences of same-aged children who either transferred to a new school or stayed in the same school during that year (i.e., transition and non-transition groups). This enables us to infer how closely the development of some gender differences in early adolescence is linked to changing schools.

The review is organized into three sections. First, we examine children's informal gendered development in their peer group, including their same-sex friendships, heterosexual interaction, and reproduction of social gender stereotypes. Second, we look at the main gender differences found in emotional health at

Table 4.1. *Summary of in-depth studies used for this chapter*

Study title	Description
The Milwaukee study 1974–1977	A two-phase repeat measures study of around 300 children either transferring to a junior high school at Grade 7 (age 12/13) or remaining in a K–8 system in Milwaukee (Simmonds & Blyth, 1987). The children were followed up when they were 14/15 years old.
Observational Research and Classroom Learning Evaluation (ORACLE) 1975–1980	A multiple methods study of 486 children transferring to age 9–13 middle schools, age 11–14 middle schools, and age 12–18 secondary schools (end number 334), in the English Midlands (Delamont & Galton, 1986; Galton, Simon, & Croll, 1980; Galton & Wilcocks, 1983).
Changing Schools 1979–1980	An ethnography of around 35 children moving from a small middle school to a large age 12–18 high school of around 2,000 pupils in the English Midlands (Measor & Woods, 1984).
Michigan Study of Adolescent Life Transitions (MSALT) 1983–1984	A four-wave repeated measures survey of around 1,850 children transferring to junior high school at Grade 7 in the Michigan area. A variety of analyses are published in academic journals (cf. Eccles et al., 1993; Feldlaufer, Midgley, & Eccles, 1988; Wigfield, Eccles, Mac Iver, Reuman, & Midgley, 1991).
ORACLE Replication Study 1996–1997	A replication of the original ORACLE study using the same system of systematic observation and survey and attainment measures to gather data from over 600 pupils, in the same school district and school systems as before, i.e., the English Midlands (Hargreaves & Galton, 2002).
Secondary and Middle School Adolescent Development (SAMSAD) study 2007–2008	A multiple methods study of Year 7 (age 11/12) children either remaining in one age 9–13 middle school (N = 86) or transferring to an age 11–16 secondary school (N = 262) in the East of England (Symonds, 2009a).

transition, necessitating a focus on self-esteem and self-consciousness. The final section overviews gender differences in how children's learning behaviors and achievement change after transition. Here we observe the influence of gender in children's experiences of classroom learning, academic self-concept, and in how they organize themselves socially and personally to achieve.

Gender differences in peer relations

Friendships

After school transition, children quickly form playground cliques of single or mixed sex (Kvalsund, 2000; Symonds, 2009a). Boys are observed to hang around either in large sports-oriented groups or in smaller special interest groups whose main interest is in activities such as playing music, computer gaming, or role playing (Measor & Woods, 1984; Swain, 2000; Symonds, 2009a). Across a 40-year period there has been little change in the type of activities boys are reported to do outside school. In the late 1970s, boys enjoyed playing football or engaging in unstructured, unsupervised activities outside school together (Measor & Woods 1984, p. 65), while in 2007, for example, Bobby liked "going out with my mates, playing football, going down the park" (Symonds, 2009a). In SAMSAD, two boys described how safety and protection were central to their friendships. As Kevin recalled, "When I first came I was a tiny bit cautious and I was just trying to work out who to make friends with and who not to make friends with," and Jacob felt that friends were important "because they make me feel slightly safer."

Rather than play sport at lunchtime, girls are observed to stand around talking in small groups (Delamont & Galton, 1986; Measor & Woods, 1984; Symonds, 2009a). In SAMSAD, Chloe and Jasmine began talking during a dance activity in the first week of term, and then quickly formed a best friend bond that lasted throughout the year. Ruby and Sam also became "best friends" in the first term, but Ruby rejected Sam's friendship in term two in order to protect her popularity with older children and boys, after Sam developed a reputation for being "mouthy" and annoying. These rapid changes in girls' friendships were documented in both transition and non-transition schools, whereas boys' friendships were observed to be more stable. As Lauren put it in the third term, "the whole of my friend list has changed" (Symonds, 2009a, p. 156).

Girls also reported becoming more analytical of each other at this age. This could lead to a more complex type of friendship conflict called "falling out" by the girls (Symonds, 2009a). Falling out is observed independently of school transition in SAMSAD (2007–2008), and in post-transition populations in ORACLE (1975–1980) and *Changing Schools* (1979–1980).

- Joanna: "It's because when you're younger you don't really fall out. Because you don't know what it is" (Symonds, 2009a, p. 161).

- Lee Anne: "If we ever fall out we just laugh our heads off and fall in again" (Delamont & Galton, 1986, p. 232).
- "Me and Jenny have fallen out with Janet you know" (Measor & Woods, 1984, p. 89).

In SAMSAD, boys did not report an increase in social analysis; instead they mentioned talking more about careers and "girls, girls, girls" (Jacob, term 2).

Heterosexual interaction

In transition and non-transition schools, early adolescent dating is commonplace (Simmons & Blyth, 1987). In *Changing Schools* and SAMSAD, girls orchestrated much of the dating activity and were often responsible for hiring and firing boys, particularly when their boyfriends ignored them (perhaps out of shyness or confusion). Relationships could be made and broken with lightning speed, some lasting for less than a day. However, not all relationships were speed dating. In SAMSAD, Gus and Yasmin had been dating for over a year and liked to hug each other, although they had never kissed.

Compared to boys, girls in the post-transition year pay more attention to heterosexual relationships (Measor & Woods, 1984; Symonds, 2009a) and rate being popular with the opposite sex as more important to them (Simmons & Blyth, 1987). Both boys and girls date more if they begin puberty earlier than their peers (Simmons & Blyth, 1987) and if they are deviant rather than conformist toward educational norms (Measor & Woods, 1984; Symonds, 2009a). In the three UK observational studies, no children reported noticing an increase in dating after school transition, although this is not to say it didn't happen. In SAMSAD, children hung around in mixed sex cliques only in the transition school, and in this school more children in the target group were dating.

Social stereotypes

Girls and boys can create gendered stereotypes by how they behave after transition. One way they do this is through what they wear. In SAMSAD, boys at transition and non-transition schools paid attention to their hairstyles and which jackets and sweaters they wore over their school uniforms. However, despite restrictions at both schools, only transition girls were observed to wear ostentatious socks, nail varnish, and jewelry. Similar observations were made in *Changing Schools*. SAMSAD girls displayed these symbols of femininity in order to convey their independence from school rules. For example, when sitting on the floor in Drama, Chloe and Stacy stretched out their legs so that their stripy socks were clearly visible below their trouser hems. Next, Chloe spent several minutes fiddling with her painted fingernails, which were splayed on the carpet for all to see, including the teacher.

School equipment can also be used to exhibit feminine appearances. In *Changing Schools*, popular girls' pencil cases were made of lilac-colored fur fabric or denim. When one girl had to borrow her little sister's toy-soldiers pencil case she made apologies for it to her friends. Similarly, over 30 years later in SAMSAD, Sam and her friends used an oversized purple fluffy pen to gain attention. In a geography lesson, Sam's friend lay on her stomach on a classroom desk while twirling the pen, and then Sam grabbed it from her and stroked and twiddled it in a manner that drew looks from the other children.

At this age, some girls desire to look more mature by emulating what older girls wear. Both *Changing Schools* and SAMSAD documented that girls reported wanting to wear revealing clothes to school discos, and being cautioned against this by their mothers and older sisters. Measor and Woods (1984) describe these girls as being "at a half-way stage" with "downward age-graded pressures ... separating them from childhood, but holding them back from fully-fledged teenage status" (p. 104).

Boys can generate a macho male stereotype through their choice of friendships, attitudes to education, and playground activities. In SAMSAD, Charlie described how this hierarchy was played out by friendship groups. The large groups of sporty boys were reputedly the most popular due to their sporting prowess (i.e., physical capabilities). Ahead of them in the pecking order were "gangs of thugs" who were to be avoided. Below the sporty boys were special interest groups followed by those who played "childish" games and at the bottom of the pile were shy social isolates (Symonds, 2009a). "Outside the playground, where the basketball court is, everyone is hanging around each other. Them two are like the highest notch. Then you go lower, lower, until the bottom. I'm in like, the middle" (Charlie, term 1). Similar groups of boys were observed in *Changing Schools* and in a study of an all-boys school at transition (Benyon, 1985).

Boys often discuss myths of toughness and aggression occurring in the post-transition school, illustrating how physical toughness is a marker of power in the new social order. Similar myths, especially the royal flush or toilet myth, are found to reoccur across a 30 year period (Mellor & Delamont, 2011). For example from *Changing Schools* and SAMSAD:

- Philip: "I've heard that there's these boys, and if you have a fight, they wear punch gloves with spikes, and they hit you and leave punch holes in your face" (Measor & Woods, 1984, p. 21).
- Charlie: "You can get picked on by the older people and they all have their threats like they are gonna chuck your head down the toilet" (Symonds, 2009a, p. 145).

Despite this, not all boys subscribe to the toughness hierarchy. Some groups choose to base their status on markers such as achievement and tend to be well adjusted if they have a stable group of like-minded friends (Symonds, 2009a).

Socially isolated boys at the bottom of the pile are often lonely and studious, or overly aggressive (Measor & Woods, 1984). The latter bully victims often have disadvantaged family backgrounds, special educational needs, and difficulty communicating and sustaining relationships in general. In ORACLE (1975–1980), a teacher described them as "loners, have few friends, tended to hang around with older boys ... seek attention by fighting, challenging older boys to fight" (Delamont & Galton, 1986, p. 89). Both studious and deviant socially isolated boys may face increased risk of adjustment problems during school transition.

Gender differences in emotional health

Studies have not yet documented an influence of school transition on how children feel about their bodies. In transition and non-transition schools, girls have rapidly declining evaluations of their body image (Petersen & Crockett, 1985; Simmons & Blyth, 1987), and in both school types, early maturing girls are found to worry about their breast development and want to stay like children (Symonds, 2009a). Feeling underdeveloped is also a problem for early adolescent girls who have lower evaluations of their body image if they develop earlier *or* later in comparison to their peers (Tobin-Richards, Boxer, & Petersen, 1983).

However, there is some evidence that transition does affect girls' self-esteem. Girls are found to have lower average self-esteem than boys across school transition (Nottelmann, 1987; Wigfield et al., 1991; Wigfield & Eccles, 1994) and to make fewer gains in self-esteem if changing schools, in comparison to remaining in a K–8 system (Zoller Booth, Chase Sheehan, & Earley, 2007). In the Milwaukee study, a greater percentage of girls had declining self-esteem if they transitioned schools at age 12 years (56%) compared to remaining in a K–8 system (40%) (Simmons & Blyth, 1987). The Milwaukee study found that the girls' self-esteem declined more if they had more life transitions including dating, puberty, geographic mobility, and school transition (Simmons et al., 1987).

The SAMSAD data can be used to test Simmons and Blyth's finding that school transition influences the development of girls' self-esteem, albeit with a smaller sample (N = 192, girls N = 106) from one transition and one non-transition school. In the SAMSAD study, school-related self-esteem was measured with a 24-item Likert-type scale constructed by Pell (Hargreaves & Galton, 2002). Highly acceptable reliability coefficients (Cronbach's alpha) of .85 in fall and .84 in summer were obtained. The fall scores were transformed into a percentage of the summer scores, yielding a percentage difference from one measurement to the next. Ceiling effects are unlikely as the 3% of the sample that scored above 95% on the original scale in fall had declined in self-esteem by summer.

A similar percentage of boys in both schools had declining self-esteem (transition = 34%, non-transition = 31%) and more had stable self-esteem if they transitioned (6% vs. none). More of both genders had increasing self-esteem if they stayed at the same school (transition boys = 60%, non-transition boys = 69%; transition girls = 57%, non-transition girls = 80%). This potential transition effect on gains in self-esteem was most pronounced for girls. The SAMSAD results concur with Simmons and Blyth (1987) by finding a far greater percentage of girls with declining self-esteem in a transition setting (39%) compared to those with no transition (13%). Also, the decline was steeper on average for girls who transitioned ($t = -4.551$, $df = 40.227$, $p < .000$).

Further analysis found that girls with higher self-esteem were more likely to be satisfied with their schoolwork by the end of the year (Pearson's $r = .37$, $p < 0.000$), while there was no association for boys. These findings suggest that gender differences in children's emotional state after transition can impact their educational attitudes and attainment.

Gender differences in learning and achievement

Working groups

In classrooms, early adolescents tend to work in single-sex cooperation groups before (Measor & Woods, 1984) and after transition (Delamont & Galton, 1986; Symonds, 2009a). In-group members help each other by offering advice and lending personal equipment, and are observed to reject the advances of opposite-sex peers who try to interact with their group (Measor & Woods, 1984). Classroom observations find that gendered segregation of working groups is greater after school transition (Hargreaves & Pell, 2002).

Comparison of the ORACLE studies reveals a greater proportion of children sitting in single-sex pairs post-transition in the late 1970s (49%) compared to the 1990s (33%), with more mixed-sex groups occurring recently (7.3% vs. 23.5%) (Hargreaves & Pell, 2002). This finding might reflect a move toward more mixed schools and working arrangements accorded by the Sex Discrimination Act that was passed in the UK in 1975. In the late 1970s, post-transition schools were observed to segregate pupils by gender in timetables, roll call, and curriculum organization, with some schools offering PE only to boys and domestic sciences to girls (Delamont & Galton, 1986). However, in SAMSAD (2007–2008) there was no gender segregation in any areas of school organization except for PE.

Academic identities

In ORACLE, the single-sex working groups had distinct academic identities that they and other children were aware of. Similar groups are observed across studies spanning several decades (Measor & Woods, 1984; Symonds, 2009a), with working groups either conforming to their school's educational values, openly rejecting them, or sitting on the fence by being a little anti-school but still managing to achieve in class. These three groups are given several titles by researchers, including gangs, goodies and jokers (Pollard, 1985) and deviants, conformists and knife-edgers (Measor & Woods, 1984).

Goodies or conformists reported that doing well at school was central to maintaining a positive self-concept. As Matthew rationalized in SAMSAD, "You feel like actually the teachers are personally interested in you and I just like to feel like that." Conformist girls in *Changing Schools* described themselves in a positive light in accordance with their placement in a top ability set: "It is a sort of privilege to be up there, you have got to be properly brainy" (Emma in Measor & Woods, 1984, p. 141). Conformist boys have reported choosing their friends carefully: for example, based on their positive attitude to work and rejection of deviant behavior (like Matthew in SAMSAD). This is no surprise as deviant boys have described their conformist peers as "soft" and working too hard (Measor & Woods, 1984).

In *Changing Schools*, academic boys engaged in knife-edge behavior to gain popularity by appearing more deviant, while more deviant boys employed these tactics to prevent themselves from appearing stupid. Kevin used knife-edge behavior in SAMSAD to avoid doing work in a high-ability set. His English teacher asked him to read a script aloud so he would stop chatting with his friend. Kevin read it at breakneck speed in a commentator's voice, enabling a quick return to his informal discussion. Knife-edger girls in *Changing Schools* messed around when they knew they could not get caught or when it did not matter: for example, by throwing Polo mints across class when the teacher couldn't see.

The development of deviant groups and learning behaviors is carefully documented in *Changing Schools*. During the first week, all children were quiet, enthusiastic about working, and did not break school rules. This was recognized by pupils and teachers as being an initial front: "They want to get a good name from the teachers" (Amy in Measor & Woods, 1984, p. 51). The front was dropped by the third week when Pete and Roy began to graffiti their belongings. Soon after, several boys deliberately challenged the boundaries of classroom rules by arriving without equipment and ignoring commands. This process of "sussing out" teachers (Benyon, 1985), also called "hypothesis-testing" (Delamont & Galton, 1986, p. 58), was also present in SAMSAD. Here, deviant boys taunted their teacher's learning skills by using serious voices to offer her silly alternatives to the rules of a learning game. Afterwards, they began fidgeting in their seats and eventually slapped and punched each other until they were reprimanded. By the second term in *Changing Schools* (1979–1980), deviant boys began to challenge teachers for center stage through interruptions and diversions. By the third term, their attitudes to teachers and school had consolidated. Roy: "Mrs Gales has us for reading, fat cow!" (Measor & Woods, 1984, p. 110).

After transition, deviant girls are noted to express their distaste for school learning through passive avoidance tactics in comparison to boys' active defiance (Delamont & Galton, 1986; Measor & Woods, 1984). As Janet put it, "Some of the girls in our class whisper and giggle, but the boys are the ones who make remarks out loud" (Measor & Woods, 1984, p. 116). In *Changing Schools*, girls who spoke loudly were rebuked by boys and labeled "mouthy" (p. 117), showing how gender stereotypes can control learning groups' behaviors. Examples of passive avoidance from girls in SAMSAD included messing around to avoid working and, by the end of the year, truanting from the transition school.

In comparison to boys, fewer deviant and more conformist girls are observed in the three post-transition studies, perhaps as girls are not under the same pressure

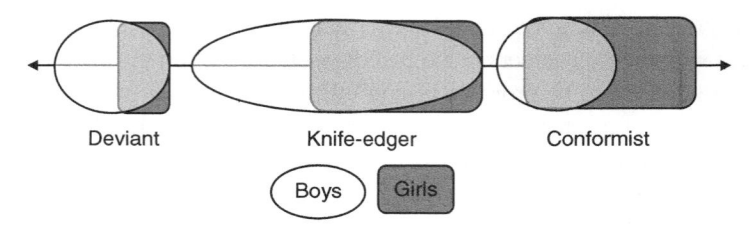

Figure 4.1 *Model of working groups*

to engage in the toughness game. Using Measor and Woods' (1984) continuum of deviant to conformist, the gender differences in UK early adolescent working groups might look a little like Figure 4.1.

The ORACLE studies note another set of academic identities by observing how often children actually work on learning tasks. The ORACLE replication study reported that more girls fitted the task-oriented profiles of *hard grinders*, *group toilers*, or *passive participants*, while more boys fitted the "task-avoidant" profiles of *routine helpers*, *distracted ghosts*, and *attention getters*. Boys got more attention from teachers when they engaged in horseplay (attention getters) or cooperated on routine tasks such as sharpening pencils and handing out textbooks (routine helpers), while girls received more attention when they were engaged in work, thus reinforcing these gendered personae. When pupils transferred to secondary school, more boys than girls moved from being task-oriented to task-avoidant. Ten years later in SAMSAD, similar behaviors were observed. For example, Indiana displayed routine helper behavior by wandering about, asking his friends about their work, and borrowing pieces of equipment. By doing so he appeared to be on task but did almost no work at all.

Attitude to English, mathematics, and science

All around us are visible gender differences in interest and engagement in careers pertaining to science, technology, and mathematics (see also Bagnoli, Demey, & Scott; Fuller & Unwin; Gutman, Sabates, & Schoon; Salmela-Aro; Weiss, Wiese, & Freund, this volume). The amount of enthusiasm that boys and girls have for these subjects at school may contribute to whether they choose to specialize in these areas in later life. Gender differences in how much children value subjects exist as early as first grade (Wigfield & Eccles, 1994). Focusing on the MSALT (US) and ORACLE (UK) studies, we explore whether these gender differences are sustained, and how they develop, for the key subjects of English, math, and science at school transition.

At the transition from Grade 6 to 7 in the US, boys rate English as being less important and useful than do girls (Wigfield & Eccles, 1994). They also like English less across transition in ORACLE – a difference that is conserved across a 30-year period (Galton, Hargreaves, & Pell, 2003). In the ORACLE replication study, both genders experienced a honeymoon period (Hargreaves, 1984) where they liked English more immediately after transition, but their liking of English declined by the end of the post-transition year (Galton et al., 2003). There was little difference between genders in how this pattern played out.

Children's attitudes toward mathematics are a different story, with few gender differences being noted in elementary school or across the transition (Wigfield & Eccles, 1994). Only in the last term before transition in ORACLE did boys like mathematics more than girls did (Galton et al., 2003). Both genders liked mathematics less and less across the pre- and post-transition years, a decline that was steeper than for any other subject.

Regarding science, in the late 1970s, girls transferring to high school explained that they disliked dissection, the smell and danger of chemicals, and having to wear safety goggles (Measor & Woods, 1984). They displayed learned helplessness by refusing to use science equipment that they perceived to be complicated or dangerous, despite being proficient at other manual work such as cooking and sewing. However, 30 years later, girls did not report these fears. In SAMSAD, Deirdre was bored by most sit down lessons, but "in science you do some practicals so that's alright" (Symonds, 2009b). There were no gender differences in how much boys and girls liked science in the ORACLE replication study, although girls liked English and mathematics more than they liked science, whereas this was not true for boys (Galton et al., 2003). After the school transition both genders liked science as much as they had done in their pre-transition schools. However, their attitudes dropped off by the end of the post-transition year.

In summary, although boys have more negative attitudes toward English, girls and boys like and value science and mathematics to a similar degree across transition. The way their attitudes develop does not differ much by gender, with declines being noted in English, science, and mathematics after school transition in the US and the UK. The ORACLE studies find that this pattern of decline is stalled in the first post-transition term for English and science, before children's liking drops off again. This temporary stability may be caused by children's enjoyment of the differences they encounter in the teaching of these subjects in comparison to their pre-transition schools. Unfortunately, these positive first encounters do not last.

Academic competencies in English and mathematics

At transition, children are often asked to evaluate how competent they are at different subjects and in academic subjects generally. They can report on their image of their competency (part of their self-image) and on their feelings about that image (part of their self-esteem) (Galton, Comber, & Pell, 2002).

Children's competency beliefs in English and mathematics can differ in gender-stereotypical ways throughout their schooling. For example, in the US, boys rate themselves as better at mathematics than do girls throughout elementary school (Wigfield & Eccles, 1994; see also Upadyaya & Eccles, this volume).

At school transition, these differences are conserved with boys feeling more competent in mathematics and less competent in English than girls (Wigfield & Eccles, 1994). Like their attitude toward subjects, both genders' competency beliefs in these subjects are found to decline across transition (Wigfield & Eccles, 1994). This may be part of a general decrease in competency beliefs noted across Grades 1 to 12 in the US, and in Australia and Germany (Marsh, 1989; Nagy et al., 2010).

Career aspirations

None of the studies reviewed looked at whether gender differences in children's feelings about different subjects impacted their future career aspirations. However, we can contrast studies from the 1970s and 2000s to show that gender differences in children's attitudes toward adult work have changed across time.

In the late 1970s, none of the boys interviewed in *Changing Schools* were supportive of their future wives working, regardless of whether their own mothers worked. In comparison, girls' career aspirations varied according to their attitudes toward schoolwork. All girls assumed that they would get married, and reported this in essays written from the perspective of an 80-year-old. No deviant girls aspired to have a career outside marriage, whereas knife-edger and conformist girls did. However, even these girls thought that they would give up their careers after marriage. Only two conformist girls wanted to continue their career after marriage, albeit in a diminished manner.

A few years earlier, early adolescent girls in the Milwaukee study were significantly more likely than boys to want future marriage and children (regardless of experiencing school transition or puberty). However, this difference disappeared when they reached 15 to 16 years old, as boys' interest in having a family grew. Across Grades 6 to 10, girls were more likely to aspire to a college placement and choose a higher salaried future job than were boys, despite their parents having lower educational expectations for them. Although they had higher aspirations than boys, half the Milwaukee girls expected to give up work when they had children.

Forty years later, no girls interviewed in SAMSAD mentioned forgoing their career in favor of being a housewife and mother. Most of the children in the target groups (16 out of 20) had made an initial (and in two cases a considered and decided) career choice in Year 7 by matching jobs they were familiar with to what they were good at and/or interested in. Although some career choices were gender-stereotyped (e.g., Deirdre wanted to be a beautician, and Gus an accountant), many were not. Matthew, Alex, Jacob, and Yasmin all wanted to be teachers, due to their successes in a particular subject or to a family history of teaching. Notably, both genders chose role models from their immediate environment, perhaps because this age group does not have much exposure to the world of work (Atherton, Cymbir, Roberts, Page, & Remedios, 2009). The SAMSAD findings may represent a generational shift in the transmission of female work roles from mothers to children, because mothers in this latter era worked, unlike those in the 1970s.

Motivation

Motivation can be seen as a system of beliefs and goals involving the self and as an emotional state. For example, at transition, Harry might set himself the goal of being placed in top set in mathematics and work hard in his lessons because he believes he can do it. Harry is buoyant about working hard because his goal is important to him, because he sees evidence of his success, and because he enjoys mathematics. One could say that Harry is intrinsically motivated because he takes personal responsibility for his goal. In contrast, if Harry's goal was prescribed and enforced by somebody else such as his teacher, he might be more extrinsically motivated to achieve it.

When quizzed on how keen they are to work in general, boys report feeling less motivated than girls across transition (Galton et al., 2002). This concurs with their work efforts, for, as described above, more boys than girls have task-avoidant work profiles and more girls are on-task in lessons (Hargreaves & Pell, 2002). In the UK, some boys try to avoid working after transition because they do not want to succeed in front of their friends (Measor & Woods, 1984) and are embarrassed to ask for help in case they look stupid (Measor & Woods, 1984; Symonds, 2009a).

Boys' reluctance to work stems from many factors. A long-standing adolescent male perspective is that working hard equates with being "soft" (Measor & Woods, 1984; Willis, 1977). In this perspective, conformity to stereotyped gender roles of masculinity (in which boys are supposed to be successful and powerful) and achievement becomes a paradox (Whitehead, 2003). Boys whose gendered identities are less secure and more stereotyped are more likely to shy away from seemingly feminine tasks such as academic achievement (Whitehead, 2006), perhaps as academic work does not involve physical prowess. Also, boys can be vulnerable to attacks on their self-esteem and by refusing to try they avoid the negative emotional consequences of failure (Covington, 1985).

Achievement

In accordance with boys' lower motivation to do schoolwork, studies from the 1970s find boys to be more at risk for slumps in achievement after changing schools. The Milwaukee study found that after transition to junior high school, only boys dipped in their grade point average. In the UK, this pattern appears for individual subjects, as a greater percentage of girls in ORACLE (1975–1980) made progress after transition in mathematics (65% vs. 55%), language skills (56% vs. 44%), and reading (73% vs. 43%).

However, the picture is more complicated in the 1990s. The ORACLE Replication Study tested the pre- and post-transition achievement of children who transferred schools at different ages. It found that more boys than girls made progress in English language and reading if they transitioned at the age of 9 and 10, while fewer boys than girls progressed in mathematics if they transitioned at age 10 (Galton et al., 2002). There were no gender differences in the percentage of boys and girls progressing in these subjects if they transitioned at age 11. This lack of gender differences in the older cohort may indicate that boys' equation of education with being non-masculine and therefore undesirable may have changed in recent years, allowing more boys the opportunity to achieve if it suits them.

Conclusions

Our review finds many gender differences occurring in early adolescence independently of school transition (Table 4.2), as the Milwaukee study, SAMSAD, and studies of pre-transition schools are able to show. During this developmental period in mixed-sex schools, boys appear to have a more rigid social hierarchy organized by markers of physical power, while girls place more emphasis on physical appearances and dating. From an evolutionary perspective, these characteristics may assist girls to develop traits that encourage pair bonding, and boys to practise skills in resource acquisition. However, the effects of these gender differences on children's emotional health are questionable, with boys being sensitive to physical victimization and girls having lower self-esteem and body image than boys. Also, we find that most children work in single-sex groups during lessons, perhaps as an extension of their playground cliques. Early adolescents are found to subscribe to gender stereotypes in their attitudes to subjects and academic competency beliefs, as are younger and older children.

At school transition, some of these gender differences are influenced by children's adaptation to their new social and academic environment (Table 4.2). Girls can become more obsessed with their physical appearances and with dating, which is unsurprising given that, for the first time, their school peers include older teenagers with more advanced sexual behaviors. With transition also comes a more rapid decline in self-esteem for more girls in comparison to those of the same age who do not transfer. When boys encounter new teachers, some challenge them for power while others do not, thus defining their membership of deviant, knife-edger, and conformist working groups. In general, fewer boys are on-task in class than girls, or make academic progress across the transition year. The picture here is that at transition, girls increase their focus on looking and acting older and are more vulnerable to declines in emotional health, while boys are especially at risk of disengaging from school.

Where data is available, we can see a lessening in some of the general gender differences across time (Table 4.2). First, girls' attitudes toward science and

Table 4.2. *Trends in gender differences*

Key area	Phenomenon	1974–1984	1996–2008
Development independent of school transition			
Peer relations	Boys socialize in large "sporty" groups or small "specialist" groups	✓	✓
	Girls mostly socialize in smaller cliques inclusive of "best friends"	✓	✓
	Friendship groups are gender-segregated	✓	✓
	Girls' friendships keep changing	✓	✓
	Girls begin to "fall out" with each other	✓	✓
	Both genders engage in "speed dating" and longer-term dating	✓	✓
	Girls are more interested in heterosexual relationships than are boys	✓	✓
Emotional health	Girls have lower self-esteem than boys	✓	✓
Learning and achievement	Gender-stereotyped competence beliefs	✓	✓
	Gender-stereotyped attitudes to subjects	✓	–
	Gender-segregated working groups	✓	–
Development moderated by school transition			
Peer relations	Girls pay more attention to physical appearances and dating	✓	✓
Emotional health	Girls have more declines in self-esteem than do boys	✓	✓
Learning and achievement	Boys "suss out" teachers by challenging them for power	✓	✓
	New gender-stereotyped pro-/anti-learning profiles develop	✓	✓
	More boys adopt anti-learning personae than do girls	✓	✓

Key area	Phenomenon	1974–1984	1996–2008
	Boys make less academic progress than do girls	✓	–
	Both genders decline in attitude toward key subjects	?	✓
No pre-transition data available, but present at transition			
Learning and achievement	Girls want to work after marriage	✓	+
	Gender-stereotyped career choices	✓	–

Key: ✓ phenomenon is observed in that era; – phenomenon has decreased; + phenomenon has increased; ? phenomenon was not recorded by studies used in the review in that era.

working after marriage appear to be more positive in the 2000s than in the 1970s. This may have been brought about by increased acceptance of women working in STEM fields and girls' observations of married women working. Second, there are fewer single-sex working groups in class, and boys have begun to catch up to girls in terms of their academic progress across transition. Here we might be seeing a decline of the traditional boys' attitude that schoolwork is for girls. In the UK at least, this attitude traces back to the mid-1900s and before, where boys left school at the age of 14 in search of manual labor (Willis, 1977). Our main finding, however, is that the multitude of gender differences recorded by studies are persistent over time, suggesting consistency of biological and social influences on how gender plays out at school transition.

References

Atherton, G., Cymbir, E., Roberts, K., Page, L., & Remedios, R. (2009). *How young people formulate their views about the future: Exploratory research* (Research Report DCSF-RR152). London: Department for Children, Schools and Families.

Bandura, A. (1977). *Social learning theory*. Englewood Cliffs, NJ: Prentice Hall.

Bem, S. L. (1981). Gender schema theory: A cognitive account of sex typing. *Psychological Review*, 88(4), 354–364.

Benyon, J. (1985). *Initial encounters in the secondary school: Sussing, typing and coding*. Lewes: Falmer Press.

Coleman, L., & Coleman, J. (2002). The measurement of puberty: A review. *Journal of Adolescence*, 25, 535–550.

Comber, C. (2001). *The academic underachievement of boys and the impact of educational transition*. Unpublished doctoral thesis, University of Leicester.

Covington, M. V. (1985). The self-worth theory of achievement motivation: Findings and implications. *The Elementary School Journal*, 85(1), 5–20.

Dahl, R. E. (2004). Adolescent brain development: A period of vulnerabilities and opportunities. *Annals of the New York Academy of Sciences*, 1–22.

Delamont, S., & Galton, M. (1986). *Inside the secondary classroom*. London: Routledge & Kegan Paul.

Eccles, J. S. (1999). The development of children ages 6 to 14. *The Future of Children: When School Is Out*, 9(2), 30–44.

Eccles, J. S., Midgley, C., Wigfield, A., Buchanan, C. M., Reuman, D., Flanagan, C., & Mac Iver, D. (1993). Development during adolescence: The impact of stage-environment fit on young adolescents' experiences in schools and in families. *American Psychologist*, 48(2), 90–101.

Epstein, S. (1973). The self-concept revisited: Or a theory of a theory. *American Psychologist*, 28, 404–416.

Fechner, P. Y. (2003). The biology of puberty: New developments in sex differences. In C. Hayward (Ed.), *Gender differences at puberty* (pp. 17–28). Cambridge University Press.

Feldlaufer, H., Midgley, C., & Eccles, J. S. (1988). Student, teacher, and observer perceptions of the classroom before and after the transition to junior high school. *Journal of Early Adolescence*, 8(2), 133–156.

Galton, M., Comber, C., & Pell, T. (2002). The consequences of transfer for pupils: Attitudes and attainment. In L. Hargreaves & M. Galton (Eds.), *Transfer from the primary classroom, 20 years on* (University of Cambridge ed., pp. 131–158). London, New York: Routledge Falmer.

Galton, M., Hargreaves, L., & Pell, T. (2003). Progress in the middle years of schooling: Continuities and discontinuities at transition. *Education 3–13*, 31(2), 9–19.

Galton, M., Simon, B., & Croll, P. (1980). *Inside the primary classroom*. London: Routledge & Kegan Paul.

Galton, M., & Wilcocks, J. (1983). *Moving from the primary classroom*. London: Routledge & Kegan Paul.

Giedd, J. N., Blumenthal, J., Jeffries, N. O., Castellanos, F. X., Liu, H., Zijdenbos, A., et al. (1999). Brain development during childhood and adolescence: A longitudinal MRI study. *Nature Neuroscience*, 2(10), 861–863.

Gray, J., Galton, M., McLaughlin, C., Clarke, B., & Symonds, J. (2011). *The supportive school: Wellbeing and the young adolescent*. Newcastle-upon-Tyne: Cambridge Scholars Publishing.

Hargreaves, D. J. (1984). *Improving secondary schools*. London: Inner London Education Authority.

Hargreaves, L., & Galton, M. (2002). *Transfer from the primary classroom 20 years on*. London: Routledge Falmer.

Hargreaves, L., & Pell, T. (2002). Patterns of pupil behavior in the transition schools. In L. Hargreaves & M. Galton (Eds.), *Transition from the primary classroom, 20 years on* (pp. 159–184). London, New York: Routledge Falmer.

Hill, J. P., & Lynch, M. E. (1983). The intensification of gender-related role expectations during early adolescence. In J. Brooks-Gunn & A. C. Petersen (Eds.), *Girls at puberty: Biological and psychosocial perspectives* (pp. 201–228). New York, London: Plenum Press.

Jackson, C., & Warin, J. (2000). The importance of gender as an aspect of identity at key transition points in compulsory education. *British Educational Research Journal*, 26(3), 375–391.

Kvalsund, R. (2000). The transition from primary to secondary level in smaller and larger rural schools in Norway: Comparing differences in context and social meaning. *International Journal of Educational Research*, 33(4), 401–424.

Lenroot, R. K., Gogtay, N., Greenstein, D. K., Wells, E. M., Wallace, G. L., Clasen, L. S., et al. (2007). Sexual dimorphism of brain developmental trajectories during childhood and adolescence. *NeuroImage*, 36(4), 1065–1073.

Markus, H., & Wurf, E. (1987). The dynamic self-concept: A social psychological perspective. *Annual Review of Psychology*, 38, 299–337.

Marsh, H. W. (1989). Age and sex effects in multiple dimensions of self-concept: Preadolescence to early adulthood. *Journal of Educational Psychology*, 81(3), 417–430.

Measor, L., & Woods, P. (1984). *Changing schools*. Milton Keynes: Open University Press.

Mellor, D., & Delamont, S. (2011). Old anticipations, new anxieties? A contemporary perspective on primary to secondary transfer. *Cambridge Journal of Education*, 41(3), 331–346.

Nagy, G., Watt, H. M. G., Eccles, J. S., Trautwein, U., Lüdtke, O., & Baumert, J. (2010). The development of students' mathematics self-concept in relation to gender: Different countries, different trajectories? *Journal of Research on Adolescence*, 20(2), 482–506.

Nottelmann, E. D. (1987). Competence and self-esteem during transition from childhood to adolescence. *Developmental Psychology*, 23(3), 441–450.

Petersen, A. C., & Crockett, L. J. (1985). Pubertal timing and grade effects on adjustment. *Journal of Youth and Adolescence*, 14, 191–206.

Pollard, A. (1985). *The social world of the primary school*. London: Cassell.

Roderick, M. (2003). What's happening to the boys? Early high school experiences and school outcomes among African American male adolescents in Chicago. *Urban Education*, 38, 538–607.

Simmons, R. G., & Blyth, D. A. (1987). *Moving into adolescence: The impact of pubertal change and school context* (Vol. 2). New Brunswick, London: Transaction Publishers.

Simmons, R. G., Burgeson, R., Carlton-Ford, S., & Blyth, D. A. (1987). The impact of cumulative change in early adolescence. *Child Development*, 58(5), 1220–1234.

Sisk, C. L., & Foster, D. L. (2004). The neural basis of puberty and adolescence. *Nature Neuroscience*, 7(10), 1040–1047.

Swain, J. (2000). "The money's good, the fame's good, the girls are good": The role of playground football in the construction of young boys' masculinity in a junior school. *British Journal of Sociology of Education*, 21, 95–109.

Symonds, J. E. (2009a). *Constructing stage-environment fit: Early adolescents' psychological development and their attitudes to school in English middle and secondary school environments*. Faculty of Education, University of Cambridge. Retrieved from www.dspace.cam.ac.uk/handle/1810/223866.

(2009b). Unpublished data from: *Constructing stage-environment fit: Early adolescents' psychological development and their attitudes to school in English middle and secondary school environments*. Doctoral thesis, Faculty of Education, University of Cambridge.

Tanner, J. M., Whitehouse, R. H., Marubini, E., & Resele, L. F. (1976). The adolescent growth spurt of boys and girls of the Harpenden Growth Study. *Annals of Human Biology*, 3(2), 109–129.

Tobin-Richards, M. H., Boxer, A. M., & Petersen, A. C. (1983). The psychological significance of pubertal change: Sex differences in perceptions of self during early adolescence. In J. Brooks-Gunn & A. C. Petersen (Eds.), *Girls at puberty: Biological and psychosocial perspectives* (pp. 127–154). New York, London: Plenum Press.

Whitehead, J. M. (2003). Masculinity, motivation and academic success: A paradox. *Teacher Research*, 38, 147–160.

(2006). Starting school: Why girls are already ahead of boys. *Teacher Development*, 10(2), 249–270.

Wigfield, A., Eccles, J. S., Mac Iver, D., Reuman, D. A., & Midgley, C. (1991). Transitions during early adolescence: Changes in children's domain-specific self-perceptions and general self-esteem. *Developmental Psychology*, 27(4), 552–565.

Wigfield, A., & Eccles, J. S. (1994). Children's competence beliefs, achievement values, and general self-esteem: Change across elementary and middle school. *Journal of Early Adolescence*, 14(2), 107–138.

Willis, P. (1977). *Learning to labour: How working class kids get working class jobs.* New York: Columbia University Press.

Zoller Booth, M., Chase Sheehan, H., & Earley, M. A. (2007). Middle grades' school models and their impact on early adolescent self-esteem. *Middle Grades Research Journal*, 2(1), 73–97.

PART III

Career planning during adolescence

5 What should I do with my life? Motivational, personal, and contextual factors in mastering the transition of graduating from high school

David Weiss, Bettina S. Wiese and Alexandra M. Freund

Abstract

The transition from high school to college, an apprenticeship, or the workforce is very demanding for adolescents. In this chapter, we explore the factors that contribute to successfully adapting to the many demands of this transition. Building on findings from developmental, social, and vocational psychology, we explore the role of three types of factors for mastering this transition: (1) motivational factors (goal selection and pursuit), (2) personal attributes and attitudes (personality and gender-related attitudes), and (3) context variables (parent modeling). Regarding motivational factors, we build on the model of selection, optimization, and compensation (SOC) and investigate the importance of the selection, pursuit, and maintenance of goals for adapting to the transition. As for personal attributes and attitudes, we argue that traditional gender-related attitudes, although less influential for educational choices, can help to buffer the insecurities adolescents face during this period. Finally, turning to contextual factors, we discuss the influence of parental work participation in different phases of the family life cycle on adolescents' planning of their future career- and family-related lives.

Graduating from high school: an important transition in late adolescence

Adolescence and emerging adulthood is the time of life when young people experience new opportunities for action (Arnett, 2000). This is a life phase marked by the responsibility of making many decisions that will have a continued and strong impact on one's future life (Freund, 2011). During the years of emerging adulthood, for instance, many individuals obtain the level of education that builds the foundation for their later careers (e.g., Chisholm & Hurrelmann, 1995; see also Schoon & Silbereisen, 2009). In fact, career-related decisions and transitions represent a major developmental task during this life stage.

The study was made possible by a grant to the second and third author from the Jacobs Foundation (Zurich). We gratefully acknowledge this support. This publication benefited also from the support of the Swiss National Centre of Competence in Research "LIVES – Overcoming vulnerability: Life course perspectives" financed by the Swiss National Science Foundation.

Transitions are "points in the life course when roles are transformed, redefined, or left behind for new ones" (Perrig-Chiello & Perren, 2005, p. 170) and create opportunities for individuals to design their future life course (Salmela-Aro, 2009). One major transition in late adolescence occurs upon graduation from high school (e.g., Tomasik, Hardy, Haase, & Heckhausen, 2009). In this chapter, we focus on this important transition from high school to college or the workforce. We examine how adolescents deal with their new freedom and autonomy in making important life decisions by selecting and pursuing personal goals. Moreover, we focus on individual and social factors that shape adolescents' attitudes as well as their career- and family-related goals. We will focus on how adolescents successfully master the transition from high school rather than considering more problematic pathways (e.g., high school dropout). Specifically, we present a new perspective highlighting the role of motivational factors, personal attributes and attitudes, and context variables for managing this central transition in adolescence.

The transition from high school to college or to the workforce holds many opportunities and chances for late adolescents. These changes necessitate important life decisions. This can be very challenging, as adolescents have to choose between – sometimes rather vague and uncertain – alternatives (e.g., "Should I go to college or apply for an apprenticeship?") with ever-increasing specificity (e.g., "Should I major in education, biology, or history?"). When it comes to planning and decision making, adolescents may feel overwhelmed by the possibilities that lie before them. To master the transition from high school to life thereafter, they need to set and pursue personal goals. In this chapter, we present a set of studies that explores the factors contributing to successfully adapting to the many demands of this transition. On the basis of these results, we explain how motivational factors, personal attributes and attitudes, as well as social-contextual variables shape adolescents' adjustment and their development of educational and family-related goals.

Adolescence is a period of life in which individuals achieve motivational competence and extend various self-regulatory skills (Lerner, Freund, De Stefanis, & Habermas, 2001). These developmental gains help them to meet the educational, occupational, and social challenges of this life stage. In the following, we focus on the specific self-regulatory processes of selection, optimization, and compensation, which contribute positively to adolescents' adaptation to the transition from high school to college or an apprenticeship. In particular, we propose an age-specific pattern of strategies that allow for successful goal selection and pursuit. Moreover, we examine motivational factors that explain the adoption of gender-related attitudes. Further, we focus on how gender-related attributes affect goals among male and female students. Finally, we demonstrate how social factors such as the family context shape adolescents' goals. We highlight adolescents' individual experience of their family life as an important moderating variable. In this chapter, we present various factors located on different levels of analysis (e.g., individual and social-contextual level) that are important to successfully negotiate

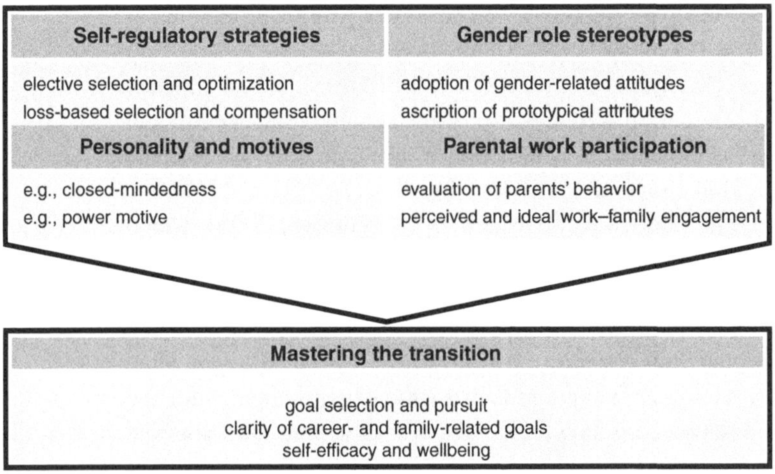

Self-regulatory strategies	Gender role stereotypes
elective selection and optimization loss-based selection and compensation	adoption of gender-related attitudes ascription of prototypical attributes
Personality and motives	**Parental work participation**
e.g., closed-mindedness e.g., power motive	evaluation of parents' behavior perceived and ideal work–family engagement

Mastering the transition
goal selection and pursuit clarity of career- and family-related goals self-efficacy and wellbeing

Figure 5.1 *Psychological factors relevant to mastering the transition from high school to college or an apprenticeship*

career transitions in adolescence.[1] Figure 5.1 presents an overview of the psychological factors relevant to mastering the transition from high school to college or an apprenticeship.

Selecting, pursuing, and maintaining goals for adapting to the transition from high school to college or an apprenticeship

The developmental period between childhood and adulthood is a time when adolescents are motivated to acquire new skills and enter environments that allow maximum access to resources (Lerner et al., 2001). Specifically, in this period young people experience novel and various opportunities for action (Arnett, 2000; Silbereisen, Eyferth, & Rudinger, 1986). Adolescents' emerging ability to anticipate future outcomes enables them to represent goals and motivates them to take action to attain these goals. Specifically during adolescence, individuals develop basic psychological requirements for self-regulation, such as thinking about the past, present, and future ("diachronic thinking," Habermas & Bluck, 2000; Montangero, 1996), and an increased ability to delay gratification and thus commit to long-term goals in the presence of attractive short-term gains

---

[1] Besides a review of results published by different authors from the fields of developmental, social, and vocational psychology, we also report findings from a longitudinal study that investigated the transition from high school to college or the workforce in Switzerland with N = 520 high school graduates (64.1% female, mean age of 19 years). They completed three questionnaires: (1) just before graduating from high school, (2) 3 months, and (3) 9 months after graduation (retention rate was approx. 70%). For a detailed description of the sample and the study, see Freund et al. (2013); Wiese and Freund (2011), and Weiss et al. (2012).

(Funder & Block, 1989; Mischel, Shoda, & Peake, 1988). Moreover, practicing and planning (Ericsson & Lehmann, 1996; Smith, 1996) as well as establishing control beliefs (Skinner, Chapman, & Baltes, 1988) and a sense of self-efficacy (Bandura, 1997, 2006) are major skills necessary for achieving autonomy and successfully managing the demands of adulthood. At the same time, adolescents are susceptible to increased egocentrism, risk-taking (Greene, Krcmar, Walters, Rubin, & Hale, 2000), and peer pressure (Gardner & Steinberg, 2005), which might have detrimental effects on decision making and goal pursuit. Therefore, adolescents need to identify and select the "right" developmental paths in accordance with their individual motives, values, personality, and abilities. How can adolescents effectively plan their future in a period of life full of challenges when the complexity of choices is increasing and their own decisions entail – for the first time – serious, long-term consequences? Adolescents need to find answers to difficult questions such as "What should I do with my life?" "What do I want in life?" and "How do I get what I want in life?"

The *selection*, *optimization*, and *compensation* model (SOC; Baltes, 1997; Baltes & Baltes, 1990; Freund & Baltes, 2000, 2002) addresses developmental strategies that people can use to manage constraints and opportunities within developmental transitions. The SOC model represents a meta-theory, which specifies the dynamic interplay of strategy use for effective adaptation to changing circumstances across the life-span. Specifically, the SOC model defines developmental strategies that foster positive development in times of biological, psychological, and social changes. In a nutshell, this theory focuses on the antecedents and consequences of adaptive goal selection and goal pursuit reflected in high levels of self-efficacy, growth, and wellbeing.

The process of *selection* describes the development of and commitment to personal goals. Given that resources such as time and energy are limited (even for adolescents who have a lot of time and energy at their disposal), people need to choose specific goals and identify the means by which to concentrate their resources in order to accomplish these goals. Since goals motivate and direct behavior, selecting a goal is the most central and apparently the most difficult step in the transition from high school to college or the workforce. Developing and committing to a hierarchy of personal goals has been described as *elective selection*. With increasing age, adolescents become progressively more realistic, prioritize their goals, and focus on fewer goals (Hirschi & Vondracek, 2009). During the transition from high school to the workforce, elective selection comprises exploring and seeking new information in order to realize future opportunities. With respect to early career development, it is a very important task for adolescents to systematically explore their interests, motivation, and capabilities as well as the different career pathways and occupational domains that are open to them (see Kracke & Schmitt-Rodermund, 2001). Nurmi, Salmela-Aro, and Koivisto (2002) showed in a longitudinal study with adolescents from vocational schools that assigning a high priority to education-related goals is of high importance in adolescence. Those who rated their educational goals as highly important were more likely to find an adequate position after high school and less likely to face unemployment.

Adolescents are likely to be confronted with obstacles along the difficult road from high school to college or an apprenticeship and may experience setbacks after initial goal selection, necessitating *loss-based selection*. This process refers to a person's re-evaluation of their goals, focusing on their most important goals or lowering the level of aspiration in response to hindrances. An example of loss-based selection can be found in a study by Heckhausen and Tomasik (2002) with German adolescents in a vocational school: when the deadline for finding an apprenticeship was approaching, these adolescents gradually adjusted their goal of getting their ideal apprenticeship to more feasible but less prestigious alternative options.

Planning the future, although of great importance for managing one's life in late adolescence, is but a first step in mastering the transition from high school to college or the workforce. Sticking to one's goals might be a greater challenge for adolescents than for adults. *Optimization* describes the process of individuals' striving to make the most of their selected goals. This involves identifying and acquiring the means for goal attainment (i.e., internal and external resources) and the implementation of goal-relevant actions. For example, in order to reach their educational or career goals, adolescents need to acquire the necessary skills for goal attainment, to repeat and to practice the initiated goal-directed actions, to be persistent, and to invest time and resources.

Compensation is an alternative response to loss-based selection when one encounters setbacks during goal pursuit or losses that endanger the maintenance of goals. In contrast to loss-based selection (which is about changing the goal), compensation maintains the goal but changes the means of goal pursuit. This may involve the substitution of means that are no longer available (e.g., taking a part-time job to help pay one's tuition when one's parents' financial support is inadequate) or increasing resource investments (e.g., allotting more time for studying after having failed an exam in one's first semester at college). Although compensation for losses might seem less important during a time of life when resources are plentiful and losses do not occur as frequently as in old age, adolescents are also prone to encounter losses or setbacks that require compensation (Lerner et al., 2001).

Table 5.1 summarizes some examples of specific strategies of elective selection, loss-based selection, optimization, and compensation that might be helpful for successfully dealing with academic and career transitions in late adolescence.

Importantly, developmental self-regulation does not take place in a social vacuum; instead, individual development is also shaped by social-contextual influences. That is, individual self-regulation occurs within normative conceptions of societal influences and constraints (Freund, Nikitin, & Ritter, 2009; Wrosch & Freund, 2001). Thus, age-related expectations influence adolescents' selection of educational, occupational, and family-related goals. Beyond age-graded social expectations, macro-structural constraints such as youth unemployment rates

Table 5.1. *Examples of specific SOC-related strategies in the context of the transition from high school to college or an apprenticeship*

Elective selection	Loss-based selection	Optimization	Compensation
- Decide whether to pursue higher education or vocational training - Explore one's own interests, motivation, and capabilities - Identify careers that fit one's own interests and capabilities	- If one cannot get an apprenticeship in the desired field in one's own geographical area, expand search to other areas - If one does not get into medical school, consider nursing as an alternative profession	- Invest effort into preparing for final examinations in order to get the best grades possible - Fill out job applications - Take job application training	- Take on a part-time job to help finance college tuition if parents' financial support is inadequate - If study group to prepare for final examinations disbands, ask parents to administer quizzes

also play an important role for planning one's professional and family-related future. By negotiating societal and personal constraints, adolescents can select goals that best match their individual and social circumstances.

Taken together, in order to successfully manage the transition from high school to college or work, adolescents need to coordinate the processes of goal selection, to optimize efforts to reach the selected goals, and to compensate in situations when goals cannot be achieved. During adolescence, the development of personal goals, commitment to goals, investment in goal pursuit, maintenance of goal commitment, and implementation are of great importance for mastering the career-related transition. First, adolescents have to select those career opportunities that best match their interests, motives, and personal capabilities as well as structural constraints. For example, as a first step, a high school student needs to identify content domains of occupations that fit his or her individual interests and capabilities (e.g., "I like helping other people. What careers target helping others?"). This first step is very much in line with Holland's (1985) person–environment matching approach, which is popular in career counseling. He divided personality as well as work environments into six categories (i.e., realistic, investigative, artistic, social, enterprising, conventional) and placed high importance on matching the person's characteristics with those of the jobs (e.g., a very social person best matches a social job such as social worker or teacher). Holland's approach has been criticized because it assumes high stability of both the characteristics and interests of a person and the requirements and affordances of a particular job. From a developmental perspective, it seems highly unlikely that a person's interests and values will not change across adulthood. Moreover, in modern times, jobs also undergo changes in the competencies that are required and the activities they entail. This critique notwithstanding, Holland's model stresses the importance of becoming acquainted with one's likes, dislikes, interests, and abilities as well as occupational requirements in order to be able to make informed decisions as a central step in professional development. Based on this knowledge, an adolescent can then specify alternatives within a certain professional domain (e.g., a social profession), taking into account the required investments in training or education (e.g., nurse, physician) as well as the short- and long-term career prospects. In this context, an adolescent will need to decide between pursuing higher academic education (e.g., going to medical school) or entering the vocational track (e.g., becoming a nurse). Oftentimes there might be several options that fit the adolescent's preferences (e.g., medical doctor, clinical psychologist) necessitating a prioritization. This step also requires a careful comparison of the requirements of the college education or apprenticeship (e.g., admission to medical school in German-speaking countries requires very good grades). If one does not meet these requirements, an adaptive strategy would be to consider a career in a related profession with different or lower requirements (e.g., in nursing).

Research shows that SOC strategies are associated with positive outcomes across adulthood (for a summary, see Freund, 2008). For instance, Freund and Baltes (2002) found a positive relationship between the self-reported SOC and various indicators of subjective wellbeing such as positive emotions, personal growth, and meaning in life in a sample of participants aged 14 to 89 years. Moreover, Wiese, Freund, and Baltes (2002) showed in a longitudinal study that young adults who engaged in the use of SOC strategies achieved increases in subjective wellbeing and subjective career success over time. Furthermore, Abele and Wiese (2008) found that college graduates who used the strategies of elective selection and optimization were more likely to develop specific career management strategies (e.g., specific career planning activities), which, in turn, showed positive associations with career satisfaction and objective career success (e.g., income, leadership position). Gestsdottir and Lerner (2007) demonstrated that SOC strategy use is an important predictor of positive development in early adolescence. Their study with pre-adolescents (fifth and sixth grade; $M = 10.9$ and $M = 12.1$ years of age, respectively) revealed positive associations between SOC indicators of positive development (i.e., psychological wellbeing) and negative associations between SOC and problem behavior.

Previous research has shown that young adults (relative to older adults) are more motivated to attain gains and growth than to prevent losses (Ebner, Freund, & Baltes, 2006; Freund, 2006). Freund and Ebner (2005) suggested that this might be partly due to social expectations and developmental goals that are primarily concerned with gains and growth during this phase in life. This is also true for late adolescence, when graduating from high school, going to college or starting an apprenticeship, and finding a romantic partner are central tasks. Therefore, self-regulatory processes geared toward gains, namely, elective selection and optimization, should be particularly beneficial for adapting to the transition from high school to college or work. However, in many European countries the self-regulatory processes are currently constrained by extremely high youth unemployment rates (adolescents and young adults under the age of 25; e.g., in 2012 53.2% in Spain, 55.3% in Greece; see Eurostat, 2013).

In a longitudinal study, we explored the role of SOC strategies for indicators of adaptation to the transition from high school (i.e., adolescents' vocational goal clarity, wellbeing, and self-efficacy) and found support for this expectation (Weiss, Wiese, & Freund, 2011). Adolescents' engagement in SOC behaviors positively predicted the experience of self-efficacy and positively contributed to career goal clarity. As expected, a more differentiated analysis of the SOC subcomponents revealed that *elective selection* and *optimization* were the strongest predictors for career goal clarity. Turning to self-efficacy beliefs, again, optimization was of central predictive importance, but elective selection was not. The ability to persistently invest resources into one's goals (i.e., optimization) as well as the ability to adjust one's goals when one encounters setbacks or when goals are blocked (i.e., loss-based selection) predicted self-efficacy beliefs across the transition.

Taken together, it appears that gain-related self-regulatory strategies are particularly important for successfully negotiating career development transitions in adolescence: optimization and elective selection emerged as the most important factors for adolescents' development of career goal clarity during the transition from high school. Optimization also played a crucial role for increasing and maintaining perceptions of self-efficacy during the transition from high school to college or the workforce. This indicates that exploration and seeking new information in order to realize one's goals are particularly beneficial to adapt to the transition from high school. However, it appears also important to be able to deal with setbacks and obstacles in order to face a long-term career with an enduring sense of personal efficacy.

Motivational factors in predicting the adoption of gender-related attitudes during the transition

As mentioned above, adolescents' career-related choices are embedded in a social context. According to Eccles (2011), one important social-contextual factor is socially shared gender-related expectations (see also Abele & Spurk, 2011). Gender can be regarded as a social category that becomes socially and psychologically meaningful in early childhood (Crouter, Whiteman, McHale, & Osgood, 2007). At a very young age (2–3 years), children begin to rely on gender categories and are able to identify men and women (e.g., Fagot & Leinbach, 1993). Research shows that 8-year-old children describe themselves using gender-role characteristics (Katz & Walsh,

1991). Social learning theory (Bandura, 1977) explains gender-role behavior as a result of cumulative experiences in which important social role models such as parents, teachers, and peers shape children's gender-related behaviors. Social norms entail different expectations about the typical behavior of men and women and constitute the basis for gender stereotypes. Gender stereotypes refer to beliefs and cognitive representations including prescriptions of certain attributes (Deaux, 1985). Specifically, they encompass physical characteristics, personality traits, abilities, work roles, and even career paths (Abele, 2003; Eagly, 1987; Sczesny, Bosak, Neff, & Schyns, 2004). Women are ascribed attributes such as warmth, emotionality, and sensitivity, while men are viewed as competent, self-confident, and assertive. Hence, women are ascribed more communal attributes, which refer to group participation and cooperation with others, while men are ascribed attributes that imply self-enhancement and self-assertion (Bakan, 1966). Importantly, the ascription of predominantly agentic attributes to men and mainly communal attributes to women forms the basis of gender-role expectations (Eagly, 1987; Eagly & Steffen, 1984; Glick & Fiske, 2001). From early adolescence on, girls are more likely to report higher levels of expressiveness, and boys, higher levels of instrumentality (McHale, Shanahan, Updegraff, Crouter, & Booth, 2004; see also Fabes et al.; Kriesi & Buchmann, this volume). Ascriptions of gender-related attributes even tend to increase during adolescence as has been predicted by the Gender-Intensification Hypothesis (Hill & Lynch, 1983).

Gender-related attributes are linked to perceptions of becoming a man or a woman (Prentice & Carranza, 2002). Specifically, these gender-related attributes become part of adolescents' self-conceptions. Research has focused on how gendered socialization affects career-related choices. In fact, adolescents may conform to gender-related norms and expectations when deciding against or in favor of educational and career options (Eccles, 2011; Lips, 2004; Wigfield & Eccles, 2001). Through socializing, girls learn that they are good in interpersonal situations and care for others. In contrast, boys learn that they have a strong instrumental orientation and should avoid expressions of weakness ("Boys don't cry!"). Through internalization and self-stereotyping, these gender-related behavioral patterns are incorporated in people's self-concept and transformed into personal behavior. Importantly, gender differences in self-ascribed levels of instrumentality and expressivity have significant implications for mastering developmental transitions. In line with this argument, previous research has demonstrated that higher levels of instrumentality have a positive impact on self-esteem and wellbeing (Bussey & Bandura, 1999; Heppner, Walther, & Good, 1995; Whitley, 1983). Furthermore, higher levels of instrumentality are negatively related to anxiety, depression, and self-esteem in adolescent boys and girls (Towbes, Cohen, & Glyshaw, 1989).

In the context of their longitudinal study on the transition from high school to college or the workforce, Freund, Weiss, and Wiese (2013) investigated the interplay of goal clarity and gender-related motives, attributes, and attitudes.

Gender-related attributes predicted adolescents' goal clarity and aspirations. Specifically, instrumentality and expressivity positively predicted career-related goal clarity, which, in turn, predicted an increase in life satisfaction across time. As expected, the boys in this study described themselves as more instrumental than girls and the girls described themselves as more expressive than boys. Similarly, boys as compared to girls indicated that they have a higher power and a lower affiliation motive. No differences emerged between boys and girls for career goal clarity; however, girls were higher in family-related goal clarity.

Although empirical evidence suggests that there are gender differences in self-ascribed gender-related attributes, people do not always automatically accept and internalize gender stereotypes. Depending on whether or not adhering to these stereotypes carries potential disadvantages, individuals might resist adopting such stereotypes. From an intergroup perspective, *traditional gender ideology* denotes the definition of gender roles legitimizing an unequal distribution of resources, status, and power between men and women. Even today women are seen as holding – and actually tend to hold – lower-status positions, whereas men are seen as holding – and, again, actually tend to hold – higher-status positions. Perceived status differences between men and women result from intergroup comparison processes (Tajfel, 1981). Because members of privileged groups are more likely to endorse beliefs that protect their group-based advantaged position (Guimond, Dambrun, Michinov, & Duarte, 2003; Schmitt & Wirth, 2009), men try to protect their privileged position. By contrast, members of disadvantaged groups are often found to be motivated to improve their social position by eliminating their disadvantage (Guimond & Dube-Simard, 1983; Tajfel & Turner, 1986). It has consistently been shown that women are more likely to reject traditional gender ideology in order to improve their disadvantaged situation (Eagly, Diekman, Johannesen-Schmidt, & Koenig, 2004; Grant & Brown, 1995; Kelly & Breinlinger, 2006). In other words, the endorsement of traditional gender ideology is beneficial for men because they occupy the privileged position in the gendered intergroup context. In contrast, for women, traditional gender ideology represents a barrier to the attainment of equal status with men. In line with this theorizing, the results of the study on high school students showed that, on average, female students were less likely than male students to endorse traditional gender roles and non-egalitarian attitudes (Freund et al., 2013). Moreover, longitudinal research has shown that girls become less traditional during adolescence whereas boys become increasingly more likely to endorse traditional gender attitudes as they grow older (Galambos, Almeida, & Petersen, 1990). Thus, the gender-intensification effect (Hill & Lynch, 1983) might be linked to boys' motivation to maintain their privileged position. That girls have the opposite motivation (i.e., to change their disadvantaged position) might be a reason why, up to now, research has only confirmed the gender-intensification hypothesis for boys (Crouter et al., 2007).

Individual differences in the endorsement of traditional gender-role attitudes

A further moderator in the relationship between adolescents' sex- and gender-related attitudes is that of explicit motives. Explicit motives can be defined as personal values and reasons for action that are acquired through socialization (McClelland, 1980). One important explicit motive is the personal striving for power. Because explicit motives are associated with preferences and behavioral choice (Brunstein, 2008), they may be predictors of the endorsement of gender roles. More specifically, we posit that power motives are likely to be negatively associated with egalitarian attitudes for boys, because boys' power motives might increase their tendency to promote non-egalitarian and traditional gender attitudes. This would help them to justify and maintain higher power positions compared to girls. This hypothesis is based on the functional assumption that people generally promote attitudes and ideologies that serve their self-interests. In other words, boys with a strong power motive might also be highly motivated to maintain gender-group-based privileges.

Against this backdrop, it seems surprising that some women accept or even endorse traditional gender ideology that benefits men and discriminates against women. The phenomenon that people sometimes endorse ideologies even at their own or their group's expense has received much attention from various scholars (Jost & Banaji, 1994; Marx & Engels, 1845/1998; Scott, 1990). Weiss, Freund, and Wiese (2012) addressed this phenomenon in the context of educational and occupational transitions and investigated whether adopting disadvantageous beliefs about one's group might be adaptive under certain circumstances. By adopting a functional perspective, they argued that a strong belief system such as traditional gender ideology serves personal goals. For some women, traditional gender ideology may serve as a guideline for action that protects their sense of control and self-efficacy in times of change and uncertainty (e.g., transitions). They hypothesized that the endorsement of traditional gender ideology might be beneficial for girls who are low in openness for new experiences in order to cope with insecurities associated with the transition from high school to college or the workforce. Conversely, girls high in openness who endorse traditional gender ideology should perceive a decrease in self-efficacy because endorsing traditional gender ideology may hinder them from pursuing and realizing their career goals. Supporting these hypotheses, experimental findings reveal that transitional uncertainty impairs perception of control and subjective wellbeing among people with low levels in openness to new experiences. In addition, latent-growth analyses with the longitudinal data of Swiss high school graduates showed that endorsing traditional gender ideology contributed to the self-efficacy of girls (but not boys) low in openness to experience. Moreover, this positive change in self-efficacy led to an increase in their subjective wellbeing. By contrast, girls with high levels in openness who endorsed traditional gender ideology experienced a decrease of self-efficacy and subjective wellbeing during the transition. Taken together, these findings suggest that endorsing an ideology that provides strong behavioral guidelines can help some people to deal with the uncertainty inherent in developmental transition and to provide a sense of control even if this ideology discriminates against one's ingroup. At the same time, it poses a threat to those who strive to change their disadvantaged position and, thus, the predominant social structure.

The impact of parental work participation on adolescents' perception of future work-related choices

The social environment provides adolescents with information concerning future work roles. On the one hand, an egalitarian view that both genders are (and should be) involved to some degree in the work and the family domain is commonly shared. On the other hand, children are likely to be confronted with a more traditional gender-role division at home, with their mothers being less engaged in work (e.g., having a part-time position in German-speaking countries) and having the main responsibility for the household and childcare while their fathers are full-time "bread winners." In the following, we will focus on how the way parents coordinate their work and family roles may affect their children's beliefs about how to best combine family and work life. These beliefs may exert an important influence on adolescents' career-related preferences and choices.

Social role theory (Eagly, 1987; Eagly, Wood, & Diekman, 2000) argues that the division of labor in society is the major factor that shapes gender stereotypes, which, in turn, affect people's educational and career plans. Accordingly, adolescents' understanding of how men and women should organize their family and work lives is shaped by their observations and experience of the responsibilities of their parents. In fact, there are studies that point to the predictive roles of parental behavior for adolescents' future work involvement plans. In a study with female adolescents, Marks and Houston (2002) showed that mothers' preschool work pattern had a significant impact on plans to combine work and motherhood. Keith (1988) found that adolescents from two-career families were likely to desire egalitarian roles when becoming parents. Note also, however, that a number of studies failed to demonstrate associations between maternal employment and adolescent's gender-role attitudes (e.g., O'Neal Weeks, Wise, & Duncan, 1984; Willetts-Bloom & Nock, 1994). This might be partly due to a neglect of the question about how adolescents evaluate their parents' behaviors.

Wiese and Freund (2011) presented a *reflected-modeling* perspective stressing the complex nature that accounts for adolescents' representations of – and even their own decisions about – how to integrate their future family and work lives. According to this perspective, one important factor in predicting adolescents' attitudes and plans regarding combining work and family are their evaluations of their parents' behavior. Children and adolescents not only observe their parents'

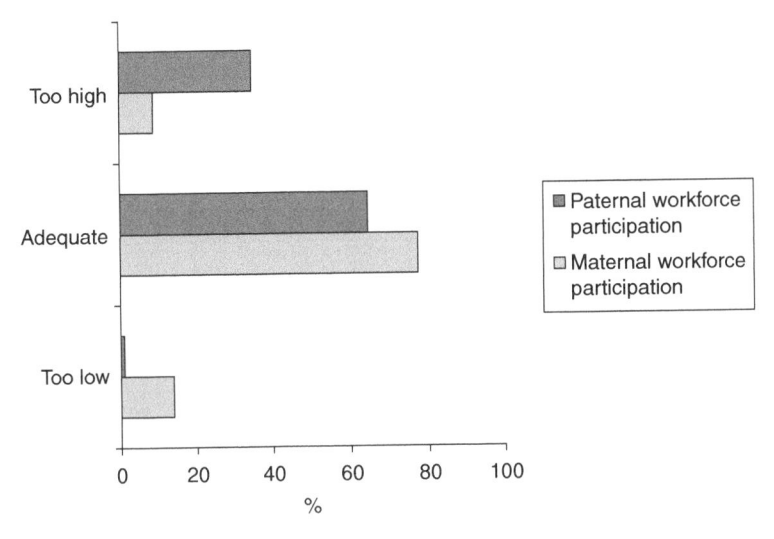

Figure 5.2 *Discrepancies between actual and ideal parental workforce participation during the preschool years (based on data from Wiese & Freund, 2011)*

gender-related behavior regarding work and family; their parents' behaviors also have a direct bearing on them. These experiences might influence adolescents' attitudes toward what constitutes the ideal engagement of men and women in the work and the family domains. When forming future plans regarding how to combine work and family, adolescents may consider whether or not they themselves, during different phases of their childhood (i.e., preschool years, school years), would have preferred their parents to be involved more or less at home or at work. This process, which probably also encompasses preferences for future partners' work involvement, goes beyond simple social modeling but takes cognitive-evaluative processes into account.

In one study of high school graduates, adolescents first indicated whether each of their parents worked full-time, part-time, or stayed at home during their preschool and their school years (Wiese & Freund, 2011). In a second step, to assess retrospective work involvement preferences, adolescents were asked to indicate the degree of parental work involvement they would have wished for during their childhood. In a third step, groups were built to characterize the degree and direction of discrepancy between perceived and ideal parental work involvement (i.e., no discrepancy, too low, too high; see Figure 5.2 for the results for the preschool years). There was a high level of convergence between adolescents' perceptions of parents' actual working behavior and adolescents' retrospective ideals. The largest discrepancy between actual and ideal parental work involvement was found with respect to fathers' work involvement during the preschool years. About one third of the adolescents would have preferred their fathers to have worked fewer hours. With respect to adolescents' own work involvement plans and their preferences for their future partners' work involvement, part-time positions were reported to be attractive for both male

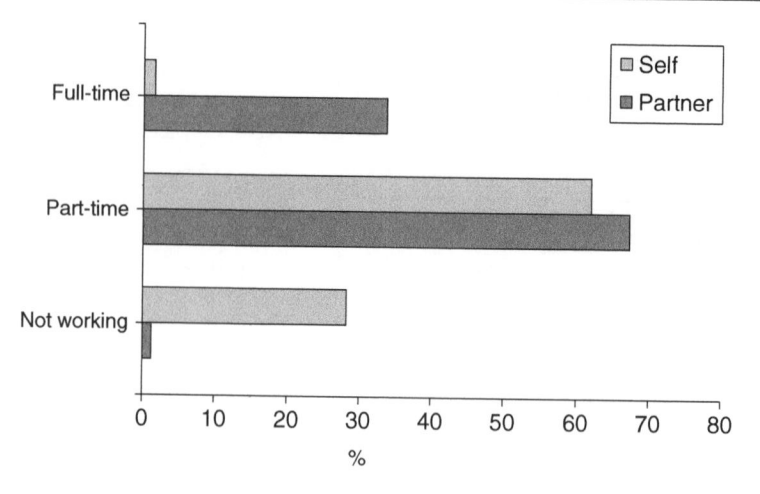

Figure 5.3 *Female adolescents' preferred future workforce participation for themselves and their future partners when they have preschool children (based on data from Wiese & Freund, 2011)*

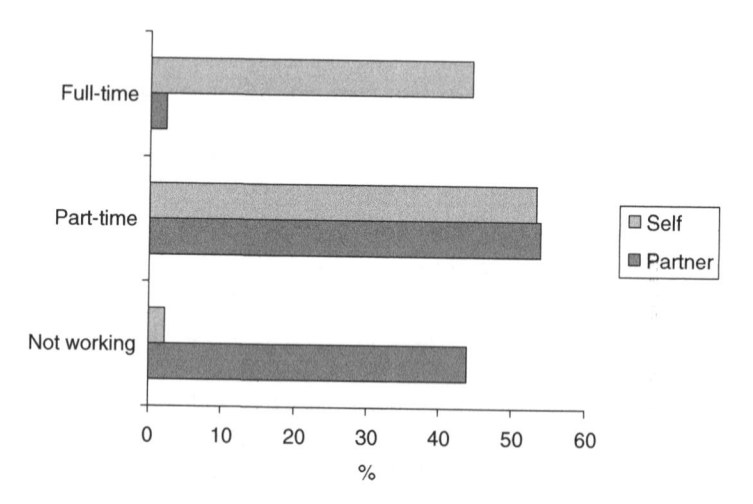

Figure 5.4 *Male adolescents' preferred future workforce participation for themselves and their future partners when they have preschool children (based on data from Wiese & Freund, 2011)*

and female adolescents, at least during the preschool years (see Figures 5.3 and 5.4). Of course, plans for working part-time during specific phases of the family life cycle may not persist when one actually has one's own children, especially among boys. Adolescents have no experience with the financial requirements for supporting a family or with (implicit) organizational rules regarding working hours. In addition, there may also be internal barriers that become more salient when they actually have children. As mentioned above, many boys still adhere to rather traditional views concerning the central role of mothers during the childrearing years.

How was the preferred degree of the adolescent's own work involvement related to childhood experiences at home? Wiese and Freund (2011) found that same-sex parents served as the main role models for their children, whereas opposite-sex parents served as the main role models for the preferred degree of work participation for future life partners, thereby supporting a gender-matching hypothesis. Specifically, adolescents' preferences for their future partners' work involvement reflected the opposite-sex parents' ideal and actual work history. However, adolescents' own plans were not mere imitations of their parents' behaviors but, supporting the reflected role-model hypothesis, adolescents' plans were strongly influenced by their evaluation of their parents' behaviors. There was only one exception to the overall finding: girls' future work involvement plans with preschool children were equally predicted by their mother's actual as well as ideal work involvement. Female adolescents may take the structural constraints into account that both their mothers as well as they themselves will have to face regarding childcare institutions and social expectations. If this interpretation is true, women's motivation for very time-demanding leadership careers is unlikely to increase even among the next generation. This further adds to the necessity of investments in the availability of high-quality institutional childcare as well as in political initiatives to encourage girls and young women not only to invest in higher education but also to value an egalitarian role share between men and women.

In conclusion, parental work participation and adolescents' subjective evaluation of their work–family experiences during childhood shaped high school students' future vocational plans in terms of preferences for personal and partner work involvement during the childrearing years. However, these dynamics might be different for adolescents who entered the workforce much earlier in their lives. In addition, differences of gendered work involvement in certain contexts should also affect adolescents' future vocational plans. Finally, positively evaluated parental role models might encourage personal initiative in terms of adolescents' career choice and career planning but the likelihood of actually achieving career-related goals is restricted by socio-structural constraints (e.g., unemployment rates, high tuition fees). Obviously, such socio-structural constraints are not under the control of adolescents themselves but need to be negotiated on a political level.

Conclusion

The transition from high school to college or the workforce is a major step in adolescents' journey to adulthood. During this time, adolescents have to develop, set, and pursue goals in order to master the challenges and constraints of this most critical and vital time of life. In this chapter, we have presented a selective review of research findings published over the last few years as well as recent findings from a larger research project with high school graduates.

Taken together, the results draw a complex picture of adolescents' adjustment to the transition. In particular, central factors that shape adolescents' choices and adaptation to the transition from high school to college or the workforce are the self-regulatory strategies of selection, optimization, and compensation, as well as personal motives, gender stereotypes, and self-ascribed attributes. Empirical findings highlight the importance of understanding the dynamics of social-contextual factors and individual difference variables that moderate the impact of these influences. It is crucial to consider societal norms and status differences as well as motives (e.g., power) and personality differences (e.g., openness) when explaining individual developmental trajectories. Thus, the findings reported in this chapter highlight motivational and contextual influences that contribute to the successful management of central life transitions of adolescence. There is growing evidence that adolescents actively negotiate their career and family roles in the transition from high school to college or the workforce, thereby setting the course of their future career and family lives.

References

Abele, A. E. (2003). The dynamics of masculine-agentic and feminine-communal traits: Findings from a prospective study. *Journal of Personality and Social Psychology*, 85, 768–776.

Abele, A. E., & Spurk, D. (2011). The dual impact of gender on objective career success: Longitudinal effects of the gender-self-concept and the timing of parenthood. *International Journal of Behavioral Development*, 35, 225–232.

Abele, A. E., & Wiese, B. S. (2008). The nomological network of self-management strategies and career success. *Journal of Occupational and Organizational Psychology*, 81, 733–749.

Arnett, J. J. (2000). Emerging adulthood: A theory of development from the late teens through the twenties. *American Psychologist*, 55, 469–480.

Bakan, D. (1966). *The duality of human existence: An essay on psychology and religion.* Chicago, IL: Rand McNally.

Baltes, P. B. (1997). On the incomplete architecture of human ontogeny: Selection, optimization, and compensation as foundation of developmental theory. *American Psychologist*, 52, 366–380.

Baltes, P. B., & Baltes, M. M. (1990). Psychological perspectives on successful aging: The model of selective optimization with compensation. In P. B. Baltes & M. M. Baltes (Eds.), *Successful aging: Perspectives from the behavioral sciences* (pp. 1–34). New York: Cambridge University Press.

Bandura, A. (1977). *Social learning theory.* Englewood-Cliffs, NJ: Prentice-Hall.
  (1997). *Self-efficacy: The exercise of control.* New York: Freeman.
  (2006). Adolescent development from an agentic perspective. In F. Pajares & T. Urdan (Eds.), *Self-efficacy beliefs of adolescents* (pp. 1–43). Greenwich, CT: Information Age.

Brunstein, J. C. (2008). Implicit and explicit motives. In J. Heckhausen & H. Heckhausen (Eds.), *Motivation and action* (pp. 227–246). New York: Cambridge University Press.

Bussey, K., & Bandura, A. (1999). Social cognitive theory of gender development and differentiation. *Psychological Review*, 106, 676–713.

Chisholm, L., & Hurrelmann, K. (1995). Adolescence in modern Europe: Pluralized transition patterns and their implications for personal and social risks. *Journal of Adolescence*, 18, 129–158.

Crouter, A. C., Whiteman, S. D., McHale, S. M., & Osgood, D. W. (2007). Development of gender attitude traditionality across middle childhood and adolescence. *Child Development*, 78, 911–926.

Deaux, K. (1985). Sex and gender. *Annual Review of Psychology*, 36, 49–81.

Deaux, K., & LaFrance, M. (1998). Gender. In D. Gilbert, S. T. Fiske, & G. Lindzey (Eds.), *Handbook of social psychology* (4th ed., pp. 788–827). New York: McGraw-Hill.

Eagly, A. H. (1987). *Sex differences in social behavior: A social-role interpretation.* Hillsdale, NJ: Erlbaum.

Eagly, A. H., Diekman, A. B., Johannesen-Schmidt, M. C., & Koenig, A. M. (2004). Gender gaps in sociopolitical attitudes: A social psychological analysis. *Journal of Personality and Social Psychology*, 87, 796–816.

Eagly, A., & Steffen, V. J. (1984). Gender stereotypes stem from distributions of women and men into social roles. *Journal of Personality and Social Psychology*, 46, 735–754.

Eagly, A. H., & Wood, W. (1999). The origins of sex differences in human behavior: Evolved dispositions versus social roles. *American Psychologist*, 54, 406–423.

Eagly, A. H., Wood, W., & Diekman, A. B. (2000). Social role theory of sex differences and similarities: A current appraisal. In T. Eckes & H. M. Trautner (Eds.), *The developmental social psychology of gender* (pp. 123–174). Mahwah, NJ: Erlbaum.

Ebner, N. C., Freund, A. M., & Baltes, P. B. (2006). Developmental changes in personal goal orientation from young to late adulthood: From striving for gains to maintenance and prevention of losses. *Psychology and Aging*, 21, 664–678.

Eccles, J. S. (2011). Gendered educational and occupational choices: Applying the Eccles et al. model of achievement-related choices. *International Journal of Behavioral Development*, 35, 195–201.

Ericsson, K. A., & Lehmann, A. C. (1996). Expert and exceptional performance: Evidence of maximal adaptation to task constraints. *Annual Review of Psychology*, 47, 273–305.

Eurostat (2013). *Unemployment rate by gender and age, 2007–2012 statistics explained.* Retrieved July 8, 2013, from http://epp.eurostat.ec.europa.eu/statistics_explained.

Fagot, B. I., & Leinbach, M. D. (1993). Gender-role development in young children: From discrimination to labeling. *Developmental Review*, 13, 205–224.

Freund, A. M. (2006). Age-differential motivational consequences of optimization versus compensation focus in younger and older adults. *Psychology and Aging*, 21, 240–252.

———(2008). Successful aging as management of resources: The role of selection, optimization, and compensation. *Research on Human Development*, 5, 94–106.

———(2011). The role of gender in school-related transitions and beyond: Introduction to the special section. *International Journal of Behavioral Development*, 35, 193–194.

Freund, A. M., & Baltes, P. B. (2000). The orchestration of selection, optimization, and compensation: An action-theoretical conceptualization of a theory of developmental regulation. In W. J. Perrig & A. Grob (Eds.), *Control of human behavior, mental processes and consciousness* (pp. 35–58). Mahwah, NJ: Erlbaum.

Freund, A. M., & Baltes, P. B. (2002). Life-management strategies of selection, optimization, and compensation: Measurement by self-report and construct validity. *Journal of Personality and Social Psychology, 82*, 642–662.

Freund, A. M., & Ebner, N. C. (2005). The aging self: Shifting from promoting gains to balancing losses. In W. Greve, K. Rothermund, & D. Wentura (Eds.), *The adaptive self: Personal continuity and intentional self-development* (pp. 185–202). Ashland, OH: Hogrefe & Huber.

Freund, A. M., Nikitin, J., & Ritter, J. O. (2009). Psychological consequences of longevity: The increasing importance of self-regulation in old age. *Human Development, 52*, 1–37.

Freund, A. M., Weiss, D., & Wiese, B. S. (2013). Graduating from high school: The role of gender-related attitudes, attributes, and motives for a central transition in young adulthood. *European Journal of Developmental Psychology, 10*, 580–596.

Funder, D. C, & Block, J. (1989). The role of ego-control, ego-resiliency, and IQ in delay of gratification in adolescence. *Journal of Personality and Social Psychology, 57*, 1041–1050. doi: 10.1037/0022-3514.57.6.1041.

Galambos, N. L., Almeida, D. M., & Petersen, A. C. (1990). Masculinity, femininity, and sex role attitudes in early adolescence: Exploring gender intensification. *Child Development, 61*, 1905–1914.

Gardner, M., & Steinberg, L. (2005). Peer influence on risk taking, risk preference, and risky decision making in adolescence and adulthood: An experimental study. *Developmental Psychology, 41*, 625–635.

Gestsdottir, S., & Lerner, R. M. (2007). Intentional self-regulation and positive youth development in early adolescence: Findings from the 4-H study of positive youth development. *Developmental Psychology, 43*, 508–521.

Glick, P., & Fiske, S. T. (2001). An ambivalent alliance: Hostile and benevolent sexism as complementary justifications for gender inequality. *American Psychologist, 56*, 109–118.

Grant, P. R., & Brown, R. (1995). From ethnocentrism to collective protest: Responses to relative deprivation and threats to social identity. *Social Psychology Quarterly, 58*, 195–211.

Greene, K., Krcmar, M., Walters, L. H., Rubin, D. L., Hale, J., & Hale, L. (2000). Targeting adolescent risk-taking behaviors: The contributions of egocentrism and sensation-seeking. *Journal of Adolescence, 23*, 439–461.

Guimond, S., Dambrun, M., Michinov, N., & Duarte, S. (2003). Does social dominance generate prejudice? Integrating individual and contextual determinants of intergroup cognitions. *Journal of Personality & Social Psychology, 84*, 697–721.

Guimond, S., & Dube-Simard, L. (1983). Relative deprivation theory and the Quebec nationalist movement: The cognitive-emotion distinction and the personal-group deprivation issue. *Journal of Personality and Social Psychology, 44*, 526–353.

Habermas, T., & Bluck, S. (2000). Getting a life: The emergence of the life story in adolescence. *Psychological Bulletin*, 126, 748–769.

Heckhausen, J., & Tomasik, M. J. (2002). Get an apprenticeship before school is out: How German adolescents adjust vocational aspirations when getting close to a developmental deadline. *Journal of Vocational Behavior*, 60, 199–219.

Heppner, P. P., Walther, D. J., & Good, G. E. (1995). The differential role of instrumentality, expressivity, and social support in predicting problem-solving appraisal in men and women. *Sex Roles*, 32, 91–108.

Hill, J. P., & Lynch, M. E. (1983). The intensification of gender-related role expectations during early adolescence. In J. Brooks-Gunn & A. C. Petersen (Eds.), *Girls at puberty: Biological and psychosocial perspectives* (pp. 201–228). New York: Plenum.

Hirschi, A., & Vondracek, F. W. (2009). Adaptation of career goals to self and opportunities in early adolescence. *Journal of Vocational Behavior*, 75, 120–128.

Holland, J. L. (1985). *Making vocational choices: A theory of vocational personalities and work environments* (2nd ed.). Englewood Cliffs, NJ: Prentice Hall.

Jost, J. T., & Banaji, M. R. (1994). The role of stereotyping in system-justification and the production of false consciousness. *British Journal of Social Psychology*, 33, 1–27.

Katz, P. A., & Walsh, P. V. (1991). Modification of children's gender-stereotyped behavior. *Child Development*, 62, 338–351.

Keith, P. M. (1988). The relationship of self-esteem, maternal employment, and work–family plans to sex role orientations of late adolescence. *Adolescence*, 13, 959–966.

Kelly, C., & Breinlinger, S. (2006). Identity and injustice: Exploring women's participation in collective action. *Journal of Community and Applied Social Psychology*, 5, 41–57.

Kracke, B., & Schmitt-Rodermund, E. (2001). Adolescents' career exploration in the context of educational and occupational transitions. In J. Nurmi (Ed.), *Navigating through adolescence: European perspectives* (pp. 141–165). New York: Routledge.

Lerner, R. M., Freund, A. M., De Stefanis, I., & Habermas, T. (2001). Understanding developmental regulation in adolescence: The use of the selection, optimization, and compensation model. *Human Development*, 44, 29–50.

Lips, H. M. (2004). The gender gap in possible selves: Divergence of academic self-views among high school and university students. *Sex Roles*, 50, 357–372.

Marks, G., & Houston, D. M. (2002). The determinants of young women's intentions about education, career development and family life. *Journal of Education and Work*, 15, 321–336.

Marx, K., & Engels, F. (1998). *The German ideology*. New York: Amherst. [Original work published 1845.]

McClelland, D. C. (1980). Motive dispositions. The merits of operant and respondent measures. In L. Wheeler (Ed.), *Review of personality and social psychology* (pp. 10–41). London: Sage.

McHale, S. M., Shanahan, L., Updegraff, K. A., Crouter, A. C., & Booth, A. (2004). Developmental and individual differences in girls' sex-typed activities in middle childhood and adolescence. *Child Development*, 75, 1575–1593.

Mischel, W., Shoda, Y., & Peake, P. K. (1988). The nature of adolescent competencies predicted by preschool delay of gratification. *Journal of Personality and Social Psychology*, 54, 687–696.

Montangero, J. (1996). *Understanding changes in time: The development of diachronic thinking in 7- to 12-year-old children*. London: Taylor & Francis.

Nurmi, J.-E., Salmela-Aro, K., & Koivisto, P. (2002). Goal importance, and related agency-beliefs and emotions during the transition from vocational school to work: Antecedents and consequences. *Journal of Vocational Behavior*, 60, 241–261.

O'Neal Weeks, M., Wise, G. W., & Duncan, C. (1984). The relationship between sex-role attitudes and career orientations of high school females and their mothers. *Adolescence*, 19, 595–607.

Perrig-Chiello, P., & Perren, S. (2005). Biographical transitions from a midlife perspective. *Journal of Adult Development*, 12, 169–181.

Prentice, D. A., & Carranza, E. (2002). What women and men should be, shouldn't be, are allowed to be, and don't have to be: The contents of prescriptive gender stereotypes. *Psychology of Women Quarterly*, 26, 269–281.

Salmela-Aro, K. (2009). Personal goals and well-being during critical life transitions: Channelling, selection, co-agency and adjustment. *Advances in Life Course Research*, 14, 63–73.

Schmitt, M. T., & Wirth, H. W. (2009). Evidence that gender differences in social dominance orientation result from gendered self-stereotyping and group-interested responses to patriarchy. *Psychology of Women Quarterly*, 33, 429–436.

Schoon, I., & Silbereisen, R. K. (Eds.). (2009). *Transitions from school to work: Globalisation, individualisation, and patterns of diversity*. New York: Cambridge University Press.

Scott, J. (1990). *Domination and the arts of resistance: Hidden transcripts*. New Haven, CT: Yale University Press.

Sczesny, S., Bosak, J., Neff, D., & Schyns, B. (2004). Gender stereotypes and the attribution of leadership traits: A cross-cultural comparison. *Sex Roles*, 51, 631–645.

Silbereisen, R. K., Eyferth, K., & Rudinger, G. (Eds.). (1986). *Development as action in context: Problem behavior and normal youth development*. New York: Springer.

Skinner, E. A., Chapman, M., & Baltes, P. B. (1988). Control, means-ends, and agency beliefs: A new conceptualization and its measurement during childhood. *Journal of Personality and Social Psychology*, 54, 117–133.

Smith, J. (1996). Planning about life: A social-interactive and life-span perspective. In P. B. Baltes & U. M. Staudinger (Eds.), *Interactive minds: Life-span perspectives on the social foundation of cognition* (pp. 242–275). New York: Cambridge University Press.

Tajfel, H. (1981). *Human groups and social categories*. Cambridge University Press.

Tajfel, H., & Turner, J. C. (1986). The social identity theory of intergroup behavior. In S. Worchel & W. Austin (Eds.), *The social psychology of intergroup relations* (pp. 7–24). Chicago, IL: Nelson-Hall.

Tomasik, M. J., Hardy, S., Haase, C. M., & Heckhausen, J. (2009). Adaptive adjustment of vocational aspirations among German youths during the transition from school to work. *Journal of Vocational Behavior*, 74, 38–46.

Towbes, L. C., Cohen, L. H., & Glyshaw, K. (1989). Instrumentality as a life-stress moderator for early versus middle adolescents. *Journal of Personality and Social Psychology*, 57, 109–119.

Weiss, D., Wiese, B. S., & Freund, A. M. (2011). *Keeping on track or throwing the towel? Adolescents' self-regulatory strategy use in mastering life transitions.* Paper presented at the Success and Well-Being Conference in Basel, Switzerland.

Weiss, D., Freund, A. M., & Wiese, B. S. (2012). Mastering developmental transitions in young and middle adulthood: The interplay of openness to experience and traditional gender ideology on women's self-efficacy and well-being. *Developmental Psychology*, 48, 1774–1784.

Whitley, B. E., Jr. (1983). Sex role orientation and self-esteem: A critical meta-analytic review. *Journal of Personality and Social Psychology*, 44, 765–778.

Wiese, B. S., & Freund, A. M. (2011). Parents as role models: Parental behavior affects adolescents' plans for work involvement. *International Journal of Behavioral Development*, 35, 218–224.

Wiese, B. S., Freund, A. M., & Baltes, P. B. (2002). Subjective career success and emotional well-being: Longitudinal predictive power of selection, optimization and compensation. *Journal of Vocational Behavior*, 60, 321–335.

Wigfield, A. L., & Eccles, J. S. (2001). *Development of achievement motivation.* San Diego, CA: Academic Press.

Willetts-Bloom, M. C., & Nock, S. L. (1994). The influence of maternal employment on the gender role attitudes of men and women. *Sex Roles*, 30, 371–389.

Wrosch, C., & Freund, A. M. (2001). Self-regulation of normative and non-normative developmental challenges. *Human Development*, 44, 264–283.

6 Gendered happiness gap? Adolescents' academic wellbeing pathways

Katariina Salmela-Aro

Abstract

The aim of this chapter is to present recent research findings on gendered academic wellbeing obtained by applying both person- and variable-oriented approaches in the context of the stage-environment-fit theory and the lifespan model of motivation. The research formed part of the ongoing FinEdu longitudinal study, where all the students in the same city in Finland were followed from the end of comprehensive school at age 15 to young adulthood at age 23. The variable-oriented results showed that school burnout increased in high school after comprehensive school. Analysis of gendered pathways showed that cynicism increased, particularly among boys on the academic track, whereas feelings of inadequacy increased among girls. Moreover, among girls on the vocational track, feelings of inadequacy as a student decreased. Applying a person-oriented approach among those on the academic track revealed four groups or typologies: engaged, engaged–exhausted, cynical, and burned out. At the beginning of high school, more cynical boys, fewer cynical girls, and more engaged boys were found than would be expected by chance. In the final year of high school, there were more engaged–exhausted girls, fewer engaged–exhausted boys, and fewer engaged boys than would be expected by chance.

Introduction

The majority of young people manage adolescence without severe problems (Graber & Brooks-Gunn, 1996; Powers, Hauser, & Kilner, 1989). However, some have difficulties in adapting to the transitions and changes that characterize this age period (Rutter, 1990). A gender difference has also been noted. Girls more commonly experience depressive symptoms and other internalized symptoms, while boys more commonly experience more externalized symptoms, such as problem behavior, than girls (Masten et al., 1999). During adolescence, academic demands at school increase and adolescents become more aware of individual differences in abilities and achievement (Renick & Harter, 1989). Recently, it has been suggested that educational transitions may play a destabilizing role in academic wellbeing (Salmela-Aro & Tynkkynen, 2012; Salmela-Aro, Kiuru, & Nurmi, 2008; Tram & Cole, 2006; see also Symonds, Galton, & Hargreaves, this volume). The transition from comprehensive school to either an academic or vocational track is one of the key educational transitions in adolescence and thus a challenge for academic wellbeing. Academic wellbeing is approached in this chapter through the assessment of school engagement and school burnout (Salmela-Aro & Upadyaya, 2012). School burnout is defined along three dimensions: exhaustion due to school demands, cynical and detached attitude toward school, and feelings of inadequacy as a student (Salmela-Aro & Näätänen, 2005; Salmela-Aro, Kiuru, Leskinen, & Nurmi, 2009), whereas school engagement is defined as energy, dedication, and absorption toward school (Salmela-Aro & Upadyaya, 2012). Based on the stage-environment-fit theory (Eccles & Midgley, 1989) and the life-span model of motivation (Salmela-Aro, 2009), positive outcomes, such as increasing engagement and decreasing burnout, might result if the changes in school opportunities are in alignment with the changes in adolescents' needs, while a negative developmental fit may lead to a decrease in engagement, alienation, and cynicism. In the present chapter I review recent findings on academic wellbeing among girls and boys during key educational transitions in adolescence and young adulthood with the aim of addressing the issue of gendered happiness pathways.

Schooling in Finland

Finnish children start their education in kindergarten during the year of their sixth birthday. One year later, at age 7, they move to compulsory comprehensive school, where they continue for the next 9 years. Up until age 16, all Finnish adolescents receive a similar basic education. After comprehensive school, adolescents' educational trajectories begin to diverge. About 50% of all adolescents enter senior high schools and 42% vocational schools, 2% stay on for a voluntary 10th grade, and 6% exit formal education. Average academic achievement in the ninth grade is the minimum requirement for admission to senior high school. Senior high school graduation, in turn, is a bridge to further education and, most likely, higher education. Secondary vocational education serves as a route to working life in academically less demanding occupations, and also to tertiary-level education, most likely vocational education. Thus, educational choices at the end of comprehensive school channel young Finns onto either an academic or a vocational track (OECD, 1998). Finnish girls graduate from senior high schools and enter universities more often than boys. Education in Finland is state-provided and tuition is free.

Life-span model of motivation

The 4-C model, proposed by Salmela-Aro (2009), describes the regulation of critical life transitions in terms of four processes: channeling, choices, co-regulation, and compensation. First, the environments, such as education in which individuals grow up, set age-graded norms and standards that structure individuals' development and the timing of critical life transitions (channeling). Transitions, such as educational transitions, *channel* their engagement. Second, as also argued by number of contemporary developmental psychologists (e.g., Baltes, 1997; see also Heckhausen; Weiss, Wiese, & Freund, this volume), young people actively produce their engagement (choices). Third, young people's engagements are also embedded in their social relations with their parents, peers, and teachers (co-regulation). Finally, young people often need to adjust their engagements in order to maintain or regain wellbeing (compensation) (Salmela-Aro & Suikkari, 2008; Tomasik & Salmela-Aro, 2012). Young people may, however, also prepare themselves for possible setbacks (Salmela-Aro, Mutanen, Koivisto, & Vuori, 2010). The engagement process approached in this chapter is that of school-related engagement, whereas disengagement is conceptualized through the process of school burnout, in which disengagement is a key concept.

Academic wellbeing during adolescence

In general most adolescents view their lives positively (Gilman & Huebner, 2003). However, some young people suffer from school-related difficulties. Earlier results have shown that about 13–15% of adolescents suffer from school burnout at the end of comprehensive school at age 15 to 16 (Salmela-Aro & Tynkkynen, 2012). Our results showed further that school burnout increased for students who entered an academic track after comprehensive school (Salmela-Aro et al., 2008).

Gender might play a key role in determining young people's trajectories of academic wellbeing during middle and late adolescence (Ge, Conger, & Elder, 2001; Nolen-Hoeksema & Girgus, 1994). Previous research has found gender differences in school adjustment, particularly during middle adolescence. For example, girls have been found to experience higher levels of stress than boys (e.g., Ge, Lorenz, Conger, Elder, & Simons, 1994; Jose & Ratcliffe, 2004) and more depressive symptoms (e.g., Hoffmann, Powlishta, & White, 2004; Nolen-Hoeksema & Girgus, 1994; Pomerantz, Altermatt, & Saxon, 2002). There is some evidence to suggest that girls respond more negatively to competitive learning conditions. In line with this, research shows that girls not only perceive more life events as stressful, but also are more vulnerable to their negative effects (Ge et al., 1994; Kessler & McLeod, 1984; Salmela-Aro et al., 2008). Moreover, girls tend to perform better at school than boys (e.g., Dwyer & Johnson, 1997; Pomerantz et al., 2002) and to attribute greater importance to academic achievement than boys (Berndt & Miller, 1990; Murberg & Bru, 2004). Turning to boys, courses at school are often taught in a manner that boys might find either dull or irrelevant (Eccles & Midgley, 1989), possibly leading them to disengage from school.

The transition from comprehensive school to either an academic or a vocational track or to working life is the key educational change during adolescence in many European educational systems, although the actual age of the transition varies widely across countries. The track taken determines the quality and kinds of learning opportunities a student receives (Oakes, Gamoran, & Page, 1992). It also determines exposure to different peers and thus, to a certain degree, the social relationships that young people form (Fuligni, Eccles & Barber, 1995). Comprehensive schools are frequently referred to as "neighborhood" schools, where the students spend most of the school day with one set of peers and teachers, both of whom live in their neighborhood. Upper secondary schools are in most cases larger than comprehensive schools. In addition, as adolescents approach upper secondary high school graduation, they experience increasing pressure to be academically successful (Lee & Larson, 2000). School also provides an important developmental context for adolescents' psychological needs of competence, autonomy, and relatedness, as well as mattering (Eccles, 2004).

School transitions can be understood with the help of the stage-environment-fit theory (Eccles & Midgley, 1989) and the life-span model of motivation (Salmela-Aro, 2009). According to the stage-environment-fit theory (Eccles & Midgley, 1989), positive outcomes will result if the changes in school opportunities are in alignment with adolescents' needs. In contrast, unfavorable outcomes will result if adolescents' needs are not matched by the opportunities provided by school. Eccles and Midgley (1989) proposed that negative developmental changes might result if schools do not provide developmentally appropriate educational environments for adolescents and that negative developmental fit may lead to alienation and cynicism. For example, some students might feel the need to be related to others, but the size of the school increases after comprehensive school and it becomes more difficult to receive support and mentoring. In addition, the need to feel competent is more challenging as the demands and workload increase. Students might be expected to be more motivated to learn if the material they were asked to master was appropriate to their current level of competence and interests, and if they could feel competent. According to the life-span model of motivation (Salmela-Aro, 2009), approaching the school transition channels students' engagement. However, young people also use active agency in their transition-related choices and in their related engagement and disengagement processes.

There is strong evidence of a decline in academic motivation, attachment to school, and academic achievement across the school transition in early adolescence, i.e., the transition to middle school or junior high school (Eccles & Midgley, 1989). However, most of these studies have been conducted in the United States. Moreover, less is known about what happens in the subsequent school transition, in middle and late adolescence, from comprehensive school to senior high school (academic or vocational track), which are the typical school transition patterns in the Nordic countries. Previous studies conducted in Finland confirmed that school transitions are a period during which changes in school adjustment and wellbeing can occur (Salmela-Aro & Tynkkynen, 2012). When adolescents make the transition to an academic track, they might perceive their school environment as more competitive. This in turn might lead girls to experience exhaustion and feelings of inadequacy as a student, and boys, who are more prone to externalize, to experience a cynical attitude toward school.

Gendered changes in academic wellbeing during educational transitions

In a recent study using data collected for the ongoing FinEdu longitudinal study (Salmela-Aro & Tynkkynen, 2012), we investigated whether the transition from comprehensive school to either an academic or a vocational track and graduation from upper secondary education contributed differently to school-related burnout in girls and boys. Based on the stage-environment-fit Theory, it was assumed that the entry to an academic track would increase school burnout in girls and boys as the demands increase, while the entry to a vocational track might lead to a decrease in burnout, owing to the decrease in academic challenges, which in turn increases feelings of competence. In addition, during the transition from comprehensive school to their subsequent educational tracks adolescents are able to experience autonomy and to strive toward their own goals, which might increase their school engagement after the transition.

The broad aim of the FinEdu longitudinal study is to examine adolescents' life-planning and wellbeing during the educational transitions from middle adolescence to adulthood. At the beginning of the study, the participants were ninth-graders (median age = 15) facing the transition to post-comprehensive schooling. All the ninth-grade students in a medium-sized town (population = 88,000) in Central Finland were recruited for the study (N = 954). At present, six waves have been carried out. Two measurements were carried out before the transition to senior secondary (academic track) or vocational (vocational track) education: one at the beginning of the ninth grade, which is the final term of comprehensive school, and the other at the end of the ninth grade. Two further post-transition measurements were carried out during post-comprehensive schooling: the first was half a year after the transition and the second was 1 year later. Moreover, two measurements were carried out after the transition from secondary education. At the last two measurement times, the participants were aged 21 and 23. The majority of the participants (99%) were Finnish-speaking, 1% of them having some other mother tongue. This ratio agrees well with the figures for ethnic minorities at the national level.

Attrition analyses were carried out to examine attrition between the measurements by comparing the adolescents who participated in the study at each measurement point ($N = 469$) with those who had missing data at some measurement point ($N = 389$). The results indicated a small selection effect with respect to the life satisfaction variables. Those who did not answer at all the measurement points scored slightly lower on life satisfaction. However, there was no selection effect for attained educational track between those who did not answer at all the measurement points and those who did. To take into account missingness between the data collections we used the missing data procedure as implemented in Mplus (Muthén & Muthén, 1998–2007). Mplus Version 5 was used for all analyses, adopting the standard MAR approach (assuming *missing at random*).

School burnout was assessed with the School Burnout Inventory developed by Salmela-Aro and Näätänen (2005; Salmela-Aro et al., 2009) and according to adolescents' self-reports for the previous month. The scale consists of nine unidimensional items measuring three components of school burnout: (1) exhaustion at school (e.g., *I feel overwhelmed by my schoolwork*; *I brood over matters related to my schoolwork a lot during my free time*); (2) cynicism toward the meaning of school (e.g., *I feel lack of motivation in my schoolwork and often think of giving up*; *I feel that I am losing interest in my schoolwork*); and (3) sense of inadequacy at school (e.g., *I often have feelings of inadequacy in my schoolwork*). The Cronbach's alpha reliability for the scale is high, varying between .80 and .90. Academic achievement was measured by asking the participants to report their grade point average (GPA). GPA ranged from 4 (lowest) to 10 (highest). Self-reported GPA has shown a correlation of .96 with actual GPA (Holopainen & Savolainen, 2005). The participants' educational track after comprehensive school was measured by the following questions: (1) "Are you in education at the moment?" (1 = yes, 0 = no); (2) "If you are in education, what is the name of your school?" Next, an educational track variable was created by contrasting academic track with vocational track. The number of participants who had dropped out of the educational system 1 year after comprehensive school was 21 (3%). They were included in the data.

To examine changes in school burnout during the educational transition from comprehensive school to the two educational tracks, Latent Growth Curve Modeling for school burnout, incorporating only statistically significant parameters, was used (Salmela-Aro & Tynkkynen, 2012). The results showed that the two growth components (i.e., level and linear change) described the shape of the change well. The linear change of school burnout was statistically significant, indicating that school burnout increased during the transition. The results for the variances of the growth components showed significant individual variation in school burnout both in level and in linear change, indicating the presence of significant individual differences in these two growth components. Moreover, the covariance between the intercept and linear trend was negative, suggesting that the lower the initial level of school burnout, the greater its increase across the transition. In addition, the intercept of school burnout was higher among girls. The results showed that the slope among both boys and girls on the academic track was significant, suggesting that school burnout strongly increased for students on the academic track. The increase was higher among boys, indicating that, on this track, the difference between girls and boys decreased. In turn, on the vocational track, school burnout decreased among girls. To summarize, school burnout was highest among girls on the academic track. However, school burnout increased strongly among boys on the academic track. School burnout also increased among girls on the academic track, whereas it decreased among girls on the vocational track.

Gendered groups in school burnout and engagement

We also expected to find gendered heterogeneity in academic wellbeing during high school. To examine this we used a person-oriented approach focusing on patterns of school burnout and school engagement. Using the FinEdu data, our aim was to identify heterogeneous groups. Conducting a latent profile analysis, we identified four distinct groups (see Tuominen-Soini & Salmela-Aro, 2014); these were labeled engaged, engaged–exhausted, cynical, and burned out. Most of the students were engaged. The engaged group (44%) scored relatively low on all the burnout dimensions and high on schoolwork engagement. Students in the engaged–exhausted group (28%) scored high on exhaustion and sense of inadequacy despite high levels of school engagement. Two groups of students were disengaged. Students in the burnout group (14%) were characterized by relatively high levels of school burnout in all three components: exhaustion, cynicism, and inadequacy, and students in the cynical group (14%) scored particularly high on the cynicism component.

We examined these four groups for possible gender differences and also whether the groups changed over the high school years. Using configural analysis, we identified three types and three antitypes. At the beginning of senior high school, more cynical boys and fewer cynical girls were identified than could be expected by chance. In addition the proportion of engaged boys was greater than expected by chance. In the final year of senior high school, more engaged–exhausted girls and fewer engaged–exhausted boys were identified than expected by chance. Finally, the results showed fewer engaged boys at the end of senior high school than expected.

The engaged students valued school, were doing well in school, and had the lowest levels of academic withdrawal and avoidance orientation. The engaged–exhausted students were more exhausted and more stressed by their educational aspirations, more preoccupied with possible failure in school, and expressed more depressive symptoms compared to the engaged students. The cynical and burnout students displayed less adaptive patterns of academic wellbeing and motivation. They attributed lower value to school and showed lower academic achievement and a higher avoidance orientation compared to the engaged and engaged–exhausted students. The cynical students, however, differed from the burned-out students in that they were less exhausted, less stressed, and less worried about failing in school. Moreover, with respect to more general wellbeing, this group also displayed higher self-esteem and a lower level of depressive symptoms.

In the engaged group, more students than expected were aspiring to a university degree and fewer students than expected were aspiring to a polytechnic degree. The burned-out students were more likely than expected to pursue a polytechnic degree and less likely than expected to pursue a university degree. The cynical students were also less likely to pursue a university degree. Six years later, the engaged students were more likely than predicted by chance to be attending university, and the engaged–exhausted students were more likely to be attending a polytechnic. Among the former 3rd-year high school students, the engaged students were more likely than predicted by chance to be attending university or to have already completed a university degree by that time.

In general, over a quarter of high school students experience rather high levels of engagement and exhaustion simultaneously, even though it has been suggested that, overall, the higher the level of engagement, the less school burnout adolescents should experience (Salmela-Aro et al., 2009). On the other hand, girls have been shown to experience higher levels of both engagement (Salmela-Aro & Upadyaya, 2012) and exhaustion (Salmela-Aro et al., 2008) than boys and, indeed, girls were overrepresented in the engaged–exhausted group in high school. Boys, instead, were overrepresented in the cynical group. Interestingly, in the first year of high school, there were more engaged boys than expected, while in the 3rd year there were fewer engaged boys than expected. Also, there were more engaged–exhausted girls in the 3rd year of high school. These findings reflect the stressfulness of academic studies during the final year of high school and imply that there might be unfavorable developmental shifts in academic wellbeing in the course of studying at high school.

Discussion

The present chapter focused on the role of educational transitions from comprehensive school to either an academic or a vocational track in contributing to girls' and boys' academic wellbeing in the context of the stage-environment-fit Theory (Eccles & Midgley, 1989) and life-span model of motivation (Salmela-Aro, 2009). The results showed a lower level of school burnout among boys than girls. However, school burnout increased among both boys and girls on the academic track, while among girls on the vocational track burnout decreased. Analysis of gendered pathways revealed that, among those on the academic track, cynical attitudes toward school increased, particularly among boys, whereas among girls feelings of inadequacy as a student increased. Based on findings from the person-oriented approach, most of the students were engaged. However, compared to boys, more girls were identified as engaged–exhausted, while more boys belonged to the cynical group. Thus, there is some evidence of a gender gap in academic wellbeing during educational transitions.

The adolescent phase can be characterized by a high level of developmental change and discontinuity. Moreover, during adolescence, developmental changes seem to vary by gender. Adolescents experience more autonomy and independence as they move out of the comprehensive school system. However, stress exposure also increases during adolescence (Ge et al., 1994). As adolescents approach upper secondary high school graduation, they experience increasing pressure to be academically successful (Lee & Larson, 2000). However, there seem to be gender differences in the trajectories of school-related stress during upper secondary high school. The results showed that, among girls, feelings of inadequacy as a student increased on the academic track but decreased on the vocational track. Among boys, those on the academic track showed the strongest increases in cynical attitude toward school and feelings of inadequacy as a student. These trends suggest that boys put increasing academic pressure on themselves as they approach high school graduation. Consistent with this idea, studies on young adults suggest that the gender gap in academic wellbeing declines during the transition to young adulthood (Galambos, Barker, & Krahn, 2006; Needham, 2007).

In Finland, all students follow the same comprehensive school curriculum. This might reasonably be assumed to mean that the match between the material they are asked to master and their current level of competence is poor for those who show a low level of academic skills. However, this situation changes when adolescents with lower-level academic skills or interests make the transition to vocational school, where the focus is more on practical training than on academic learning. In turn, it can be assumed that comprehensive schools are relatively less demanding for adolescents with high academic skills. However, when they make the transition to the academic track (which is very demanding in Finland), this may lead to poor fit between the demands of the academic environment and their level of competence, at least for some senior high school students. The demands and norms of Finnish senior high schools can be both challenging and stressful: young people often face unfamiliar academic expectations, changes in sources of social support, and demanding social norms as well as a group of students with all-round high academic skills. Adolescence can be a risk period for developing school burnout. The findings suggest that increased school burnout during adolescence might vary by gender. Consequently, one has to be cautious when interpreting the results in relation to adjustment and maladjustment at school, if gender has not been taken into account.

The stage-environment-fit theory (Eccles, 2004; Eccles & Midgley, 1989) offers one explanation for the result: depending on the ability of the new school environment to meet the individual needs of the students, wellbeing among young people may either improve or decline following a major educational transition (see also Ash & Huebner, 2001). Eccles (2004) argued that schools need to change in developmentally appropriate ways if they are to provide the kind of social context that will continue to motivate students' engagement as they mature. To the extent that this does not happen, adolescents disengage, first psychologically and then physically, from school as they mature through adolescence. The results also lend support to the big-fish-little-pond effect (BFLPE), according to which attending academically selective high schools negatively affects academic self-concept (Marsch, Trautwein, Lüdtke, Baumert, & Koller, 2007). However, one has to bear in mind that, besides a major educational transition, adolescents face several other key transitions during this age period, such as neurobiological, social, and autonomy transitions (Caspi, 2002; Erikson, 1968; Lefkowitz, 2005; Masten et al., 1999; Schulenberg, Maggs, & O'Malley, 2003; Shanahan, 2000; Shiner & Masten, 2002; see also Symonds et al., this volume), which might have contributed to the changes in school engagement in this study. In addition to educational transitions, there are various genetic and biological factors, such as puberty and environmental risk factors (e.g., stressful life events; Bagwell, Newcomb, & Bukowski, 1998), and cognitive vulnerabilities (e.g., dysfunctional attitudes, negative attributional style, and ruminative response style; for a review, see Hankin & Abramson, 2001) that might also be connected to school burnout.

A happiness gap seems to exist between girls and boys: early adolescence might be harder on girls but this gap seems to narrow during late adolescence. Previous research has explained girls' higher vulnerability to low wellbeing by changes in hormonal levels (Angold, Costello, Erkanli, & Worthman, 1999), entering puberty early (Ge et al., 2001), being more reactive to stress and negative life events (Crick & Zahn-Waxler, 2003), having a higher tendency toward ruminative coping styles (Broderick, 1998; Burwell & Shirk, 2007; Nolen-Hoeksema, 1994), and lower body satisfaction (Barker & Galambos, 2003). However, the picture seems to change during late adolescence. Boys and girls are shown to differ in the ways in which they adjust their self-perceptions according to external feedback on their academic ability (Crosnoe, Riegle-Crumb, & Muller, 2007). Girls, particularly, feel bad when they do not measure up to the standards set by their peers and family, whereas no special sensitivity to their more intimate contexts appears to exist among boys. Furthermore, girls and boys differ in their attributions for failing a class (Crosnoe et al., 2007). One explanation for this result is that girls find new academic and social challenges more positive than boys after the transition to post-compulsory education (Cole, Martin, Peeke, Seroczynski, & Fier, 1999). However, more research is needed on this topic.

Limitations

A number of limitations should be taken into account in any effort to generalize the results of the present study. First, all the measures included in the present study were based on self-report measures, which are not always the most valid or reliable method of data collection (Shaffer, 2002). The fact that the study was wholly based on adolescents' self-reports means that the data are subject to common-method variance. Accordingly, it would have been important to have had register data on achievement as well as information on the neurobiological and hormonal changes taking place during this age period. In addition, we did not have information about other transitions, such as puberty, which might also have taken place at around this age. Future studies are needed to examine the role of burnout trajectories during other educational transitions and educational and occupational trajectories across a more extended period. The present study was carried out in Finland and thus one has to be cautious in generalizing the results to other school contexts. However, many European countries have a similar educational system, in which students attend comprehensive school and then go on to an academic or a vocational track. Moreover, it is very likely that those who dropped out of the educational system are the same adolescents who dropped out of this longitudinal data collection, and this bias should be taken into account as a possible limitation of this study. Moreover, third variables, such as family problems, may affect both academic progress and engagement. This should be taken into account in future studies. Finally, our results do not allow us to propose any causal explanations, and thus more research is needed to examine possible reverse paths from school performance and burnout and engagement.

Implications for future research and practice

As most of the longitudinal research conducted among adolescents has focused on the negative side of adolescent development, there is evident need for longitudinal studies focusing on adolescents' strengths and wellbeing (Rich, 2003). In addition, there is a need to take into account the different changes adolescents experience, such as hormonal changes and their impact on academic wellbeing. Moreover, future studies should be conducted more intensively during stable time periods in secondary education in order to be able to examine if changes in trajectories take place in stable as well as in transitional periods. For future studies, more intensive data need to be collected, for example by means of diary methods, to reveal in greater detail the development of adolescents' academic wellbeing during educational transitions (Huebner, Funk, & Gilman, 2000). The results also have some practical implications. On the basis of our study, adolescence seems to be a period of possibility, during which changes in school engagement and school burnout can take place. Early interventions should, in particular, target adolescents who exhibit increasing school burnout in order to prevent the accumulation of problems. Person-oriented research revealed different groups of students, engaged, engaged–exhausted, cynical, and burned out. These different groups would benefit from different interventions. Engaged students can serve as a role models for those who are disengaged or burned out. Students who are engaged but exhausted could benefit from positive feedbak and a less competitive school environment. They could also benefit from mindfulness practices in which they focus on the present rather than ruminate on future challenges. Cynical students could benefit from interventions focusing on the meaning of school for future pathways. The same students might also benefit if they could build motivation around their out-of-school interests. Finally, burned-out students could benefit from supportive interventions that would prevent them from dropping out.

References

Angold, A., Costello, E. J., Erkanli, A., & Worthman, C. M. (1999). Pubertal changes in hormone levels and depression in girls. *Psychological Medicine*, 29, 1043–1053.

Ash, C., & Huebner, E. S. (2001). Environmental events and life satisfaction reports of adolescents. *School Psychology International*, 22, 20–36.

Bagwell, C. L., Newcomb, A. F., & Bukowski, W. M. (1998). Preadolescent friendship and peer rejection as predictors of adult adjustment. *Child Development*, 69, 140–153.

Baltes, P. B. (1997). On the incomplete architecture of human ontogeny: Selection, optimization, and compensation as foundation of developmental theory. *American Psychologist*, 52, 366–380.

Barker, E. T., & Galambos, N. L. (2003). Body dissatisfaction of adolescent girls and boys: Risk and resource factors. *The Journal of Early Adolescence*, 23, 141–165.

Berndt, T. J., & Miller, K. E. (1990). Expectancies, values, and achievement in junior high school. *Journal of Educational Psychology*, 82, 319–326.

Broderick, P. C. (1998). Early adolescent gender differences in the use of ruminative and distracting coping strategies. *Journal of Early Adolescence*, 18, 173–191.

Burwell, R. A., & Shirk, S. R. (2007). Subtypes of rumination in adolescence: Associations between brooding, reflection, depressive symptoms, and coping. *Journal of Clinical Child and Adolescent Psychology*, 36, 56–65.

Caspi, A. (2002). Social selection, social causation and developmental pathways: Empirical strategies for better understanding how individuals and environments are linked across the life course. In L. Pulkkinen & A. Caspi (Eds.), *Paths to successful development: Personality in the life course* (pp. 281–301). Cambridge University Press.

Cole, D. A., Martin, J. M., Peeke, L. A., Seroczynski, A. D., & Fier, J. (1999). Children's over- and underestimation of academic competence: A longitudinal study of gender differences, depression and anxiety. *Child Development*, 70, 459–473.

Crick, N. R., & Zahn-Waxler, C. (2003). The development of psychopathology in females and males: Current progress and future challenges. *Development and Psychopathology*, 15, 719–742.

Crosnoe, R., Riegle-Crumb, C., & Muller, C. (2007). Gender, self-perception, and academic problems in high school. *Social Problems*, 54, 118–138.

Dwyer, C. A., & Johnson, L. M. (1997). Grades, accomplishments, and correlates. In W. W. Willingham & N. S. Cole (Eds.). *Gender and fair assessment* (pp. 127–156). Mahwah, NJ: Lawrence Erlbaum Associates.

Eccles, J. S. (2004). Schools, academic motivation, and stage-environment fit. In R. M. Lerner & L. D. Steinberg (Eds.), *Handbook of adolescent psychology* (2nd ed., pp. 125–153). Hoboken, NJ: John Wiley & Sons.

Eccles, J. S., & Midgley, C. (1989). Stage/environment fit: Developmentally appropriate classrooms for early adolescents. In R. Ames & C. Ames (Eds.), *Research on motivation in education* (Vol. 3, pp. 139–181). New York: Academic Press.

Erikson, E. H. (1968). *Identity: Youth and crisis*. Oxford: Norton & Co.

Fuligni, A. J., Eccles, J. S., & Barber, L. B. (1995). The long-term effects of seventh-grade ability grouping in mathematics. *Journal of Early Adolescence*, 15, 58–89.

Galambos, N., Barker, E., & Krahn, H. (2006). Depression, self-esteem and anger in emerging adulthood: Seven-year trajectories. *Developmental Psychology*, 42, 350–365.

Ge, X., Conger, R. D., & Elder, G. H., Jr. (2001). Pubertal transition, stressful life events, and the emergence of gender differences in adolescent depressive symptoms. *Developmental Psychology*, 37, 404–417.

Ge, X., Lorenz, F. O., Conger, R. D., Elder, G. H., & Simons, R. L. (1994). Trajectories of stressful life events and depressive symptoms during adolescence. *Developmental Psychology*, 30, 467–483.

Gilman, R., & Huebner, E. S. (2003). A review of life satisfaction research with children and adolescents. *School Psychology Quarterly*, 18, 192–205.

Graber, J. A., & Brooks-Gunn, J. (1996). Transitions and turning points: Navigating the passage from childhood through adolescence. *Developmental Psychology*, 32, 768–776.

Hankin, B. L., & Abramson, L. Y. (2001). Development of gender differences in depression: An elaborated cognitive vulnerability-transactional stress theory. *Psychological Bulletin*, 127, 773–796.

Hoffmann, M. L., Powlishta, K. K., & White, K. (2004). An examination of gender differences in adolescent adjustment: The effect of competence on gender role differences in symptoms of psychopathology. *Sex Roles: A Journal of Research*, 50, 795–810.

Holopainen, L., & Savolainen, H. (2005). Unpublished raw data. University of Joensuu and University of Jyväskylä, Finland.

Huebner, E. S., Funk, B. A., & Gilman, R. (2000). Cross-sectional and longitudinal psychosocial correlates of adolescent life satisfaction reports. *Canadian Journal of School Psychology*, 16, 53–64.

Jose, P. E., & Ratcliffe, V. (2004). Stressor frequency and perceived intensity as predictors of internalizing symptoms: Gender and age differences in adolescence. *New Zealand Journal of Psychology*, 33, 145–154.

Kessler, R. C., & McLeod, J. D. (1984). Sex differences in vulnerability to undesirable life events. *American Sociological Review*, 49, 620–631.

Lee, M., & Larson, R. (2000). The Korean "examination hell": Long hours of studying, distress, and depression. *Journal of Youth and Adolescence*, 29, 249–271.

Lefkowitz, E. S. (2005). "Things have gotten better": Developmental changes among emerging adults after the transition to university. *Journal of Adolescent Research*, 20, 40–63.

Marsch, H., Trautwein, U., Lüdtke, O., Baumert, J., & Koller, O. (2007). The Big-Fish-Little-Pond Effect: Persistent negative effects of selective high schools on self-concept after graduation. *American Psychologist*, 44, 631–634.

Masten, A. S., Hubbard, J. J., Gest, S. D., Tellegen, A., Garmezy, N., & Ramirez, M. (1999). Competence in the context of adversity: Pathways to resilience and maladaptation from childhood to late adolescence. *Development and Psychopathology*, 11, 143–169.

Murberg, T. A., & Bru, E. (2004). School-related stress and psychosomatic symptoms among Norwegian adolescents. *School Psychology International*, 25, 317–332.

Muthén, L., & Muthén, B. O. (1998–2007). *Mplus user's guide* and *Mplus version 5*. Retrieved from www.statmodel.com.

Needham, B. (2007). Gender differences in trajectories of depressive symptomatology and substance use during the transition from adolescence to young adulthood. *Social Science and Medicine*, 65, 1166–1179.

Nolen-Hoeksema, S. (1994). An interactive model for the emergence of gender differences in depression in adolescence. *Journal of Research on Adolescence*, 4, 519–534.

Nolen-Hoeksema, S., & Girgus, J. S. (1994). The emergence of gender differences in depression during adolescence. *Psychological Bulletin*, 115, 424–443.

Oakes, J., Gamoran, A., & Page, R. N. (1992). Curriculum differentiation: Opportunities, outcomes, and meanings. In P. W. Jackson (Ed.), *Handbook of research on curriculum* (pp. 570–608). New York: Macmillan.

OECD. (1998). Getting started, settling in: The transition from education to the labour market. *Employment Outlook*, 60, 81–122.

Pomerantz, E. M., Altermatt, E. R., & Saxon, J. L. (2002). Making the grade but feeling distressed: Gender differences in academic performance and internal distress. *Journal of Educational Psychology*, 94, 396–404.

Powers, S. I., Hauser, S. T., & Kilner, L. A. (1989). Adolescent mental health. *American Psychologist*, 44, 200–208.

Renick, M. J., & Harter, S. (1989). Impact of social comparisons on the developing self-perceptions of learning disabled students. *Journal of Educational Psychology*, 81, 631–638.

Rich, G. J. (2003). The positive psychology of youth and adolescence. *Journal of Youth and Adolescence*, 32, 1–3.

Rutter, M. (1990). Psychosocial resilience and protective mechanisms. In J. E. Rolf, A. Masten, D. Cicchetti, K. H. Neucherterlein, & S. Weintraub (Eds.), *Risk and protective factors in the development of psychopathology* (pp. 181–214). Cambridge University Press.

Salmela-Aro, K. (2009). Personal goals and well-being during critical life transitions: The 4 C's – channeling, choice, co-agency and compensation. *Advances in Life Course Research*, 14, 63–73.

Salmela-Aro, K., Kiuru, N., Leskinen, E., & Nurmi, J.-E. (2009). School burnout inventory: Reliability and validity. *European Journal of Psychological Assessment*, 25, 48–57.

Salmela-Aro, K., Kiuru, N., & Nurmi, J.-E. (2008). The role of educational track in adolescents' school burnout. *British Journal of Educational Psychology*, 78, 663–689.

Salmela-Aro, K., Mutanen, P., Koivisto, P., & Vuori, J. (2010). Adolescents' future education-related personal goals, concerns and internal motivation during the "Towards Working Life" group intervention. *European Journal of Developmental Psychology*, 7, 445–462.

Salmela-Aro, K., & Näätänen, P. (2005). *BBI-10: Koulu-uupumusmittari – School burnout inventory.* Helsinki: Edita.

Salmela-Aro, K., & Suikkari, A-M. (2008). Letting go of your dreams: Adjustment of child-related goal appraisals and depressive symptoms during infertility treatment. *Journal of Research in Personality*, 42, 988–1003.

Salmela-Aro, K., & Tynkkynen, L. (2012). Gendered pathways in school burnout among adolescents. *Journal of Adolescence*, 35, 929–939.

Salmela-Aro, K., & Upadyaya, K. (2012). Schoolwork engagement inventory: Energy, dedication and absorption (EDA). *European Journal of Psychological Assessment*, 28, 60–67.

Schulenberg, J. E., Maggs, J. L., & O'Malley, P. M. (2003). How and why the understanding of developmental continuity and discontinuity is important: The sample case of long-term consequences of adolescent substance abuse. In J. T. Mortimer & M. J. Shanahan (Eds.), *Handbook of the life course* (pp. 413–436). New York: Kluwer Academic/Plenum Publishers.

Shanahan, M. J. (2000). Pathways to adulthood in changing societies: Variability and mechanisms in life course perspective. *Annual Review of Sociology*, 26, 667–692.

Shaffer, D. R. (2002). *Developmental psychology: Childhood and adolescence* (6th ed.). Belmont, CA: Wadsworth/Thomson Learning.

Shiner, R. L., & Masten, A. S. (2002). Transactional links between personality and adaptation from childhood through adulthood. *Journal of Research in Personality*, 36, 580–588.

Tomasik, M. J., & Salmela-Aro, K. (2012). Knowing when to let go at the entrance to university: Beneficial effects of compensatory secondary control after failure. *Motivation and Emotion*, 36, 170–179.

Tram, J. M., & Cole, D. A. (2006). A multimethod examination of the stability of depressive symptoms in childhood and adolescence. *Journal of Abnormal Psychology*, 115, 674–686.

Tuominen-Soini, H., & Salmela-Aro, K. (2014). Schoolwork engagement and burnout among Finnish high school students and young adults: Profiles, progressions and educational outcomes. *Developmental Psychology*, 50, 649–662.

7 Uncertainty in educational and career aspirations: gender differences in young people

Leslie Morrison Gutman, Ricardo Sabates and Ingrid Schoon

Abstract

Drawing upon data from two British age cohorts born in 1970 and 1990, this chapter examines gender and socio-historical differences regarding uncertainty in the educational and career aspirations of young people. Despite differences in the age of assessment and measurement, findings suggest that similar background characteristics are associated with uncertain aspirations in the two age cohorts. Males were more uncertain of their educational aspirations than were females. Uncertainty was also associated with growing up in a relatively disadvantaged family, with parents who did not expect their children to continue in education, as well as with low academic attainment, low levels of school motivation, and lack of belief in one's own ability. However, findings indicated differences in the associated outcomes of uncertain aspirations between the two age cohorts. In the earlier-born cohort, young people with uncertain aspirations were more likely to be not in education, employment, or training (NEET), while there were no differences in NEET due to uncertain aspirations in the later-born cohort. The findings point toward a female advantage regarding certainty in aspirations as well as a prolonged period of career exploration in the later-born cohort.

Introduction

In recent years, researchers have highlighted the increasing uncertainty of young people regarding their education and career development, attributed to changes in the global market (Kalleberg, Reskin, & Hudson, 2000; Mills & Blossfeld, 2003). Globalization has tightened the availability of jobs, particularly for those aged 16 to 24 (Bynner, 2001; Danziger & Ratner, 2010). Young people are now under increasing pressure to continue in full-time education and acquire formal qualifications in order to succeed in a competitive labor market, and educational and career routes have become more complicated and protracted (Blossfeld, 2005; Bynner, 2005). These changes are likely to generate uncertainty for young people who lack the knowledge and experience concerning established routes to success, especially those from more disadvantaged backgrounds (Appadurai, 2004).

The preparation of this chapter was supported by a grant from the Economic and Social Research Council (ESRC) – grant reference RES-000-22-3849.

Young men and women are likely to have different responses to such uncertainty (Mills & Blossfeld, 2003). Decreased employment opportunities, lower wages, increased debt, and higher housing prices have made it more difficult for young men to assume the responsibilities of adulthood including marriage and supporting a family, which may be associated with greater uncertainty about their future prospects (Danziger & Rouse, 2007). In contrast, relatively greater economic benefits of college and improved labor market opportunities entail that young women are more likely to invest in their education and careers rather than partnership and parenthood (Danziger & Rouse, 2007; Goldin, Katz, & Kuziemko, 2006).

While there is a wealth of evidence that high educational and career aspirations during adolescence increase educational achievement, occupational prestige, and wage attainments in adulthood (Clausen, 1993; Schoon & Parsons, 2002; Sewell & Hauser, 1975), relatively little research has focused on young people with uncertain aspirations (i.e., those who do not know what they want to do for their future educational and career choices), especially regarding gender differences in uncertainty (Gutman & Schoon, 2012; Gutman, Schoon, & Sabates, 2012). In this chapter, we address this evidence gap and examine to what extent males and females differ regarding uncertainty in their aspirations, taking into account the antecedents as well as associated outcomes of uncertain educational and career aspirations. We focus on the aspirations of young people, which can be distinguished from career expectations. While expectations are considered to reflect more realistic evaluations of available opportunities, aspirations tap more into the hopes of what one wants to achieve (Gottfredson, 1981).

Our study adopts a developmental-contextual approach (Schoon, 2006; Vondracek, Lerner, & Schulenberg, 1983), taking into account multiple and interlinked levels of influence on career development, the importance of formative years in shaping later development, the role of individual agency involving preference and capabilities, as well as co-regulation by significant others (e.g., parents, teachers, or career advisers). We furthermore take into account that career choice is highly sensitive to historical and economic conditions (Mortimer, Zimmer-Gembeck, Holmes, & Shanahan, 2002). To assess similarities and differences in associations across a changing socio-historical context, we draw upon two age cohorts: the 1970 British Cohort Study (BCS70) and the Longitudinal Study of Young People in England (LSYPE) born in 1989/1990. Comparing experiences in two age cohorts enables us to examine gender differences across contexts and to establish generalizability of findings.

The role of a changing socio-historical context

The two age cohorts examined in this chapter grew up during two distinct periods regarding the development of the post-compulsory education and training system in England, and changing expectations with regards to educational participation. The 1970 cohort reached compulsory school leaving age (i.e., age

16) in the mid-1980s, following a major economic recession at the beginning of the decade. Compared internationally, the participation rate in England was low with less than 50% of learners staying on in education after the age of 16 (Machin & Vignoles, 2006). It was only at the end of the 1980s that the English education and training system changed gear toward higher levels of educational participation, both beyond the age of 16 and in relation to higher education. The 1989/1990 age cohort, on the other hand, reached school leaving age during a period of economic growth. By 2004 (when they were aged 14/15), expectations to stay on in education and training beyond age 16 had become more or less the norm, regardless of social background or previous academic attainment (Schoon, 2010). In 2008, however, the 1989/1990 age cohort found itself in the midst of a sustained economic recession, providing a further impetus to education participation given the rising unemployment rates for 18- to 24-year-olds (Office for National Statistics, 2010). We thus expect increasing aspirations for higher education – but also increasing uncertainty regarding career opportunities for the later-born cohort.

Antecedents of uncertain educational and career aspirations

To gain a better understanding of the antecedents of uncertain aspirations, we examine a number of demographic and social factors that have been related to the formation of aspirations in previous studies.

Family socioeconomic status

Young people from working-class backgrounds generally report lower educational aspirations than their more privileged peers, even after controlling for academic ability (Kerckhoff, 2003; Schnabel, Alfeld, Eccles, Koller, & Baumert, 2002; Schoon, 2010). Young people from lower socioeconomic backgrounds also report greater uncertainty in their aspirations than those from higher socioeconomic backgrounds (Croll, Attwood, Fuller, & Last, 2008; Gutman & Schoon, 2012). Evidence also suggests that the negative influence of economic hardship on teenage job aspirations is stronger for males than females (Schoon, Martin, & Ross, 2007). We thus would expect that young men from relatively disadvantaged family backgrounds may have greater uncertainty regarding their career aspirations than women in similar circumstances.

Parental expectations

Parental expectations are another important influence on young people's aspirations, indicating the importance of co-regulation and the interactions between the young person and significant others (Eccles & Wigfield, 2002; Goodman & Gregg, 2010; Schoon, 2006). Children whose parents have higher expectations for them also tend to have higher aspirations for themselves (Mau & Bikos, 2000; Rhea & Otto, 2001; Schoon, 2010). However, using data from the LSYPE, Schoon (2010) found that teen and parental expectations are less strongly associated among girls than among boys, suggesting that compared to girls, boys might be more dependent on parental support and encouragement when deciding about their future.

Prior attainment

Aspirations (both of oneself and of one's parents) are also shaped by previous attainment. Aspirations may be raised for young people who do well in school, whereas they may be lowered for those who have poor school performance (Jencks, Crouse, & Mueser, 1983; Mau & Bikos, 2000; Sacker, Schoon, & Bartley, 2002). However, Schoon (2010) found that the association between academic attainment and education expectations was stronger for boys than for girls, suggesting that girls' aspirations may be less strongly influenced by their previous academic attainment than are boys.

School motivation and perceived ability

School motivation has also been associated with higher career aspirations and exam performance (Schoon et al., 2007). Young people who have uncertain aspirations about their educational plans are more likely to report lower school motivation than young people who plan to continue in school (Croll et al., 2008; Gutman et al., 2012). Furthermore, research has demonstrated that perceptions of one's own ability predict the occupational and academic aspirations of children and young people (Bandura, Barbaranelli, Caprara, & Pastorelli, 2001). Girls tend to have higher school motivation but lower perceptions of their abilities compared to boys (Bandura et al., 2001; Schoon et al., 2007). We thus expect that for males the association between school motivation and uncertain aspirations may be stronger than for females, while for females the association between self-perceived ability and uncertainty may be stronger than for males.

Career advice

Evidence also suggests that information about educational and career options and opportunities is associated with the aspirations of young people, particularly those who lack opportunities for more established routes to success (Wigfield, Lutz, & Wagner, 2005). For the older cohort, career advice was provided in the school through teachers and career officers, as well as through special youth training schemes. In 2001 a special career advice service, *Connexions*, was introduced in the United Kingdom, offering both individual support and career advice to young people. Connexions is especially targeted toward the most disengaged and disadvantaged groups, i.e., 16–18-year-olds who are not in education, employment, or training (NEET) (Hoggart & Smith, 2004). These services were discontinued in 2010, yet they were on offer for young people in the later-born cohort during secondary schooling. We would expect that in both cohorts the usefulness of the career advice, as perceived by the students, might be associated with lower uncertainty in aspirations (see also Gutman & Schoon, 2012; Gutman et al., 2012).

Consequences of uncertain educational and career aspirations

Different viewpoints exist concerning the role of uncertainty on the educational and career outcomes of young people. According to Kerckhoff (2003), uncertainty may lead to prolonged schooling without the attainment of qualifications and floundering in the labor market. Arnett (2004), on the other hand, views uncertainty as part of a formative period for adolescents who are exploring possible life directions without detrimental consequences. This may be particularly true for certain groups of young people, especially young people from relatively privileged backgrounds who can more easily afford a period of extended exploration (Bynner, 2005). Furthermore, females may benefit from more flexibility in their aspirations as their career trajectories tend to be more complex than those of males because of multiple and competing commitments regarding family and work-related roles (Schoon et al., 2007; Vondracek et al., 1983).

Recent research, however, indicates that uncertainty in educational aspirations is associated with negative educational outcomes (Croll, 2009; Gutman et al., 2012). In the British Household Panel Survey (BHPS), among those born between 1979 and 1989, for example, Croll (2009) found that uncertainty at age 13 about whether to continue in education past compulsory schooling age was highly predictive of their actual behavior 3 years later. In LSYPE, Gutman et al. (2012) found that 15-year-olds who were uncertain about continuing in school past compulsory schooling age had lower scores on their school exams at age 16 and were less likely to continue in education at age 18.

For uncertainty in career aspirations, there is also evidence that uncertainty at age 16 may place young people at risk of outcomes such as lower educational attainment, difficulties in establishing oneself in the labor market (as indicated by NEET between the ages of 16 and 18), later employment instability, and a wage penalty (Staff, Harris, Sabates, & Briddell, 2010; Yates, Harris, Sabates, & Staff, 2011). These findings were observed among young people born between 1970 and 1974. In the more recent LSYPE cohort, however, uncertain career aspirations at age 13/14 were associated with better educational outcomes for disadvantaged young people who remained in the education system beyond the age of 16, offering greater flexibility to explore career options while still being engaged in educational pursuits (Gutman & Schoon, 2012). Together, these findings indicate that the consequences of uncertainty may depend on the individual characteristics and age of the young person as well as the socio-historical context in which they mature.

Research questions

Previous research examining uncertain aspirations suggests that there is likely to be variation in the both the background characteristics and consequences of uncertainty. In this chapter, we are interested in exploring the gender differences in uncertain aspirations in two different age cohorts growing up in distinct social and economic periods. In order to do this, we examine background characteristics including socioeconomic background, prior academic attainment, parental educational expectations, school motivation, perceived ability, and usefulness of career advice, as well as being NEET between the ages of 16 and 18.

In summary, we address the following questions, comparing evidence in two age cohorts:

1. What background characteristics are associated with uncertainty in educational and occupational aspirations, and do those differ by gender and by period?
2. Do young men and women with uncertain aspirations have a greater likelihood of becoming NEET relative to those who hold high aspirations? Has this association changed in a changing socio-historical context?

Method

Data

The study was based on the 1970 British Cohort Study (BCS70) and the Longitudinal Study of Young People in England (LSYPE) born in 1989/1990. BCS70 comprises data collected from large nationally representative samples of over 16,000 individuals born in a single week in 1970 who have been followed from birth to adulthood (Elliott & Shepherd, 2006). Data sweeps have taken place at birth and when cohort members were aged 5, 10, 16, 26, 30, 34, and 38 years, using personal interviews and self-completion questionnaires.[1] At age 16, when questions about aspirations for the future were asked, the study was affected by a teacher strike. This led to a reduced sample, which did not, however, differ greatly from the target population, despite a slight underrepresentation of males and the most disadvantaged (Elliott & Shepherd, 2006).

[1] For more details, see www.cls.ioe.ac.uk.

LSYPE is a panel study of over 21,000 young people born between September 1, 1989 and August 31, 1990. Sample members were all young people in year 9 (age 13/14) or equivalent in all schools in England in February 2004. Annual face-to-face interviews had been conducted with young people and their parents since 2004, and linkage was available to other administrative data, such as those held on the National Pupil Database.[2] Special sample weights were applied to account for differential selection probabilities and non-response bias. We use information from the first five waves of the dataset, from ages 13/14 to 17/18 years.

As in all longitudinal studies, LSYPE experienced sample loss between the multiple waves. The analytic sample in both age cohorts comprises cohort members for whom we have complete data.

Measures

Table 7.1 provides the means, standard deviations, and percentages for each of the measures.

Uncertain aspirations

Uncertain educational aspirations were measured differently and at different ages in the two age cohorts. In the LSYPE, young people were asked at age 13/14 whether they wanted to continue in school after age 16. Responses included: 1 = yes, continue in education; 2 = no, leave education; 3 = don't know. In order to create a measure of uncertainty for continuing in education past compulsory schooling age, responses were dummy-coded into a dichotomous variable, differentiating those with uncertain aspirations (1) and those who wanted to continue in education (0), excluding those who were certain about leaving school. In BCS70 cohort members were asked at age 16 whether they planned to continue in education after age 18. Responses included: 1 = yes; 2 = no; and 3 = I do not know. As for the LSYPE, responses were also recoded into those who were certain about continuing in education after age 18 and those who were uncertain about this. We excluded young people who were certain about leaving school at age 18. Notice that in LSYPE children were asked about uncertainty about continuing beyond compulsory education, whereas for BCS70 uncertainty was about continuing in higher education.

Uncertain career aspirations were also assessed differently in the two age cohorts. In the LSYPE, young people were asked at age 13/14: "Do you have any ideas of the kind of job you want to do after full-time education?" Response alternatives included "yes," "no," and "do not know." Our measure of uncertain career aspirations differentiates between those who had an

---
[2] For more information, see www.esds.ac.uk /longitudinal/access/lsype/ L5545.asp.

Table 7.1. *Descriptive statistics for all variables in analysis*

Description	Unit	LSYPE males Mean (SD)	LSYPE females Mean (SD)	BCS70 males Mean (SD)	BCS70 females Mean (SD)
Main predictor variables					
Uncertainty in educational aspirations	%	6.40[a]	4.70	23.08[a]	20.03
Uncertainty in career aspirations	%	22.40[a]	18.60	8.29	7.34
Control variables					
Parental social background					
Professional, managerial	%	41.80[a]	43.70	38.42	36.64
Skilled	%	33.30	32.00	47.36	48.47
Semi-skilled, unskilled	%	18.30	17.00	12.01	12.58
Unemployed, never worked	%	6.60	7.30	2.20	2.31
Ethnic background (non-white British or European)	%	31.90[a]	34.00	4.43	4.67
Maths test scores at age 10/11 (standardized)	#	0.06[a] (1.02)	0.03 (0.97)	0.30[a] (0.87)	0.14 (0.81)
Reading test scores at age 10/11 (standardized)	#	−0.15[a] (1.02)	0.17 (0.94)	0.22 (0.84)	0.25 (0.81)
Parental expectations	%	67.40[a]	79.20	24.05	25.77
School motivation (standardized)	#	−0.05[a] (1.00)	0.05 (0.99)	−0.07[a] (0.87)	0.15 (0.85)
Perceived ability (standardized)	#	0.11[a] (0.97)	−0.11 (1.01)	0.12[a] (0.74)	−0.08 (0.76)
Usefulness of information from career advice	#	3.44 (0.73)	3.42 (0.72)	2.56 (1.10)	2.43 (1.06)
Outcome variables					
NEET at 17/18	%	6.10[a]	5.40	5.29	5.69

Note: [a] Significant gender differences using ANOVA test. %: frequencies in percent; #: mean (standard deviation).

idea about their future job and those who had no ideas or did not know. In addition it was possible to identify the status of the aspired-for occupation by coding up the open-ended question: "What job do you want to do after you have finished full-time education?" using the National Statistics Socio-economic Classification (NS-SEC). In our coding we differentiated professional and managerial occupations versus others (i.e., skilled, semi-skilled, and unskilled occupations). In order to create a measure of uncertainty for career aspirations, responses were dummy-coded into a dichotomous variable, differentiating those with uncertain aspirations (1) and those who had aspirations for a professional career (0), excluding those who were certain about having a skilled or semi-skilled occupation. For the BCS70, cohort members were asked at age 16 to report the kind of jobs they would like to do later on in life. There were several pre-formulated response alternatives, ranging from professional occupations, managerial, teaching, administrative posts, to semi- or unskilled jobs. One of the possible response alternatives was "I cannot decide," which was our measurement of uncertainty in career aspirations for BCS70 cohort members. We also selected young people who had aspirations for professional occupations in later life. Notice that uncertainty in future jobs referred to jobs after completing full-time education in LSYPE, whereas for BSC70 it referred to jobs later in life. In both cohorts we identified young people with high career aspirations, i.e., aspiring for a professional or managerial job, and we compared them to those who were uncertain in their career aspirations.

It is important to highlight that the age of assessment and the wording and meaning of the questions regarding educational and occupational aspirations differed between the two datasets, and that the data cannot be directly compared. Instead we focused on functional equivalence, and did not make statistical comparisons between the cohorts. Nevertheless, we were still able to discuss similarities and differences in the background characteristics and outcomes associated with uncertainty in aspirations.

Background characteristics

Parental social background was measured using operational categories of NS-SEC aggregated to produce the approximate Social Class based on Occupation (see Standard Occupational Classification, 1991). Six categories were aggregated into four groups differentiating professional and managerial occupations; skilled occupations; semi-skilled and unskilled occupations; as well as being unemployed or never worked.

Ethnic background was gathered from young people, enabling us to examine differences between white (0) versus other (1) young people. In BCS70 there are only about 5% of ethnic minority youths, reflecting the ethnic composition at the time of their birth (Ferri, Bynner, & Wadsworth, 2003), not allowing us to break up the groups further. LSYPE is more ethnically diverse, as there has been oversampling for ethnic minority groups. For both cohorts we used a similar coding scheme differentiating between white versus other for comparison purposes.

Prior achievement was measured using assessments for the student's math and reading ability at age 10/11. In BCS70, specially designed assessments were used to test academic abilities (see Schoon, 2006). In LSYPE, Key Stage 2 test scores from the National Pupil Database were accessed. The test data has been z-standardized to enable comparison across cohorts.

Parental expectations were measured as parents' education expectations for their child. In LSYPE, parents were asked when their child was 13/14 what they would expect their child to do when reaching school leaving age (i.e., age 16). High parental expectations were assigned to parents who expected the cohort member to stay in education after age 16. In BCS70 parents were asked about their expectations regarding further education beyond age 18 when their child was aged 16. High parental expectations were assigned to parents who expected the cohort member to stay in education after age 18.[3]

School motivation was measured with the same 5-item academic motivation scale in both cohorts (sample items: *School is a waste of time*; *I like being at school*) yet different response formats were used. Questions were assessed at age 13/14 for the LSYPE and at age 16 for BCS70. Scores were z-standardized for further analysis and a high score indicates positive school motivation in both cohorts.

Perceived ability measured the young person's perceptions of his/her own abilities in school subjects (sample items: *How good are you at maths?*; *How good are you in English?*). Questions were assessed at age 13/14 for the LSYPE and at age 16 for BCS70. Questions were z-standardized to enable comparison across cohorts.

Usefulness of career advice assessed the perceptions of the young person regarding career advice given at school. In the LSYPE, young people at age 13/14 were asked whether they found it useful to talk about plans for future study with Connexions (a governmental organization that provides advice and information for young people) and their teachers. In the BCS70, young people at age 16 responded as to whether they found the information and advice provided by career officers or youth training schemes useful. In both studies the same response format was used (a Likert scale ranging from 1 = not at all useful to 4 = useful).

---

[3] The difference in parental expectations between LSYPE and BCS70 is due to the nature of uncertainty in educational aspirations for young people mentioned above. In LSYPE, uncertainty refers to staying on after completion of compulsory schooling whereas in BCS70 uncertainty refers to education after age 18.

Outcomes

NEET status between the ages of 16 and 18 was a dichotomous variable. In the LSYPE, a young person was defined as NEET if they were not in part-time or full-time education, employment, or training at Wave 4 (assessed when young people were age 16/17) and/or Wave 5 (assessed when most young people were age 17/18). In BCS70, "NEET status" is defined as spending a combined total of 6 months (or one quarter of the 24 months between ages 16 and 18) outside of work, education, or training. Young people who worked part-time were not counted as NEET using employment histories between ages 16 and 18 (see Bynner & Parsons, 2002; Yates et al., 2011).

Analytic strategy

For the descriptive statistics, ANOVA was used to examine gender differences in all of the variables included in the analysis. To investigate background factors that predict uncertainty in educational and career aspirations, we employed a logit model. This estimation technique is useful for understanding which factors increase (or decrease) the probability of being uncertain (see Greene, 2008). In particular, we estimated the likelihood of being uncertain relative to being certain with high aspirations. We only used young people with high ambitions as our reference or comparison group given previous research showing the importance of high ambitions for future outcomes. For educational aspirations, we compared young people who were uncertain in their educational plans to those who were hoping to continue in education. For career aspirations, we compared young people who were uncertain in their career plans to those who were hoping to have a professional or managerial career. The reduced subsamples regarding educational aspirations included 1,111 males and 1,516 females in BCS70, and 1,766 males and 1,898 females in LSYPE. Regarding career aspiration the subsamples comprised 764 males and 1,211 females in BCS70 and 1,972 males and 2,007 females in LSYPE.

Models were examined separately for males and females and separately for each cohort. Estimated parameters from the logit model were transformed using the exponential function to estimate the odds ratio. An odds ratio greater than 1 indicates that the factor is positively associated with the probability of being uncertain in aspirations whereas an odds ratio less than 1 indicates that the factor is negatively associated with the probability of being uncertain in aspirations (Wooldridge, 2002). For the outcome variable, we used logit models, as NEET is binary. Parameters were transformed into odds ratios for ease of interpretation. All our models included a measure of uncertainty as the main explanatory variable and all background factors as control variables. Models were examined separately for males and females.

Findings

Gender differences in measures

Table 7.1 presents the descriptive statistics for all of the variables used in the analysis. It has to be kept in mind that the sample only comprises those with high aspirations and those who are uncertain. There were significant gender differences in most of these variables. In both cohorts, males expressed more uncertainty in their educational aspirations than females and the more recently born cohort males expressed more uncertainty regarding their career aspirations than females. These findings suggest that males in general may be more susceptible to uncertainty in their aspirations than are females. Regarding demographic background variables, females in LSYPE were more likely than males to have parents who had professional or managerial occupations, but there was no difference in other occupations in LSYPE and no differences in BCS70. Females in LSYPE were also more likely to be non-white compared to males; but this was not the case for BCS70. As established in previous studies, males tend to have higher math scores than females, while females tend to have higher reading scores than males (Else-Quest, Hyde, & Linn, 2010; Hyde, 2007; Maccoby, 2000). In LSYPE parents with daughters reported higher educational expectations than parents with sons. In support of previous research (Bandura et al., 2001; Eccles, 2009; Schoon et al., 2007), males had higher perceptions of their ability, whereas females showed higher levels of school motivation than males. For the outcomes, males were more likely to be NEET than females in LSYPE.

Background characteristics of uncertain aspirations

The background characteristics for being uncertain about educational aspirations relative to having high aspirations for continuing in education are shown in Table 7.2, and the background factors for being uncertain about career aspirations relative to having high aspirations for a professional or managerial career are shown in Table 7.3. Despite differences in assessment, there are similarities in both cohorts. For both cohorts and for men and women, the findings highlight the importance of personal academic beliefs and motivation for certainty in young people's aspirations. Young people who believe that they can achieve and who are motivated to do so were less likely to be uncertain about their future goals than those who did not believe in their abilities and who were disengaged from school. Parents' expectations about their children's future were also important factors for certainty in aspirations, highlighting the importance of co-regulation with significant others. These results were significant even though prior ability was taken into account for both cohorts. Furthermore, higher math and reading scores were not

Table 7.2. *Predicting uncertain educational aspirations (odds ratios contrasting uncertainty relative to aspiring to stay in education in LSYPE and BCS70)*

	LSYPE		BCS70	
Variables	Males uncertain	Females uncertain	Males uncertain	Females uncertain
Parental social background				
Skilled	1.074	1.605**	1.949**	1.933**
Semi and unskilled	1.323*	1.474*	2.785**	1.830**
Unemployed	1.010	1.746**	1.728	1.341
Ethnicity (non-white)	0.646**	0.657*	0.243**	0.957
Maths z-score @ 10	0.946	0.881	0.949	0.777*
Reading z-score @ 10	0.836*	0.838	0.665**	0.665**
High parental expectations	0.239**	0.208**	0.491**	0.408**
School motivation	0.606**	0.821	0.638**	0.712**
Perceived ability	0.709*	0.689*	0.652**	0.734**
Useful career advice	0.906	0.952	0.977	0.975
Pseudo R^2	0.149	0.140	0.129	0.128
Observations	1,766	1,898	1,111	1,516

Notes: Estimated odds ratio using logit model. Reference category "stay in education post 16 for LSYPE" and "stay in education post 18 for BCS70." Asterisks * and ** indicate statistical significance at .05 and .01 level, respectively. Measurements of uncertainty in aspirations, math, and reading scores at age 10 are different in the datasets.

consistently associated with less uncertainty. For example, higher math scores were significantly associated with lower levels of uncertainty in educational aspirations among females in BCS70 and with higher uncertainty regarding occupational aspirations among females in LSYPE, but were not associated with uncertainty among males in either sample. Therefore ability perceptions, expectations, and motivation appear to be more consistent than actual ability in shaping certainty in young people's aspirations for their future educational and career development.

Demographic variables were also associated with uncertainty in aspirations, although not in a consistent manner. For uncertain educational aspirations, young people in both cohorts whose parents were from semi-skilled and unskilled occupations had a greater risk of uncertain educational aspirations than those whose parents were from professional occupations. In BCS70, young people whose parents had skilled occupations, relative to those whose parents worked in professional or managerial occupations, had a greater odds ratio of uncertain educational aspirations at age 16. In LSYPE, however, where educational aspirations were measured at age 14, this only applied for girls.

Table 7.3. *Predicting career aspirations (odds ratio for uncertainty relative to aspiring for a professional or managerial job in LSYPE and BCS70)*

	LSYPE		BCS70	
Variables	Males uncertain	Females uncertain	Males uncertain	Females uncertain
Skilled	1.079	0.985	2.011**	1.994**
Semi and unskilled	1.109	0.933	3.376**	2.049**
Unemployed	1.281	1.101	1.168	2.278
Ethnicity (non-white)	1.072	1.399**	0.637	0.907
Maths z-score @ 10	1.023	1.200**	0.782	1.086
Reading z-score @ 10	0.877*	0.736**	0.890	0.862
High parental expectations	0.763**	0.593**	0.571*	0.761
School motivation	0.824**	0.805**	0.333**	0.527**
Perceived ability	0.751**	0.780**	0.533**	0.670**
Useful career advice	0.957	0.852**	0.849	0.868
Pseudo R^2	0.065	0.077	0.273	0.134
Observations	1,972	2,007	764	1,211

Notes: Estimated odds ratio using logit model. Reference category "professional or managerial occupation." Asterisks * and ** indicate statistical significance at .05 and .01 level, respectively. Measurements of uncertainty in aspirations, math, and reading scores at age 10 are different in the datasets.

For career aspirations, parental occupational status was only associated with career uncertainty of young people in BCS70, not in LSYPE. This finding might reflect a general trend toward higher career aspirations in the more recent cohorts, regardless of parental occupational status (Schoon, 2010), or increasing career uncertainty, which cuts across all social classes (Blossfeld, 2005).

In terms of ethnicity, in LSYPE non-white cohort members were more certain regarding their educational aspirations than white cohort members, and in BCS70 non-white males were more certain than white males, although for females we did not find the same association. This finding resonates with previous research indicating higher educational aspirations, higher levels of school motivation, and a positive academic self-concept among ethnic minority pupils in the LSYPE cohort, and the marginalization of white males regarding educational attainment (Strand, 2007). Regarding occupational aspirations, however, we find that non-white females in LSYPE express greater uncertainty than white females, potentially indicating the need for occupational guidance especially for females from ethnic minority backgrounds (also given the negative associations between perceived usefulness of career guidance and uncertainty among females in LSYPE).

Table 7.4. *Odds ratio (standard error) for association of uncertainty in aspirations and NEET status in LSYPE and BCS70*

	LSYPE		BCS70	
Variables	Males	Females	Males	Females
Uncertain education aspirations vs. certainty high aspirations	1.267	1.306	3.462*	1.063
Controls	Yes	Yes	Yes	Yes
Observations	1,766	1,898	939	1,366
Uncertain career aspirations vs. certainty high aspirations	1.140	.880	4.183**	2.540*
Controls	Yes	Yes	Yes	Yes
Observations	1,972	2,007	655	1,113

Notes: Estimated parameters using logit model. Models for uncertainty in educational aspirations and uncertainty in career aspirations estimated separately. Asterisks * and ** indicate statistical significance at .05 and .01 level, respectively. Measurements of uncertainty in aspirations are different in the datasets. Control variables include parental social background, math and reading skills, parental education expectations, school motivation, perceived ability and usefulness of career advice.

Later outcomes of uncertain aspirations

As shown in Table 7.4, taking into account the control variables, uncertainty in career aspirations was associated with a higher likelihood of NEET for male and female cohort members born in 1970. This result is consistent with the findings by Yates et al. (2011). We further find that young males in BCS70 who were uncertain about pursuing higher education were over 3 times more likely to spend time in NEET than male cohort members who had high, certain educational aspirations, while for females in BCS70 this association was not significant (perhaps because they were more likely to be teenage parents, as pointed out by Bynner & Parsons, 2002). For LSYPE there were no negative consequences of uncertain educational or career aspirations either for males or females over and above the control variables included in the model.

There are a number of possible explanations for this finding. First, there is the age difference when questions about career aspirations were asked in the two cohorts (age 16 in BCS70 and age 14 in LSYPE). At age 16, there may be more detrimental consequences for young people in BCS70 who are uncertain about their educational or career paths. At age 13/14, however, young people in LSYPE may not be facing any critical junctures in terms of their immediate decision making, and they might have changed their aspirations as they came closer to school leaving age. Second, the differences in findings might reflect the different socio-historical context of the two age cohorts. Young men and women in BCS70 reached the end of compulsory schooling at the height of a major economic recession, while in LSYPE they reached the same milestone just before the economic crisis of 2008, and hence might have had more training or employment opportunities after leaving school early. Furthermore, it could be that for the later-born cohort the process of career exploration has become more prolonged, especially given the generally extended education participation of young people.

Gender differences

Our findings reveal several gender differences. First, males expressed more uncertainty in their educational aspirations than females in both cohorts, and males expressed more uncertainty in their career aspirations than females in LSYPE. Furthermore, the negative consequences of educational and career uncertainty were worse for males than females in BCS70. These findings suggest that males in general may be more susceptible to uncertainty in their aspirations than females.

While low perceptions of ability were a significant predictor of uncertainty for males and females in both cohorts, low levels of school motivation, which was associated with more uncertainty in educational aspirations among young people in BCS70, also appeared to matter for the educational certainty of males but not females in LSYPE. Despite mean-level differences, perceptions of ability appear to be equally important for certainty in aspirations for both males and females, while school motivation appears to be more significant for the educational aspirations of males, especially in the more recently born cohort. This finding suggests that compared to young males, young females today are more likely to be engaged and motivated in school regardless of their future educational plans. Nevertheless, school motivation was a significant factor for both males and females in both cohorts regarding certainty in their career aspirations.

In addition, there was also a gender-diverse pattern related to math and reading test scores. As established in previous studies, males generally had higher average math scores than females, while females generally had higher average reading scores than males (Else-Quest et al., 2010; Hyde, 2007; Maccoby, 2000). Interestingly, good reading ability was significantly associated with less uncertainty in educational aspirations for boys and girls in BCS70 and less uncertainty for boys in LSYPE. High math ability, on the other hand, was significantly associated with less uncertainty in educational aspirations but only among girls in BCS70. Similar findings were found regarding career aspirations: while good reading ability was significantly associated with less uncertainty for boys and girls in LSYPE, high math ability was associated with greater uncertainty for girls in LSYPE only. This may suggest that females who are high-achievers in math may have more uncertainty regarding which careers they should pursue which may have implications for STEM subjects. Although not entirely consistent across both cohorts and aspirations, after taking into account the other variables in the model, math appears more significant for females than for males in the later born cohort in making their career decisions, while regarding education aspirations among males in the later born cohort reading appears to be more important. This finding suggests an interesting twist to previous studies examining gender differences in math and English attainment, ability concepts, and their implications for career aspirations (Marsh, Trautwein, Lüdtke, Köller, & Baumert, 2005; Marsh & Yeung, 1998; Moller, Pohlmann, Köller, & Marsh, 2009).

Career advice was also found to be associated with less uncertainty for females in LSYPE only. Females who perceived advice from teachers and Connexions as useful were less likely to report uncertainty in their career aspirations. Although not causal, this finding provides some reassurance that policies providing specialized career advice are useful for the career aspirations for females at least. On the other hand, the lack of significance for males in LSYPE and males and females in BCS70 potentially suggests the need for more appropriate guidance regarding educational and occupational opportunities for young people who do not intend to pursue an academic career. However, as this measure is based on the young person's perceptions of the usefulness of career advice, we cannot claim that either the presence or absence of career advice was (or was not) associated with certainty in their aspirations.

Interestingly, non-white females were more likely to be uncertain about their career aspirations than white females in LSYPE. In interpreting this finding, it has to be kept in mind that the sample for LSYPE has been oversampled for minority ethnic groups (33%). Although further analysis is needed to explore the differences in aspirations that have been found among minority ethnic groups in LSYPE (see Strand, 2007, for example), our finding may reflect issues of stereotypic gender roles that hinder females of certain ethnic groups from striving for traditionally male-dominated work roles (see Gutman & Akerman, 2008), and potentially the need for specific career advice to overcome cultural and gendered stereotypes.

Limitations and conclusions

There are many strengths of our research, among which are the large-scale national representative datasets, their longitudinal nature, and the possibility to measure uncertainty in aspirations as well as outcomes for young people. However, the limitations concern the fact that our measurements of uncertainty were not directly comparable between the two age cohorts, as they were collected at different ages and with different questions. In addition, BCS70 contains missing item responses, which in our case were dealt with by mean imputation for continuous variables and additional dummy categories for categorical variables.

Another potential limitation is the use of only one group of young people as a comparison group, those with high, certain aspirations. To remedy this, we also examined differences in background factors and associated outcomes between young people who were uncertain and those who had low and certain aspirations, for example, not wanting to continue into higher education or aspiring to a semi-skilled or unskilled occupation. In general, we found that young people who were uncertain about their educational and career plans had higher school motivation than those young people who were certain about leaving education. With one notable exception, however, we did not find any differences in the likelihood of NEET between those young people who were uncertain about their educational and career aspirations and those who had low, certain aspirations. In BCS70, young males who were uncertain about their job aspirations had a higher likelihood of NEET compared with young males who aspired to skilled occupations.

In conclusion, we find multiple and interlinked influences shaping uncertainty in aspirations among men and women. The findings suggest a vital role of socio-demographic background and individual resources, such as academic attainment, school motivation, and belief in one's own abilities, that are required to make decisions about one's future career. Those lacking in these resources are more likely to be uncertain about their futures, and potentially more at risk of negative outcomes, compared to those young people who hold certain aspirations. Males appear to be more susceptible to uncertainty than females. Furthermore, in the earlier-born cohort, the subsequent consequences regarding the experience of NEET are worse for males than for females. Regarding NEET, we could confirm the link between uncertainty in aspirations and negative outcomes in BCS70 only. It might be that LSYPE is not yet old enough to feel the negative consequences, as the majority are staying on in education, doing A-levels or some similar course at a school or college, compared to just over half of the BCS70 cohort. The recently born cohort might also be exploring their options and possibilities, especially when considering the higher percentage who expressed uncertain career aspirations as compared to the earlier-born cohort. Uncertainty about future career options has become more commonplace and therefore may even have beneficial consequences for certain adolescents (see Gutman & Schoon, 2012), although more evidence regarding longer-term outcomes is still required.

The evidence presented here calls for guidance especially for those young people who do not have the necessary resources for an academic career. Such guidance may wish to target males and females in different ways, given our findings. Females, for example, may benefit from increased support in math, or discussions about how best to use their math skills in various study options, occupations, or career tracks. Females may also profit from career mentorship and advice, especially those young women from some ethnic groups who may have fewer opportunities for career development and experience of guidance. Males, on the other hand, may benefit from encouraging school motivation and strengthening their reading ability. Future studies should also further examine the association between math and reading and maybe other domains (see Chow & Salmela-Aro; Wang & Kenny, this volume), gender differences in how these abilities are valued, and variations in how they determine later outcomes and potentially act as protective resources for girls and boys, respectively.

References

Appadurai, A. (2004). The capacity to aspire: Culture and the terms of recognition. In V. Rao & M. Walton (Eds.), *Culture and public action* (pp. 59–84). New York: Russell Sage Foundation.

Arnett, J. J. (2004). *Emerging adulthood: The winding road from the late teens through the twenties*. Oxford University Press.

Bandura, A., Barbaranelli, C., Caprara, G. V., & Pastorelli, C. (2001). Self-efficacy beliefs as shapers of children's aspirations and career trajectories. *Child Development*, 72, 187–206.

Blossfeld, H. P. (2005). *Globalization, uncertainty and youth in society*. London: Routledge.

Bynner, J. (2005). Rethinking the youth phase of the life course: The case for emerging adulthood. *Youth and Society*, 8, 367–384.

(2001). British youth transitions in comparative perspective. *Journal of Youth Studies*, 4, 5–23.

Bynner, J., & Parsons, S. (2002). Social exclusion and the transition from school to work: The case of young people not in employment education or training (NEET). *Journal of Vocational Behaviour*, 60, 289–309.

Clausen, J. A. (1993). *American lives: Looking back at the children of the Great Depression*. Berkeley: University of California Press.

Croll, P. (2009). Educational participation post-16: A longitudinal analysis of intentions and outcomes. *British Journal of Educational Studies*, 57(4), 400–416.

Croll, P., Attwood, G., Fuller, C., & Last, K. (2008). The structure and implications of children's attitudes to school. *British Journal of Educational Studies*, 56(4), 382–399.

Danziger, S., & Ratner, D. (2010). Labor market outcomes and the transition to adulthood. *The Future of Children*, 20, 133–158. doi:10.1353/foc.0.0041.

Danziger, S., & Rouse, C. (2007). *The price of young adulthood*. New York: Russell Sage Foundation.

Eccles, J. (2009). Who am I and what am I going to do with my life? Personal and collective identities as motivators of action. *Educational Psychologist*, 44(2), 78–89.

Eccles, J. S., & Wigfield, A. (2002). Motivational beliefs, values and goals. *Annual Review of Psychology 2002*, 53, 109–132.

Elliott, J., & Shepherd, P. (2006). Cohort profile of the 1970 British Birth Cohort (BCS70). *International Journal of Epidemiology*, 35, 836–843.

Else-Quest, N. M., Hyde, J. S., & Linn, M. C. (2010). Cross-national patterns of gender differences in mathematics: A meta-analysis. *Psychological Bulletin*, 136(1), 103–127.

Ferri, E., Bynner, J., & Wadsworth, M. (2003). *Changing Britain, changing lives: Three generations at the turn of the century*. London: Institute of Education.

Goldin, C., Katz, L., & Kuziemko, I. (2006). The homecoming of American college women: The reversal of the college gender gap. *The Journal of Economic Perspectives*, 20, 133–156.

Goodman, A., & Gregg, P. (2010). *Poorer children's educational attainment: How important are attitudes and behaviour?* York: Joseph Rowntree Foundation.

Gottfredson, L. S. (1981). Circumscription and compromise: A developmental theory of occupational aspirations. *Journal of Counseling Psychology (Monograph)*, 28, 545–579. doi: 10.1037/0022-0167.28.6.545.

Greene, W. (2008). *Econometric analysis* (6th ed.). Englewood Cliffs, NJ: Prentice Hall.

Gutman, L. M., & Akerman, R. (2008). *Determinants of aspirations*. London: Centre for Research on the Wider Benefits of Learning, Institute of Education.

Gutman, L. M., & Schoon, I. (2012). Uncertain career aspirations: Gender differences among adolescents living in England. *Journal of Vocational Behavior*, 80, 608–618.

Gutman, L. M., Schoon, I., & Sabates, R. (2012). Uncertain aspirations for continuing in education: Antecedents and associated outcomes. *Developmental Psychology*, 48, 1707–1718.

Hoggart, L., & Smith, D. I. (2004). *Understanding the impact of Connexions on young people at risk* (Research Report No. RR607). London: DfES.

Hyde, J. S. (2007). New directions in the study of gender similarities and differences. *Current Directions in Psychological Science*, 16, 259–263.

Jencks, C., Crouse, J., & Mueser, P. (1983). The Wisconsin model of status attainment: A national replication with improved measures of ability and aspiration. *Sociology of Education*, 56, 3–19.

Kalleberg, A. L., Reskin, B. F., & Hudson, K. (2000). Bad jobs in America: Standard and non-standard employment relations and job quality in the United States. *American Sociological Review*, 65(2), 256–278.

Kerckhoff, A. C. (2003). From student to worker. In J. T. Mortimer & M. Shanahan (Eds.), *Handbook of the life course* (pp. 251–267). New York: Kluwer Academic/Plenum Publishers.

Little, R. J. A., & Rubin, D. B. (2002). *Statistical analysis with missing data* (2nd ed.). Hoboken, NJ: Wiley.

Maccoby, E. E. (2000). Perspectives on gender development. *International Journal of Behavioral Development*, 24(4), 398–406.

Machin, S., & Vignoles, A. (2006). *Education policy in the UK*. London: The Centre for the Economics of Education. Retrieved from http://cee.lse.ac.uk/cee%20dps/ceedp57.pdf.

Marsh, H. W., Trautwein, U., Lüdtke, O., Köller, O., & Baumert, J. (2005). Academic self-concept, interest, grades, and standardized test scores: Reciprocal effects models of causal ordering. *Child Development*, 76(2), 397–416.

Marsh, H. W., & Yeung, A. S. (1998). Longitudinal structural equation models of academic self-concept and achievement: Gender differences in the development of math and English constructs. *American Educational Research Journal*, 35(4), 705–738.

Mau, W. C., & Bikos, L. H. (2000). Educational and vocational aspirations of minority and female students: A longitudinal study. *Journal of Counseling and Development*, 78, 186–194.

Mills, M., & Blossfeld, H. P. (2003). Globalization, uncertainty, and changes in early life courses. *Zeitschrift für Erziehungswissenschaft*, 6, 188–218.

Moller, J., Pohlmann, B., Köller, O., & Marsh, H. W. (2009). A meta-analytic path analysis of the internal/external frame of reference model of academic achievement and academic self-concept. *Review of Educational Research*, 79(3), 1129–1167.

Mortimer, J. T., Zimmer-Gembeck, M. J., Holmes, M., & Shanahan, M. J. (2002). The process of occupational decision making: Patterns during the transition to adulthood. *Journal of Vocational Behavior*, 61, 439–465.

Office for National Statistics. (2010, May). *Labour market statistics*. Retrieved from www.statistics.gov.uk/pdfdir/lmsuk0510.pdf.

Rhea, A., & Otto, L. B. (2001). Mothers' influences on adolescents' educational outcome beliefs. *Journal of Adolescent Research*, 16, 491–510.

Sacker, A., Schoon, I., & Bartley, M. (2002). Social inequality in educational achievement and psychosocial adjustment throughout childhood: Magnitude and mechanisms. *Social Science and Medicine*, 55, 863–880.

Schoon, I. (2006). *Risk and resilience: Adaptations in changing times*. Cambridge University Press.

(2010). Planning for the future: Changing education expectations in three British cohorts. *Historical Social Research*, 35(2), 99–119.

Schoon, I., Martin, P., & Ross, A. (2007). Career transitions in times of social change: His and her story. *Journal of Vocational Behaviour*, 70, 78–96.

Schoon, I., & Parsons, S. (2002). Teenage aspirations for future careers and occupational outcomes. *Journal of Vocational Behavior*, 60(2), 262–288.

Schnabel, K. U., Alfeld, C., Eccles, J. S., Köller, O., & Baumert, J. (2002). Parental influence on students' educational choices in the United States and Germany: Different ramifications – same effect? *Journal of Vocational Behavior*, 60(2), 178–198.

Sewell, W. H., & Hauser, R. M. (1975). *Education, occupation, and earnings: Achievement in the early career*. New York: Academic Press.

Staff, J., Harris, A., Sabates, R., & Briddell, L. (2010). Uncertainty in early occupational aspirations: Role exploration or aimlessness? *Social Forces*, 2, 659–683.

Standard Occupational Classification. (1991). *Social classifications and coding methodology* (Vol. 3). London: OPCS/HMSO.

Strand, S. (2007). *Minority ethnic pupils in the Longitudinal Study of Young People in England (LSYPE)* (Research Report No. RR002). London: Department for Children, Schools and Families (DCSF). Retrieved from www.dfes.gov.uk/research/data/uploadfiles/DCSF-RR002.pdf.

Vondracek, F. W., Lerner, R. M., & Schulenberg, J. E. (1983). The concept of development in vocational theory and intervention. *Journal of Vocational Behavior*, 23, 179–202.

Wigfield, A., Lutz, S. L., & Wagner, A. L. (2005). Early adolescents' development across the middle school years: Implications for school counselors. *Professional School Counseling*, 9, 112–119.

Wooldridge, J. W. (2002). *Econometric analysis of cross section and panel data*. Cambridge, MA: MIT Press.

Yates, S., Harris, A., Sabates, R., & Staff, J. (2011). Early occupational aspirations and NEETs: A study of the impact of uncertain and misaligned aspirations and social background on young people's entry into NEET status. *Journal of Social Policy*, 40(3), 513–534.

8 The challenges facing young women in apprenticeships

Alison Fuller and Lorna Unwin

Abstract

Participation in government-supported apprenticeship programs in the UK is characterized by stereotypical gender imbalances. This chapter draws on secondary data analysis of official statistics on young people's participation in vocational education and training (VET) and apprenticeship, and evidence from a study of the attitudes of 14- and 15-year-olds in England and Wales to the labor market. The discussion reveals the deep-rooted nature and continuing influence of gendered stereotypes in relation to what men and women can and cannot do in the world of work. This chapter argues that while patterns of take-up in apprenticeship mirror unequal conditions in the labor market and society more widely, initiatives in some European countries indicate that there are steps that can be taken to help young women gain access to occupations that provide better prospects in terms of pay and career progression.

Introduction

This chapter discusses the extent to which vocational education and training (VET) policies and practices, and particularly apprenticeships, perpetuate or help to alleviate the levels of gender segregation that can be found in the labor market. While it draws mainly on data from the United Kingdom (UK), the chapter raises questions that will be pertinent in many other countries. This chapter argues that while VET mirrors conditions in the labor market and wider society, and hence cannot of itself solve the gender segregation problem, there are steps that can be taken to support young women to enable them to gain access to and benefit from areas of VET that provide better prospects in terms of pay and career progression. At the same time, such steps will also be helpful for young men who aspire to careers in occupations traditionally regarded as "female."

As well as looking within the labor market for the causes of gender segregation, it is also necessary to consider the extent to which young people themselves reflect gendered attitudes toward their chosen pathways in life. Despite considerable advances in the life chances of women and the breaking down of barriers across the labor market, it is salutary to note how segregated some occupational

---

The preparation of this chapter was supported by the ESRC LLAKES Centre – grant reference RES-594-28-0001.

areas remain. Part of this chapter draws on data from a study (Beck, Fuller, & Unwin, 2006a, 2006b) of the attitudes of 14- and 15-year-olds in England and Wales toward the labor market in order to demonstrate the deep-rooted nature and continuing influence of gendered stereotypes in relation to what men and women can and cannot do in the world of work. Much of the literature on the gendered nature of education and training and career choice focuses on the social justice dimension, but in this chapter we also raise an economic argument. If young men and women continue to be reluctant to cross gender lines when it comes to forging their employment trajectories, it could be argued that employers are missing out on potential talent.

There is a new urgency to the problem of gender segregation in VET in the UK as a result of: (a) legislative change, and (b) the current economic crisis. At the moment, young people can leave school at 16 and enter the labor market. New legislation brought in under the previous Labour government, however, means that in 2013 young people will be required to remain in some form of education or officially recognized training until the age of 17, and this will rise to 18 in 2015. Recent provisional figures for England (DfE Statistical First Release (SFR), June 2012) indicate that by the end of 2011 about a third (32.8%) of 16-year-olds enter some form of VET (either work-based training or a full-time course leading to a vocational qualification at Levels 1, 2, or 3) after completing compulsory schooling and a further 0.5% enter jobs (and are not registered on government-supported training programs). At age 17, 34.8% are in VET and 2.5% enter jobs, while at age 18, the proportion in VET provision falls to 23.8%, with a far higher proportion, 15.8%, going into jobs. The proportion of young people (aged 16–18) classed as NEET (not in education, employment, or training) was 8.1% in 2011. In order to achieve the goal of ensuring that all young people remain in some form of officially recognized education or training to the age of 18, policymakers will need to look to VET to absorb the increased participation. Without significant attempts to break down current forms of gender segregation in VET, however, the raising of the participation age could further disadvantage young women. The continued consequences of and fall-out from the recent economic crisis must also be taken into account. Since 2008, youth unemployment among 16- to 24-year-olds has risen dramatically in the UK (standing at just over one million; ONS August 2012) and may rise further as a consequence of the planned cuts to public-sector expenditure. Female-dominated areas of the labor market such as health and social care and childcare will be hit hard by the reduction in public-sector jobs.

Women and the labor market

As we argued at the start of this chapter, the issues we are raising are common across many countries. Occhionero and Nocenzi (2009), in their recent review of employment structures in the European Union (EU), note that "structural factors and cultural stereotypes still contribute to a 'gender divide' in the workplace" (p. 155). Drawing on data from the most recent report from the Commission of the European Communities (2009), the following points indicate that, although women continue to perform better in general in education than men, they have a less privileged position in the labor market:

Employment

- Female employment in the EU stands at 58.3% (up from 51.1% in 1997), but varies from 36.9% to 73.2% between Member States.
- The average gap in employment rates between women and men is narrowing (from 17.1 percentage points in 2000 to 14.2 points in 2007), but this gap is doubled in the case of women with children under the age of 12.
- The percentage of women employees working part-time was 31.2% in 2007, 4 times the male rate – more than six million EU women in the 25 to 49 age group say they are obliged not to work or to work only part-time because of their family responsibilities.
- Occupational and sectoral segregation has remained almost unchanged in most Member States over the last few years, indicating that the increase in female employment has taken place in sectors (particularly service sectors) already dominated by women. There is a persistent gender pay gap across the countries of the EU (17.4% on average).

One positive and seemingly contradictory statistic (in light of the above picture) comes from Eurostat (2008) data for 2003, which suggests that women (aged 25–64) do, however, have the edge over men in relation to continuing training once in employment – 23% compared to 19% of men. Similarly, data from the UK records that women in full-time jobs are more likely to receive training than their male colleagues, though women in part-time jobs still have fewer opportunities than men. However, the sustainability of this picture is challenged by the reduction in public-sector employment. This is because the incidence of training and development is generally higher in the public than in the private sector, and female employees in the public sector have been beneficiaries of this factor (Davies, Gore, Shury, Vivian, & Winterbotham, 2012).

The growth in female employment has to be placed in the context of continued horizontal segregation (jobs concentrated in certain industries and occupations) and vertical segregation (women restricted to certain levels). Yet, despite this reality, research suggests that the career aspirations of girls have been rising. A recent study of the career plans of high school students in OECD countries shows that "girls are determined to enter many occupations formerly thought of as strongly preferred by boys," and hence "the traditional perceptions of the gender-typed occupational choices have ceased being an accurate representation of what young women aspire to" (Sikora & Saha, 2009, p. 399). The authors note, however, the dangers of girls aiming too high (in contrast to boys who will opt for more vocationally oriented careers) as they will eventually confront the realities of gender differentiation in the labor market.

Research shows that the greater the level of women's education, the more likely they are to participate in the labor market; an effect that is much stronger for women than men. A significant recent paper exploring gender inequality in the Netherlands, Sweden, and the United States has found that less educated women are less likely to enter paid work (Evertsson et al., 2009). The authors argue that women with more education can get better-paid, more meaningful and interesting jobs because, crucially, they have more exposure, through education, to "gender-egalitarian ideologies." This has major implications for VET as in most countries girls and young women (and their male peers) have limited exposure to debates about gender equality in relation to vocational training opportunities.

Apprenticeship and gender segregation in the UK

Apprenticeship, involving both males and females, has a long history in the UK, stretching back to medieval times when craft guilds were formed in a range of occupations to both protect their skills and knowledge and train new entrants to ensure continuity and development. In relation to this chapter, the contemporary manifestation of apprenticeship took shape in 1994 when the then Conservative government under the Prime Minister, John Major, decided that the State should play a much bigger role in the organization and funding of apprenticeships. This followed long-standing concerns about the relatively small number of people in the UK with intermediate (technician-level) skills as compared with other advanced industrial countries. To address this, the Major government introduced the "Modern Apprenticeship" (MA). This was aimed at 16- to 24-year-olds and was positioned as a Level 3 (intermediate/technician) program (see Unwin & Wellington, 2001).[1]

The use of the term "apprenticeship" was a deliberate attempt to set the new program apart from existing "youth training" schemes, which had struggled to shake off an image of low quality (Gospel & Fuller, 1998). Importantly for this chapter, the use of the term "modern" was also chosen to signal that this new form of apprenticeship would break through the gendered nature of apprenticeship up to that point. The MA would be available to young women as well as young men, and would achieve this by being available in a much greater range of

---

[1] The education system in the UK is organized in "levels," with Level 1 as entry level, Level 2 as five good grades (or vocational equivalent) at General Certificate of Secondary Education (GCSE) (examination taken by 16-year-olds), Level 3 as two A-level passes (or vocational equivalent), Level 4 and 5 as sub-bachelor degree level, and Level 6 as bachelor degree level.

occupations (e.g., retail, business, and administration) than had previously been the case for apprenticeship. After the New Labour government came to power in 1997, it decided to abandon the previous government's policy and rebranded all youth training schemes as "Apprenticeships," thus encompassing existing Level 2 programs, and extending the age limit to beyond 24, as well as introducing a "Young Apprenticeship" program for 14- to 16-year-olds. Since the May 2010 General Election, the Coalition Government has further increased government support for post-16 Apprenticeships, although in March 2011, the Department for Education (DfE) announced the withdrawal of the Young Apprenticeship program from September 2011. Apprenticeship is the responsibility of the UK's devolved administrations.

In England, the following levels of "apprenticeship" are currently available for 16- to 24-year-olds and for people over the age of 24:

- Higher Apprenticeship (UK qualification Level 4/5/6)
- Advanced Apprenticeship (UK qualification Level 3)
- Intermediate Apprenticeship (UK qualification Level 2)

The vast majority of apprentices are pursing either the Level 2 or 3 program. Just under 3 out of 10 (29%) apprenticeship starters were in the 16 to 18 age group, 31% were aged 19 to 24, and the remaining 40% were in the 25 and over age group (DfE, February 2012). The age profile of those starting apprenticeships has changed dramatically in the past few years. In 2004/2005, the first year to include apprentices aged 25 or over, less than 1% of starts were in this age group, but 6 years later (2010/2011) the proportion had risen to 40%. Within that same period the number of apprenticeship starts rose strongly from 189,000 to 457,200.

We have published critiques and analyses of the contemporary manifestation of apprenticeship in the UK (see, inter alia, Fuller & Unwin, 2003, 2008, 2009, 2011). In order to concentrate on the gender dimension in this chapter, we now provide a contemporary picture of the segregated nature of government-supported apprenticeship. For the first time in 2010/2011, the figures indicated that the majority of those starting an apprenticeship were female. After hovering at about 49% for several years, the increase in the female share of apprenticeship starts rose strongly to 54% in 2010/2011 (DfE, February 2012).

Apprenticeships are available in over 150 occupational sectors, but two thirds are in 12 sectors. Table 8.1 presents the 10 sectors with the highest number of apprentices starting their program in 2008/2009 and 2010/2011, and the proportion of starts that are female. The period covers the 3 years since around the beginning of the economic crisis.

It can be seen from Table 8.1 that while the traditional craft sectors (engineering and construction) are still available, the presence of the other sectors reflects the major shift in the British economy from manufacturing to services. The table shows that the number of people starting apprenticeships in the service sectors has grown dramatically since 2008–2009, while the number of starts in the

Table 8.1. Starts in the 10 most populated apprenticeship sectors by gender (England 2008/2009–2010/2011)

Sector framework	2008–2009 Female	% female (rounded)	2010–2011 Total starts	Female	% female (rounded)	Total starts (position in 2010–2011 top 10 in brackets)
Customer Service	15,520	69	22,500	33,380	62	53,970 (1)
Business Administration	16,810	93	18,100	29,710	76	38,900 (4)
Children's Care	16,730	97	17,200	25,730	94	27,410 (7)
Construction	270	2	16,800	230	1	15,590 (10)
Hospitality	9,080	54	16,800	15,300	51	29,810 (5)
Hairdressing	14,620	90	16,200	15,030	91	16,450 (9)
Engineering	430	3	15,300	940	5	18,330 (8)
Health and Social Care	10,600	86	12,300	44,320	83	53,720 (2)
Retail	7,240	66	10,900	28,030	68	41,410 (3)
Management	6,110	62	9,900	17,740	60	29,790 (6)
Total	97,410	61	158,700	210,410	65	325,380

Source: Fuller and Davey (2010) for 2008/2009 starts and from SFR February 2012 for 2010/2011 starts.

Table 8.2. *Percentage of female apprentices in five sectors*

Sector framework	2002–2003 female (%)	2010–2011 female (%)
Construction	1	1
Early Years (childcare)	97	94
Engineering	4	5
Information Technology	15	12
Plumbing	1	2

traditional sectors has remained more constant. The growth in female apprentices is a direct result of this shift. However, while the majority of apprentices are now female, the distribution across the sectors remains a major area of concern. Despite some reduction in the size of the gender imbalance in several of the service sectors since 2008–2009, female apprentices are still much more likely to be found in the service sectors where pay, qualification levels, and career prospects tend to be lower (Fuller & Davey, 2010). Their participation in male-dominated sectors remains very low. In 2003, the UK's Equal Opportunities Commission (EOC) launched a General Formal Investigation (GFI) into the gender segregation in apprenticeship in England, focusing on five sectors. Table 8.2 shows the percentage of female apprentices in these five sectors for 2002/2003 and for 2010/2011.

The findings presented in Table 8.2 show that little progress has been made in changing gender-stereotypical participation in the five occupational sectors that were included in the EOC's GFI nearly 10 years ago. Two sectors, plumbing and engineering, indicate a slightly increasing female share, although this is from a very low base. In the case of IT, it is difficult to make an accurate comparison because of changes in the relevant frameworks. Given the benefits (career prospects and financial) associated with those employed in sectors dominated by male participation, there is a strong equity case renewing efforts to reduce the gender imbalance. The lack of males participating in childcare apprenticeships continues to reflect deep-seated concerns in society about the risks (e.g., relating to potential child abuse) involved (Beck et al., 2006b), as well as wider issues relating to the status and salaries accruing to childcare workers.

Recent work by Fuller and Davey (2010) for the Equality and Human Rights Commission's Triennial Review has focused on gender participation in apprenticeship in Scotland and Wales. In Scotland, government-supported apprenticeship is still called the Modern Apprenticeship and at the time of Fuller and Davey's research remained as only a Level 3 program.[2] The majority of participants are males aged 16 to 19. Participation in the MA in Scotland is more male

---

[2] Scotland now offers four levels of Modern Apprenticeship from Level 2 through to Level 5; more information is available at www.skillsdevelopmentscotland.co.uk/our-services/modern-apprenticeships/ma-frameworks.aspx.

Table 8.3. *Modern Apprenticeship Scotland: 16–19, top 11 frameworks and gender – in training, 2008–2009*

Sector framework	Age 16–19 (n)	Female share (%)
Construction	6,432	1
Engineering	3,059	2
Electrotechnical	2,585	1
Plumbing	1,507	1
Business Administration	902	91
Early Years Care	784	99
Hospitality	387	46
Customer Service	371	67
Hairdressing	333	95
Health and Social Care	71	87
Management	43	35

Source: Fuller and Davey (2010).

Table 8.4. *Modern Apprenticeship Scotland: aged 20+, top 11 frameworks and gender – in training, 2008–2009*

Sector framework	Age 20+ (n)	Female share (%)
Construction	1,212	3
Electrotechnical	651	1
Engineering	568	3
Management	373	47
Plumbing	268	2
Health and Social Care	251	85
Hospitality	239	46
Early Years Care	168	98
Business Administration	87	87
Customer Service	54	67
Hairdressing	38	95

Source: Fuller and Davey (2010).

dominated than the Advanced Apprenticeship in England. This is because the largest apprenticeship sectors in Scotland are construction, electrotechnical, engineering, and plumbing – all sectors traditionally dominated by males. Tables 8.3 and 8.4 present participation by sector, age group, and gender.

In Wales, government-supported apprenticeship is currently available to those aged 16 and over at Levels 2, 3, and 4/5, known as the Foundation Apprenticeship, Apprenticeship, and Higher Apprenticeship, respectively. At the time of Fuller and Davey's research the majority of apprentices (60%) in Wales were participating in the Foundation Apprenticeship. In contrast with Scotland, the majority of apprentices are female (54%) and a minority of all apprentices are aged 16 to 19. Data on apprenticeship and gender and other equality groups in Wales is

Table 8.5. *Sector subject area by MA/FMA and gender in Wales (2007–2008)*

Sector subject area	MA	Female share N	%	FMA N	Female share N	%
Retailing and Customer Service	1,230	875	71	4,910	3,240	66
Leisure, Sport, and Travel	375	145	39	510	185	36
Hospitality	670	360	54	2,085	1,310	63
Hair and Beauty	500	465	93	1,495	1,365	91
Health Care and Public Services	4,835	4,000	83	5,700	4,950	87
Media and Design	30	25	83	*	*	
Agriculture	155	30	19	305	55	18
Construction	2,205	25	1	3,215	75	2
Engineering	2,410	70	3	1,480	135	9
Manufacturing	95	35	37	2,145	485	22
Transportation	35	*		180	5	3
Management and Professional	2,290	1,395	61	850	465	55
Business Administration	3,185	2,475	78	3,885	2,695	69
Sector Unknown/Not Confirmed	270	5	2	680	100	15
Total	18,275	9,885	54	27,410	15,070	55

* The data is "disclosive or not sufficiently robust for publication" (see Fuller & Davey, 2010).
Source: Fuller and Davey (2010).

only available by broad sector subject areas rather than by sector frameworks as in Scotland and England.[3] This means that the percentage share for females in Wales cannot be compared directly with the figures presented for the other two countries (see Table 8.5). Nonetheless, the pattern of gender imbalance across sectors in Wales is similar to that in Scotland and England.

Qualifications, pay, and career prospects

It could be argued that the sectoral/occupational gender segregation found in contemporary apprenticeships simply reflects the realities of the labor market. There are, however, three significant reasons why we should be concerned about this continued situation. First, there is the issue of apprenticeship wages. In the UK, apprentices aged 16 to 18 are not eligible for the minimum

---

[3] See www.statswales.wales.gov.uk.

wage, but employers are required to pay them and 19-year-olds in the first year of their apprenticeship a minimum of £2.65 an hour (from October 1, 2012). This rate falls below the threshold for National Insurance contributions, which means that apprentices are not eligible for statutory sick pay or statutory maternity pay. Recent data for apprenticeship pay shows that, while the median pay gap between men and women for the whole economy in April 2007 was 11%, for apprentices it was 21% (Fong & Phelps, 2007). The average pay for male apprentices was £186 compared to £147 for females. In the two highest-paid sectors (electrotechnical and engineering manufacture), the vast majority of apprentices were males, whereas in the three lowest-paid sectors (hairdressing, health and social care, and early childcare and early years education), the vast majority of apprentices were female. In the electrotechnical sector, the average net pay in 2007 was £210 a week, compared to £109 a week in hairdressing. Fong and Phelps (2007) also found evidence that, within some sectors, some female apprentices were paid less than their male peers, and hairdressing and childcare, both female dominated, had the highest rates (11%) of underpayment of apprentices.

In addition to being financially disadvantaged, women are also more likely to be restricted to sectors where it is difficult to progress. The service sectors, where women dominate, tend to offer far more Level 2 than Level 3 apprenticeships. To progress beyond Level 2 can be difficult in sectors where less value is placed on qualifications and where the vocational knowledge being deployed is less codified and the skills tend to be regarded as "soft" or "interpersonal" and hence equated with so-called feminine attributes (e.g., Evans, 2006; Faulkner, 2000). In the UK, Level 3 is important in that it can provide access to advanced further education and, critically, to higher education. This is a complicated picture due to the way in which vocational (and particularly competence-based qualifications) and academic (general education) qualifications are currently structured in the UK, but the point here is that apprentices in certain sectors are in danger of not acquiring the level and type of qualification that will enable them to progress both educationally and in the labor market (Fuller & Unwin, 2012).

Young people's attitudes to apprenticeship and their career prospects

As part of the EOC's investigation of gender segregation in apprenticeship, we carried out research with 14- and 15-year-olds in schools in England and Wales, with employers who were recruiting and training apprentices, and with other key informants associated with apprenticeships and the transition of young people from education to the labor market. We conducted the research using both quantitative and qualitative methods (see Beck et al., 2006a, 2006b; Fuller, Beck, & Unwin, 2005a). In England, we conducted a telephone survey of 162 employers, a questionnaire survey of 1,281 14- and 15-year-olds in eight schools, eight focus groups – one per school – and two group "events" with a sample of employers, training providers, and young people.

The research revealed the deep-rooted nature of the stereotypical attitudes still held by young people. The following quotations are indicative of the young people's responses when asked why they thought "male jobs" were better paid:

> ... because they put more work in, the work is more physical. They are totally different jobs, so they should be paid better. (Male student)
>
> ... cos it's more technical stuff you need to learn ... whereas more caring stuff you don't need ... to learn ... but it's more sort of inside you as well, it's more built in to you so they don't pay you much. (Female student)

These views were reinforced by the attitudes of some of the employers we interviewed, as the following comment illustrates:

> We want someone who's got ... not exactly plumbing in their blood but real enthusiasm. (Plumbing employer)

The implication here is that the employer would think it more likely that a young man, perhaps with relatives in plumbing, would have plumbing "in his blood." A vocational teacher emphasized the importance of generational attitudes: "they're very strong family traditions with fathers, sons, uncles, brothers all going into the family business."

The young people in our research were able to articulate the strength of deep-rooted gender stereotyping, but also spoke about the realities of actually crossing gender lines. The survey responses showed that the majority of girls and boys agreed with the statement that apprenticeship is "equally suited to boys and girls." Asked if they would consider entering non-traditional jobs, the majority of girls (80%) and boys (55%) said yes. In the focus groups, they also said that they would consider taking an apprenticeship in a non-traditional sector, but were not actually doing this because they did not want to. This raises the intriguing paradox that, on the one hand, young people believe they have the freedom to make a radical choice, but they stop short of actually doing so by justifying the choice they make as being based on what they really want. This suggests that despite their seemingly confident and assertive sense of having the autonomy to choose, ultimately they retreat back into traditional gendered pathways. Part of the problem lies with the limited provision in UK schools and colleges of careers advice and guidance, and of opportunities to discuss and debate the roles of men and women in society and equal opportunities more generally.

Many pupils, but particularly boys, held gender-stereotyped attitudes toward a range of occupations, although they regarded some occupations and jobs as being much less stereotyped (e.g., teacher, shop worker, police officer). In the focus groups, girls and boys spoke of their fears about crossing gender lines, but boys were much more cautious: 63% of boys (37% of girls) agreed that "as a young person you don't want to stand out from the crowd by doing a job normally done by the opposite sex." Boys were worried about being teased, especially about their sexuality, if they trained for a traditionally female occupation (see also Simpson, 2004). One girl captured the fears of her male peers:

Government	Increase participation targets
Schools	Keep majority of young people in full-time education
Training providers	Meet quotas/fill places
Connexions (careers service)	Reduce NEET figures
Job Centre Plus (employment agency)	Place people in jobs
Employers	To recruit as needed
Parents	"Do what's right for my child"

Figure 8.1 *Key stakeholder priorities*

> It's like if you had a 20 year old [boy] ... being like a child minder or like looking after 2 year olds or something, all his friends would be like "ha ha ha look at you looking after all these little people" ... and you don't like talk to anyone and you don't get out enough and stuff you're like a wuss and stuff and they make you feel stupid.

Our respondents said they would be more inclined to try out non-traditional occupations if:

- they received extra money to train;
- the pay rates were better;
- there was an opportunity (through "tasters") to try out working and training in non-traditional sectors before making a commitment;
- more of their sex made the same choice.

One of the most striking findings from our research was that none of the stakeholders in the education and training system in the UK appeared to have ultimate responsibility for tackling gender segregation in VET or education more generally. In Figure 8.1, we identify the range of key stakeholders in a position to influence and guide young people's decision making and indicate the main priority for each of these groups. The figure shows different primary concerns for each stakeholder and that challenging gender segregation is not the priority for any of them.

Tackling gender segregation

In order to help both girls and boys aspire to non-traditional areas of work (and, crucially, to select corresponding VET programs), research suggests that they need to be exposed to gender-awareness activities as early as possible in their school (possibly preschool) careers. A review of gender-related work in UK primary schools found that a range of mixed strategies could be effective: single-sex settings help to increase the self-confidence of girls and/or encourage them to experiment with non-gender-traditional activities; or to provide a setting for boys to tackle aspects of traditional forms of masculine attitudes and behavior; while mixed groups encouraged cross-gender friendships (EPPI, 2002). It also found that teachers could reduce stereotypical curriculum preferences, particularly with younger children, and could confront stereotypical attitudes and behavior through discussion and awareness of the perspectives of the opposite sex.

A Danish EQUAL project (Youth, Gender, and Career) was deliberately aimed at intervening at an early stage when young people "dream" about their future careers.[4] Courses were run for parents of students in years 7 to 10 (ages 12 to 16) of lower secondary school. They provided parents with information on current and future labor market trends and prospects to encourage them to adjust their stereotyped approaches to both work and educational choices. Parents and children filled in forms about their attitudes to gender stereotyping and these were used to trigger "family discussions" about each other's expectations. Similarly, in a Spanish EQUAL project in Barcelona, it was decided to introduce guidance and anti-stereotyping methods as early as kindergarten and primary school.

Young people are rational human beings and base their decisions on what Hodkinson, Sparkes, and Hodkinson (1996) usefully called their "horizons for action." In asking girls and boys (or even adults) to consider breaking through the deep-rooted gender stereotyping of occupations, it is presumed they will be prepared to take risks. In a review of young people's attitudes to gender equality and balance in 2000, Tinklin, Croxford, Ducklin, and Frame (2005) concluded that they did understand the equal opportunities message and believed that males and females should have the same opportunities and expectations in their future work and family lives. They were, however, very conscious of continuing inequalities, which they saw in the world around them and in their personal lives.

The career choices and perceptions of young people are influenced by a range of actors, including parents, siblings, friends, teachers, and careers officers. Friends appear to be particularly important, while the role of careers guidance practitioners can be overestimated. The media and the Internet also play an important role in the formation of young people's attitudes. These attitudes are often formed, however, in the absence of robust information about the realities of contemporary occupations and workplaces. To counter this, it is important to:

---

[4] The EU-funded EQUAL program "focused on supporting innovative, transnational projects aimed at tackling discrimination and disadvantage in the labour market. These projects were created to generate and test new ideas with the aim of finding new ways of fighting all forms of discrimination and inequality within and beyond the labour market." This included a focus on improving gender equality. For more information, including the results for participating Member States, go to: http://ec.europa.eu/employment_social/equal_consolidated/index.html (accessed August 23, 2012).

- bring "role models" (adults working in non-traditional roles) into schools and colleges to show young people that, for example, there are female engineers and construction workers, as well as male carers and hairdressers;
- develop work experience (or "taster") opportunities that allow young people to try out non-traditional jobs;
- develop short programs that allow young people to sample different types of apprenticeships;
- encourage schools and colleges to use their partnerships with employers to ensure teachers and careers guidance practitioners are up-to-date with their knowledge of the world of work (see Francis, Osgood, Dalgety, & Archer, 2005).

It is clear that the strategies listed above should be brought together so that a holistic package of methods can be delivered. A German EQUAL project, in an area of the country that has seen considerable economic change, has introduced a multilevel strategy aimed at girls and young women: vocational information and guidance workshops at the end of lower secondary school; a training scheme for teachers to support them in encouraging non-traditional vocational choices; coaching and mentoring for female apprentices in technical occupations; and a program to help trainers to provide optimal support to trainees. Similarly, an innovative EQUAL project in the Netherlands sought to reach out beyond educational settings and use television to target men and boys through the use of commercials.

Although many of the initiatives referred to above can have an impact on young people's attitudes, they can often be seen as tangential to the main areas of their school or college activity, and they will not, necessarily, extend beyond the classroom. A particularly innovative approach has been taken in an EQUAL project in Barcelona. This involved the development of a curriculum approach in primary and secondary schools to challenge traditional gender roles. Gender issues were not "taught," but introduced through household processes (e.g., cooking, baking, or ironing) to explain certain phenomena in chemistry and physics. The project reports how boys realized the value of unpaid female work and the need for men to accept more responsibilities at home. Female pupils saw science as a possible career choice.

In many countries, schools and colleges are expected to take responsibility for ensuring they promote social inclusion and cohesion agendas. A review of gender equality in Scottish schools (Condie & Kane, 2006) highlighted the way in which, ironically, consideration of gender issues can become marginalized within a broader inclusion agenda. This is where a whole-curriculum approach could be valuable so that the discussion of gender issues takes a natural place within teaching and learning more generally. The needs and concerns of teachers are, of course, central to such developments. The Scottish Review found that teachers responded much more positively to tackling gender inequality when they had a degree of ownership over the development of gender-awareness strategies and were supported by practical guidance and advice.

Conclusions

Despite the considerable attention in both policy making (at all levels) and the research literature that has addressed and continues to address gender equality and balance, there are no systematic international, comparative reviews of how to tackle inequality in education and training. The closest we have to an international overview are the documents produced by the EQUAL (2005) projects, which form part of the EU's strategy "for more and better jobs and for ensuring that no-one is denied access to them" and co-funds projects in all EU Member States. Since they began in 2001, some EQUAL projects have included a focus on young people's career decision making (see EQUAL, 2005, for a summary of evidence). In most cases, initiatives to encourage young people to consider non-traditional occupations form part of a broader project. While European and other countries have different education and training systems preparing young people for the transition into work, they all need to address the challenge of addressing gender inequalities. It would be very valuable if EQUAL could produce a separate report that distils the evidence related to the initiatives aimed at young people in a range of European countries and reflects on their generalizability across national systems. This would enable the lessons and ideas to be made more visible for policy makers and practitioners concerned with gender equality and balance in VET.

Even within countries, there is surprisingly little publicly available evidence of what initiatives have been effective. Most studies are based on small-scale, localized initiatives. While these are helpful in providing ideas for strategies, it is not possible to judge the extent to which they have a lasting influence as many are funded on a short-term basis. A further key problem is that there is hardly any evidence about strategies aimed specifically at boys and young men. Despite these problems, however, it is possible to highlight a number of strategies that appear to have some common currency across countries.

The evidence presented here indicates that overcoming gender inequalities and helping young people to change their attitudes to the choices they make in relation to both education and careers requires a multi-faceted, innovative, and sophisticated approach, beginning as early as possible and extending well into adult life. It requires the commitment and involvement of everyone in society, and continuous monitoring. Above all, young people's decisions need to be treated with respect for they often reflect an understanding of the realities of the world rather than ignorance. An EU Fifth Framework project (involving research in Germany, Finland, Greece, Portugal, and the UK), completed in 2004, offers important insights into these complexities (see Heidegger et al., 2004). The research explored the part played by gender in the vocational education and training experiences of young adults (aged 16–19 years) entering specific occupations in childcare, electrical engineering, food preparation, and service, and of older adults (e.g., women returners) changing occupations. It had a particular focus on studying the extent to which the development of key competences (and associated qualifications) in Europe plays a role in perpetuating gender imbalances;

the concern here is that so-called interpersonal competences are also often held to be "female skills." It found that both VET institutes and workplaces need to do a great deal to improve their performance in relation to gender equality and balance (see also Evans, 2006).

As far as apprenticeship is concerned, the challenge of gender segregation has and always will be considerable due to the continued segregation in the labor market. As the consequences of the current economic crisis continue to have an impact, this challenge will be even greater as government concentrates its efforts on trying to ensure apprenticeship places are available, regardless of whether they are equally accessible to men and women.

References

Beck, V., Fuller, A., & Unwin, L. (2006a). Safety in stereotypes? The impact of gender and "race" on young people's perceptions of their post-compulsory education and labour market opportunities. *British Educational Research Journal*, 32(5), 667–686.

Beck, V., & Unwin, L. (2006b). Increasing risk in the "scary" world of work? Male and female resistance to crossing gender lines in apprenticeships in England and Wales. *Journal of Education and Work*, 19(3), 271–289.

Commission of the European Communities. (2009). *Report from the Commission to the Council, the European Parliament, the European Economic and Social Committee and the Committee of the Regions: Equality between women and men, 2009*. Brussels: Commission of the European Communities.

Condie, R., & Kane, J. (2006). *Review of strategies to address gender inequalities in Scottish schools*. Insight 31. Edinburgh: Scottish Executive Education Department.

Davies, B., Gore, K., Shury, J., Vivian, D., & Winterbotham, M. (2012). *UK Commission's employer skills survey 2011*. Wath-on-Dearne and London: UK Commission for Employment and Skills.

Department for Education (DfE). (2012). *Participation in education, training and employment by 16–18 year olds in England* (SFR 12/2012). London: Department for Education.

The Data Service. (2010). *Post-16 education & skills: Learner participation, outcomes and level of highest qualification held* (DS/SFR6 March). Coventry: The Data Service.

EQUAL. (2005). *Success stories: Development partnerships working against discrimination and inequality in Europe*. Luxembourg: Office for Publications of the European Communities.

European Training Foundation (ETF). (2006). *Gender mainstreaming in education and employment*. Turin: European Training Foundation.

Eurostat. (2008). *The lives of women and men in Europe*. Luxembourg: Office for Publications of the European Communities.

Evans, K. (2006). Achieving equity through "gender autonomy": The challenges for VET policy and practice. *Journal of Vocational Education and Training*, 58(4), 393–408.

Evertsson, M., England, P., Mooi-Reci, I., Hermsen, J., de Bruijn, J., & Cotter, D. (2009). Is gender inequality greater at lower or higher educational levels? Common patterns in the Netherlands, Sweden, and the United States. *Social Politics: International Studies in Gender, State and Society,* 16(2), 210–241.

Evidence for Policy and Practice Information and Co-ordinating Centre (EPPI). (2002). *A systematic review of classroom strategies for reducing stereotypical gender constructions among girls and boys in mixed-sex UK primary schools.* London: Institute of Education.

Faulkner, W. (2000). Dualisms, hierarchies and gender in engineering. *Social Studies of Science,* 30, 759–792.

Fong, B., & Phelps, A. (2007). *Apprenticeship pay: 2007 survey of earnings by sector* (DIUS Research Report 08-05). London: Department for Innovation, Universities and Skills.

Francis, B., Osgood, J., Dalgety, J., & Archer, L. (2005). *Gender equality in work experience placements for young people* (Working Paper Series 27). Manchester: Equal Opportunities Commission.

Fuller, A., & Davey, G. (2010). *Equality groups and apprenticeship: Equality and Human Rights Commission Triennial Review* (Research Report). Retrieved from www.equalityhumanrights.com/uploaded_files/triennial_review/triennial_review_adult_learning.pdf.

Fuller, A., & Unwin, L. (2003). Creating a "modern apprenticeship": A critique of the UK's multi-sector, social inclusion approach. *Journal of Education and Work,* 16(1), 5–25.

(2008). *Towards expansive apprenticeships: A commentary for the ESRC's Teaching and Learning Programme.* London: Institute of Education.

(2009). Change and continuity in apprenticeship: The resilience of a model of learning. *Journal of Education and Work,* 22(5), 405–416.

(2011). Vocational education and training in the spotlight: Back to the future for the UK's coalition government? *London Review of Education,* 9(2), 191–204.

(2012). *Banging on the door of the university: The complexities of progression from apprenticeship and other vocational programmes in England* (Monograph No. 14). Retrieved from www.skope.ox.ac.uk/sites/default/files/Monograph%2014.pdf.

Fuller, A., Beck, V., & Unwin, L. (2005a). *Employers, young people and gender segregation (England)* (Working Paper Series No. 28). Manchester: Equal Opportunities Commission.

Fuller, A., & Unwin, L. (2005b). The gendered nature of apprenticeship: Employers' and young people's perspective. *Education and Training,* 47(4/5), 298–311.

Gospel, H., & Fuller, A. (1998). The modern apprenticeship: New wine in old bottles? *Human Resource Management Journal,* 8, 5–22.

Heidegger, G., Kampmeier, A., Evans, K., Figueira, E., Heikkinen, A., & Patiniotis, N. (Eds.). (2004). *Gender and qualification: Transcending gendering features of key qualifications for improving options for career choice and enhancing human resource potential* (EU Research on Social Sciences and Humanities Report). Brussels: European Commission.

Hodkinson, P., Sparkes, A., & Hodkinson, H. (1996). *Triumphs and tears: Young people, markets, and the transition from school to work.* London: David Fulton Publishers.

Occhionero, M., & Nocenzi, M. (2009). Gender inequalities: The integrated approach to the gender dimension in Europe. *International Review of Sociology*, 19(1), 155–169.

Office for National Statistics. (2012). *Labour market statistics, August 2012*. Retrieved from www.ons.gov.uk/ons/dcp171778_273802.pdf.

Sikora, J., & Saha, L. J. (2009). Gender and professional career plans of high school students in comparative perspective. *Educational Research and Evaluation*, 15(4), 385–403.

Simpson, R. (2004). Masculinity at work: The experiences of men in female dominated occupations. *Work, Employment and Society*, 18(2), 349–368.

Tinklin, T., Croxford, L., Ducklin, A., & Frame, B. (2005). Gender and attitudes to work and family roles: The views of young people at the millennium. *Gender and Education*, 17(2), 129–142.

Unwin, L., & Wellington, J. (2001). *Young people's perspectives on education, training and employment*. London: Kogan Page.

PART IV

Choosing a science career

9 Do teenagers want to become scientists? A comparison of gender differences in attitudes toward science, career expectations, and academic skill across 29 countries

John Jerrim and Ingrid Schoon

Abstract
In this chapter we investigate how boys' and girls' ability and attitudes toward science differ as they approach the end of compulsory schooling. We begin by comparing their performance on an internationally standardized test, before investigating the proportion of boys and girls aspiring to a scientific career. Results are compared across a set of 29 developed countries. Gender differences in science achievement tests completed at age 15 are small, yet boys and girls wish to enter very different careers. In all 29 countries boys are more likely than girls to expect entry into careers involving physical science or mathematics, while girls prefer a career in life sciences and the health professions.

Introduction

Over the past 15 to 20 years, educational attainment has risen dramatically across all developed countries. Whereas in 1995 only one in five children living in OECD countries completed university, this figure has almost doubled to one in three today (OECD, 2008, table A3.2). One particularly noticeable feature in almost every country in the developed world is the rising trend of women now outnumbering men in accessing tertiary education (OECD, 2008). However, men and women are not evenly distributed among the different disciplines. Compared to boys, girls are less likely to study a subject relating to the natural sciences (especially physics), technology, engineering, or math (STEM) (OECD, 2008, table A3.5). This is despite the STEM disciplines offering the greatest economic rewards. For example, Black, Sanders, and Taylor (2003) show that in the United States social science, art, education, and humanities graduates earn roughly 30% less than economists, mathematicians, scientists, and engineers. A similar picture is evident in Europe, where STEM graduates tend to have higher earnings than non-STEM graduates (DIUS, 2009).

If going into the STEM fields is so lucrative, why are girls less likely than boys to pursue careers in these fields? Several possible explanations emerge, including differences in cognitive abilities, the importance boys and girls place on different skills, the pressure and support they receive from their parents, and their own expectations about the future (see also Chow & Salmela-Aro; Parker, Nagy, Trautwein, & Lüdtke; Perez-Felkner, McDonald, & Schneider; Wang & Kenny, this volume). In this chapter we examine differences in abilities, preferences, and expectations among 15-year-old boys and girls across 29 OECD countries, drawing on evidence collected for the Programme for International Student Assessment (PISA) in 2006.

The study is guided by assumptions formulated in the expectancy-value model developed by Eccles (Parsons) et al. (1983). The model highlights the important role of values and expectations in shaping achievement-related choices. We begin by considering how cognitive ability differs between young men and women across three academic domains (reading, math, and natural sciences). Girls' reluctance to study advanced math, the physical sciences, and engineering at university could also be due to a lack of academic preparation in these subjects during secondary school (see Perez-Felkner et al.; Wang & Kenny, this volume). Alternatively, it could be that girls are performing as well as boys in these subjects, but that their comparative advantage (i.e., being better at English than at math) lies elsewhere (see Chow & Salmela-Aro; Parker et al.; Wang & Kenny, this volume). We then move on to consider whether boys and girls differ in the value they place on the aforementioned subjects (Eccles, 2007, 2009). According to the expectancy-value model, it is possible that even though boys and girls are equally able to complete STEM qualifications at university, boys are disproportionately more likely to follow such pathways as they see these skills as more important or relevant to their lives (see also Chow & Salmela-Aro; Perez-Felkner et al.; Wang & Kenny, this volume). It is therefore important to take into account academic attainment and preferences across domains rather than just mathematics or science.

Finally, we turn to young people's expectations of the future. There exists a host of evidence from across the social sciences that aspirations and expectations have a substantial impact upon young people's educational and occupational attainment (Cowan, 2011; Eccles 2009; Morgan, 2004, 2005; Schoon, 2006; Sewell, Haller, & Ohlendorf, 1970). For example, Schoon, Ross, and Martin (2007) showed that young males in the United Kingdom (UK) who aspired to a STEM occupation at age 16 were around 3 to 4 times more likely than other males without STEM-related aspirations to be working in a STEM career by age 30. For women the odds were even higher (4 times for young women born in 1958 and 7 times for women born in 1970). Likewise, Harper and Haq (2001) showed that gender differences in career aspirations during adolescence partly explained the uneven distribution of men and women across different occupations 15 years later. Similarly, Gupta (1993, 1994) found that gender differences in these occupational preferences explained a large amount of the variance in gender differences in certain types of jobs (see also Chow & Salmela-Aro and Bagnoli, Demey & Scott, this volume). Meanwhile, Kleinjans (2009) suggested that taste for competition is related to men and women's occupational decisions. Hence, when deciding their future educational paths, boys and girls may be aiming for different jobs, especially in highly developed countries that can more easily absorb the economic costs of pursuing gender-stereotypic preferences (Charles, 2011; Eccles, 2009). Indeed, it could be that girls are more likely to want to become artists and writers than scientists or engineers. Gottfredson (2002) suggested that such gender-type aspirations are developed by children when they are relatively young, approximately between the ages of 9 and 13. Gutman and Akerman (2008) argued that, even at this young age, girls "may not choose careers in math or physical sciences that have traditionally been dominated by males" (p. 5).

Hence there is ample evidence to suggest that there will be strong gender differences in occupational preferences by age 15 (McDaniel, 2010) and that such preferences are important for the educational pathways that boys and girls take (Eccles, 2007, 2009). The aim of this chapter is to establish the size of this gender difference in aspirations toward STEM occupations across a range of OECD countries using data collected for PISA. We also examine whether there are differences in aspirations within certain types of science professions (e.g., physical versus life science) and if there is a single pattern in preferences that can be generalized across the developed world (or, conversely, whether some countries are able to buck the trend).

Comparative analysis

The comparative focus of this chapter provides an overview of gender differences in attainment, preferences, and aspirations toward STEM-related occupations across a range of 29 developed countries. We do not formally try to explain why such cross-national variation may occur, but rather offer a set of plausible explanations that will hopefully encourage further research in this area. This chapter is thus of an exploratory nature, describing general patterns that hold across countries, rather than explicitly testing a firm set of a priori hypotheses about differences that occur between specific nations. We proceed by discussing the PISA data in the next section. Results are presented in the third section, with conclusions following in the final section.

The data

Data are drawn from the Programme for International Student Assessment (PISA), an OECD study of 15-year-olds' cognitive ability that is held every 3 years. Here we use the 2006 wave, which tested children's ability in science, reading, and math across 29 industrialized nations. We chose the 2006 wave because the majority of questions in this wave examined science skills. In each country, a minimum of 150 schools was included in the sample, selected with probability proportional to size. Students were then randomly selected from within these schools. Average response rates of both schools and pupils were high (roughly 90%), though this did vary moderately between countries (OECD, 2007a provides further detail). Sampling weights are applied throughout the analysis to adjust for unit non-response. The achieved sample size, across all the countries considered, is 251,278.

The primary goal of PISA is to provide cross-nationally comparable estimates of children's functional ability in reading, science, and mathematics. Children's answers to the PISA test questions were scaled by the survey organizers into five "plausible values" for each of the three domains. The assumption is that children's ability remains unobserved but the answers to the test questions provide an indication of their underlying skill. Hence these five values indicate possible levels of children's true ability (see OECD, 2007a for further information). The assessments were made on a continuous scale, and variables have a mean of 500 points and a standard deviation of 100 across all OECD countries. To aid interpretation, the OECD states that 40 PISA test points are approximately equal to 1 additional year of schooling (for further details, see OECD, 2010, p. 110).

The PISA study also collected information on young people's attitudes toward various subjects (including math, science, and reading) and their career expectations. In a first step we examine gender differences in the achievement tests, before we move to the issue of values and expectations.

Results

Gender differences in academic attainment

How did boys and girls differ in their academic attainment, especially regarding their scores in science, math, and reading? Figure 9.1 illustrates gender differences in the 2006 PISA science assessment.[1] This assessment covers a range of topics from the physical, biological, and environmental sciences. Data are taken directly from the survey organizers' calculations (OECD, 2007b). Positive figures indicate that the average mark for boys is higher than that for girls. The thin line running through the center of each bar illustrates the estimated 95% confidence interval.

The most striking aspect of Figure 9.1 is that, in the vast majority of countries, the difference in science test performance between boys and girls is relatively small and statistically insignificant. In only six countries (UK, Luxembourg, Denmark, Netherlands, Mexico, Switzerland) do boys score significantly higher

---

[1] The PISA 2006 conceptualization of "scientific knowledge" comprises knowledge of science (knowledge of the natural world across the major fields of physics, chemistry, biological sciences, Earth and space science, and science-based technology) as well as knowledge about science (i.e., knowledge of the means [scientific enquiry] and goals [scientific explanation] of science). This broad definition differs from one grounded on school science programmes, based only on the disciplines of science (Cresswell & Vayssettes, 2006). Sample questions are available from www.oecd.org/pisa/38709385.pdf.

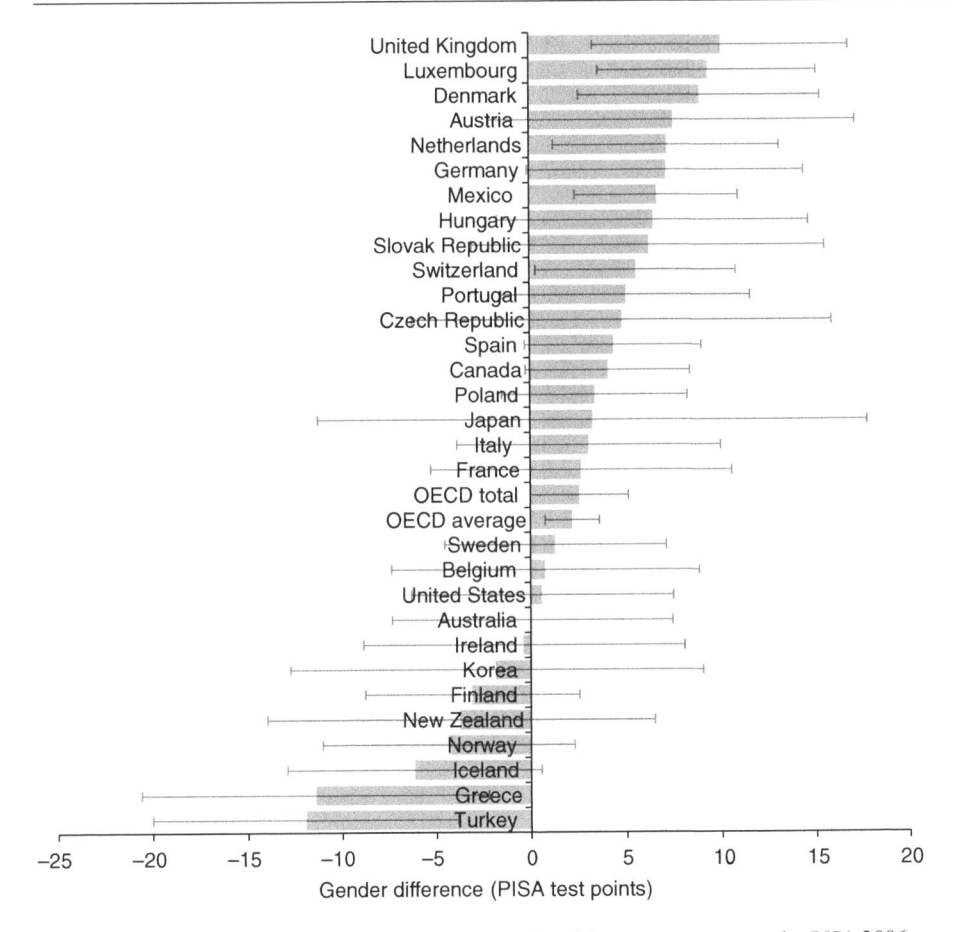

Figure 9.1 *Difference between boys' and girls' average scores on the PISA 2006 science test*

Notes:

a Positive numbers indicate where boys' average performance was greater than girls'. Negative numbers indicate where girls out-performed boys.

b The thin line through the center of each bar represents the estimated 95% confidence interval.

c Data taken from OECD (2007) report, Table 2.1c. Retrieved from www.oecd.org/document/2/0,3343,en_32252351_32236191_39718850_1_1_1_1,00.html.

marks than girls, with the opposite holding true in just two countries (Greece and Turkey), i.e., in these two countries girls score higher marks than boys in the science assessment. Indeed, in over two thirds of cases the estimated difference between boys and girls is less than 10 PISA test points (i.e., less than 0.10 of an international standard deviation). When pooling observations from all countries together, boys tend to outperform girls by just 0.02 of a standard deviation (a rather small amount). It therefore seems unlikely that the low participation of women in STEM courses and careers is due to a lack of academic ability.

Do we find a similar pattern for other subjects? Figure 9.2 illustrates that gender differences in reading skills are much more apparent, with girls outperforming boys in every country. This gap is sizeable given that the OECD average is 40 PISA test points (equivalent to roughly 1 year of schooling). Again cross-national variation is modest. Gender differences only stand out as particularly small in the Netherlands (25 PISA test points) and as particularly large in Iceland, Finland, and Greece (50 PISA test points). Results from Figures 9.1 and 9.2 thus suggest that although 15-year-old girls are as able as boys in terms of their STEM skills, it is in other areas (e.g., reading) where they hold a *comparative* advantage to boys. Hence although academic ability in science should not be a barrier to girls entering STEM professions, it is notable that their comparative advantage seems to be in other areas (e.g., reading).

How do boys and girls differ in how they value the sciences?

As part of the PISA 2006 study, children completed a background questionnaire that included questions about their attitudes toward various subjects. For instance, respondents were asked:

> "In general, how important do you think it is for you to do well in the subjects below?" [reading, math, and science]

Four tick-box options were provided, ranging from "very important" to "not important at all." We converted this information into a simple (if crude) index, with children scoring one point if they said "not very important" and up to four points for "very important."

Even though boys and girls may be equally able in science, they may attach different importance to the subject (see Chow & Salmela-Aro; Parker et al.; Wang & Kenny, this volume). Figure 9.3 illustrates differences between boys and girls in how they value different academic domains (see notes to Figure 9.3 for how these scores were calculated).

Results for boys can be found on the y axis, with analogous figures for girls on the x axis. The 45-degree line represents where boys and girls place the same value on science. If a country sits above this line, it indicates that boys attach more importance to science than girls. The opposite is true for nations that sit below this line.

The most notable feature of Figure 9.3 is how closely all countries sit to the 45-degree line. For instance, in the United States (US) boys rate the importance of STEM skills as 3.4 out of 4, while girls give a slightly higher mark (3.5). In Germany the average score is slightly lower at 3.3, but again there is little variation by gender (3.26 for girls and 3.34 for boys). Indeed, the findings suggest that across these 29 OECD countries there is little evidence that girls attach less importance to STEM skills than boys.

This issue is explored further in Figure 9.4, where we compare the importance boys and girls place on science and math skills to those for reading and literacy.

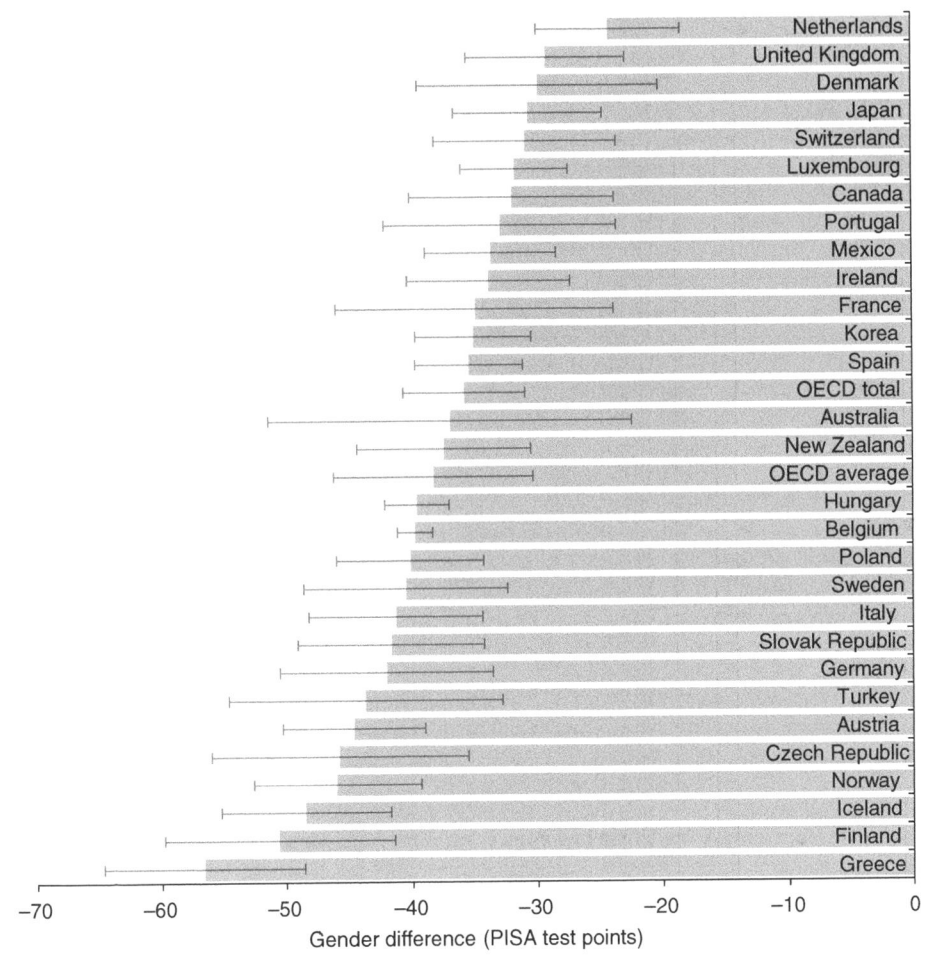

Figure 9.2 *Difference between boys' and girls' average scores on the PISA 2006 reading test*
Notes:
a See notes to Figure 9.1.
b Data taken from OECD (2007) report, Table 6.1c. Retrieved from www.oecd.org/document/2/0,3343,en_32252351_32236191_39718850_1_1_1_1,00.html.

The former can be found on the *y* axis, with the latter on the *x* axis. The left-hand panel indicates results for boys, while the left-hand panel shows the results for girls.

Starting with boys, it is interesting to note that only eight countries sit above the line and only five significantly so at the 5% level. Hence there is very little evidence that boys actually value STEM subjects as more important than reading. Indeed, in roughly half the countries considered (most notably the Czech Republic and Slovakia, but also the UK, Australia, and Sweden) boys value literacy skills more highly than STEM.

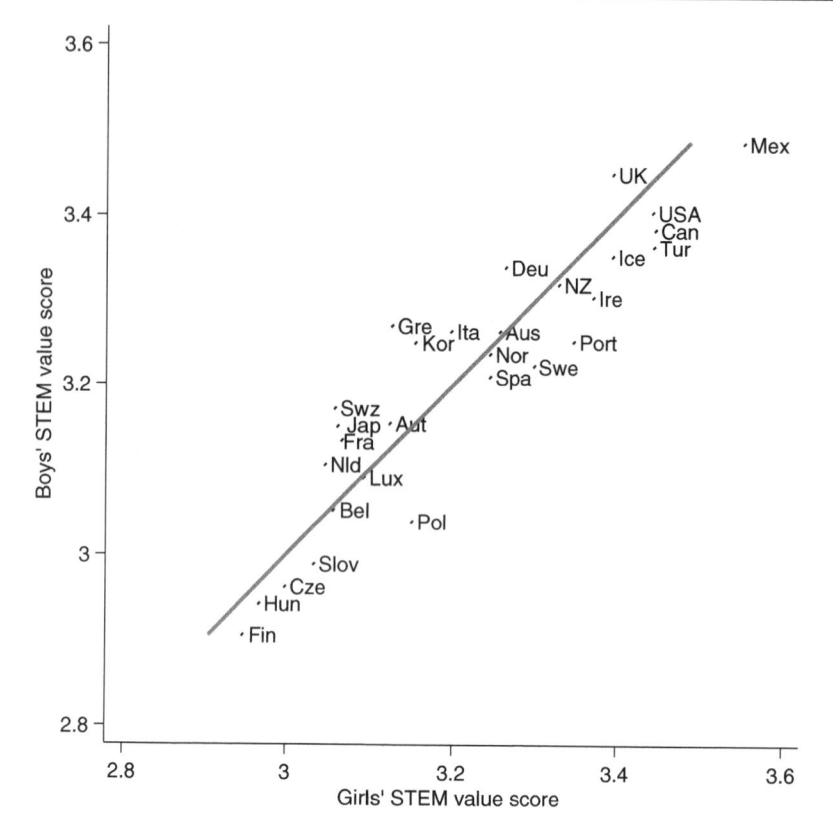

Figure 9.3 *A comparison of the importance and value boys and girls place upon science*

Notes:

a Children's "STEM" score is based on how important children believe it is to do well in science and math. They were asked to rate this on a 4-point scale, from "very important" to "not very important at all." We treat these responses as a linear index, and average the score for science and math.

b The 45-degree line illustrates where there is no difference between boys and girls.

c See Table 9.1 for country abbreviations.

Yet the magnitude of this difference pales in comparison to that shown by girls (right-hand panel), where points sit much further below the 45-degree line. Indeed, in all 29 OECD countries, girls rate reading as more important than science and math, with the difference statistically significant at the 5% level in all but one country (Portugal). The implication is that, whereas boys rate STEM skills only marginally less important than literacy, girls tend to attach much greater value to the latter. That is, boys and girls do not differ in the value they place upon STEM skills, yet young women attach greater importance to literacy than STEM.

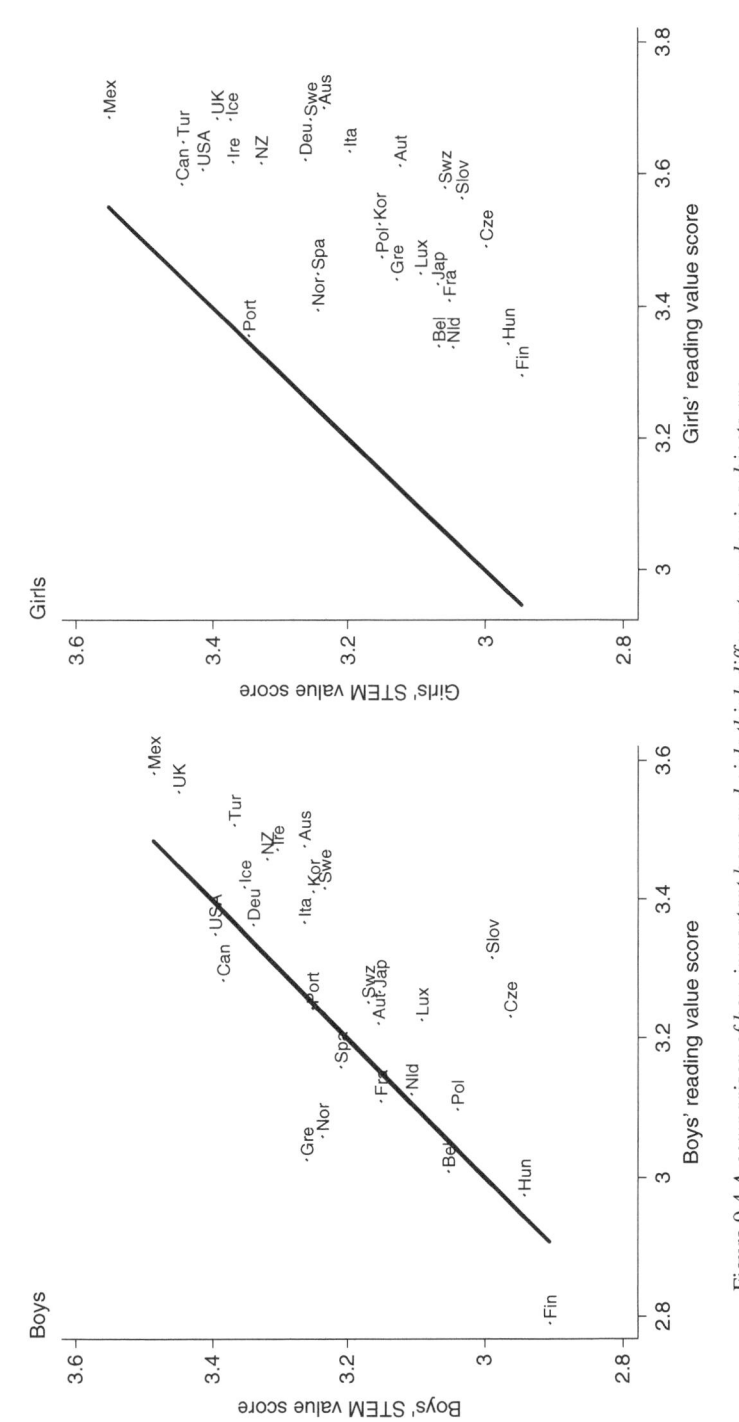

Figure 9.4 A comparison of how important boys and girls think different academic subjects are

Notes: See notes to Figure 9.3.

Gender differences in expectations toward scientific careers

We now turn to gender differences in adolescents' occupational expectations, focusing on their desire to enter a professional science career. The 15-year-olds were asked about their future occupational goals. Specifically, they were asked to provide a job title in response to the following question in an open text field:

> "What kind of job do you expect to have when you are about 30 years old?"
> *Write the job title.*

Reported occupations were converted by the survey organizers into four-digit ISCO codes. This is an internationally comparable categorization used by the International Labour Organization (ILO) to place occupations into one of 390 different groups dependent on the skill level and specialization required. The ISCO categorization does not include codes for skilled trades or science teachers.[2]

One difficulty is that roughly one in five children did not provide a valid response. Missing data are particularly high (around one third of cases) in Germany, Austria, Hungary, and Japan. Our exploration of this non-response suggests it is not random, and different factors are associated with missingness in the different countries. The reader should therefore note that differential response patterns could be driving some of the cross-national variation found. We have, however, checked the robustness of results by creating and applying a set of additional inverse probability weights. The checks suggest that the findings reported in the subsequent sections remain robust.

The reader may also ask whether the question put to the children is capturing expectations or aspirations. The terms "expectations" and "aspirations" are often used interchangeably, as they are different yet interlinked concepts (e.g., see Croll, 2008; Schneider & Stevenson, 1999). While aspirations capture what one would like to happen, expectations describe a more realistic evaluation of what one thinks will happen, taking into account one's abilities as well as available opportunity structure (Gutman & Akerman, 2008; Ritchie, Flouri, & Buchanan, 2004). The question in PISA asked young people what they *expect* to happen in the future, yet does seem to generate responses that are more idealistic than realistic. For instance, 1 in 10 US children report that they expect to become a doctor, a further 6% a lawyer, and 4% a professional sportsperson or entertainer. This lack of clarity over whether the question is capturing children's aspirations or expectations could influence some of the substantial results presented in the following section.

We begin by estimating a multinomial logistic regression model. This is a statistical method that enables analysts to relate a series of predictor variables (e.g.,

---

[2] Further details can be found on the ISCO website www.ilo.org/public/english/bureau/stat/isco/isco88/index.htm.

gender, academic achievement) to a categorical outcome variable. Estimates from such models help us to understand how strong the association is between a factor of interest (e.g., gender) and a given outcome (e.g., aspiration toward a STEM career), holding constant a range of other factors (e.g., taking into account that boys and girls differ in their academic abilities). In the first set of estimates, the outcome variable takes one of three possible values. Zero indicates that the child does not expect to enter a professional occupation, 1 that they want to work in a professional science career (either a physical or health scientist, as defined in Appendix 9.1), and 2 that they want to become a professional in another field. Full definitions of these groups (and the exact occupations they include) can be found in Appendix 9.1. Gender enters as a dummy variable, with a value of 0 for girls and 1 for boys. We also control for PISA reading, math, and science test scores, and a combined indicator of family background (comprising measures of parental occupation, parental education, and household possessions – a proxy for wealth). PISA survey weights are applied in all models. The complex survey design (children clustered within schools) is taken into account via an adjustment to the standard errors.

Our discussion shall focus upon the comparison between children expecting to become a *science professional* versus entering another profession (i.e., outcome 1 versus outcome 2). Results are presented as "odds ratios." To help readers interpret findings, an odds ratio of 2 means that boys are (approximately) twice as likely to expect entry into a science profession as girls. A value of 3 would mean they are 3 times more likely (and so forth).

Boys are generally much more likely than girls to expect entry into a science career (compared to working in some other type of profession). In every country (bar Japan), the estimated odds ratio is greater than 1, with statistical significance reaching at least the 5% level on 26 out of 29 occasions. This result therefore seems to generalize across several different settings; boys are more likely to expect to enter a science profession (versus some other professional career) than girls – even after taking into account differences in academic ability across several domains as well as family background.

Yet it is also interesting to note that there is a reasonable degree of cross-national variation in these estimates. The low ranking of the US particularly stands out; the odds ratio of 1.5 is the fourth smallest in the developed world and significantly below 14 other countries (significant at the 5% level). In interpreting that finding one should bear in mind that, even in the US, boys are 50% more likely to aspire to a STEM occupation than girls. In contrast, the odds ratio is much higher in Eastern European countries (3.0 in Hungary and Poland and 3.5 in the Slovak Republic) and some Southern European countries (e.g., Spain and Italy). One may speculate that this could be due to the traditional family values in these countries, and perhaps greater stereotyping of what are considered to be male and female roles. It is also interesting to see that Finland is near the top of the international ranking, significantly above some other Northern European nations (like Norway and Sweden). This finding might suggest that in some advanced countries career

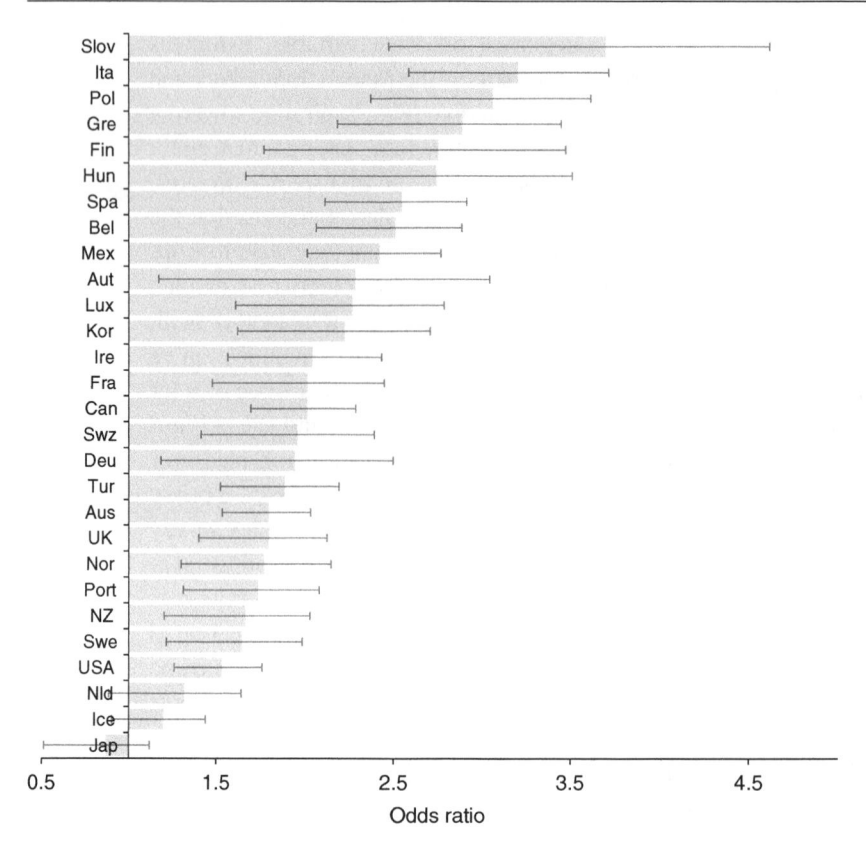

Figure 9.5 *Estimated odds ratio of whether boys are more likely than girls to expect to become a science professional*
Notes:
a These results illustrate the odds ratio for expecting to become a science professional versus entering a non-science profession based on a multinomial logistic regression of children's occupational expectations. Variables included in the model are a dummy variable for gender, the PISA ESCS indicator of family background, and children's scores on the PISA math, reading, and science assessment.
b Odds ratio greater than 1 indicates that boys more likely to expect entry into a science profession than girls.
c The line running through the center of each bar refers to the estimated 95% confidence interval.
d A list of country abbreviations can be found in Table 9.1.

choice and outcomes can be more gender stereotyped and have to be considered within the social contexts in which they emerge (Charles, 2011).[3]

---

[3] Although the confidence intervals of certain countries may overlap in Figure 9.5, this does not by itself mean that there is not a statistically significant difference. Rather a formal test for differences between groups is required (e.g., a two-sample t-test). See Maghsoodloo and Huang (2010) for a discussion of this issue and the related literature.

In a next step we consider gender differences between specific types of science-based careers. In particular, we re-estimate the model above, but now define the dependent variable as one of *four* possible outcomes (non-professional, *physical* science professional, health science professional, and other professional). Table 9.1 illustrates differences between boys and girls in the likelihood of (a) wanting to enter a physical science/mathematics profession, and (b) wanting to enter a health science profession, relative to the other professional group. As previously, odds ratios greater than 1 indicate that boys are more likely to expect entry into a science career than girls.

The most striking feature of Table 9.1 is the very large odds ratios for physical sciences – boys are much more likely than girls to expect to enter this type of career. For instance, an odds ratio of 8 for the US suggests that boys are approximately 8 times more likely to expect to enter the physical sciences (relative to the other professional group) than girls. Indeed, there are instances where the estimated odds ratio is approaching 10. Interestingly, the same pattern does not emerge for "life science" occupations. Here the estimated odds ratio is actually below 1 in 24 out of the 29 countries, with the difference being statistically significant at the 5% threshold in 13 countries. Hence in several countries it is girls who are more likely to expect to work in the health sciences than other occupations (although this pattern does not generalize across every single OECD nation).

It is again interesting to discuss the cross-national variation in these estimates, with some nations standing out from the rest. Notice, in particular, results for the US. The odds ratio for boys regarding a career in the physical sciences is the third *biggest* in the OECD, meaning that boys are particularly likely to expect to enter a physical science career. This is in contrast to the analysis presented in Figure 9.5 (looking at science occupations when broadly defined) where the estimated odds ratio was the third *lowest*. Similarly, whereas the US previously stood out in comparison to countries like Finland and Italy (Figure 9.5), Table 9.1 illustrates that this is only the case for life sciences; in terms of physical sciences the estimated odds ratio in these nations is roughly the same.

Thus although the US may not be very gender-stereotyped when STEM aspirations are broadly defined, there remain very big differences in career preferences between boys and girls when it comes to specific fields (e.g., mathematics, advanced engineering, computer programming). This is important for public policy, as several leading bodies have claimed that there are labor supply shortages in such industries (National Academy of Science, 2007), and that these industries are particularly important for economic growth (Pakes & Sokoloff, 1996). STEM occupations are also careers with high wages and economic returns (Black et al., 2003). It has already been shown that, at age 15, girls are as able academically as boys to pursue science careers. Closing the aspirations gap, and thus increasing the number of girls taking college courses leading to these professions, may therefore be important for the competitiveness of the US economy.

Table 9.1. *Expectations of entering a health or physical science occupation versus a non-science profession (odds ratios)*

	Physical science			Life science		
	Odds ratio	Upper CI	Lower CI	Odds ratio	Upper CI	Lower CI
Iceland ("Ice")	2.4	3.2	1.7	0.6	0.8	0.5
Turkey ("Turk")	3.5	4.6	2.7	0.9	1.2	0.7
Japan ("Jap")	3.6	5.6	2.3	0.3	0.5	0.2
Greece ("Gre")	3.9	5.0	3.0	1.5	2.1	1.2
Sweden ("Swe")	4.1	5.6	2.9	0.7	0.9	0.5
Germany ("Deu")	4.1	6.4	2.7	0.7	1.1	0.5
Norway ("Nor")	4.2	5.6	3.2	0.5	0.8	0.4
Netherlands ("Nld")	4.4	6.7	2.9	0.4	0.6	0.3
Luxembourg ("Lux")	5.1	7.7	3.4	0.9	1.2	0.7
Austria ("Aut")	5.2	8.6	3.1	0.9	1.4	0.5
Switzerland ("Swz")	5.4	7.3	3.9	0.4	0.5	0.3
New Zealand ("NZ")	5.5	7.6	4.0	0.7	1.0	0.5
Mexico ("Mex")	5.6	6.6	4.7	1.1	1.4	0.9
France ("Fra")	5.7	7.8	4.2	0.6	0.9	0.4
Korea ("Kor")	5.8	8.0	4.2	0.9	1.2	0.7
Portugal ("Port")	5.9	7.9	4.4	0.7	0.9	0.5
Spain ("Spa")	6.7	8.2	5.5	0.9	1.1	0.7
Australia ("Aus")	6.9	8.5	5.6	0.7	0.8	0.6
Canada ("Can")	7.0	8.6	5.7	0.9	1.1	0.8
Poland ("Pol")	7.2	9.1	5.7	0.9	1.2	0.6
Belgium ("Bel")	7.3	9.1	5.9	0.8	1.0	0.6
United Kingdom ("UK")	7.9	11.0	5.7	0.6	0.8	0.5
Ireland ("Ire")	8.6	12.2	6.0	0.6	0.8	0.5
Hungary ("Hun")	8.7	13.3	5.7	0.6	0.9	0.4
Finland ("Fin")	8.9	12.8	6.1	1.1	1.6	0.7
Italy ("Ita")	9.0	11.3	7.2	1.2	1.5	1.0
USA ("USA")	9.1	12.0	6.9	0.6	0.8	0.5
Czech Republic ("Cze")	9.3	14.7	5.9	1.0	1.5	0.7
Slovak Republic ("Slov")	9.8	14.3	6.7	0.7	1.1	0.5

Notes: Figures greater than 1 indicate that boys are more likely to expect to enter that occupation than girls; "Upper CI" and "Lower CI" refer to the estimated 95% confidence interval of the odds ratio; results refer to the likelihood of a child expecting to enter a science profession relative to a non-science profession; data ordered by the estimated odds ratio for physical sciences.

Summary and conclusion

Women now outnumber men in tertiary education participation in almost every country within the developed world (OECD, 2008). Yet women are still underrepresented within certain disciplines, most notably physical science, technology, engineering, and mathematics. Consequently, relatively few women go on to become professionals working in STEM careers. This is a problem of genuine policy relevance, given the shortage of STEM graduates in many countries, and the importance of having a workforce with these skills for technological innovation and economic growth.

Our exploration of the data suggests that, in the vast majority of countries, the difference between boys' and girls' academic achievement in science at age 15 is small. Furthermore, females perform much better than boys in reading tasks. Interestingly, there is no obvious gender difference in the importance boys and girls place on science and math skills (see also Chow & Salmela-Aro; Parker et al.; Perez-Felkner et al.; Wang & Kenny, this volume), although boys value science and math over literacy skills while girls prefer reading over math and science. Regarding future career plans, boys are much more likely than girls to expect entry into a scientific career.

Variations in individual preferences and occupational expectations in secondary school are thus potential explanations as to why men and women disproportionately choose rather distinct educational and occupational pathways. The contribution of this chapter has been to document the size of the gender gap in academic achievement, values, and occupational expectations across a wide range of developed countries.

Our results suggest that at age 15 boys and girls are equally able academically in science and attach the same importance to being competent in science and math. This holds true across the vast majority of OECD countries, with gender differences in PISA science test scores being generally small and statistically insignificant. However, in almost every developed country, girls believe that it is more important to be a good reader than to be proficient in science and math. Furthermore, girls significantly outperform boys in reading ability in each of the 29 countries included in this study. Girls score about 40 points better than boys, which corresponds to approximately 1 year of schooling. These findings highlight the importance of taking into account attainment and preferences across domains (Eccles, 1994, 2007; see also Parker et al.; Chow & Salmela-Aro; Wang & Kenny, this volume), rather than focusing on gender difference in one subject area like math, which has often been identified as a critical filter for selecting a career in science fields (Sells, 1980).

The findings also suggest that individual preferences can have important implications for choices regarding tertiary education, subject choices, and subsequent career paths (see also Chow & Salmela-Aro; Parker et al.; Wang & Kenny; Bagnoli, Demey, & Scott, this volume). Regarding future career plans, boys are much more likely than girls to expect entry into a scientific career (relative to working in some other professional occupation). Yet this result needs to be clarified in terms of the exact *type* of scientific occupation one considers (see also Schoon et al., 2007; Bagnoli et al.; Parker et al., this volume). It seems that girls are generally *more* likely than boys to expect entry into a career with a large biological or health component, while they are less likely than boys to want a job in either math, computing, or the physical sciences.

Although women are as well qualified as men to follow STEM pathways, their *comparative* gender advantage and preferences seem to be in other areas (e.g., in language and literacy, health or life sciences). It is therefore perhaps a rational decision for many females to follow non-STEM careers. Career choices can, however, also be more than practical economic decisions. They also represent acts of identity construction and self-affirmation (Eccles, 2009). They furthermore have to be understood against the wider socio-historical context in which they emerge.

Although some developed countries do not stand out as very gender-stereotyped nations in terms of STEM aspirations – at least when STEM has been broadly defined – aspirations toward specific STEM careers are very heavily male dominated in the US, the UK, and Finland compared to other countries such as Iceland or Greece (particularly regarding math, physical science, and computing). It might be that some developed countries have a less gender-stereotypical conception of science-related occupations. A challenge for educators and parents would be to not only raise the value of science skills for both girls and boys, so that more boys and girls consider these skills important enough to acquire and then to consider careers that make use of these skills, but also to improve awareness of strength in math and science skills among females. Furthermore, men and women need to be more aware of persisting inequalities in economic returns associated with gender-typical occupations, and should be provided with information and guidance about career opportunities in different STEM occupations.

If teenage preferences and expectations do indeed have a *causal* impact upon young people's choice of college major and their career trajectory, then reducing or closing gender gaps in values and expectations will potentially be beneficial for gender equity. Specifically, this may help to (1) equalize labor market outcomes (e.g., pay) between men and women and (2) increase the labor supply in important, high-value STEM industries. It has been argued that in order to thrive in the modern, knowledge-based economies it is vital that cultural values gradually shift toward a more egalitarian and less gender-biased direction (Inglehart & Norris, 2003). Regardless of their economic efficiency, egalitarian values are spreading globally through international organizations, social movements, and professional associations (Meyer, Boli, Thomas, & Ramirez, 1997; Ramirez & Wotipka, 2001).

However, changing values is only part of the story in achieving gender equity. To initiate change it is also important to raise awareness of existing inequalities (see Hoskins & Janmaat, this volume) and to take an active stance in changing institutional structures. Major strides toward increasing equality in access to education and the labor market have been made, and the movement toward more egalitarian and less gendered institutions, educational systems, and labor markets might be accelerated by economic pressures, such as worldwide shortages of science and technology workers.

References

Black, D., Sanders, S., & Taylor, L. (2003). The economic reward for studying economics. *Economic Inquiry*, 41(3), 365–377.

Charles, M. (2011). A world of difference: International trends in women's economic status. *Annual Review of Sociology* (Vol. 37, pp. 355–371). Palo Alto, CA: Annual Reviews.

Cowan, B. (2011). Forward-thinking teens: The effects of college costs on adolescent risky behavior. *Economics of Education Review*, 30(5), 813–825.

Cresswell, J., & Vayssettes, S. (2006). *Assessing scientific, reading and mathematical literacy: A framework for PISA 2006*. Paris: Organisation for Economic Co-operation and Development (OECD).

Croll, P. (2008). Occupational choice, socio-economic status and educational attainment: A study of the occupational choices and destinations of young people in the British Household Panel Survey. *Research Papers in Education*, 23, 243–268.

Department for Innovation, University and Skills (DIUS). (2009). *The demand for science, technology, engineering and mathematics (STEM) skills*. Retrieved from www.dius.gov.uk/research_and_analysis/~/media/publications/D/DIUS_RR_08_14.

Eccles, J. S. (1994). Understanding women's educational and occupational choices: Applying the Eccles et al. model of achievement-related choices. *Psychology of Women Quarterly*, 18(4), 585–609.

(2007). Where are all the women? Gender differences in participation in physical science and engineering. In S. J. Ceci & W. M. Williams (Eds.), *Why aren't more women in science? Top researchers debate the evidence* (pp. 199–210). Washington, DC: American Psychological Association.

(2009). Who am I and what am I going to do with my life? Personal and collective identities as motivators of action. *Educational Psychologist*, 44(2), 78–89.

Eccles (Parsons), J., Adler, T. F., Futterman, R., Goff, S. B., Kaczala, C. M., Meece, J. L., & Midgley, C. (1983). Expectancies, values and academic behaviors. In J. T. Spence (Ed.), *Achievement and achievement motives: Psychological and sociological approaches* (pp. 75–146). San Francisco, CA: W. H. Freeman.

Gottfredson, L. (2002). Gottfredson's theory of circumscription, compromise, and self-creation. In D. Brown & Associates (Eds.), *Career choice and development* (4th ed., pp. 85–148). San Francisco, CA: Jossey-Bass.

Gupta, N. (1993). Probabilities of job choice and employer selection and male–female occupational differences. *American Economic Review*, 83(2), 57–61.

(1994). A specification test of the determinants of male–female occupational differences. *Economics Letters*, 44(1–2), 197–203.

Gutman, L., & Akerman, R. (2008). *Determinants of aspirations* (Department for Children, Schools and Families (DCSF) Research Report 27). Retrieved from http://eprints.ioe.ac.uk/2052/1/Gutman2008Determinants.pdf.

Harper, B., & Haq, M. (2001). Ambition, discrimination, and occupational attainment: A study of a British cohort. *Oxford Economic Papers*, 53(4), 695–720.

Inglehart, R., & Norris, P. (2003). *Rising tide: Gender equality and cultural change around the world*. New York: Cambridge University Press.

Kleinjans, K. (2009). Do gender differences in preferences from competition matter for occupational expectations? *Journal of Economic Psychology*, 30(5), 701–710.

Maghsoodloo, S., & Huang, C. (2010). Comparing the overlapping of two independent confidence intervals with a single confidence interval for two normal population parameters. *Journal of Statistical Planning and Inference*, 140(11), 3295–3305.

McDaniel, A. (2010). Cross-national gender gaps in educational expectations: The influence of national-level gender ideology and educational systems. *Comparative Education Review*, 54(1), 22–50.

Meyer, J. W., Boli, J., Thomas, G. M., & Ramirez, F. O. (1997). World society and the nation state. *American Journal of Sociology*, 103(1), 144–181.

Morgan, S. (2004). Methodologist as arbitrator: Five methods for black–white differences in the causal effect of expectations on attainment. *Sociological Methods and Research*, 33(1), 3–53.

(2005). *On the edge of commitment: Educational attainment and race in the United States*. Stanford University Press.

National Academy of Science. (2007). *Rising above the gathering storm: Energizing and employing America for a brighter economic future*. Washington, DC: Committee on Science, Engineering and Public Policy. Retrieved from www.nap.edu/openbook.php?record_id=11463.

Organisation for Economic Co-operation and Development (OECD). (2007a). *PISA 2006 technical report*. Paris: Organisation for Economic Co-operation and Development (OECD).

(2007b). *Learning for tomorrow's world: First results from PISA 2006*. Paris: Organisation for Economic Co-operation and Development (OECD).

(2008). *Education at a glance 2008: OECD indicators*. Paris: Organisation for Economic Co-operation and Development (OECD).

(2010). *PISA 2009 results: Learning to learn – Student engagement strategies and practices* (Vol. 3). Paris: Organisation for Economic Co-operation and Development (OECD).

Pakes, A., & Sokoloff, K. (1996). Science, technology and economic growth. *PNAS*, 93(23), 12655–12657.

Ramirez, F. O., & Wotipka, C. M. (2001). Slowly but surely? The global expansion of women's participation in engineering fields of study, 1972–92. *Sociology of Education*, 74, 231–251.

Ritchie, C., Flouri, E., & Buchanan, A. (2004). *Aspirations and expectations*. National Parenting and Family Institute. Retrieved from http://familyandparenting.web-platform.net/Filestore/Documents/publications/aspirations.pdf.

Schneider, B., & Stevenson, D. (1999). The ambitious generation. *Educational Leadership*, 57, 23–25.

Schoon, I. (2006). *Risk and resilience: Adaptations in changing times*. Cambridge University Press.

Schoon, I., Ross, A., & Martin, P. (2007). Science related careers: Aspirations and outcomes in two British cohort studies. *Equal Opportunities International*, 26(2), 129–143.

Sells, L. W. (1980). The mathematics filter and the education of women and minorities. In L. Fox, L. Brody, & D. Tobin (Eds.), *Women and the mathematical mystique:*

Proceedings of the Eighth Annual Hyman Blumberg Symposium on Research in Early Childhood Education (pp. 66–75). Baltimore, MD: Johns Hopkins University Press.

Sewell, W., Haller, A., & Ohlendorf, G. (1970). The educational and early occupational status attainment process: Replication and revision. *American Sociological Review*, 35(6), 1014–1027.

Appendix 9.1: Assignment of ISCO codes to scientific occupations

(a) Definition of physical, mathematical and engineering professions

Physical, mathematical, and engineering science professionals conduct research, improve or develop concepts, theories and operational methods, or apply scientific knowledge relating to fields such as physics, astronomy, meteorology, chemistry, geophysics, geology, mathematics, statistics, computing, architecture, engineering, and technology. Tasks performed by workers in this sub-major group usually include: conducting research, enlarging, advising on or applying scientific knowledge obtained through the study of structures and properties of physical matter and phenomena, chemical characteristics and processes of various substances, materials and products, and of mathematical, statistical and computing concepts and methods; advising on, designing and directing construction of buildings, towns and traffic systems, or civil engineering and industrial structures, as well as machines and other equipment, and advising on and applying mining methods, and ensuring their optimum use; surveying land and sea and making maps; studying and advising on technological aspects of particular materials, products and processes, and on efficiency of production and work organization; preparing scientific papers and reports. Supervision of other workers may be included.

Sub-occupational groups

    2111 Physicists and astronomers
    2112 Meteorologists
    2113 Chemists
    2114 Geologists and geophysicists
    2121 Mathematicians and related professionals
    2122 Statisticians
    2131 Computer systems designers and analysts
    2132 Computer programmers
    2139 Computing professionals not elsewhere classified
    2141 Architects, town and traffic planners
    2142 Civil engineers
    2143 Electrical engineers
    2144 Electronics and telecommunications engineers
    2145 Mechanical engineers

2146 Chemical engineers
2147 Mining engineers, metallurgists, and related professionals
2148 Cartographers and surveyors
2149 Architects, engineers, and related professionals not elsewhere classified

(b) Definition of health and life science professional

Life science and health professionals conduct research, improve or develop concepts, theories and operational methods, or apply scientific knowledge relating to fields such as biology, zoology, botany, ecology, physiology, biochemistry, microbiology, pharmacology, agronomy, and medicine.

Tasks performed by workers in this sub-major group usually include: conducting research, enlarging, advising on or applying scientific knowledge obtained through the study of all forms of human, animal and plant life, including specific organs, tissues, cells and micro-organisms and the effect of environmental factors, or drugs and other substances, on them; studying human, animal or plant illnesses, advising on and applying preventive, curative and nursing measures, or promoting health; preparing scientific papers and reports. Supervision of other workers may be included.

Sub-occupational groups

2211 Biologists, botanists, zoologists, and related professionals
2212 Pharmacologists, pathologists, and related professionals
2213 Agronomists and related professionals
2221 Medical doctors
2222 Dentists
2223 Veterinarians
2224 Pharmacists
2229 Health professionals (except nursing) not elsewhere classified
2230 Nursing and midwifery professionals

(c) Definition of other professionals

Other professionals conduct research, improve or develop concepts, theories and operational methods, or apply knowledge relating to information dissemination and organization of business, as well as to philosophy, law, psychology, politics, economics, history, religion, languages, sociology, other social sciences, and to arts and entertainment.

Tasks performed by workers in this sub-major group usually include: dealing with information dissemination and operational methods relating to organization of business; application of the law; enlarging, advising on or applying knowledge obtained through the study of individual or group behavior, language development, and philosophical, political, economic, juridical, educational, social, religious and other doctrines, concepts, theories, systems and organizations, from a current and historical perspective; conceiving and creating or performing works of art; preparing scholarly papers and reports. Supervision of other workers may be included.

It should be noted that, depending on the specific tasks and degree of responsibility in executing them, as well as on the national educational and training requirements, it may be appropriate to classify some of the occupations that are identified here into Sub-major group 34, Other associate professionals. This is particularly relevant to the occupations classified into Unit group 2446, Social work professionals.

Occupations in this sub-major group are classified into the following minor groups:

      231 College, university, and higher education teaching professionals
      232 Secondary education teaching professionals
      233 Primary and preprimary education teaching professionals
      234 Special education teaching professionals
      235 Other teaching professionals
      2411 Accountants
      2412 Personnel and careers professionals
      2419 Business professionals not elsewhere classified
      2421 Lawyers
      2422 Judges
      2429 Legal professionals not elsewhere classified
      2431 Archivists and curators
      2432 Librarians and related information professionals
      2441 Economists
      2442 Sociologists, anthropologists, and related professionals
      2443 Philosophers, historians, and political scientists
      2444 Philologists, translators, and interpreters
      2445 Psychologists
      2446 Social work professionals
      2451 Authors, journalists, and other writers
      2452 Sculptors, painters, and related artists
      2453 Composers, musicians, and singers
      2454 Choreographers and dancers
      2455 Film, stage, and related actors and directors
      2460 Religious professionals

10 Predicting career aspirations and university majors from academic ability and self-concept: a longitudinal application of the internal–external frame of reference model

Philip Parker, Gabriel Nagy, Ulrich Trautwein and Oliver Lüdtke

Abstract

Science, technology, engineering, and mathematics university majors are critical pathways toward prestigious careers, yet women are still underrepresented in many of these domains. In this chapter, we review the role that self-beliefs play in the development of educational aspirations and attempts to realize those aspirations at the end of secondary school. In particular, we use the internal/external frame of reference model to explore the potential of achievement and self-concept profiles as predictors of university major aspirations and attainment as one possible explanation for gender differences in these domains. After reviewing previous research in this area, we provide a research example using a large longitudinal database from Germany (N = 1,881). Results suggest that (a) high math achievement and self-concept predicted math-intensive university major choice and lower likelihood of entering verbal-intensive majors (and vice versa); (b) there appeared to be a continuum of university majors such that strong mathematics achievement and self-concept profiles predicted entry into hard sciences, while the opposite profile predicted entry into the humanities with biology and medicine displaying more mixed patterns; and (c) after controlling for achievement and self-concept there were still important gender differences in university majors. Implications for theory and practice are discussed.

Introduction

The issues of career aspirations and choice of university majors are particularly important for research exploring gender differences in science, technology, engineering, and mathematics (STEM) fields. Aspirations and study choice provide the basis from which individuals enter these occupational arenas and/or obtain access to higher degrees and thus more advanced positions in these fields. Sells (1976) identified mathematics in school as a critical filter for entering a career in the sciences, as differences in math achievement accounted for gender differences in training and careers in STEM-related fields across the life-span (see also Sells, 1980). Math as a critical filter suggests that math ability is associated with entry into many university majors, with poor achievement and/or failure to undertake advanced mathematics courses effectively barring individuals from many prestigious careers (Ma & Johnson, 2008; Shapka, Domene, & Keating, 2006). This has important implications particularly for females, as empirical research findings suggest that women are generally less likely than men to undertake advanced course selection in mathematics (Nagy et al., 2008; Parker et al., 2012) and generally have lower math achievement scores (e.g., Wigfield, Battle, Keller, & Eccles, 2002). Interestingly, however, studies on gifted populations of students indicate that fewer females enter the physical sciences, mathematics, and technology professions despite having the requisite ability (Eccles & Harold, 1992). This evidence suggests that achievement alone is insufficient to explain gender differences in these fields (see also Chow & Salmela-Aro; Jerrim & Schoon; Perez-Felkner, McDonald, & Schneider; Wang & Kenny, this volume).

Many theories of career and academic choice highlight the importance of psychological factors over and above academic achievement, including math self-concept, interest, and values that provide information on the appraised appropriateness of particular achievement-related choices (e.g., Bandura, Barbaranelli, Caprara, & Pastorelli, 2001; Eccles, 1994; Marsh & Yeung, 1997; Wigfield et al., 2002). Furthermore, research and theory suggest that focusing solely on predictors associated with a single domain provides a limited perspective for predicting and explaining gendered career-relevant outcomes. The internal/external frame of reference model proposed by Marsh (1986, 1990b) explicitly focuses on such intraindividual cross-domain comparison, with recent research indicating that associations between math and verbal domains are useful for predicting achievement-related choices and aspirations (Marsh & Yeung, 1997; Nagy, Trautwein, Baumert, Köller, & Garrett, 2006; Nagy et al., 2008; Parker et al., 2012; see also Chow & Salmela-Aro, this volume). As yet, this model has rarely been applied to career-relevant variables such as university majors and aspirations, despite its potential relevance.

Math and gendered differences in STEM fields

The role of mathematics as a critical filter to later prestigious careers developed as a hypothesis to explain gender differences regarding the enrollment of women in STEM-related university majors (Sell, 1976). While this hypothesis originally developed in relation to a broad set of STEM fields, in recent years there has been considerable progress in closing the gender gap in some STEM domains (Brotman & Moore, 2008). Largely, this progress has occurred within biological and medical sciences where more females than males undertake and/or aspire to careers in these areas (Eccles, 1994; Keeves & Kotte, 1992; Nagy et al., 2006; Schoon, Ross, & Martin, 2007; see also Jerrim & Schoon; Bagnoli,

Demey, & Scott, this volume). This suggests that the traditional idea of gender differences across all STEM domains is misleading. Rather considerable gender gaps continue to exist in some science fields, most prominently the physical sciences, mathematics, engineering, and technology (hereafter PME) (Brotman & Moore, 2008; Camp, Gilleland, Pearson, & Vander Putten, 2009; Chinn, 1999; Eccles, 1994; Eccles & Harold, 1992; Jones, Howe, & Rua, 2000; Rosenbloom, Ash, Dupont, & Coder, 2008).

Much research has found that math achievement is critical in predicting a variety of career paths and is a potential mechanism to explain the continued gender differences in PME fields (e.g., Ma & Johnson, 2008). Indeed, both multinational and longitudinal research has suggested an important link between school math ability and achievement-related choices both in school and for later career pathways (Nagy et al., 2008; Parker et al., 2012; Schoon, 2001; Schoon et al., 2007). Models of achievement-related choices, however, have suggested that the role of math achievement is insufficient to explain gender differences in PME fields and have indicated the importance of psychological factors such as self-concept, self-efficacy, or interest as central determinates of career-relevant choices and aspirations (Bandura et al., 2001; Eccles, 1994). In relation to self-concept, considerable support is now present in the literature to suggest its important role both regarding academic and career-relevant choices and outcomes and as a predictor of these outcomes over and above achievement (e.g., Camp et al., 2009; Marsh & Yeung, 1997; Nagy et al., 2008; Parker, Marsh, Ciarrochi, Marshall, & Abduljabbar, 2014; Parker et al., 2012; Schoon et al., 2007).

Self-concept factors associated with academic and career choice

Importantly, these results generally support theoretical models that suggest that stereotypical self-evaluations including self-concept mediate the role of ability in predicting various achievement-related choices (Bandura et al., 2001; Eccles, 1994; Marsh & Yeung, 1997). Indeed, Bandura et al.'s (2001) review of the literature suggests that when ability and achievement are controlled for stereotypical self-evaluations, they continue to be strong predictors of a number of career-relevant choices and aspirations. Stereotypical self-evaluations, in part, suggest that there are important gender differences in achievement-relevant self-perceptions over and above gender differences in achievement. Indeed, research suggests that domain-specific academic self-beliefs not only differ by gender but also strongly predict achievement-related choices after controlling for achievement (e.g. Nagy et al., 2006, 2008; Parker et al., 2012).

These gender differences suggest that males consistently report higher levels of mathematics self-concept, while females report higher levels of verbal self-concept (for a review, see Marsh, 1990a). Research and theory suggest that gender differences in self-concept incorporate not only differences in achievement but also stereotypical self-evaluations informed by the individual's social context (socialization, parental expectations, cultural climate, stereotypical gender roles), all of which are thought to be influential in explaining paths (see Eccles, 1994; Rosenbloom et al., 2008; Shapka et al., 2006; Wigfield et al., 2002). These models also emphasize the importance of taking into account self-beliefs in multiple domains rather than just in mathematics. This is consistent with Eccles (1994), who suggested the limited picture that emerges from only considering the influences of math-relevant variables when exploring achievement-related choices. As such, self-concept is not just an important predictor of career-relevant choices; it also provides a framework for predicting and interpreting gender difference in career-relevant outcomes like PME aspirations and university majors.

Internal/external frame of reference model

Marsh's (1986, 1990b) internal/external frame of reference (I/E) model provides a potential framework for analyzing the association between achievement and academic self-concept factors across multiple domains in predicting career-relevant variables. The model also has the potential for framing gender difference in such outcomes as it focuses on domains known to have stable gender differences – verbal (favoring females) and math (favoring males) (Marsh, 1990a). The model focuses on self-concept, which is hypothesized to be a multidimensionally and hierarchically arranged construct consisting of a number of self-perceptions relating to socially relevant domains of interest (Marsh & Hau, 2004; Shavelson, Hubner, & Stanton, 1976). While this model has traditionally been used to explain self-concept formation (Marsh, 1990a, 1990b), more recent research has begun to use the model as a framework for explaining academic choices (Marsh & Yeung, 1997; Nagy et al., 2006, 2008; Parker et al., 2012). The basic I/E model was developed to account for several paradoxical self-concept findings including: (a) the moderate correlation between achievement measures and general academic self-concept; (b) the observations that math and verbal self-concepts are only weakly related despite math and verbal achievement being moderately to strongly related; and (c) the negative correlations between achievement in one domain and self-concept in another domain (Marsh, 1990b).

In relation to these empirical findings, Marsh (1986, 1990b; see also Parker et al., 2013) suggested that domain-specific academic self-beliefs generally emerge as the result of two competing frames of reference. The moderate to strong correlation between domain-specific self-concept and achievement within a subject area can be explained by an external frame of reference where students evaluate their ability in a subject in reference to their peers. In such cases, class tests and other comparative achievement indicators provide information on which individuals can make self-relevant judgments. The low correlation between math and verbal self-concept, however, is explained by an internal frame of reference where individuals' achievement in different subject areas is compared relative

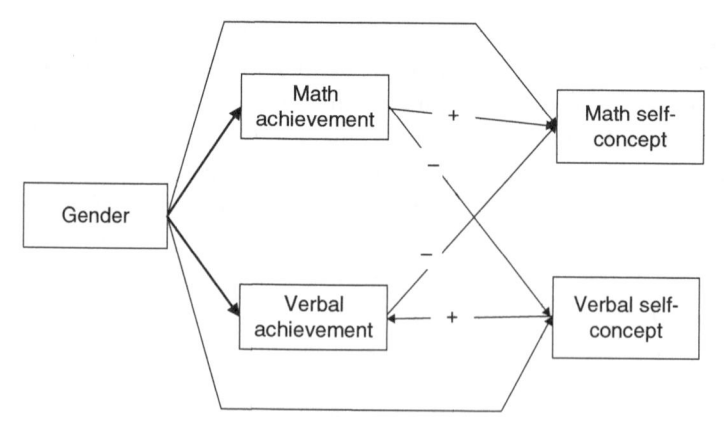

Figure 10.1 *Internal/external model*

to each other – a so-called ipsative effect (Marsh, 1990b). That is, individuals tend to compare their performance in multiple domains where better performance in one domain (e.g., math) results in a higher self-concept for that field than for other fields (e.g., English) – even if objective performance in both fields is relatively low. Alternatively, higher math performance would be expected to be associated with lower English self-concept even if performance in English is comparatively high (Marsh & Hau, 2004).

Thus, it would be expected on the basis of the I/E model that higher mathematics achievement would have a negative relationship with verbal self-concept and vice versa. This model and the expected relationships between achievement and self-concept have received widespread cross-cultural support (Marsh & Hau, 2004). Importantly, this model can incorporate both gender differences in math and verbal self-concept (Marsh, 1990a), and differences in stereotypical self-evaluations with gender contributing to differences in self-concept even after achievement differences are controlled for (Nagy et al., 2008; see Figure 10.1).

While the model has consistent empirical support (see Marsh & Hau, 2004), it has been applied to achievement-related choices in only a few cases. The results of these studies, however, confirm I/E predictions suggesting that (a) high levels of math self-concept predict math achievement-related decisions such as taking or aspiring to an advanced course in mathematics, (b) higher English self-concept is negatively related to taking such courses even after controlling for achievement in both fields, and (c) the introduction of self-concept as a predictor reduces the importance of achievement in predicting achievement-related choices (Marsh & Yeung, 2001; Nagy et al., 2006, 2008; Parker et al., 2012). Consistent with not only the I/E model but also other models of achievement-related choice (e.g. Bandura et al., 2001; Eccles, 1994), we thus assume that the effect of achievement on choice may be mediated by self-beliefs and evaluations. In the following section, this assumption, with a focus on the I/E model, will be tested in predicting career-relevant choices and outcomes particularly in relation to the high math-relevant PME fields.

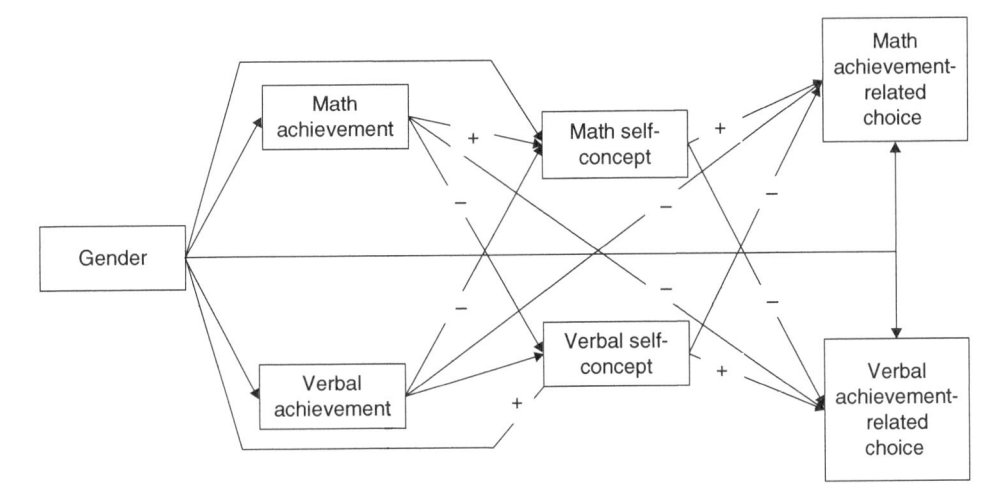

Figure 10.2 *Extended I/E model*

A research example

While the I/E model is well supported in academic settings (Marsh & Hau, 2004) and has been found to predict academic-relevant choices such as advanced course selection (Marsh & Yeung, 1997; Nagy et al., 2006, 2008), the model has rarely been used to predict career-relevant choices and pathways. Furthermore, research using this model to predict outcomes has typically been cross-sectional in nature. This is especially relevant in the current research where the transition from school to a career path introduces a number of new influences (e.g., university experiences and culture) that may lessen the importance of I/E processes formed in school. Thus we provide a research example that resolves some of the limitations in the current research, and illustrate many of the concepts discussed above. We explore whether the I/E model predicts career aspirations concurrently in school and also whether this model has a longitudinal influence on career-related outcomes after school (see Figure 10.2). In particular, we test the role of the I/E model in predicting university majors 2 years later in a sample of German young people.

This was done through several steps. First, gender differences were explored in domain-specific achievement and self-concept. Second, gender differences in university majors were explored. The current research went beyond typical distinctions between science and non-science fields given the increasing participation of women in biological and medical sciences, as well as the continued gender gap regarding the mathematics, physics, and engineering fields (see Parker et al., 2012). We differentiated between four study domains: (a) physical sciences, math, and engineering; (b) life, biological, and medical sciences; (c) law and business; and (d) humanities. These domains closely map groupings found in the ISCO-88 occupational coding scheme (Elias, 1997). Third, the research explored the I/E model via structural equation modeling, to see if the relationships between gender, self-concept, and achievement expected by the I/E framework were present in this dataset. Finally, gender and verbal and math self-concept and achievement were used to predict career aspirations at school and later university majors. Several specific hypotheses were made: (a) that high levels of math achievement and self-concept would predict aspirations and university majors in PME over other fields; (b) that English achievement and self-concept would predict aspirations and university majors in fields other than PME; (c) that the introduction of self-concept would result in achievement becoming a less important predictor; and (d) that these processes would predict not only concurrent career aspirations but also longitudinal university majors 2 years later. It was expected that the incorporation of gender differences in math and English self-concept factors with these I/E predictions would provide a useful frame for exploring gender differences in aspirations and university majors, particularly in reference to PME fields.

Method

Participants

The current research utilized data from the ongoing project *Transformation of the Secondary School System and Academic Careers* (TOSCA) conducted in Germany at the Max Planck Institute of Human Development in Berlin and the University of Tübingen. The data for this particular project comes from the second cohort of this project, which began in 2006, from schools that represent the university or college track in Germany (*Gymnasium*). The second wave was completed in 2008 when participants were at university. In total, 1,881 participants completed measures of self-concept and math and English achievement, and reported on their career aspirations at Time 1 and reported their university majors at Time 2. Participants' average age at Time 1 was 19.76 ($SD = 1.12$). The sample was weighted toward females (58%). Such a bias has been found in previous research with German university-track students, suggesting that these samples tend to reflect more selective populations of males than females (see Nagy et al., 2006). The analytic sample of 1,881 participants came from a much larger database of 5,030 young adults attending a *Gymnasium* in 2006. The 1,881 participants were chosen because they had provided information at Time 2 indicating that they were at university or other tertiary colleges in 2008 and were undertaking majors in professional fields.

Materials

Achievement

The mathematics achievement test administered was taken from the Third International Mathematics and Science Study (TIMSS; e.g., Baumert, Bos,

& Lehmann, 2000). Reliability estimates indicated good internal consistency (α = .88). English achievement was assessed using a shortened research version of the Test of English as a Foreign Language (TOEFL), as used in the Institutional Testing Program. The instrument comprised three components (listening comprehension, structure and written expression, reading comprehension). Reliability of the achievement measure was good (α = .95).

Self-concept

Math and English self-concept were measured using the German version (Schwanzer, Trautwein, Lüdtke, & Sydow, 2005) of the Self-Description Questionnaire (SDQ) III (Marsh & O'Neill, 1984). The SDQ III is a multidimensional self-concept instrument for late adolescents and young adults and includes a number of domain-specific factors based on the Shavelson et al. (1976) model. Previous research with the German SDQ instruments indicates excellent construct validity and reliability (Marsh, Trautwein, Lüdtke, Köller, & Baumert, 2006; Schwanzer et al., 2005). From the 17 scales in the SDQ III (German), only the math self-concept factor (e.g., *I was always good in mathematics*) and the English self-concept factor (e.g., *I am good at English*) were used. Participants responded to each item on a 4-point (agree–disagree) response scale. Internal consistency for the current sample was .91 for math self-concept and .93 for English self-concept.

Career aspirations and university majors

At Time 1, participants were asked to report on their long-term career aspirations. At Time 2, participants were asked to report on their university major. In both cases the responses were coded based on the ISCO-88 system (Elias, 1997). The study participants were then divided into four groups: (a) math, physics, and engineering (hereafter PME); (b) life, biological, and medical science (hereafter biological/medical sciences); (c) humanities and social sciences (hereafter humanities); and (d) law, economics, and business (hereafter law/business).

Analysis

Analysis was conducted in several steps. First, gender differences in math and English achievement and self-concept, career aspirations, and realized university majors were explored. Second, profiles on the I/E achievement and self-concept variables for career aspirations and university majors were assessed using a set of univariate ANOVAs. In addition, the relationship between self-concept and achievement was explored in relation to the I/E model using Structural Equation Modeling (SEM). Finally, multinomial logit models were used in Mplus to explore the role of math and English achievement and self-concept in predicting career aspirations and later university majors. All variables observed (achievement scores) and latent (self-concept) factors were z-standardized to the same scale so that odds ratios could be directly compared. Full-information-

Table 10.1. *Gender differences in self-concept and achievement*

	Males		Females		
	Mean	SD	Mean	SD	Cohen's d
Math self-concept	2.84	.81	2.55	.83	−.35***
English self-concept	2.92	0.82	2.87	0.86	−0.06
English achievement^	.17	.99	−.13	.98	−.31***
Math achievement^	.19	.91	−.22	.87	−.46***

	Percentage male		Percentage female		Odds ratio: males	
	Aspire	UM	Aspire	UM	Aspire	UM
PME	44.8	47.4	7.0	17.0	10.8	4.4
Biology/medical	15.0	10.3	21.3	12.7	0.7	0.8
Humanities	26.0	16.8	55.7	44.2	0.3	0.3
Law/business	14.2	25.5	16.0	26.1	0.9	1.0

Notes:^ English and math tests scores are standardized.
Aspire = Career aspirations; UM = University majors.
* $p < .05$, ** $p < .01$, *** $p < .001$.

maximum-likelihood estimation was implemented for the small amount of missing data (< 5%) relating to achievement and self-concept factors.

Results and discussion

Gender differences, career aspirations, and university majors

Table 10.1 illustrates the gender differences in career aspirations present at Time 1. The gender difference observed in previous research (e.g., OECD, 2011) was present in this sample with only 7% of females indicating a desire to work in PME fields. In contrast, PME was the most popular career aspiration for males, with 45% indicating that they aspired to work in this field. Humanities represented the opposing gender pattern to PME with 56% of females but only 26% of males aspiring to careers in the humanities. A greater percentage of females than males aspired to work in the fields of biological/medical sciences, athough the difference was moderate (males 15%; females 21%). Finally, law/business was the least gender-typed aspiration (males 14%; females 16%). For university majors, gender differences generally followed the same pattern as career aspirations, although differences were smaller.[1] While the increased participation

---

[1] The match between career aspirations at Time 1 and university majors at Time 2 was explored (see Table 10.2). Importantly, career aspirations in school were a strong predictor of what young adults would go on to study in university 2 years later (Kappa = .62). Important for the current research's focus on PME, aspirations and majors in this field were the most closely related over time, with 90% of young adults who aspired to PME careers studying university majors in these

of women in many professional fields, particularly biological/medical sciences, was observed, the continued and considerable gender differences in PME favoring males (and in humanities favoring females) was apparent (Wigfield et al., 2002). These results, including the higher rate of women taking on humanities majors, are consistent with trends in the US (Bowen, Chingos, & McPherson, 2009) and internationally (OECD, 2011). Many hypotheses have been developed to explain such gender differences. One recent hypothesis is that the difference is due, at least in part, to differences in achievement and/or academic self-concept profiles (e.g., Eccles, 1994; Lubinski & Benbow, 2006).

Gender differences, career aspirations, university majors, and the I/E model

Achievement and self-concept profiles by gender

Analysis then moved to explore the predictors of career aspirations and university majors in terms of gender differences and mean profiles across aspiration and university major groups. Gender differences in the central constructs generally followed those expected for mathematics but were less apparent for English (see Table 10.1). Males tended to achieve higher scores on the math achievement test ($d = -.46, p < .001$) and were higher on math self-concept ($d = -.35, p < .001$). Males also recorded higher scores on the English-language test ($d = -.31, p < .001$) but there was no significant difference on English self-concept despite achievement differences ($d = .06$, n.s.).[2] These results, however, need to be understood in the context of the German education system. As Nagy et al. (2008) has pointed out, *Gymnasium* (university-track) entry is more selective for boys than it is for girls. Put simply, *Gymnasium* schools draw female students from a wider band of achievement than they do males. This is supported when exploring the Programme for International Student Assessment (PISA) results for 2003 (for math) and 2009 (for reading). The PISA reports, which consist of a random sample of the total German secondary school population (rather than just those in the university-track schools), show that females outperform males in verbal domains (OECD, 2004; see also Jerrim & Schoon, this volume). For all secondary school students there is a gender difference in mathematics favoring males, but, while significant, it is smaller than the difference noted in this chapter.

---

fields at university. The humanities also displayed a close match between career aspirations and university majors. Aspiring to biological/medical sciences was the least predictive with only 56% who aspired to this field undertaking university majors in this area 2 years later. The significant role of aspirations in predicting actual university majors is strongly consistent with the Wisconsin model of educational and status attainment.

[2] The lack of gender differences favoring females may reflect the nature of the sample where German university-track schools have a smaller and more selective male population (Nagy et al., 2006).

Table 10.2. *Time 1 career aspirations and Time 2 university majors*

Career aspirations percentage	University majors percentage			
	PMES	BMS	Law/business	Humanities
PMES	**90.0**	4.7	2.1	3.2
BMS	17.2	**55.6**	13.6	13.6
Law/business	15.6	5.6	**68.2**	10.6
Humanities	6.0	2.2	9.0	**82.8**

Note: Chi-square (9) = 1,068, p < .001. Kappa = .6.

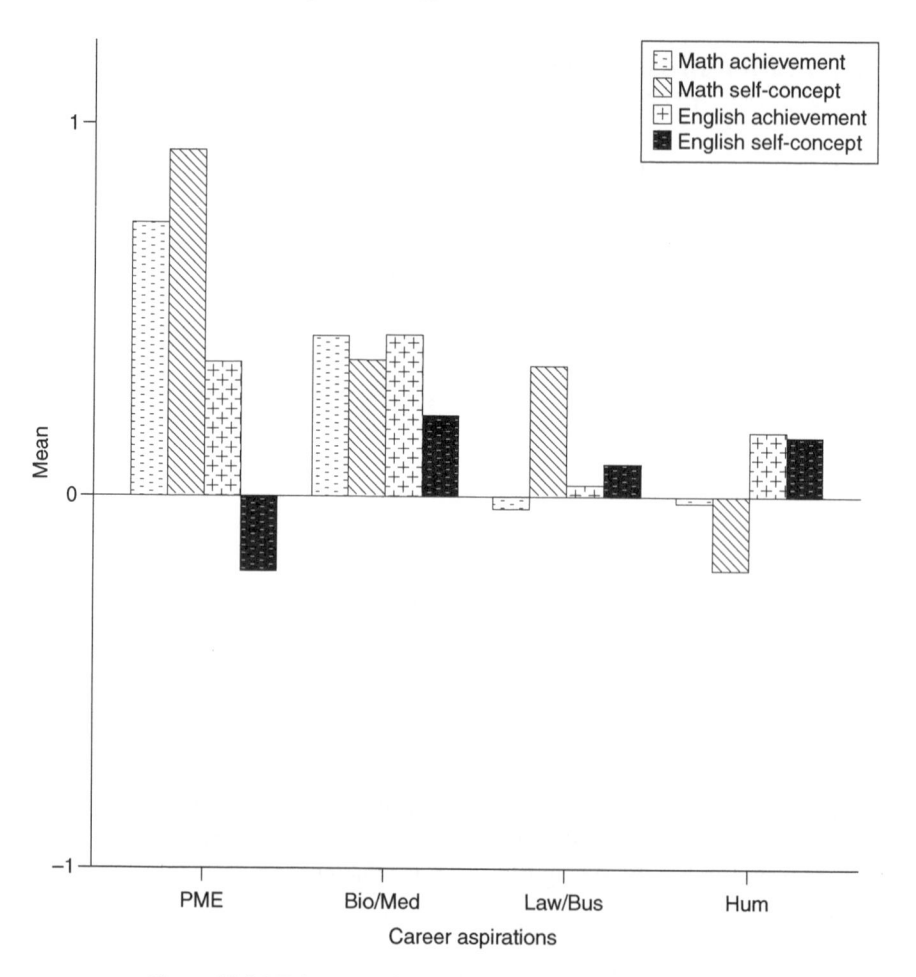

Figure 10.3 *I/E factor profiles for career aspiration groups*

Achievement and self-concept profiles by college major

Standardized mean profiles on I/E factors were also explored across the four academic fields on aspirations and university majors (see Figures 10.2 and 10.3). As expected, individuals who aspired to and who undertook majors

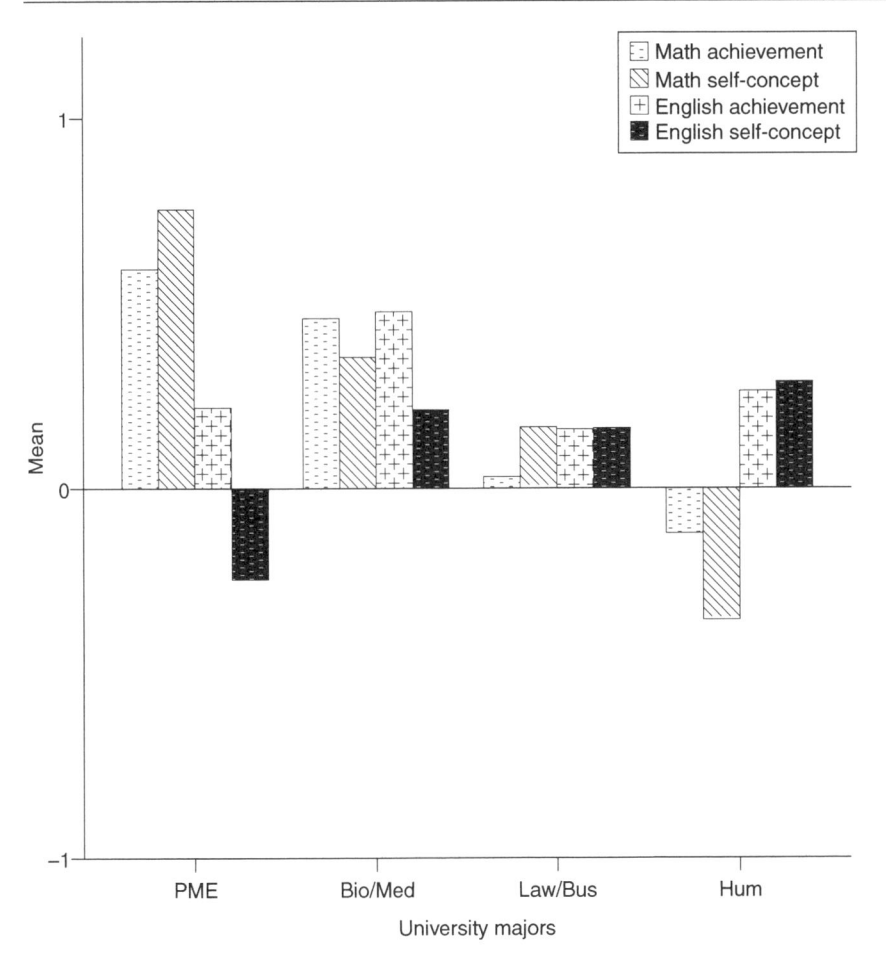

Figure 10.4 *I/E factor profiles for university major groups*

in PME fields had the highest math achievement and self-concept but comparatively lower levels of English achievement and the lowest levels of English self-concept. Humanities displayed the opposite pattern: we found the lowest levels of math achievement and self-concept for both aspiration and university major groups. Interestingly, the biological/medical sciences groups showed relatively high levels of both math and English achievement and self-concept, with the highest English achievement scores and the second highest mathematics scores. Univariate ANOVAs indicated all I/E predictors were significantly different across groups ($p < .001$). Importantly, in relation to career aspirations, group membership predicted considerable variance in math-relevant predictors (math achievement $R^2 = .12$; math self-concept $R^2 = .18$). Group membership also explained small, yet statistically significant amounts of variance in English variables (English achievement $R^2 = .02$; English self-concept $R^2 = .02$). In relation to university majors, group membership explained large amounts of variance in math variables (math achievement $R^2 = .11$; math self-concept $R^2 = .24$) but also statistically significant levels in English variables (English achievement $R^2 = .01$; English self-concept $R^2 = .05$).

Mean profiles on math and English achievement and self-concept indicated that the PME group was the only group to consistently display higher math achievement scores and self-concept levels than English achievement and self-concept for both career aspirations at school and later university majors. Most other groups displayed the opposite pattern, with higher levels of English achievement and self-concept than corresponding math factors. However, those who aspired to and studied biological/medical sciences displayed relatively similar levels of both math and English self-concept and achievement. These profiles suggest a continuum of career choice ranging from fields with high math and relatively lower verbal influences in PME, to fields with a balance of math and verbal in the biological and medical sciences, through to those outcomes that are more dominated by verbal influences, in particular law and business and the humanities. The degree to which math-dominated university majors are associated with gender, achievement, and academic self-concept was explored next.

I/E predictors of career aspirations and university majors[3]

Two stepwise multinomial logit models were run, one for Time 1 I/E factors predicting career aspirations at school and one for Time 1 I/E factors predicting Time 2 university majors (see Table 10.3). Each multinomial logit model consisted of a series of steps. Step 1 included gender as the sole predictor. Step 2 included gender and math and English achievement. Finally, Step 3 included gender, math and English achievement and self-concept. In all models the PME group was used as the reference group. Results are presented in odds ratios.

The first stepwise model used gender and I/E predictors at Time 1 to predict career aspirations in school. In the first step gender was found to be a significant

---

[3] An SEM model was used to explore the validity of the I/E model in the current sample. This model explored the role of gender on English and math achievement and self-concept and the relationship between achievement measures and domain-specific academic self-concept. This model provided a good fit to the data (chi-square = 468, df = 38, RMSEA = .08, CFI = .97) and supported the hypotheses drawn from I/E and self-concept theory. In particular, gender predicted both achievement and self-concept. Gender difference in achievement favored males (males coded 0, females coded 1) in both math ($\beta = -.24, p < .001$) and English ($\beta = -.12, p < .001$). Controlling for gender differences in achievement, gender predicted self-concept in expected patterns with males being higher in math self-concept ($\beta = -.11, p < .001$), and females, despite lower levels of achievement, were higher in English self-concept ($\beta = .06, p < .001$). In relation to the associations between achievement and self-concept, findings strongly supported I/E predictions in the following three ways. First, math achievement was a strong predictor of math self-concept ($\beta = .61, p < .001$), while English achievement was a strong predictor of English self-concept ($\beta = .65, p < .001$). Second, math achievement was a moderate negative predictor of English self-concept ($\beta = -.21, p < .001$), and English achievement was a statistically significant negative predictor of math self-concept ($\beta = -.14, p < .001$). Finally, the association between math and English self-concept controlling for achievement paths was moderate and negative ($r = -.21, p < .001$).

Table 10.3. *Multinomial logit odds ratios for career aspirations*

	Step 1				Step 2				Step 3			
	Bio	Law	Hum		Bio	Law	Hum		Bio	Law	Hum	
	Career aspirations											
Gender (F = 1)	2.66***	3.66***	2.98***		2.40***	3.42***	3.00***		2.46***	3.06***	3.47***	
Math test					.37***	.36***	.64***		.50***	1.11	.86	
English test					1.14	1.41**	1.48**		.73	.99	.92	
Math SC									.70	.44***	.26***	
English SC									2.11***	1.78***	1.60*	
	University majors											
Gender (F = 1)	1.69***	2.69***	1.84***		1.56***	2.52***	1.90***		1.55***	1.88***	2.42***	
Math test					.45***	.36***	.76**		.68***	1.15	.83	
English test					1.33***	1.73***	1.64***		.86	1.19	1.08	
Math SC									.58***	.52***	.27***	
English SC									2.04***	1.62***	1.79***	

Notes: Reference group is PME.
S1 = Step 1 with only gender as a predictor.
S2 = Step 2 with gender and achievement measures as predictors.
S3 = Step 3 with gender, achievement, and self-concept as predictors.
* $p < .05$, ** $p < .01$, *** $p < .001$.
SC = self-concept. All predictors standardized.

predictor of career aspirations. Females were significantly more likely to aspire to be in any field other than PME, particularly in relation to humanities (*or* = 3.66, *p* < .001). The second step indicated that higher math achievement decreased the odds that an individual would aspire to any other field than PME, while English achievement increased the odds that an individual would aspire to a different field than PME with the exception of biological/medical sciences (*or* = 1.14, n.s.). In the final step, math and English self-concept were introduced into the model, resulting in a considerable decrease in the predictive effects of achievement. Indeed, the effect of achievement predicting career aspirations was weakened to non-significant levels in all cases with the exception of math achievement predicting aspirations in PME over biological/medical sciences (*or* = .50, *p* < .001). Importantly, the results for the self-concept factors closely followed I/E prediction where it was found that higher math self-concept increased the odds that an individual would aspire to a career in PME over humanities (*or* = .26, *p* < .001) and law/business (*or* = .44, *p* < .001). In contrast, higher English self-concept increased the odds that a person would have career aspirations in biological/medical science (*or* = 2.11, *p* < .001), law/business (*or* = 1.78, *p* < .001), and humanities (*or* = 1.60, *p* < .001) rather than in PME.

Using the same strategy as for career aspirations at school, I/E factors at school were used to longitudinally predict university majors 2 years later. Gender was found to be a strong predictor of university majors, with results ranging from females being one-and-a-half times more likely (Step 1: *or* = 1.69; Step 3: *or* = 1.55) to study biological/medical sciences than PME to females being almost two-and-a-half times more likely to study humanities (Step 1: *or* = 2.69; Step 3: *or* = 2.46) than PME. In Step 2, achievement tests were observed to be a predictor of all university major groups with high math achievement decreasing the odds that an individual would study biological/medical sciences (*or* = .45, *p* < .05), humanities (*or* = .36, *p* < .001), or law/business (*or* = .77, *p* < .001) over PME. In contrast, English achievement increased the odds that an individual would study any one of these fields over PME. In the final step, domain-specific self-concept was introduced into the model. Again the introduction of self-concept considerably reduced the effects of achievement, with only math achievement predicting PME university majors over biological/medical science majors being the only remaining significant effect (*or* = .68, *p* < .001). Results for self-concept also matched I/E predictions, suggesting that high English self-concept significantly increased the odds that an individual would go on to study in a field other than PME, particularly in relation to biological/medical sciences (*or* = 2.04, *p* < .001) and humanities (*or* = 1.79, *p* < .001) but also in law/business (*or* = 1.62, *p* < .01). High math self-concept was associated with a much greater likelihood that individuals would study PME over any other field, particularly regarding the humanities (*or* = .27, *p* < .001), but also in biological and medical sciences (*or* = .58, *p* < .001) and law/business (*or* = .52, *p* < .001).

With the relationships between constructs following patterns expected on the basis of the I/E model, multinomial logit models likewise supported the

Table 10.4. *Loglikelihood difference test of constrained multinomial logit models versus free model*

Constrained parameters	df	Loglikelihood difference test Career aspirations	University majors
All parameters constrained	14	184***	342***
Biological/medical sciences and law/business constrained	9	99***	147***
Humanities and biological/medical sciences constrained	9	169***	321***
Humanities and law/business constrained	9	167***	321***

Note: Loglikelihood difference test produces values on a chi-squared distribution. Significant value indicates constraining paths to be equal significantly reduces the fit of the model compared to a model in which all parameters are free to vary. *** $p < .001$.

hypotheses. These multinomial models suggested that math factors increased the odds that an individual would have aspirations in and study PME fields. Likewise, English achievement and self-concept decreased these odds.

The findings also supported several central models of career-relevant choices. Self-beliefs were expected to mediate the relationship between achievement (and other gendered socio-cultural influences) and outcomes (Bandura et al., 2001; Eccles, 1994; Marsh & Yeung, 1997). This was confirmed as the introduction of self-concept generally resulted in achievement becoming a non-significant predictor. The finding suggests that stereotypical self-evaluations play a central role in achievement-related aspirations and choices. From an I/E perspective the importance of self-concept as a predictor is due to self-concept containing information not only from an external frame of reference, tied closely to achievement scores, but also an internal frame of reference that consists of information drawn from individuals' internal comparison of their performance across a range of subject areas (Marsh, 1986, 1990b; Marsh & Yeung, 1997). Furthermore, Eccles (1994) suggests that self-evaluation factors contain information about socialization, gender roles, and parental expectations, all of which impact on individuals' views about the nature of certain fields and whether these fields are more or less appropriate when compared to other fields. This is also consistent with Bandura et al. (2001), who emphasized the importance of self-beliefs as a product of a range of achievement and socio-cultural factors and as central determinates of a range of career outcomes.

For gender, the results suggest two things. First, gender-stereotypical self-evaluations appeared to be more important and accounted for more of the effect of gender than achievement. Second, even when controlling for achievement and self-concept, gender still had a strong and significant effect on university major choice. This indicates that the effect of gender on university major selection is more complicated than simply differences in achievement and self-beliefs, and likely includes task value, gender socialization, and other psychological and contextual factors (see Eccles, 1994).

Constrained multinomial logit models

A final set of analyses were run in which parameters were constrained to be equal in predicting aspirations and university majors in fields other than PME. This provided an opportunity to explore whether odds ratios for I/E factors predicting non-PME appraisals and university majors differed across biological/medical sciences, humanities, and law/business. Results suggested that constraining parameters across groups resulted in a significantly worse-fitting model than one in which all parameters were free to vary for both career aspirations (loglikelihood (14) = 184, $p < .001$) and university majors (loglikelihood (14) = 339, $p < .001$). Follow-up tests indicated that all groups differed from the PME reference group in significantly different ways (see Table 10.4). We used a series of line graphs of standardized multinomial regression coefficients to explore these differential effects. These graphs suggest that math achievement and English self-concept were the most important factors in predicting biological/medical science aspiration and university major group membership over PME group membership (see Figures 10.5 and 10.6). In contrast, math self-concept and, to a lesser degree, English self-concept, but not achievement, were most important for predicting law/business and humanities membership. Interestingly, math self-concept was a more important predictor for the humanities, while English self-concept was more important for law/business. These profiles were relatively consistent for both career aspiration and the university major outcomes.

These results reveal that math and English achievement and self-concepts distinguished biological/medical sciences, humanities, and law/business from PME in significantly different ways. In particular, it appeared that lower math achievement and higher English self-concept were key factors in choosing biological and medical sciences over PME. Interestingly, this suggests that the mediating role of self-concepts may be less important for biological/medical sciences than PME where math achievement remained a significant predictor of both concurrent aspirations at school and longitudinal university majors. Likewise, the relative importance of math or English variables as predictors differed across groups. English self-concept was relatively more important for predicting aspirations and entry into law/business over PME, while math self-concept was more important for the humanities. This suggests that both of the central predictions of this chapter drawn from the I/E model – the mediating role of self-concept and the ipsative processes between math and English variables – predicted career-relevant variables in different ways depending on the fields of interest.

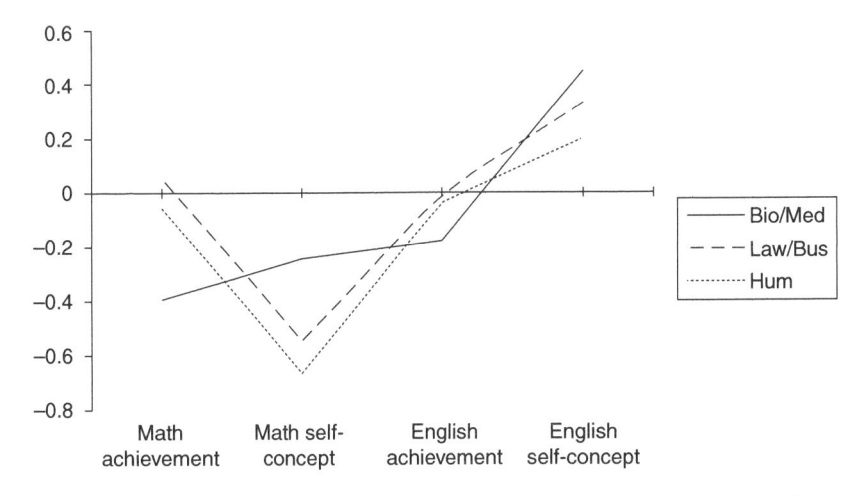

Figure 10.5 *Profile of standardized multinomial regression weights for career aspiration groups*

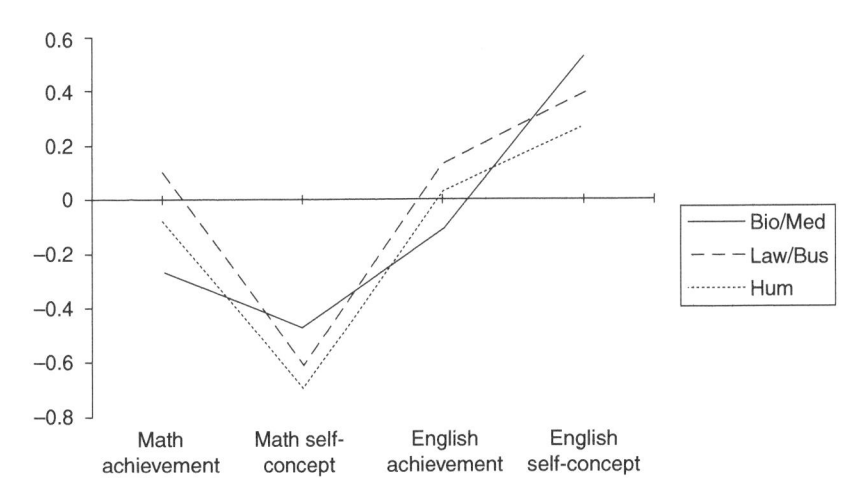

Figure 10.6 *Profile of standardized multinomial regression weights for university major groups*

Summary and conclusions

The finding of this research example illustrates the limitations of considering math achievement alone as a critical filter into the physical sciences for women. Indeed, math achievement was reduced to a non-significant significant predictor of PME aspirations and university in all cases but the biological/medical sciences when academic self-concept was introduced. It is important to note, however, that math self-concept was the strongest predictor in the current research, indicating that it may be a more critical filter to PME careers than math achievement. While math self-concept was clearly an important factor, the current results indicate that considering variables in a single domain may not be sufficient in providing an explanation of differences in career paths such as why individuals choose PME over biological/medical sciences (see also Chow & Salmela-Aro; Jerrim & Schoon; Wang & Kenny, this volume). Such a model has important substantive and applied implications for explaining gender differences in career aspirations and university majors. This is particularly the case when the results are placed in the context of gender difference in self-concept.

Eccles (1994) states that gender differences in career paths can reflect legitimate decisions by females to choose occupational arenas that best reflect their interests, attitudes, and values. Indeed, Eccles (1994, p. 605) indicates that female choices not to enter male-dominated fields are both "reasonable and predictable." Crucially, however, such choices have implications for PME fields and suggest that society as a whole may suffer from the loss of women's talent and perspectives when they do not enter fields such as PME (Eccles, 1994).

Importantly, this chapter points to the importance of self-perceptions at school as a target for intervention and policy. First, the self-concept factors used in this research were formed in school and predicted achievement-related choices both concurrently, for career aspirations at school, and longitudinally, for university majors. Second, these self-concept factors were stronger predictors of both appraisals and university majors than achievement. Finally, SEM results indicated that gender contributes to differences in self-perceptions, with males higher on math self-concept and females higher on English self-concept, after controlling for achievement differences (see note 3). Taken together, these findings indicate that stereotypical self-evaluations formed in school (both low math and high English) may be a barrier to females entering PME fields.

Therefore, strategies to improve female participation in PME arenas should take into consideration the importance of academic self-perceptions and the importance of school experiences in forming these perceptions. Importantly, given the positive effect of high math self-concept on PME aspirations and university majors and the parallel negative effect of high English self-concept, any program aiming to increase PME participation must carefully target programs by acknowledging a multidimensional approach to academic self-concept (O'Mara, Marsh, Craven, & Debus, 2006) and acknowledge the integrated effect that multiple academic (and indeed other life) domains outside mathematics have on young adults' achievement-related choices (Eccles, 1994). Indeed, highlighted by this research is the idea that individuals use profiles across a range of domains rather than strengths in a particular area in order to make achievement-related choices (see Eccles, 1994; Chow & Salmela-Aro, this volume). As such, useful strategies may include increasing the salience of strengths in mathematical skills, knowledge, and abilities of females who are gifted in these areas, and by suggesting that such individuals may be more suited to careers in PME fields rather than in traditional gender-stereotyped occupations.

In some cases the introduction of self-concept into the model reduced the direct effect of gender on aspirations and university majors, suggesting that academic self-concept may be one important mechanism that explains gender differences in gendered aspirations and university majors. However, one of the most interesting findings was that there were still considerable gender differences after controlling for achievement and self-concept. This suggests that other gender-relevant choice mechanisms are at work. Eccles' (1994) achievement-related choices model suggests some additional pathways that were not explored here but are likely to help account for the remaining gender difference effect. First, in the work of Eccles math and verbal self-concept can largely be categorized as expectancies of success (see Nagengast et al., 2011). In Eccles' model the effects of such expectations on achievement-related choice (such as university majors) are hypothesized to be moderated by task values. Significant gender differences have also been observed in such task values (Chow & Salmela-Aro, 2011, and this volume) and thus such constructs are likely to be of interest to future research. Another mechanism that may help explain gender differences in aspirations and college majors that was not studied here is the role of gender socialization (Eccles, 1994). Taken together, gender differences in aspirations and college majors appear to be the result of a multi-causal system. Thus, while research progresses by identifying and studying components of this system, like the research example used here, policy and practice are likely to benefit most from considering a broader picture, synthesizing research from a number of different perspectives.

References

Bandura, A., Barbaranelli, C., Caprara, G. V., & Pastorelli, C. (2001). Self-efficacy beliefs as shapers of children's aspirations and career trajectories. *Child Development, 72,* 187–206.

Baumert, J., Bos, W., & Lehmann, R. (Eds.). (2000). *TIMSS/III. 2: Mathematische und physikalische Kompetenzen am Ende der gymnasialen Oberstufe* (Vol. 2). Opladen: Leske + Budrich.

Bowen, W. G., Chingos, M. M., & McPherson, M. S. (2009). *Crossing the finish line: Completing college at America's public universities.* Princeton University Press.

Brotman, J., & Moore, F. (2008). Girls and science: A review of four themes in the science education literature. *Journal of Research in Science Teaching, 45,* 971–1002.

Camp, A., Gilleland, D., Pearson, C., & Vander Putten, J. (2009). Women's path into science and engineering majors: A structural equation model. *Educational Research and Evaluation, 15,* 63–77.

Chinn, P. (1999). Multiple worlds/mismatched meanings: Barriers to minority women engineers. *Journal of Research in Science Teaching, 36,* 621–636.

Chow, A., & Salmela-Aro, K. (2011). Task-values across subject domains: A gender comparison using a person-centered approach. *International Journal of Behavioral Development, 35,* 202–209.

Eccles, J. (1994). Understanding women's educational and occupational choices. *Psychology of Women Quarterly*, 18, 585–609.

Eccles, J., & Harold, R. (1992). Gender differences in educational and occupational patterns among the gifted. In N. Colangelo, S. Assouline, & D. Amronson (Eds.), *Talent development: Proceedings from the 1991 Henry B. and Jocelyn Wallace National Research Symposium on Talent Development* (pp. 3–29). Unionville, NY: Trillium Press.

Elias, P. (1997). Occupational classification (ISCO-88): Concepts, methods, reliability, validity and cross-national comparability. *OECD Labour Market and Social Policy Occasional Papers*.

Jones, M., Howe, A., & Rua, M. (2000). Gender differences in students' experiences, interests, and attitudes toward science and scientists. *Science Education*, 84, 180–192.

Keeves, J., & Kotte, D. (1992). Disparities between the sexes in science education: 1970–84. In J. Keeves (Ed.), *The IEA study of science III* (pp. 141–164). New York: Pergamon.

Lubinski, D., & Benbow, C. P. (2006). Study of mathematically precocious youth after 35 years: Uncovering antecedents for the development of math-science expertise. *Perspectives on Psychological Science*, 1, 316–345.

Ma, X., & Johnson, W. (2008). Mathematics as the critical filter: Curricular effects on gendered career choices. In H. Watt & J. Eccles (Eds.), *Gender and occupational outcomes: Longitudinal assessments of individual, social, and cultural influences*. Washington, DC: American Psychological Association.

Marsh, H. (1986). Verbal and math self-concepts: An internal/external frame of reference model. *American Educational Research Journal*, 23, 129.

(1990a). Influences of internal and external frames of reference on the formation of math and English self-concepts. *Journal of Educational Psychology*, 82, 107–116.

(1990b). A multidimensional, hierarchical model of self-concept: Theoretical and empirical justification. *Educational Psychology Review*, 2, 77–172.

Marsh, H., & Hau, K. (2004). Explaining paradoxical relations between academic self-concepts and achievements: Cross-cultural generalizability of the internal/external frame of reference predictions across 26 countries. *Journal of Educational Psychology*, 96, 56–67.

Marsh, H. W., & O'Neill, R. (1984). Self description questionnaire III: The construct validity of multidimensional self-concept ratings by late adolescence. *Journal of Educational Psychology*, 21, 153–174.

Marsh, H., Trautwein, U., Lüdtke, O., Köller, O., & Baumert, J. (2006). Integration of multidimensional self-concept and core personality constructs: Construct validation and relations to well-being and achievement. *Journal of Personality*, 74, 403–456.

Marsh, H., & Yeung, A. (1997). Coursework selection: Relations to academic self-concept and achievement. *American Educational Research Journal*, 34, 691.

(2001). An extension of the internal/external frame of reference model: A response to Bong (1998). *Multivariate Behavioral Research*, 36, 389–420.

Nagengast, B., Marsh, H. W., Scalas, L. F., Xu, M. K., Hau, K. T., & Trautwein, U. (2011). Who took the "×" out of expectancy-value theory? A psychological mystery, a substantive-methodological synergy, and a cross-national generalization. *Psychological science*, 22, 1058–1066.

Nagy, G., Garrett, J., Trautwein, U., Cortina, K., Baumert, J., & Eccles, J. (2008). Gendered high school course selection as a precursor of gendered careers: The mediating role of self-concept and intrinsic value. In H. Watt & J. Eccles (Eds.), *Gender and occupational outcomes: Longitudinal assessments of individual, social, and cultural influences* (pp. 115–143). Washington, DC: American Psychological Association.

Nagy, G., Trautwein, U., Baumert, J., Köller, O., & Garrett, J. (2006). Gender and course selection in upper secondary education: Effects of academic self-concept and intrinsic value. *Educational Research and Evaluation*, 12, 323–345.

OECD. (2004). *Education at a glance: OECD indicators*. Paris: OECD.

(2011). *Learning for tomorrow's world: First results from PISA 2003*. Paris: OECD.

O Mara, A., Marsh, H., Craven, R., & Debus, R. (2006). Do self-concept interventions make a difference? A synergistic blend of construct validation and meta-analysis. *Educational Psychologist*, 41, 181–206.

Parker, P. D., Marsh, H. W., Ciarrochi, J., Marshall, S., & Abduljabbar, A. S. (2014). Juxtaposing math self-efficacy and self-concept as predictors of long-term achievement outcomes. *Educational Psychology*, 43(1), 29–48.

Parker, P. D., Marsh, H. W., Lüdtke, O., & Trautwein, U. (2013). Differential school contextual effects for math and English: Integrating the Big-Fish-Little-Pond Effect and the Internal/external Frame of Reference. *Learning and Instruction*, 23, 78–89.

Parker, P. D., Schoon, I., Tsai, Y.-M., Nagy, G., Trautwein, U., & Eccles, J. S. (2012). Achievement, agency, gender, and socioeconomic background as predictors of postschool choices: A multicontext study. *Developmental Psychology*, 48(6), 1629–1642. doi: 10.1037/a0029167.

Rosenbloom, J., Ash, R., Dupont, B., & Coder, L. (2008). Why are there so few women in information technology? Assessing the role of personality in career choices. *Journal of Economic Psychology*, 29, 543–554.

Schoon, I. (2001). Teenage job aspirations and career attainment in adulthood: A 17-year follow-up study of teenagers who aspired to become scientists, health professionals, or engineers. *International Journal of Behavioral Development*, 25, 124–132.

Schoon, I., Ross, A., & Martin, P. (2007). Science related careers: Aspirations and outcomes in two British cohort studies. *Equal Opportunities International*, 26, 129–143.

Schwanzer, A., Trautwein, U., Lüdtke, O., & Sydow, H. (2005). Entwicklung eines Instruments zur Erfassung des Selbstkonzepts junger Erwachsener. *Diagnostica*, 51, 183–194.

Sells, L. (1976). *The mathematics filter and the education of women and minorities*. Paper presented at the Annual Meeting of the American Association for the Advancement of Science, Boston, MA.

(1980). Mathematics: The invisible filter. *Engineering Education*, 70, 340–341.

Shapka, J., Domene, J., & Keating, D. (2006). Trajectories of career aspirations through adolescence and young adulthood: Early math achievement as a critical filter. *Educational Research and Evaluation*, 12, 347–358.

Shavelson, R. J., Hubner, J. J., & Stanton, G. C. (1976). Self-concept: Validation of construct interpretations. *Review of Educational Research*, 46, 407–441.

Wigfield, A., Battle, A., Keller, L., & Eccles, J. (2002). Sex differences in motivation, self-concept, career aspiration, and career choice: Implications for cognitive development. In A. McGillicuddy-De Lisi & R. De Lisi (Eds.), *Biology, society, and behavior: The development of sex differences in cognition* (pp. 93–124). Greenwich, CT: Ablex.

11 Does priority matter? Gendered patterns of subjective task values across school subject domains

Angela Chow and Katariina Salmela-Aro

Abstract

This chapter examines patterns in subjective task values across different school subjects from a person-centered perspective. According to the Eccles expectancy-value model of behavioral choice, individuals' perceived values on school subjects or activities, the so-called *subjective task values* (STVs or simply *task values*), are important motivational sources that play an influential role in shaping behaviors and choices over and above ability concepts and actual capabilities (Eccles (Parsons), 1983; Eccles, Wigfield, & Schiefele, 1998). Going beyond previous studies that focused on associations between STVs and outcomes within one particular school subject area, we compare how boys and girls in a sample of Finnish high school students ($N = 398$) prioritize values across three subject domains, including (1) math and science, (2) Finnish, and (3) social sciences. Moreover, the relationships between these priority patterns and their educational aspirations to hard sciences are examined. It is argued that focusing on gender differences in internal hierarchies (i.e., the ordering of preferences) can help to improve our understanding of gender differences in educational aspirations and subsequent career paths.

Introduction

A student who values math highly may not value English to the same extent. Subjective task values (STVs) are a domain-specific construct that varies across school subjects (Eccles (Parsons), 1983; see also Jerrim & Schoon; Parker, Nagy, Trautwein, & Lüdtke; Wang & Kenny, this volume). The STV of an activity comprises four major components: attainment value, intrinsic value, utility value, and perceived cost (Eccles (Parsons), 1983; Eccles et al., 1998). Attainment value is the perceived importance of performing well in a task, and it is closely related to an individual's perception of how relevant the task is to own identity. Intrinsic value is also known as interest value, which refers to the expected enjoyment of engaging in a task. Utility value is defined as the perceived usefulness of a task in achieving any goals or obtaining any rewards. The perceived cost refers to the anticipated effort needed for the task completion as well as what individuals are willing to give up for participating in a task: for example, spending time reading a book instead of hanging out with friends.

This study was funded by the Academy of Finland (134931) and the Jacobs Foundation.

There are two major possible ways to describe gender differences in STVs. For example, in a hypothetical study, boys in a sample on average rated math as "4" and English as "3" along a 7-point scale (from 1 = very low to 7 = very high), while girls from the same sample on average rated math as "4" and English as "6." First, we may compare their STVs on each subject. Accordingly, we can say that girls placed a higher value on English than did boys, but they shared the same level of STV on math. This research approach is named a variable-centered approach, which aims to describe the relationships between variables (e.g., the correlations between gender and STVs on a specific school subject). Variable-centered studies take variables as the main conceptual and analytical units, and the research questions are answered in terms of the empirical relationships between the variables (Bergman & El-Khouri, 2003; Niemivirta, 2002; Wohlwill, 1973).

Alternatively, we may compare how boys and girls prioritize the values for math and English. From this perspective, we can say boys valued math more than English, while girls had an opposite profile in that they valued English more than math. Such a comparison was done based on a person-centered approach, which aims to understand individuals as *"functioning wholes"* instead of the *"summation of variables"* (Bergman, 2001, p. 29). Contrary to the variable-centered approach, the person-centered approach takes individuals as the main units of analysis. More specifically, person-centered studies on STVs were designed to identify homogeneous groups of learners according to their STVs across an array of school subjects and to reveal the characteristics of individuals from different STV groups (Chow, Eccles, & Salmela-Aro, 2012; Chow & Salmela-Aro, 2011; Viljaranta, Nurmi, Aunola, & Salmela-Aro, 2009). As shown in the above example, using a person-based versus a variable-based approach to compare individuals' STVs may lead to very different research findings.

Most previous studies on STVs employed a variable-centered approach for examining gender differences in STVs on individual school subjects and subsequent outcomes related to the corresponding subject domains. For example, in the subject area of math, Updegraff, Eccles, Barber, and O'Brien (1996) found that boys placed higher values on math than did girls, which in turn accounted for why they subsequently took more high school math courses. However, research examining students' STVs for different school subjects simultaneously from a person-centered perspective has been rarely conducted (see Chow et al., 2012; Chow & Salmela-Aro, 2011; Viljaranta et al., 2009 for exceptions; see also Parker et al.; Wang & Kenny, this volume). There is a lack of understanding of gender differences in STV profiles among students and how these profiles may relate to subsequent behaviors and choices.

This chapter aims to highlight the importance of person-centered approaches for gaining a better understanding of gender differences in STV profiles across school subjects and to demonstrate how information on STV profiles can help to understand subsequent outcomes, specifically regarding educational aspirations toward STEM (science, technology, engineering, and math) majors at university. In this chapter, we intentionally focus on hard sciences because gender imbalance disfavoring girls in these fields has been an enduring problem that deserves more research attention (Jacobs, 2005; Xie & Shauman, 2003; Zarrett & Malanchuk, 2005).

We will first provide a review on gender differences in STVs and educational aspirations. This will be followed by a discussion on the importance of researching gender differences in STV profiles across school subjects. Lastly, a study that employed a person-centered approach for examining students' STVs across three subject domains (math and science, Finnish, and social sciences) will be presented, so as to showcase how this type of study can help to provide a more thorough understanding of gender differences in STVs. Moreover, this study also tested if STV profiles could contribute to explaining gender differences in educational aspirations to STEM.

Gender differences in math and physical science

Gender difference in STVs for math and physical science has been an important topic over 3 decades. Studies conducted in the 1980s and early 1990s found that boys attach greater personal importance to math than girls (Meece, Wigfield, & Eccles, 1990; Updegraff et al., 1996). This partially explained why male students are more likely than girls to take high school math courses and to major in hard sciences in university.

Nevertheless, some recent studies comparing means on STVs for math and science have found no significant differences between boys and girls (Jacobs, Lanza, Osgood, Eccles, & Wigfield, 2002; Simpkins, Davis-Kean, & Eccles, 2006). The results suggested a possible narrowing of the gender gap. Yet, despite the fact that at the mean level gender differences in math and science valuation have become smaller or insignificant, gender imbalance in both career choice and educational aspirations to hard sciences continues to exist (Jacobs, 2005; Jerrim & Schoon, this volume). It seems that the variable-centered approach of comparing math or science valuation between boys and girls at a subject-specific level is insufficient in substantially capturing the gendered characteristics of STVs. Thus, it is timely and important to investigate STV patterns across school subjects from a person-centered perspective.

Intraindividual hierarchical patterns of subjective task values

Students' STVs on school subjects play an influential role in shaping subsequent behaviors and choices. From a variable-centered perspective, a higher level of STV on math is associated with a stronger aspiration to STEM (Eccles (Parsons), 1983). Alternatively, from a person-centered perspective, students who place higher STVs on math and science than the other school subjects also have a stronger aspiration to hard sciences (Chow et al., 2012). The rank orderings of STVs across subjects of individuals (*intraindividual hierarchical patterns* of STVs; Eccles, 2011) are crucial in the choice-making process of individuals. Choices and preferences are made within a context of complex social realities (Schwartz,

2004), where choosing one option means forfeiting another (Eccles (Parsons), 1983; Eccles, 2011). For example, undergraduates who choose to major in computer engineering are going to spend much of their time in this field with very little time left for taking courses in other areas such as fine arts and history. Thus, researching how students prioritize the STVs of various subjects is important for understanding why individuals pick one particular educational option rather than another. Instead of merely taking STVs of a specific subject domain as a predictor for educational aspirations, the STV patterns of how this school subject is ranked in relation to other subjects should also be taken into account. In terms of gender comparison, rather than only examining if boys and girls differ in terms of their STVs within a school subject domain, it is also important to investigate gender differences in the intraindividual hierarchical patterns of STVs across domains.

Examining task-value patterns across subjects: empirical findings

To illustrate the applicability of the person-centered approach in bringing about a deeper understanding of gender difference in STV profiles and how these differences are related to the gendered educational aspiration, we present a study that examined the patterns of students' STVs across three subject domains (math and science, Finnish, and social sciences) and the respective gender differences. We hypothesized that (1) the intraindividual hierarchy of STVs across subjects is different for males and females, and (2) students with different STV patterns differ in their educational aspirations.

Participants and measures

The study was part of a larger research project titled *Finnish Educational Transition Studies* (FinEdu), which is an ongoing longitudinal study of the transition to adulthood in Finland. FinEdu commenced in 2004, and its sample consisted of all the ninth-graders (age = 16) from all nine lower secondary schools in a city in central Finland. We focused on those participants who were followed through to the 2nd year in high school (age = 18). If students had data on at least one of their STV ratings for each subject area at their 1st year in high school and also on their educational aspirations at their 2nd year in high school, they were included in the final sample (N = 398).

Subjective task values

Students' STVs for three school subject domains were measured, including (1) math and science, (2) Finnish, and (3) social sciences. Following the expectancy-value model (Eccles (Parsons), 1983), the participants were asked to rate (1) the importance, (2) the usefulness, and (3) the level of interest of these three subject domains, based on a 7-point scale (1 = not at all; 7 = very much). The Cronbach alphas for these three items of math and science, Finnish, and social sciences were .82, .86, and .79 respectively. The means of these three items on each subject domain were used as the STV scores.

Educational aspirations for physical and IT-related sciences

An open-ended question was asked to collect information regarding the field that the participants would like to major in at the postsecondary school level. The open-ended responses on educational aspirations were coded according to the *Classification of Educational/Occupational Field* issued by the Ministry of Education and Culture of Finland (2004), differentiating nine categories: (1) humanities and education (include teaching science and math in high school), (2) culture, (3) social sciences, business, and administration, (4) math and physical science, (5) computer and engineering, (6) natural resources and the environment, (7) social, medicine, nursing, and sports, (8) tourism, catering, and domestic services, and (9) military, police, and firefighters (see Appendix 11.1 for details). Then, a binary variable was generated to indicate if the participants aspired to major in physical or information technology (IT)-related sciences: *physical or IT-related sciences* (combining the fourth and fifth categories; coded 1) versus *all other fields* (the other seven categories; coded 0).

Grade point average (GPA)

The participants were asked to report their GPA at Grade 9. The mean value for GPA was 8.64 ($SD = .55$; minimum = 6.9 and maximum = 9.9).

Table 11.1 shows the means and standard deviations of the measures, and their intercorrelations. At the mean level, the STVs for the three subjects are quite similar, ranging from 5.22 to 5.29. STVs for math and science did not correlate with those of the other two subject domains. A significant positive correlation was found between STVs for Finnish and social sciences ($r = .49$, $p < .001$). Gender (girls coded 0 and boys coded 1) was negatively correlated with STVs for Finnish ($r = -.34$, $p < .001$) and STVs for social sciences ($r = -.16$, $p < .001$), indicating that girls placed a higher value on these domains than did boys. In contrast, gender was positively correlated with STVs for math and science ($r = .21$, $p < .001$), indicating that boys had higher STVs for math and science. Gender was positively correlated with educational aspirations for physical and IT-related sciences ($r = .41$, $p < .001$) but negatively correlated with GPA ($r = -.18$, $p < .001$).

Application of latent profile analysis

To meet the methodological challenges of examining students' STVs across different domains simultaneously, we employed a latent profile analysis

Table 11.1. *Correlations among measures*

Variable	M	SD	1	2	3	4	5	6
STVs								
1. Math and science	5.25	1.31	–	–.05	–.00	.21***	.19***	.26***
2. Finnish	5.29	1.33		–	.49***	–.34***	.12*	–.26***
3. Social sciences	5.22	1.12			–	–.16***	.06	–.23***
Other measures								
4. Gender	0.40	0.49				–	–.18***	.41***
5. GPA	8.64	0.55					–	–.01
6. Educational aspirations to physical and IT-related sciences	0.21	0.41						

Notes: Gender coded: girl = 0 and boy = 1.
*** $p < .001$, * $p < .05$.

(LPA) to identify distinct types of STV patterns, according to their STVs across the three subject domains. LPA is a statistical procedure that estimates the number of latent homogeneous groups in a heterogeneous sample according to the pattern of observed responses (Vermunt & Magidson, 2002). LPA is exploratory in nature, which means there are no specific a priori assumptions regarding the number or distribution of groups (Nylund, Bellmore, Nishina, & Graham, 2007). Typically, in running LPA, a series of models is specified. The best-fitting model is then selected based on the goodness-of-fit indices and conceptual considerations such as the interpretability of the latent groups in the solutions (Aldridge & Roesch, 2008; Herman, Ostrander, Silva, March, & Walkup, 2007; Tuominen-Soini, Salmela-Aro, & Niemivirta, 2008).

Bayesian Information Criterion (BIC) and Akaike's Information Criterion (AIC) are the two goodness-of-fit indices that have been widely used to evaluate the quality of LPA models (e.g., Marsh, Lüdtke, Trautwein, & Morin, 2009; Smith & Shevlin, 2008). Recent simulation research (Nylund, Asparouhov, & Muthén, 2007) found that BIC outperforms the other indexes in determining model fit. Therefore we employed BIC as the key referencing indicator. A model with a lower BIC value was considered to provide a better fit to the data. In addition, the latent class probabilities, which indicated how parsimoniously individuals were assigned to their respective classes, were also considered. We also took into account the results of the Vuong-Lo-Mendell-Rubin likelihood ratio test (Lo, Mendell, & Rubin, 2001), which indicated whether or not an additional class led to a significant increase in fit. Lastly, following Marsh et al. (2009) and

Bowen, Lee, and Weller (2007), the size of the smallest group of an acceptable solution should at least exceed 5% of the sample.

If a variable is known to be influential to the outcome measures, in order to achieve a more accurate classification and estimation of the data, this variable should be included in LPA as a covariate (Lubke & Muthén, 2007; Muthén, 2002). As both previous academic achievement and gender have been identified as important antecedent factors of STVs, they are specified as the covariates in the LPA procedures in our work.

Typology of task-value patterns

Table 11.2 lists the key goodness-of-fit indices of the one- to four-class solutions. The BIC index of the three-class solution was lowest (BIC = 3,786.06). In addition, the p value of the Vuong-Lo-Mendell-Rubin likelihood ratio test indicated that increasing the number of classes from two to three significantly improved the model fit, but not from three to four. Accordingly, we decided that the three-class solution was optimal. The average probabilities of individuals being parsimoniously assigned into their respective classes were .87 (Class 1), .92 (Class 2), and .93 (Class 3), which further indicated the robustness of the three-class model.

The three groups were labeled according to how math and science were ranked in relation to other subjects (see Figure 11.1): (1) *High Math and Science*, (2) *Moderately High Math and Science*, and (3) *Moderately Low Math and Science*, which accounted for 8.8%, 36.7%, and 54.5%, respectively, of the sample. Figure 11.1 lists the STV scores of the groups on each subject. Interestingly, the STVs for math and sciences among the three groups were not significantly different (see Table 11.3). However, each group was characterized by a unique pattern of how math and science are valued in relation to the other two subjects. The *High Math and Science* group placed a particularly high value on math and science, but not on the other two subjects. The *Moderately High Math and Science* group placed a slightly higher value on math and science than on the other two subjects. In contrast, the *Moderately Low Math and Science* group placed a slightly lower value on math and science than they did on the other two subjects.

A gender comparison of task-value patterns across subjects

The distribution of boys and girls among the three STV groups is listed in Table 11.4. The *High Math and Science, Moderately High Math and Science*, and *Moderately Low Math and Science* groups accounted for 2.9%, 29.2%, and 67.9% of girls and 17.7%, 48.1%, and 34.2% of boys, respectively. A significant relationship between gender and STV group membership was evidenced by the cross-tabulation with chi-square test, $\chi^2 = 52.95$, $N = 398$, $df = 2$, $p < .001$. Regression analyses using gender to predict group memberships found

Table 11.2. *Fit indices for latent profile analysis models*

No. of classes	No. of parameters	Log likelihood	AIC	BIC	p-VLMR	Class size ≤5%	Latent class probabilities 1st	2nd	3rd	4th
1	10	−2,562.68	5,145.36	5,185.22	—	0	—	—	—	—
2	12	−1,873.63	3,771.27	3,819.10	.00	0	.93	.88	—	—
3	18	−1,839.15	3,714.30	3,786.06	.00	0	.87	.92	.93	—
4	24	−1,825.93	3,699.86	3,795.54	.15	0	.92	.86	.83	.86

Note: AIC = Akaike Information Criterion; BIC = Bayesian Information Criterion; *p*-VLMR = *p* values for the Vuong-Lo-Mendell-Rubin likelihood ratio test for *K* versus *K*−1 classes.

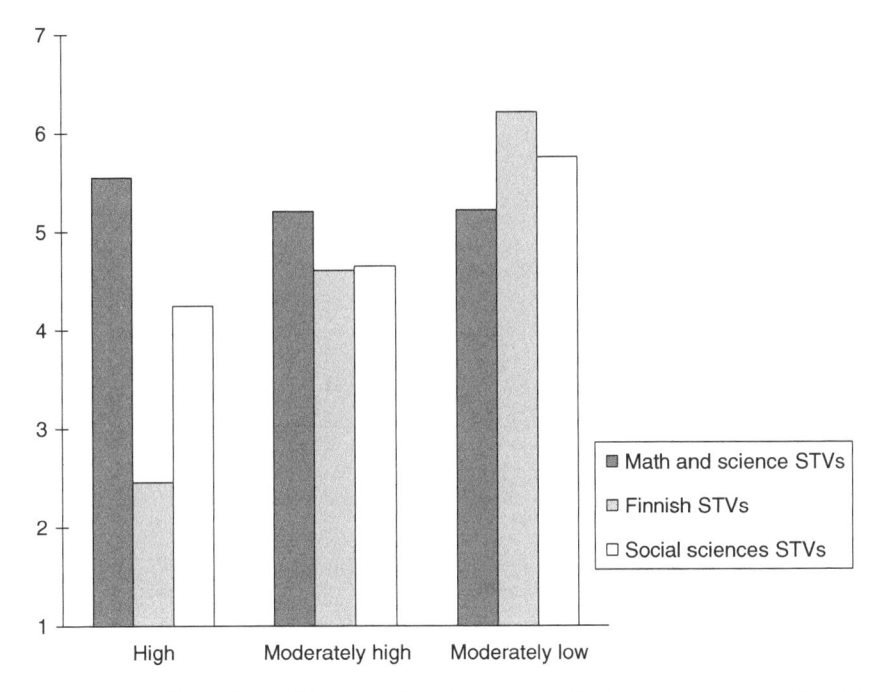

Figure 11.1 *Subjective task-value scores of the three groups across the subject domains. Ranking of math and science in relation to other subjects.*

Table 11.3. *Mean differences in subject task values and grade point average across the three groups*

	STV groups							
	High Math and Science		Moderately High Math and Science		Moderately Low Math and Science			
Variable	M	SD	M	SD	M	SD	F(2, 391)	η^2
STVs								
Math and science	5.57[a]	1.24	5.20[a]	1.30	5.22[a]	1.33	1.19	.01
Finnish	2.39	0.68	4.56	0.60	6.25	0.52	895.99***	.82
Social sciences	4.20	1.13	4.64	0.97	5.77	0.89	84.31***	.30
GPA	8.51[a]	0.46	8.61[a]	0.54	8.69[a]	0.57	2.32	.01

Note: Means within a row sharing the same subscripts are not significantly different at the $p < .05$ level.*** $p < .001$.

that even after controlling for academic achievement, boys were more likely than girls to fall into the *High Math and Science* and *Moderately High Math and Science* groups, $Exp(B) = 6.88, p < .001$ and $Exp(B) = 2.23, p < .001$. In contrast, boys were significantly less likely than girls to fall into the *Moderately Low Math*

Table 11.4. *Gender distribution and grade point average of girls and boys from the three subjective task-value groups*

	High Math and Science	Moderately High Math and Science	Moderately Low Math and Science
Girls			
N	7	70	163
% within girls	2.9%	29.2%	67.9%
GPA Mean (SD)	8.54ª (.51)	8.73ª (.48)	8.73ª (.56)
Boys			
N	28	76	54
% within boys	17.7%	48.1%	34.2%
GPA Mean (SD)	8.50ª (.46)	8.50ª (.56)	8.56ª (.61)

Note: Means within a row sharing the same subscripts are not significantly different at the $p < .05$ level.

and Science group, $Exp(B) = .25$, $p < .001$. These results indicated that, when comparing the intraindividual hierarchical patterns of STVs among students with the same academic achievement (as indicated by GPA), it is more likely for boys to rank math and science higher than the other subjects, but girls tend to give a low ranking to math and science.

Linking task-value group membership to educational aspiration

Lastly, we examined the relationships between STV patterns, gender, and educational aspirations for physical and IT sciences, controlling for GPA and STVs for math and science. Table 11.5 lists the results for each step of the regression analysis. The chi-square (χ^2) generated by Omnibus Tests indicated the significance of the overall model.

Gender and GPA were first entered in Step 1. The model was significant, $\chi^2 = 67.72$, $N = 398$, $df = 2$, $p < .001$. Only gender was a significant predictor, $Exp(B) = 9.46$, $p < .001$. Next, STV for math and science was added to the model, yielding a significantly improved model, $\chi^2 = 83.64$, $N = 398$, $df = 3$, $p < .001$. STV for math and science was a significant predictor, $Exp(B) = 1.68$, $p < .001$, indicating a higher STV on these subjects is associated with a stronger aspiration toward physical and IT-related science. Lastly, in Step 3, STV group membership was entered, which further improved the model, $\chi^2 = 91.70$, $N = 398$, $df = 5$, $p < .001$. Compared to the *Moderately Low Math and Science* group, the *High Math and Science* and *Moderately High Math and Science* groups had significantly higher educational aspirations for physical and IT-related science, $Exp(B) = 2.82$, $p < .05$ and $Exp(B) = 2.15$, $p < .05$, respectively.

The decrease in regression coefficients of gender from Step 1 to Step 2 indicated a possible mediation effect of STV group membership on the associations

Table 11.5. *Regression analysis predicting educational aspirations for physical and IT-related science fields*

Step and predictor	Step 1 Exp(B)	Step 1 95% CI for Exp(B)	Step 2 Exp(B)	Step 2 95% CI for Exp(B)	Step 3 Exp(B)	Step 3 95% CI for Exp(B)	χ^2	$\Delta\chi^2$
Step 1							67.72***	—
Gender	9.46***	5.22–17.13	7.77***	4.25–14.22	6.06***	3.23–11.35		
GPA	1.54	.94–2.53	1.17	.69–1.97	1.21	.70–2.08		
Step 2							83.64***	15.92***
Math and science task value			1.68***	1.28–2.21	1.73***	1.30–2.28		
Step 3							91.70***	8.06*
STV groups								
High vs. Mod. Low					2.82*	1.16–6.83		
Mod. High vs. Mod. Low					2.15*	1.16–3.97		

Note: Exp(B) = exponential odds ratio; 95% CI = 95% confidence interval; $\Delta\chi^2$ = change in chi-square. High = High Math and Science; Mod. High = Moderately High Math and Science; Mod. Low = Moderately Low Math and Science (reference group).
*** $p < .001$, ** $p < .01$, * $p < .05$.

between gender and educational aspirations (Baron & Kenny, 1986). A follow-up bootstrap test was conducted to further determine the significance of such a possible mediation using Mplus statistical package Version 6.1 (Muthén & Muthén, 2010). The bootstrap test controlling for GPA and STVs for math and science found a significant indirect effect of gender on educational aspirations through the mediation of STV group membership ($B = .26$, $SE = .12$, $p < .05$). Given that the direct effects of gender on educational aspirations were still significant (B of gender $= 1.05$, $SE = .17$, $p < .001$), these results indicated that STV group membership partially mediated the associations between gender and aspirations to major in the physical and IT-related science fields.

Gendered patterns in subjective task-value profiles and aspirations for hard sciences

Our study employed a person-centered approach to examine gender differences in STVs across school subjects. Boys were significantly more likely to favor math and science over other subjects, whereas girls were significantly more likely to favor other subjects over math and science. Employing variable-centered approaches, earlier studies conducted in the 1980s and early 1990s consistently found significant gender differences favoring boys in perceived importance for math and science. More recent gender-comparative studies on STVs, however, yield no significant results (Jacobs et al., 2002; Simpkins et al., 2006). Despite these recent studies suggesting a possible narrowing or disappearing of the gender gap in math and science valuation, the present study using a person-centered approach shows that boys and girls still differ in how they prioritize math and science in relation to other school subjects.

To date, there are only a handful of person-centered studies on students' STVs (Chow et al., 2012; Chow & Salmela-Aro, 2011; Viljaranta et al., 2009). Nevertheless, in congruence to the present study, all these studies pointed to similar gender differences in intraindividual hierarchical patterns of STVs. For example, in a comparative study on high school students in the US and Finland (ages = 15.5 and 17, respectively) by Chow et al. (2012), boys in both samples tended to value math and science higher than the other school subjects, and girls in both samples tended to value math and science lower than the other school subjects. In another study by Viljaranta et al. (2009), a sample of ninth-graders (age = 16) in Finland was classified into groups according to their STVs across five subject areas (math and science, Finnish, foreign languages, social sciences, and, lastly, the non-academic subjects such as music). Boys were overrepresented in an STV group that placed the highest priority on math and science. Drawing on a sample of ninth-graders in Finland, Chow and Salmela-Aro (2011) also found gender differences in STV patterns across school subjects: on average, boys placed higher value on math and science than on language, and vice versa for girls.

Evidenced by extensive studies from the variable-centered tradition, students' STVs play an influential role in shaping subsequent behaviors and choices (e.g., Atwater, Wiggins, & Gardner, 1995; Crombie et al., 2005; Durik, Vida, & Eccles, 2006; Simpkins et al., 2006; Wigfield & Guthrie, 1997). For example, Simpkins et al. (2006) found that the STVs for math of a US sample of 10th-graders significantly predicted the total number of high school math courses they subsequently took. In the domain of literacy, Durik et al. (2006) found that the STVs for reading of fourth-graders in the US predicted how many English courses they took in high school, and also their subsequent aspirations for jobs requiring high literacy skills measured 8 years later. These studies usually focused on the associations between STVs and subsequent outcomes within a specific school subject domain.

Alternatively, research employing a person-centered approach examined the intraindividual hierarchical patterns of STVs across school subjects (e.g., Chow et al, 2012; Chow & Salmela-Aro, 2011). As pointed out by Eccles (2011), when selecting among several alternatives, picking one option means forfeiting alternatives. As such, individuals are expected to pick the choice that they value most. This is empirically supported by our current study. We found that STV patterns were a significant predictor of educational aspirations for hard sciences. The two groups of students who prioritized math and science over other school subjects were more likely to aspire to major in hard sciences than the group with an opposite priority pattern. Importantly, it should be noted that in addition to gender and academic achievement, STVs for math and science were also controlled in our analyses, indicating that STV patterns independently predicted education aspirations over and above the other variables included in the model, highlighting the importance of STV profiles in shaping the educational aspirations of high school students. This finding is particularly important from a developmental perspective, because high school is a critical time for students to make important educational and occupational choices. The preferences and choices that high school students make can affect the future educational/career opportunities available to them and, thus, shape their career trajectories. For example, in Finland, university applicants have to apply for specific university majors and take the entrance exams conducted by the respective university departments. As these entrance exams are highly competitive, applicants who wish to major in physical and IT-related sciences usually should already have completed the advanced courses in math or other related courses in high school.

Limitations and implications

This current study should be considered in light of its limitations. First, we focused on STVs but did not include *expectancies for success* in our study – another important variable in the expectancy-value model (Eccles (Parsons), 1983). Although it is not unusual for research drawing on the expectancy-value model to focus only on STVs (e.g., Chow et al., 2012; Chow & Salmela-Aro, 2011; Viljaranta et al., 2009; Yli-Piipari, Kiuru, Jaakkola, Liukkonen, & Watt, 2011), further studies are recommended to extend our understanding of the effects of these two factors on outcomes when they are considered simultaneously. Moreover, our study measured STVs for math and science together. A more appropriate research design should measure STVs for math, physical science, and biological science in three independent scales. Also, we used self-reported overall GPA scores instead of the achievement scores of individual school subjects in our study, which should also be noted as a limitation of our study.

Despite these limitations, together with other person-centered studies on STVs across school subjects (e.g., Chow et al., 2012; Chow & Salmela-Aro, 2011; Viljaranta et al., 2009), our work illustrates the applicability of employing a person-centered approach in examining STVs. Using latent profile analysis, the study participants were reliably classified into unique STV profiles. It revealed gender differences in intraindividual hierarchical patterns of STVs across school subjects. Also, the study found associations between STV profiles and subsequent educational aspirations to hard sciences.

In addition to the gender imbalance problem in the physical and IT-related science career fields, quite a number of countries, such as the US and Finland, are experiencing a shortage of labor supply in these STEM fields (Herzig, 2004; Jacobs, 2005). Seeking ways to remedy these problems has been an important policy concern. This study demonstrated that the tendencies for individuals to enter these fields can be traced back to their STV profiles across school subjects in adolescence, which underscores the importance of early intervention efforts in adolescence for encouraging more individuals to pursue hard science careers. In addition, we found that gender differences in educational aspirations toward hard sciences were partially rooted in STV profiles. To overcome the problem of the shortage of labor in the hard sciences industry, more attention should be paid to how students rank math and science in relation to other subjects, especially among girls. To boost the utility and attainment values that girls attach to jobs related to hard sciences and increase the number of girls considering these careers, vocational education programs should provide more detailed images of the nature of jobs in these fields and to make clearer connections between careers in these fields with the work values of young women.

References

Aldridge, A., & Roesch, S. (2008). Developing coping typologies of minority adolescents: A latent profile analysis. *Journal of Adolescence*, 31, 499–517.

Atwater, M. M., Wiggins, J., & Gardner, C. M. (1995). A study of urban middle school students with high and low attitudes toward science. *Journal of Research in Science Teaching*, 32, 665–677.

Baron, R. M., & Kenny, D. A. (1986). The moderator–mediator distinction in social psychological research: Conceptual, strategic, and statistical considerations. *Journal of Personality and Social Psychology*, 51, 1173–1182.

Bergman, L. R. (2001). A person approach in research on adolescence: Some methodological challenges. *Journal of Adolescent Research*, 16, 28–53.

Bergman, L. R., & El-Khouri, B. M. (2003). A person-oriented approach: Methods for today and methods for tomorrow. *New Directions for Child and Adolescent Development*, 101, 25–38.

Bowen, N. K., Lee, J.-S., & Weller, B. (2007). Childreport social environmental risk and protection: A typology with implications for practice in elementary schools. *Children & Schools*, 29, 229–242.

Chow, A., Eccles, J., & Salmela-Aro, K. (2012). Task value profiles across subjects and aspirations to physical and IT-related sciences in the United States and Finland. *Developmental Psychology*, 48(6), 1612–1628.

Chow, A., & Salmela-Aro, K. (2011). Task values across subject domains: A gender comparison using a person-centred approach. *International Journal of Behavioral Development*, 35(3), 202–209.

Crombie, G., Sinclair, N., Silverthorn, N., Byrne, B., DuBois, D., & Trinneer, A. (2005). Predictors of young adolescents' math grades and course enrollment intentions: Gender similarities and differences. *Sex Roles*, 52, 351–367.

Durik, A. M., Vida, M., & Eccles, J. S. (2006). Task values and ability beliefs as predictors of high school literacy choices: A developmental analysis. *Journal of Educational psychology*, 98(2), 382–393.

Eccles, J. S. (2011). Gendered educational and occupational choices: Applying the Eccles et al. model of achievement-related choices. *International Journal of Behavioural Development*, 35(3), 195–201.

Eccles, J. S., Wigfield, A., & Schiefele, U. (1998). Motivation to succeed. In W. Damon & N. Eisenberg (Eds.), *Handbook of child psychology: Social, emotional, and personality development* (5th ed., No. 3, pp. 1017–1095). New York: Wiley.

Eccles (Parsons), J. S. (1983). Expectancies, values, and academic behaviours. In J. T. Spence (Ed.), *Achievement and achievement motives: Psychological and sociological approaches* (pp. 75–146). San Francisco, CA: W. H. Freeman.

Herman, K. C., Ostrander, R., Silva, S., March, J., & Walkup, J. (2007). Empirically derived subtypes of adolescent depression: Latent profile analysis of co-occurring symptoms in the Treatment for Adolescents with Depression Study (TADS). *Journal of Consulting and Clinical Psychology*, 75, 716–728.

Herzig, A. H. (2004). Becoming mathematicians: Women and students of color choosing and leaving doctoral mathematics. *Review of Educational Research*, 74, 171–214.

Jacobs, J. E. (2005). Twenty-five years of research on gender and ethnic differences on math and science career choices: What have we learned? *New Directions for Child and Adolescent Development*, 110, 85–94.

Jacobs, J. E., Lanza, S., Osgood, D. W., Eccles, J. S., & Wigfield, A. (2002). Changes in children's self-competence and values: Gender and domain differences across grades one through twelve. *Child Development*, 73, 509–527.

Lo, Y., Mendell, N., & Rubin, D. (2001). Testing the number of components in a normal mixture. *Biometrika*, 88, 767–778.

Lubke, G. H., & Muthén, B. (2007). Performance of factor mixture models as a function of model size, criterion measure effects, and class-specific parameters. *Structural Equation Modeling*, 14, 26–47.

Marsh, H. W., Lüdtke, O., Trautwein, U., & Morin, A. J. S. (2009). Classical latent profile analysis of academic self-concept dimensions: Synergy of person- and variable-centered approaches to theoretical models of self-concept. *Structural Equation Modeling*, 16, 191–225.

Meece, J. L., Wigfield, A., & Eccles, J. S. (1990). Predictors of math anxiety and its influence on young adolescents' course enrollment intentions and performance in mathematics. *Journal of Educational Psychology*, 82, 60–70.

Ministry of Education and Culture. (2004). *Classification of educational field*. Retrieved from www.minedu.fi/export/sites/default/OPM/Koulutus/koulutusjaerjestelmae/liitteet/koulutusluokitukset.pdf.

Muthén, B. (2002). Beyond SEM: General latent variable modeling. *Behaviormetrika*, 29, 81–117.

Muthén, L., & Muthén, B. (2010). *Mplus (version 6.1)*. Los Angeles, CA: Muthén & Muthén.

Niemivirta, M. (2002). Individual differences and developmental trends in motivation: Integrating person-centered and variable-centered methods. In P. R. Pintrich & M. L. Maehr (Eds.), *Advances in motivations and achievement: Vol. 12. New directions in measures and methods* (pp. 241–275). Amsterdam: JAI Press.

Nylund, K., Asparouhov, T., & Muthén, B. (2007). Deciding on the number of classes in latent class analysis and growth mixture modeling. A Monte Carlo simulation study. *Structural Equation Modeling*, 14, 535–569.

Nylund, K., Bellmore, A., Nishina, A., & Graham, S. (2007). Subtypes, severity, and structural stability of peer victimization: What does latent class analysis say? *Child Development*, 78(6), 1706–1722.

Schwartz, B. (2004). *The paradox of choice: Why more is less*. New York: HarperCollins.

Simpkins, S. D., Davis-Kean, P. E., & Eccles, J. S. (2006). Math and science motivation: A longitudinal examination of the links between choices and beliefs. *Developmental Psychology*, 42(1), 70–83.

Smith, G. W., & Shevlin, M. (2008). Patterns of alcohol consumption and related behaviour in Great Britain: A latent class analysis of the Alcohol Use Disorder Identification Test (AUDIT). *Alcohol & Alcoholism*, 43(5), 590–594.

Tuominen-Soini, H., Salmela-Aro, K., & Niemivirta, M. (2008). Achievement goal orientations and subjective well-being: A person-centered analysis. *Learning and Instruction*, 18, 251–266.

Updegraff, K. A., Eccles, J. S., Barber, B. L., & O'Brien, K. M. (1996). Course enrollment as self-regulatory behavior: Who takes optional high school math courses? *Learning and Individual Differences*, 8, 239–259.

Vermunt, J. K., & Magidson, J. (2002). Latent class cluster analysis. In J. A. Hagenaars & A. L. McCutcheon (Eds.), *Applied latent class analysis* (pp. 89–106). Cambridge University Press.

Viljaranta, J., Nurmi, J.-E., Aunola, K., & Salmela-Aro, K. (2009). The role of task values in adolescents' educational tracks: A person-oriented approach. *Journal of Research on Adolescence*, 19(4), 786–798.

Wigfield, A., & Guthrie, J. T. (1997). Relations of children's motivation for reading to the amount and breadth of their reading. *Journal of Educational Psychology*, 89, 420–432.

Wohlwill, J. F. (1973). *The study of behavioral development*. Orlando, FL: Academic Press.

Xie, Y., & Shauman, K. (2003). *Women in science*. Cambridge, MA: Harvard University Press.

Yli-Piipari, S., Kiuru, N., Jaakkola, T., Liukkonen, J., & Watt, A. (2011). The role of peer groups in male and female adolescents' task values and physical activity. *Psychological Reports*, 108(1), 75–93.

Zarrett, N. R., & Malanchuk, O. (2005). Who's computing? Gender and race differences in young adults' decisions to pursue an information technology career. *New Directions for Child & Adolescent Development*, 110, 65–84.

Appendix 11.1

Coding scheme for the educational fields to which respondents aspired

1. Humanities and education
    1.1 Leisure and youth work
    1.2 Linguistics
    1.3 History and archeology
    1.4 Philosophy
    1.5 Education and psychology
    1.6 Teaching and education
    1.7 Theology
    1.8 Other humanities and education training
2. Culture
    2.1 Crafts and design
    2.2 Communication and information science
    2.3 Literature
    2.4 Theater and dance
    2.5 Music
    2.6 Visual arts
    2.7 Culture and arts research
    2.8 Other cultural training
3. Social sciences, business and administration
    3.1 Business and trade
    3.2 Economics
    3.3 Management
    3.4 Statistical science
    3.5 Social science
    3.6 Political science
    3.7 Law

   3.8 Other social sciences, business management and administration training
4. Science
   4.1 Mathematics
   4.2 Data processing
   4.3 Space and astronomy
   4.4 Physics
   4.5 Chemistry
   4.6 Geography
   4.7 Other science education
5. Computer and engineering
   5.1 Architecture and construction
   5.2. Machinery, metal, and energy technology
   5.3 Electrical and automation engineering
   5.4 Computer programming
   5.5 Graphic and communication technologies
   5.6 Food and biotechnology
   5.7 Processing, chemical, and materials technology
   5.8 Textile and clothing technology
   5.9 Automotive and transport engineering
   5.10 Other technology and communications sector
6. Natural resources and environment
   6.1 Farming
   6.2 Gardening
   6.3 Fishing
   6.4 Forestry
   6.5 Nature and the environment
   6.6 Other natural resources and environmental education
7. Life science and medicine
   7.1 Social work
   7.2 The health sector
   7.3 Social and health issues (cross-cutting programs)
   7.4 Dentists and other dental care
   7.5 Rehabilitation and physical
   7.6 Tech health
   7.7 Pharmaceutical and other medical care
   7.8 Medicine
   7.9 Biology
   7.10 Veterinary medicine
   7.11 Beauty care
   7.12 Other social, health, and physical education
8. Tourism, catering, and domestic services
   8.1 The tourism industry
   8.2 Accommodation and catering

　　　　8.3　　　　　Domestic and consumer services
　　　　8.4　　　　　Cleansing services
　　　　8.5　　　　　Other tourism, catering, and economics education
9.　　Military, police, and firemen
　　　　9.1　　　　　Military and border guards
　　　　9.2　　　　　Firefighters and rescue officers
　　　　9.3　　　　　Police
　　　　9.4　　　　　Prison officers
　　　　9.5　　　　　Other Ministry of Education organized outside the field of education
　　　　9.6　　　　　Other Ministry of Education sector

12 Gender differences in personal aptitudes and motivational beliefs for achievement in and commitment to math and science fields

Ming-Te Wang and Sarah Kenny

Abstract

In this chapter we examine gender differences in a variety of personal aptitudes and motivational beliefs that move individuals toward or away from STEM fields. The overarching goal of this chapter is to understand how individual intellectual aptitudes interact with motivational beliefs to account for individual and gender differences in STEM interests and choices. Specifically, we aim to address three questions: (1) What are the gender differences in mathematics and verbal abilities, math ability self-concept, personal values, and desired job characteristics at 12th grade? (2) Do adolescent intellectual aptitudes in mathematics and verbal areas at 12th grade predict their future college major selection? (3) How do individual differences in motivational factors discriminate between individuals who select college majors in STEM versus non-STEM fields while holding math and verbal ability constant? Answers to these questions will guide future research and interventions designed to promote individual motivation and capacity to pursue STEM careers.

Introduction

Throughout the past 30 years, considerable research has been dedicated to understanding how educators and policy makers can increase the size of the science, technology, engineering, and mathematics (STEM) workforce in the United States (US) (Kuenzi, Mathews, & Magnan, 2006). Research in this field is particularly relevant during the current time of economic crisis and mass unemployment. Not only does the success of the United States in the current global economy depend on the pool of available STEM talent (National Science Board, 2010), but STEM fields are "open for business" and have the potential to provide employment security for young people facing an uncertain future in the job market. However, many young people (women and ethnic minorities in particular) are struggling with math and science subjects, and are not embarking upon the pathways leading to STEM occupations (see also Perez-Felkner, McDonald, & Schneider, this volume). For instance, in recent years women have been awarded only 27% of doctoral degrees in mathematics, 15% in physics, 20% in computer science, and 18% in engineering. In order for policies intended to encourage women to join STEM fields to be effective, we need to understand what *motivates* both males and females to pursue and achieve in these fields. Previous research has shown that cultural, contextual, and social patterns, such as learning experiences in school and gender stereotypes, are important for development of motivation in math and science domains (Ceci & Williams, 2010; see also Chow & Salmela-Aro; Parker, Nagy, Trautwein, & Lüdtke; Perez-Felkner et al.; Schoon & Eccles, this volume). Reviewing a broad array of socialization processes is outside the scope of one chapter. Instead, we will focus on the well-documented gender differences in a variety of personal aptitudes and motivational beliefs that move individuals toward or away from STEM fields. Specifically, we aim to address three questions:

1. What are the gender differences in mathematics and verbal abilities, math ability self-concept, personal values, and desired job characteristics at 12th grade?
2. Do adolescent intellectual aptitudes in mathematics and verbal areas at 12th grade predict their future college major selection?
3. How do individual differences in motivational factors discriminate between individuals who select college majors in STEM versus non-STEM fields while holding math and verbal ability constant?

The overarching goal of this chapter is to understand how individual intellectual aptitudes interact with motivational beliefs to account for individual and gender differences in STEM interests and choices. Knowledge gained through this chapter will guide future research and interventions designed to promote individual motivation and capacity to pursue STEM careers. We begin with a brief review of the theoretical framework and empirical research on the impact of intellectual aptitudes, personal beliefs and attitudes on educational and career choices. We then present an empirical study that investigates the psychological factors leading to college major selection in STEM. We finish with a discussion of the implications of our research in terms of encouraging engagement of greater numbers of females in STEM disciplines.

Theoretical and empirical framework

Expectancy-value theory

According to Eccles' expectancy-value theory (Eccles, 1983, 2009), the career pathway is composed of a series of choices and achievements that commence in childhood and adolescence. Educational and career choices, regarding course enrollment and college majors, for example, are most directly related to an individual's ability, perceived competence (e.g., expectations for success), and the subject task value they attach to the various options they see as available. Specifically, the subject task value includes *interest value* (liking or enjoyment), *utility value* (the instrumental value of the task for helping to fulfill personal goals), *attainment value* (the link between the task and one's sense of self and identity), and *cost* (what may need to be sacrificed if a specific choice is made). When individuals feel confident that they can learn and be successful in particular subject areas such as math and science, they are more likely to persist and engage in deeper-level cognitive strategies; this in turn is associated with increased academic achievement and course taking (Wang, 2012; Wigfield & Eccles, 2002). Value-related beliefs are predictive of achievement and academic engagement (Schiefele, 2001) but are even stronger predictors of choice behaviors and beliefs, such as STEM career aspirations (Eccles, 2009; Wang & Eccles, 2013; see also Chow & Salmela-Aro; Parker et al., this volume). Thus, both perceived competence and subjective task value (motivational beliefs) are essential for encouraging adolescents to pursue careers in STEM areas (see Eccles, 2007).

The decision to choose one career over another – occupational choice – is influenced by a relative within-person hierarchy of expectations for success and subjective task values across the set of options being considered (Eccles, 1994, 2005, 2009; see also Chow & Salmela-Aro, this volume). Gaining insight into the development of these hierarchies allows us to understand the predictive power of these motivational beliefs in influencing individual educational and occupational choice. In addition, when examining educational and career choices, such as selection of a STEM college major, it is important to take into account all potential individual differences that factor into performance and commitment, and not to disregard any personal attributes that are known to be important (Lubinski & Benbow, 2007). Studying only one type of attribute may lead to an underestimation of male versus female disparities in career choices. For instance, in the case of gender differences in participation in math and science, although males and females do not differ in general intelligence, they do differ in their specific ability patterns, ability self-concept, interest, and life values (Ceci & Williams, 2010; Wang, Eccles, & Kenny, 2013; see also Chow & Salmela-Aro; Parker et al., this volume). Here we review the evidence on intellectual aptitudes, personal mindsets, ability self-concept levels, and task values, which in part explain male versus female disparities in educational and career choices in STEM fields.

Intellectual aptitudes

A recent meta-analysis has demonstrated that on average girls are doing as well as boys in math in the general school population (Hyde, Lindberg, Linn, Ellis, & Williams, 2008). Girls and boys appear to each have their own unique strengths and weaknesses, with girls possessing stronger verbal skills (Ceci & Williams, 2010; Park, Lubinski, & Benbow, 2008) and earning slightly higher grades in high school math and science classes (National Center for Education Statistics, 2012), and with boys outscoring girls by a small margin on high-stakes math tests such as the mathematics section of the Scholastic Assessment Test (SAT) and the American College Testing (ACT) (Halpern et al., 2007) – two of the most commonly used standardized tests for college admissions in the United States. Boys also generally outnumber girls by a ratio of 2:1 on the right-tail of the math ability distribution (Hyde et al., 2008) and are clearly overrepresented in math-intensive fields, leading some researchers to suggest that boys have an innate skill-set that favors an orientation toward math-intensive fields. For example, mental rotation (the ability to rotate mental representations of two-dimensional and three-dimensional objects) is important in fields such as engineering, chemistry, and physics (Hyde, 2007), and has been shown to be an important mediator of gender differences in SAT mathematics, and other exam performance, over and above mathematics self-confidence (Casey, Nuttall, & Pezaris, 1997, 2001). Differences in mental rotation ability have been demonstrated in children as young as kindergarten (Casey et al., 2008). Some studies also suggest that boys have an advantage in spatial ability (the capacity to think about objects in three dimensions and to draw conclusions about those objects from limited information) (e.g., Voyer, Voyer, & Bryden, 1995). However, building with Lego and computer games (stereotypically male play activities) have been shown to improve mental rotation ability (e.g., Quaiser-Pohl, Geiser, & Lehmann, 2005) and spatial ability can also be improved with training in both genders (Baenninger & Newcombe, 1989; Vasta, Knott, & Graze, 1996), countering the argument that boys have an innately superior ability. Dramatic increases in the number of girls achieving very high scores on mathematics tests (30 years ago there were 13 boys for every girl who scored above 700 on the SAT math exam at age 13; today it is about four boys for every girl) (Hill, Corbett, & St. Rose, 2010) also suggest that ability levels in general are not static, but rather respond to educational and societal change. In summary, a range of recent studies suggests that intellectual aptitude, at least by itself, is not an overriding factor in the underrepresentation of women in math-intensive fields (Ceci & Williams, 2010; Wang & Degol, 2013).

However, aptitude patterns can affect career choice. Mathematically gifted people appear to be drawn to engineering, math, and computer science, while those who are verbally gifted appear to be drawn to the social sciences and humanities (Lubinski & Benbow, 2007; Wang et al., 2013; see also Chow & Salmela-Aro; Parker et al., this volume). In addition, among females and males of comparable outstanding math aptitude, females are more likely to outperform males in verbal ability (Wang et al., 2013), suggesting that such females may have a wider choice of careers – including both STEM and non-STEM fields – to choose from. For example, Wai, Lubinski, and Benbow (2005) tracked high math ability individuals who expressed a desire to pursue either a math- or science-related college major, finding that many women in this group had switched from math/science majors into non math-intensive majors such as law. On average, these females possessed both high verbal and mathematical ability. In a similar vein, Wang and colleagues recently found that mathematically able individuals who also had high verbal skills were less likely to pursue STEM careers than individuals who had high math skills but moderate verbal skills (Wang et al., 2013). Notably, in this study, more females than males were identified in the high verbal and high math ability group. Perhaps it is not surprising that mathematically talented young women who are equally verbally talented are drawn to equally ambitious non-STEM fields. These women have the opportunity to weigh the pros and cons of both STEM and non-STEM career pathways, and consider the potential of each to fulfill important life goals.

Mindset

Personal beliefs or mindset regarding math ability may, to a certain extent, dictate performance. Students who view intellectual ability as a gift (a fixed mindset) question their ability and lose motivation when setbacks or challenges (such as a difficult exam) are encountered. Conversely, students who view intellectual ability as a quality that can be developed are more inclined to seek alternative strategies in the face of difficulty (e.g., Mueller & Dweck, 1998). Dweck and her colleagues found that interventions teaching students that intelligence is malleable promote a positive change in math class motivation and in math grades (Blackwell, Trzesniewski, & Dweck, 2007). Valian (2007) suggests that the US school system adopts a "fixed mindset" approach where ability is treated as an unchanging entity. Japanese girls, she points out, educated in a country in which a "growth mindset" is promoted, outperform US boys by 62 points. Interestingly, stereotype threat (when awareness of negative stereotypes influences students to perform according to those stereotypes) has been found to have little or no effect on females who have a growth mindset (Blackwell et al., 2007; Good, Aronson, & Inzlicht, 2003).

Ability self-concept

Important predictors of behavioral choice include expectations for success, confidence in one's abilities to succeed (ability self-concept), and personal efficacy (Eccles, 2009; Eccles, Wigfield, & Schiefele, 1997; Wigfield, Eccles, Schiefele, Roeser, & Davis-Kean, 2006). People are more likely to select activities for which they have high expectations for success and feel efficacious – internal factors, which may vary across subject domains (Eccles, Barber, Updegraff, & O'Brien, 1998). Much research has confirmed the role that perceived incompetence or poor math ability self-concept plays in females' underperformance in mathematics (Durik, Vida, & Eccles, 2006; Eccles et al., 1998; Valian, 2007; Parker et al., this volume). High school boys tend to assess their math competence more highly than girls with similar math grades and test scores (Correll, 2001; Nagy et al., 2008). Both girls and boys who rate their math competence higher are more likely to enroll in advanced math courses, choose a quantitative college major, and, subsequently, a STEM-related career (Dweck, 2008). However, it should be noted that ability self-concept is a necessary but not entirely sufficient predictor of educational and career choices (Joyce & Farenga, 2000; Shapka, 2009; Updegraff, Eccles, Barber, & O'Brien, 1996). Proficiency in a given activity does not necessarily mean that the activity is experienced as fulfilling or enjoyable, nor does it guarantee that an individual will pursue it. In addition to these facets of ability self-concept, expectancy-value theory suggests that career choices also depend on the value one attaches to various occupational characteristics.

Interest value

Research has found that interest in math and science is associated with the number of math and science courses taken in high school (Atwar, Wiggins, & Gardner, 1995; Joyce & Farenga, 2000; Meece, Wigfield, & Eccles, 1990). A number of studies indicate that boys report higher interest in math, although boys and girls regard math as equally important (Frenzel, Goetz, Pekrun, & Watt, 2010; Wang & Eccles, 2012; see also Chow & Salmela-Aro; Jerrim & Schoon, this volume). Jacobs, Davis-Kean, Bleeker, Eccles, and Malanchuk (2005) found that children with higher math ability self-concept were more likely to be interested in math but also found, in contrast to the above studies, that math interest did not predict involvement in math or science activities. Girls' "liking" of math appears to decrease through middle school and high school, whereas boys' "liking" of math remains the same (Eccles & Harold, 1992; Koller, Baumert, & Schnabel, 2001; see also Bagnoli, Demey, & Scott, this volume). This pattern holds true for self-concept as well, as girls begin to demonstrate progressively lower self-concept relative to boys beginning in middle school through high school and college (Pajares, 2005). Expectancy-value theory suggests that the relationship between interest and ability self-concept is such that interest is influenced by the belief that one can succeed in a given field (Eccles, 1983). For Eccles and others (e.g., Pajares, 2005; Wang, 2012), interest and ability self-concept are intimately interlinked. Therefore, girls' interest in math is decreased by their lower math self-concepts relative to boys.

Occupational value

Gendered differences in occupation and lifestyle values (e.g., work–family balance and relationships with others) are equally important contributing factors to women's underrepresentation in STEM careers (Ferriman, Lubinski, & Benbow, 2009; see also Abele; Bagnoli et al.; Heckhausen; Weiss, Wiese, & Freund, this volume). Studies indicate that females' and males' different work preferences and occupational aspirations are already formed and visible in adolescence (e.g., Diekman, Clark, Johnston, Brown, & Steinberg, 2011; Eccles, 2007; Frome, Alfeld-Liro, & Eccles, 1996). Females generally prefer occupations that are geared toward social interactions, while males prefer work with things, machines, and tools (Ruble & Martin, 1998; Su, Rounds, & Armstrong, 2009). Although men and women with similar ability profiles achieve college degrees at the same rate, mathematically capable women are more likely than their male counterparts to pursue pathways in "people fields," such as the humanities and biological or health sciences, relative to engineering and physical sciences, while the inverse is true for men (Benbow, Lubinski, Shea, & Eftekhari-Sanjani, 2000; Lubinski, Webb, Morelock, & Benbow, 2001; Schoon, Ross, & Martin, 2007; see also Chow & Salmela-Aro; Parker et al., this volume).

Other research indicates that female gravitation toward "people fields" appears to be an altruistic as well as a social orientation. For example, women have been shown to place more value on jobs that allow them to help others and do something worthwhile for society (communion/affiliative orientation), while men place more value on jobs that allow them to have power, be financially successful, and become famous (agentic/power-based orientation) (Abele & Spurk, 2011; Eccles, Barber, & Josefowicz, 1999). Hill and colleagues (2010) have suggested that math-intensive fields do not afford, or are not seen as affording, the interaction with other people that women value. A recent study demonstrated that when a STEM career was presented to females as more communal, their interest in the field increased (Diekman et al., 2011). Indeed, biomedical, civil, and environmental engineering (which are more likely to be associated with helping people) attract higher numbers of women than other areas such as mechanical or nuclear engineering (Gibbons, 2009). These findings indicate that different individual gendered interests in working with people versus things may play a crucial role in women's underrepresentation in STEM fields.

Lifestyle value

Research indicates that work–family balance is an additional important factor in women's decisions not to enter math-intensive fields, or to leave math-intensive fields for other fields (Hill et al., 2010; see also Abele; Bagnoli et al.; Heckhausen; Weiss et al., this volume). Trower (2008) reported that math-intensive careers are not perceived by women to allow for a work–family balance. Ceci and Williams (2010) referred to a woman's decision to have both a family and a STEM career as a "collision course." It appears that the decision to have a family has the potential to be detrimental to women's STEM careers. This may be because women believe it to be more important to make occupational sacrifices for the family than do men (Eccles et al., 1999). Women have also been shown to prefer more home-centered lifestyles, whereas men prefer more work-committed lifestyles (Hakim, 2006). It is difficult for women who must balance a STEM career and care for a family to attain the same level of productivity as men. For example, research shows that faculty in STEM fields who work more than 60 hours a week are more likely to publish, whereas women with children in STEM fields are more likely to work fewer than 60 hours a week (Jacobs & Winslow, 2004). It has also been pointed out that STEM fields are characterized by rapid technological change that requires continual development of expertise, perhaps to a greater degree than other fields, thus making it difficult for people to take a leave of absence, such as maternity leave (Lubinski & Benbow, 2007). Hence, female underrepresentation in STEM careers may be partially explained by gendered preferences in the balancing of home life and work life.

Empirical evidence from the Michigan Study of Adolescent Life Transitions

Bringing together the different assumptions regarding gender differences in career choice, we now present some findings from our most recent studies that aim to understand how individuals choose between different college majors. First, we examined gender differences in mathematics and verbal abilities, math ability self-concept, personal values, and desired job characteristics at 12th grade (approximately ages 17 and 18). We then tested whether adolescent intellectual aptitudes in mathematics and verbal areas at 12th grade predicted their future college major selection in STEM versus non-STEM fields. Finally, we examined how individual differences in motivational factors discriminated between individuals who selected college majors in STEM versus non-STEM fields while holding math and verbal ability constant.

Sample description

The sample was 1,200 intellectually able, college-bound students in Southeastern Michigan in the United States drawn from the Michigan Study of Adolescent Life Transitions (MSALT). This longitudinal study began with a sample of approximately 3,000 sixth-graders (ages 12 and 13) in 12 different school districts. These districts serve primarily working-class and middle-class small city communities. The sample is predominantly white (95% Caucasian and 5% African American). Approximately 2,000 of these adolescents (52% females; 97% Caucasian) have been tracked well into their early adulthood years with standard survey questions. All of the survey instruments employed here have been used in a variety of studies and have well-established reliability and validity.

Gender differences in ability and motivational beliefs

We found evidence of gender differences in math and verbal ability, math ability self-concept, lifestyle, and work style values as revealed by individual t-tests (see Table 12.1). Specifically, females at 12th grade had higher verbal scores but lower math scores than males. With regard to motivational factors, females at 12th grade were less confident of success in math than males although there was no gender difference in math interest. When asked to rate how important each of a series of job- and life-related values were to them, females placed more value on putting family needs before work, working with people, and altruism. In contrast, males placed more value on working with things, making money, and seeking out high-risk and high-status tasks. We did not find gender differences in careerism, suggesting that it is not the ambition that distinguishes the gender patterns, but rather differences in expectations for success and in beliefs as to what kind of work and lifestyle would allow for overall life goal fulfillment. But do these differences explain gender differences in college major selection?

Table 12.1. *Descriptive characteristics of the study sample*

	Female (N = 612) M (SD)	Male (N = 588) M (SD)	Difference test
Aptitude at 12th grade:			
Math ability	4.21 (1.38)	4.35 (1.23)	5.61**
Verbal ability	2.87 (1.23)	3.06 (1.32)	12.96***
Motivational beliefs at 12th grade:			
Math ability self-concept	3.73 (1.09)	4.61 (1.05)	13.00***
Math interest	3.95 (1.18)	4.02 (1.12)	0.96
Value family needs	4.74 (1.02)	3.91 (1.04)	12.44***
Careerism	4.71 (1.06)	4.69 (1.05)	0.77
Value working with people	4.38 (1.05)	3.42 (1.16)	13.78***
Vale working with things	3.35 (1.06)	3.95 (1.02)	9.12***
Altruism	4.73 (0.98)	4.12 (1.11)	9.21***
Value material wealth	3.72 (1.11)	4.35 (1.09)	9.06***
Value risk taking	3.65 (1.11)	4.26 (1.03)	9.01***
Value high status	3.53 (1.00)	3.92 (1.00)	6.17***
Course enrollment at 10th–12th grade:			
Number of math courses taken	4.12 (1.65)	4.06 (1.52)	0.60
Family characteristics:			
Family SES (family income and parent education)	0.57 (1.02)	0.58 (1.02)	0.16
College major:			
Selection of STEM college major[a]	0.18	0.37	157.36***

Notes: Superscript a represents dichotomous variable so the mean is the percentage of females and males who are in these majors; STEM = science, technology, engineering, and mathematics (0 = non-STEM occupation, 1 = STEM occupation); ** $p < .01$, *** $p < .001$.

Gender differences in math and verbal ability pattern

We conducted latent profile analysis to identify categorical latent classes of students as indicated by their math and verbal aptitudes in 12th grade. Logistic regression analysis was then used to examine group differences in the likelihood of selecting college majors in STEM versus non-STEM fields. We found that a five-profile solution provided the best-fitting model for this data based on conventional indices (AIC = 7,215.23, BIC = 7,431.52, entropy = .86). We focused primarily on the comparison of the first two groups: students with high math and high verbal abilities versus students with high math but moderate

Percentage of selecting STEM college major

- High math/high verbal (63% females, 37% males): 43% [a]
- High math/average verbal (30% females, 70% males): 62% [b]
- Average math/average verbal (47% females, 53% males): 25% [c]
- Low math/high verbal (71% females, 29% males): 7% [d]
- Low math/low verbal (37% females, 63% males): 0% [d]

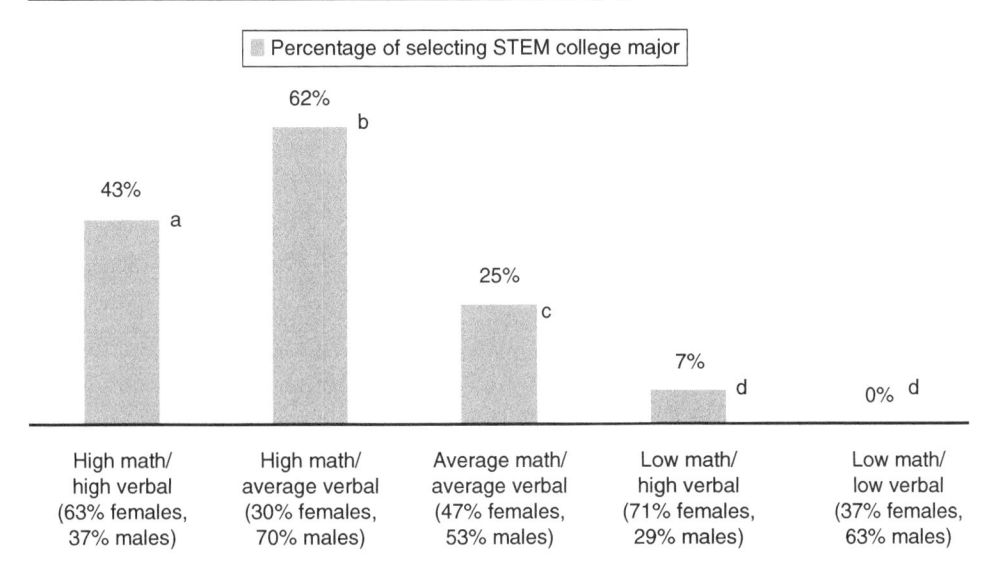

Figure 12.1 *Predicting STEM vs. non-STEM college major from math and verbal scores*
Notes: χ^2 (4, N = 1,200) = 43.54, $p < .001$; Means with the same superscript were not significantly different at $p < .05$ level.

verbal abilities. As hypothesized, the high math/high verbal students were less likely to select college majors in STEM (43%) than were high math/moderate verbal students (62%), χ^2 (1, N = 1,200) = 12.47, $p < .001$ (see Figure 12.1). More females were in the high math/high verbal group than males (63% females), whereas more males were in the high math/moderate verbal group than females (70% males). Thus mathematically capable individuals who were also high in verbal skill were more likely to pursue college majors outside of STEM.

Ability patterns play a role in choice, with students choosing to focus on their area of strength. Recent studies show that verbally gifted people appear to be drawn to the social sciences and humanities, and mathematically gifted people appear to be drawn to engineering, math, and computer science (Lubinski & Benbow, 2007; Wang et al., 2013). Therefore, it is not surprising that the high math/moderate verbal ability students would be drawn to fields that require strong quantitative skills, as demonstrated in this study. It is noteworthy that this high math/moderate verbal ability grouping was 74% male. In contrast, the high math/high verbal group was only 35% male (65% female). Students in this group presumably have a greater range of career pathways to choose from, perhaps allowing them to feel they are in a better position to consider factors such as personal values and job characteristics than those who did not possess such choice (i.e., those with high math but moderate or low verbal ability). Given that high math/high verbal students were less likely to choose STEM college majors, it is likely that non-STEM fields may be seen as affording greater accommodation of personal values and life goals (e.g., Diekman et al., 2011; Lips, 1992; Wang et al., 2013; Ware & Lee, 1988). We will explore this hypothesis later.

It is also possible that frame of reference effects, which cause an internal comparison of abilities and influence verbal and math self-concepts (Marsh, 1987), are influencing the high math/high verbal group gravitation toward non-STEM fields (see also Parker et al., this volume). Studies have shown that better verbal skills lead to higher English self-concepts but slightly lower math self-concepts, and vice versa (Marsh, 1986, 1990). Indeed, Marsh (1990) found that self-concepts were extremely sensitive to even small differences in frame of reference contexts. Consequently, it is possible that a weakened math self-concept causes students to rely more heavily on their verbal skills, and to give English a more integral role in their developing identity than math or science. However, numerous questions arise from such an assumption: for example, what are the trajectories of mathematically talented young girls in high school; and how do we promote reliance on math ability over verbal ability?

Our findings lead us to suggest that it is not lack of ability that is driving females to pursue non-STEM careers; rather it is an abundance of choice (Wang et al., 2013). Here, it appears that the arguably more balanced ability profiles of female students afford them greater opportunity than males to consider both STEM and non-STEM college majors. This finding may go some distance in explaining female underrepresentation in STEM fields. However, it is important not to rule out the potentially detrimental effects of frame of reference effects. Students whose verbal skills are even slightly better than their math skills may underestimate their high math ability. Individuals are more likely to choose a given pathway if they feel confident in their capacity to succeed in the area, and so it is possible that a lessened math self-concept or a heightened English self-concept may have interfered with some participants' motivation to pursue STEM college majors. We discuss additional motivational factors contributing to participants' occupational choice below.

Gender differences in STEM college major selection

We used logistic regression analyses, run separately for male and female participants, to determine which personal values, expected math efficacy, and math interest better discriminated adolescents who chose a college major in STEM from those who did not. As hypothesized, both females and males who expected to do well in math and placed low value on working with people (female college major: $\beta = -.668$, $SE = .120$, $p < .001$, odds ratio = .513; male college major: $\beta = -.397$, $SE = .115$, $p < .001$, odds ratio = .672) were more likely to select college majors in STEM than those who expected to do less well and valued working with people at 12th grade, when holding math and verbal abilities constant (see Table 12.2). Consistent with previous studies, high math ability self-concept and low people orientation appear to move both genders toward STEM pathways (Correll, 2001; Su et al., 2009), and males in our study rated their level of math ability self-concept higher and level of people orientation

Table 12.2. *Logistic regression analysis predicting individual STEM versus non-STEM college major from aptitude, motivational beliefs, course enrollment, and family socioeconomic status at 12th grade*

Independent variable	Female (N = 612) Selection of STEM college major β (SE)	Odds ratio (OR)	Male (N = 588) Selection of STEM college major β (SE)	Odds ratio (OR)
Aptitude at 12th grade:				
Math ability	**.290 (.07)***	**1.336**	**.364 (.08)***	**1.439**
Verbal ability	−.068 (.07)	.934	−.040 (.05)	.961
Motivational beliefs at 12th grade:				
Math ability self-concept	**.494 (.08)***	**1.639**	**.580 (.09)***	**1.786**
Math interest	.044 (.05)	1.045	.057 (.06)	1.058
Value family needs	**−.481 (.11)***	**.618**	.032 (.09)	1.033
Value working with people	**−.668 (.12)***	**.513**	**−.397 (.11)***	**.672**
Value working with things	.072 (.06)	1.075	**.654 (.08)***	**1.924**
Altruism	−.060 (.10)	.942	−.052 (.08)	.949
Careerism	.036 (.04)	1.037	.024 (.07)	1.024
Value material wealth	−.040 (.05)	.961	−.052 (.04)	.949
Value risk taking	.000 (.01)	1.000	.024 (.05)	1.024
Value high status	−.032 (.04)	.969	−.016 (.04)	.984
Course enrollment at 10th–12th grade:				
Number of math courses taken	**.420 (.10)***	**1.522**	**.456 (.09)***	**1.578**
Family characteristics:				
Family income and parent education	**.190 (.06)***	**1.209**	**.186 (.06)***	**1.204**
Constant	.426 (.16)***	NA	.395 (.13)***	NA

Notes: β (SE) = standardized coefficient (standard errors); STEM = science, technology, engineering, and mathematics (0 = non-STEM college major, 1 = STEM college major); * $p < .05$, *** $p < .001$. Significant findings are highlighted in bold.

lower than females at 12th grade. These findings may in part explain gender differences in decisions to pursue STEM careers.

In addition to math ability self-concept and people orientation, higher value on fulfilling family obligations before work also pushed females away from STEM college majors (female college major: $\beta = -.481$, $SE = .115$, $p < .001$, odds ratio = .618), and females placed more value on family than males at 12th grade (see Table 12.2). Interestingly, the effect of family value was not evident for males (see also Bagnoli et al., this volume). One must question why family values do not arise here for both males and females. It is likely that societal expectations and processes of gender socialization cause females to rate family as more important than males (Powell & Greenhaus, 2010). Previous research indicates that women who rate family as important are less likely to choose a science path, whereas men's family and science career choices are not generally associated (Lips, 1992; Ware & Lee, 1988). In addition, a range of studies referred to earlier in this chapter suggest that the STEM pathway is less than hospitable to prioritization of the family (e.g., Ceci & Williams, 2010; Jacobs & Winslow, 2004). Our findings indicate that in order to encourage women to pursue STEM pathways, measures to improve math ability self-concept among girls are important, but not sufficient. Rather, the complexity of career choice and factors feeding into decisions to pursue STEM must be accounted for. For example, it is imperative that STEM fields evolve to accommodate family values and plans. In addition, increasing public awareness of the people-oriented aspects of STEM-related careers would likely appeal to the intrinsic interests of talented young women who are choosing pathways that are more explicitly linked with community and affiliation.

Conclusion

Gender differences in personal attributes relevant to commitment to and excellence in STEM fields include but are not limited to personal aptitude patterns, academic ability self-concept, interest, occupational values, and lifestyle values. These differences may contribute to the underrepresentation of females in STEM even when holding math and verbal ability and family demographic characteristics constant. Our findings indicate that gender equity in the provision of educational and occupational opportunity may not be sufficient to ensure similar educational and career outcomes. It is not surprising that differential aptitudes and motivational beliefs lead to differential educational and career choices. This may to some extent explain why, despite similarity in math and science course-taking patterns and achievement in high school, females are still underrepresented in mathematics, physical, engineering, and computer sciences, as opposed to social, biological, and medical sciences.

It is not in the interest of society to encourage young women to pursue pathways that do not accommodate their values and life goals. However, it is possible that young women are lacking the information on which to base their STEM or non-

STEM career decisions. Furthermore, there is an array of research that alludes to unequal treatment of girls in the home, school, and in the wider cultural context (Ceci & Williams, 2010), which likely contributes to the gender gap in math and science career motivation. Although important, we do not have the scope to expand upon these factors here. However, it is clear that the underrepresentation of women in STEM fields is caused by a complex interaction of both psychological and socio-cultural factors. Our findings illustrate the importance of taking personal choice and life goals and values into account when addressing the gender gap in STEM fields. In order to address these motivational factors, STEM fields must adapt and evolve to accommodate the needs and goals of women. The capacity of STEM fields to address altruistic and communal goals must also be highlighted in the public domain. There are numerous measures that could be implemented in order to advance the field in this direction. For example, providing young mothers with job flexibility and support, and running campaigns to increase public awareness of the work that STEM professionals do and how it benefits society, would likely make the field more attractive to women. It is important to note, however, that these measures must be combined with others that tackle entrenched stereotypes, low ability self-concept, and other factors detrimental to young girls' motivation to pursue STEM education and career pathways.

References

Abele, A. E., & Spurk, D. (2011). The dual impact of gender and the influence of timing of parenthood on men's and women's careers development: Longitudinal findings. *International Journal of Behavioral Development*, 35, 225–232.

Atwar, M. M., Wiggins, J., & Gardner, C. M. (1995). A study of urban middle school students with high and low attitudes toward science. *Journal of Research in Science Teaching*, 32, 665–677.

Baenninger, M., & Newcombe, N. (1989). The role of experience in spatial test performance: A meta-analysis. *Sex Roles*, 20, 327–343.

Benbow, C. P., Lubinski, D., Shea, D. L., & Eftekhari-Sanjani, H. (2000). Sex differences in mathematical reasoning ability: Their status 10-years later. *Psychological Science*, 11, 474–480.

Blackwell, L. S., Trzesniewski, K. H., & Dweck, C. S. (2007). Implicit theories of intelligence predict achievement across and adolescent transition: A longitudinal study and an intervention. *Child Development*, 78, 246–263.

Casey, B. M., Andrews, N., Schindler, H., Kersh, J. E., Samper, A., & Copley, J. (2008). The development of spatial skills through interventions involving block building activities. *Cognition and Instruction*, 26, 269–309.

Casey, M. B., Nuttall, R. L., & Pezaris, E. (1997). Mediators of gender differences in mathematics college entrance test scores: A comparison of spatial skills with internalized beliefs and anxieties. *Developmental Psychology*, 33, 669–680.

Casey, M. B., & Pezaris, E. (2001). Spatial-mechanical reasoning skill versus mathematics self-confidence as mediators of gender differences on mathematics subsets using cross-national gender-based items. *Journal for Research in Mathematics Education*, 32, 28–57.

Ceci, S. J., & Williams, W. M. (2010). *The mathematics of sex: How biology and society conspire to limit talented women*. New York: Oxford University Press.

Correll, S. J. (2001). Gender and the career choice process: The role of biased self-assessments. *American Journal of Sociology*, 106, 1691–1730.

Diekman, A. B., Clark, E. K., Johnston, A. M., Brown, E. R., & Steinberg, M. (2011). Malleability in communal goals and beliefs influences attraction to STEM careers: Evidence for a goal congruity perspective. *Journal of Personality and Social Psychology*, 101, 902–918.

Durik, A. M., Vida, M., & Eccles, J. S. (2006). Task values and ability beliefs as predictors of high school literacy choices: A developmental analysis. *Journal of Educational Psychology*, 98, 382–393.

Dweck, C. (2008). *Mindsets and math/science achievement*. New York: Carnegie Corporation of New York, Institute for Advance Study, Commission on Mathematics and Science Education.

Eccles, J. S. (1983). Female achievement patterns: Attributions, expectancies, values, and choice. *Journal of Social Issues*, 1–26.

(1994). Understanding women's educational and occupational choices: Applying the Eccles et al. model of achievement-related choices. *Psychology of Women Quarterly*, 18, 585–609.

(2005). Studying gender and ethnic differences in participation in math, physical science, and information technology. In J. E. Jacobs & S. D. Simpkins (Eds.), *Leaks in the pipeline to math, science, and technology careers: New directions for child and adolescent development* (No. 110, pp. 7–14). San Francisco, CA: Jossey-Bass.

(2007). Families, schools, and developing achievement-related motivations and engagement. In J. E. Grusec & P. D. Hastings (Eds.), *Handbook of socialization* (pp. 665–691). New York: The Guilford Press.

(2009). Who am I and what am I going to do with my life? Personal and collective identities as motivators of action. *Educational Psychologist*, 44, 78–89.

Eccles, J. S., Barber, B., & Josefowicz, D. (1999). Linking gender to educational, occupational, and recreational choice: Applying the Eccles et al. model of achievement-related choices. In J. T. Spence (Ed.) *Sexism and stereotypes in modern society: The gender science of Janet Taylor Spence* (pp. 153–191). Washington, DC: APA.

Eccles, J. S., Barber, B. L., Updegraff, K., & O'Brien, K. M. (1998). An expectancy-value model of achievement choices: The role of ability self-concepts, perceived task utility and interest in predicting activity choice and course enrollment. In A. K. L. Hoffmann, K. A. Renninger, & J. Baumert (Eds.), *Interest and learning: Proceedings of the Seeon Conference on Interest and Gender* (pp. 267–280). Kiel, Germany: Institute for Science Education at the University of Kiel.

Eccles, J. S., & Harold, R. D. (1992). Gender differences in educational and occupational patterns among the gifted. In N. Colangelo, S. G. Assouline, & D. L. Amronson (Eds.), *Talent development: Proceedings from the 1991 Henry B. and Jocelyn Wallace National Research Symposium on Talent Development* (pp. 3–29). Unionville, NY: Trillium Press.

Eccles, J. S., Wigfield, A., & Schiefele, U. (1997). Motivation to succeed. In W. Damon (Ed.), N. Eisenberg (Series Ed.), *Handbook of child psychology: Social, emotional, and personality development* (5th ed., Vol. 3, pp. 1017–1095). New York: Wiley.

Ferriman, K., Lubinski, D., & Benbow, C. P. (2009). Work preferences, life values, and personal views of top math/science graduate students and the profoundly gifted: Developmental changes and gender differences during emerging adulthood and parenthood. *Journal of Personality and Social Psychology*, 97, 517–532.

Frenzel, A. C., Goetz, T., Pekrun, R., & Watt, H. M. G. (2010). Development of mathematics interest in adolescence: Influences of gender, family and school context. *Journal of Research on Adolescence*, 20, 507–537.

Frome, P. M., Alfeld-Liro, C., & Eccles, J. (1996, March). *Why don't young women want to pursue male-typed occupational aspirations? A test of competing hypotheses*. Paper presented at the biennial meeting of the Society for Research on Adolescence, Boston, MA.

Gibbons, M. T. (2009). Engineering by the numbers. In *Profiles of engineering and engineering technology colleges*. Washington, DC: American Society for Engineering Education. Retrieved from http://people.ku.edu/~dginther/working%20papers/w12691.pdf.

Good, C., Aronson, J., & Inzlicht, M. (2003). Improving adolescents' standardized test performance: An intervention to reduce the effects of stereotype threat. *Applied Developmental Psychology*, 24, 645–662.

Hakim, C. (2006). Women, careers, and work–life preferences. *British Journal of Guidance and Counseling*, 34, 279–294.

Halpern, D. F., Benbow, C. P., Geary, D. C., Gur, R. C., Hyde, J. S., & Gernsbacher, M. A. (2007). The science of sex differences in science and mathematics. *Psychological Science in the Public Interest*, 8, 1–51.

Hill, C., Corbett, C., & St. Rose, A. (2010). *Why so few? Women in science, technology, engineering, and mathematics*. Washington, DC: AAUW.

Hyde, J. S. (2007). Women in science: Gender similarities in abilities and sociocultural forces. In S. J. Ceci & W. M. Williams (Eds.), *Why aren't more women in science? Top researchers debate the evidence* (pp. 131–145). Washington, DC: American Psychological Association.

Hyde, J. S., Lindberg, S. M., Linn, M. C., Ellis, A. B., & Williams, C. C. (2008). Gender similarities characterize math performance. *Science*, 321, 494–495.

Jacobs, J. E., Davis-Kean, P., Bleeker, M., Eccles, J. S., & Malanchuk, O. (2005). "I can, but I don't want to": The impact of parents, interests, and activities on gender differences in mathematics. In A. Gallagher & J. Kaufman (Eds.), *Gender differences in mathematics* (pp. 246–263). Cambridge University Press.

Jacobs, J. E., & Winslow, S. E. (2004). Overworked faculty: Job and stresses and family demands. *Annals of American Political and Social Scientist*, 596, 104–129.

Joyce, B. A., & Farenga, S. J. (2000). Young girls in science: Academic ability, perceptions and future participation in science. *Roeper Review*, 22, 261–262.

Koller, O., Baumert, J., & Schnabel, K. (2001). Does interest matter? The relationship between academic interest and achievement in mathematics. *Journal for Research in Mathematics Education*, 32, 448–470.

Kuenzi, J. J., Mathews, C., & Mangan, B. (2006). *Science, technology, engineering, and mathematics (STEM) education issues and legislative options.* Washington, DC: Congressional Research Service.

Lips, H. M. (1992). Gender- and science-related attitudes as predictors of college students' academic choices. *Journal of Vocational Behavior, 40,* 62–81.

Lubinski, D., & Benbow, C. P. (2007). Sex differences in personal attributes for the development of scientific expertise. In S. J. Ceci & W. M. Williams (Eds.), *Why aren't more women in science? Top researchers debate the evidence* (pp. 79–100). Washington, DC: APA.

Lubinski, D., Webb, R. M., Morelock, M. J., & Benbow, C. P. (2001). Top 1 in 10,000: A 10-year follow-up of the profoundly gifted. *Journal of Applied Psychology, 86,* 718–729.

Marsh, H. W. (1986). Verbal and math self-concepts: An internal/external frame of reference model. *American Educational Research Journal, 23,* 129–149.

—— (1987). The big-fish-little-pond effect on academic self concept. *Journal of Educational Psychology, 79,* 280–229.

—— (1990). Influences of internal and external frames of reference on the formation of math and English self-concepts. *Journal of Educational Psychology, 82,* 107–116.

Meece, J., Wigfield, A., & Eccles, J. S. (1990). Predictors of math anxiety and its consequences for young adolescents' course enrollment intentions and performance in mathematics. *Journal of Educational Psychology, 82,* 60–70.

Mueller, C. M., & Dweck, C. S. (1998). Praise for intelligence can undermine children's motivation and performance. *Journal of Personality and Social Psychology, 75,* 33–52.

Nagy, G., Garrett, J. L., Trautwein, U., Cortina, K. S., Baumert, J., & Eccles, J. S. (2008). Gender and high school course selection in Germany and the US: The mediating role of self-concept and intrinsic value. In H. Watt & J. Eccles (Eds.), *Gender and occupational outcomes* (pp. 115–143). Washington, DC: APA.

National Center for Education Statistics. (2012). *Higher education: Gaps in access and persistence study* (Table E-42-2). Washington, DC: Author. Retrieved from http://nces.ed.gov/pubs2012/2012046/tables/e-42-2.asp.

National Science Board. (2010). *Preparing the next generation of STEM innovators: Identifying and developing our nation's human capital.* Arlington, VA: Author. Retrieved from www.nsf.gov/nsb/publications/2010/nsb1033.pdf.

Pajares, F. (2005). Gender differences in mathematics self-efficacy beliefs. In A. M. Gallagher & J. C. Kaufmann (Eds.), *Gender differences in mathematics: An integrative psychological approach* (pp. 294–315). New York: Cambridge University Press.

Park, G., Lubinski, D., & Benbow, C. P. (2008). Ability differences among people who have commensurate degrees matter for scientific creativity. *Psychological Science, 19,* 957–961.

Powell, G. N., & Greenhaus, J. H. (2010). Sex, gender and decisions at the family/work interface. *Journal of Management, 36,* 1011–1039.

Quaiser-Pohl, C., Geiser, C., & Lehmann, W. (2005). The relationship between computer-game preference, gender, and mental-rotation ability. *Personality and Individual Differences, 40,* 609–619.

Ruble, D. N., & Martin, C. (1998). Gender development. In N. Eisenberg, (Ed.) *Handbook of child psychology: Social, emotional, and personality development* (5th ed., Vol. 3, pp. 858–932). New York: Wiley.

Schiefele, U. (2001). The role of interest in motivation and learning. In J. M. Collis & S. Messick (Eds.), *Intelligence and personality: Bridging the gap in theory and measurement* (pp. 163–194). Mahwah, NJ: Erlbaum.

Schoon, I., Ross, A., & Martin, P. (2007). Science related careers: Aspirations and outcomes in two British cohort studies. *Equal Opportunities International*, 26, 129–143.

Shapka, J. D. (2009). Trajectories of math achievement and math competence over high school and postsecondary education: Effects of an all-girl curriculum in high school. *Educational Research and Evaluation*, 15, 527–541.

Su, R., Rounds, J., & Armstrong, P. I. (2009). Men and things, women and people: A meta-analysis of sex differences in interests. *Psychological Bulletin*, 135, 859–884.

Trower, C. A. (2008). *Competing on culture: Academia's new strategic imperative.* Unpublished presentation. Retrieved from www.advance.iastate.edu/conference/conferencepdf/2008_10-11trower_ppt.pdf.

Updegraff, K. A., Eccles, J. S., Barber, B. L., & O'Brien, K. M. (1996). Course enrollment as self-regulatory behavior: Who takes optional high school math courses? *Learning and Individual Differences*, 8, 239–259.

Valian, V. (2007). Women at the top in science and elsewhere. In S. J. Ceci & W. M. Williams (Eds.), *Why aren't more women in science? Top researchers debate the evidence* (pp. 27–39). Washington, DC: APA.

Vasta, R., Knott, J. A., & Graze, C. E. (1996). Can spatial training erase the gender differences on the water level task? *Psychology of Women Quarterly*, 20, 549–567.

Voyer, D., Voyer, S., & Bryden, M. P. (1995). Magnitude of sex differences in spatial abilities: A meta-analysis and consideration of critical variables. *Psychological Bulletin*, 117, 250–270.

Wai, J., Lubinski, D., & Benbow, C. P. (2005). Creativity and occupational accomplishments among intellectually precocious youths: An age 13 to age 33 longitudinal study. *Journal of Educational Psychology*, 97, 484–492.

Wang, M. T. (2012). Educational and career interests in math: A longitudinal examination of the links between perceived classroom environment, motivational beliefs, and interests. *Developmental Psychology*, 48, 1643–1657.

Wang, M. T., & Degol, J. (2013). Motivational pathways to STEM career choices: Using expectancy–value perspective to understand individual and gender differences in STEM fields. *Developmental Review*, 33(4), 304–340.

Wang, M. T., & Eccles, J. S. (2012). Adolescent behavioral, emotional, and cognitive engagement trajectories in school and their differential relations to educational success. *Journal of Research on Adolescence*, 22, 31–39.

(2013). School context, achievement motivation, and academic engagement: A longitudinal study of school engagement using a multidimensional perspective. *Learning and Instruction*, 28, 12–23.

Wang, M. T., Eccles, J. S., & Kenny, S. (2013). Not lack of ability but more choice: Individual and gender differences in STEM career choice. *Psychological Science*, 24, 770–775.

Ware, N. C., & Lee, V. E. (1988). Sex differences in choice of college science majors. *American Educational Research Journal, 25,* 593–614.

Wigfield, A., & Eccles, J. S. (2002). The development of competence beliefs and values from childhood through adolescence. In A. Wigfield & J. S. Eccles (Eds.), *Development of achievement motivation* (pp. 92–120). San Diego, CA: Academic Press.

Wigfield, A., Eccles, J. S., Schiefele, U., Roeser, R. W., & Davis-Kean, P. (2006). Development of achievement motivation. In N. Eisenberg (Ed.), *Handbook of child psychology* (6th ed., Vol. 3, pp. 933–1002). New York: Wiley.

13 What happens to high-achieving females after high school? Gender and persistence on the postsecondary STEM pipeline

Lara Perez-Felkner, Sarah-Kathryn McDonald and Barbara Schneider

Abstract

Although progress has been made in reducing gender inequality in postsecondary education, in the US and in other countries, gender gaps remain in the science, technology, engineering, and mathematics (STEM) fields judged so critical to economic competitiveness. Using the Education Longitudinal Study of 2002, we examine the influence of young women and men's secondary school experiences of on their subsequent courses of study in college. In particular, we use this large-scale study to examine the effect of the psychological indicators (such as deep interest or absorption in the subject matter) suggested to be important predictors of persistence in small-scale studies of women specializing in STEM fields at the postsecondary level. Focusing the analysis on high-achieving youth who have completed the secondary school STEM pipeline course sequences, we find that academic preparation in secondary school is the critically important consideration in keeping US boys on the STEM pipeline midway through their undergraduate postsecondary educational experience. African American boys who have completed these sequences are the most likely to declare STEM majors and Latino males are least likely, net of nativity status. For high-achieving girls on the whole, however, course taking is insufficient to keep them on the STEM pipeline. Their orientation toward mathematics and external supports from engaged family, school staff, and friends are powerful predictors of their persistence in STEM at the postsecondary level.

Introduction

Many explanations have been articulated for why female students are less likely to pursue science, technology, engineering, and mathematics (STEM)

This material is based upon work supported by the National Science Foundation under Grant Nos. 0815295, 1232139, and DRL-1108778. Any opinions, findings, and conclusions or recommendations expressed in this material are those of the authors and do not necessarily reflect the views of the National Science Foundation. The first author has also been supported by a grant from the American Educational Research Association, which receives funds for its "AERA Grants Program" from the National Science Foundation under NSF Grant No. DRL-0941014, and the Pathways to Adulthood Programme, which is supported by the Jacobs Foundation.

majors in college. Particularly powerful has been the recognition that failure to complete specific mathematics and science course sequences in secondary school is predictive of postsecondary transitions and outcomes. Also influential are differences in actual and perceived abilities that lead many to conclude they are less well-suited to succeed in certain STEM fields (see also Chow & Salmela-Aro; Parker, Nagy, Trautwein, & Lüdtke; M. Wang & Kenny, this volume). Together this evidence suggests that young women who perceive themselves as less able to perform well in math and science, and complete fewer advanced mathematics and science courses in high school, would be less likely than those women who perceive themselves as more able, and who are better prepared to remain in the STEM pipeline. Similarly girls and boys who complete advanced courses in science and mathematics by the time they graduate from secondary school would seem especially well prepared to declare a STEM major in postsecondary school.

This chapter assesses the links between high school experiences and tendencies to remain on the STEM pipeline in postsecondary programs of study. In particular, we explore whether the academic and subjective experiences of students on the STEM pipeline in secondary school differ from those of students off the pipeline, and assess to what extent these experiences vary by gender.

Gender differences in science participation

Countries across the globe have made considerable progress toward the goal of decreasing disparities between women's and men's average education levels. In the early 1990s, males in Organization of Economic Co-operation and Development (OECD) countries were more likely than females to obtain postsecondary degrees (Vincent-Lancrin, 2008). By the mid-1990s, the trend began to change. In the US, females were as likely as males to graduate with a postsecondary degree (US Department of Education, 1995, p. 1). Gender parity was achieved among OECD countries in 2008 when the average proportion of females aged 25 to 64 with university-level education was the same as that found in the population overall (21%) (OECD, 2010, tables A1.3a–c).

Progress has also been made in the STEM fields judged so critical to economic competitiveness. In the US, for example, important gains were made at the undergraduate level in the four decades from 1966 to 2006. The percentage of bachelor's degrees earned by women more than doubled in the biological and agricultural sciences (increasing from 25 to nearly 60%), nearly tripled in chemistry (increasing from 18 to 52%), and approximately quadrupled in the earth, atmospheric, and ocean sciences (moving from 9 to 41%) and physics (from 5 to 21%) (Hill, Corbett, & St. Rose, 2010, p. 9).

With these gains, women were receiving nearly one half of the undergraduate degrees in mathematics and chemistry, and the majority of the bachelor's degrees in biology. However, much remains to be done to close persistent – in some cases, widening – gender gaps in other STEM fields in the US and other countries. US women were still gaining less than a third of the bachelor's degrees in physics in 2007, and only a small fraction of the degrees awarded in engineering. In computer science there was actually a decreasing proportion of undergraduate degrees awarded to women (Hill et al., 2010, pp. 9–10).

This troubling pace toward gender equity across the STEM fields is not unique to the US. Less than one quarter of the entering postsecondary student population in OECD countries are women in mathematics and computer science (24%) and engineering, manufacturing, and construction (23%).[1] These patterns of enrollment are often foreshadowed by students' expectations while still in secondary school. In US high schools, more adolescent boys than adolescent girls expect they will pursue STEM majors in higher education, especially in the more quantitative sciences, despite the fact that female high school students have been more likely than males to report that they expect to attend and graduate from college since the 1990s (Burke, 2007; Goldin, Katz, & Kuziemko, 2006). Consistent with these educational expectations and female underrepresentation in STEM fields in postsecondary institutions, women constitute a substantially smaller proportion than men of the US labor force in key STEM fields, including computer and information sciences (where only 26% of those employed are women), chemistry (23%), physics/astronomy (14%), electrical engineering (9%), aerospace engineering (8%), and mechanical engineering (7%).[2] Women, however, averaged a little over half (51%) of those entering postsecondary majors in the life sciences and agriculture.

This chapter examines the reasons for this persistent underrepresentation of women in specific STEM fields, starting with experiences in secondary education, which are then linked to participation in science fields during postsecondary education. Using data from the Education Longitudinal Study of 2002 (ELS), the most recent US representative sample of adolescents designed to capture high school to postsecondary transitions, we explore the secondary school experiences of young women and men, and the impact of these experiences on their subsequent courses of study in college.[3] Specifically, we consider whether efforts to further increase young women's preparation in mathematics and science in secondary school are likely on their own to keep more women on the STEM pipeline midway through the typical 4-year US undergraduate postsecondary school experience. Our study takes into account that preparation for science courses during secondary school is often conflated with ability, as students with a particular aptitude for a subject are often those who choose to pursue advanced studies in this area. We thus take into account variations in academic ability as well as a number of other possible confounding factors associated with the school experience.

---

[1] Countries differ with respect to their gender gaps in STEM fields. In mathematics and computer science, women ranged from 9% (in Belgium) to 44% (in Greece); see OECD (2010, table A2.6). (Web only, percentage of new entrants into tertiary education and proportion of females, by field of education, 2008.)

[2] Authors' calculations, based on data on employment in science and engineering careers provided in NSF (2009, table H-5): "Employed scientists and engineers, by occupation, highest degree level, and sex: 2006."

[3] ELS presently includes a base-year student survey in 2002 and two follow-ups in 2004 and 2006. In 2002, 15,400 students were included in the sample. This dataset also includes information from parents, students' teachers, and their schools. In 2002, 750 schools completed the base-year questionnaire.

Key dimensions of the US secondary school experience: school academic supports and opportunities

Students' experiences in secondary school are conditioned by a variety of factors, some unique to the school, some to the student, some to broader familial, neighborhood, and other cultural and social forces. In attempting to parse the relative impacts on students' postsecondary educational choices, it is helpful to distinguish school-level academic supports and opportunities from a wide range of individual-level factors that prior research has shown to have powerful influences on students' interest in STEM, in high school and beyond.

Considerable research supports the association between finishing advanced-level math and science classes and enrolling in and completing college (Adelman, 1999, 2006; Trusty & Niles, 2003). Completing mathematics and science pipeline courses impacts students' grades, test scores, college selectivity, and entrance into a STEM field in postsecondary education. Calculus and physics are both considered particularly important preparation for postsecondary STEM coursework. Although girls are less likely to complete physics than are boys, they complete calculus – perhaps strategically, to help them excel on college entrance examinations and increase their chances of admission to selective postsecondary institutions (Riegle-Crumb, 2010).

Selecting courses can be complicated, especially for students planning STEM careers. The most appropriate sequence of secondary school courses can be unclear to students (Schneider & Stevenson, 1999). Recognizing this, many schools and districts have made concerted efforts to increase students' understandings of the most appropriate courses to take in secondary school, if not earlier.[4] Still, rates and patterns of advanced course taking vary widely at both the individual and school levels. Affluent students tend to take more advanced mathematics and science coursework than their less socioeconomically advantaged peers; similarly, white and Asian students take more advanced courses compared to underrepresented minority students (Dalton, Ingels, Downing, & Bozick, 2007; Riegle-Crumb, 2006). High schools that serve high percentages of minority and low-income youth less commonly offer advanced math and science courses to their students (Adelman, 2006).

Another critical source of support for students as they navigate the demands of their secondary school courses and plan for their futures is provided by adult members of the school community. Teachers in particular can bolster students' educational attainment and persistence. Particularly important to students are their interpretations of their teachers' expectations for and behaviors toward them, especially teachers' positive or negative reinforcement of students' academic behaviors and ambitions. Students may withdraw academically when

---

[4] Research suggests that middle school should be the primary site for developing STEM ambitions; to be prepared to enter the mathematics pipeline, students should be encouraged to take the more advanced mathematics courses available to them (e.g., Algebra 1) (McDonough, 2004).

they encounter teacher and school attitudes that they perceive as being uncaring or holding low expectations for their academic performance and careers (Valenzuela, 1999). Students' perceptions of the degree to which teachers and peers regard their academic potential can explain differences in their postsecondary enrollment (Perez-Felkner, in press).

Girls are typically perceived as "better" students, harder working and easier to discipline (Jones & Myhill, 2004; Mickelson, 1989). While boys may receive less praise than girls for their overall academic performance, they appear to receive more support from parents and teachers for their interests and ambitions in STEM (Gunderson, Ramirez, Levine, & Beilock, 2012). In short, gendered differences in support may be less evident overall but still persist in some scientific fields. Thus it is critical to gauge the academic support students receive on the basis of self-reports of teachers' expectations, interest, praise, and whether or not they feel put down in class.

Individual-level factors influencing STEM interests and postsecondary choices

It has been suggested that young women's achievement on mathematics and science tests may help to explain why a smaller proportion of women than men pursue certain STEM majors in college. Females are less likely to score in the highest tail of the distribution of both mathematics and science standardized test scores and college entrance examinations. While the gender gap in test scores on the mathematics section of the SAT college entrance examination has narrowed over the years, the percentage of high-scoring boys (i.e., those achieving a score of 700 or better) continues to exceed the percentage of high-scoring girls (Wai, Cacchio, Putallaz, & Makel, 2010).

Influencing female students' assessments of their academic abilities may be the input they receive or perceive from others. High-performing students may attract more interest from college recruiters able to provide STEM fellowship and scholarship aid. As the number of high-performing women is more limited, it can reinforce negative perceptions of female ability to successfully pursue STEM careers in college. For example, teachers and counselors may base the messages they give on teachers' test results and overlook other factors relevant to the appropriateness of pursuing a STEM career (NSF, 2000).

Unpacking and redressing factors that contribute to students' under-assessments of their academic capabilities may be important in tackling the gendered differences that remain in STEM fields. Females' career pursuits have been found to be strongly associated with self-assessments of ability, in particular for STEM careers (Correll, 2001; see also Chow & Salmela-Aro; Parker et al.; Wang & Kenny, this volume). Self-assessments are shaped by local and societal beliefs about women's abilities and career opportunities, especially in the quantitative sciences (Correll, 2004; Ridgeway & Correll, 2004; Eccles (Parsons) et al., 1983).

When teachers emphasize process, memorization, and facts in isolation from the social context and real-world application of scientific or mathematical concepts, girls may still work hard in order to do well, but fail to develop a true passion that can be carried forward to a future university major. Students who express deep interest in particular subject domains (i.e., computer science) prior to postsecondary education have been found to persist in those fields (Margolis & Fisher, 2002; Singh, Allen, Scheckler, & Darlington, 2007). In a qualitative study of women who initially selected computer science majors in university, the authors found that these women reported enjoying working with computers, but came to doubt their identity as computer scientists; compared to their male classmates, they felt that they did not belong, were "guests in a male-hosted world," and did not feel the same "total absorption" (an all-consuming passion for working with computers and robotics in both work time and free time) that their male counterparts reported (Margolis & Fisher, 2002, p. 72).

Interlinked lives

The ongoing relationships among adolescents' psychological and social dispositions and their environments – including their interactions with family, peers, and school staff – can profoundly shape their interests and actions regarding college plans, particularly toward STEM fields. Students' expectations of themselves are shaped in important ways by the expectations others have for and communicate to them, the encouragement they receive from others, their adult and peer role models, and their experiences of broader social environments. Girls have been found to be more academically engaged overall; however, their engagement in mathematics and science in particular is less well understood. Past research has suggested that females underestimate their abilities in content areas in which their gender is not well represented (Correll, 2004).

Adults in the school community (including teachers, counselors, and coaches) are powerful influencers of student expectations. Thus the amount of time students spend interacting with such adults and the nature of these interactions are important in aligning adolescents' ambitions toward college and pursuit of postsecondary plans. It is important then to consider how these interactions vary within and across schools. Particularly relevant are the college advising resources available to students in school. Limited resources exist in many urban disadvantaged schools to help students learn about careers and postsecondary choices; this problem is partially attributable to their low numbers of STEM-trained teachers. Girls may, however, be more likely in disadvantaged secondary schools to achieve in math and science. Recent research suggests that girls in these schools may be receiving more attention and support from their teachers for pursuing STEM careers; African American and Latina girls in these schools complete more advanced mathematics course sequences in comparison to their African American or Latino male peers (Riegle-Crumb, 2006).

Important as their interactions with adults in the high school are, students may enter secondary school with deeply ingrained expectations and beliefs resulting from their internalization of broader social and cultural factors. When these include negative perceptions of STEM – e.g., science and mathematics are for males (Farland-Smith, 2009; Hill et al., 2010) – even the most dedicated adult proponents of STEM in high school (e.g., teachers and counselors) may find them hard to shift. Children as young as 5 have been found to evaluate their behavior according to these gender stereotypes (Eccles & Hoffman, 1984; Huston, 1985). Significantly, parents' socialization messages have been found to have long-term effects on young adults' occupational outcomes, in particular for girls (Chhin, Bleeker, & Jacobs, 2008).

Such socialization may help to explain why young women may still shy away from a career in math or science, even when they choose to pursue STEM majors in college. Women may choose other occupations because they perceive traditionally male-dominated fields to be oriented around competition (Hill et al., 2010). Women are more likely than men to report being motivated to pursue careers in which they help others or can use their skills to generate social benefits (Margolis & Fisher, 2002). In a recent study of Australian adolescents, girls' estimation of the "usefulness" of math was found to be highly predictive of their aspirations to mathematics careers; boys' view of the utility of math bore no effect on their pursuit of math careers (Watt, 2008). Some adolescent girls report viewing careers in computer science as "materialistic" male pursuits in which boys "fool around" with often-violent games (AAUW, 2000, p. 8). Females have generally been found to focus on the quality of their and others' lives in evaluating their educational and career options, as opposed to males who focus more on status rewards (Mickelson, 2003).

School peers also serve a critical role in forming adolescents' ambitions toward postsecondary schools and careers. College-oriented peer cultures can form in schools with high concentrations of students planning to enroll in postsecondary institutions; these cultures can serve to disseminate information and skills to facilitate the alignment of these college ambitions with the behaviors that assist in their realization (Schneider, 2007). The opportunity to develop a science identity may be stalled, perhaps permanently, by peers' and adults' explicit and implicit messages to young girls that science is for boys. Carlone (2004) suggests supportive communities help students embrace a "science identity," for example, that one is a "science person." Farland-Smith (2009) demonstrated that when middle school girls were exposed to female scientists as role models, they developed positive attitudes toward scientific careers and orientations toward pursuing a career in the sciences.[5]

Parents' expectations for their children's education influence students' academic and career aspirations, which in turn have been shown to influence

---

[5] The lack of female role models in university STEM departments has also been used to explain gender disparities in STEM majors. Only 20% of faculty in science and engineering departments are female (Dworkin, Kwolek-Folland, Maurer, & Schipani, 2008). These ratios are similar across

their career development (Schoon & Parsons, 2002). In the past, parents had lower expectations for their daughters. Today that is no longer the case (Schoon, 2010). In fact, as we will show, parents have higher expectations for females. In considering the impacts of students' educational expectations, identities, and role models on their STEM interests and postsecondary choices, we are particularly interested in how high school students are influenced by their understandings of their parents' expectations for them, the advice and guidance they receive from school staff, and the role models their peers present.

Factors influencing pursuit of a STEM major

Studies of female underrepresentation in STEM subjects in higher education tend to employ small samples of youth at select colleges and universities who are already enrolled in STEM coursework or even STEM majors. Less common are large-scale, prospective studies of youth that capture the periods prior to and through their commitment to a STEM concentration at the tertiary level. Large-scale, nationally representative, longitudinal studies such as the Education Longitudinal Study of 2002 (ELS) provide important opportunities to explore patterns of STEM persistence and attrition at the tertiary level.

ELS follows a cohort of students from secondary school through their transitions to work or postsecondary education, providing information about young people's aspirations, course taking, high school experiences, future plans, and academic achievement. This enables analyses of the influence of family background and school contexts' influence on students' college matriculation and pursuit of STEM majors. Importantly the study allows us to evaluate the degree to which students report engaging in conversations with adults about their courses and about college.

An open question is whether the psychological indicators (such as deep interest or absorption in the subject matter) suggested to be important predictors of persistence in small-scale studies of women specializing in STEM fields at the tertiary level (e.g., Margolis & Fisher, 2002) would be present in large-scale studies. This is particularly relevant with respect to the question of whether females are responding to education policies emphasizing science and mathematics at the secondary level. With its data on the academic experiences of male and female students from their sophomore year in high school into postsecondary education and the labor market, ELS allows us to explore two questions: (1) To what extent are the academic and subjective experiences of students on the STEM pipeline in secondary school different from those of

most STEM fields. Studies have further suggested that STEM professors may contribute to an environment perceived to be hostile or unsupportive for women (Baron-Cohen, 2009; Goodman et al., 2002).

students off the pipeline? and (2) Do these experiences vary by gender, and are these differences sustaining, as evidenced by the college major declared 2 years after high school?

Relating high school experiences to females' and males' tendencies to remain on the STEM pipeline in postsecondary programs of study is complicated, especially when considering not only individual cognitive and social factors but the family and high school contextual factors that are likely to influence choices. We suspect that differences in both individual and contextual factors interact with gender and are likely to influence not only choices but also sustaining interest in postsecondary school. The following analyses take both the individual and contextual factors into account to examine postsecondary matriculation and pursuit of a STEM major, with a special emphasis on females and males. The primary dependent measure indicates whether or not female or male students declare a STEM major 2 years out of secondary school.[6] Analyses also consider whether females and males with high levels of high school STEM preparation are enrolled in a 2- or 4-year college or university.

Assessing gendered differences

To begin, a series of descriptive analyses are conducted to examine if there are differences in the performance and academic experiences of students on and off the STEM pipeline in high school. Generally, it is assumed students *in* the STEM pipeline are those who, by the end of secondary school, have completed coursework in science and mathematics that would prepare them to be eligible for STEM major coursework in postsecondary education. We define *being on the STEM pipeline in secondary school* as successful completion of (1) at least 1 year of physics and chemistry and (2) at least 3 years of high-school-level math coursework, such as completing Algebra 2. Conversely, students described here as *not* in the STEM pipeline are those who have not met one or both of these criteria.

In considering the potential impacts of academic abilities and achievement on students' STEM interests and postsecondary choices, two indicators of students' academic ability are included in the model. The first is overall academic ability over time, administered by examinations given by the US National Center for Educational Statistics (NCES). The second is high school grade point aver-

---

[6] This variable was measured by the US National Center for Educational Statistics (NCES) for only those respondents who enrolled in postsecondary institutions, as reported in the chapter's descriptive results. For the multinomial analysis, however, all respondents are incorporated into the model to prevent sample bias from missing data. Respondents not enrolled in postsecondary education are coded as "0" for not declaring a STEM major. To include a fuller analytic sample of male and lower socioeconomic status respondents, we recoded those missing on the basis of a "legitimate skip" as "not declaring STEM major" because they are not on track to complete a STEM major 2 years after high school. These models were additionally estimated with the original coding scheme and similar results were obtained.

age (GPA) from their 12th-grade academic transcripts (excluding non-academic courses).

Other student factors include expectations held by 10th-grade students and their parents for their education (how far they will go in school), how frequently students talk with their parents about college and courses, and how frequently they speak with school staff (counselors, teachers, and coaches) about college. In addition to how often they seek out advice from adults, we measure their beliefs about the ability to learn to be good in math, to understand the degree to which they might view academic challenges in mathematics. Further, we examine students' perceptions of the efficacy of their secondary school math and science training for postsecondary education.

School contextual measures include: (1) student responses regarding their plans to take the ACT or SAT college entrance examinations, aggregated to the school level; (2) the proportion of 2003 graduates enrolling in a 2-year college or university; and (3) the proportion of 2003 graduates enrolling in a 4-year college or university.[7] A composite measure of school quality is created, coded into four quartiles based on the proportion of students planning to take the SAT/ACT and percentage of 2003 graduates enrolling in 4-year colleges.

Analyses are conducted on the full sample of ELS students and a subsample of those who were on the STEM pipeline in secondary school as defined above. The experiences and outcomes of these two groups are compared with a special focus on gender differences both during and after high school. Additionally, a series of logistic multilevel models are estimated to examine the relationships among their individual and school-level characteristics and the odds of declaring a STEM major 2 years after secondary school. These analyses employ a hierarchical linear modeling (HLM) approach to consider students' nested positions within schools, by estimating individual-level attributes as predictors at level 1 and school-level attributes as predictors at level 2.[8]

Odds ratio comparisons demonstrate the degree to which each predictor affects the probability of declaring a STEM major 2 years after high school, for males

---

[7] These school-level variables were generated from the 10th- and 12th-grade school administrator files.

[8] The following logistic hierarchical linear models are used to calculate the odds of declaring a STEM major 2 years after high school:
Level-1 (student-level):
Odds of STEM major (2006) = $\beta_0 + \beta_1$ Student background characteristics $_{ij} + \beta_2$ Student abilities, academic experiences, and achievement in high school $_{ij} + \beta_3$ Student educational expectations, identities, and role models in high school $_{ij} + \beta_4$ Student engagement in high school $_{ij} + \beta_5$ Academic supports in high school $_{ij} + \beta_6\ q_{ij}$
Level-2 (school-level):
$\beta_{1ij} = \gamma_{(0-\text{fixed})} + \gamma_1$ High School Characteristics $_{ij} + \gamma_3\ s_{ij}$
$\beta_{2ij} = \gamma_{(0-\text{fixed})} + \gamma_1$ High School Characteristics $_{ij} + \gamma_3\ s_{ij}$
$\beta_{3ij} = \gamma_{(0-\text{fixed})} + \gamma_1$ High School Characteristics $_{ij} + \gamma_3\ s_{ij}$
$\beta_{4ij} = \gamma_{(0-\text{fixed})} + \gamma_1$ High School Characteristics $_{ij} + \gamma_3\ s_{ij}$
$\beta_{5ij} = \gamma_{(0-\text{fixed})} + \gamma_1$ High School Characteristics $_{ij} + \gamma_3\ s_{ij}$

Table 13.1. *Descriptive characteristics of sample population by STEM pipeline course taking*

	Full analytic sample		
	STEM N = 4,632 $\bar{X}$ (SD)	Non-STEM N = 9,508 $\bar{X}$ (SD)	
Student background characteristics[a]			
Race and ethnicity			
White and/or Asian	0.773 (0.419)	0.650 (0.477)	***
Black/African American	0.106 (0.307)	0.159 (0.366)	***
Latino/Hispanic	0.114 (0.318)	0.178 (0.383)	***
Foreign-born	0.087 (0.281)	0.073 (0.260)	**
Family composition	0.748 (0.434)	0.657 (0.475)	***
Number of siblings	2.052 (1.399)	2.433 (1.567)	***
Socioeconomic status	0.300 (0.718)	−0.119 (0.685)	***
Student abilities, academic experiences, and achievement in high school			
Overall academic ability	0.558 (0.959)	−0.277 (0.921)	***
Math ability	0.563 (0.946)	−0.289 (0.916)	***
Hours spent per week on extracurricular activities	2.577 (1.263)	2.147 (1.246)	***
Hours spent per week on math homework	3.404 (2.143)	3.031 (2.350)	***
Math pipeline completion[b]	7.167 (0.781)	4.774 (1.409)	***
Science pipeline completion[b]	6.503 (0.500)	4.364 (1.163)	***
GPA (all academic courses only)[b]	6.326 (1.245)	4.255 (1.642)	***
Total AP/IB Science courses[b]	0.385 (0.604)	0.021 (0.151)	***
Student educational expectations, identities, and role models in high school[c]			
College educational expectations	5.658 (1.203)	4.890 (1.484)	***

Table 13.1. (*cont.*)

	Full analytic sample		
Parent expectations (10th)	5.564 (1.179)	4.955 (1.467)	***
Parent volunteering in school (10th)	0.359 (0.480)	0.251 (0.434)	***
Talk with parents about courses (12th)	2.216 (0.655)	2.059 (0.683)	***
Talk with parents about college (12th)	2.419 (0.636)	2.273 (0.686)	***
Talk to school staff about college			
Counselor	0.599 (0.490)	0.473 (0.499)	***
Teacher	0.317 (0.465)	0.270 (0.444)	***
Coach	0.099 (0.298)	0.076 (0.265)	***
Most people can learn to be good in math	2.952 (0.663)	2.955 (0.696)	
Friends' plans to attend 4-year college	3.647 (0.999)	3.084 (1.100)	***
Student engagement in high school			
Engagement (keeps studying even if difficult)	2.913 (0.866)	2.556 (0.865)	***
Gets absorbed in math	2.617 (0.799)	2.439 (0.810)	***
Student experience of school academic climate 9th through 12th			
Academic support from teachers	2.922 (0.492)	2.819 (0.526)	***
High school characteristics[d]			
Urban	0.328 (0.470)	0.273 (0.446)	***
Suburban	0.499 (0.500)	0.513 (0.500)	*
Rural	0.172 (0.378)	0.213 (0.410)	***
% enrolled in dropout prevention program	2.735 (1.340)	2.701 (1.274)	
% minority	31.099 (30.416)	34.752 (30.439)	***
Plans to take SAT or ACT	2.589 (0.294)	2.427 (0.315)	***
% enroll in 2-year college or university	3.314 (0.961)	3.523 (0.869)	***

	Full analytic sample		
% enroll in 4-year college or university	4.714	4.262	***
	(1.068)	(1.066)	
Transition outcomes			
Does not complete high school	0.034	0.075	***
	(0.181)	(0.263)	
High school graduate or equivalent (GED)	0.141	0.358	***
	(0.348)	(0.479)	
Attend 2-year college or university	0.142	0.297	***
	(0.349)	(0.457)	
Attend 4-year college or university	0.718	0.335	***
	(0.450)	(0.472)	
Postsecondary experience[e]			
For those enrolled in postsecondary			
College selectivity rank	2.858	1.892	***
	(1.133)	(1.057)	
Social or behavioral sciences major, 2 years after high school	0.135	0.100	***
	(0.342)	(0.301)	
STEM major 2 years after high school	0.406	0.290	***
	(0.491)	(0.454)	
Biological or bio-medical sciences	0.091	0.036	***
	(0.287)	(0.186)	
Clinical or health sciences	0.110	0.159	***
	(0.313)	(0.366)	
Physical sciences (chemistry, physics, or related sciences)	0.028	0.005	***
	(0.164)	(0.074)	
Engineering	0.103	0.031	***
	(0.305)	(0.173)	
Computer science	0.027	0.030	
	(0.162)	(0.171)	
Mathematics (including statistics)	0.018	0.004	***
	(0.132)	(0.063)	
Other sciences (agricultural, architectural, and technology)	0.030	0.024	
	(0.170)	(0.154)	

Table 13.1. (*cont.*)

	Full analytic sample		
Perceives that high school math prepared for postsecondary	2.465 (0.614)	2.257 (0.677)	***
Perceives that high school science prepared for postsecondary	2.274 (0.679)	2.085 (0.721)	***

Source: US Department of Education, National Center for Education Statistics, Educational Longitudinal Study of 2002 (ELS: 2002).

Notes: Data are weighted to population means. Significant differences were calculated using t-tests. ^ $p < 0.10$, * $p < 0.05$, ** $p < 0.01$, *** $p < 0.001$.

a. Family composition was coded 1 for married or marriage-like relationships and 0 for all other nonmissing categories. SES and academic ability are constructed by NCES. SES is a standardized z-score ranging from −2.11 to 1.82.

b. These measures were generated by NCES from the Transcript File. Math and science pipeline measures were also generated by NCES and range from 1 (no course in the subject) to 8 (most advanced courses) and 1 (no course in the subject) to 7 (most advanced courses), respectively. The STEM pipeline subsample consists of respondents who were coded 6 or higher on both the math and science pipelines. GPA is coded 0 (0.00 to 0.50) to 8 (more than 4.00), includes only academic courses, honors weighted. Total AP/IB science courses is coded 0 (no courses) to 2 (two or more courses).

c. Students' and parents' educational expectations in the 10th grade are coded 1 (less than high school diploma) to 7 (doctorate). Parent expectations and volunteering were obtained from the 10th-grade parent survey. Talking with parent variables correspond to students' 12th-grade responses, ranging from 1 (never) to 3 (often).

d. The first four outcomes in this category are mutually exclusive. The variable "Does not complete high school" is a dummy: 0 (high school graduates) and 1 (those who did not receive a high school diploma, including GED recipients). SAT/ACT plans are derived by averaging 12th-grade responses, aggregated to the school level and averaged within each school cluster, ranging continuously from 0 (not planning to take) to 2 (have taken). Percentage enrolled corresponds to administrator-reported proportions of high school graduates' postsecondary enrollments.

e. College selectivity rank, ranging from 1 (least selective) to 4 (most) is based on Carnegie Institution rankings.

and females. While ELS asks only those respondents enrolled in postsecondary education about their declared major, we include those not attending postsecondary school in our logistic HLM analyses to better understand the national sample's postsecondary transitions into STEM.

On and off the STEM pipeline in secondary school

Table 13.1 presents a set of descriptive analyses that compare the experiences of girls and boys on the STEM pipeline in high school with those who were not, and their subsequent pathways into postsecondary school majors. Comparisons were determined using ANOVA and Bonferroni tests for statistical significance.

Looking at Table 13.1, those on the STEM pipeline have notably higher socioeconomic backgrounds than those who are not. Racial and ethnic differences emerged as well. Of those on the STEM pipeline, only 11% are black or Latino, compared to those not on the STEM pipeline, of whom 16% are black and 18% are Latino. Students still on the pipeline in 12th grade scored higher than their non-STEM pipeline peers on 10th-grade examinations of their math and overall academic ability.

The STEM pipeline group also spent on average 26 more minutes per week on extracurricular activities and an extra 22 more minutes per week on math homework. Those off the pipeline on average completed only the lower-level "middle academic" math sequence, equivalent with Algebra 2, whereas their peers on the STEM pipeline completed pre-calculus. In science, STEM pipeline students on average completed Chemistry 1 and Physics 1, compared to their non-STEM peers who on average completed only general biology.

Clear differences were apparent between students on and off the STEM pipeline in secondary school with respect to their educational expectations, identities, and role models, with one exception: differences in beliefs that most people can learn to be good in math existed *within* rather than between groups, by gender. Those on the STEM pipeline reported considerably higher expectations for their education (between bachelor's and master's completion) than did their non-STEM peers (slightly less than a bachelor's degree). Interestingly, parents of students off the STEM pipeline had slightly higher expectations for their children than did the students themselves; while for students on the STEM pipeline, their parents' expectations were slightly lower than their own. Those on the pipeline were also more likely to talk with their parents about high school courses and college than were their non-STEM peers.

The same pattern holds for students' discussions with school staff about college. Perhaps because of the social composition of their academic courses, students on the STEM pipeline in high school were more likely to have friends planning to attend a 4-year college than their non-STEM peers. Rounding out the profile of STEM students, those on the STEM pipeline were significantly more engaged in their academic studies – including total absorption in math – more often than those not on the STEM pipeline. They also experienced higher levels of academic support from their teachers.

Students on the STEM pipeline were more likely to be enrolled in urban and rural schools than their non-STEM peers. Their schools were also more oriented toward college. Their 12th-grade classmates had taken or planned to take the College Board exams at higher rates than the 12th-grade non-STEM peers. Moreover, of the schools attended by STEM pipeline students, the previous year's graduates enrolled in 4-year colleges or universities at significantly higher proportions (just under 50%) than those from schools where the majority were non-STEM pipeline students. As expected, students who completed the more rigorous coursework that placed them on the STEM pipeline had a greater tendency to attend 4-year colleges and enroll in STEM majors. Some 72% of those on the STEM pipeline enrolled in a 4-year college. They tended to enroll in more selective postsecondary institutions compared to those off the pipeline, of whom only 34% enrolled in 4-year colleges. Students on the STEM pipeline in secondary school were significantly more likely than all other students to enroll in STEM majors at the tertiary level, with the exception of two majors: computer science and other sciences (agricultural, architectural, and technology), whose applied appeal might make them more accessible to those with less rigorous course backgrounds. Both of these categories had strong gender differences, favoring males. As expected, STEM course pipeline completers had a higher tendency to report that they perceived their secondary school math and science coursework as good preparation for their postsecondary studies.

Gendered differences in secondary school

Using similar analytic procedures, we next examine the differences between female and male students on the STEM pipeline in secondary school (see Table 13.2). One of the more unusual findings is that in the subsample of students who are not on a STEM pipeline, females complete more rigorous course sequences than their male peers. With respect to those who are on the STEM pipeline, the gendered differences are more pronounced, in the opposite direction. Males completed slightly more rigorous math sequences than girls and had significantly higher scores on 10th-grade tests of math ability. Within this group, girls spent more hours per week on both math homework and extracurricular activities and had significantly higher grade point averages in their academic classes overall. Interestingly, STEM girls are from less socioeconomically advantaged families. Similar trends are evidenced in the non-STEM subsample, with the exception of coursework.

Educational expectations, identities, and role models

Earlier we noted that those on the STEM pipeline reported considerably higher expectations for their education than did their non-STEM peers. Looking more closely at those on the STEM pipeline, we find that girls have significantly higher expectations for their education, as do their parents for them (echoing previously discussed research findings, e.g., Smith, 2002).[9] Boys, meanwhile, have a significantly greater tendency to believe that most people can learn to be good in math, a worldview that could bolster their self-confidence and resilience in challenging courses. Girls' self-confidence and resilience, in turn,

---

[9] Recall that these results represent *general* educational expectations, that is, how far in school parents expect their children to go. We do not have a similar measure for how long parents expect their children to persist in STEM.

Table 13.2. *Descriptive characteristics of sample population by STEM pipeline course taking and gender*

	STEM pipeline				Non-STEM			
	Females $\bar{X}$ N = 2,515	(SD)	Males $\bar{X}$ N = 2,445	(SD)		Females $\bar{X}$ N = 5,202	(SD)	Males $\bar{X}$ N = 5,208	(SD)	
---	---	---	---	---	---	---	---	---	---
Student background characteristics[a]									
Race and ethnicity									
White and/or Asian	0.775	(0.418)	0.771	(0.420)		0.650	(0.477)	0.650	(0.478)	
Black/African American	0.101	(0.301)	0.111	(0.314)		0.156	(0.363)	0.162	(0.369)	
Latino/Hispanic	0.118	(0.323)	0.110	(0.313)		0.183	(0.183)	0.174	(0.379)	
Foreign-born	0.081	(0.273)	0.093	(0.290)		0.080	(0.272)	0.065	(0.247)	**
Family composition	0.746	(0.435)	0.751	(0.433)		0.660	(0.474)	0.654	(0.476)	
Number of siblings	2.070	(1.420)	2.034	(1.379)		2.490	(1.579)	2.377	(1.553)	**
Socioeconomic status	0.266	(0.724)	0.335	(0.709)	***	−0.132	(0.698)	−0.107	(0.672)	^
Student abilities, academic experiences, and achievement in high school									
Overall academic ability	0.537	(0.917)	0.578	(1.000)		−0.253	(0.893)	−0.301	(0.948)	**

Table 13.2. (cont.)

	STEM pipeline		Non-STEM	
Math ability	0.487 (0.914)		−0.331 (0.894)	−0.248 (0.936) ***
Hours spent per week on extracurricular activities	2.600 (1.226)		2.141 (1.208)	2.154 (1.283)
Hours spent per week on math homework	3.648 (2.184)	***	3.258 (2.393)	2.810 (2.285) ***
Math pipeline completion[b]	7.132 (0.781)	**	4.925 (1.377)	4.626 (1.425) ***
Science pipeline completion[b]	6.517 (0.500)	<	4.481 (1.100)	4.250 (1.211) ***
GPA (all academic courses only)[b]	6.572 (1.111)	***	4.649 (1.608)	3.865 (1.581) ***
Total AP/IB Science courses[b]	0.375 (0.603)		0.024 (0.165)	0.018 (0.136)
Student educational expectations, identities, and role models in high school[c]				
College educational expectations	5.805 (1.107)	***	5.172 (1.402)	4.608 (1.510) ***
Parent expectations (10th)	5.627 (1.154)	***	5.093 (1.441)	4.809 (1.479) ***
Parent volunteering in school (10th)	0.371 (0.483)	<	0.268 (0.443)	0.234 (0.424)
Talk with parents about courses (12th)	2.289 (0.647)	***	2.125 (0.673)	1.987 (0.686) ***
Talk with parents about college (12th)	2.501 (0.602)	***	2.357 (0.660)	2.180 (0.703) ***

Talk to school staff about college					
Counselor	0.624	0.574	***	0.525	0.422 ***
	(0.484)	(0.495)		(0.499)	(0.494)
Teacher	0.322	0.312		0.287	0.254 ***
	(0.467)	(0.463)		(0.452)	(0.435)
Coach	0.085	0.113	***	0.056	0.096 ***
	(0.279)	(0.317)		(0.229)	(0.294)
Most people can learn to be good in math	2.891	3.018	***	2.903	3.013 ***
	(0.648)	(0.673)		(0.697)	(0.691)
Friends' plans to attend 4-year college	3.765	3.527	***	3.204	2.966 ***
	(0.949)	(1.033)		(1.086)	(1.102)
Student engagement in high school					
Engagement (keeps studying even if difficult)	2.945	2.878	*	2.583	2.527 **
	(0.844)	(0.888)		(0.878)	(0.848)
Gets absorbed in math	2.582	2.654	**	2.399	2.484 ***
	(0.781)	(0.817)		(0.806)	(0.813)
Student experience of school academic climate 9th through 12th					
Academic support from teachers	2.958	2.884	***	2.847	2.791 ***
	(0.463)	(0.518)		(0.507)	(0.541)
High school characteristics[d]					
Urban	0.326	0.331		0.278	0.269
	(0.469)	(0.471)		(0.448)	(0.443)
Suburban	0.508	0.490		0.508	0.518
	(0.500)	(0.500)		(0.500)	(0.500)
Rural	0.165	0.179		0.214	0.213
	(0.372)	(0.384)		(0.410)	(0.409)

Table 13.2. (cont.)

	STEM pipeline	Non-STEM	
% enrolled in dropout prevention program	2.701 (1.335)	2.712 (1.300)	2.690 (1.248)
% minority	31.278 (30.498)	34.431 (30.589)	35.065 (30.292)
Plans to take SAT or ACT	2.592 (0.294)	2.445 (0.315)	2.409 (0.314)	***
% enroll in 2-year college or university	3.341 (0.966)	3.524 (0.877)	3.522 (0.861)
% enroll in 4-year college or university	4.691 (1.0899)	4.266 (1.065)	4.257 (1.067)
Transition outcomes			
Does not complete high school	0.027 (0.162)	0.041 (0.198) **	0.088 (0.283) ***
High school graduate or equivalent (GED)	0.117 (0.322)	0.165 (0.372) ***	0.409 (0.492) ***
Attend 2-year college or university	0.140 (0.347)	0.143 (0.350)	0.287 (0.452) *
Attend 4-year college or university	0.745 (0.436)	0.690 (0.463) ***	0.293 (0.455) ***
Postsecondary experience[e]			
For those enrolled in postsecondary			
College selectivity rank	2.882 (1.117)	2.832 (1.151)	1.942 (1.079)	1.829 (1.027) ***

Social or behavioral sciences major, 2 years after high school	0.139 (0.346)	0.131 (0.337)	***	0.116 (0.320)	0.077 (0.266) ***
STEM major 2 years after high school	0.367 (0.482)	0.451 (0.498)	***	0.304 (0.460)	0.267 (0.443) *
Biological or biomedical sciences	0.098 (0.297)	0.082 (0.275)		0.039 (0.194)	0.031 (0.173)
Clinical or health sciences	0.172 (0.377)	0.038 (0.191)	***	0.224 (0.417)	0.061 (0.240) ***
Physical sciences (chemistry, physics, or related sciences)	0.027 (0.161)	0.029 (0.168)		0.004 (0.064)	0.007 (0.086)
Engineering	0.027 (0.162)	0.193 (0.395)	***	0.006 (0.079)	0.068 (0.252) ***
Computer science	0.010 (0.101)	0.046 (0.210)	***	0.011 (0.102)	0.059 (0.236) ***
Mathematics (including statistics)	0.010 (0.098)	0.027 (0.162)	***	0.004 (0.060)	0.004 (0.067)
Other sciences (agricultural, architectural, and technology)	0.024 (0.153)	0.036 (0.187)	<	0.017 (0.129)	0.036 (0.185) ***

Table 13.2. (cont.)

	STEM pipeline	Non-STEM	
Perceives that high school math prepared for postsecondary	2.460 (0.622)	2.471 (0.606)	2.239 (0.690)	2.280 (0.660)	*
Perceives that high school science prepared for postsecondary	2.260 (0.685)	2.288 (0.673)	2.101 (0.721)	2.065 (0.721)	^

Source: US Department of Education, National Center for Education Statistics, Educational Longitudinal Study of 2002 (ELS: 2002).

Notes: Data are weighted to population means. Significant differences were calculated using t-tests. ^ $p < 0.10$, * $p < 0.05$, ** $p < 0.01$, *** $p \leq 0.001$.

a. Family composition was coded 1 for married or marriage-like relationships and 0 for all other nonmissing categories. SES and academic ability are constructed by NCES. SES is a standardized z-score ranging from −2.11 to 1.82.

b. These measures were generated by NCES from the Transcript File. Math and science pipeline measures were also generated by NCES and range from 1 (no course in the subject) to 8 (most advanced courses) and 1 (no course in the subject) to 7 (most advanced courses), respectively. The STEM pipeline subsample consists of respondents who were coded 6 or higher on both the math and science pipelines. GPA is coded 0 (0.00 to 0.50) to 8 (more than 4.00), includes only academic courses, honors weighted. Total AP/IB science courses is coded 0 (no courses) to 2 (two or more courses).

c. Students' and parents' educational expectations in the 10th grade are coded 1 (less than high school diploma) to 7 (doctorate). Parent expectations and volunteering were obtained from the 10th-grade parent survey. Talking with parent variables correspond to students' 12th-grade responses, ranging from 1 (never) to 3 (often).

d. The first four outcomes in this category are mutually exclusive. The variable "Does not complete high school" is a dummy: 0 (high school graduates) and 1 (those who did not receive a high school diploma, including GED recipients). SAT/ACT plans are derived by averaging 12th-grade responses, aggregated to the school level and averaged within each school cluster, ranging continuously from 0 (not planning to take) to 2 (have taken). Percentage enrolled corresponds to administrator-reported proportions of high school graduates' postsecondary enrollments.

e. College selectivity rank, ranging from 1 (least selective) to 4 (most) is based on Carnegie Institution rankings.

may be increased through the support they receive from their parents; girls' parents are more actively engaged in their education than are boys' parents, and girls are more likely than boys to report that their parents volunteer in the school. Girls report talking to their parents about both classes and college significantly more frequently than boys do, consistent with research indicating girls have stronger and more frequent communication with their families (Kao, 2004; Stattin & Kerr, 2000). Girls are also more likely to talk with school guidance counselors about college compared to boys, whereas boys are more likely to talk with their coaches about college than are their female peers. Girls' friends were also more likely to be attending 4-year colleges than were boys' friends, echoing female students' greater engagement of adult role models in their college and course planning. These boy–girl differences are again consistent with those in the non-STEM pipeline group.

Girls have a greater tendency to keep studying when the material is difficult than boys, especially in the non-STEM group. Despite their diligence, this significantly lower tendency to become "totally absorbed" in math, even in the STEM pipeline group, foreshadows why girls in the STEM pipeline group do not enter STEM majors as much as do their male peers. One might expect females to enroll in STEM majors more readily than males, given their qualifications and ambitions, but this is not the case.

At the postsecondary level, STEM pipeline females are more likely to enroll in social or behavioral sciences after high school than males and are highly significantly less likely to enroll in STEM majors. Only 37% of these females declare STEM majors, compared to 45% of their male counterparts. Within the STEM fields, females tend to enroll in the clinical or health sciences (17% of females compared to 4% of males) rather than engineering (3% of females compared to 19% of males) and computer science (1% of females compared to 5% of males). Gender differences do not, however, exist in declaring a biological science or a physical science major. Using this data on secondary school experiences, we conduct a series of analyses to determine the characteristics of females who stay on the STEM pipeline in postsecondary school and what factors are most predictive of their persistence.

On and off the STEM pipeline in postsecondary education

Recognizing these gendered differences, we conducted a logistic HLM analysis to investigate the degree to which these differences helped explain persistence in a STEM major 2 years after high school graduation. Table 13.3 reports on the two-level logistic HLM regression models. We conducted separate logistic HLM models for each subgroup, estimating the proportion of variance in choosing a STEM major that can be attributed to student- and high-school-level

Table 13.3. Likelihood of declaring a STEM major 2 years after high school, by STEM pipeline and gender

	Declaring a STEM major					
	STEM pipeline			Non-STEM[f]		
	Females OR (SE)		Males OR (SE)		Females OR (SE)		Males OR (SE)	
Student background characteristics[a]								
Race (reference: White/Asian)								
Black/African American	1.011 (0.006)	*	2.181 (0.013)	***	1.317 (0.005)	***	1.277 (0.007)	***
Latino/Hispanic	0.741 (0.004)	***	0.374 (0.002)	***	0.922 (0.003)	***	1.148 (0.006)	***
Foreign-born	0.727 (0.003)	***	1.548 (0.006)	***	1.118 (0.004)	***	0.177 (0.002)	***
Family composition	1.092 (0.004)	***	0.965 (0.004)	***	1.302 (0.003)	***	1.269 (0.005)	***
Socioeconomic status	0.795 (0.001)	***	0.859 (0.002)	***	0.917 (0.001)	***	0.814 (0.002)	***
Student abilities, academic experiences, and achievement in high school								
Overall academic ability	0.628 (0.001)	***	0.869 (0.002)	***	0.794 (0.001)	***	0.702 (0.002)	***
Hours spent per week on extra-curricular activities	0.941 (0.001)	***	0.952 (0.001)	***	1.005 (1.005)	***	1.114 (0.001)	***
Hours spent per week on math homework	1.003 (0.001)	***	0.875 (0.001)	***	0.969 (0.969)	***	0.993 (0.001)	***
Math pipeline completion[b]	1.302 (0.002)	***	1.292 (0.003)	***	1.193 (0.001)	***	1.287 (0.002)	***

Science pipeline completion[b]	1.402	***	1.569	***	1.102	***	1.266	***
	(0.003)		(0.004)		(0.001)		(0.002)	
GPA (all academic courses only)[b]	1.211	***	1.400	***	1.118	***	1.520	***
	(0.002)		(0.002)		(0.001)		(0.002)	
Student educational expectations, identities, and role models in high school[c]								
College educational expectations	1.355	***	1.073	***	1.283	***	1.093	***
	(0.002)		(0.002)		(0.001)		(0.002)	
Parent expectations (10th)	1.101	***	0.902	***	0.965	***	1.121	***
	(0.002)		(0.001)		(0.001)		(0.001)	
Parent volunteering in school (10th)	0.990	***	0.746	***	0.663	***	1.527	***
	(0.002)		(0.002)		(0.002)		(0.005)	
Talk with parents about courses (12th)	1.379	***	1.056	***	0.999		0.922	***
	(0.003)		(0.002)		(0.002)		(0.002)	
Talk with parents about college (12th)	0.853	***	0.894	***	0.956	***	1.102	***
	(0.002)		(0.002)		(0.002)		(0.003)	
Talk to school staff about college								
Counselor (12th)	0.853	***	0.872	***	1.065	***	1.259	***
	(0.002)		(0.003)		(0.003)		(0.005)	
Teacher (12th)	0.774	***	1.055	***	0.991	***	1.270	***
	(0.002)		(0.003)		(0.002)		(0.004)	
Coach (12th)	0.829	***	0.618	***	0.738	***	0.875	***
	(0.003)		(0.003)		(0.003)		(0.004)	
Most people can learn to be good in math	1.064	***	1.338	***	1.057	***	1.125	***
	(0.002)		(0.003)		(0.002)		(0.003)	
Friends plan to attend 4-year college (12th)	1.128	***	0.918	***	0.960	***	0.915	***
	(0.002)		(0.002)		(0.001)		(0.002)	

Table 13.3. (cont.)

	Declaring a STEM major					
Student engagement in high school						
Engagement (keeps studying even if difficult)	1.233	***	1.087	**	1.042	***
	(0.002)		(0.002)		(0.001)	
Gets absorbed in math	1.216	***	1.242	***	0.982	***
	(0.002)		(0.002)		(0.001)	
Student experience of school academic climate 9th through 12th						
Academic support from teachers (10th)	0.981	***	0.727	***	1.153	***
	(0.003)		(0.002)		(0.002)	
High school characteristics[d]						
Urbanicity (reference: Suburban)						
Urban	1.025	***	0.908	***	0.956	***
	(0.003)		(0.003)		(0.002)	
Rural	1.262	***	2.050	***	1.282	***
	(0.004)		.0076656		(0.003)	
School quality level (reference: Highest)						
Lowest	0.714	***	0.826	***	1.019	***
	(0.003)		(0.004)		(0.003)	
Low–middle	1.041	***	0.844	***	1.001	
	(0.003)		(0.003)		(0.003)	
Middle–high	0.845	***	0.651	***	1.238	***
	(0.002)		(0.002)		(0.004)	
% minority	1.001	***	1.005	***	1.001	***
	(0.000)		(0.000)		(0.000)	

0.967	***
(0.002)	
1.389	***
(0.003)	
0.627	***
(0.002)	
0.722	***
(0.003)	
0.771	***
(0.003)	
0.852	***
(0.004)	
0.981	***
(0.004)	
1.340	***
(0.006)	
1.000	
(0.000)	

Hierarchical linear model statistics[e]			
Level 1 variance component	0.002	0.002	0.600
Level 2 variance component	−12.257	−12.458	−1.020
Intraclass correlation	0.000	0.000	0.099
Log likelihood	−2,409,920 ***	−2,025,653 ***	
		−3,634,946 ***	−1,843,654 ***
N observations	2,359	800	1,696	1,292
N clusters	381	357	550	502

Source: US Department of Education, National Center for Education Statistics, Educational Longitudinal Study of 2002 (ELS: 2002).

Notes: Data are weighted to population means. Significant differences were calculated using t-tests. ^ $p < 0.10$, * $p < 0.05$, ** $p < 0.01$, *** $p \leq 0.001$.

a. Family composition was coded 1 for married or marriage-like relationships and 0 for all other nonmissing categories. SES and academic ability are constructed by NCES. SES is a standardized z-score ranging from −2.11 to 1.82. Number of siblings was also included in the analysis but the comparisons were not significant. Results are available by request.

b. These measures were generated by NCES from the Transcript File. Math and science pipeline measures were also generated by NCES and range from 1 (no course in the subject) to 8 (most advanced courses) and 1 (no course in the subject) to 7 (most advanced courses), respectively. The STEM pipeline subsample consists of respondents who were coded 6 or higher on both the math and science pipelines. GPA is coded 0 (0.00 to 0.50) to 8 (more than 4.00), includes only academic courses, honors weighted.

c. Students' and parents' educational expectations in the 10th grade are coded 1 (less than high school diploma) to 7 (doctorate). Parent expectations and volunteering were obtained from the 10th-grade parent survey. Talking with parent variables correspond to students' 12th-grade responses, ranging from 1 (never) to 3 (often).

d. SAT/ACT plans are derived by averaging 12th-grade responses, aggregated to the school level and averaged within each school cluster, ranging continuously from 0 (not planning to take) to 2 (have taken). Percentage enrolled corresponds to administrator-reported proportions of high school graduates' postsecondary enrollments.

e. College selectivity rank, ranging from 1 (least selective) to 4 (most) is based on Carnegie Institution rankings.

f. The null hypothesis is rejected for both models: the likelihood-ratio test of rho = 0 is significant, $p < 0.001$ for each model.

differences.[10] The odds ratios (OR) for predictors represent how these independent variables relate to the likelihood of females' and males' pursuit of a STEM major 2 years after high school.

It has been argued that increasing college preparatory mathematics coursework requirements has detrimental effects on the academic performance of underrepresented minority students and bears no positive effect on their college matriculation (Allensworth, Nomi, Montgomery, & Lee, 2009). We find, however, that, holding all other variables in the model constant, African American youth who have completed the secondary school pipeline courses are more likely to persist to a STEM major in college than are their white and Asian peers. African American males were more than twice as likely as white and/or Asian males to continue on a STEM pipeline. Foreign-born males were 55% more likely than otherwise similar white and/or Asian males to major in a STEM field. The odds of persistence in STEM were lower for Latino males and females. This disadvantage was strongest for males, however, who were 63% less likely to declare a STEM major than their white and Asian peers.

Looking more closely at the effects of course taking within the STEM pipeline sample, we find that for every additional high-school-level mathematics course completed in secondary school, the odds of remaining in STEM increased about 30% for females and males. Completing science pipeline courses in high school similarly increased the odds of remaining on the STEM pipeline in college, especially for males, whose odds increased about 57%. For females, every additional science pipeline course completed was associated with a 40% increase in odds of remaining on the STEM pipeline.

Students' academic abilities and overall academic performance also influenced males' and females' pursuit of a STEM major. Students demonstrating greater academic ability in the 10th grade were less likely to remain on the STEM pipeline in college; this tendency was particularly strong for females. It is important to remember, however, that the academic ability variable is an overall measure, which does not give particular weight to the math and science domains. Unlike this 10th-grade measure of academic potential, however, increases in students' academic performance (their GPA) increase their odds of majoring in a STEM field. This is especially the case for males, whose odds increase 40% for every one-unit increase in GPA. Here again, males who succeed academically are more likely than otherwise similar females to major in STEM, even within this subsample of those who completed STEM college preparatory coursework.

Particularly salient for female and less so for male college students who are STEM majors were the educational expectations, identities, and role models reported while they were in high school. For every one-unit increase in educational expectations, the odds of declaring a STEM major increased 36% for

---

[10] This model can be referred to as a two-level hierarchical *generalized* linear model (HGLM) with a binary outcome. See Bryk and Raudenbush (2002) and Rabe-Hesketh and Skrondal (2008) for further discussion of HGLM.

girls and 7% for boys. Controlling for all other variables in the model, talking to parents about courses also increased the odds of remaining in STEM in college; again, more positively impacting females than males. A one-unit increase in talking with parents about high school courses was associated with a 38% increase in odds for remaining in STEM for girls, and a 6% increase in odds for boys. However, talking about college (as opposed to high school) with parents had a negative impact on both females and males. These results suggest that for this highly prepared subsample, conversations with parents about specific subjects are more important than more general discussions of academic futures.

How do females on and off the secondary STEM pipeline differ with respect to declaring a STEM major?

Girls on the pipeline see almost four times the return from each additional advanced science course than non-pipeline girls do. Their odds of persisting in STEM increase 40% for each additional science course completed. Girls who were not on the secondary school STEM pipeline still see a benefit, however, with their odds of moving onto the STEM pipeline at the postsecondary level increasing 10% for each additional science course. The gap between these females decreases with respect to the push they each receive for each additional mathematics course completed. STEM females' odds of persisting in STEM increase by 30%, while those of non-STEM females increase by 19%.

Differences emerge between these groups with respect to talking with family and in-school adults about their coursework and their futures. Informational exchanges between females on the STEM pipeline and their parents and adults in school serve as strong predictors of females' persistence in STEM. Specifically, talking with parents about courses positively predicts declaring a STEM major for STEM females with no strong effect for females off the pipeline. For girls on the pipeline, every one-unit increase in talking with parents about courses (e.g., from "sometimes" to "often") increases their odds of declaring a STEM major by 38%, compared to girls not on the pipeline, whose odds remain the same. When it comes to speaking with adults about college generally, however, girls on the STEM pipeline decrease their odds at greater levels than their non-pipeline counterparts with every one-unit increase in talking with counselors and teachers about college.

If teachers and counselors are discouraging girls from pursuing STEM careers, the effect is greatest for those girls on the STEM pipeline. Interestingly, although less than 10% of girls talk to their coaches about college (see Table 13.2), for those that do, the negative effect is stronger for girls not on the STEM pipeline. In a related finding, STEM pipeline girls who report academic support from teachers are less likely to major in STEM, as compared to all other girls, who are more likely to major in a STEM field. On the other hand, having friends planning to attend a 4-year college is a more powerful, and positive, predictor for STEM pipeline females (odds increase 13%) than for non-pipeline model females (odds decrease 4%).

Next, we turn to girls' engagement in school and their experience of the academic climate. For every one-unit increase in their academic engagement and deep interest in math, STEM pipeline girls are considerably more likely to declare STEM majors than are their non-pipeline counterparts. For example, STEM pipeline girls who "often" keep studying when the material is difficult are 23% more likely to persist to declare a STEM major than those who keep studying only "sometimes." For a girl who is not on the pipeline, the same increase would make her only 4% more likely to move onto the pipeline by declaring a STEM major. Similarly, absorption in math increases the odds of a STEM major much more so than it does for non-STEM girls. STEM pipeline girls who "strongly agree" that they get totally absorbed in math are 22% more likely to declare a STEM major than those who only "agree." The same one-unit change in absorption decreases the odds by 2% for girls who are not on the STEM pipeline.

Overall, school-level predictors are more significant for STEM pipeline girls than for non-STEM pipeline girls. The level 2 variance component is significantly lower for girls who are not on the STEM pipeline and the level 1 variance component is significantly higher. Therefore, for girls on the STEM pipeline, there is less variation between girls in the same school and more variation across schools. The effect of the school is weaker for girls who were not on the STEM pipeline.

How do boys on and off the secondary STEM pipeline differ with respect to declaring a STEM major?

The greatest differences between predictors of boys' declaration of a STEM major pertain to their individual background and school characteristics. Race affects boys similarly but the magnitude is significantly higher for boys who completed the advanced STEM pipeline courses in secondary school. Their odds of majoring in STEM in college more than double if they are African American, as compared to non-STEM pipeline boys whose odds increase by only 28%. For boys on the STEM pipeline in high school, being Latino dramatically reduces odds by 63%, as compared to an increase of 15% for all other boys. Being foreign-born also dramatically affects the odds of declaring a STEM major, although differently for those on and off the STEM pipeline in high school. Specifically, foreign-born males on the STEM pipeline are 55% more likely than those who are native-born to declare a STEM major in college. However, for males already off the STEM pipeline in high school, being foreign-born decreases the odds of declaring a STEM major by 82%.

With respect to their school characteristics, being from a rural school more than doubles the odds of declaring a STEM major for STEM pipeline boys, as compared to a decrease of 22% for all other boys. With the exception of non-STEM pipeline boys, enrollment in a rural secondary school improves the odds of declaring a STEM major, for all subsamples studied. This finding is consistent with research that suggests students in urban schools receive qualitatively different, and often less effective, mathematics and science instruction than their suburban and rural peers (Schmidt, Cogan, Houang, & McKnight, 2009, p. 72). Students' classroom experiences in science have also been found to impact their postsecondary aspirations (J. Wang, 1999; J. Wang & Staver, 2001).

Conclusions

Our findings suggest that academic preparation in secondary school is the critically important consideration in keeping US males on the STEM pipeline midway through their undergraduate postsecondary educational experience, with race and ethnicity providing an additional impetus for African American males and posing an additional obstacle for Latino males. Based on our analyses, however, US women need something more. Rigorous math and especially science course taking in secondary school are important predictors of female university students' persistence in STEM, but on its own such course taking is insufficient to keep young women on the STEM pipeline.

Our analyses underscore the critical role of external supports (e.g., received from parents, or through positive role models that their peers provide) to young women's persistence in STEM studies. While not altogether surprising in light of the relatively recent inroads that have been made in equalizing gendered differences in higher educational attainment more generally, this is a sobering finding that reminds us that absent seismic external forces, social and cultural climates tend to change slowly and incrementally. Until this evolutionary change process is complete, additional external supports are likely to be necessary to sustain females across the life course in imagining and achieving significant roles for themselves in previously male-dominated fields of study and work domains.

Others have demonstrated the importance of personal supports and a wide range of factors affecting subjective perceptions in sustaining females' interest, persistence, and success in STEM fields and careers, including: perceived similarity to others in a field; stereotypes embodied in physical environments (e.g., the physical characteristics of classrooms); encouragement from peers, mentors, and role models; and positive relationships with advisors (Anderson-Rowland, Bernstein, & Russo, 2007; Cheryan & Plaut, 2010; Cheryan, Plaut, Davies, & Steele, 2009; Rohlfing et al., 2009). In addition to these proximal influences, recent research suggests that more fundamental differences in the status and welfare of women have a powerful role to play in explaining the cross-national variability in gender gaps that persist (Else-Quest, Hyde, & Linn, 2010).

Against this background, we should perhaps not be surprised that the supports teenage girls perceive and receive midway through their time in secondary school would have such a crucial influence on their educational choices midway through their postsecondary educational experience. Important progress has been made toward the goals of decreasing disparities between women's and men's average education levels, and diminishing the gendered differences in the STEM fields so critical to economic competitiveness. Sustaining this progress and closing the gaps that remain seem likely to require continued dedicated efforts to provide the social and emotional supports instrumental in keeping well-qualified women on a STEM trajectory.

References

Adelman, C. (1999). *Answers in the toolbox: Academic intensity, attendance patterns, and bachelor's degree attainment*. US Department of Education, Office of Educational Research and Improvement. Washington, DC: Government Printing Office.

(2006). *The toolbox revisited: Paths to degree completion from high school through college*. Washington, DC: US Department of Education.

Allensworth, E., Nomi, T., Montgomery, N., & Lee, V. E. (2009). College preparatory curriculum for all: Academic consequences of requiring algebra and English I for ninth graders in Chicago. *Educational Evaluation and Policy Analysis*, 31(4), 367–391.

American Association of University Women (AAUW). (2000). *Tech-savvy: Educating girls in the new computer age*. Washington, DC: American Association of University Women Educational Foundation.

Anderson-Rowland, M., Bernstein, B., & Russo, N. F. (2007). Encouragers and discouragers for domestic and international women in doctoral programs in engineering and computer science. *Proceedings of the American Society for Engineering Education (ASEE) 2007 Annual Conference*, Honolulu, Hawaii, June 2007. Retrieved October 19, 2010, from http://soa.asee.org/paper/conference/paper-view.cfm?id=5665.

Baron-Cohen, S. (2009). Why so few women in math and science? In C. Sommers (Ed.), *The science on women and science*. Washington, DC: American Enterprise Institute for Public Policy Research.

Bozick, R., & Ingels, S. J. (2007). *Mathematics coursetaking and achievement at the end of high school: Evidence from the education longitudinal study of 2002 (ELS:2002)* (NCES 2008–319). Washington, DC: National Center for Education Statistics, Institute of Education Sciences, US Department of Education.

Bryk, A. S., & Raudenbush, S. W. (2002). *Hierarchical linear models: Applications and data analysis methods* (2nd ed.). Thousand Oaks, CA: Sage Publications.

Burke, R. (2007). Women and minorities in STEM: A primer. In R. J. Burke & M. C. Mattis (Eds.), *Women and minorities in science, technology, engineering and mathematics* (pp. 3–27). Northampton, MA: Edward Elgar Publishing.

Carlone, H. (2004). The cultural production of science in reform-based physics: Girls' access, participation, and resistance. *Journal of Research in Science Teaching*, 41(4), 392–414.

Cheryan, S., & Plaut, V. C. (2010). Explaining underrepresentation: A theory of precluded interest. *Sex Roles*, 63, 475–488. Retrieved October 19, 2010, from http://depts.washington.edu/sibl/Publications/Cheryan%20Plaut%20Sex%20Roles%20(2010).pdf.

Cheryan, S., Plaut, V. C., Davies, P. G., & Steele, C. M. (2009). Ambient belonging: How stereotypical cues impact gender participation in computer science. *Journal of Personality and Social Psychology*, 97(6), 1045–1060. Retrieved October 19, 2010, from http://depts.washington.edu/sibl/Publications/Cheryan,%20Plaut,%20Davies,%20&%20Steele%20(2009).pdf.

Chhin, C. S., Bleeker, M. M., & Jacobs, J. E. (2008). Gender-typed occupational choices: The long-term impact of parents' beliefs and expectations. In H. M. G. Watt & J. S. Eccles (Eds.), *Gender and occupational outcomes: Longitudinal assessments of individual, social, and cultural influences* (pp. 215–234). Washington, DC: American Psychological Association.

Correll, S. J. (2001). Gender and the career choice process: The role of biased self-assessments. *The American Journal of Sociology*, 106(6), 1691–1730.

(2004). Constraints into preferences: Gender, status, and emerging career aspirations. *American Sociological Review*, 69(1), 93–113.

Dalton, B., Ingels, S., Downing, J., & Bozick, R. (2007). *Moving beyond the basics: Advanced mathematics and science coursetaking in the high school classes of 1982, 1992, and 2004* (NCES 2007–312). National Center for Education Statistics, Institute of Education Sciences, US Department of Education. Washington, DC: US Government Printing Office.

Dworkin, T. M., Kwolek-Folland, A., Maurer, V., & Schipani, C. A. (2008). Pathways to success for women scientists in higher education in the US. In S. Grenz, B. Kortendiek, M. Kriszio, & A. Löther (Eds.), *Gender equality programmes in higher education: International perspectives* (pp. 69–86). Wiesbaden, Germany: VS Verlag.

Eccles, J., & Hoffman, L. (1984). Sex roles, socialization, and occupational behavior. In H. W. Stevenson & A. E. Siegel (Eds.), *Child development research and social policy* (Vol. 1, pp. 367). University of Chicago Press.

Eccles (Parsons), J. S., Adler, T., Futterman, R., Goff, S., Kaczala, C., Meece, J., et al. (1983). Expectancies, values, and academic behaviors. In J. T. Spence (Ed.), *Achievement and achievement motives: Psychological and sociological approaches* (pp. 75–146). San Francisco, CA: W.H. Freeman.

Else-Quest, N. M., Hyde, J. S., & Linn, M. C. (2010). Cross-national patterns of gender differences in mathematics: A meta-analysis. *Psychological Bulletin*, 136(1), 103–127. Retrieved October 19, 2010, from www.apa.org/pubs/journals/releases/bul-136-1-103.pdf.

Farland-Smith, D. (2009). Exploring middle school girl's science identities: Examining attitudes and perceptions of scientists when working "side-by-side" with scientists. *School Science and Mathematics*, 109(7), 415–427.

Geary, D. (1996). Sexual selection and sex differences in mathematical abilities. *Behavioral and Brain Sciences*, 19(2), 229–284.

Goldin, C., Katz, L., & Kuziemko, I. (2006). The homecoming of American college women: The reversal of the college gender gap. *The Journal of Economic Perspectives*, 20(4), 133–156.

Goodman, I., Cunningham, C., Lachapelle, C., Thompson, M., Bittinger, K., Brennan, R., et al. (2002). *Final report of the Women's Experiences in College Engineering Project*. Cambridge, MA: Goodman Research Group.

Gunderson, E., Ramirez, G., Levine, S., & Beilock, S. (2012). The role of parents and teachers in the development of gender-related math attitudes. *Sex Roles*, 66(3), 153–166. doi: 10.1007/s11199-011-9996-2.

Hill, C., Corbett, C., & St. Rose, A. (2010). *Why so few? Women in science, technology, engineering, and mathematics*. Washington, DC: American Association of University Women.

Huston, A. C. (1985). The development of sex typing: Themes from recent research. *Developmental Review*, 5(1), 1–17.

Ingels, S., & Dalton, B. (2008). *Trends among high school seniors, 1972–2004* (NCES 2008- 320). Washington, DC: National Center for Education Statistics, Institute for Education Sciences, US Department of Education.

Kao, G. (2004). Parental influences on the educational outcomes of immigrant youth. *International Migration Review*, 38(2), 427–449.

Jones, S., & Myhill, D. (2004). Seeing things differently: Teachers' constructions of underachievement. *Gender and Education*, 16(4), 531–546. doi: 10.1080/0954025004200030041l.

Margolis, J., & Fisher, A. (2002). *Unlocking the clubhouse: Women in computing*. Cambridge, MA: MIT Press.

McDonough, P. (2004). *The school-to-college transition: Challenges and prospects*. Washington, DC: American Council on Education.

Mickelson, R. A. (1989). Why does Jane read and write so well? The anomaly of women's achievement. *Sociology of Education*, 62(1), 47–63.

——— (2003). Gender, Bourdieu, and the anomaly of women's achievement redux. *Sociology of Education*, 76(4), 373–375.

National Science Foundation (NSF). (2000). *Land of plenty: Diversity as America's competitive edge in science, engineering, and technology*. Washington, DC: National Science Foundation.

——— (2009). *Women, minorities, and persons with disabilities in science and engineering: 2009 (NSF 09-305)*. Arlington, VA: National Science Foundation.

Organisation for Economic Co-operation and Development. (2010). *Education at a Glance 2010*. Paris: OECD.

Perez-Felkner, L. (in press). Perceptions and Resilience in Underrepresented Students' Pathways to College. [Feature Article]. *Teachers College Record*, 117(8), 1–69.

Rabe-Hesketh, S., & Skrondal, A. (2008). *Multilevel and longitudinal modeling using Stata* (2nd ed.). College Station, TX: Stata Corp.

Ridgeway, C. L., & Correll, S. J. (2004). Unpacking the gender system: A theoretical perspective on gender beliefs and social relations. *Gender and Society*, 18(4), 510–531.

Riegle-Crumb, C. (2006). The path through math: Course sequences and academic performance at the intersection of race-ethnicity and gender. *American Journal of Education*, 113(1), 101–122.

(2010). More girls go to college: Exploring the social and academic factors behind the female postsecondary advantage among Hispanic and white students. *Research in Higher Education*, 51, 573–593.

Rohlfing, J., Kube, E., Yabko, B., Murguia, E., Bekki, J., & Bernstein, B. (2009). Improving STEM doctoral students' relationships with their advisors: Web-based training in interpersonal problem-solving skills. *Proceedings of the American Society for Engineering Education (ASEE) 2009 Annual Conference*. Retrieved October 19, 2010, from http://soa.asee.org/paper/conference/paper-view.cfm?id=10868.

Schmidt, W. H., Cogan, L. S., Houang, R. T., & McKnight, C. (2009). *Equality of educational opportunity: A myth or reality in US schooling*. Lansing, MI: The Education Policy Center at Michigan State University.

Schneider, B. (2007). *Forming a college going culture in US public high schools*. Seattle, WA: Bill and Melinda Gates Foundation.

Schneider, B., & Stevenson, D. (1999). *The ambitious generation: America's teenagers, motivated but directionless*. New Haven, CT: Yale University Press.

Schoon, I. (2010). Planning for the future: Changing education expectations in three British cohorts. *Historical Social Research–Historische Sozialforschung*, 35(2), 99–119.

Schoon, I., & Parsons, S. (2002). Teenage aspirations for future career and occupational outcomes. *Journal of Vocational Behavior*, 60(2), 262–288.

Singh, K., Allen, K. R., Scheckler, R., & Darlington, L. (2007). Women in computer-related majors: A critical synthesis of research and theory from 1994 to 2005. *Review of Educational Research*, 77(4), 500–533.

Smith, R. C. (2002). Gender, ethnicity, and race in school and work outcomes of second-generation Mexican-Americans. In M. M. Suarez-Orozco & M. M. Paez (Eds.), *Latinos: Remaking America* (pp. 110–125). Berkeley: University of California Press.

Stattin, H., & Kerr, M. (2000). Parental monitoring: A reinterpretation. *Child Development*, 71(4), 1072–1085.

Trusty, J., & Niles, S. G. (2003). High-school math courses and completion of the bachelor's degree. *Professional School Counseling*, 7, 99–107.

US Department of Education, Office of Educational Research and Improvement. (1995). *Findings from The Condition of Education 1995. No. 5: The Educational Progress of Women* (NCES 95–768). Washington, DC: US Department of Education. Retrieved October 12, 2010, from http://nces.ed.gov/pubs/96768.pdf.

Valenzuela, A. (1999). *Subtractive schooling: US Mexican youth and the politics of caring*. Albany, NY: State University of New York Press.

Vincent-Lancrin, S. (2008). The reversal of gender inequalities in higher education: An ongoing trend. In Organisation for Economic Co-operation and Development (Ed.). *Higher education to 2030: Vol. 1: Demography* (pp. 265–298). Paris: Organisation for Economic Co-operation and Development.

Wai, J., Cacchio, M., Putallaz, M., & Makel, M. C. (2010). Sex differences in the right tail of cognitive abilities: A 30 year examination. *Intelligence*, 38(4), 412–423. doi: http://dx.doi.org/10.1016/j.intell.2010.04.006

Wang, J. (1999). A structural model of student career aspiration and science education. *Research in Schools*, 6(1), 53–63.

Wang, J., & Staver, J. (2001). Examining relationships between factors of science education and student career aspirations. *The Journal of Education Research*, 94(5), 312–319.

Watt, H. M. G. (2008). What motivates females and males to pursue sex-stereotyped careers? In H. M. G. Watt & J. S. Eccles (Eds.), *Gender and occupational outcomes: Longitudinal assessments of individual, social, and cultural influences* (pp. 87–114). Washington, DC: American Psychological Association.

14 Young people, gender, and science: does an early interest lead to a job in SET? A longitudinal view from the BHPS youth data

Anna Bagnoli, Dieter Demey and Jacqueline Scott

Abstract

This chapter examines the role of teenage career aspirations in predicting later outcomes. In particular we focus on young adolescent males and females who show an interest in SET (science, engineering, and technology) careers. We present the results of secondary analysis that we carried out on the British Youth Survey, which is part of the British Household Panel Survey. Looking at data from a recent cohort, we investigate trends in aspirations over time. Our analysis focuses on four research questions: first, identifying young people's future aspirations, more specifically their aspirations to get into SET, and the ways in which these relate to family background and gender; second, looking at whether an early interest in science leads to having a SET job as an adult; third, investigating the extent to which young people who aspire to a career in SET may be seeking to reproduce family patterns by following in the footsteps of their parents; and fourth, looking at how those young people who express an interest in SET speak of their career ambitions in relation to family aspirations. Before presenting the results of the analysis we clarify the different working definitions for SET occupations that we adopt in this study. We first present the quantitative cross-sectional and longitudinal results that link youth and adult data in the sample. Second, we present results of the qualitative analysis of future aspirations. Finally, we draw some policy implications concerning possible ways of improving the image of science to reduce the gender gap and encourage more young people to aspire to SET careers.

Introduction and background

In recent years a number of Organisation for Economic Co-operation and Development (OECD) reports have highlighted how, according to the Programme for International Student Assessment (PISA), there are marked differences in science competencies across countries (OECD, 2006; see also Jerrim &

This project was funded by the Nuffield Foundation with a Small Grant, EDU37680, from January to April 2010. Corresponding author is Jacqueline Scott.

Schoon, this volume). In addition, while there is no overall significant difference observed between boys and girls in science competence as measured by PISA, girls do less well than boys in some countries like the UK, France, Poland, Austria, Denmark, and Korea; while in other countries including the United States, Norway, and New Zealand, girls out-perform boys (DES, 2007). Although the PISA assessment of scientific literacy is not without its critiques (e.g., Sadler & Zeidler, 2009), governments, including that of the UK, take such comparative statistics seriously (DES, 2007). In the UK there has been considerable concern about young people's apparent disaffection from science (Roberts, 2002). However, as highlighted in a review of the literature on young people's attitudes to science (Osborne, Simon, & Collins, 2003), this concern is not new, and dates back to at least the end of the 1960s, when the 1968 Dainton report spoke of a "swing from science" (Ormerod with Duckworth, 1975). Trends in young people's educational qualifications in science can be misleading if they do not take into account how cohort size varies across time. Analysis of trends in A-level sciences in England, Northern Ireland, and Wales shows that participation in biology, chemistry, and physics in the period 2000–2007 has stayed relatively stable, with none of these subjects being chosen by more than 12% of the population of 17-year-olds (Royal Society, 2008). Such a low take-up of science is problematic for an economy that relies on science and technology.

If the low interest in science is general for all young people, the picture for girls is particularly dismal. Girls seem to be put off early on from scientific studies, and even though the overall number of girls studying scientific subjects has increased in recent years, in some disciplines, like physics, they remain underrepresented (Greenfield, 2002). For example, in 2006, the percentage of male A-level students taking physics was 5.7%, compared to only 1.3% of girls, whereas for biology the equivalent percentages for boys and girls were 7.1 and 5.9 respectively (DES, 2007). The gender differences become increasingly marked with the progression of scientific careers, with women dropping out from every stage at a much higher rate than men, a phenomenon known as the "leaky pipeline" (Jensen, 2005; see also Perez-Felkner, McDonald, & Schneider, this volume). In economic terms, such trends are problematic, since a fall in the supply of people with the necessary skills and qualifications can make it difficult for the UK economy to successfully compete on a global level. Equally, the underutilization of women's talents and the absence of diversity in the SET workforce may be severely limiting the advancement of a knowledge-based economy in terms of innovation and quality. Educational choices about whether to embark on or leave science have crucial ramifications, not least in terms of gender equality. The reduced number of women entering the labor market with scientific skills is one key factor associated with the persistence of a UK gender pay gap (Purcell & Elias, 2008).

This concern about the declining interest in science among young people motivated several countries to implement policies aimed at increasing human resources in SET. In the UK, the government piloted after-school science and engineering clubs in March 2007, as well as a STEM Communication Campaign in 2008 (OECD, 2008). According to the Relevance of Science Education (ROSE) study, an international investigation that started in 2001, most young people in England, despite considering science and technology as important to society, do not like science education as much as other subjects. They view it as "important but not for me" (Jenkins & Pell, 2006). The same study also found persistent gender differences in the attitudes expressed by boys and girls toward science and technology, the subjects that they were interested in learning, what they regarded as important in future employment, and the kind of research they would pursue as a scientist. The contrast between an appreciation of science and its value to society on the one hand, and the perceived lack of relevance of science as far as one's own studies and career are concerned on the other hand, has been found by several studies, among them the recent Eurobarometer survey on Young People and Science (Gallup Organization, 2008). This Eurobarometer survey revealed that young people (aged 15–25) in the UK were well below the EU average in their interest in science and technology topics. Research has also consistently demonstrated that interest in science declines in the early years of secondary schooling, between the ages of 11 and 14, the so-called "age 14 dip" (Bennett & Hogarth, 2009; Osborne et al., 2003).

The role of structure and agency

If girls' disaffection with science can be traced back so early in life, investigating the aspirations of girls and boys about their future and how this may influence their educational and career choices is important if we are to understand the gender imbalance that characterizes the SET sector. Studying young people's agency has to go hand in hand with an appreciation of the impact of structural conditions on their life choices, including the extent to which young people are free to "choose." It has been widely shown that class of origin is associated with educational outcomes. Family socioeconomic background has a strong impact on young people's life choices, and education is one crucial mechanism through which families transmit advantage or disadvantage to their children (Scott, 2004; Sullivan, 2007). However, this should not lead us to an over-deterministic view of young people's life chances, for young people's aspirations and actions do matter. Some succeed despite disadvantaged starting conditions (Scott & Chaudhary, 2003).

In recent years, the investigation of social reproduction and social stratification has been affected by a "cultural turn," and there has been a growing interest in exploring the cultural dimensions of class, i.e., non-material aspects of advantage, such as tastes, values, etc. Such studies often draw on Bourdieu's notions of cultural capital and habitus (Devine & Savage, 2005). Sullivan (2001, 2007) investigated cultural capital through a variety of measures, concluding that it is a useful explanatory concept, and a mechanism through which privileged families, particularly the professional middle class, ensure educational advantage to their children. Families in which parents are educated will more easily provide a context in which education is valued (Brookes, 2003; Scott, 2004). Particularly in some professions, young people may actively reproduce existing family patterns in their choice of occupation (Devine, 2010). North American evidence shows that the educational and occupational attainments of children are related to the education and occupation of both parents, with parental characteristics being stronger for same-sex children (Lampard, 2007). The effects of maternal employment have been widely investigated, and there is evidence that working mothers provide positive role models to their daughters, and are linked to girls' higher educational achievement and ambitions (Scott, 2004).

Gendered aspirations

An interest in a career in science is formed relatively early in life, and this is particularly true in the case of girls, for whom an early interest in science seems to be a good predictor of subsequent choice of SET studies (Schoon, Ross, & Martin, 2007). By contrast, boys may just "drift" into science. SET careers are regarded as more gender appropriate for boys/men, and it is thus easier for boys to think of themselves as working in science-related fields and aspire to a job in SET. The association between the cultures of science and technology and dominant forms of masculinity is long-standing (Wajcman, 2004). Subtle gender dynamics, reproducing normative gender identities, may alienate girls and women from pursuing scientific careers, by emphasizing their position as "outsiders," and not belonging to the field (Faulkner, 2007).

At school, teachers may unwittingly reproduce gender stereotypes in the assumptions they make about girls' and boys' abilities in science, and dissuade girls from even entering scientific studies (Shepardson & Pizzini, 1992; see also Perez-Felkner et al. and Upadyaya & Eccles, this volume). Already from an early age young people's academic interests, abilities, and motivation may be significantly influenced by what their teachers perceive and expect them to be (Eccles et al., 1983). Several studies have found teachers' expectations to be gender-biased and to rate pupils' abilities on the grounds of stereotypical views of gender-appropriate subjects (see Upadyaya & Eccles, this volume). Gender stereotyping and underrepresentation of women in textbooks may also play a part in reproducing the gender gap in science (Good, Woodzicka, & Wingfield, 2010). According to Buck, Plano Clark, Lesley-Pelecky, Lu, and Cerda-Lizarraga (2007), the stereotypical scientist as a white male in a lab coat wearing glasses described by students investigated by Mead and Metraux in US high schools in the 1950s (Mead & Metraux, 1957) remains potent for young female eighth-graders (aged 13–14). Buck et al. (2007) suggest that appropriate female scientist role models can encourage girls to enter science professions.

In a study on role models in the media commissioned by the UK Resource Centre for Women in Science, Engineering and Technology (UKRC), it was found that female scientists were either ignored or portrayed in sex-stereotypical ways, as either ultra-glamorous, or masculine and frumpy (Kitzinger, Haran, Chimba, & Boyce, 2008). Thus the media portrayals of women in science tended to be confined to "boffins or bimbos" (Chimba & Kitzinger, 2010). As pointed out by Steinke (2004), the media may be crucial in encouraging girls to take up science, since for many girls this will be their only exposure to female scientists. Both websites and films are likely to be particularly important. Whereas purposive websites can be constructed to provide appropriate women in science role models that are designed to heighten female career aspirations for science, adolescent girls are more likely to encounter female scientists in popular films. Research by Steinke (2005) has shown that more recent movies, from the 1990s onwards, represent female scientists in non-stereotypical ways, highlighting both their femininity and their intelligence. However, female scientists in films also appear to be mostly single and without children (Steinke, 2005), as well as marginalized by the scientific community (Flicker, 2003).

In our qualitative research we explore how family and career clashes are differentially perceived by adolescent boys and girls. While a woman's career is often seen as in conflict with motherhood, having a career is a crucial component of being a good father (see also Abele, this volume). According to Scott (2004), children even as young as 11 are aware that education and career on the one hand, and motherhood and family on the other, poses conflicts for women, but not for men. In this earlier research using the British Household Panel Survey, the acceptance of traditional gender roles was found to pose a barrier to girls' educational attainment. This finding might initially seem at odds with research using the 1958 and 1970 British Cohort studies, which suggest that women are more ambitious in their occupational aspirations than men and more likely to participate in further education (Schoon & Polek, 2011). Despite the greater ambition of women, gender inequalities in adult life remain potent, in part because of the "incomplete revolution" in women's roles that make motherhood and career incompatible (Esping-Andersen, 2009). Young women are likely to be aware of tensions between family life and SET careers that do not apply for young men.

Researching young people's aspirations for SET jobs

In this project, we are using quantitative and qualitative data analysis of the youth data from the British Household Panel Survey (BHPS) to investigate young people's aspirations for careers in SET, in relation to four research questions that are suggested by our review of the existing literature:

1. What are young people's aspirations to enter SET careers and how do they relate to gender and family background?
2. Does an early interest in science lead young people to enter SET related jobs?

3. To what extent are young people who aspire to SET careers seeking to reproduce family patterns by following in the footsteps of their parents?
4. Are there qualitative differences in the way young adolescent males and females view family and career that can help interpret gender differences in SET aspirations?

Suitable panel data have only just become available in the UK that allow us to examine trends in science-related aspirations for a nationally representative sample of young adolescent males and females. Much of the existing trend data for the UK has been derived to date from educational subject-choice statistics, which are only crude proxies for job aspirations. In addition, most of the European and international literature that is concerned with the underrepresentation of women in SET and the "leaky pipe" phenomenon (PRAGES, 2009) have focused on adult university and career pathways that follow secondary education. This is far too late in developmental terms to uncover the processes and mechanisms, associated with gender differences in job aspirations in early adolescence, which underpin the later underrepresentation of women in science, engineering, and technology.

Our next section introduces the British Household Panel Survey (BHPS), which we use for our cross-sectional and longitudinal quantitative analysis of young people's reports of their job aspirations (aged 11–15), and subsequent SET occupations in young adulthood (aged 16–28). The interpretation of our quantitative analysis is aided by a qualitative analysis of gender differences to an open-ended question asked of the BHPS youth, about what they would like to be doing with their lives in 10 years' time.

The British Household Panel Survey and the British Youth Survey

The BHPS (Taylor, Brice, Buck, & Prentice-Lane, 2010) is an ongoing longitudinal study that began in 1991 and annually surveys a nationally representative sample of the UK population consisting of 5,000 households. Each study year is referred to as a "wave," thus 1991 is wave 1 and 1994 is wave 4. Since 1994 the BHPS has also involved all young people in the sampled families between the ages of 11 and 15, through a dedicated survey known as the British Youth Survey (BYS). At age 16 the young people enter the adult panel of BHPS. The data that have been collected about young people are relatively under-utilized, but are an important resource for studying trends and characteristics of the younger generations.

The BHPS has collected a wealth of data about young people that provides some context for understanding their aspirations. In order to explore young people's interest in SET, including studying science or having a science-related job in the future, we focus our analysis on the responses to two questions: "What

Table 14.1. *Sample size for each wave, Youth Study, British Household Panel Survey 1994–2005*

Wave	4	5	6	7	8	12	13	14	15	Total
Males	146	376	362	364	474	414	412	406	367	3,321
Females	126	334	347	326	443	483	458	430	435	3,382
Total	272	710	709	690	917	897	870	836	802	6,703

job would you like to do when you have left school?" and "What would you like to be doing with your life in about ten years' time from now?" The job question is coded from an occupational classification scheme and the responses are analyzed quantitatively. The life-in-the-future question is open-ended, and requires a more in-depth qualitative investigation. Our analysis seeks to bring these quantitative and qualitative results together.

There are limitations in the data, in that there is no question regarding the different subjects studied by young people at school. Thus, unfortunately, we are unable to examine directly educational choices, or distinguish those studying science. Despite this limitation, one advantage of the BHPS is that it allows a longitudinal analysis and we can see how aspirations evolve over the life course and whether earlier aspirations influence actual job status in early adulthood.

The job question was asked in waves 4 to 8 (1994–1998) and waves 12 to 15 (2002–2005) of boys and girls aged 11 to 15, with the exception of wave 4 when it was asked of 14- to 15-year-olds only. Table 14.1 provides an overview of the sample size in each wave for males and females separately (3,321 girls and 3,382 boys), yielding a total of 6,703.

For adolescents who provided a valid answer to the occupational aspiration question in more than one wave, it is possible to analyze stability in aspirations. We examine changes in aspirations over a 3-year period using a combined-wave approach. The number of cases for whom we can analyze 3-year stability and change is 1,511. It is also possible to link young people's job aspirations to their actual occupations in early adulthood. Some of the young people present in wave 4 (1994) became eligible for the adult interview in wave 5 (1995), when they reached the age of 16, and we pooled the adult files for waves 5 to 17 (1995–2007). Out of 3,201 young people for whom we have at least one valid answer on the job aspirations question, 2,530 (79%) are included in at least one of the adult interviews for waves 5 to 17. For 1,832 out of 2,530 (72%) at least one job was recorded in one of these adult files, between the ages of 16 and 28. Out of these 1,832, 49% are boys, 51% are girls. In addition, we can link the youth data with information concerning their parents' educational and occupational status. In this chapter, our focus is on SET occupations and the next section outlines the procedure we followed for defining a job as SET or not.

Defining SET

Providing a definition of what can be considered SET jobs is not entirely straightforward. Several occupations require some sort of scientific and technical training, but they are not usually classified as SET. This is the case, for instance, for science teachers, army officers, or air pilots. In order to decide what could be categorized as SET we looked up various definitions, including those by the UK Resource Centre for Women in SET (UKRC), the International Standard Classification of Occupations (ISCO), the Department of Trade and Industry (DTI), and the Institute of Employment Rights (IER). There are three different definitions provided in the United Nations Educational, Scientific, and Cultural Organization (UNESCO) toolkit in terms of recommendations by the OECD *Frascati Manual*, and the *Canberra Manual*. Definitions vary both in terms of the subject areas that are categorized as SET, and in terms of the inclusion or not of technical and skilled occupations, which require fewer qualifications. All of these definitions classify the main occupational groups in SET in similar ways, but differ about whether to include health-related occupations and skilled trades in the definition. Jerrim and Schoon, in this volume, use the ISCO categorization, distinguishing life science and health professionals from the mathematical, engineering, or physical science professionals.

Our decision was to adopt a different working definition of SET in this study. A first "strict" definition of SET excludes health-related occupations, and includes technical occupations and skilled trades. A second, "wide" definition of SET includes health-related occupations as well. The occupational groups that we include in the two definitions are indicated in Appendix 14.1. There are two main classifications. Standard Occupational Classification (SOC) 1990, which is used for the quantitative analysis in the BHPS, distinguishes 374 occupation unit groups. The classification was extensively revised as SOC 2000 to include the substantial changes in SET occupations associated with technological change, including the growth of the IT industry. This resulted in the occupations being reclassified with five additional occupational groupings: Information and Communications Technology (ICT) professionals; research professionals; draught persons and building inspectors; and IT service delivery occupations. An additional category – therapists – was included in the wide definition of SOC 2000.

Quantitative analysis of SET aspirations: cross-sectional analysis

"What job would you like to do when you have left school?"

In order to investigate aspirations for SET by gender as well as changes in aspirations over time, we constructed a variable indicating whether a young person aspires to a SET career or not for each wave that the question was asked and for both SET definitions, strict and wide.

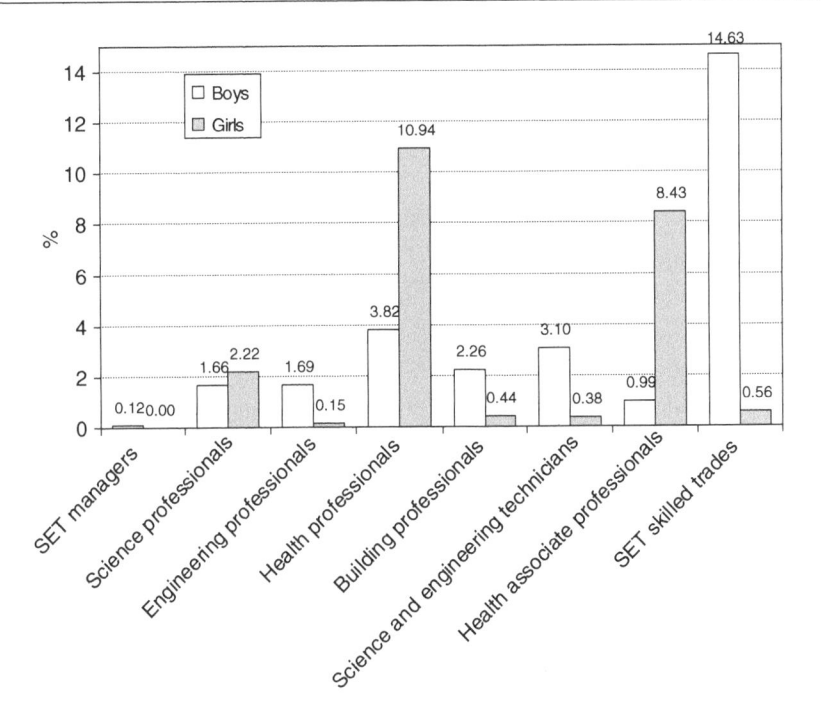

Figure 14.1 *Aspiration for SET, breakdown by SET groups and gender (N = 6,703)*

The results of the cross-sectional analysis indicate that more boys than girls aspire to a SET career, although this gender difference is much higher for the strict SET definition than for the wide SET definition. For all waves combined, 24% of boys and 4% of girls aspire to SET, using the strict definition. When considering the wide SET definition, which includes health-related professions, however, the number of girls expressing SET aspirations is far closer to that of boys. For all waves combined, 28% of boys aspire to a SET career, compared to 23% of girls (N = 6,703).

When these boys' and girls' aspirations for careers in the wide SET definition are broken into major SET groups, we can see from Figure 14.1 that boys' and girls' interests are clearly differentiated. Boys want to do a skilled trade (14.63%) and also want to be health professionals (3.82%) or science and engineering technicians (3.10%), whereas girls are overwhelmingly attracted to health or health-associated professions (10.94% and 8.43% respectively).

We looked in more detail at the types of jobs mentioned for each occupational group in SET by gender (based on first mentions from the 1,721 young people who aspired to a SET occupation). Table 14.2 shows the jobs most frequently mentioned by boys and girls in each occupational group. Thus if we look at health professionals, for instance, we can see that a popular occupation among both boys and girls is that of veterinarian, although this occupation is far more frequently chosen by females (138 responses among girls over a total of 782

Table 14.2. *Most frequent SET occupations by gender, based on first mentions of those aspiring to SET careers (N = 1,721)*

SET occupational group	Boys (N = 939)	Girls (N = 782)
SET managers	IT managers (2)	n/a
Science professionals	Biological scientists and biochemists (27)	Biological scientists and biochemists (26)
Engineering professionals	Mechanical engineers (7)	Other engineers and technologists n.e.c. (1)
Health professionals	Veterinarians (30)	Veterinarians (138)
Building professionals	Architects (29)	Architects (5)
Science and engineering technicians	Computer analysts/programmers (38)	Computer analysts/programmers (4)
Health associate professionals	Occupational and speech therapists, psychotherapists, therapists n.e.c. (4)	Nurses (68)
SET skilled trades	Motor mechanics, auto engineers (93)	Motor mechanics, auto engineers (3)

and 30 among boys over a total of 939). In the health associate category nursing dominates the female mentions (68 responses). Skilled trades are almost entirely cited by boys (93 boys and 3 girls).

Figure 14.2 shows the changes in SET aspirations over time, according to both the strict and wide definitions, from 1994 through to 2005 (the dotted lines between 1998–2002 show the gap when the job aspiration question was not asked). There appears to be an increase in SET aspirations over time, which is most pronounced for boys. For instance, 20.6% of boys wanted a job in SET in wave 4 (1994) according to the strict definition, and 26.0% according to the wide. In wave 15 (2005), the numbers are 31.6% and 36.2%, for the strict and wide definitions respectively. The corresponding figures for girls are 3.2% and 5.8% in wave 4, and 15.9% and 24.8% in wave 15. Thus the increase among girls is less marked than among boys.

Changes in aspirations over time

In our longitudinal analysis we created a variable that indicates whether the first answer to the question "What job would you like to do when you left school?" refers to a SET career or not, according to the wide definition. This allows us to examine the age at which the preference for a SET job was first mentioned and we can also look at the proportion of boys and girls expressing an aspiration for a SET career by age. It is important to note that, since these young people are followed over time, it is possible that they provide an answer to this

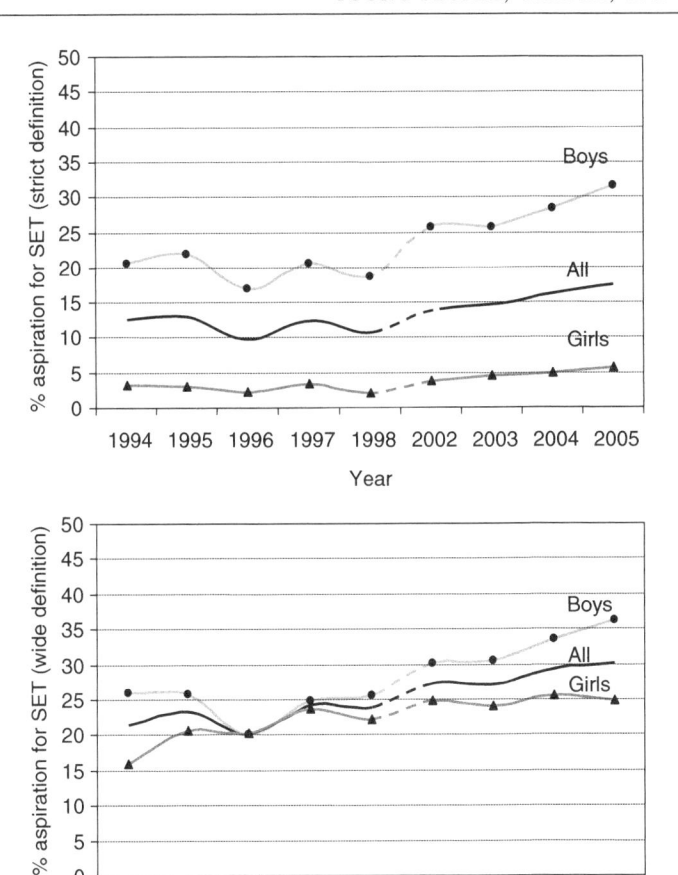

Figure 14.2 *Trends in aspiration for SET over time, by gender, for strict and wide definitions (N = 6,703)*
Source: British Household Panel Survey (1994–1998, 2002–2005).

question on more than one occasion, for instance in wave 5 at the age of 11 and in wave 6 at the age of 12. In this analysis, if there is more than one valid response, we prioritize the response given at the youngest age. Because of small sample sizes in each wave, we have pooled waves 4 to 8 (1994–1998) and waves 12 to 15 (2002–2005) for this analysis.

In Figure 14.3 it appears that the proportion of boys stating they want a job in SET increases by age, whereas for girls it increases between ages 11 and 12 but then decreases. At age 13, using the wide definition of SET, 24.1% of girls and 28.1% of boys say they want a career in SET, compared to 15.1% and 34.6% at age 15 for girls and boys respectively. Girls' and boys' interests start to diverge quite early in adolescence (age 13). This is about the age at which they are required to make General Certificate of Secondary Education (GCSE) subject

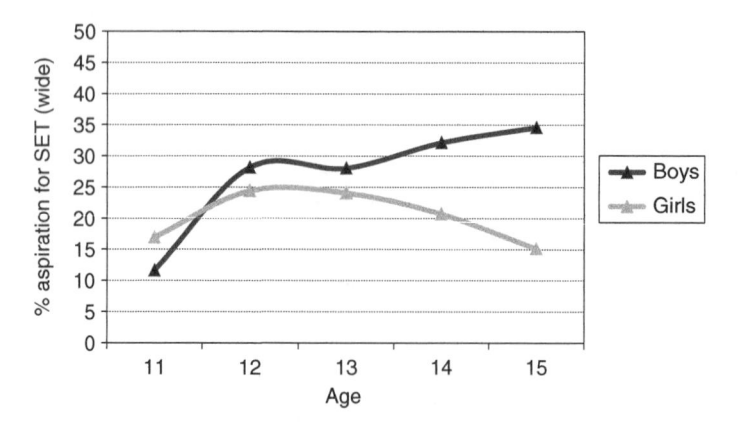

Figure 14.3 *Aspiration for SET, by gender and age (11–15) (wide SET definition) (N = 3,201)*

choices. Thus this early divergence of interests by gender is likely to be important in shaping future careers.

We also examine the stability of young people's job aspirations, by seeing how they changed or remained the same across three waves (N = 1,511). The change includes change toward and away from SET. Figure 14.4 shows the percentage of change in aspirations between three waves for the strict and wide definition. An important difference between Figure 14.3 and Figure 14.4 is that for the analysis for Figure 14.4 the sample is in addition restricted to those who provided a valid response to the young people's job aspirations question in three successive waves. The results of this analysis suggest that aspirations are relatively stable between successive waves: if we consider the wide SET definition, around one fourth of boys and girls changed their aspiration toward or away from SET between three waves (Figure 14.4). Furthermore, even on the wide definition, boys seem to be slightly more likely than girls to change their job aspiration, though the differences between the genders are very small.

The results of additional analysis (not shown) indicate that among boys two thirds of the changes are toward a SET career, whereas the majority of girls change their aspirations away from a SET career. This seems to confirm what we found earlier with regards to job preference in relation to age (Figure 14.3), that boys are more likely to aspire to a career in SET as they get older, whereas the opposite is true for girls.

Teenage aspirations as predictors of adult career outcomes

In answering our second research question: "Does an early interest in science lead young people to enter SET-related jobs?" we examined the relationship between young people's job aspirations and their occupation in early

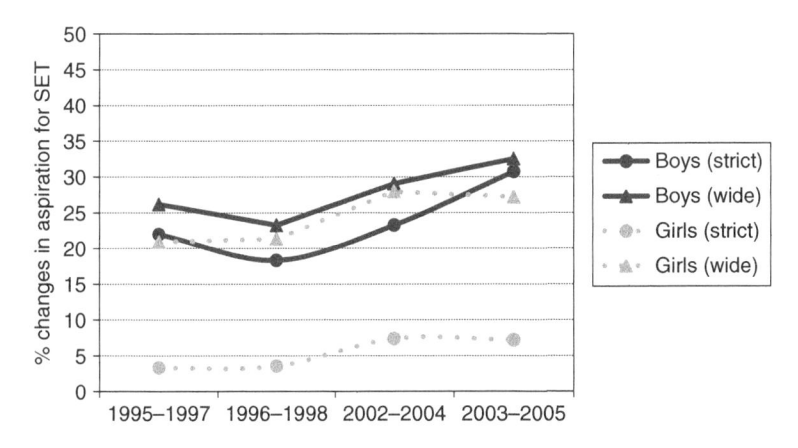

Figure 14.4 *Change in aspiration for SET across 3-year intervals, by gender for strict and wide definitions (N = 1,511)*

Table 14.3. *Cross-tabulation of SET aspirations and SET occupations (N = 1,832)*

SET occupations by age 28							
SET aspirations at age 11–15		Boys (N = 897)		Girls (N = 935)		Total (N = 1,832)	
		No	Yes	No	Yes	No	Yes
	No	506	152	694	28	1,200	180
		76.9%	23.1%	96.1%	3.9%	87.0%	13.0%
	Yes	162	77	204	9	366	86
		67.8%	32.2%	95.8%	4.2%	81.0%	19.0%

adulthood. Of those for whom we have adult job information (between the ages of 16 and 28), 25% of boys entered a SET occupation later on (according to both the strict and wide definitions), compared to 2% and 4% of the girls for the strict and wide definitions respectively. The absence of women relative to men in SET careers is stark.

In Table 14.3 we look at the relationship between SET aspirations in youth and SET occupations in young adulthood. For both boys and girls, the proportion who are in a SET occupation as adults is slightly higher among those who aspired to a SET career during adolescence. Of the boys who expressed a preference for a job in SET, 32.2% are in a SET-related job as young adults, compared to 23.1% of those who did not aspire to a SET career (boys N = 897). The percentages for girls are much smaller and only 4.2% of those who originally expressed a wish to work in SET eventually have a SET job as adults, compared to 3.9% of those who did not mention a SET interest in their youth (girls N = 935). These differences are statistically significant for men ($p < .01$) but not for women. Schoon, Ross, and Martin (2007) also found that teenage occupational aspirations are a strong predictor for entering a SET-related occupation by the early 30s, although this was found for both men and women. We found considerably higher proportions of teenage girls aspiring to a SET career (see Figure 14.2) compared to Schoon, Ross, and Martin (2007). One possible explanation for the different findings in the two studies could therefore be that the group of teenage girls who expressed an aspiration to work in a SET occupation in our study is more heterogeneous in terms of occupations in young adulthood. The sample in the current study is also younger and the sample sizes are considerably smaller compared to Schoon et al. (2007).

Parental role modeling

Our third research question asked: "To what extent are young people who aspire to science careers reproducing family patterns or 'inheriting' a SET route from their parents?" In order to explore this question we linked the youth data to the parental data in BHPS, specifically the occupational and educational backgrounds of the mother and father. This allowed us to investigate the relationship between family socioeconomic background and young people's SET aspirations. Because of quite high missing data due to families where the father is absent, we were only able to match on 2,360 fathers and 3,071 mothers. These numbers were further reduced by missing data on parental education and occupation, and thus we report only some preliminary and rather tentative findings.

We initially found no discernible relationship between parental education and children's set aspirations. This was unexpected since we had assumed that more highly educated parents would stimulate their children to pursue higher education, including fields such as science and engineering. The explanation appears to be that the inclusion of skilled trades, for which higher education is not required, suppressed the expected relationship. Once skilled trades were removed, we found the expected positive relation between the fathers' education and SET aspirations for boys. For girls the relationship is less clear. Moreover, fathers' educational influence appears to be stronger than mothers' education. Regarding occupation, when the father is in a SET-related job this enhances the likelihood of both daughters and sons aspiring to SET careers. Furthermore, girls whose mother has a SET job are slightly more likely to aspire to a SET career themselves, whereas this is not true for boys. However, this finding should be interpreted with considerable caution, as numbers of mothers in SET careers are small, with only 6% of mothers working in SET, compared to 30% of fathers.

Thus exploring intergenerational influence in SET aspirations is difficult with this dataset using quantitative analysis. However, our qualitative analysis using the verbatim responses of young people concerning their future aspirations may provide some insights into how gendered patterns at home and in society at large can shape boys' and girls' thinking about their future careers and families.

Qualitative analysis of young people's aspirations

To examine young adolescent girls' and boys' perceptions of the relationship between a career in SET and family aspirations, we carried out a qualitative analysis of an open-ended question on future aspirations, asking "What would you like to be doing with your life in about ten years' time from now?" Our analysis is based on the 710 valid responses of young people aged 13–15 who were asked this question in 2002 and 2003, combining the two waves. The qualitative data were already pre-coded, with up to two mentions allowed. This initial coding distinguishes between different aspiration domains, including career, education, family, material ownership, and leisure, in addition to other, more general aspirations.

No gender difference is found with regards to the prioritizing of career: boys and girls are about equally split in indicating career in their answers (girls 51%; boys 49%). The responses focusing on family, which include aspirations to be married or partnered and to have children, show a small gender difference. Two thirds of those who indicate family as a priority are girls (66%), although almost half of those who identify both family and career as priorities are boys. There are slight gender differences also in the prioritizing of education. The majority of answers expressing aspirations to pass exams or get good qualifications are by girls (70%), and again the majority of mentions about wanting a degree and to go to university or college are by girls (60%).

Aspirations for SET and the career/family interface

In order to get a sense of the interest young people have in pursuing a scientific career we could not rely on the pre-coded data, since the classification adopted with regard to career only captures large categories, such as "having a particular career" or "having a good job." It was thus necessary to read the verbatim answers, which we linked to the quantitative youth data. Starting from the young people's own words made it possible to distinguish the different types of careers they mentioned, and we re-coded the responses to focus specifically on those that indicated an interest in studying or working in SET in the future.

In our qualitative coding of SET careers we could be more inclusive than in the earlier quantitative analysis, and code as SET some occupations that could not be counted as such, when restricted to the earlier occupational classification scheme. For example, science teacher is not identified in SOC 1990 as a SET occupation, nor is air pilot, despite the fact that such a profession requires scientific and technical training. In order to maximize cases, we decided that whenever young people mentioned more than one job in their aspirations, we coded them as SET if one of these jobs was SET. If they indicated more than one SET career, we coded them according to the one that seemed to be prioritized, usually if it was mentioned first, or if it was given more emphasis in the answer. When young people indicated no particular job, but mentioned studies that they were interested in pursuing, we coded all studies as SET or not.

In total, 17% of young people indicated they have SET-related aspirations (127/710). We then examined how these SET-related responses are associated with the pre-coded mentions of career and family, looking particularly at the relationship between the two. For this analysis we included all careers mentioned by young people, and not only those that focus on SET. It emerged from these data that, when mentioning career among their aspirations, girls show an explicit awareness of timing issues and the potential conflict between career and family that is not apparent in the responses of boys. In the following examples, two girls explicitly point out that, even though they may aspire to have a partner or have children at some point in the future, they intend to have a "career first":

> *I would like to be a marine biologist/singer with a family (not sure about the family because I would like to get a stable career first) but certainly would like to be married or in a stable relationship.*

> *I would like to be in school training to be a doctor but having time to have some fun with my friends. I would not want to be married or have children. It is a bit too soon I want to have a career first.*

Other girls indicate how, before thinking about forming a family, it is not only important to finish university studies, but also to put off a serious partnership that might conflict with career:

> *I would definitely like to go into sixth form the university and study to become a vet. I would like to travel so I could maybe work as a vet in 3rd world countries for a year or so. I would like to have a family but not before I had got university degrees sorted out. I think I would like children but I cannot be sure yet.*

> *I would like to be training for being a qualified paramedic. I would also like to be in a stable relationship but nothing too serious that would affect my career.*

Another young adolescent female expresses her aspirations for the future by balancing family and career ambitions on the basis of the rewards she may be able to get in the world of work:

> *I don't know yet it depends on the job I do. If I found a job which would be very important to me than I would probably wait and have children/get married later on once my career is sorted out. If I found a job which I don't like I would probably have children and get married earlier.*

Thus for all five girls the timing for a family may not only be dictated by finishing one's studies or getting a stable job and career, but more generally by the extent to which the dimension of work may be experienced as fulfilling in one's life. Boys express similar aspirations to have a family in the future. However, there is a qualitative gender difference in the way they express themselves. Boys' aspirations are often worded much more vaguely, in terms of why they may or may not want a family and there is little awareness of family–work tensions:

> *In 10 years I would like to be in a City working as a doctor in a nice house and maybe even a family.*

In this boy's future scenario, the job is clear, and so are the location and the home. The desire for a family is left vague. An expression that is recurrent in the young people's words when thinking about their future is the notion of "settling down," something that they may either envisage doing, or otherwise aim to avoid or defer, like the boy in the following example:

> *Finish teaching course etc. Go into teaching not settle with a family quite yet. Have a good social life go out with friends at weekends.*

In this case, settling down is something not to be done "quite yet." This may be read as a similar aspiration to that expressed by the girls: in 10 years' time it is too soon to have a family, and one wants to have a "career first." What is interesting, however, is that neither boy gives any explanation as to why the time is not right. Reading these quotations suggests that, when manifesting an interest in having both a career and a family in the future, both boys and girls might have similar aspirations, and wish for family formation to happen once their careers and studies are sorted out. Even though boys' and girls' wishes may be similar, they are expressed differently. While girls point out the reasons why they may want a family only later on in life, boys have no similar need to specify that they want to have a "career first": this may be taken for granted in their expected life-plan, and timing does not appear for them to be an issue. There is no suggestion from boys' answers that having a family could be the cause of conflict with their careers, something that instead surfaces quite clearly from the girls' responses. Already at this early age girls have obviously learned about gender inequalities and different gender expectations in the home/work interface and their aspirations fit into a gendered script that assumes conflict between family and career as the norm.

Conclusions and policy implications

In sum, analysis of the youth data from the BHPS has shown that more boys than girls aspire to a SET job. Boys also aspire to work in all SET sectors, while girls are mainly interested in health-related occupations, a domain that is mentioned far more frequently by girls than by boys; and in being science professionals, in particular chemists and biologists, occupations that appear to attract similar numbers of boys and girls. We have also seen that aspirations for SET have generally increased over time since 1994, when the youth survey started. Moreover, this increase is more pronounced for boys than for girls. Job aspirations are also reasonably stable during adolescence. For those who do change aspirations, change is gender-specific, with boys changing *toward* SET and girls diverting their interests *away from* SET jobs. This points toward an early divergence in the interests of boys and girls, which begins about age 13.

The longitudinal picture emerging from these data indicates that once these young people become adults there are very strong gender differences in their occupational choice by gender. Of all the boys who ever answered the question on job aspirations, 25% are working in SET once adults. The proportion of girls is extremely low – less than 2% if we consider the strict definition, and less than 4% for the wide definition. Those young people who did express an interest in SET are also more likely to have a SET job in young adulthood: their ratio compared to those who did not aspire to a SET career is 19% versus 13%, for men and women combined. Thus our analyses show that if governments are concerned with the shortage of SET skills in the population, the underrepresentation of women in SET, and the "leaky pipe" phenomenon (PRAGES, 2009), they need to promote policies that address the disaffection with science in early adolescence.

There have been interesting studies in both the UK and US investigating the role of class and parental role models in shaping professional occupations (e.g., Devine, 2010) using purposive samples of parents in professional occupations, rather than nationally representative samples. There have also been informative longitudinal studies looking at the links between teenage aspirations and occupational outcomes (e.g., Schoon & Parsons, 2002; Schoon, Martin, & Ross, 2007). However, our analysis adds evidence about the SET aspirations and career outcomes of a younger sample, representative of young people in Britain, growing up in the last decade of the twentieth century and the first decade of the new millennium. Our exploratory quantitative analysis linking BHPS youth data to data about their parents' education and occupation suggests that paternal parental education is positively linked to SET aspirations, as far as professional jobs are concerned (the higher the fathers' education, the more likely the children, and particularly the sons, will aspire to a SET professional job). In terms of occupation, those young people whose fathers work in SET are more likely to aspire to work in SET themselves. We had very few cases of mothers working in SET, but our analysis does suggest that the mother can be a role model for her daughter's aspirations, something that Kiernan (1996) also found, although not specifically for SET.

The results of our quantitative analysis matter because they indicate that early on in life, already at age 13, the aspirations of boys and girls start to diverge and girls abandon their scientific interests. While the literature has consistently found a sharp decline in the interest young people manifest for science in the early years of secondary schooling, between the ages of 11 and 14 (Bennett & Hogarth, 2009; Osborne et al., 2003), our data indicate this decline is gender-specific. It must be pointed out, however, that our data only refer to young people's job aspirations, and not to the way they feel toward the science they study at school. Nevertheless, this indication of girls' estrangement from scientific careers confirms the concerns highlighted in the Greenfield report (2002). Girls' early abandonment of science is extremely important in terms of educational choices, future employment prospects, and gender equality. Dropping science at 13, at a time when young people are required to make important choices regarding their future course of studies, has a strong impact on the educational trajectories they will follow and the sort of jobs they will eventually be able to aim for. As Purcell and Elias (2008) have pointed out, the reduced number of women entering the labor market with scientific skills is one important factor associated with the persistence of a gender pay gap, since many of the better-remunerated jobs are those in the SET sector.

Girls' early loss of interest in SET might also be related to perceived conflict between career and family aspirations. The qualitative data suggest that, when thinking about their future, girls (aged 13–15) are more likely than boys of the same age to anticipate potential conflict between career and family aspirations and feel they have to indicate whether they want to concentrate on "career first." Our analysis suggests that young adolescents are all too conscious of the gendered division of paid and unpaid labor in terms of how males and females tend to specialize respectively in careers and home life. Young adolescent girls express an awareness of work–family conflicts that boys do not perceive. For boys, careers in science are a positive advantage for their future status as family breadwinners; whereas for girls SET careers are something to embark on before starting a family of one's own and are problematic thereafter. To mend the gendered "leaky pipe" that affects female dropout rates from science from early adolescence onwards implies a need to reduce gender inequalities in family-related care. The UK has much ground to make up before young adolescent females can view SET (or other demanding careers) as compatible with family life. A gender gap in SET is, however, still present even in those Scandinavian or former socialist societies that have, to some extent, adopted work–family policies that minimize gender inequalities (Charles, 2011).

Our findings reinforce the importance of policies that aim to improve young people's relationship to science and strengthen their focus on science at this crucial stage in the educational career. In particular, policies should strive to maintain and enhance girls' interest in science. In addition to specific interventions at this stage, there may, however, be a more substantial need to change the curriculum as a whole, and the ways in which scientific subjects are presented to young people. As pointed out in the review evidence gathered by Murphy and Whitelegg for the Institute of Physics (2006), teaching and learning should be continuously informed by, and sensitive to, the influence of gender representations. Evidence from interventions also suggests that a context-based or humanistic approach to physics lessons is beneficial for the motivation of girls and also of boys: young people are interested in knowing about the wider social context in which science operates, and in learning about the social applications in their school lessons. As Osborne et al. (2003) point out, it is ironic if science, with its promise of freedom from the hold of traditions, is taught in an authoritarian, dogmatic, and non-reflexive way. They suggest more space for practical work and for developing students' sense of control and autonomy.

The fact that the scientific interests of girls tend to be limited to health-related occupations, something that our research has confirmed, highlights how girls are more easily attracted to occupations that have a clear social and caring dimension (see also Perez-Felkner et al.; Wang & Kenny, this volume). A social dimension is also present in other scientific professions, including that of engineer; however, engineering is largely portrayed in the media and popular culture as a masculine profession that is concerned with objects, not people (Faulkner, 2007). It seems that many of the scientific occupations, especially those in the physical sciences, have an image issue, which makes them appear to young people, and particularly to girls, as inappropriate because of not requiring any social skills. It would therefore be crucial for the teaching of science to highlight the variety of skills that may be required in scientific occupations. Science teaching should focus on engaging with images of contemporary scientists, and not just the "great men of the past" (Osborne et al., 2003). Engaging with women scientists in a way that might allow girls to identify with them could be crucial to attracting more girls into scientific education (Buck et al., 2007). Changing the image of science and of scientists should therefore be a priority, and the media may have a crucial role in this, since it may provide "vicarious contact" with female scientists (Steinke, 2004). This goes hand in hand with the need to emphasize the social context of science and the wide range of skills that characterize SET occupations. Hopefully such an image change would narrow the gender gap in SET aspirations and increase the pool of people interested in pursuing SET careers.

References

Bennett, J., & Hogarth, S. (2009). Would you want to talk to a scientist at a party? *International Journal of Science Education*, 31(14), 1975–1998.

Brooks, R. (2003). Young people's higher education choices: The role of family and friends. *British Journal of Sociology of Education*, 24(3), 283–297.

Buck, G. A., Plano Clark, V., Lesley-Pelecky, D., Lu, Y., & Cerda-Lizarraga, P. (2007). Examining the cognitive processes used by adolescent girls and women scientists in identifying science role models: A feminist approach. *Science Education*, 92(4), 688–707.

Charles, M. (2011). A world of difference: International trends in women's economic status. *Annual Review of Sociology*, 37, 355–371. Palo Alto: Annual Reviews.

Chimba, M., & Kitzinger, J. (2010). Bimbo or boffin? Women in science: An analysis of media representations and how female scientists negotiate cultural contradictions. *Public Understanding of Science*, 19(5), 609–624.

DES (Department for Education and Skills). (2007). *Gender and education: The evidence on pupils in England*. Retrieved from http://www.education.gov.uk/rsgateway/DB/RRP/u015238/index.shtml.

Devine, F. (2010). Class reproduction, occupational inheritance and occupational choice. In J. Scott, R. Crompton, & C. Lyonette (Eds.), *Gender inequalities in the 21st century* (pp. 40–58). Cheltenham: Edward Elgar.

Devine, F., & Savage, M. (2005). The cultural turn, sociology and class analysis. In F. Devine, M. Savage, J. Scott, & R. Crompton (Eds.), *Rethinking class: Cultures, identities and lifestyles* (pp. 1–23). Houndmills: Palgrave Macmillan.

Eccles, J. S., Adler, T. F., Futterman, R., Goff, S. B., Kaczala, C. M., Meece, J., & Midgley, C. (1983). Expectancies, values, and academic behaviours. In T. J. Spence (Ed.), *Achievement and academic motives* (pp. 75–146). New York: Freeman.

Esping-Andersen, G. (2009). *The incomplete revolution*. Cambridge: Polity.

Faulkner, W. (2007). "Nuts and bolts and people": Gender-troubled engineering identities. *Social Studies of Science*, 37(3), 331–356.

Flicker, E. (2003). Between brains and breasts: Women scientists in fiction film – On the marginalisation and sexualisation of scientific competence. *Public Understanding of Science*, 12(3), 307–318.

Gallup Organization. (2008). *Flash barometer: Young people and science*. Retrieved from http://ec.europa.eu/public_opinion/flash/fl_239_en.pdf.

Good, J. J., Woodzicka, J. A., & Wingfield, L. C. (2010). The effects of gender stereotypic and counter-stereotypic textbook images on science performance. *The Journal of Social Psychology*, 150(2), 132–147.

Greenfield, S. (2002). *SET FAIR: A report on women in science, engineering and technology from Baroness Greenfield CBE to the Secretary of State for Trade and Industry*. Retrieved from www.vitae.ac.uk/cms/files/Greenfield-review-SET-Fair-November-2002.pdf.

Jenkins, E. W., & Pell, R. G. (2006). *The Relevance of Science Education Project (ROSE) in England: A summary of findings*. Retrieved from http://roseproject.no/network/countries/uk-england/rose-report-eng.pdf.

Jensen, K. S. H. (2005). *Women working in science, engineering and technology. Higher education and industry – A literature review*. Retrieved from www.cse.salford.ac.uk/dfe/literaturereviewMay.doc.

Kiernan, K. (1996). Lone motherhood, employment and outcomes for children. *International Journal of Law, Policy and the Family*, 10(3), 233–249.

Kitzinger, J., Haran, J., Chimba, M., & Boyce, T. (2008). *Role models in the media: An exploration of the views and experiences of women in science, engineering and technology*. Retrieved from www.cardiff.ac.uk/jomec/resources/Kitzinger_Report_1.pdf.

Lampard, R. (2007). Is social mobility an echo of educational mobility? Parents' educations and occupations and their children's occupational attainment. *Sociological Research Online*, 12(5). Retrieved from www.socresonline.org.uk/12/5/16.html.

Mead, M., & Metraux, R. (1957). Image of the scientist among high school students: A pilot study. *Science*, 126, 384–390.

Murphy, P., & Whitelegg, E. (2006). *Girls in the physics classroom: A review of the research on the participation of girls in physics*. London: Institute of Physics. Retrieved from http://oro.open.ac.uk/6499/1.

OECD. (2006). *PISA 2006: Science competencies for tomorrow's world: Vol. 1. Analysis*. Retrieved from www.oecd-ilibrary.org/content/book/9789264040014-en.

(2008). *OECD Science, technology and industry outlook.* Retrieved from www.oecd.org/sti/oecdsciencetechnologyandindustryoutlook.htm.

Ormerod, M. with Duckworth, D. (1975). *Pupils' attitudes to science: A review of research.* Windsor: N.F.E.R. Publishing Company Ltd.

Osborne, J., Simon, S., & Collins, S. (2003). Attitudes towards science: A review of the literature and its implications. *International Journal of Science Education*, 25(9), 1049–1079.

Potter, E. F., & Rosser, S. V. (1992). Factors in life science textbooks that may deter girls' interest in science. *Journal of Research in Science Teaching*, 29, 669–686.

PRAGES (Practising Gender Equality in Science). (2009). *Guidelines for gender equality programmes in science.* Retrieved from www.retepariopportunita.it/Rete_Pari_Opportunita/UserFiles/Progetti/prages/pragesguidelines.pdf.

Purcell, K., & Elias, P. (2008). Achieving equality in the knowledge economy. In J. Scott, S. Dex, & H. Joshi (Eds.), *Women and employment: Changing lives and new challenges* (pp. 19–49). Cheltenham: Edward Elgar Publishing.

Roberts, G. (2002). *SET for success: The supply of people with science, technology, engineering and mathematics skills – The report of Sir Gareth Roberts' Review.* Retrieved from http://webarchive.nationalarchives.gov.uk/+/http:/www.hm-treasury.gov.uk/d/robertsreview_introch1.pdf.

Royal Society. (2008). *Science and mathematics education, 14–19: A "state of the nation" report on the participation and attainment of 14–19 year olds in science and mathematics in the UK, 1996–2007.* Retrieved from http://royalsociety.org/uploadedFiles/Royal_Society_Content/Influencing_Policy/Education/Reports/SNR2_-_full_report.pdf.

Sadler, T. D. & Zeidler, D. L. (2009). Scientific literacy, PISA and socioscientific discourse: Assessment for progressive aims of science education. *Journal of Research in Science Teaching*, 46(8), 909–921.

Schoon, I., Martin, P., & Ross, A. (2007). Career transitions in times of social change: His and her story. *Journal of Vocational Behavior*, 70(1), 78–96.

Schoon, I., & Parsons, S. (2002). Teenage aspirations for future careers and occupational outcomes. *Journal of Vocational Behavior*, 60(2), 262–288.

Schoon, I., & Polek, E. (2011). Teenage career aspirations and adult career attainment: The role of gender, social background and general cognitive ability. *International Journal of Behavioral Development*, 36(3), 210–217.

Schoon, I., Ross, A., & Martin, P. (2007). Science related careers: Aspirations and outcomes in two British cohort studies. In J. Scott, & J. Nolan (Eds.), New technologies and gendered divisions of labour: Problems and prospects for equality in the public and private spheres. *Equal Opportunities International* [special issue], 26 (2), 129–143.

Scott, J. (2004). Family, gender and educational attainment in Britain: A longitudinal study. *Journal of Comparative Family Studies*, 35(4), 565–589.

Scott, J., & Chaudhary, C. (2003). *Beating the odds: Youth and family disadvantage.* Leicester: The National Youth Agency.

Shepardson, D. P., & Pizzini, E. L. (1992). Gender bias in female elementary teachers' perceptions of the scientific ability of students. *Science Education*, 76(2), 147–153.

Steinke, J. (2004). Science in cyberspace: Science and engineering World Wide Web sites for girls. *Public Understanding of Science*, 13(1), 7–30.

(2005). Cultural representations of gender and science. *Science Communication*, 27(1), 27–63.

Sullivan, A. (2001). Cultural capital and educational attainment. *Sociology*, 35(4), 893–912.

(2007). Cultural capital, cultural knowledge and ability. *Sociological Research Online*, 12(6). Retrieved from www.socresonline.org.uk/12/6/1.html.

Taylor, M. F. (Ed.), with Brice, J., Buck, N., & Prentice-Lane, E. (2010). *British Household Panel Survey user manual: Vol. A. Introduction, technical report and appendices*. Colchester: University of Essex.

Wajcman, J. (2004). *Technofeminism*. Cambridge: Polity.

Appendix 14.1

A. SET occupations (strict definition) from SOC 1990

SET Managers e.g. Production, works and maintenance managers; Managers in building and contracting; Clerks of works; Managers in mining and energy industries; Computer systems and data processing managers

Science Professionals e.g. Chemists; Biological scientists and biochemists; Physicists, geologists and meteorologists; Other natural scientists n.e.c.

Engineering Professionals e.g. Civil, structural, municipal, mining and quarry engineers; Mechanical engineers; Electrical engineers; Electronics engineers; Software engineers; Chemical engineers; Design and development engineers; Process and production engineers; Planning and quality control engineers; Other engineers and technologists n.e.c.

Building Professionals e.g. Architects; Town planners; Building, land, mining, and "general practice" surveyors

Science & Engineering Technicians e.g. Laboratory technicians; Engineering technicians; Electrical/electronics technicians; Architectural and town planning technicians; Building and civil engineering technicians; Other scientific technicians n.e.c.; Draughtspersons; Building inspectors; Quantity and marine surveyors; Computer analysts/programmers

SET Skilled Trades e.g. Bricklayers, masons; Roofers, slaters, tilers, sheeters, cladders; Plasterers; Glaziers; Builders, building contractors; Scaffolders, stagers, steeplejacks, riggers; Floorers, floor coverers, carpet fitters and planners, floor and wall tillers; Painters and decorators; Other construction trades n.e.c.; Tool makers, tool fitters, and markers-out; Metal working production and maintenance fitters; Precision instrument makers and repairers; Other machine tool setters and setter-operators n.e.c. (inc. CNC setter-operators); Production fitters (electrical/electronic); Electricians, electrical maintenance fitters; Electrical engineers (not professional); Telephone fitters; Cable jointers, lines repairers; Radio, TV and video engineers; Computer engineers, installation and maintenance; Other electrical/electronic trades n.e.c.; Smiths and forge workers; Welding trades; Motor mechanics, auto engineers (inc. road patrol engineers); Coach and vehicle body builders; Vehicle body repairers, panel beaters; Auto electricians; Tire and exhaust fitters; Carpenters and joiners; Coach painters, other spray painters; Other machinery mechanics

B.   SET occupations (wide definition) from SOC 1990

As in A above with additional categories as follows:

Health Professionals e.g. Medical practitioners; Pharmacists/pharmacologists; Ophthalmic opticians; Dental practitioners; Veterinarians

Health Associate Professionals e.g. Nurses; Midwives; Medical radiographers; Physiotherapists; Chiropodists; Dispensing opticians; Medical technicians, dental auxiliaries; Occupational and speech therapists, psychotherapists, therapists n.e.c.; Environmental health officers; Other health associate professionals n.e.c.

C.   SET occupations (strict definition) from SOC 2000

SET Managers e.g. Production, works, and maintenance managers; Managers in construction; Managers in mining and energy; Information and communication technology managers; Research and development managers

Science Professionals e.g. Chemists; Biological scientists and biochemists; Physicists, geologists and meteorologists

Engineering Professionals e.g. Civil engineers; Mechanical engineers; Electrical engineers; Electronics engineers; Chemical engineers; Design and development engineers; Production and process engineers; Planning and quality control engineers; Engineering professionals n.e.c.

ICT Professionals e.g. IT Strategy and planning professionals; Software professionals

Research Professionals e.g. Scientific researchers; Researchers n.e.c.

Building Professionals e.g. Architects; Town planners; Quantity surveyors; Chartered surveyors (not quantity surveyors)

Science & Engineering Technicians e.g. Laboratory technicians; Electrical/electronics technicians; Engineering technicians; Building and civil engineering technicians; Quality assurance technicians; Science and engineering technicians n.e.c.

Draughtspersons and Building Inspectors e.g. Architectural technologists and town planning technicians; Draughtspersons; Building inspectors

IT Service Delivery Occupations e.g. IT operations technicians; IT user support technicians

SET skilled trades subfields e.g. Metal forming, Welding and related trades; Metal machining, Fitting, and instrument making trades; Vehicle trades; Electrical trades; Construction trades; Building trades

D.   SET occupations (wide definition) from SOC 2000

As in C above with additional categories as follows:

Health Professionals e.g. Medical practitioners; Psychologists; Pharmacists/pharmacologists; Ophthalmic opticians; Dental practitioners; Veterinarians

Health Associate Professionals e.g. Nurses; Midwives; Paramedics; Medical radiographers; Chiropodists; Dispensing opticians; Pharmaceutical dispensers; Medical and dental technicians

Therapists e.g. Physiotherapists; Occupational therapists; Speech and language therapists; Therapists n.e.c.

15 Motivational affordances in school versus work contexts advantage different individuals: a possible explanation for domain-differential gender gaps

Jutta Heckhausen

Abstract
In the last decade, girls have attained similar achievement levels in mathematics and natural sciences as boys. Girls also value mathematics or sciences as highly as boys do. However, women are still not attaining equivalent career success in professional fields associated with mathematics and natural sciences, such as engineering and computer science. One possible explanation for the disassociation between school-based motivation and achievement in mathematics and sciences, on the one hand, and successful entry and pursuit of science-related careers, on the other hand, might be that the two achievement contexts – school and work/career – require different motivational self-regulatory skills to be most effective. The chapter discusses a set of individual differences in various components of motivational self-regulation, ranging from opportunity-congruent goal selection to implicit and explicit motives, volitional commitment, and goal disengagement and self-protection. To date, we have only scarce empirical evidence about gender differences in these components of motivational self-regulation. However, the stark contrasts between the self-regulatory requirements in the highly structured school versus the low structured work domain present a fascinating research area to begin to explain the gender gap between the two domains of achievement behavior.

Introduction

In the last decade, girls in most countries have caught up with boys regarding achievement in mathematics and other STEM fields (i.e., science, technology, engineering, and mathematics) (Hyde, Lindberg, Linn, Ellis, & Williams, 2008). Cross-national analyses suggest that remaining gender gaps in math performance are associated with gender inequities in society reflected in such indicators as gender distributions in school enrollment, research jobs, and seats in parliament (Else-Quest, Hyde, & Linn, 2010). Moreover, boys no longer value mathematics or sciences more than girls do (Wigfield & Eccles, 2002, see also Chow & Salmela-Aro; Jerrim & Schoon; Parker, Nagy, Trautwein, & Lüdtke; Wang & Kenny, this volume). However, men are still more successful in entering and pursuing professional careers in STEM fields, such as engineering and computer science (Schoon, Martin, & Ross, 2007; see also Bagnoli, Demey, & Scott, this volume).

Researchers have scrambled to explain this incongruence between gender similarities in school-based motivation and achievement and gender divergence in career success for the STEM fields. Some research, especially coming from a sociological approach, has focused on social contextual factors such as parental socioeconomic status (SES) and aspirations, SES- and gender-differential resources and opportunities (see review in Schoon et al., 2007; Schoon & Silbereisen, 2009; see also Bagnoli et al., this volume). The present chapter leaves these aspects aside and focuses selectively on the potential school versus work differential effect of individual differences in processes of motivational self-regulation. In the search for an explanation of the gender gap in career achievement given the equal attainments in school, one would have to look for factors that have little influence on school performance, but become consequential in the world of work outside the highly regulated educational institutions of high school and college. The motivational theory of life-span development provides a conceptual framework for examining the role of individual differences in motivation as sources of differentially effective agency in different life course contexts, specifically here school versus work life. I will argue that in the less structured and less regulated world of work and career, individual differences in four aspects of achievement motivation and self-regulation will have greater consequences than in the highly structured school context. Those four aspects pertain to (1) how multi-faceted and flexible a person's achievement goals are, (2) whether the general achievement motive is activated in a wider range of achievement contexts or is more focused on the career domain, (3) whether a person has strong explicit and/or implicit achievement motives and the degree to which implicit and explicit achievement-related motives are congruent, and (4) the capacity to organize one's action cycles into discrete phases of goal engagement and of goal disengagement in accordance with the control opportunities in the current developmental context. Overall, the empirical research regarding gender differences in these four aspects of achievement motivation and self-regulation is not yet well developed and thus provides ample exciting avenues for future empirical investigations into the causes for the baffling domain-differential gender differences.

A motivational theory of life-span development

Human life-span development reflects comparatively vast individual variations. One of the major challenges for life-span developmental psychology is to explain how, given the vast ontogenetic potential and life course variability for humans, most individuals manage to lead consistent and meaningful lives that follow productive paths into and throughout adulthood (Heckhausen, 1999; Heckhausen, Wrosch, & Schulz, 2010). Three major factors of influence contribute to the structuredness of human life courses: (1) biology of maturation and aging, (2) societal institutions and social structure, and (3) the individual as an active agent in his/her own development. Biological and societal influences bring about an age-graded sequence of developmental tasks that provides both constraint and supportive structure to the individual's life-span developmental agency. Opportunities are not distributed evenly across the life course. Instead they cluster around certain transitions, one of which is the transition from school or college to employment and work.

Our approach to the regulation of life-span development focuses on the impressive adaptive capacity of individuals to optimize development across major changes in the life course (Heckhausen, 1999; Heckhausen & Schulz, 1995; Heckhausen et al., 2010). Individuals substantially contribute to regulating their own development by pursuing developmental goals that organize how much time and effort they invest in their life course. Individual differences in the self-regulatory capacities that are required to do this developmental regulation successfully should have major consequences on how well the individual fares in his/her life course, particularly during times of transition and in domains of life that require a great amount of individual agency.

The motivational theory of life-span development (Heckhausen et al., 2010) proposes that the major criterion of adaptive development is the overall *primary control* realized in a life course; that is, the extent to which the individual realizes control over his/her life and immediate social environment across different domains of life (work, family, leisure) and throughout their life course. This underlying goal of maximizing primary control is realized best if the individual is aware and adjusts goal choices on changes in opportunities and constraints to goal striving as they move from school to college, to work, from family of origin to finding a long-term romantic partner, building a family, and so on. Biological maturation and aging as well as societal institutions (e.g., education, labor market, retirement) set up a general life-span trajectory of control capacity that resembles an inverted U-shaped curve, composed of a steep increase during childhood and adolescence, a peak and plateau in young adulthood and middle age, and a continuous decline in old age (see Figure 15.1). Adaptive developmental agency should reflect these changes in opportunities for growth and risks for decline. And indeed, when looking at adult age group differences in goals reflecting striving for gains versus goals reflecting avoidance of losses, we find a decrease of growth-approach goals and an increase in loss-avoidance goals from young to middle to old age (see Figure 15.2).

The general life course trajectory of first increasing and then decreasing opportunities is overlaid with more domain-specific trajectories of improving and declining chances for achieving specific developmental goals (e.g., build a family, enter a professional career) (see Figure 15.3). Societal institutions and structures, such as the educational system, the labor market, and vocational career patterns, set up critical transitions (e.g., school entry, promotions, retirement) and sequential constraints (e.g., educational qualifications as prerequisites for certain

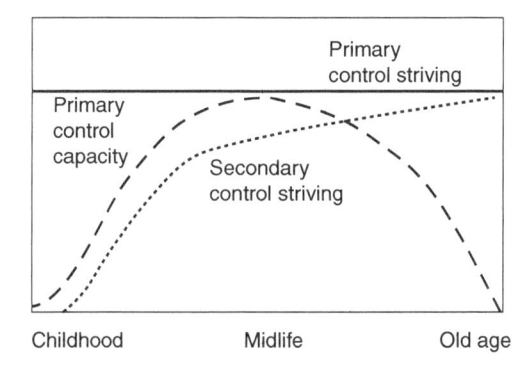

Figure 15.1 *Hypothetical life-span trajectories for primary control potential and primary and secondary control striving (from Heckhausen, 1999)*

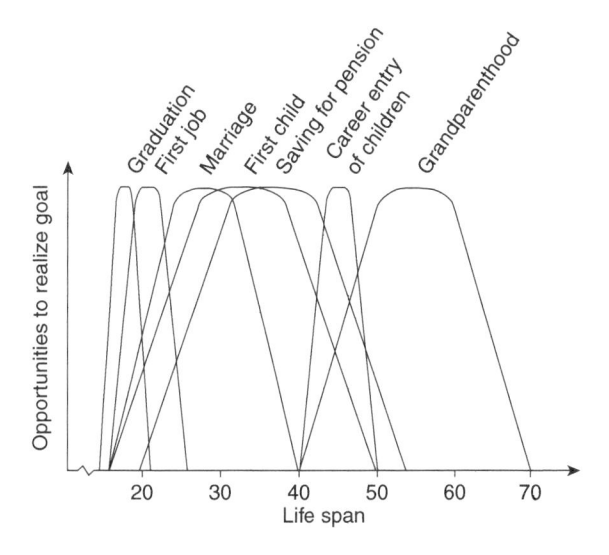

Figure 15.2 *Age-graded sequencing of opportunities to realize various developmental goals (from Heckhausen, 2000)*

careers). These transitions with their shifts in opportunities are both challenges to the individual and chances to optimize one's goal striving in congruence with the changes in the developmental ecology. In this process, some developmental goals for which opportunities have vanished (e.g., get into a top-ranked college after admission period is over) have to be given up forever, a phenomenon captured in the construct of "developmental deadline" (Heckhausen, Wrosch, & Fleeson, 2001; Wrosch & Heckhausen, 1999). The individual has to develop the capacity to identify the degree of controllability present in a given social and developmental ecology, and then adjust his or her goal selection to it. This might involve disengaging from futile or illusory goals, adjusting the goals to fit the reach of one's capacity for primary control (i.e., control of one's social and material environment) and re-engage with this newly adjusted goal. These motivational

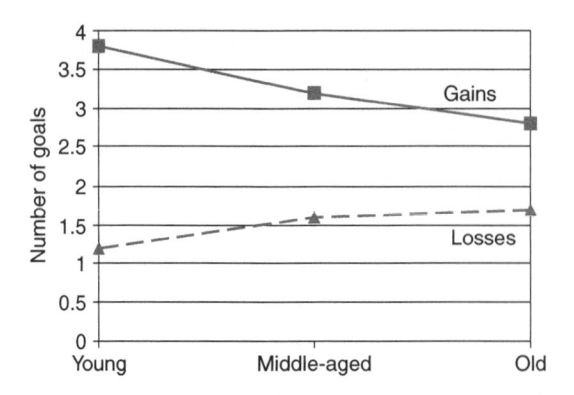

Figure 15.3 *Striving for gains and avoiding losses in developmental goals across age groups (from Heckhausen, 1997)*

adaptations are challenging and individuals differ in the degree to which they master them. I will return to this issue in the section on "Action Cycles of Goal Engagement and Disengagement in Congruence with Context Opportunities."

School and work: two contrasting social contexts for individual agency

What are the motivational challenges an individual agent faces in school versus in the domain of paid work? Let us turn first to the social and institutional context of K–12 schools. The school classroom provides a highly structured set of demands and opportunities. It is typically not the student but the teacher (or school authority) who sets the curriculum, pace of progress, and level of difficulty in homework, tests, and exams. Achievement demands are standardized; performances are closely monitored and can easily be compared between individuals. Thus, educational institutions, especially schools K–12, but also colleges, provide few degrees of freedom for the individual agent to truly engage their achievement motive. Traditional schools leave little room to generate self-chosen goals in congruence with one's achievement motive (Heckhausen & Heckhausen, 2011; see also Eccles & Roeser, 2011; Wigfield, Eccles, Schiefele, Roeser, & Davis-Kean, 2006) and to regulate one's own progress through action phases of goal engagement and goal disengagement or adjustment.

In contrast, the world of work, especially during the process of career entry, is much less structured and thus can reflect individual differences in motivation and action regulation to a greater extent. During job searches, individuals can exert more or less persistence, and show more or less capacity to realize when a lowering or enhancing of aspirations is called for, or when to move on from a given non-optimal job to search for a better job en route to the desired career. Because the social institutions involved in young adults' early career building (e.g., vocational training schools) in most countries provide little structure (Hamilton, 1990; Heinz, 1999), they leave the majority of decisions, calibrations, and regulations to the individual agent.[1] Based on this reasoning, one can predict that individual differences in motivational preferences and self-regulation should play a much larger role in early careers compared to school and college.

Achievement goal orientations

The achievement goal construct was based on the work of several motivational researchers, including Carol Ames, Carol Dweck, Marty Maehr, and John Nicholls (see review in Elliot, 2005). According to current achievement goal theory, individuals differ in the degree to which they prefer mastery-oriented goals or performance-oriented goals, and also in the degree to which they are oriented toward approaching success versus avoiding failure. Here we will focus on the distinction between mastery and performance goals. Mastery goals pertain to the incentive of improving one's competence (i.e., getting better) in the task-relevant behavior. In contrast, performance goals are extrinsic to the activity and geared toward maximizing favorable evaluations of the self, particularly in comparison to others (i.e., doing better than others). Early theorists agreed on the notion that mastery goals were superior to performance goals in motivating successful achievement behavior. Numerous empirical studies indeed showed achievement behavior and achievement emotions of mastery-oriented students to be superior to achievement behavior and emotions in performance-oriented students (see summary in Barron & Harackiewicz, 2001). However, the actual academic performance was less consistently related to students' mastery orientation (Harackiewicz, Barron, Tauer, & Elliot, 2002).

With respect to initially shunned performance goals, over the years, evidence has accumulated regarding their widespread spontaneous use (see review in Senko, Hulleman, & Harackiewicz, 2011) and their potential adaptive effects, particularly when coupled with a positive perception of own competence and/or an approach (rather than an avoidance) orientation (Harackiewicz, Barron, & Elliot, 1998; Witkowski & Stiensmeier-Pelster, 1998). This evidence gave rise to a "multiple goal perspective" (Barron & Harackiewicz, 2001; see also review in Elliot, 2005) that proposes that different achievement goals and notably *combinations* of achievement goals may promote better achievement and wellbeing outcomes in different settings. To date, considerable evidence supports this view. For instance, combinations of mastery and (approach) performance goals (i.e., showing oneself as more competent than others) seem to be particularly motivating in the workplace (Farr, Hofmann, & Mathieu, 1993), in sports settings (Fox, Goudas, Biddle, Duda, & Armstrong, 1994), but also in the school context (Pintrich, Conley, & Kempler, 2003).

---

[1] Exceptions are a small number of countries with highly structured vocational training systems such as Germany and Poland (Hamilton, 1990; Heinz, 1999).

Empirical research on gender differences in achievement goals is scarce. The available evidence either indicates no gender differences in achievement goals (Meece, Glienke, & Burg, 2006) or it suggests that in the school context girls are more oriented toward mastery goals than boys (Anderman & Young, 1994; Pajares, Britner, & Valiante, 2000), whereas boys are more oriented toward performance goals (Pajares & Cheong, 2003).

Implicit and explicit motives

In recent years, motivational researchers have differentiated between two types of motives, implicit and explicit motives (Brunstein, 2011; McClelland, Koestner, & Weinberger, 1989). *Implicit motives* are what traditional motivational psychology identifies as *need*, for instance *need (n) for* Achievement, *n* Affiliation, *n* Power (Heckhausen & Heckhausen, 2011). They are acquired early in life during the preverbal period and thus inaccessible to introspection. Assessment of implicit motives requires the use of non-self-reflective methods, specifically the projective method of thematic apperception (TAT). Implicit motives energize, direct, and select "*operant*" (McClelland, 1980) behavior that is instrumental for satisfying the respective motive (e.g., improving one's mastery in the case of *n* Achievement). Implicit motives predict behaviors that are more spontaneous and self-initiated, such as effort expenditure, spontaneous mastery activity, attention, and learning with regard to motive-relevant materials and activities. Such *operant* behavior is less likely to adhere to external prompts or constraints. In this regard, the classroom and school setting in general is ironically inhospitable to the implicit achievement motive (Heckhausen & Heckhausen, 2011; for the junior high school context, see Wigfield et al., 2006), whereas career striving with less structured challenges offers plenty of cues and incentives for a strong implicit achievement motive.

In contrast, *explicit motives*, sometimes also referred to as (explicit) *goals*, reflect the individual's self-concept, that is the way an individual sees him/herself and wants to present the self to themselves and others (Brunstein, 2011; McClelland et al., 1989). They are best assessed using self-report measures such as questionnaires about goals. Explicit motives influence behavior that is under conscious and deliberate control, and are *respondent* to external stimulation or prompts, such as a questionnaire, classroom setting, or in a clearly delineated decision situation (McClelland, 1980). In unstructured situations such as seeking a job or investing in a career, explicit goals can function as effective tools, but will not help with seeking out opportunities and maintaining effort across longer time periods and unforeseen obstacles.

Interestingly, implicit and explicit motives appear to constitute distinct and independent motivational systems that are only weakly correlated (Schultheiss & Brunstein, 2001). Moreover, and most importantly for the issue of context-differential behavior, implicit and explicit motives are selectively useful in different situational settings (Brunstein, 2011). For example, implicitly but not explicitly assessed achievement motives predicted greater effort expenditure and faster learning when people were given tasks but not told to try to do well (Biernat, 1989; deCharms, Morrison, Reitman, & McClelland, 1955). Moreover, in the not so closely structured domain of career, high implicit achievement motive, but not explicit achievement motive, predicts occupational, economic, and business success (McClelland, 1961), sometimes in combination with high implicit power motive (McClelland & Boyatzis, 1982). In addition, implicit motives are enticed when task-inherent incentives (e.g., production output) are present. In contrast, extrinsic questionnaire-assessed motives were enticed by the presence of social achievement incentives such as school grades (Brunstein & Maier, 2005; Spangler, 1992). In sum, implicit motives are more effective for navigating less structured situations or life-transitions in accordance with the individual's motive strengths, whereas explicit motives are most effective when a situation is well structured and requires specific responses and decisions.

Most interestingly, it makes a difference whether implicit and explicit motives are congruent or not (see review in Brunstein, 2011; Langan-Fox, Samkeu, & Canty, 2009). People whose implicit and explicit (goals) motives are congruent report better psychological wellbeing and life satisfaction (Brunstein, Schultheiss, & Grassman, 1998; see review in Brunstein, Schultheiss, & Maier, 1999; Brunstein, 2011), whereas implicit/explicit motive incongruence was associated with low emotional wellbeing (Baumann, Kaschel, & Kuhl, 2005; Brunstein et al., 1998).

The relation between implicit and explicit motives is a relatively recent area of research and to date little is known about gender differences in this regard. Given the findings of the differential effectiveness of explicit and implicit motives in more (for explicit motives) or less (for implicit goals) structured achievement contexts, gender differences in this regard could contribute to the differential success of men and women in school versus work contexts.

Domain-focus of achievement motive

Another aspect of achievement motivation pertains to the breadth versus selective focus of the achievement motive on certain domains of competence. Classical achievement motivation theory does not speak to this issue (Brunstein & Heckhausen, 2011) and interest theory (Krapp, 2002) addresses intrinsic attraction to certain content domains, but not whether the need for achievement is triggered by these content domains. However, from an everyday lay perspective on motivational psychology we know that different individuals have different domains of achievement behavior that "make them tick." It seems likely that these domains differ in the profile of incentives they provide in terms of activity-inherent, outcome-related, or consequence-related incentives. Particularly interesting are differences in activity-intrinsic versus activity-extrinsic indicators of success. Some individuals may rely more on activity-intrinsic indicators such as experiences of flow (Rheinberg, 2008) or meeting one's personal achievement standards and experiencing the emotion of pride, whereas others may be adept at extracting information about their own competence from extrinsic feedback, such as social comparison with classmates or co-workers, praise from a superior (e.g., teacher, boss), career advancement, or salary.

Very little is known about such individual differences in which people see available incentives given the same level of achievement motive. However, some early empirical evidence on gender differences in achievement behavior indicated that men high in achievement motive exhibit achievement behavior in more narrowly constrained domains of career and leadership, whereas women high in achievement motive showed broader achievement behavior in domains beyond career and leadership (Stewart & Chester, 1982). Based on two studies of need achievement in the years 1957 and 1976, Veroff (1982; Veroff, Reuman, & Feld, 1984) reports that for men in the United States, high n Achievement is associated with preferring work to leisure and viewing work as fulfilling one's major life goal. In contrast, women with high n Achievement in the late 1950s and even mid-1970s were more likely to participate in challenging leisure activities and view leisure as their major life goal. Moreover, Veroff reported that women's need achievement scores increased between the two assessments in 1957 and 1976, whereas men's scores remained stable. Veroff concluded that the expression of achievement motivation reflects changes in societal opportunities for the two gender groups. In the relevant period, the 1960s and early 1970s, the Women's Movement had greatly expanded accepted domains for women's achievement behavior.

Moreover, women may use ways of creating achievement challenges for themselves in alternative achievement domains in societies that do not offer such opportunities in careers accessible to women if the highest-status careers provide fewer such opportunities for women. For example, senior year women's high n Achievement predicted employment in a teaching career 14 years later (Jenkins, 1987). Those highly achievement-motivated women who worked in achievement-compatible careers increased their achievement motivation over time, whereas those who had ended up in achievement-incompatible careers valued career advancement less, saw fewer status mobility routes, had career interruptions, and became more involved in homemaking and mothering than in work. Individuals' life social context can thus arouse or suppress achievement motivation over time or channel it into a different domain that is more in line with societally accepted gender roles.

Finally, cultural norms regarding accepted achievement domains for women may require a stronger achievement and or power motive than men have to have in the same careers. Evidence for this notion stems from a study of women managers in the 1980s that found women enrolled in MBA programs had higher n Achievement and n Power scores than men enrolled in the same programs (Chusmir, 1985). It seems that during times of strong societal discouragement of women from high achievement and power careers, it takes an extra push of implicit motive(s) to overcome the societal hurdles (Duncan & Peterson, 2010).

```
                    ┌──────────────┐              ┌──────────────────┐
                    │  Rubicon:    │              │    Deadline:     │
                    │ Goal decision│              │Loss of opportunities│
                    └──────┬───────┘              └────────┬─────────┘
                           │                               │
                           ▼         Goal engagement       ▼
                              Not urgent      Urgent
```

Optimize opportunity match, consequences, and diversity	Selective primary control Selective secondary control	Increased selective primary and secondary control Compensatory primary control	After failure: Compensatory secondary control
			After success: Capitalize on success; new action cycle.

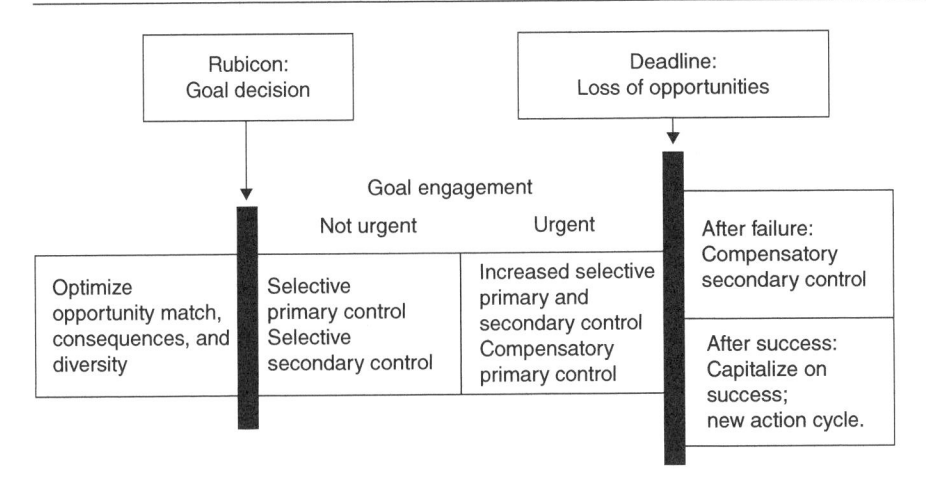

Figure 15.4 *Action-phase model of developmental regulation (from Heckhausen, 1999)*

Women today entering science, engineering, and computer science careers may have to come up against similar obstacles and may have received an extra boost of an exceptionally strong achievement motive.

Action cycles of goal engagement and goal disengagement in congruence with context opportunities

Successful development critically depends on whether an individual is able to regulate his/her own motivational investment in on-time goals that match the developmental opportunities of a given social ecology (e.g., school, internship, entry-level position, senior position in a company's hierarchy). The individual needs to select, pursue, and adapt his/her developmental goals to reflect changes in life course opportunities.

Figure 15.4 shows the action-phase model of developmental regulation (see detailed discussion in Heckhausen et al., 2010). The developmental action-cycle starts out with a phase of *optimized goal choice*, during which the individual has to weigh the pros and cons of different developmental goal pursuits in terms of their value and expected opportunities for success, as well as the consequences they have on other goal pursuits that are concurrent or may be activated in the future. For example, pursuing a high-engagement career has lots of potential benefits, but may hamper one's opportunities to build a family. Such career–family trade-offs are particularly difficult for women, who come up against biological constraints in child-bearing (Heckhausen et al., 2001; Wiese & Freund, 2000). Once a person has made a decision about which goal to pursue, s/he enters the volitional phase of goal pursuit, during which behavior (selective primary control) and motivated cognition (selected secondary control) is strongly biased toward persistence and strengthening of goal pursuit. The volitional commitment becomes particularly pronounced during phases of urgent goal pursuit when the remaining time to reach that goal (the deadline) runs out. During the urgency phase, individuals will be more motivated to even use means of compensatory primary control by requesting help from other people or by finding new or detour-like strategies to reach the goal when the usual strategies fail. Once the deadline of declining and insufficient opportunities has been passed, the individual has to master a radical shift from high volitional engagement with an urgent goal to disengagement from that goal. In the process of disengagement and thereafter, it may be necessary to use strategies of self-protective thought in order to not suffer a depletion of self-esteem and hopefulness for future goal pursuits. Such self-protective compensatory strategies include thoughts to avoid self-blame and attributions to external factors, re-evaluation of the value of the original goal, and social comparisons with people who were also not successful or even worse off than oneself.

These shifts from optimized goal choice to volitional goal engagement to disengagement and self-protection require a highly developed capacity to self-regulate one's motivational processes. People differ in the extent to which they master the various components of the progression through the action phases. Those individuals will fare best who can stay ahead of the game and anticipate emergent opportunities for goal pursuits, activate behavioral and motivational strategies of goal engagement, disengage from goals that have become unattainable and/or too costly in a new developmental ecology, and replace old and futile goals with goals that are still or newly attainable in the new context.

There are individual differences in the extent to which people respond to changes in opportunities and to newly arising constraints with appropriate goal choices, goal engagement, and goal disengagement. Opportunity–goal congruency is an achievement of individuals' motivational self-regulation. Those who are more competent in this regard have more positive developmental outcomes in terms of both objective attainments (e.g., educational qualifications, entry in vocational career) and subjective wellbeing. Most of our evidence to date is with regard to goal adaptations in middle-aged and older adults (Heckhausen et al., 2010). However, we also have evidence that German adolescents as young as 16 years of age can calibrate their vocational aspirations to the accessible vocational training market (Heckhausen & Tomasik, 2002; Tomasik, Hardy, Haase, & Heckhausen, 2009). In contrast, US youth in California fared best in terms of attaining long-term educational goals when they started with greatly optimistic goals that seemed hardly realistic at the time of their graduation from high school (Heckhausen & Chang, 2009).

Regarding the employment of selective secondary control strategies (i.e., strategies to enhance one's volitional commitment to a goal, for example, by boosting its perceived value or controllability) of enhancing one's volitional commitment to a goal, we have evidence that they make a difference when youth are facing a particularly burdensome life situation. Poulin and Heckhausen (2007) found that for those adolescents who had recently experienced a very severe life event (i.e., death or life-threatening illness of family member, divorce of parents), only those who used selective secondary strategies of enhancing volition were able to keep up their primary control striving for a vocational training position.

Research in this area has not identified gender differences in youth's usage of various control and self-regulatory strategies to date. However, one study uncovered a differential effectiveness of goal engagement strategies for girls compared to boys (Haase, Heckhausen, & Köller, 2008). In this study of German youth, girls searching for vocational training positions in the context of the German vocational training and labor market were more likely to find a position if they combined behavioral investments in primary control striving (e.g., write job applications) with volitional self-management to enhance goal commitment (e.g., focus on how important it is to find a job; Haase et al., 2008). Both girls and boys profited from such goal engagement in terms of their subjective wellbeing.

As mentioned, gender differences were not found in usage of compensatory secondary control strategies, that is, in strategies of goal disengagement and self-protection. However, the studies were conducted either in a clearly structured educational system (the California system of community colleges and universities) or in the similarly clearly structured German system of vocational training (apprenticeships). It was unknown if gender differences would emerge in the realm of job and career search, where individuals need to take greater self-initiative to achieve desirable outcomes. There is some evidence in research on older adults for women's greater propensity and competence to use compensatory secondary strategies, such as goal adjustment and self-protection (Chipperfield, Perry, Bailis, Ruthig, & Chuchmach, 2007). If such gender differences were to be found among young job seekers and career beginners, they might set up women for less persistence along ambitious career paths that are riddled with setbacks and uncertain decision points.

Summary

Effective achievement striving in the school and the work contexts may require different self-regulatory and motivational processes. The school context is more structured and facilitates explicit goal setting and feedback as well as social comparison. The context of work and career is less well structured in terms of the sequential requirements, timing of initiatives (e.g., when to move on to the next and better job), and criteria for success. As a consequence, the two achievement contexts may favor different individuals who hold greater strength in structured versus unstructured achievement striving. A set of individual differences in motivational self-regulation was discussed that may be relevant: (a) whether an individual is primarily oriented toward mastery or performance goals or able to use both kinds of goals flexibly as needed in a given achievement setting; (b) whether the general achievement motive is activated in a wider range of achievement contexts or is more focused on the career domain; (c) whether a person has strong explicit and/or implicit achievement motives and the degree to which implicit and explicit achievement-related motives are congruent; and (d) the capacity to organize one's action cycles into discrete phases of goal engagement and of goal disengagement in accordance with the control opportunities in the current developmental context. To date, we know very little about gender or other group (e.g., ethnic, social class) differences in these components of motivational self-regulation. However, initial evidence suggests that based on their strengths and weaknesses in motivational self-regulation, girls and women are better in more structured contexts such as school, whereas boys and men hold an advantage in the less structured domain of work and career. We still know far too little to be confident about this conclusion, but it is an intriguing possibility that warrants further research. This line of research has the potential to guide interventions to enable individuals of either gender to use their motivational capacities and specializations and mindsets as productively as possible in multiple contexts of work, family, community, and leisure.

References

Anderman, E. M., & Young, A. J. (1994). Motivation and strategy use in science: Individual differences and classroom effects. *Journal of Research in Science Teaching*, 31, 811–831.

Barron, K. E., & Harackiewicz, J. M. (2001). Achievement goals and optimal motivation: Testing multiple goal models. *Journal of Personality and Social Psychology*, 80, 706–722.

Baumann, N., Kaschel, R., & Kuhl, J. (2005). Striving for unwanted goals: Stress-dependent discrepancies between explicit and implicit achievement motives reduce subjective well-being and increase psychosomatic symptoms. *Journal of Personality and Social Psychology*, 89, 781–799.

Biernat, M. (1989). Motives and values to achieve: Different constructs with different effects. *Journal of Personality*, 57, 69–95.

Brunstein, J. C. (2011). Implicit and explicit motives. In J. Heckhausen & H. Heckhausen (Eds.), *Motivation and action* (2nd ed., pp. 227–246). New York: Cambridge University Press.

Brunstein, J., & Heckhausen, H. (2011). Achievement motivation. In J. Heckhausen & H. Heckhausen (Eds.), *Motivation and action* (2nd ed., pp. 137–183). New York: Cambridge University Press.

Brunstein, J. C., & Maier, G. W. (2005). Implicit and self-attributed motives to achieve: Two separate but interacting needs. *Journal of Personality and Social Psychology*, 89, 205–222.

Brunstein, J. C., Schultheiss, O. C., & Grassman, R. (1998). Personal goals and emotional well-being: The moderating role of motive dispositions. *Journal of Personality and Social psychology*, 75, 494–508.

Brunstein, J. C., & Maier, G. W. (1999). *The pursuit of personal goals: A motivational approach to well-being and life adjustment*. Thousand Oaks, CA: Sage Publications.

Chipperfield, J. G., Perry, R. P., Bailis, D. S., Ruthig, J. C., & Chuchmach, L. P. (2007). Gender differences in use of primary and secondary control strategies in older adults with major health problems. *Psychology and Health*, 22, 83–105.

Chusmir, L. H. (1985). Motivation of managers: Is gender a factor? *Psychology of Women Quarterly*, 9, 153–159.

deCharms, R., Morrison, H. W., Reitman, W., & McClelland, D. C. (1955). Behavioral correlates of directly and indirectly measured achievement motivation. In D. C. McClelland (Ed.), *Studies in motivation* (pp. 414–423). New York: Appleton-Century-Crofts.

Duncan, L. E., & Peterson, B. E. (2010). Gender and motivation for achievement, affiliation-intimacy, and power. In J. C. Chrisler & D. R. McCreary (Eds.), *Handbook of gender research in psychology: Vol. 2. Gender research in social and applied psychology* (pp. 41–62). New York: Springer.

Eccles, J. S., & Roeser, R. W. (2011). Schools as developmental contexts during adolescence. *Journal of Research on Adolescence*, 21, 225–241.

Elliot, A. J. (2005). A conceptual history of the achievement goal construct. In A. J. Elliot & C. S. Dweck (Eds.), *Handbook of competence and motivation* (pp. 52–72). New York: Guilford Publications.

Else-Quest, N. M., Hyde, J. S., & Linn, M. C. (2010). Cross-national patterns of gender differences in mathematics: A meta-analysis. *Psychological Bulletin*, 136, 103–127.

Farr, J. L., Hofmann, D. A., & Mathieu, J. E. (1993). Job perception, job satisfaction relations: An empirical comparison of three competing theories. *Organizational Behavior and Human Decision Processes*, 56(3), 370–387.

Fox, K., Goudas, M., Biddle, S., Duda, J. L., & Armstrong, N. (1994). Children's task and ego goal profiles in sport. *British Journal of Educational Psychology*, 64, 253–261.

Haase, C. M., Heckhausen, J., & Köller, O. (2008). Goal engagement during the school-to-work transition: Beneficial for all, particularly for girls. *Journal of Research on Adolescence*, 18, 671–698.

Hamilton, S. F. (1990). *Apprenticeship for adulthood: Preparing youth for the future*. New York: Free Press.

Harackiewicz, J. M., Barron, K. E., & Elliot, A. J. (1998). Rethinking achievement goals: When are they adaptive for college students and why? *Educational Psychology*, 33, 1–21.

Harackiewicz, J. M., Barron, K. E., Tauer, J. M., & Elliot, A. J. (2002). Predicting success in college: A longitudinal study of achievement goals and ability measures as predictors of interest and performance from freshman year through graduation. *Journal of Educational Psychology*, 94, 562–575.

Heckhausen, J. (1997). Developmental regulation across adulthood: Primary and secondary control of age-related challenges. *Developmental Psychology*, 33, 176–187.

(1999). *Developmental regulation in adulthood: Age-normative and sociostructural constraints as adaptive challenges.* Cambridge University Press.

(2000). *Motivational psychology of human development: Developing motivation and motivating development.* Oxford: Elsevier.

Heckhausen, J., & Chang, E. S. (2009). Can ambition help overcome social inequality in the transition to adulthood? Individual agency and societal opportunities in Germany and the United States. *Research in Human Development*, 6, 1–17.

Heckhausen, J., & Heckhausen, H. (2011). Motivation and development. In J. Heckhausen & H. Heckhausen (Eds.), *Motivation and action* (2nd ed., pp. 384–443). New York: Cambridge University Press.

Heckhausen, J., & Schulz, R. (1995). A life-span theory of control. *Psychological Review*, 102, 284–304.

Heckhausen, J., & Tomasik, M. J. (2002). Get an apprenticeship before school is out: How German adolescents adjust vocational aspirations when getting close to a developmental deadline. *Journal of Vocational Behavior*, 60, 199–219.

Heckhausen, J., Wrosch, C., & Fleeson, W. (2001). Developmental regulation before and after a developmental deadline: The sample case of "biological clock" for child-bearing. *Psychology and Aging*, 16, 400–413.

Heckhausen, J., Wrosch, C., & Schulz, R. (2010). A motivational theory of lifespan development. *Psychological Review*, 117, 32–60.

Heinz, W. R. (1999). *From education to work: Cross-national perspectives.* Cambridge University Press.

Hyde, J. S., Lindberg, S. M., Linn, M. C., Ellis, A., & Williams, C. (2008). Gender similarities characterize math performance. *Science*, 321, 494–495.

Jenkins, S. (1987). Need for achievement and women's careers over 14 years: Evidence for occupational structure effects. *Journal of Personality and Social Psychology*, 53, 922–932.

Krapp, A. (2002). Structural and dynamic aspects of interest development: Theoretical considerations from an ontogenetic perspective. *Learning and Instruction*, 12, 383–409.

Langan-Fox, J., Samkeu, M. J., & Canty, J. M. (2009). Incongruence between implicit and self-attributed achievement motives and psychological well-being: The moderating role of self-directedness, self-disclosure and locus of control. *Personality and Individual Differences*, 47, 99–104.

McClelland, D. C. (1961). *Achievement and society.* Princeton, NJ: Van Nostrand.

(1980). Motives dispositions: The merits of operant and respondent measures. In L. Wheeler (Ed.), *Review of personality and social psychology* (pp. 87–113). New York: Wiley.

McClelland, D. C., & Boyatzis, R. E. (1982). The leadership motive pattern and long-term success in management. *Journal of Applied Psychology*, 67, 737–743.

McClelland, D. C., Koestner, R., & Weinberger, J. (1989). How do self-attributed and implicit motives differ? *Psychological Review*, 96, 690–702.

Meece, J. L., Glienke, B. B., & Burg, S. (2006). Gender and motivation. *Journal of School Psychology*, 44, 351–373.

National Center for Education Statistics (NCES). (2008, February). *Ten years after college: Comparing the employment experiences of 1992–93 Bachelor's degree recipients with academic and career-oriented majors – Postsecondary education descriptive analysis report* (NCES 2008–1550. Washington, DC: Dept. of Education.

Pajares, F., Britner, S. L., & Valiante, G. (2000). Relation between achievement goals and self-beliefs of middle school students in writing and science. *Contemporary Educational Psychology*, 25, 406–422.

Pajares, F., & Cheong, Y. F. (2003). Achievement goal orientations in writing: A developmental perspective. *International Journal of Educational Research*, 39, 437–455.

Pintrich, P. R., Conley, A. M., & Kempler, T. M. (2003). Current issues in achievement goal theory and research. *International Journal of Educational Research*, 39, 319–337.

Poulin, M., & Heckhausen, J. (2007). Stressful events compromise goal striving during a major life transition. *Motivation and Emotion*, 31, 300–311.

Rheinberg, F. (2008). Intrinsic motivation and flow. In J. Heckhausen & H. Heckhausen (Eds.), *Motivation and action* (pp. 323–383). New York: Cambridge University Press.

Schoon, I., Martin, P., & Ross, A. (2007). Career transitions in times of social change: His and her story. *Journal of Vocational Behavior*, 70, 78–96.

Schoon, I., & Silbereisen, R. K. (Eds.). (2009). *Transitions from school to work: Globalisation, individualisation, and patterns of diversity*. New York: Cambridge University Press.

Schultheiss, O. C., & Brunstein, J. C. (2001). Assessment of implicit motives with a research version of the TAT: Picture profiles, gender differences and relations to other personality measures. *Journal of Personality Assessment*, 77, 71–86.

Senko, C., Hulleman, C. S., & Harackiewicz, J. M. (2011). Achievement goal theory at the crossroads: Old controversies, current challenges, and new directions. *Educational Psychologist*, 46, 26–47.

Spangler, W. (1992). Validity of questionnaire and TAT measures of need for achievement: Two meta-analyses. *Psychological Bulletin*, 112, 140–154.

Stewart, A. J., & Chester, N. L. (1982). Sex differences in human social motives: Achievement, affiliation and power. In A. J. Stewart (Eds.), *Motivation and society* (pp. 172–218). San Francisco, CA: Jossey-Bass.

Tomasik, M. J., Hardy, S., Haase, C. M., & Heckhausen, J. (2009). Adaptive adjustment of vocational aspirations among German youths during the transition from school to work. *Journal of Vocational Behavior*, 74, 38–46.

Veroff, J. (1982). Assertive motivations. In A. J. Stewart (Eds.), *Motivation and society*. San Francisco, CA: Jossey-Bass.

Veroff, J., Reuman, D., & Feld, S. C. (1984). Motives in American men and women across the adult life span. *Developmental Psychology*, 20, 1142–1158.

Wiese, B. S., & Freund, A. M. (2000). The interplay of work and family in young and middle adulthood. In J. Heckhausen (Ed.), *Motivational psychology of human development: Developing motivation and motivating development* (pp. 233–249). New York: Elsevier Science.

Wigfield, A., & Eccles, J. S. (2002). The development of competence beliefs, expectancies for success, and achievement values from childhood through adolescence. In A. Wigfield & J. S. Eccles (Eds.), *The development of achievement motivation* (pp. 91–120). San Diego, CA: Academic Press.

Wigfield, A., Eccles, J. S., Schiefele, U., Roeser, R., & Davis-Kean, P. (2006). Motivation. In N. Eisenberg (Ed.), *Handbook of child psychology* (6th ed., Vol. 3, pp. 933–1002). New York: Wiley.

Witkowski, T., & Stiensmeier-Pelster (1998). Performance deficits following failure: Learned helplessness or self-esteem protection? *British Journal of Social Psychology*, 37, 59–71.

Wrosch, C., & Heckhausen, J. (1999). Control processes before and after passing a developmental deadline: Activation and deactivation of intimate relationship goals. *Journal of Personality and Social Psychology*, 77, 415–427.

PART V

Longer-term consequences of early experiences

16 The life course consequences of single-sex and co-educational schooling

Alice Sullivan and Heather Joshi

Abstract

This chapter reports on a study examining whether attending single-sex rather than co-educational secondary school made a difference to the lives of a cohort of men and women born in Britain in 1958. The project aimed to assess the impact of single-sex secondary schooling, not just on short-term and narrowly academic outcomes, but also on longer-term social, psychological, and economic outcomes. In a generally gendered environment for adults, did it make any difference to have been to a gender segregated school, and in what way? This chapter provides an overview of our findings, and a discussion of the implications for policy and for future research.

Background

Controversies about co-education at secondary schools in Britain began at the end of the nineteenth century and continue to the present. However, the arguments for and against co-education have changed over time, with changing gender differences in educational aspirations and attainment, while the number of single-sex schools has declined steadily. The evidence regarding single-sex schools must therefore be placed in historical context.

Traditionally, single-sex secondary schooling was the norm. However, in the 1920s, "progressives" began to argue that co-education could help overcome "sex antagonisms," improve the quality of marriage and help prevent homosexuality (Brice, 1980; Dyhouse, 1985; Faraday, 1989). In the 1960s and 1970s, Dale (1969, 1971, 1974) reported that boys, girls, and especially teachers were happier in co-educational secondary schools, where boys did better academically. Benn and Simon (1970) used this in support of comprehensive schooling, which they believed should be a common school for *all* children. Others in the same period continued to support single-sex schools for religious reasons and/or to control (mainly girls') sexual behavior – to guard against early sexual relationships and premarital pregnancy.

This work was funded by ESRC Award RES-000-22-1085. Thanks are due to the National Child Development Study survey members for their contribution over many years. We would also like to thank our late colleague, Professor Diana Leonard (1941–2010), who was PI of the project.

In the 1970s and 1980s, feminists reasserted that single-sex schools were better for girls, even if co-education might be better for boys (Spender & Sarah, 1980). Girls were said to get more attention from teachers and a fairer share of resources when boys were not present; and the heads of girls' schools suggested their schools encouraged girls' ambitions (Shaw, 1976). This was countered by arguments that it was the school sector (private, grammar, or comprehensive) that mattered most (Bone, 1983). If it seemed that girls did better if they went to single-sex schools, this was because single-sex schools were likely to be longer established, academically selective, and recruited from higher socioeconomic groups.

Today the concern is more narrowly with GCSE examination results and which type of school (or type of grouping within mixed schools) produces the best performances (Smithers & Robinson, 2006; Spielhofer, Benton, & Schagen, 2004). Single-sex classes are being tried in mixed schools in the hope of raising boys' performance in particular (Warrington & Younger, 2001; Younger & Warrington, 2006), reflecting increasing concerns about boys' "underachievement" in school.

Deeply held opinions on single-sex and co-educational schooling continue and there is a lack of rigorous research evidence. Most available data is based on small-scale, synchronous studies or is anecdotal. The project we report on here aimed to make a long overdue assessment of the short- and long-term effects of single- and mixed-sex schooling, using evidence from a large and nationally representative longitudinal study. This has followed individuals from birth, through the education system, and into adulthood. We have been able to control for crucial confounding variables (such as prior academic attainment and social class) and to provide information on the longer-term impacts of schooling, which have never previously been tested. We have reported the results of this study in various places (Leonard, Joshi, & Sullivan, 2007; Sullivan, 2006, 2009; Sullivan, Joshi, & Leonard, 2010, 2011, 2012). The purpose of the current chapter is to provide an overview of our findings regarding the effects of single-sex schooling in different life domains. This evidence adds to our understanding of the way in which school contexts can influence gendered aspirations and attainment.

Research questions

Arguments in favor of and against single-sex schooling have been put forward from a range of different perspectives, with some feminists on either side of the debate. Hypotheses emerging from the views of commentators are varied and conflicting. Single-sex schooling will improve the academic attainments of girls or of boys or both, or will be detrimental to both sexes. Single-sex schooling will produce confident and successful women, or women who cannot compete with men. It will lead to difficult relationships between the sexes, or to more equal relationships (Leonard, 1996).

Before addressing the potential consequences of attending a single-sex school, it was crucial to examine the issue of the ways in which boys and girls attending single-sex schools differed from their peers at co-educational schools, particularly in terms of key characteristics such as family background and cognitive test scores. We went on to examine outcomes from age 16 to age 42, and our findings can be divided into four main areas:

- During schooling we focused on happiness/wellbeing at school, truancy, and academic self-evaluation.
- Academic attainment was measured at ages 16, 18, and 33: We examined attainment in secondary school examinations and later degree success, and the gender segregation of subjects studied.
- We examined occupational outcomes in mid-life (age 42), namely labor market participation, occupational status, wages, and occupational gender segregation.
- Also in mid-life, we looked at social outcomes such as attitudes to gender roles, marriage, and the domestic division of labor.

In each case the experience of men and women is compared, and we assess whether outcomes are linked to single-sex and co-educational schooling once potential confounding variables have been controlled.

Data and methods

The National Child Development Study (NCDS) is a longitudinal study of a single cohort born in Great Britain (i.e., England, Scotland, and Wales, but not Northern Ireland) in one week in 1958 (Power & Elliott, 2006). The NCDS is a continuing, multidisciplinary longitudinal study, with data relating to health, education, wellbeing, family formation, and labor market participation, among other things. The cohort members have been followed up throughout their lives, including at age 50 in 2008 and 55 in 2013'.

The initial sample was designed to be nationally representative of all children in Great Britain, and achieved a sample size of 17,414 (Bynner & Joshi, 2007). By the third follow-up, when the children were aged 16, 14,761 remained in the study. Hawkes and Plewis' (2006) examination of attrition and non-response in the NCDS finds systematic yet modest predictability in attrition, wave non-response, and missing education data, thus supporting the assumption of ignorable non-response. Neither parental education nor social class were significant predictors of non-response. The distribution of educational qualifications gained by the cohort members by age 33 was closely in line with other data sources (Dale & Egerton, 1997).

Previous studies of the effects of single-sex schooling have been criticized for inadequate controls for prior attainment and family background. Given the concentration of single-sex schools in the private and selective sectors, it is important to control for such potential sources of bias. The NCDS gives exceptionally rich information on various aspects of the respondents, their schools, and their parents, allowing crucial confounding variables to be controlled. The parents were interviewed at the childhood data collections, providing information on social background, parents' education, and other characteristics.

Data were also collected directly from the children through tests and questionnaires administered at school at the ages of 7, 11, and 16. Extensive information on academic examination results was collected directly from the schools. From the age of 16 onwards, the respondents themselves were interviewed.

The NCDS cohort took a range of cognitive tests at ages 7 and 11, allowing us to control for prior attainment in an unusually fine-grained way (Steedman, 1980, 1983b, 1983c).

The sample is not clustered, i.e., pupils are not sampled within schools. The sample consists of all children born in Great Britain in the relevant week. Many schools would be represented by a single cohort member. It is therefore neither possible nor necessary to apply a multilevel statistical model to these data. A further limitation is that, due to the small numbers of ethnic minority individuals included in the NCDS, it is not possible to conduct analyses according to ethnic group. Some 98% of the NCDS sample was white (at the 1969 survey).

Results

1. Who attended single-sex schools in 1974?

The NCDS cohort experienced a state secondary education system that was in transition from the tripartite to the comprehensive system. Under the tripartite system, children sat an exam around age 11 (called "the Eleven plus") that determined whether, in the September following their 11th birthday, they would attend an academically selective Grammar or Technical school, or a Secondary Modern school, designed for the majority of pupils. Comprehensive schools were intended to replace this selective system with all-ability schools. Some 58% of the NCDS respondents attended comprehensive schools, but 11% still attended Grammar and Technical schools, 22% attended Secondary Modern schools, and 6% attended Private and Direct Grant schools. Private schools are fee-paying schools. Direct Grant schools were fee-paying, but had a proportion of state-funded places. Henceforth, we refer to Grammar and Technical schools as "grammar schools," and Private and Direct Grant schools as "private schools." Taking the NCDS sample as a whole, 24% of boys and 27% of girls aged 16 attended single-sex schools. However, there was great variation between school sectors. Within the private sector, single-sex schooling was the norm, with 78% of private school pupils attending single-sex schools. In the state sector, however,

67% of grammar school pupils against 26% of secondary modern and 11% of comprehensive school pupils went to single-sex schools. There were also more boys than girls at mixed schools in the private, secondary modern, comprehensive, and special sectors. The latter catered for a small number of pupils with special needs, and these are excluded from all subsequent analyses. More boys than girls attended such schools, and there were especially few girls at single-sex special schools.

There was also substantial regional variation in the extent of provision of single-sex schooling in 1974. Single-sex schooling was most common in London and the South East, with 49% of pupils (51% of girls and 46% of boys) attending single-sex schools. These were common throughout the state sector, even among comprehensives. Single-sex schooling was least common in Scotland, catering for only 6% of girls and 7% of boys in the study.

We modeled attendance at a single-sex school in order to identify which children were more likely to go to one. The results of separate binary regression analyses for boys and girls are reported in Table 16.1. Single-sex schools were more academically and socially selective than co-educational schools, reflecting their being more prevalent in the private and grammar sectors. Within each school sector, only modest differences in who attended single-sex versus co-educational schools were found, which is reassuring in terms of dealing with selection bias. School sector attended (i.e., private, comprehensive, secondary modern, or grammar) and region were the key predictors of individuals experiencing single-sex schooling. The effect of social class was fully captured by the school sector variable. For boys, but not for girls, test scores at age 11 were significantly positively linked to attending a single-sex school. For both sexes, there was an interaction between test scores at age 11 and private schooling, in line with the greater academic selectivity of single-sex schools within the private sector.

In summary, comprehensive schools were generally less likely to be single-sex than the other types of school, but within each school sector, children who attended single-sex and co-educational schools were similar.

2. Did single-sex schooling have any impact on: liking school, behavior, and wellbeing during adolescence?

Our second set of research questions related to the points stressed by Benn and Simon (1970) and Dale (1969, 1971, 1974) concerning the supposed greater happiness and wellbeing of boys and girls in mixed-sex schools, as well as their supposed better behavior.

At age 16, the NCDS cohort members were asked to respond to the statement "I do not like school." Figure 16.1 shows a breakdown of responses to this statement according to the pupil's sex and whether they attended a single-sex or co-educational school.

Table 16.1. *Attendance at a single-sex school, contrasted with attendance at a mixed school, binary logistic regression*

	Girls		Boys	
	B	S.E.	B	S.E.
Region		***		***
North Western	1.984	.206***	1.904	.208***
North	.191	.262	.250	.263
East, West Riding	.909	.236***	1.089	.230***
North Midlands	1.066	.229***	1.255	.228***
East	1.283	.224***	1.154	.227***
London South East	2.657	.201***	2.565	.200***
South	1.591	.228***	1.574	.228***
South West	1.312	.230***	.935	.234***
Midlands	1.292	.218***	1.196	.219***
Wales	.788	.265***	.910	.262***
Scotland				
Father's class				
Missing	.157	.134	.207	.134
Employer, manager (1)	.267	.208	−.152	.222
Employer, manager (2)	.121	.152	.048	.154
Professional	.250	.198	−.271	.197
Own account	.166	.206	.048	.203
Non-manual	.282	.141*	−.003	.146
Skilled manual	.101	.115	.055	.117
Unskilled manual				
Parents' education		**		**
Missing	.354	.101***	.320	.103**
19+	.198	.146	.111	.152
17–18	−.042	.116	−.073	.119
16	.052	.104	.000	.107
Left school pre-16				
Cognitive test score age 11	.004	.003	.004	.003*
Secondary school sector		***		***
Private	2.002	.608***	.986	.505
Grammar	1.564	.500**	3.092	.517***
Secondary modern	1.116	.256***	.811	.247***
Comprehensive				
Interactions				
Test Score*School		**		***
Test score*Private	.025	.010*	.037	.009***
Test score*Grammar	.014	.008	−.005	.008
Test Score*Secondary modern	−.009	.006	.000	.005
Constant	−3.685	.282	−4.064	.279
N	6,052		6,263	
Chi-square	2,035.487	***	1,924.798	***

Note: 371 students at special schools and schools outside standard categories excluded.

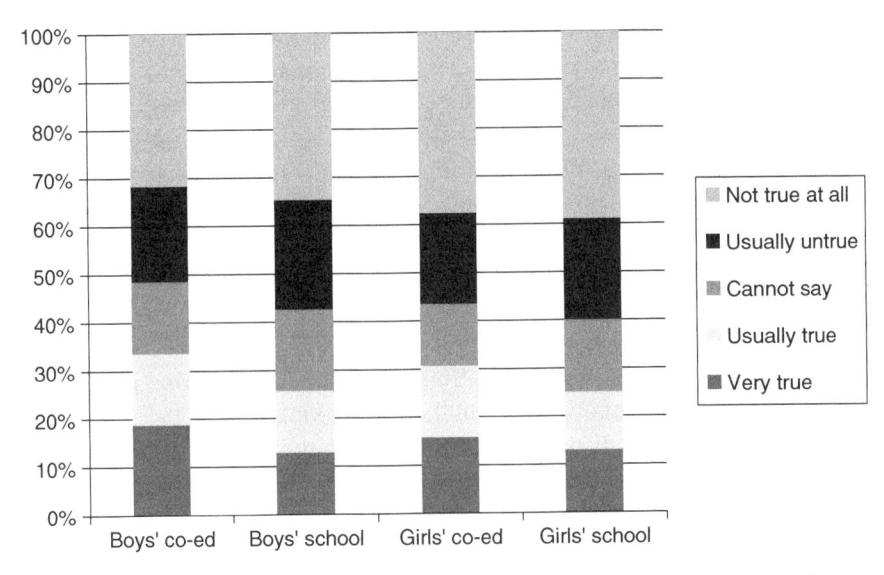

Figure 16.1 *Pupils' responses to "I do not like school," at age 16 (1974)*
N = 11,688

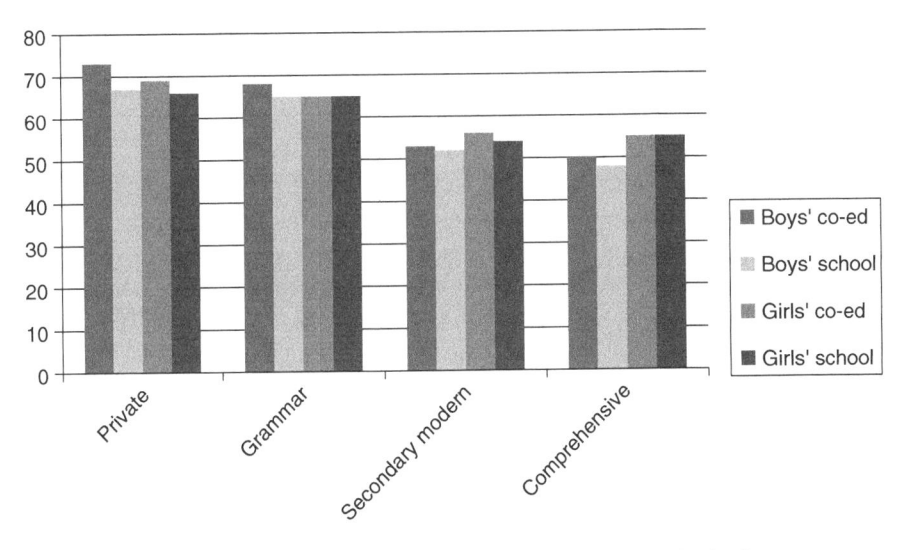

Figure 16.2 *Percentage liking school at age 16 by type of school*
N = 11,688

Figure 16.1 appears to show that pupils were happier in single-sex schools. However, this is misleading because pupils in private and grammar schools were generally more likely to say that they liked school. Figure 16.2 above shows the proportions of pupils responding "usually untrue" or "not true at all" to the statement "I do not like school" (i.e., those who generally liked school) by type of school.

Pupils at private and grammar schools were most likely to say that they liked school, and pupils at comprehensives were slightly less likely to like school than pupils at secondary moderns. Girls liked school more than boys at comprehensives, but this was not true at private and grammar schools.

Within each school sector, there was therefore a slight tendency for both boys and girls at co-ed schools to be more positive about school than those in single-sex schools. This is in line with Dale's findings from his various surveys of grammar and former grammar school pupils. However, we found the differences to be slight in each sector and we did not find that girls were "decidedly happier" in mixed schools (cf. Dale, 1971).

Binary logistic regression analysis (reported in Sullivan et al., 2012) showed that, conditioning on background controls, the link between liking school and being at a single-sex school was statistically significant for boys, but not for girls. In addition, school sector showed statistically significant differences for boys (positive private, grammar, and secondary modern parameters) but not for girls.

Pupils were asked whether they had truanted at all during the last year. Both boys and girls were less likely to report truanting from private and grammar schools. Single-sex schooling was also significantly associated with a lower likelihood of reported truanting, conditioning on school sector and other background controls. These findings are based on a binary logistic regression analysis reported in Sullivan et al. (2012).

Both mothers and teachers reported on the child's behavioral adjustment using the Rutter aggression and anxiety scales (Rutter, Tizard, & Whitmore, 1970). We have used the mother's report since the teacher's report may be conditioned by the school context. We found no impact of single-sex schooling on scores for either anxiety or aggression, based on regression analysis reported in Sullivan et al. (2012).

In summary, for boys, single-sex schooling was linked to a dislike of school. It is intriguing that school sector was linked to the chances of liking school for boys but not for girls, with boys being less happy at comprehensive schools. Although we can only offer tentative explanations for this finding, it does point to the possibility that ostensibly the same school structures and practices can be experienced differently by boys and girls. Research that fails to analyze outcomes for girls and boys separately will not pick up on the intersection of gender and school structures in producing outcomes, whether these are purely academic or wider. It is also notable that a great deal of research was carried out on the question of the effects of comprehensivization on academic outcomes, but, as far as we are aware, little attention has been given to the question of pupils' enjoyment within the different school sectors.

We found that both sexes were less likely to truant from single-sex schools. It is possible that pupils truanted from school as a direct consequence of the presence of the opposite sex. However, this may be more likely to reflect the different cultural and disciplinary regimes prevailing within single-sex and co-educational

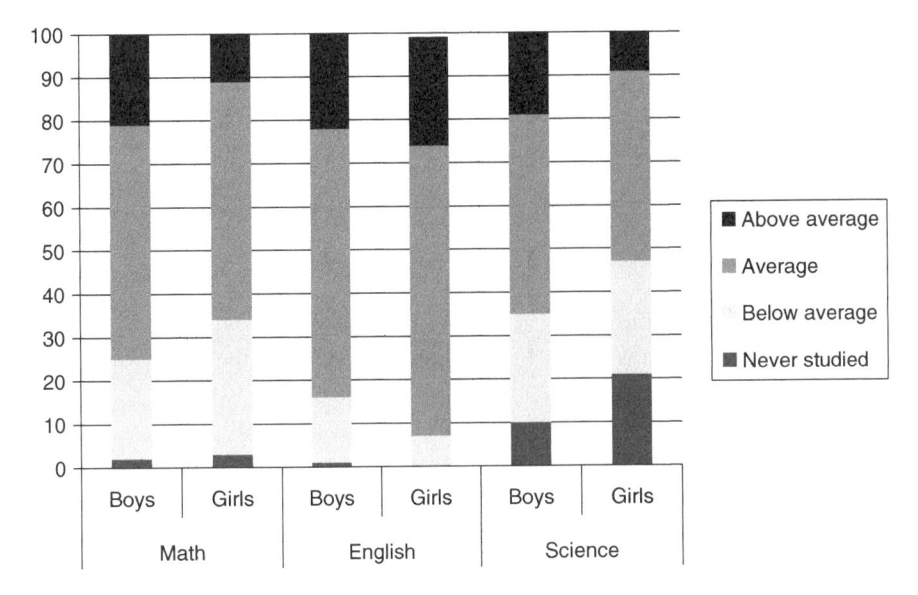

Figure 16.3 *Self-concept in math, English, and science*

schools at the time. It is possible that this also in turn accounts for boys' greater dislike of single-sex schools.

3. Was single-sex schooling linked to academic self-concept in different subject areas?

The cohort members were asked to rate their own academic abilities in a range of academic subjects. Figure 16.3 shows boys' and girls' evaluations of their own abilities in math, English, and science. Boys rated themselves more highly in math and science, while girls rated themselves more highly in English. Some 21% of girls and 10% of boys stated that they had never studied science.

These gender gaps in self-concept were moderated by single-sex schooling. In regression analyses conditioning on background controls (Sullivan, 2009), including verbal and non-verbal test scores at ages 7 and 11, we found that girls at single-sex schools were less likely than co-educated girls to see themselves as below average in math and science, and less likely to see themselves as above average in English. Boys at single-sex schools were more likely than co-educated boys to see themselves as above average in English. This confirms feminist arguments of the 1970s: gender stereotypes are exacerbated in mixed schools. The gender gap in self-confidence is smaller in the single-sex sector. These analyses were also replicated for the 1970 British Cohort Study (BCS70) (Sullivan, 2006).

To the extent that single-sex schooling affected academic self-concept, it generally promoted the gender-atypical. Conversely, co-educational schooling reinforced gendered self-concepts among pupils.

4. Did boys and/or girls get better overall academic results in single-sex schools?

This is the one area in which the cohort studies have previously been used to look at differences between single-sex and co-educational schooling, although Steedman's (1983a) analyses were limited to exam results at age 16. Our analysis of academic attainment at O- (Ordinary) level at age 16 and A- (Advanced) level at age 18 is limited to schools in England and Wales, since Scotland has different qualifications.

In Britain, pupils sit public examinations at age 16, the legal school-leaving age for this cohort. Separate exams were set for different subjects, and the most able students would have sat exams in around eight subjects. There were two sets of public examinations: O-levels were intended for the most academically able, and CSEs (Certificate of Secondary Education) for the less able. O-level grades ranged from A to G, with A–C grades being treated here as a pass. A top-grade CSE (grade 1) was deemed equivalent to a grade C at O-level. Here we examine the chance of getting five or more passes at O-level A–C or CSE1. This was the typical benchmark for progression to further academic-track education, for which grades D and E in O-level, while technically not failures, were not seen as adequate.

The raw figures suggest an enormous advantage for single-sex schools in examination attainment at 16 in 1974. Of co-ed boys, 15% achieved five or more passes, compared to 37% of single-sex boys. For girls, the gap was even wider: 14% of co-educated girls achieved five or more passes, compared to 42% of single-sex educated girls.

However, these raw differences are extremely misleading, given the concentration of single-sex schools within the private and selective sectors. Once school sector is taken into account, the difference in exam results between single-sex and co-educational schools appears generally more modest (Figure 16.4).

The results of a binary logistic regression analysis controlling for a relevant background controls are reported in Sullivan et al. (2010). This analysis shows an advantage for girls at single-sex schools, but no statistically significant effect of single-sex schooling for boys.

We examined whether single-sex schooling was associated with the likelihood of gaining passes in specific subject disciplines. In general, a higher proportion of girls achieved passes in English and modern languages, while a higher proportion of boys achieved passes in math, physics, and chemistry.

Figure 16.5 shows the number of exam passes in math, physics, and chemistry gained by the subset of boys and girls at co-ed and single-sex schools who gained at least one pass at O-level/CSE1. Girls at girls' schools were more likely to get O-levels in all three subjects, and less likely to get O-levels in none of them. Boys at boys' schools were no more likely than co-ed boys to get three passes, but were more likely to get one pass, and correspondingly less likely to get none.

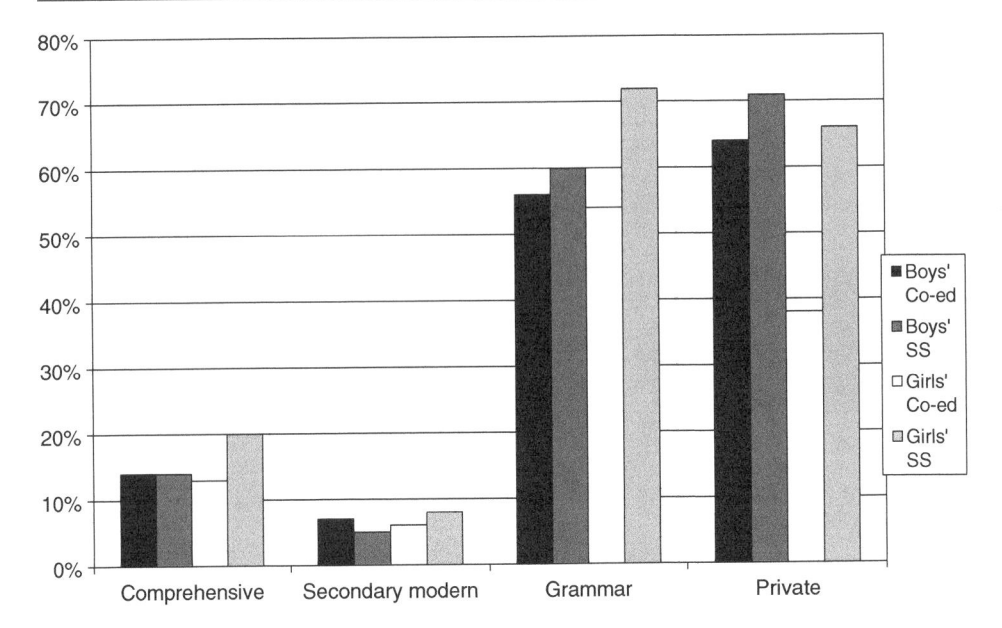

Figure 16.4 *Five or more O-level passes*

Figure 16.5 shows the number of passes in English, French, and an additional modern language gained by boys and girls at co-ed and single-sex schools. Boys at boys' schools were more likely than co-educated boys to get two or three passes in these subjects, while girls at single-sex schools were more likely to get two passes, but no more likely to get three.

We modeled these outcomes using a partial proportional odds model (Sullivan et al., 2010). Once appropriate controls were included in the model, we found a positive girls' school effect and a negative boys' school effect on the number of passes gained in math, physics, and chemistry. We also found positive differentials of single-sex schooling for English and modern languages for both boys and girls. Overall, the results confirm that girls did better in math and science, and boys did better in languages, at single-sex schools. That is to say, co-education was associated with increased gender differentiation.

The information we have about the curriculum available to the cohort members is limited, but at age 16 they were asked to report on whether they had "ever studied" a range of subjects: math, science, English, art, music, practical subjects, and sports.

We found that, conditioning on background controls (Sullivan, 2009), girls were more likely to report never having studied math and science, but single-sex schooling made no difference to their chance of ever studying these subjects. Girls at single-sex schools were more likely than girls at mixed schools to have studied art and music, suggesting that girls' schools sought to cater to girls' perceived interests, rather than trying to provide access to a gender-atypical

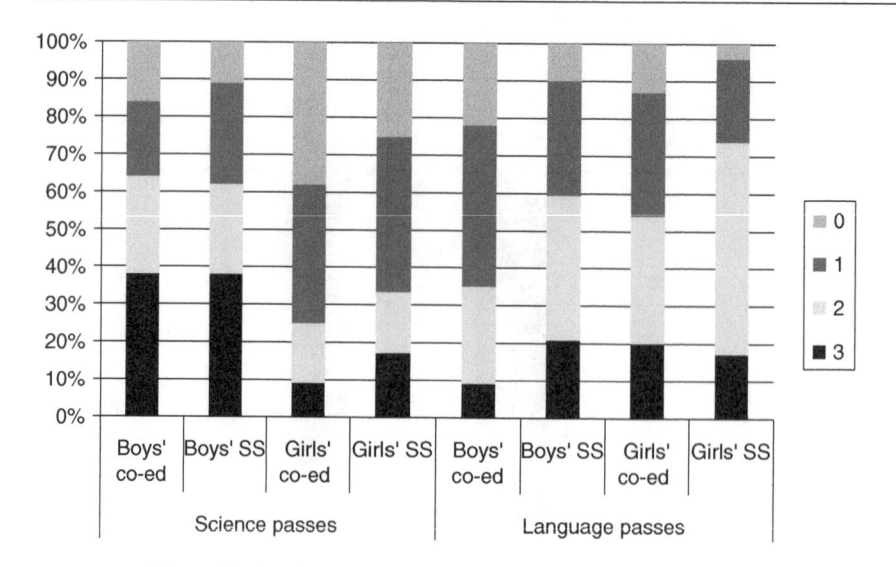

Figure 16.5 *O-level subject passes*
Note: Cohort members with at least one pass in any subject. "Science" = physics, chemistry, math. "Languages" = English, French, another modern language.

curriculum. In contrast, boys at single-sex schools were more likely never to have studied practical subjects and sports.

A minority of students stayed on at school from 16 to 18, and studied for A-level exams. Some 14.6% of boys and 14.3% of girls gained one or more A-level passes (at grades A to E) by 1976. Binary logistic regression analyses (Sullivan et al., 2010) revealed no statistically significant difference in the likelihood of gaining one or more A-level passes (at grades A to E) at a single-sex or co-educational school, for either boys or girls. However, there were substantial differences in the *subjects* that boys and girls passed at A-level at single-sex and co-educational schools.

Figure 16.6 shows that girls at single-sex schools were more likely than co-educated girls to get at least one A-level in math, physics, or chemistry. Boys at single-sex schools were slightly less likely than co-educated boys to get any A-levels in these subjects. Girls at both co-educational and girls' schools had similar chances of getting an A-level in English or a modern language. Boys at boys' schools were more likely than co-ed boys to get an A-level in these subjects.

The pattern shown in these graphs is confirmed by logistic regression analyses reported by Sullivan et al. (2010). Boys were significantly more likely to get an A-level in English or a modern language if they went to a boys-only school. Girls were significantly more likely, and boys significantly less likely, to get an A-level in math, physics, or chemistry if they attended a single-sex school.

In summary, girls at single-sex schools were substantially more likely than their co-educated peers to achieve a high level of examination success at age

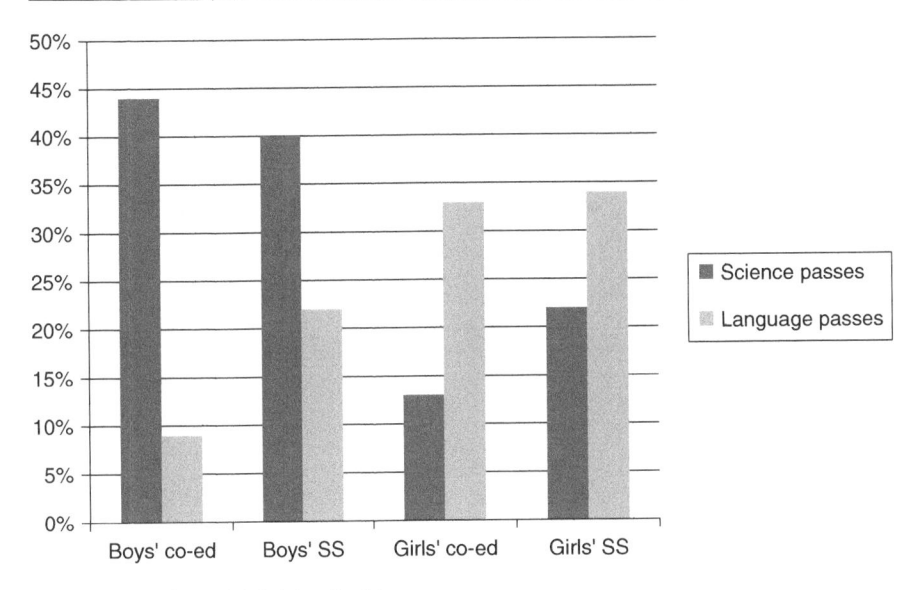

Figure 16.6 *A-level subject passes*
Notes: Includes only pupils who achieved at least one A-level pass.

16, but boys were neither significantly advantaged nor disadvantaged in terms of overall examination attainment by attending single-sex schools. One interpretation of this would be that boys tend to be relatively disruptive in class, and therefore girls receive less attention from teachers when there are boys present. Single-sex schools were associated with attainment in gender-atypical subject areas for both boys and girls. This supports the view that co-educational schools tended to exacerbate the problems of sex-stereotyping rather than remedy them. This may be due to peer pressures in the presence of the opposite sex.

5. Was there an impact of single-sex schooling on post-school qualifications?

Here we used the national sample again, including Scotland. Cohort members were asked about any new qualifications they had gained at each wave of the survey. Single-sex schooling was not significantly associated with either the chance of getting a degree by the age of 33, or having no qualifications by then, once school sector had been controlled (Sullivan et al., 2010).

The subject area of the highest qualification gained (reported by the cohort member) was significantly related to single-sex schooling. Because the cell sizes for each individual subject area were small, we grouped subjects according to whether they were "male-dominated," "female-dominated," or "integrated," "integrated disciplines" being defined as those with no more than 60% of one sex (coding due to Dale & Egerton, 1997). Figure 16.7 shows that women who had attended girls' schools were more likely than co-educated women to have

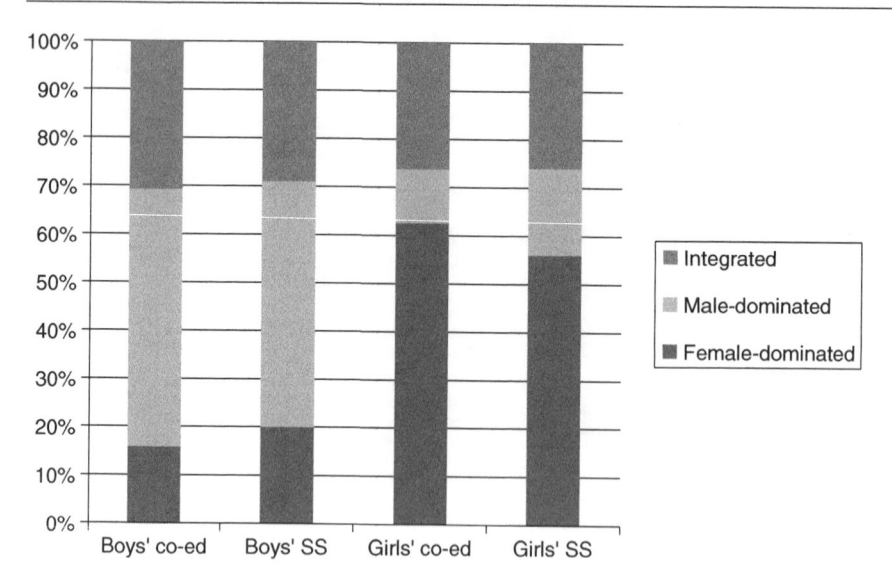

Figure 16.7 *Sex composition of highest qualification age 33*

"male-typed" highest qualifications; and men who went to boys' schools were more likely than co-educated men to have "female-typed" qualifications.

Regression analyses (Sullivan et al., 2010) confirmed that, other things equal, girls were significantly more likely to study "male-dominated" subjects, and less likely to study "female-dominated" subjects, if they had attended single-sex schools.

So, having been to a single-sex school was not linked, except through selective schooling, to the chances of an individual getting a degree or other post-school qualification, but it did influence the subject area of that qualification.

In summary, single-sex schooling was not linked to the level of qualification achieved by age 33, but was linked to the subject area of the qualification, suggesting long-term consequences of the stronger sex-stereotyping of the subject options taken by boys and girls in co-educational schools.

6. Did single-sex schooling have any impact on aspects of personal wellbeing in adult life?

To assess mental health and general wellbeing, we looked at the responses given at age 42 to the "malaise inventory," a 24-item scale designed to assess tendency to depression (Rutter et al., 1970). The items in this scale range from relatively minor symptoms, e.g., "Do you often have bad headaches?" to severe problems, e.g., "Have you ever had a nervous breakdown?"

Linear regression analysis (Sullivan et al., 2012) showed that, conditioning on background controls, there was a significant interaction between school sector and single-sex schooling. Men who had attended single-sex boys' schools in the private and grammar sectors suffered from slight but statistically significantly higher levels of malaise compared to their peers from comprehensive schools.

In summary, it is interesting that men who had attended selective and private single-sex schools were at greater risk of depression than men who had attended comprehensive single-sex schools. However, more important from our point of view is the absence of any overall difference for either men or women in their depression risk according to whether they attended a single-sex or co-educational school.

7. Did single-sex schooling have any impact on adult domestic life and views on gender equality?

In the 1958 cohort, the vast majority of those who formed any partnership eventually married. We found no link between single-sex schooling and the chances of marriage by the ages of 33 or 42.

We looked for evidence of same-sex relationships in household composition, but such cases were far too rare – only 21 men and 22 women reported living with same-sex partners at age 42 – to be a reliable indicator of sexual preference, let alone a basis for analysis. We are therefore unable to comment on whether co-education did provide the "clean, healthy natural atmosphere" so commended by its early advocates (see Dyhouse, 1985, on the Progressive Education Movement).

Cohort members who were married or cohabiting were asked to rate the quality of their relationship from 1 (extremely happy) to 7 (extremely unhappy). They were also asked whether they ever regretted marrying or cohabiting with their partner, and whether they would marry/cohabit with the same person if they could have their time again. We modeled this outcome using binary logistic regression (modeling "extremely happy" in contrast to any other response) and found that the coefficient for single-sex schooling was negative for both sexes, but not statistically significant for men. For women, it just achieved statistical significance at the 0.05 level (Sullivan et al., 2012).

In addition, we examined the risk of divorce or separation by age 42 for those who had ever been married. Men who had been to single-sex schools were somewhat more likely to have divorced or separated (except in the private sector) than those in co-educational schools (see Figure 16.8).

Regression analyses (Leonard et al., 2007; Sullivan et al., 2012) conditioning on background controls show that there was a statistically significant increased risk of divorce or separation for men from single-sex schools. For women, however, there was no significant link.

At age 33, cohort members who were married or cohabiting were asked whether they or their partner most often carried out a range of household tasks: cooking the main meal, laundry, cleaning, shopping, etc. We found no significant link between single-sex schooling and later domestic division of labor.

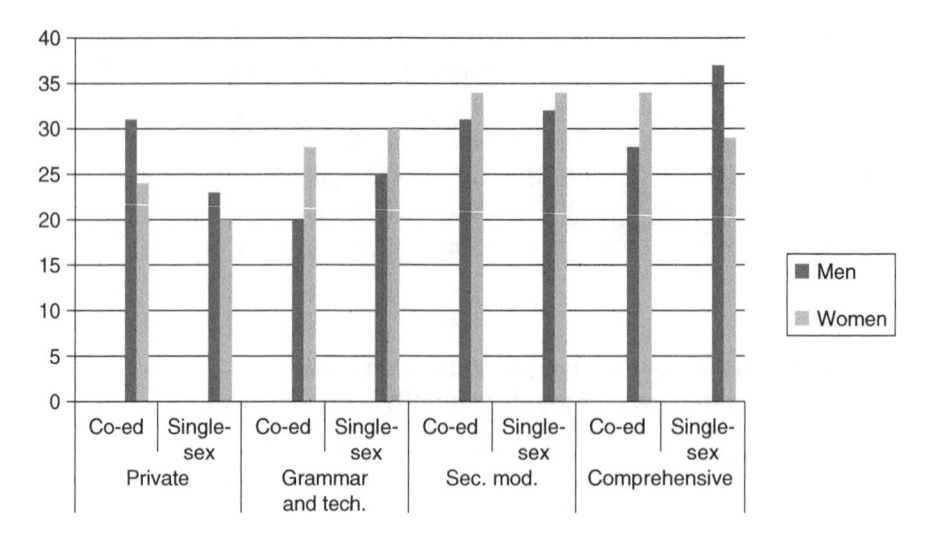

Figure 16.8 *Divorce or separation by age 42, by gender and school sector*

At age 33, cohort members also responded to a series of Likert questions regarding their attitudes toward gender and work, such as "there should be more women bosses," "men and women should do the same jobs," "where both partners work full-time, housework should be shared equally," etc. We again found no link between single-sex schooling and attitudes to gender roles on these measures.

Regression analyses on outcomes for men and women show no link between single-sex schooling and either the chance of having a child by age 42, or age of first childbearing. In particular, despite the concerns of religious opponents of mixed schooling for adolescents, we found no significant deterrent effect of single-sex schooling on teenage parenthood for either girls or boys.

Overall, there were a large number of outcomes for which we could show no effect of attending a single-sex school. Perhaps surprisingly, teenage pregnancy was no more or less likely for respondents from single-sex schools. There was no difference in the likelihood of having children, or in the age of first childbirth, according to whether the respondent had been to a single-sex or a co-educational school. Neither attitudes to working women nor the domestic division of labor were linked to attendance at a single-sex school, for either men or women. There was little link between single-sex schooling and reported relationship quality for either sex (there was a marginally significant dip in quality for women who had been to girls' schools). However, for men, there was a statistically significant link between single-sex schooling and divorce. This lends some support to those who have expressed concerns about the impact of single-sex schooling on later relationships between the sexes, though it is unclear why this impact on divorce should be limited to men.

Table 16.2. *Economic activity at 42, by gender*

Main economic activity	Men (%)	Women (%)	Total (N)
Full-time employment	88	45	7,514
Part-time employment	2	34	2,107
Family	1	13	791
Unemployed including govt. scheme	3	2	269
Full-time education	0.2	1	58
Disabled or sick	5	5	533
Retired or other	1	1	108
Total N	5,608	5,772	11,380

8. Was single-sex schooling associated with any labor-market outcomes at age 42 (year 2000)?

Women's labor market participation and whether they were working, and whether jobs were full- or part-time, is shown in Table 16.2. Of women born in 1958, 45% were in full-time employment at age 42, 34% were in part-time employment, and 13% were at home looking after their families (88% of men were in full-time work).

We modeled women's likelihood of being in (a) full-time employment, (b) part-time employment, and (c) being at home with the family (Sullivan et al., 2011). Conditioning on relevant background controls, single-sex schooling was not significantly associated with any of these outcomes.

Socioeconomic status is based on the individual's current or most recent job at age 42, categorized according to the National Statistics Socio-economic Classification (NS-SEC). NS-SEC is an occupational schema, and determines class position in terms of employment relations (Goldthorpe & McKnight, 2006). Figure 16.9 shows the socioeconomic class of the cohort members' current or most recent occupation at age 42. Women were underrepresented among employers, managers, and professionals, as well as skilled manual and own-account workers. Women were overrepresented among junior non-manual and personal service workers and ancillary professionals (this category includes teachers and nurses).

Although the NS-SEC occupational classification cannot be viewed as a straightforward hierarchy, the first three categories, comprising employers, managers, and professionals, are generally seen as relatively high status, and often referred to as the "service class" or "salariat." We modeled entry to the salariat by age 42 in order to assess whether single-sex schooling was linked to this outcome, conditioning on controls for prior characteristics (Sullivan et al., 2011). We found no significant link between single-sex schooling and access to the salariat for either men or women.

[Bar chart showing social class categories with Men and Women bars, x-axis 0 to 30]

- Employers and managers, large
- Employers and managers, small
- Professionals
- Ancillary professionals
- Own account
- Foremen and supervisors
- Junior non-manual
- Personal service
- Skilled manual
- Unskilled manual

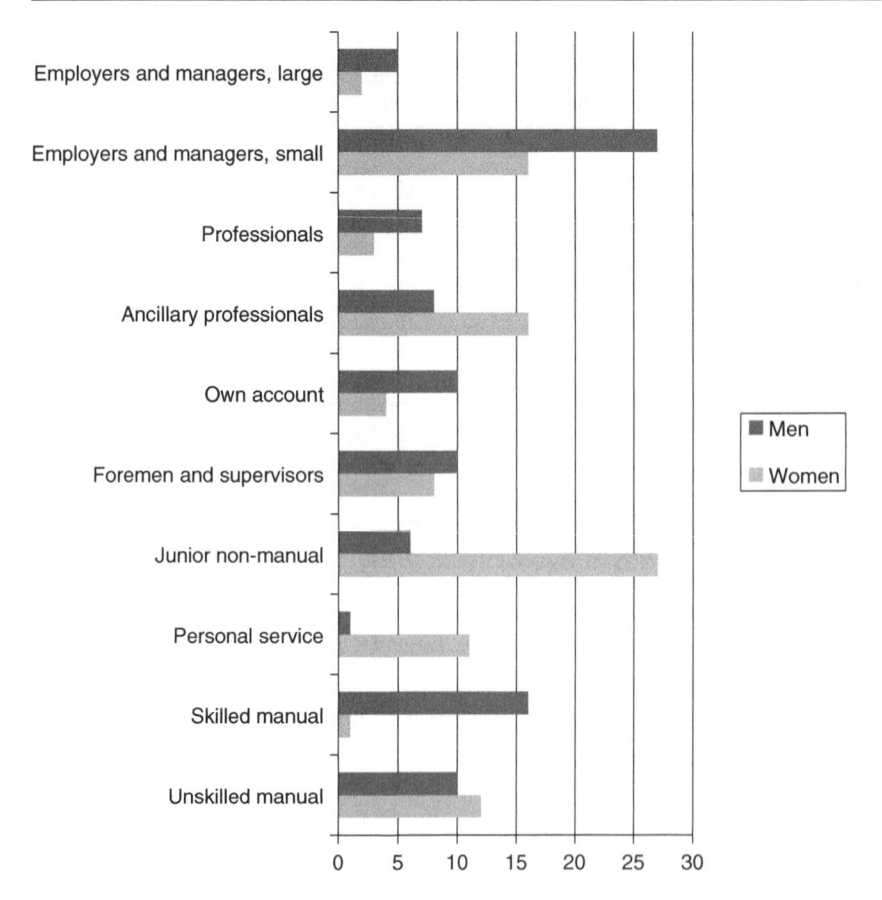

Figure 16.9 *Social class of cohort member at current or most recent job by age 42 by gender*

Many occupations are highly sex-segregated. We used the classification of occupational segregation proposed by Hakim (1998), where occupations with 25% to 54% women are described as "integrated." The asymmetry, that 25% women is considered integrated, but 25% men is considered women-dominated, is designed to reflect the fact that there were fewer women than men in the labor market. This definition is not necessarily suitable for all times or places. Figure 16.10 shows the proportions of men and women from single-sex and co-educational schools who were in women-dominated, men-dominated, or integrated jobs at age 42.

Figure 16.10 gives the impression that men and women who went to single-sex schools went on to have a less sex-segregated experience of the labor market, since single-sex educated men and women were relatively likely to be found in "integrated" occupations. However, the integrated occupations also tended to be higher status than the sex-segregated occupations. Thus, the fact that the single-sex schools were found disproportionately in the private and grammar sectors largely accounts for the apparent effect of single-sex schooling.

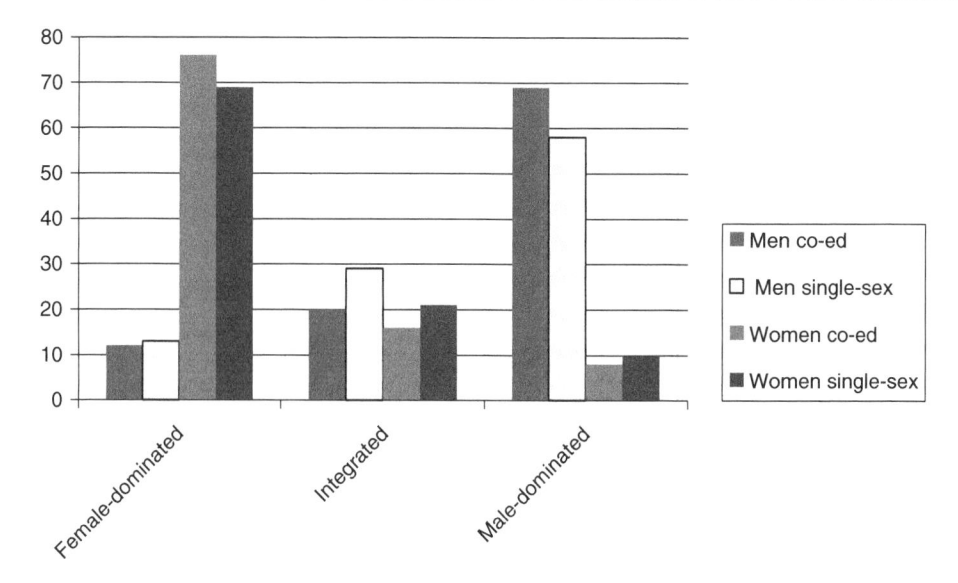

Figure 16.10 *Occupational segregation (Hakim's classification) at current or most recent job by age 42*
Note: Includes only those currently employed at age 42.

In regressions controlling for pupils' background characteristics (Sullivan et al., 2011), no significant effect of single-sex schooling on occupational segregation at age 42 was found. We modeled the likelihood of the cohort members being in (a) integrated, (b) male-dominated, and (c) female-dominated occupations, using logistic regression, and ran separate regressions for men and women.

Figure 16.11 shows the mean hourly wages of men and women in paid employment (reported by the cohort members), according to whether they had attended single-sex or co-educational schools, and according to school sector. Women were paid substantially less than men; but across school sectors, women who had attended single-sex schools gained higher wages.

Regression analyses (Sullivan et al., 2011) confirm that, conditioning on background controls, there was a statistically significant positive association between single-sex schooling and wages for women, but not for men. Women who had been to girls' schools received a pay premium of about 5% at age 42 compared to other women. This advantage was accounted for by their superior examination results at age 16. It may seem surprising that single-sex schooling should have had a positive impact on women's wages, despite having no statistically significant impact on access to the salariat or to integrated or male-dominated occupations. It is likely that these variables are too broad to pick up the effect identified by the more fine-grained wages variable.

Our analyses also established that men gained more advantage than women from having attended private schools and from having fathers with higher social class jobs. This implies that the study of social mobility needs to take account of gendered processes.

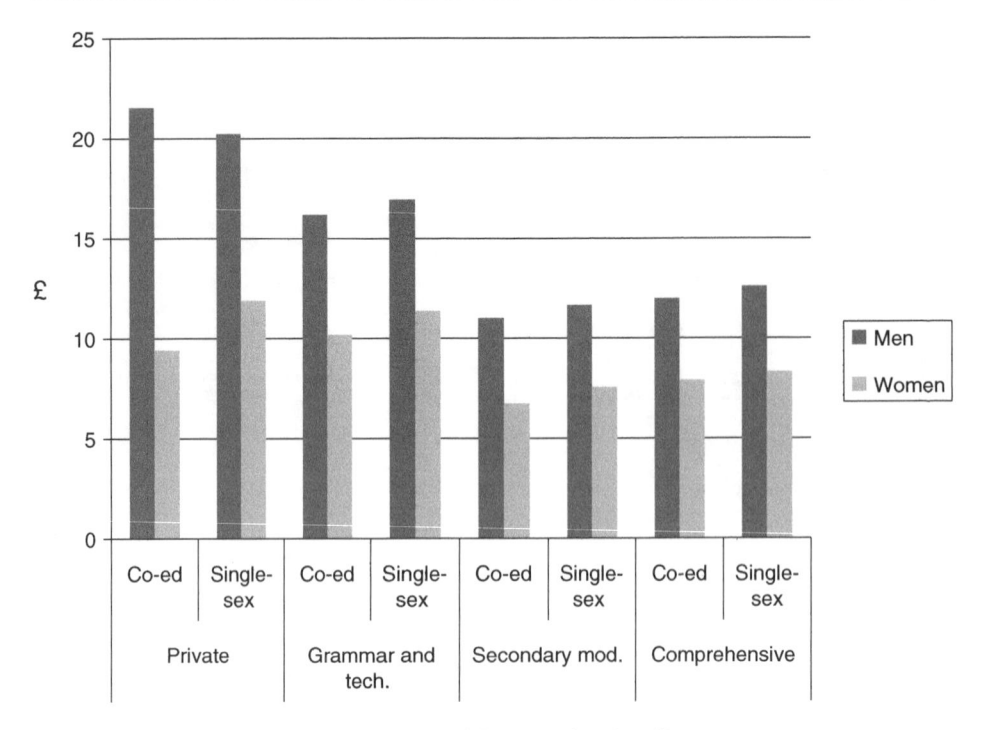

Figure 16.11 *Hourly wages (£) of those employed at 42*

Overall, while the men and women of the 1958 cohort had different experiences of paid work and its remuneration at age 42, we found little evidence that having attended a single-sex secondary school had a direct impact on labor market success, or occupational segregation. For men, we found a lasting advantage from having attended a private school, but nothing directly attributable to having been educated with or without girls. Among girls, we did find a long-term legacy of having been to a single-sex rather than a co-educational school. Women who had been to girls' schools received a pay premium of about 5% at age 42 compared to other women. This advantage was accounted for by their superior examination results at age 16.

Summary and conclusion

Twice as many graduates in the 1958 cohort had been to single-sex schools as the rest of the cohort (46% versus 22%). This tells us that a co-educational background is less common for the currently middle-aged elite than for most of their contemporaries. However, this reflects the socially selective nature of the single-sex schools, rather than their single-sexness in itself. This confirms the importance of controlling adequately for selection bias, something that previous studies of single-sex education have rarely been able to do.

We found that single-sex schooling had a positive impact on academic outcomes at age 16 for girls, and no impact at all for boys. Single-sex schooling was not independently linked to the likelihood of gaining A-level or degree-level qualifications.

However, we did find that single-sex schooling was in itself related to girls getting qualifications in math and sciences and boys getting qualifications in English and modern languages. Also, girls at girls' schools were more confident than co-educated girls in their abilities in math and sciences, while boys at boys' schools were relatively confident in their abilities in English. So, single-sex schooling moderated the effect of gender-stereotyping in terms of self-concept and choice of field of study.

For boys, single-sex schooling was also linked to a dislike of school, and a greater chance of divorce by age 42. For girls, the picture was more positive, as single-sex schooling was linked to higher wages by 42. For both sexes, a wide range of outcomes were not related to single-sex schooling. Perhaps most surprisingly, there was no link to attitudes toward gender roles.

It is generally positive research findings that generate the most interest. However, it is important not to lose sight of the fact that most of our results showed no significant difference between people who had attended single-sex and co-educational schools. Overall, then, we can conclude that single-sex schooling had less impact on many of the outcomes considered here than might have been expected by either the proponents or the opponents of single-sex schooling.

Of course, our results relate to schooling in a particular historical period in Britain, and clearly both co-educational and single-sex schools have changed since the 1970s. Equally, both co-educational and single-sex schools differ in different national contexts. One major change in Britain is that many single-sex schools now have mixed "sixth forms" (the non-compulsory final 2 years of schooling, from the ages of 16 to 18). This allows pupils to mix with the opposite sex before leaving school, and may make future relationship difficulties less likely.

What implications does our study have for today's debates? The fact that girls fared better academically in single-sex than in co-educational schools during the 1970s cannot be taken to imply that this must still be the case. The British birth cohort surveys of 1946, 1958, and 1970 have documented the changing relative educational achievements of males and females, alongside changes in the role of women within the labor market and the wider society (Makepeace, Joshi, Woods, & Galinda-Rueda, 2003). It is not widely recognized that, in terms of overall educational qualifications at 16, girls were fractionally ahead of boys even in 1974, when the 1958 cohort were 16. This is despite the fact that many of the parents and teachers of that generation would not have thought that academic qualifications were as important for girls as they were for boys. Girls' achievement at 16 was in spite of their subordinate status, and boys still achieved higher levels of post-compulsory qualifications. Girls' marginal average advantage at the 5+ A–C benchmark was entirely driven by girls in girls' schools, as co-educated girls were slightly less likely to achieve this benchmark than co-educated boys.

The fact that girls are now outperforming boys in terms of academic attainment at school has been an enormous political issue in countries including Great Britain, the US, and Australia. It is plausible to infer that, in Britain, this gap would be even larger had it not been for the decline in single-sex schooling. Yet it is important to point out that, if we can extrapolate from our findings, an increase in the provision of single-sex schooling would have improved girls' academic attainments, but not at the expense of the boys, as boys in boys' schools did just as well as co-educated boys.

Hubbard and Datnow (2002) point out that single-sex schooling needs to be driven by an agenda of gender equity for both boys and girls. Of course, we can say the same for co-educational schooling. Our findings have implications for co-educational as well as single-sex schools. In both of these contexts, there is a need to move beyond seeing girls' versus boys' achievement as a zero sum game, where female success must imply male failure. Broader gender issues should not be forgotten: notably, the issue of the ways in which both girls and boys may be trammeled by sex stereotypes during their school years, which set them on divergent pathways in their later lives and careers. The fact that co-education has exacerbated the gendered nature of students' attainments, not just at school, but also in terms of their post-school qualifications, suggests that gendered norms regarding education are not immutable, and can be influenced by the context of schooling. The fact that boys and girls still tend to pursue highly gendered educational trajectories suggests that more needs to be done within co-educational schools to challenge this.

From a policy perspective, social impacts need to be considered alongside the academic and economic outcomes. Our work suggests that girls who had attended single-sex schools fared well in examinations at age 16 compared to girls who had attended co-educational schools, and that girls who had attended girls' schools also went on to earn higher wages later in life. Also, self-concept and participation in math and science, English and modern languages, were more starkly gendered for boys and girls in the co-educational schools. Clearly, single-sex schooling had advantages for this cohort, especially for the girls. The difficulty is to weigh these advantages against the social disadvantages, which are more apparent for boys than for girls, including a dislike of school and a raised risk of divorce. For a previous generation of "progressive" educationalists, the answer to this dilemma was clear – boys' wellbeing trumped girls' academic attainment. However, these social disadvantages may not be an inevitable consequence of single-sex schooling. No doubt social outcomes varied by individual school, and it is unfortunate that our data do not allow us to investigate such variability. We are also conscious that our findings raise many questions regarding the daily lived experiences underpinning the aggregate differences that we observe here. We hope that future research will be able to take up the issues raised by our findings and develop them, bringing in both quantitative and qualitative longitudinal school- and pupil-level data.

References

Benn, C., & Simon, B. (1970). *Half way there: Report on the British comprehensive school reform*. London: Penguin.

Bone, A. (1983). *Girls and girl-only schools: A review of the evidence*. Manchester: Equal Opportunities Commission.

Brice, I. (1980). The early coeducation movement in English secondary education. *Melbourne Studies in Education*, 134–177.

Bynner, J., & Joshi, H. (2007). Building the evidence base from longitudinal data: The aims, content and achievements of the British Birth Cohort Studies. *Innovations*, 20(2), 159–179.

Dale, A., & Egerton, M. (1997). *Highly educated women: Evidence from the National Child Development Study*. London: HMSO.

Dale, R. (1969). *Mixed or single-sex school?* (Vol. 1). London: Routledge & Kegan Paul.

(1971). *Mixed or single-sex school?* (Vol. 2). London: Routledge & Kegan Paul.

(1974). *Mixed or single-sex school?* (Vol. 3). London: Routledge & Kegan Paul.

Dyhouse, C. (1985). Feminism and the debate over coeducational/single-sex schooling: Some historical perspectives. In J. Purvis (Ed.), *The education of girls and women*. Leicester: History of Education Society.

Faraday, A. (1989). Lessoning lesbians: Girls' schools, co-education and anti-lesbianism between the wars. In C. Jones & P. Mahony (Ed.), *Learning our lines*. London: The Women's Press.

Goldthorpe, J., & McKnight, A. (2006). The economic basis of social class. In S. Morgan, D. B. Grusky, & G. S. Fields (Eds.), *Mobility and inequality: Frontiers of research from sociology and economics*. Stanford University Press.

Hakim, C. (1998). *Social change and innovation in the labour market*. Oxford University Press.

Hawkes, D., & Plewis, I. (2006). Modelling non-response in the National Child Development Study. *Journal of the Royal Statistical Society, A*, 169, 479–491.

Hubbard, L., & Datnow, A. (2002). Are single-sex schools sustainable in the public sector. In A. Datnow & L. Hubbard (Eds.), *Gender in policy and practice: Perspectives on single-sex and co-educational schooling* (pp. 109–132). New York: Routledge Falmer.

Leonard, D. (1996). The debate around coeducation. In S. Kemal, D. Leonard, M. Pringle, & S. Sadeque (Eds.), *Targeting underachievement: Boys or girls?* (pp. 21–29). London: Institute of Education.

Leonard, D., Joshi, H., & Sullivan, A. (2007). *Single-sex and co-educational schooling: Lifecourse consequences?* ESRC report. Swindon: ESRC.

Makepeace, G., Joshi, H., Woods, L., & Galinda-Rueda, F. (2003). From school to the labour market. In E. Ferri, J. Bynner, & M. Wadsworth (Eds.), *Changing*

Britain, changing lives: Three generations at the turn of the century (pp. 29–104). London: Bedford Way Papers.

Power, C., & Elliott, J. (2006). Cohort profile: 1958 British birth cohort (National Child Development Study). *International Journal of Epidemiology*, 35(1), 34–41.

Rutter, M., Tizard, J., & Whitmore, K. (1970). *Education, health and behaviour*. London: Longmans.

Shaw, J. (1976). Finishing school: Some implications of sex-segregated education. In D. L. Barker & S. Allen (Eds.), *Sexual divisions and society: Process and change* (pp. 133–149). London: Tavistock.

Smithers, A., & Robinson, P. (2006). *The paradox of single-sex and co-educational schooling*. University of Buckingham.

Spender, D., & Sarah, E. (Eds.). (1980). *Learning to lose: Sexism and education*. London: Women's Press.

Spielhofer, T., Benton, T., & Schagen, S. (2004). A study of the effects of school size and single-sex education in English schools. *Research Papers in Education*, 19(2), 133–159.

Steedman, J. (1980). *Progress in secondary schools*. London: National Children's Bureau.

(1983a). *Examination results in mixed and single sex schools: Findings from the National Child Development Study*. Manchester: Equal Opportunities Commission.

(1983b). *Examination results in selective and non-selective schools*. London: National Children's Bureau.

(1983c). *Examination results in selective and non-selective schools: Vol. 2. Appendices*. London: National Children's Bureau.

Sullivan, A. (2006). *Academic self-concept, gender and single-sex schooling in the 1970 cohort*. CLS Working Paper. London: Centre for Longitudinal Studies.

(2009). Academic self-concept, gender, and single-sex schooling. *British Educational Research Journal*, 35(2), 259–288.

Sullivan, A., Joshi, H., & Leonard, D. (2010). Single-sex schooling and academic attainment at school and through the lifecourse. *American Educational Research Journal*, 47(1), 6–36.

(2011). Single-sex schooling and labour market outcomes. *Oxford Review of Education*, 37(3), 311–332.

(2012). Single-sex and co-educational schooling: What are the social and family outcomes, in the short and longer term? *Longitudinal and Life Course Studies*, 3(1), 137–157.

Warrington, M., & Younger, M. (2001). Single-sex classes and equal opportunities for girls and boys: Perspectives through time from a mixed comprehensive school in England. *Oxford Review of Education*, 27(3), 339–356.

Younger, M., & Warrington, M. (2006). Would Harry and Hermione have done better in single-sex classes? A review of single-sex teaching in co-educational schools in the United Kingdom. *American Educational Research Journal*, 43(4), 579–620.

17 Pathways to educational attainment in middle adulthood: the role of gender and parental educational expectations in adolescence

Miia Bask, Laura Ferrer-Wreder, Katariina Salmela-Aro and Lars R. Bergman

Abstract

In this chapter, we apply the expectancy-value model of motivation, particularly the family socialization aspect of the model (Eccles (Parsons) et al., 1983; Eccles, 1994, 2007; Wigfield & Eccles, 2002) to address a number of key questions regarding gender differences in adult attainment, in particular educational attainment. When some individuals in the work force of today were children, what kinds of expectations did they have for themselves? What expectations did their parents have for them? Did these expectations vary for girls and boys? Were parents' expectations about their children's future education related to the actual education that these adolescents later attained in midlife? How did the child's academic ability and characteristics of the family figure into this picture? We present original empirical findings, drawing on data collected for a Swedish longitudinal study that spans from childhood to middle adulthood. In line with the expectancy-value model of motivation, the family's socioeconomic status (SES) was identified as an important predictor of several outcomes. Consistent with the model, for both genders, the family's SES and parental educational expectations in middle adolescence predicted middle adult educational attainment. The importance of grades differed by gender in that the mathematics grade was a statistically significant predictor of middle adult educational attainment for males, while for females grades in Swedish were a statistically significant predictor of middle adult educational attainment. In this chapter, we situated these study findings in the wider pertinent scholarly literature and discussed the implications of our results as they might relate to efforts to promote equitable and optimal life chances for the current generation of European girls and boys.

Educational attainment in Europe

In several post-industrial societies, there is evidence of increased participation in university education (e.g., Beck-Domzalska, 2007; Côté & Allahar, 2006). For example, according to a 2005 European Union (EU) Labour Force Survey, surveyed Europeans in their 30s had greater educational attainment (in upper secondary and university education[1]) than those in their 50s (Beck-Domzalska, 2007). In some cases, women's representation in this wider generational trend of increased educational attainment outstripped that of men (e.g., Beck-Domzalska, 2007; Côté & Allahar, 2006; Korpi & Stern, 2003). Considering 25 countries in the EU and associated countries, for instance, 3% units more women than men in their 30s attained a university education in 2005 (i.e., 30% of women compared to 27% of men; Beck-Domzalska, 2007). This trend towards greater university educational attainment among women in their 30s over men is in contrast to those in their 50s (see also McMunn, Webb, Bartley, Blane, & Netuveli, this volume). For this older cohort, the 3% units differential was reversed in favor of men's greater university educational attainment relative to women (i.e., 19% of women relative to 22% of men attained a university education; Beck-Domzalska, 2007). As is sometimes the case with trends across the EU, there are interesting across and within country variations (see also Jerrim & Schoon, this volume).

In Sweden, the overall trend toward increased university-level educational attainment was supported by data from the Swedish 2005 EU Labour Force Survey (Beck-Domzalska, 2007) as well as other national statistics collected on this subject (Batljan, Lagergren, & Thorslund, 2009; The Swedish National Agency for Education, 2006). Regarding cohort-based gender differences in university educational attainment, Sweden has not appeared to exactly follow EU trends of university educational attainment. Among two cohorts of Swedes born 20 years apart, for instance, more women than men attained a university education in both the older and younger cohort (9% units more women than men in their 30s and 11% units more women than men in their 50s; Beck-Domzalska, 2007).

These national trends in university educational attainment by Swedish women and men can be situated at the intersection of a particular time and place. For example, in 2005 a cohort in their 50s would have been adolescents approximately during the period from 1965 to 1975 (e.g., 10-year-olds in 1965, 15-year-olds in 1970). In this chapter, we present original research findings about the educational attainment of a Swedish cohort who were in their teens from 1965 to 1975. In particular, we use data from the Swedish Individual Development and Adaptation (IDA) cohort (Bergman & Magnusson, 1997; Magnusson, 1988; Trost & Bergman, 2004). The data for this study were collected during an interesting historical period, during which on a national level increasing numbers of Swedes were becoming involved in higher education, and during a time of growing parity between the genders in their involvement in university education. However, unlike the similarly aged cohort of 50-year-olds in the 2005 EU Labour Force Survey, this cohort was from a particular region of Sweden. Cohort members completed a personal interview and numerous questionnaires that provided

---

[1] Upper secondary education is called "*Gymnasium*" in some European countries (ISCED 3 and 4 – upper secondary and postsecondary non-tertiary education). European university education is also sometimes called tertiary education (e.g., ISCED 5 and 6 – first and second stages of tertiary education; Beck-Domzalska, 2007).

very detailed information about their life situation in midlife, including different career outcomes. Linking experiences during adolescence to achievements in middle adulthood (i.e., age 50), this chapter provides an additional perspective on the extent to which the Swedish experience in university educational attainment for women and men may or may not have departed from gender/cohort educational attainment trends in other EU countries.

The Swedish educational system

In terms of place, it is important to orient oneself to the educational system in Sweden. In the Swedish educational system, compulsory education continues until Grade 9 (approximately 16 years old), after which adolescents can elect to discontinue their education or pursue an upper secondary school educational track, for approximately 3 years (The Swedish National Agency for Education, 2009b). The upper secondary school educational tracks are geared toward an academic or vocational education. The academic track is more oriented towards preparing students for university than the vocational track (The Swedish National Agency for Education, 2009b). In Sweden during the 1960s and 1970s, family income was not necessarily higher for those who would select an academic upper secondary education compared to those with a vocational educational track (Statistics Sweden, 2010).

In recent decades, Sweden has been viewed as a country that aspires to achieve a gender-equal state with welfare policies that support both men and women to have an equal opportunity to fully participate in the educational system, labor market, and at home as parents (Korpi & Stern, 2003; The Swedish National Agency for Education, 2006). Most of the individuals in the IDA study came of age in a medium-sized and geographically southern centrally located Swedish city. This cohort grew up during a period (in the 1960s) in which there was a gender differential in favor of males compared to females in terms of university educational attainment (The Swedish National Agency for Education, 2009a). For example, more fathers of the individuals in this cohort had a university education compared to mothers (5.2% of fathers and 1.0% of mothers had a university education). However, the Swedish national educational policy documents of the time (in the 1960s when the gender revolution took place) were stressing the need for girls to pursue upper secondary and university education (The Swedish National Agency for Education, 2006).

The IDA cohort subsequently was more likely to pursue a university education than previous cohorts, and this at a time when more Swedes generally were participating in university education than prior generations. At the same time, there was increasing gender parity in university educational attainment. For example, in 1975 and 1985, this cohort would have been in their 20s to 30s and in 1985 there was almost the same number of men and women attaining a university education in Sweden. From 1985 onwards gender differences in university educational attainment in Sweden, on a national level, shifted in favor of females compared to males (The Swedish National Agency for Education, 2006), reflecting general trends of women outperforming men regarding educational attainment (see also Heckhausen; McMunn et al.; Perez-Felkner, McDonald, & Schneider, this volume).

Educational attainment through a theoretical lens

To guide the discussion of the potential importance of structural, individual, and family-level factors regarding educational attainment, Eccles and colleagues' expectancy-value model of motivation will be used (Eccles (Parsons) et al., 1983; Eccles, 1994, 2007; Wigfield & Eccles, 2002). The expectancy-value model is based on several perspectives, including expectancy-value models of behavioral choice, achievement, attribution, and social cognitive theories. This model is designed to address the question of why people make the choices that they make when it comes to education, leisure, and occupation. The model is also concerned with the explanation of differences in performance in these areas. For example, why do some people attain a university education and why do others take different paths through and out of education?

According to Eccles and colleagues, the choices made in achievement-related settings and performance are a product of a dynamic, ongoing interaction of several aspects of the child (or person), the child in relationship with socialization agents (such as parents, teachers, or peers), and other aspects of the child's context. Eccles (2007) theorized a multi-determined, dynamic developmental process. We have been selective in our treatment of this model, focusing on the role of family and parents. Parents are not the only socialization agents of importance in Eccles' model. However, parents and the family figure very prominently in our study. Therefore, we have chosen to highlight this particular aspect of the model, because it relates most directly to our own research questions. This part of the model is also called the *family socialization model* (Jacobs & Eccles, 2000), and it emphasizes the role of family processes in the child's achievement-related development.

Jacobs and Eccles (2000) explained how the family and parents may influence a child's achievement-related choices and performance. In this model, achievement-related choices and performance are influenced by characteristics of the family (e.g., demographics and resources, such as parents' education or family income) and characteristics of the child (e.g., gender, actual level of ability in a particular domain, such as the child's mathematics abilities). The model is a multiple-person, dynamic, and multi-construct model in which characteristics of the family and child interact with each other. Beliefs and behaviors are a prominent mechanism of change in the model (e.g., parents' general and child-specific beliefs). For example, parents' general beliefs involve views of how the world works (or is), including beliefs about gender roles or the value of particular occupations. Parents' child-specific beliefs involve parents' views of their child, which for instance could include an evaluation of the child's abilities in different achievement-related settings like school. Parents' evaluations in turn provide a basis for parents' expectations about their child's probable future (e.g., child-specific beliefs about whether the parent's child might pursue a particular educational track or type of profession).

Gender has been an important point of inquiry in the expectancy-value model of motivation (e.g., Eccles, 1987, 1994). Many studies conducted from the vantage point of this model deal with examining the extent of gender differences/similarities in task value, self-concept, and performance in mathematics and languages among children and adolescents (e.g., Nagy et al., 2010). For example, from this research field, it has been demonstrated longitudinally and cross-nationally (in the United States (US), Germany, and Australia) that adolescent boys had a more favorable view of their own mathematical ability relative to adolescent girls (Nagy et al., 2010; see also Chow & Salmela-Aro; Parker, Nagy, Trautwein, & Lüdtke; Wang & Kenny, this volume).

Parental beliefs, both general and child-specific, set the stage for parental action in the types of encouragement and opportunities that parents provide for their children (Chhin, Bleeker, & Jacobs, 2008). Parents' beliefs and behaviors also help to inform the task value a child gives to a particular activity, goal, or outcome (e.g., whether it would be worthwhile to try to do well on a test, or to try to get good enough grades to pursue a university-bound educational track). Through this interaction between aspects of the environment, the family, and child, the parents' and the child's beliefs and behaviors come together and are hypothesized to have a significant influence on the child when she or he is going to make a choice about how to (or whether to) approach and take part (and perhaps even succeed) in an achievement-related activity.

Performance in school-based achievement settings, gender, and parental educational expectations: the research literature

Using Eccles and colleagues' (1983) model as the conceptual guide, the focal point of this chapter involves an exploration of the role of parental educational expectations in adolescence (which could be regarded as a reflection of parents' child-specific beliefs in Eccles' model) to educational attainment in middle adulthood. According to the theory described in this chapter and as indicated by the research literature, educational attainment in adulthood has been connected to several characteristics of the family of origin as well as the childhood characteristics. Specifically, parents' SES and educational attainment as well as early indicators of ability (e.g., intellectual ability, prior academic achievement) are often found to be explanatory variables in educational achievement and attainment models (Andres & Grayson, 2003; Bleeker & Jacobs, 2004;

Ceci & Williams, 1997; Deary, Strand, Smith, & Fernandes, 2007; Ganzach, 2000; Gottfredson, 2002; Judge, Ilies, & Dimotakis, 2010). Additionally, parent and child educational expectations are significantly and positively related to one another (Ashby & Schoon, 2010; Garg, Kauppi, Lewko, & Urajnik, 2002; Schoon & Parsons, 2002; Trusty, Watts, & Erdmann, 1997).

As educational expectations are the subject of this chapter, it is useful to distinguish this construct from educational aspirations. Educational expectations and aspirations, while they might be confused in everyday language, are different psychological constructs that may also lead to distinct outcomes (Boxer, Goldstein, DeLorenzo, Savoy, & Mercado, 2011). Educational expectations are grounded in reality, reflecting evaluations of what seems most likely to happen to an individual in the future, whereas aspirations refer to perceptions of an ideal outcome or situation given optimal circumstances (Cook et al., 1996). Rytkönen, Aunola, and Nurmi (2005) examined parental educational expectations for their adolescent children, and recognized that the child's past academic performance was associated with parental educational expectations, reflecting the relationship between expectations and objective criteria. For this reason, we expected a child's academic achievement to be related to the educational expectations held for that child by her or his parents.

A case in point of the importance of family characteristics to educational attainment can be found in the results of a Canadian longitudinal study (N = 1,055; Pathways on Life's Way Project) that indicated that parents' educational attainment and father's occupation (as one latent construct) were significantly related to children's educational attainment at 5 and 10 years after high school graduation (Andres & Grayson, 2003). Similarly, in a cross-sectional analysis of middle adults in the Swedish Adoption/Twin Study on Aging, a positive correlation was found between parental SES in childhood and educational attainment measured in middle adulthood (Judge et al., 2010).[2]

Beyond family characteristics (e.g., parents' educational attainment or family income), some studies have added additional constructs in order to better understand factors that have the potential to shape pathways to educational attainment. For example, in a US study (N = 8,570; the National Longitudinal Survey of Youth [NLSY]), family income, parents' education, as well as the young person's general cognitive ability and educational expectations (measured at the ages of 15 to 23) were significantly related to educational attainment in young adulthood (measured at the ages of 27 to 34; Ganzach, 2000).

It should be reiterated that what is of most interest in the present inquiry is an investigation of whether or not parental educational expectations remain important as predictors of their children's educational attainment even with the contribution of well-known other explanatory constructs taken into consideration,

---

[2] SES in childhood was measured in this study retrospectively by participants' report of their parents' education and status of parents' occupation, as well as other financially linked aspects of family life (Judge et al., 2010).

such as parents' educational attainment, family income, child/adolescent intellectual ability, and the child's prior academic performance. Regarding prior research on this question, two studies can be highlighted that specifically deal with parental expectations for educational attainment and offer an approximate model for the current study. The two studies by Neuenschwander, Vida, Garrett, and Eccles (2007) and Zhan (2006), however, use as their main outcome variable school-based performance on standardized achievement tests rather than educational attainment in adulthood.

Zhan (2006) found in a 2-year panel longitudinal study that an index of family wealth (e.g., assets) and mother's education were related to children's educational performance 2 years later. As in the aforementioned Ganzach (2000) study, Zhan also made use of the NLSY, but in this instance analyzed and reported data from the original longitudinal study participants (women only) and one of their children (N = 1,370 children 5 to 14 years old). Educational performance was indexed in Zhan's study by standardized achievement test scores in mathematics and reading. The relation between assets and mother's education and the child's academic performance was mediated by parents' expectations for their child's educational attainment. Interestingly, for this US cohort composed of children and adolescents (in the 2000s) and their mothers, mothers had higher educational expectations if the child included in the longitudinal study was a daughter rather than a son (Zhan, 2006). Similar findings are reported using evidence from three British cohort studies (Schoon, 2010).

In a conceptually related study, Neuenschwander et al. (2007) used evidence from a cross-sectional study of 11-year-olds in the US and Switzerland (N = 3,350) to show that parents' educational expectations were related to the child's performance on standardized achievement tests and this association was found even with the child's ability taken into consideration. Additionally, the influence of family income on the child's performance on standardized achievement tests was mediated by parents' educational expectations of their child and the child's self-beliefs (i.e., self-concept of ability). There was no report in this study of analyses that would speak to the question of whether or not parental educational expectations differed by gender.

In line with Eccles' model, the extant empirical research on this topic supports the importance of family characteristics as influential in partially explaining performance in school-based achievement situations (e.g., standardized achievement tests, later educational attainment). The relevant research literature also supports the model in which multiple actors are of importance and change takes place through cognitive and behavioral processes in addition to structural constraints and opportunities. The specific relations explored in the present study have been less well studied and researchers in this field have yet to definitely address the question of whether parental expectations in adolescence remain important to adult educational attainment even when indicators of socio-cultural capital and the young person's ability and gender are taken into account. Therefore, the present study was designed to address this question.

Research questions

Based on the aforementioned theoretical model and existing research literature, three research questions were examined using data collected for the IDA study: (a) Are there significant differences in parental educational expectations for adolescent females and males? (b) Does gender moderate the expected relation between adolescent/family characteristics (i.e., intellectual ability, prior academic performance, family's SES) and parental educational expectations? (This research question follows directly from Eccles' (2007) model in which parents' child-specific beliefs may differ in accordance with characteristics of the family and adolescent.) (c) Does gender moderate the expected relation between adolescent/family characteristics, parental educational expectations, and middle adult educational attainment?

Method

Participants and procedure

These empirical findings are based on analyses with data from the IDA study (Bergman & Magnusson, 1997; Magnusson, 1988; Trost & Bergman, 2004). Data were gathered in a middle-sized Swedish city and involved three entire school grade cohorts. Each grade cohort consisted of children of different ages (in 1965 ages were 10, 13, and 15 at the first data-collection point). IDA started in 1965 with approximately 1,400 children per grade cohort (Bergman, 2000).

In this chapter, we use data from the "main group" with parent and adolescent reported data as well as school registry data collected at age 13 (year: 1968) when the pupils were in Grade 6 (N = 1,392). Additional parent and adolescent and school registry data were provided for this cohort at age 16 in Grade 9 (year: 1971). In adulthood, an assessment (including an interview) was conducted at the approximate ages of 43 years for women (year: 1998) and 47 years for men (year: 2002). The data collection for males was carried out 3–4 years later than for females. The delay was for logistical reasons since the data collection for females was so comprehensive that it was not feasible to implement a data collection at the same time for the males.

Measures collected in adolescence

School registry: gender

The sample for this analysis includes 682 females (49%) and 710 males (51%).

Parent reported: family's socioeconomic status (SES)

Participating families' SES was measured during Grade 6. This scale score represents the sum of two questions: (a) the educational level of the parent with the highest education and (b) family gross income. Highest parental education response options were from 1 (university) to 7 (compulsory school), and this item was reverse scored. The response options for the family income question were income bands that ranged from 1 (low) to 7 (high).

The family's SES scale score, which is the sum of the parent education and family income item, varied between 2 (low SES) and 14 (high SES). The mean for this sample on this scale was 7.70 (SD = 2.87). For the ANCOVA analyses, the family's SES score was trichotomized into low, medium, and high, in this case using the average of the two items in this scale (1 = low SES (1 to 2), 2 = medium SES (2.5–5.5), 3 = high SES (6–7)).

Adolescents' performance: intellectual ability

Adolescents' intellectual ability was measured in Grade 6 with a standardized intelligence test – the Differential Ability Analysis (DAA) (Härnqvist, 1961). The intellectual ability scale score used in this chapter represents the sum of six different intelligence tests including tests of verbal, logical-inductive, and spatial abilities. Härnqvist (1961) reported a test–retest reliability coefficient of 0.95 for the DAA. Participants' scores on this scale ranged from 52 (low) to 201 (high) and the mean of this sample was 147.58 (SD = 27.39).

School registry: academic achievement (mathematics)

Achievement in mathematics was assessed via Grade 6 school records. Scores on this index ranged from 1 (low) to 5 (high) and the mean in mathematics grades for this sample was 3.16 (SD = 1.05).

School registry: academic achievement (Swedish)

Adolescents' achievement in Swedish was based on school registry information from Grade 6. Scores on this index ranged from 1 (low) to 5 (high) and the mean of this sample was 3.12 (SD = .944).

Parent reported: parental educational expectations (Grades 6 and 9)

Parents reported their expectations about their child's education when the child was in the sixth and ninth grades. Parental educational expectations were measured by the sum of five items in Grade 6 (approximately 13 years old) concerning either academic or vocational education and the sum of three items in Grade 9 (approximately 16 years old). Items on this scale in Grade 6 were as follows:

- Parent's expectation for the child's educational track.
- Which educational track the parent believes the child will choose.
- Parent's expectation of the child's final education.
- What education would fit your daughter or son best?
- What kind of education is most profitable today?

Items on this scale in Grade 9 were as follows:

- Should your daughter or son continue her or his studies?
- What should your daughter or son do after the ninth grade?
- Is it suitable for your daughter or son to choose a long theoretical education?

Because these items had dissimilar response options, item responses were coded so that 1 indicated that the parent had a preference that the child would pursue a vocational education and 2 represented a preference for academic education. The Grade 6 parental educational expectations scale score, consisting of five items, varied between 5 (strong vocational preference for child) and 10 (strong academic preference for child). The mean for this sample on the Grade 6 scale was 8.41 ($SD = 2.01$). Cronbach's alpha for the Grade 6 scale was .92.

The Grade 9 parental educational expectations scale score, consisting of three items, varied between 3 (strong vocational preference for child) and 6 (strong academic preference for child). The mean on this scale for this sample was 4.76 ($SD = 1.01$). Cronbach's alpha for the Grade 9 scale was .61.

For the majority of the analyses, the parental educational expectations scale was used as a continuous variable. However, for the chi-square analyses the Grade 9 parental educational expectations scale score was trichotomized into Low = 3, Medium = 4 to 5, and High = 6.

Measure collected in middle adulthood

Educational attainment

Educational attainment in middle adulthood was determined from interviews carried out at age 43 for women and age 47 for men. Participants' responses were coded on a 13-point scale (1 = did not finish compulsory school, 2 = compulsory school completed, 3 = compulsory school plus 1 year of upper secondary school, 4 = completed 2 years of upper secondary school, 5 = completed 2 years of upper secondary school and at least 1 year of continuing education, 6 = completed 3 years of upper secondary school, 7 = completed 3 years of upper secondary school and 1 year of university, 8 = completed university education (such as nurse, kindergarten teacher, engineer), 9 = completed a bachelor's degree [120 credits], 10 = completed a master's degree [at least 160 credits, but not in a prestige program], 11 = completed a university degree with special qualification [such as physician, veterinarian, psychologist, master's in business or engineering], 12 = completed a licentiate degree, 13 = completed a doctoral degree). The mean for reported educational level was 5.65 ($SD = 2.72$).

Results

Describing parental educational expectations in adolescence

First, the focus is on describing parental educational expectations in adolescence. A Pearson's correlation between parental educational expectations at Grades 6 and 9 was significant ($r = .51$, $p < .01$). A comparison of a binary coding of responses on similar items shared across the scales in Grades 6 and 9 (i.e., academic preference coded as yes or no) showed that in Grade 6 the majority of parents (71.3%) reported an academic preference for their child's future education, while at Grade 9 an academic preference was in the minority (38.3%). The questions asked in Grades 6 and 9 were not exactly the same and we are therefore not able to draw any definite conclusions about the shift in parental expectations.

Table 17.1 shows the correlations (Pearson's r) between the study variables. These results indicated that parental expectations (Grades 6 and 9) are significantly and positively correlated with all other study variables (e.g., family SES, adolescents' intellectual ability and grades in mathematics and Swedish, educational attainment in middle adulthood).

Gender and parents' educational expectations in adolescence

To address the first research question, "Are there differences in parental educational expectations for adolescent females and males?", two Analysis of Covariance (2 × 3 ANCOVAs) tests were conducted with the fixed factors as gender (male, females) and family socioeconomic status (trichotomized as low, middle, high only for these mean difference analyses) and the dependent variable as parental educational expectations in Grade 6 and 9, respectively. Adolescents' intellectual ability and academic achievement were included as covariates in this analysis. The results of these mean difference analyses indicated that there was not a significant gender difference in the parental educational expectations in Grade 6 or 9. Other group differences were found in these analyses. To avoid redundancy, the relations between the other study variables and parental educational expectations are described in the regression analyses.

In addition to the two ANCOVAs, two Pearson chi-square tests were also conducted in order to gain additional insight into the first research question. Parental educational expectations were trichotomized into low, medium, and high for

Table 17.1. *Correlations (Pearson's r) between the main study variables*

Variables	Gender	Parental expectation (Grade 6)	Parental expectation (Grade 9)	Grades in Swedish (Grade 6)	Grades in mathematics (Grade 6)	Family SES	Intellectual ability (Grade 6)	Educational attainment (middle adulthood)
Gender	—							
Parental expectations (Grade 6)	.05	—						
Parental expectations (Grade 9)	.02	.51**	—					
Grades in Swedish (Grade 6)	.24**	.50**	.55**	—				
Grades in mathematics (Grade 6)	.04	.52**	.52**	.69**	—			
Family SES	.04	.40**	.35**	.31**	.32**	—		
Intellectual ability (Grade 6)	.07*	.50**	.44**	.64**	.67**	.32**	—	
Educational attainment (middle adulthood)	-.07*	.45**	.51**	.42**	.51**	.39**	.45**	—

Notes: SES = Socioeconomic status; ** $p<.01$; * $p<.05$.

Table 17.2. *Association between gender and parental expectations (N = 894)*

Parental expectations (Grade 9)	Males	Females
Low	70 (16%)	34 (8%)
Medium	228 (52%)	294 (65%)
High	145 (33%)	123 (27%)
Total	443	451

Note: $X^2(2) = 22.54, p < .001$.

these analyses. One chi-square test was conducted with Grade 6 parental educational expectations (trichotomized) and gender. The second chi-square test was conducted with Grade 9 parental educational expectations and gender. The Grade 6 chi-square test was not statistically significant. The Grade 9 chi-square test was statistically significant $X^2(2) = 22.54, p < .001$ (see Table 17.2). There were higher percentages of males relative to females in the lowest and highest educational expectation categories (8% units more males in the lowest category or twice as many males as females in this category, and 6% units more males in the highest category relative to females in this category). The medium educational expectation category had more females than males in it (13% units more females).

What predicts parental educational expectations in adolescence?

The second research question was as follows: "Does gender moderate the relation between adolescent/family characteristics (i.e., intellectual ability, academic performance, family's SES) and parental educational expectations?" To begin to examine this research question, four multiple regression analyses (MRAs) were conducted. In the first two MRAs, the family's SES and adolescents' gender, intellectual ability, and grades were simultaneously entered as predictor variables in the MRAs. Parental educational expectations in Grade 6 was the criterion variable for the first MRA and expectations in Grade 9 was the criterion variable for the second MRA. Results from these MRAs indicated that in Grade 6 the family's SES was the strongest predictor of parental educational expectations. Gender was not a statistically significant predictor of parental educational expectations in Grade 6. The results were somewhat different in Grade 9. Parental educational expectations were lower for girls than for boys. The strongest predictor of parental educational expectations was grades in Swedish. Intellectual ability, which was a significant predictor for Grade 6 educational expectations, was not statistically significant in Grade 9.

The same types of MRA as just described were conducted but this time separately for females and males in order to examine if the relation between the predictor and criterion variables was moderated by gender. Thus, four additional

Table 17.3. *Parental educational expectations in Grades 6 and 9. Relation to gender and adolescent/family characteristics (N = 789/701)*

Variable	Grade 6 expectations (β)	Grade 9 expectations (β)
Family's SES	.225***	.165***
Grades in Swedish	.177***	.349***
Grades in mathematics	.211***	.197***
Intellectual ability	.189***	.054
Gender♣	−.127	−.137*

Notes: ♣ = the gender variable was not standardized; SES = Socioeconomic status; β = Standardized Beta Coefficient; Grade 6 expectations: R = .618, R^2 = .382; Grade 9 expectations: R = .611; R^2 = .373; *** p < .001; * p < .05.

Table 17.4. *Multiple regression analyses separated by gender for adolescent/family characteristics predicting parental educational expectations in Grade 6*

	Parental educational expectations	
	Males (N = 388)	Females (N = 401)
Variable	β	β
Family's SES	.169***	.267***
Grades in Swedish	.295***	.046
Grades in mathematics	.171**	.254***
Intellectual ability	.177***	.211***

Notes: SES = Socioeconomic status; β = Standardized Beta Coefficient; Males/Females: R = .653/.594; R^2 = .427/.352; *** p < .001; ** p < .01.

MRAs were conducted with females and males separated in the analyses. In all four MRAs, the family's SES and adolescents' intellectual ability and grades were simultaneously entered as predictor variables. Parental educational expectations in Grade 6 was the criterion variable for two MRAs, and expectations in Grade 9 was the criterion variable for the other two MRAs (e.g., MRA 1: Females only – Predictors: family's SES, adolescents' intellectual ability and grades; Criterion: Parental educational expectations in Grade 6). Only the two MRAs for parental educational expectations in Grade 6 are described here because the pattern of the MRA results was substantively similar between the predictor and criterion variables across the four MRAs.

Table 17.4 shows the MRA results in Grade 6 for the separated genders. For both genders, the family's SES and adolescents' intellectual ability and academic performance predicted parental educational expectations in Grade 6. However, the results were nuanced in that achievement in Swedish and mathematics were important for parental expectations in Grade 6 for males. For females, achievement in mathematics but not in Swedish was important to parental educational expectations in Grade 6. Additionally, the R^2 was .43 for males and .35 for females.

Table 17.5. *Middle adult educational attainment in relation to gender and adolescent/family characteristics (N = 559)*

Variable	β
Family's SES	.199***
Grades in Swedish	.085
Grades in mathematics	.196***
Intellectual ability	.094
Parental expectations (Grade 9)	.250***
Gender ♣	−.465*

Notes: ♣ = the gender variable was not standardized; SES = Socioeconomic status; β = Standardized Beta Coefficient; R = .623; R^2 = .388; *** p < .001; * p < .05.

What predicts educational attainment in middle adulthood?

As can be seen in Table 17.1, educational attainment in middle adulthood was significantly and positively correlated with the family's SES, adolescents' intellectual ability and grades, as well as parental expectations in Grades 6 and 9.

A comparison between the effect sizes (Cohen's *d*) indicated that there was a significant difference between males and females in middle adult educational attainment (*p* < .05; *d* = .15 − Females: *M* = 5.49, *SD* = 2.66; Males: *M* = 5.88, *SD* = 2.78), with females attaining on average less education than males by middle adulthood.

The third research question was as follows: "Does gender moderate the relation between adolescent/family characteristics, parental educational expectations, and middle adult educational attainment?" To examine this research question, three MRAs were conducted. In the first MRA, the family's SES, adolescents' intellectual ability and grades, as well as parental expectations in Grades 6 and 9 were simultaneously entered as predictor variables. Middle adult educational attainment was the criterion variable. Results from this MRA indicated that parental educational expectations in Grade 6 were not statistically significant when the parental expectations scale from Grade 9 was also included as a predictor. Thus, the Grade 6 parental expectations scale was removed from the final regression equations used to examine the third research question.

Table 17.5 shows the MRA results. For the entire sample, both females and males together, the family's SES, adolescents' grades in mathematics, parental educational expectations in Grade 9, and gender predicted middle adult educational attainment, with a R^2 for the model of .39.

As a final point in our analysis, the same analysis as above was conducted but this time separately for females and males in order to check that the form

Table 17.6. *Multiple regression analyses separated by gender for adolescent/family characteristics, parental educational expectations predicting middle adult educational attainment*

	Middle adult educational attainment	
	Males (N = 244)	Females (N = 315)
Variable	β	β
Family's SES	.179***	.218***
Grades Swedish	.030	.136*
Grades mathematics	.279***	.123
Intellectual ability	.061	.118
Parental expectations (Grade 9)	.275***	.228***

Notes: SES = Socioeconomic status; β = Standardized Beta Coefficient; Males/Females: R = .645/.604; R^2 = .416/.365; *** p < .001; * p < .05.

of the relationships was similar for both genders. The gender-separated MRA results can be seen in Table 17.6. For both genders, the family's SES and parental educational expectations in Grade 9 predicted middle adult educational attainment. The importance of grades differed by gender in that the mathematics grade was a statistically significant predictor of middle adult educational attainment for males only. For females in this sample, grades in Swedish were important to middle adult educational attainment. Additionally, the R^2 for the male model was .42 and .37 for the female model.

Discussion

In this chapter, we scrutinized the role of parental educational expectations on the educational attainment of middle-aged Swedish men and women. We extended previous research by linking the role of parental educational expectations to educational attainment in adulthood. Sweden is a country that aspires to achieve gender equality in many aspects of everyday life (Korpi & Stern, 2003). Therefore, the results presented in this chapter aim to contribute new knowledge about the role of parental educational expectations to adult educational attainment in a Swedish context.

This chapter used data from the IDA longitudinal research program. Data were gathered in a middle-sized Swedish city and involved three entire school grade cohorts. Study results were presented using both parent and adolescent reported data as well as school registry data collected at ages 13 and 16. Finally, in adulthood, an assessment was conducted at the approximate ages of 43 for women and 47 for men.

The data presented in this chapter were collected during an interesting historical period, during which, on a national level, increasing numbers of Swedes were becoming involved in higher education relative to past generations, and during a time of growing parity between the genders in their involvement in university education (The Swedish National Agency for Education, 2006). However, this cohort was still growing up in a time of substantial gender-oriented structural barriers to full and equal participation in particular fields of academic study and in work life (Korpi & Stern, 2003).

The existing research literature as well as the expectancy-value model of motivation (Eccles, 1994, 2007; Wigfield & Eccles, 2002) guided the formulation of this study's research questions. According to this theory parents are influential in shaping their children's educational attainment. In the expectancy-value model of motivation, characteristics of parents (e.g., SES) and children (e.g., abilities) come together to help inform parents' beliefs about the child (e.g., educational expectations toward the child), which is hypothesized to influence children's view of themselves and of the world, and ultimately their performance in achievement-related settings (Eccles, 2007). The present study focused particularly on parents' child-related educational expectations with a special emphasis on better understanding the potential role of gender in parents' educational expectations and later adult educational attainment.

Thus, our first aim was to examine the possible differences in parental educational expectations for adolescent females and males. The results of the mean difference tests revealed no significant gender difference in the parental educational expectations for early adolescents. However, a chi-square analysis for middle adolescent boys indicated that parental expectations were polarized: in both the lowest and highest educational expectation categories there were higher percentages of males relative to females.

Our second aim was to examine the possible moderating role of gender between adolescent/family characteristics and parental educational expectations. Among early adolescents (in Grade 6, approximately 13 years old), the family's SES as well as the child's intellectual ability and grades (males both mathematics and Swedish, and females only mathematics) played a critical role in predicting parental educational expectations. Likewise, among middle adolescents (in Grade 9, approximately 16 years old), the family's SES and grades (both in mathematics and Swedish) significantly predicted parental educational expectations. Interestingly, parental educational expectations during middle adolescence were lower for girls than boys, and the strongest predictor of expectations was grades in Swedish. Overall, both in early and middle adolescence the family's SES and grades played a modest but important role in predicting parental expectations. Grades and SES together explained about a third of the variance in parental expectations. This finding was consistent with other prior relevant studies; for example, parents' educational expectations have been found to be significantly and positively related to family SES (e.g., Garg et al., 2002; Trusty & Pirtle, 1998). Although there were some significant differences in the pattern of results for boys and girls in terms of adolescent parental expectations (e.g., a chi-square and regression analysis for middle adolescents), the results for research questions 1 and 2 were characterized by gender similarity rather than consistent differences (e.g., ANCOVAs and regression analysis for early adolescents).

Our final aim was to examine if gender moderated the relation between adolescent/family characteristics, parental educational expectations, and middle adult educational attainment. The results showed for both genders that the family's SES and parental educational expectations in middle adolescence predicted adult educational attainment in midlife. Even after for controlling for conventional factors, including the family's SES, we found that for both genders parental expectations was the strongest predictive factor. Although replication studies with more contemporary cohorts of Swedish adolescents are needed to confirm the importance of parental expectations, the present results point to the promise of such expectations as a potential target for educational interventions and reform efforts.

As in the analyses conducted for research questions 1 and 2, the family's SES was of importance, and in the case of research question 3, to middle adult educational attainment. The importance of the family's SES is not surprising given that parents can serve as role models for adolescents that convey work and career values (Jacobs & Eccles, 2000). Parents with higher SES may be more supportive and engaged in their child's school, and have higher educational aspirations for them, which together may lead to higher educational expectations (e.g., Davis-Kean, 2005; Garg et al., 2002; Schoon, 2010; Trusty et al., 1997). This may explain why in Sweden educational and occupational status continues to be transferred from generation to generation despite the fact that in Sweden educational opportunities are designed to be equal. Parents' educational aspirations may also mediate the influence of SES on the child's expectations (e.g., Davis-Kean, 2005; Neuenschwander et al., 2007). Thus, in future studies adolescents' own educational expectations should be considered.

The importance of grades to middle adult educational attainment differed by gender. Mathematics was a statistically significant predictor for males, whereas grades in Swedish were of importance for females' educational attainment. The results revealed the key role of mathematics for educational attainment concerning males, whereas languages played a role for educational attainment of females. This differential finding is consistent with gender-stereotypical tracking of males and females into academic subjects and later occupations (e.g., historic female underrepresentation in STEM educational tracks and occupations; Eccles, 2009). Explanations for the sources of these gender-stereotypical findings in academic subjects are beyond the direct measurement scope of this study. However, these findings can be situated in the wider research literature on gender and parental socialization. When parents hold conventional gender stereotypes, they are more likely to be inaccurate about their child's ability and interests and to hold gender-stereotypic attributions about their child's academic performance (Eccles, 2009). Such inaccuracies can contribute to differential parent-supported experiences for boys and girls (e.g., encouragement for and provision of gender-stereotypical interests and activities; Eccles, 2009). Such gendered experiences and messages may undermine girls' confidence in their own mathematics abilities and interest and thereby enhance the probability that young women who are quite skillful at mathematics decide not to pursue advanced education and careers in mathematics-related fields (Eccles, 1987).

The Swedish educational tracking system used in *Gymnasium* may have also played an additive role to the gender-related findings on the differential importance to mathematics and Swedish to later educational attainment. Although the outcomes in this study were in the compulsory school years (Grades 6 and 9, prior to *Gymnasium*), study participants were subject to an educational system of curriculum differentiation that eventually streamed them into "higher-achievement" and "lower-achievement" *Gymnasium* curricula (e.g., "regular mathematics" and "advanced mathematics"). Such ability tracking has been found to be associated with lower-ability-stream students perceiving themselves to be less academically oriented and competent relative to higher-ability-stream students (e.g., Fuligni, Eccles, & Barber, 1995). Such tracking may have prematurely curtailed the possibility of study participants in the lower ability streams to change their academic course by gaining post-compulsory school exposure to and experience with advanced mathematics and Swedish, regardless of gender.

In summary, we found that parental expectations are important for men and women as predictors of their middle adult educational attainment (even after controlling for other important factors such as the family's SES and adolescent intellectual ability and academic achievement). Summarizing the adolescent findings, we found that in Grade 9 parental expectations were polarized: there were higher percentages of males relative to females in the lowest and highest educational expectation categories (8% units more males in the lowest category and 6% units more males in the highest category). Further, in Grade 6, the family's SES was the strongest predictor of parental educational expectations. In Grade 9, the mean parental educational expectations were lower for girls than boys and the strongest predictor of parental educational expectations was grades in Swedish. A comparison of parental expectations in Grades 6 and 9 showed that the majority of parents reported an academic preference for their child's future education in Grade 6 whereas an academic preference was in the minority in Grade 9. Thus, we observe a downgrading of parental expectations when their teens are closer to their *gymnasium* decisions (i.e., academic or vocational education). This could represent a reality check for the parents. However, the questions asked in Grades 6 and 9 were not exactly the same and we are therefore not able to draw any definite conclusions. Separate analyses for both genders showed that achievement in Swedish and mathematics were important for parental expectations in Grade 6 for the boys and that achievement in mathematics was important for the girls. Finally, when analyzing the long-term outcomes, we found that female educational attainment was on average lower than that of males. Educational attainment in middle adulthood was significantly and positively correlated with the family's SES, adolescents' intellectual ability and grades as well as parental expectations in Grades 6 and 9. Separate analyses by gender showed that for both genders, the family's SES and parental educational expectations in Grade

9 predicted middle adult educational attainment. The importance of grades differed by gender in that a mathematics grade was a significant predictor of middle adult educational attainment for males only, and Swedish was only important to female educational attainment.

Our results can be discussed in terms of present-day efforts to promote equitable and optimal life chances for the current generation of European adolescents. The research summarized in this chapter suggests that gender differences in parental expectations were important to a prior generation's educational attainment, which could be expected given the socialization history of most men and women in this generation. In the adolescent to middle adult analyses conducted for both genders together and for those conducted by gender, the results indicated that, yes, parental educational expectations remained important to educational attainment, even with the consideration of several other important predictors, including gender. In combination with other empirical work on the importance of parental educational expectations in younger cohorts to shorter-term educational outcomes (e.g., Neuenschwander et al., 2007; Zhan, 2006), parental educational expectations emerges as a promising construct for additional examination in present-day longitudinal studies.

Notwithstanding the potential importance of parental educational expectations, structural constraints were also found to be of importance in the present study findings and such factors are likely to remain important for current-day youth. Continued development of gender-equitable family and work social policies and supports are likely to facilitate both men's and women's willingness to consider a wide variety of educational and occupational choices. Understanding men's and women's educational attainment is likely to be improved by taking a broad view of the options and roles available to both men and women that they encounter within the historical and cultural milieu of the moment.

Limitations

The present study was carried out in Sweden, a country that aspires to achieve gender equality in many aspects of everyday life, with a particular cohort coming of age during a given point in history. Thus study results, while cautiously discussed in terms of present-day efforts to improve educational attainment among today's European youth, should be considered as possibly limited to this particular study's context and cohort. Generalization of study results to other contexts and cohorts awaits additional research.

Because educational choices are not made in isolation from other life choices, such as the decision to marry and have children, and the decision to balance one's occupational behaviors with one's other life roles, it would be important for future studies to consider the use of a wider measurement net than was used in the present study. It would be worthwhile to measure additional factors such as adolescents' gender-related beliefs, values, and their own educational expectations.

In future studies, it could be valuable to examine mothers' and fathers' expectations separately. In the previous studies, for example, it has been found that mothers' expectations seemed to play a stronger role in the adolescent's expectations than fathers' expectations (Trusty, 2000). Replication of the present study findings in cross-national longitudinal studies as well as the use of combined person and variable-oriented approaches also represent promising avenues for additional research on this subject.

References

Andres, L., & Grayson, J. P. (2003). Parents, educational attainment, jobs and satisfaction: What's the connection? A 10-year portrait of Canadian young women and men. *Journal of Youth Studies*, 6(2), 181–202.

Ashby, J. S., & Schoon, I. (2010). Career success: The role of teenage career aspirations, ambition value and gender in predicting adult social status and earnings. *Journal of Vocational Behavior*, 77(3), 350–360.

Batljan, I., Lagergren, M., & Thorslund, M. (2009). Population ageing in Sweden: The effect of change in educational composition on the future number of older people suffering severe ill-health. *European Journal of Ageing*, 6(3), 201–211.

Beck-Domzalska, M. (2007). The narrowing education gap between women and men. *Eurostat Statistics in Focus: Population and Social Conditions*, 130, 1–11. Luxembourg: European Communities.

Bergman, L. R. (2000). *Women's health, work, and education in a life-span perspective: Technical report 1 – Theoretical background and overview of the data collection* (Reports from the project IDA, No. 70). Stockholm: Stockholm University, Department of Psychology.

Bergman, L. R., & Magnusson, D. (1997). A person-oriented approach in research on developmental psychopathology. *Development and Psychopathology*, 9(2), 291–319.

Bleeker, M. M., & Jacobs, J. E. (2004). Achievement in math and science: Do mothers' beliefs matter 12 years later? *Journal of Educational Psychology*, 96(1), 97–109.

Boxer, P., Goldstein, S. E., DeLorenzo, T., Savoy, S., & Mercado, I. (2011). Educational aspiration–expectation discrepancies: Relation to socioeconomic and academic risk-related factors. *Journal of Adolescence*, 34(4), 609–617.

Ceci, S. J., & Williams, W. M. (1997). Schooling, intelligence and income. *American Psychologist*, 52(10), 1051–1058.

Chhin, C. S., Bleeker, M. M., & Jacobs, J. E. (2008). Gender-typed occupational choices: The long-term impact of parents' beliefs and expectations. In H. M. G. Watt & J. S. Eccles (Eds.), *Gender and occupational outcomes: Longitudinal assessment of individual, social, and cultural influences* (pp. 215–234). Washington, DC: American Psychological Association.

Cook, T. D., Church, M. B., Ajanaku, S., Shadish, Jr., W. R., Kim, J.-R., & Cohen, R. (1996). The development of occupational aspirations and expectations among inner-city boys. *Child Development*, 67(6), 3368–3385.

Côté, J. E., & Allahar, A. (2006). *Critical youth studies: A Canadian focus.* Toronto: Pearson Education.
Davis-Kean, P. E. (2005). The influence of parent education and family income on child achievement: The indirect role of parental expectations and the home environment. *Journal of Family Psychology,* 19(2), 294–304.
Deary, I. J., Strand, S., Smith, P., & Fernandes, C. (2007). Intelligence and educational achievement. *Intelligence,* 35(1), 13–21.
Eccles, J. S. (1987). Gender roles and women's achievement-related decisions. *Psychology of Women Quarterly,* 11(2), 135–172.
—— (1994). Understanding women's educational and occupational choices: Applying the Eccles et al. model of achievement-related choices. *Psychology of Women Quarterly,* 18, 585–609.
—— (2007). Families, schools, and developing achievement-related motivations and engagement. In J. E. Grusec & P. D. Hastings (Eds.), *Handbook of socialization: Theory and research* (pp. 665–691). New York: Guilford Press.
—— (2009). Who am I and what am I going to do with my life? Personal and collective identities as motivators of action. *Educational Psychologist,* 44(2), 78–89.
Eccles (Parsons), J., Adler, T. F., Futterman, R., Goff, S. B., Kaczala, C. M., Meece, J. L., & Midgley, C. (1983). Expectancies, values, and academic behaviors. In J. T. Spence (Ed.), *Achievement and achievement motives: Psychological and sociological approaches* (pp. 75–146). San Francisco, CA: Freeman.
Fuligni, A. J., Eccles, J. S., & Barber, B. L. (1995). The long-term effects of seventh-grade ability grouping in mathematics. *Journal of Early Adolescence,* 15(1), 58–89.
Ganzach, Y. (2000). Parents' education, cognitive ability, educational expectations and educational attainment: Interactive effects. *British Journal of Educational Psychology,* 70(3), 419–441.
Garg, R., Kauppi, C., Lewko, J., & Urajnik, D. (2002). A structural model of educational aspirations. *Journal of Career Development,* 29(2), 87–108.
Gottfredson, L. S. (2002). Where and why g matters: Not a mystery. *Human Performance,* 15(1–2), 25–46.
Härnqvist, K. (1961). *Manual till DBA: differentiell begåvningsanalys* [Manual to DIA: Differential intelligence analysis]. Stockholm: Skandinaviska Testförlaget.
Jacobs, J. E., & Eccles, J. S. (2000). Parents, task values, and real-life achievement-related choices. In C. Sansone & J. M. Harackiewicz (Eds.), *Intrinsic and extrinsic motivation: The search for optimal motivation and performance* (pp. 405–439). Orlando, FL: Academic Press.
Judge, T. A., Ilies, R., & Dimotakis, N. (2010). Are health and happiness the product of wisdom? The relationship of general mental ability to educational and occupational attainment, health, and well-being. *Journal of Applied Psychology,* 95(3), 454–468.
Korpi, T., & Stern, C. (2003). *Women's employment in Sweden: Globalization, deindustrialization, and the labor market experiences of Swedish women 1950–2000.* Stockholm University, Swedish Institute for Social Research.
Magnusson, D. (1988). *Individual development from an interactional perspective: A longitudinal study.* Hillsdale, NJ: Erlbaum.
Nagy, G., Watt, H. M. G., Eccles, J. S., Trautwein, U., Lüdtke, O., & Baumert, J. (2010). The development of students' mathematics self-concept in relation to

gender: Different countries, different trajectories? *Journal of Research on Adolescence*, 20(2), 482–506.

Neuenschwander, M. P., Vida, M., Garrett, J. L., & Eccles, J. S. (2007). Parents' expectations and students' achievement in two western nations. *International Journal of Behavioral Development*, 31(6), 594–602.

Rytkönen, K., Aunola, K., & Nurmi, J.-E. (2005). Parents' causal attributions concerning their children's school achievement: A longitudinal study. *Merrill-Palmer Quarterly*, 51(4), 494–522.

Schoon, I. (2010). Childhood cognitive ability and adult academic attainment: Evidence from three British cohort studies. *Longitudinal and Life Course Studies*, 1(3), 241–258.

Schoon, I., & Parsons, S. (2002). Teenage aspirations for future careers and occupational outcomes. *Journal of Vocational Behavior*, 60(2), 262–288.

Statistics Sweden. (2010). Retrieved November 1, 2010, from www.scb.se/Pages/TableAndChart____149081.aspx.

The Swedish National Agency for Education. (2006). *Gender differences in goal fulfillment and education choices* (Report 287). Stockholm: Author.

(2009a). *Universitet & högskolor: Högskoleverkets årsrapport 2009*. Retrieved May 23, 2011, from www.hsv.se/download/18.1dbd1f9a120d72e05717ffe2356/0912R.pdf.

(2009b). *What is upper secondary school?* Retrieved May 12, 2011, from www.skolverket.se/sb/d/2669.

Trost, K., & Bergman, E. (2004). *Men's work and well-being in a lifespan perspective: Technical report from the 2002–2003 data collection* (Reports from the project IDA, No. 85). Stockholm: Stockholm University, Department of Psychology.

Trusty, J. (2000). High educational expectations and low achievement: Stability of educational goals across adolescence. *Journal of Educational Research*, 93(6), 356–365.

Trusty, J., & Pirtle, T. (1998). Parents' transmission of educational goals to their adolescent children. *Journal of Research and Development in Education*, 32(1), 53–65.

Trusty, J., Watts, R. E., & Erdman, P. (1997). Predictors of parents' involvement in their teens' career development. *Journal of Career Development*, 23(3), 189–201.

Wigfield, A., & Eccles, J. S. (2002). *The development of achievement motivation*. San Diego, CA: Academic Press.

Zhan, M. (2006). Assets, parental expectations and involvement, and children's educational performance. *Children and Youth Services Review*, 28(8), 961–975.

18 How gender influences objective career success and subjective career satisfaction: the impact of self-concept and of parenthood

Andrea E. Abele

Abstract

Despite excellent educational backgrounds women are still less successful in their occupational careers than men. The present research tests hypotheses derived from a dual-impact model of gender- and career-related processes in a longitudinal study with 1,015 German professionals over a time span of 10 years. In line with predictions, parenthood had a negative influence on women's objective career success that was completely due to a reduced workload and career discontinuities during their children's early childhood. In contrast, parenthood had a slightly positive effect on men's objective career success that was independent of workload. Moreover, the participants' self-concept had an influence both on parenthood (participants with a more "communal" self-concept, e.g., warmth and empathy, were more often parents) and on career success (participants with a more "agentic" self-concept, e.g., assertiveness and independence, were more successful). Both men's and women's career satisfaction could be predicted by their degree of agency and by workload. Parents were more satisfied with their careers than non-parents, and this effect was stronger for women than for men. Implications of these findings with respect to the dual-impact model of gender and with respect to applied issues are discussed.

Introduction

Women's human capital has changed dramatically during the last 100 years in Western societies. In several countries women are better educated than men and the discrepancy favoring women still increases. Women's workforce participation has also considerably increased and the higher women's education is, the higher is their workforce participation. However, women still earn less than men, are less often promoted, and are largely underrepresented in leadership positions (Eurostat, 2005; Marini & Fan, 1997; for a review see Eby, Casper, Lockwood, Bordeaux, & Brinley, 2005). Hence, women are highly

The present research was supported by a grant from the German Research Council (AB 45/8-1/2/4/6). Thanks to Daniel Spurk, who helped with computing the structural equation models.

qualified, but these qualifications are not reflected in their occupational attainments. Women are objectively less successful in their careers than men.

The current study defines *career success* as "the positive psychological or work-related outcomes or achievements one accumulates as a result of work experiences" (Seibert, Crant, & Kraimer, 1999). It is identified through both objective attainments like income or status, and subjective evaluation, such as the feeling of career satisfaction (Abele, Spurk, & Volmer, 2011; Heslin, 2005). Using the *dual-impact model* of gender- and career-related processes (Abele, 2000, 2003; Abele & Spurk, 2011), the present research compares career success of women and men.

Many scholars have already addressed the issue of women's lower career success compared to men's (Abele, 2000, 2003; Eby et al., 2005; Kirchmeyer, 1998; Lyness & Thompson, 1997; Ng, Eby, Sorensen, & Feldman, 2005; Reitman & Schneer, 2003, 2005; Taniguchi, 1999; Watts & Eccles, 2008). *Process accounts* (for instance, Super, 1957) suggest that career development is characterized by different career patterns and that continuous career patterns usually lead to more career success than discontinuous ones. Women are assumed to be less successful in their occupational careers than men because their career patterns are often discontinuous due to childcare responsibilities (Abele & Spurk, 2009a; Gattiker & Larwood, 1990; Melamed, 1995, 1996; Tharenou, Latimer, & Conroy, 1994). *Structural approaches* distinguish between different sources of influence on career decisions and career outcomes and specifically stress the influence of human capital variables (e.g., education, social background), of individual differences (e.g., personality, expectations, goals), and of environmental variables (e.g., sponsoring, support vs. discrimination) (cf. Lent, Brown, & Hackett, 1994; Ng et al., 2005).

Specific *gender approaches* address the complex influences that being female or male has on lifetime development. The distinction between "sex" and "gender" is crucial in respective theorizing. Whereas "sex" is related to mainly biological and socio-demographic aspects, gender is related to both psychological aspects (gender identity, gender-related self-concept) and to social aspects, e.g., the social construction of gender (such as gender roles, gender-role expectations). Gender is a dynamic construct that draws on and impinges upon processes at the individual, interactional, group, institutional, and cultural levels (Deaux & LaFrance, 1998).

The dual-impact model of gendered career processes

The *dual-impact model* on gender- and career-related processes (Abele, 2000, 2003; Abele & Spurk, 2011) distinguishes between an outside perspective and an inside perspective of gender. The *outside perspective* refers to gender as a social category and to the expectations directed at people belonging to the category of "man" or "woman." The outside perspective defines the areas in which men's and women's behaviors are differentially evaluated due to different expectations. People are influenced by these outside expectations when they make family and/or career-related decisions. An example is the expectation that women are – for different reasons – less suited for leadership positions than men, and hence they receive those positions less often than men and/or if they obtain a leadership position they are evaluated less favorably than men (Eagly & Karau, 2002; Rudman & Fairchild, 2004). Another example is the expectation that "good" mothers reduce their workload while they are mothers of an infant child. Respective expectations may be a barrier to women's career success (see also Eby, Allen, & Douthitt, 1999).

The *inside perspective* refers to how an individual conceives him/herself as a man or a woman, i.e., the self-concept regarding "masculinity" and "femininity." It is now generally acknowledged that masculinity and femininity are not the endpoints of one continuum but rather two independent dimensions (Abele & Wojciszke, 2007; Bem, 1993; Spence, Helmreich, & Stapp, 1974). The gender-related self-concept of women and men is built upon both stereotypically masculine traits called *agency* (such as "decisive," "active") and stereotypically feminine traits called *communion* (such as "empathic," "warm").

The present study

The analyses presented in this chapter focus on one of the most important process factors relevant for gender-specific trends, namely the amount and continuity of workload in individuals' occupational careers. It has been shown that workload, the number of contractual hours an individual works per week, is a major determinant of objective career attainments like salary or promotions (Ng & Feldman, 2008). Hypotheses derived from the dual-impact model were tested in a prospective longitudinal study with highly educated professionals who were first contacted at career entry and then several times again until 10 years later (see Abele, 2000, 2003; Abele & Spurk, 2009a, 2011).

First, the prediction that women reduce their workload when they become mothers, whereas men do not reduce their workload when they become fathers, was tested (see also Eby et al., 2005; Kirchmeyer, 1998; Lyness & Thompson, 1997; Ng et al., 2005; Reitman & Schneer, 2003, 2005; Taniguchi, 1999). Hence, the negative effect of parenthood on women's objective career success should be completely mediated via workload. Regarding men, parenthood should either have no effect on objective career success or it might even have a positive effect, because men's roles often become more traditional after the birth of a child (Lundberg & Frankenhaeuser, 1999).

A possible moderator of these relationships could be the field of the profession because interruptions and/or reductions of work hours are more common in some fields than in others (e.g., Olson, Frieze, & Detlefsen, 1990). Therefore a distinction was made between employment in the public vs. the private sector vs. self-employment.

The second prediction was that an individual's gender-related self-concept influences both the decision to become a parent and the decision to reduce one's workload in case of parenthood. It has been shown that the agentic part of the self-concept is especially important in predicting career success and career-related behavior: people high in agency are more successful than people low in agency (Abele, 2003; Abele, Rupprecht, & Wojciszke, 2008; Astin, 1984; Betz & Fitzgerald, 1987; Corrigall & Konrad, 2007; Kirchmeyer, 1998). The communal part of the self-concept is more associated with how people build their social relationships (e.g., Feldman & Aschenbrenner, 1983; Kasen, Chen, Sneed, Crawford, & Cohen, 2006; Uchronski, 2008). It follows that a person's agency will positively predict workload and career success, whereas his/her communion will positively predict parenthood.

Finally, career success is not only an individual's objective attainment in terms of money, status, and/or promotions. Career success also means satisfaction with one's career (cf. Abele et al., 2011). A final objective of the present analyses therefore is the analysis of career satisfaction. Career satisfaction might be predicted by the agentic part of the self-concept, since agentic persons are more career-oriented (Abele, 2003; Astin, 1984; Betz & Fitzgerald, 1987; Corrigall & Konrad, 2007; Kirchmeyer, 1998). Workload should also be a determinant of career satisfaction since higher workload is correlated with more objective success (Abele et al., 2011). It is especially interesting to analyze the relationship between parenthood and career satisfaction. Regarding women, one might suggest that parenthood is negatively related to career satisfaction, because parenthood has a negative influence on women's objective career success. However, parenthood might also have a positive influence on women's career satisfaction because women nowadays want to integrate work and family and might feel more satisfied when they have both a family and employment (cf. Eby et al., 2005). Regarding men, parenthood should either not be correlated with career satisfaction or it should be positively correlated because fatherhood has no negative impact on men's objective career success.

Method

We tested these predictions with a sample of German professionals with university degrees from different fields of study. Participants completed the first questionnaire shortly after they had passed their final exams. They received the second questionnaire about 1 year later, the third one 3 years after graduation, the fourth one 7 years after graduation and the fifth one 10 years after graduation.

The following analyses were performed with 1,015 participants (428 women, 587 men; mean age $M = 37.08$, $SD = 2.23$) who had participated in all five waves. These participants are representative for the initial sample of 1,930 persons (see Abele & Spurk, 2009a). The sample comprised professionals with degrees in law (25 women, 27 men), medicine (73 women, 98 men), arts and humanities (81 women, 29 men), natural sciences (39 women, 94 men), economics (68 women,

104 men), engineering (17 women, 168 men), and teaching (125 women, 67 men). At wave 5, 30% of our participants worked in the public sector, 47% were employed in the private sector, 15% were self-employed, 6% were on parental leave (93% of them women), and 2% were unemployed.

We assessed participants' gender, age, grade point average (GPA) school attainment, and study major at wave 1. Since GPA did not differ between men and women, we will not consider it further. Among others, we also assessed whether the participant was a parent (number of children, year of birth) throughout waves 1 to 5. From waves 2 to 5 we asked our participants how many contractual hours they worked per week and we assessed their specific employment (public vs. private vs. self-employed vs. other; specific job description).

Gender self-concept was measured by means of the Personal Attributes Questionnaire at wave 1 (PAQ; Spence et al., 1974; German version Runge, Frey, Gollwitzer, Helmreich, & Spence, 1981). The communion scale comprised eight items (sample items "empathic," "emotional," "understanding"), and the agency scale comprised seven items (sample items "decisive," "independent," "self-confident"). Participants responded on 5-point scales (1 = not at all to 5 = very much).

We measured objective career success by monthly income before taxes (in 13 steps from "no income," coded as 0; "less than €500," coded as 0.5; "less than €1,000," coded as 1; and then in equal steps to "less than €10,000," coded as 10; and "more than €10,000," coded as 11) and by three variables assessing hierarchical status (permission to delegate work, 0 = *no*, 1 = *yes*; temporary project responsibility, 0 = *no*, 1 = *yes*; official leadership position 0 = *no*, 1 = *yes*). We created an objective career success index by adding the points for income and hierarchical status (scores from 0 to 14; see also Abele & Spurk, 2009b). Objective success was assessed throughout waves 2 to 5.

Finally we measured career satisfaction with a scale presented by Greenhaus, Parasuraman, and Wormley (1990). It consists of five items (sample item "I am satisfied with the success I have attained in my career so far"). Participants responded on 5-point scales (1 = *not at all* to 5 = *very much*). Here the measure for wave 5 is used.

Results and discussion

Table 18.1 reports the means and standard deviations of all variables considered here, separated between men and women. Agency was higher in men, and communion was higher in women. Both women and men, however, had higher scores in communion than in agency. There were no gender differences regarding parenthood. Women's weekly work hours were generally lower than men's. Similarly, women's objective career success was always lower than men's. Women's career satisfaction at wave 5 was also lower than men's.

Table 18.1. *Descriptive statistics: gender differences (N = 1,015)*

	Women M, SD	Men M, SD	t (1,013)
Agency t1[a]	3.44 (0.63)	3.60 (0.58)	4.25, $p < .001$
Communion t1[a]	4.06 (0.48)	3.81 (0.52)	7.70, $p < .001$
Percentage parents t1	8%	6%	$\chi^2(1) = 1.83$, n.s.
Percentage parents t2	10%	11%	$\chi^2 < 1$
Percentage parents t3	17%	21%	$\chi^2(1) = 2.32$, n.s.
Percentage parents t4	46%	45%	$\chi^2 < 1$
Percentage parents t5	59%	61%	$\chi^2 < 1$
Work hours t2[b]	34.16 (12.65)	37.19 (9.61)	5.04, $p < .001$
Work hours t3[b]	30.77 (13.72)	36.27 (9.24)	7.50, $p < .001$
Work hours t4[b]	25.10 (17.09)	38.60 (7.01)	17.24, $p < .001$
Work hours t5[b]	24.71 (16.18)	39.19 (7.48)	19.08, $p < .001$
Objective success t2[c]	2.06 (1.38)	2.79 (1.52)	7.90, $p < .001$
Objective success t3[c]	3.23 (1.86)	4.44 (1.85)	10.31, $p < .001$
Objective success t4[c]	3.71 (2.95)	6.72 (2.63)	17.08, $p < .001$
Objective success t5[c]	3.93 (3.03)	7.54 (3.03)	18.78, $p < .001$
Career satisfaction t5[a]	3.44 (0.81)	3.64 (0.73)	4.12, $p < .001$

Notes: [a] Scale from 1 to 5; [b] contractual hours worked per week; [c] scale from 0 to 14.

Objective career success

The prediction that women reduce their workload when they become a parent whereas men do not was tested with four analyses of variance (ANOVA) with gender and parenthood as factors and work hours at wave 2, wave 3, wave 4, or wave 5 as dependent variables. Gender, parenthood, and the interaction of gender by parenthood were always highly significant predictors. Figure 18.1 shows that mothers' work hours were always lower than fathers' and than childless men's and women's work hours.

Then the prediction was tested that women's objective career success is indirectly influenced by parenthood mediated by work hours, whereas men's objective career success is not or is even positively influenced by parenthood. Separate hierarchical linear regression analyses were run for men and women with objective career success at wave 5 as the outcome, parenthood as predictor in the first step, and work hours at wave 2 through wave 5 as predictors in the second step. As can be seen in Table 18.2, parenthood is a highly significant negative predictor of women's objective career success, but this influence is completely mediated by work hours. In contrast, men's objective career success is slightly positively influenced by parenthood, and – of course – by work hours. It was also tested whether these effects were the same across different fields of employment (public sector, private sector, self-employed). This was the case.

In order to test the prediction that the communal part of the gender self-concept has an influence on parenthood, binary logistic regressions were used

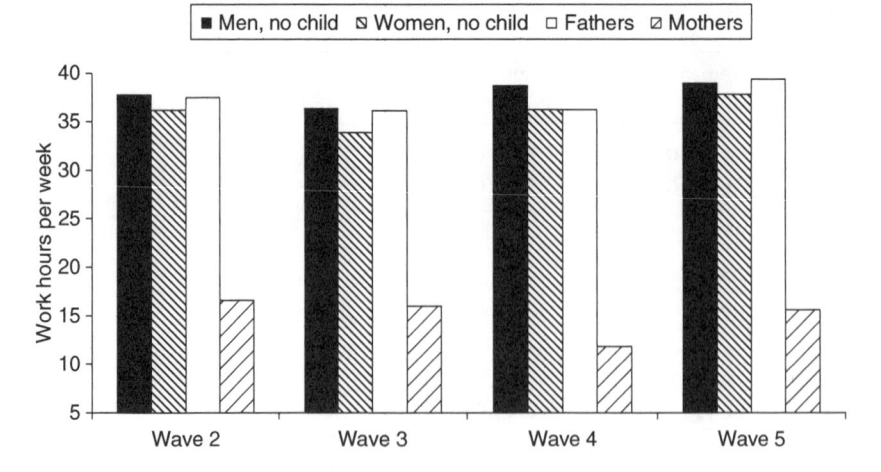

Figure 18.1 *Average work hours of women and men with and without children across waves 2 to 5*

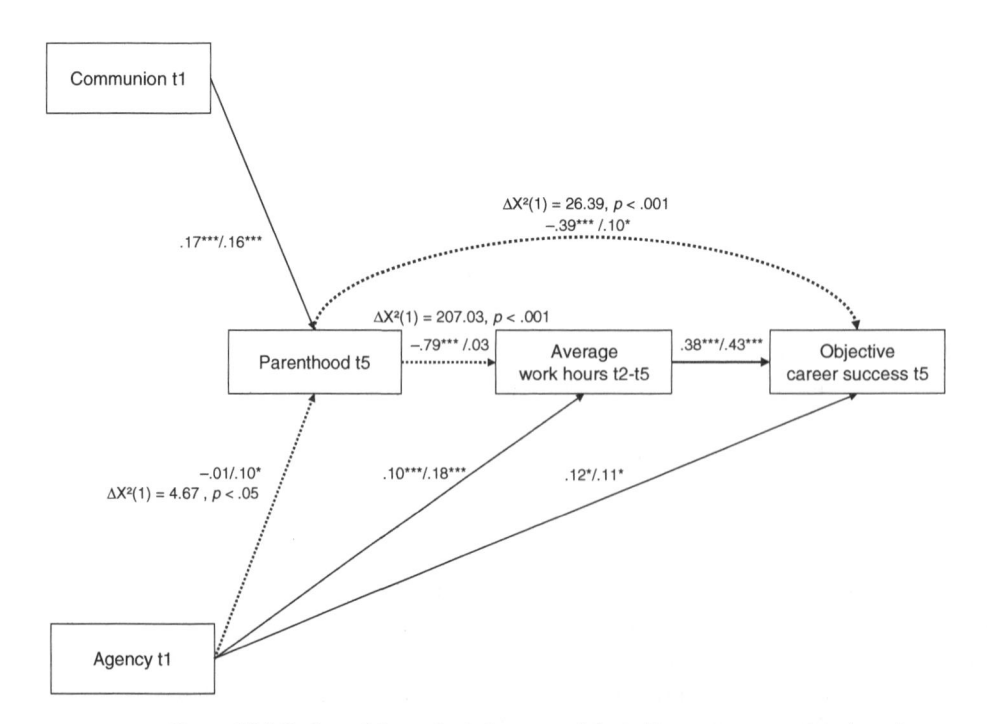

Figure 18.2 *Path models on the influences of the self-concept, parenthood, and average work hours on objective career success at wave 5 for men and women*
Notes:
χ^2 = 8.75, df = 7, CFI = 1.00, TLI = .99, RMSEA = .02
Explained variance in objective career success: R^2 = .55 for women and R^2 = .23 for men. Path coefficients for women are displayed left and path coefficients for men are displayed right of the slashes; dotted lines signify gender differences in the path coefficients, solid lines indicate no gender differences in the path coefficients; * p < .05; *** p < .001.

Table 18.2. *Objective career success at wave 5 regressed on parenthood and workload*

	Women	Men
Step 1		
Parenthood t5[a]	β = −.58***	β = .10*
	Δ R² = .33***	Δ R² = .01*
Step 2		
Parenthood t5	β = −.03	β = .08*
Work hours t2[b]	β = .08**	β = .13***
Work hours t3[b]	β = .05	β = .05
Work hours t4[b]	β = .07**	β = .17***
Work hours t5[b]	β = .72***	β = .37***
	Δ R² = .33***	Δ R² = .27***
	R² = .66***	R² = .28***

Notes: [a] Dummy coded: 0 no parent, 1 parent; [b] contractual hours worked per week; * $p < .05$, ** $p < .01$; *** $p < .001$.

with agency and communion as predictors and parenthood at wave 5 (yes/no) as outcome, again running separate analyses for men and women. In accord with the assumption, communion was a significant predictor of parenthood both for women and for men, whereas agency was not.

In order to test the prediction that the agentic part of the gender self-concept has an influence on work hours, hierarchical linear regression analyses were run with work hours at wave 5 as the outcome and with parenthood as predictor at step 1 and agency and communion as predictors at step 2, again separate analyses for men and women. In accord with the prediction, the agency part of the gender self-concept explained an additional share of variance in the workload in wave 5 over and above parenthood. Both women and men worked more when they were highly agentic. Communion had no influence.

In order to combine all these findings into one computation, a structural equation model was estimated with gender, agency, and communion at wave 1, parenthood at wave 5, work hour average over waves 2 to 5, and objective career success at wave 5. The resulting model revealed good fit indices and is graphically depicted in Figure 18.2. Path coefficients for women are displayed left, and path coefficients for men are displayed right of the slashes. Paths that do not differ between men and women are presented as solid lines, and paths that differ between men and women are presented as dotted lines. Parenthood exerted a negative effect on women's average work hours, but had no effect on men's average work hours. Average work hours strongly predicted women's and men's objective career success. Agency had a positive influence on average work hours as well as on objective career success. Furthermore, agency significantly predicted parenthood among men but not among women. Communion had a positive influence on parenthood. Overall, the model explains more variance in

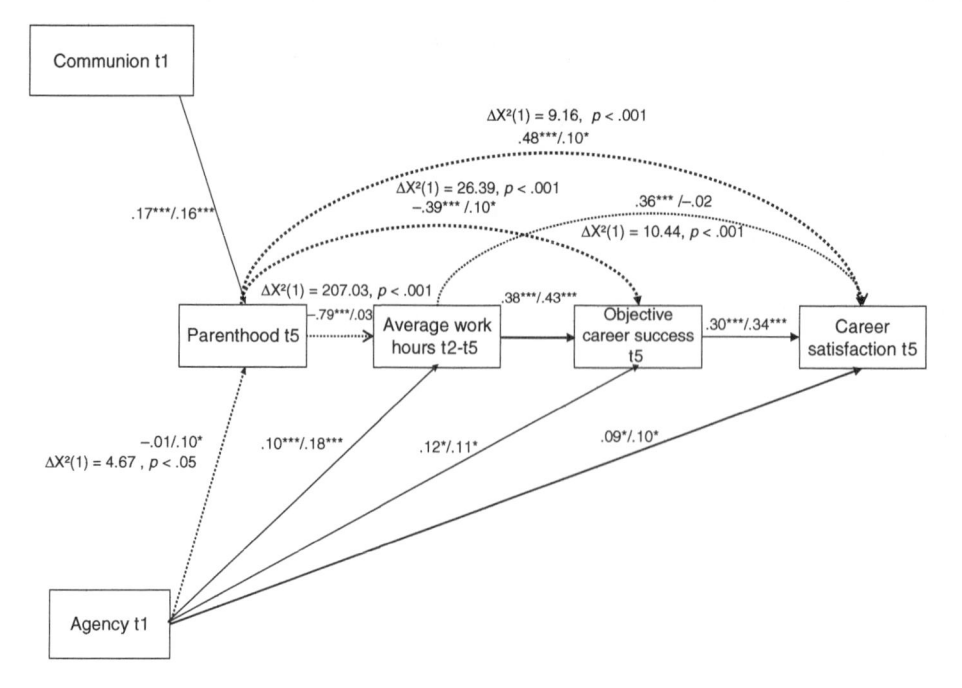

Figure 18.3 Path models on the influences of the self-concept, parenthood, and average work hours on career satisfaction at wave 5 for men and women
Notes:
$\chi^2 = 12.61$, df = 11, CFI = 1.00, TLI = .99, RMSEA = .02
Explained variance in career satisfaction: $R^2 = .15$ for women and $R^2 = .13$ for men. Path coefficients for women are displayed left and path coefficients for men are displayed right of the slashes; dotted lines signify gender differences in the path coefficients, solid lines indicate no gender differences in the path coefficients; * p < .05; *** p < .001.

wave 5 in women's objective career success (55%) than men's (23%). This is due to the stronger influence of parenthood on work hours among women than among men.

Career satisfaction

The final analysis concerned career satisfaction. We directly estimated a structural equation model and tested the same paths as in the above model for objective career success. The resulting model revealed good fit indices and is graphically depicted in Figure 18.3. Path coefficients for women are again displayed left, and path coefficients for men are displayed right of the slashes. Paths that do not differ between men and women are presented as solid lines, and paths that differ between men and women are presented as dotted lines.

Besides the already known effects (communion effects on parenthood; agency effects on average work hours; agency effects on men's parenthood; parenthood effects on women's average work hours), the model also shows that agency has a positive influence on career satisfaction. Most importantly it shows that parenthood has a positive effect on career satisfaction. This effect is even higher for women than for men. Field of employment again had no influence, i.e., the findings were the same in the public sector, the private sector, and for self-employed persons.

Conclusions

The present study showed that career interruptions and/or workload reductions due to childcare responsibilities are one of the main reasons for women's lower objective career success than men's (see also Abele & Spurk, 2011; Gattiker & Larwood, 1990; Melamed, 1995, 1996; Tharenou et al., 1994). This finding reflects the dual impact of gender, transmitted through both outside expectations and the subjective gender self-concept. Within the sample of German professionals with university degrees, there are clear expectations directed at mothers and fathers of infant children, such as that mothers should invest more time in childcare and should be more willing to reduce their occupational workload than fathers, whereas fathers should be reliable and responsible breadwinners. These expectations are independent of field of employment, as the present data show. In a previous analysis (Abele, 2005) it was found that even though quite a few women wanted to reduce their workload after the birth of a child, the percentage of women who actually did so was much higher. In a parallel fashion, even though there were some men who wanted to reduce their workload after the birth of a child the percentage of men who actually did so was negligible (Abele, 2005). Throughout the different waves of our study mothers always had a lower amount of working hours in their jobs (see Table 18.1) than fathers, whereas childless men and women did not differ considerably.

The finding that mothers reduce their workload more than fathers, however, also reflects the inside perspective of gender. Quite a few women and men want to have a division of labor that assigns – at least for the time when the child is very young – the homemaker and caregiver role to the mother and the breadwinner role to the father. In other words, women do not want to copy traditional "male" careers with a clear and unambiguous focus on the work domain at the expense of private life. They know that they have to "pay" for these work reductions in favor of the family by being objectively less successful and also being less satisfied with their careers than men without such discontinuities. However, part of mothers' career satisfaction also stems from the fact that they were able to combine work and family, as was demonstrated in the positive impact of parenthood on women's career satisfaction.

These general findings are also reflected on the level of individuals' self-concepts. Persons with a more "feminine" self-concept, i.e., higher scores on communion, were more prone to become parents; whereas persons with a more "masculine" self-concept, i.e., higher scores on agency, were more prone to work longer, were more successful, and were also more satisfied with their careers. It should be noted that these effects occurred over a time interval of 10 years. Communion measured at age 27 predicted whether participants were parents at age 37; agency measured at age 27 predicted how much participants worked throughout the 10-year interval, how successful they were, and also how satisfied they were – men's agency even predicted their parenthood. These long-lasting effects underpin the importance of the two self-concept dimensions, which have also been called the "fundamental" dimensions (cf. Abele & Wojciszke, 2007). It should also be noted that although there are still gender differences, such as that agency is higher in men and communion is higher in women, the predicted influence patterns of both self-concept dimensions are by and large the same for men and women.

The study was conducted in Germany and it may be asked if the results are specific to this country. On the one hand the "mother ideology," i.e., the reasoning that mothers should stay at home when they have children under the age of 3 years, is particularly strong in Germany. On the other hand working conditions for professionals differ only slightly between Western countries. Hence, the present findings may apply in other Western countries, as well. Moreover, as many findings come from the US or from the UK, the present German data add to the results revealed in these other countries.

Implications

What are the implications of the present data? Should career-oriented women stop having children? Women in top positions indeed often have no children (cf. Eby et al., 2005; Ng et al., 2005). However, this cannot be the solution. Societies can ill afford that their best-educated women do not become mothers. Should women stop striving for high-ranking positions? This is obviously also no solution, given that the percentage of well-educated young women is still rising and there are not enough young men suitable for respective positions. Should career-oriented mothers stop reducing their workload when they have infant children? This would require that mothers be supported by their partners, their family, or a paid nurse, and that economic policy provides for enough external childcare facilities. It is without doubt necessary and valuable when young families have a supporting network and when they have the opportunity to call on external childcare. Respective activities are highly appreciated. Nevertheless, only concentrating on childcare facilities that allow mothers to return to work as soon and as extensively as possible can only be part of the solution for the dilemma facing young mothers. Women would adapt to traditional male careers with a unanimous focus on work and with the advantages (higher objective career success) but also the disadvantages (lower work–life balance, stress, social isolation, etc.) of such traditional careers. Focusing on the traditional male career pattern as the standard might perhaps gradually lead to a change in the above "outside perspective" of gender, i.e., societal expectations directed at the roles of women and men, toward less rigidity and more flexibility. But what about the "inside perspective of gender"? Research has demonstrated that women became more and more agentic over time, but at the same time they remained high in communion (Twenge, 1997, 2001). Research has also demonstrated that women are as interested in their occupational careers as are men. However, they focus on both work and private life, and want to integrate both (Abele, 2005). One means for providing a better work–life balance is part-time work. Flexible work schedules already exist in quite a few employment sectors, and this is another "solution" to the above dilemma. However, these part-time work arrangements often still lead to dead-end careers. If flexible part-time work arrangements would also allow for career advancement and for climbing the career ladder then this would be a further solution to the work/private life balance issue. Wittenberg-Cox (2010), a woman specializing in gender issues in management, concisely pointed out that it is time to stop supporting "poor ladies" on their way to the top by providing leadership training, mentoring, or other "help." Rather, it is time to ask business representatives why they do not hire, keep, and develop the majority of talent in their countries, and, by these means, also appeal to the majority of their customers.

References

Abele, A. E. (2000). A dual impact model of gender and career-related processes and the reciprocal impact of career on gender. In T. Eckes & H-.M. Trautner (Eds.), *The developmental social psychology of gender* (pp. 361–388). Mahwah, NJ: Lawrence Erlbaum.

(2003). The dynamics of masculine-agentic and feminine-communal traits: Findings from a prospective study. *Journal of Personality and Social Psychology*, 85, 768–776.

(2005). Ziele, Selbstkonzept und Work-Life-Balance bei der längerfristigen Lebensgestaltung [Goals, self-concept and work-life balance in people's life planning]. *Zeitschrift für Arbeits- und Organisationspsychologie*, 49, 176–186.

Abele, A. E., Rupprecht, T., & Wojciszke, B. (2008). The influence of success and failure experiences on agency. *European Journal of Social Psychology*, 38, 436–448.

Abele, A. E., & Spurk, D. (2009a). The longitudinal impact of self-efficacy and career goals on objective and subjective career success. *Journal of Vocational Behavior*, 74, 53–62.

(2009b). How do objective and subjective career success interrelate over time? *Journal of Occupational and Organizational Psychology*, 82, 803–824.

(2011). The dual impact of gender and the influence of timing of parenthood on men's and women's career development: Longitudinal findings. *International Journal of Behavioral Development*, 35, 225–232.

Abele, A. E., Spurk, D., & Volmer, J. (2011). The construct of career success: Measurement issues and an empirical example. *Journal of Labour Market Research*, 43, 195–206.

Abele, A. E., & Wojciszke, B. (2007). Agency and communion from the perspective of self versus others. *Journal of Personality and Social Psychology*, 93, 751–763.

Astin, H. S. (1984). The meaning of work in women's lives: A sociological model of career choice and work behavior. *The Counseling Psychologist*, 12, 117–126.

Bem, S. (1993). *The lenses of gender: Transforming the debate on sexual inequality*. New Haven, CT and London: Yale University Press.

Betz, N. E., & Fitzgerald, L. F. (1987). *The career psychology of women*. San Diego, CA: Academic Press.

Corrigall, E. A., & Konrad, A. M. (2007). Gender role attitudes and careers: A longitudinal study. *Sex Roles*, 56, 847–855.

Deaux, K., & LaFrance, M. (1998). Gender. In D. T. Gilbert, S. T. Fiske, & G. Lindzey (Eds.), *The handbook of social psychology* (4th ed., Vol. 1, pp. 788–827). New York: McGraw-Hill.

Eagly, A. H., & Karau, S. J. (2002). Role congruity theory of prejudice toward female leaders. *Psychological Review*, 109, 573–598.

Eby, L. T., Allen, T. D., & Douthitt, S. S. (1999). The role of nonperformance factors on job-related relocation opportunities: A field study and laboratory experiment. *Organizational Behavior and Human Decision Processes*, 79, 29–55.

Eby, L., Casper, W., Lockwood, A., Bordeaux, C., & Brinley, A. (2005). Work and family research in IO/OB: Content analysis and review of the literature (1980–2002). *Journal of Vocational Behavior*, 66, 124–197.

Eurostat (2005). *European statistical data support*. Retrieved January 25, 2005, from http://epp.eurostat.cec.eu.int.

Feldman, S. S., & Aschenbrenner, B. (1983). Impact of parenthood on various aspects of masculinity and femininity: A short-term longitudinal study. *Developmental Psychology*, 19, 278–289.

Gattiker, U. E., & Larwood, L. (1990). Predictors of career achievement in corporate hierarchy. *Human Relations*, 43, 703–726.

Greenhaus, J. H., Parasuraman, S., Wormley, W. M. (1990). Effects of race on organizational experiences, job performance evaluations, and career outcomes. *Academy of Management Journal*, 33, 64–86.

Heslin, P. A. (2005). Conceptualizing and evaluating career success. *Journal of Organizational Behavior*, 26, 113–136.

Kasen, S., Chen, H., Sneed, J., Crawford, T., & Cohen, P. (2006). Social role and birth cohort influences on gender-linked personality traits in women: A 20-year longitudinal analysis. *Journal of Personality and Social Psychology*, 91, 944–958.

Kirchmeyer, C. (1998). Determinants of managerial career success: Evidence and explanation of male/female differences. *Journal of Management*, 24, 673–692.

Lent, R. W., Brown, S. D., & Hackett, G. (1994). Toward a unifying social cognitive theory of career and academic interest, choice, and performance. *Journal of Vocational Behavior*, 45, 79–122.

Lundberg, U., & Frankenhaeuser, M. (1999). Stress and workload of men and women in high-ranking positions. *Journal of Occupational Health Psychology*, 4, 142–151.

Lyness, K. S., & Thompson, D. E. (1997). Above the glass ceiling? A comparison of matched samples of female and male executives. *Journal of Applied Psychology*, 82, 359–375.

Marini, M., & Fan, P.-L. (1997). The gender gap in earnings at career entry. *American Sociological Review*, 62, 588–604.

Melamed, T. (1995). Career success: The moderating effect of gender. *Journal of Vocational Behavior*, 47, 35–60.

—— (1996). Career success: An assessment of a gender-specific model. *Journal of Occupational and Organizational Psychology*, 69, 217–242.

Ng, T. W. H., Eby, L. T., Sorensen, K. L., & Feldman, D. C. (2005). Predictors of objective and subjective career success: A meta-analysis. *Personnel Psychology*, 58, 367–408.

Ng, T. W. H., & Feldman, D. C. (2008). Long work hours: A social identity perspective on meta-analysis data. *Journal of Organizational Behavior*, 29, 853–880.

Olson, J., Frieze, I. H., & Detlefsen, E. G. (1990). Having it all? Combining work and family in a male and a female profession. *Sex Roles*, 23, 515–533.

Reitman, F., & Schneer, J. A. (2003). The promised path: A longitudinal study of managerial careers. *Journal of Managerial Psychology*, 18, 60–75.

—— (2005). The long-term negative impacts of managerial career interruptions: A longitudinal study of men and women MBAs. *Group & Organization Management*, 30, 243–262.

Rudman, L., & Fairchild, K. (2004). Reactions to counterstereotypic behaviour: The role of backlash in cultural stereotype maintenance. *Journal of Personality and Social Psychology*, 87, 157–176.

Runge, T., Frey, D., Gollwitzer, P., Helmreich, R., & Spence, J. (1981). Masculine (instrumental) and feminine (expressive) traits: A comparison between students in the United States and West Germany. *Journal of Cross-Cultural Psychology*, 12, 142–162.

Seibert, S. E., Crant, J. M., & Kraimer, M. L. (1999). Proactive personality and career success. *Journal of Applied Psychology*, 84, 416–427.

Spence, J. T., Helmreich, R. L., & Stapp, J. (1974). The personal attributes questionnaire: A measure of sex role stereotypes and masculinity femininity. *JSAS Catalog of Selected Documents in Psychology*, 4, 43–44.

Super, D. E. (1957). *The psychology of careers: An introduction to vocational development*. New York: Harper & Bros.

Taniguchi, H. (1999). The timing of childbearing and women's wages. *Journal of Marriage & the Family*, 61, 1008–1019.

Tharenou, P., Latimer, S., & Conroy, D. (1994). How do you make it to the top? An examination of influences on women's and men's managerial advancement. *Academy of Management Journal*, 37, 899–931.

Twenge, J. M. (1997). Changes in masculine and feminine traits over time: A meta-analysis. *Sex Roles*, 36, 305–325.

(2001). Changes in women's assertiveness in response to status and roles: A cross-temporal meta-analysis. *Journal of Personality and Social Psychology*, 81, 133–145.

Uchronski, M. (2008). Agency and communion in spontaneous self-descriptions: Occurrence and situational malleability. *European Journal of Social Psychology*, 38, 1093–1102.

Watts, H., & Eccles, J. (Eds.). (2008). *Gender and occupational outcomes*. Washington, DC: American Psychological Association.

Wittenberg-Cox, A. (2010). *How women mean business: A step to step guide to profiting from gender balanced business*. New York: Wiley.

PART VI

The role of context

19 Gender differences in attainment across generations from a historical perspective

Anne McMunn, Elizabeth Webb, Mel Bartley, David Blane and Gopal Netuveli

Abstract

This chapter examines gender differences in socioeconomic attainment and wellbeing among English men and women born in the first half of the 20th century using the English Longitudinal Study of Ageing (ELSA). We find a fairly traditional picture of gender difference. Women's attainment in education and occupational class was significantly and substantially lower than that of men, and there was no evidence of a decrease in these gender differences with each subsequent birth cohort. A steadily decreasing gender differential was seen in the number of years men and women spent in paid work, however. Relationships between family forms and socioeconomic attainment ran in opposite directions for men and women. Non-normative family forms, such as never having lived with a spouse/partner or not having children, were associated with higher socioeconomic attainment for women, but lower socioeconomic attainment for men. Results suggest that recent reductions seen in gender inequality have been not so much a gentle shift over the course of the century, but the result of relatively swift and dramatic social change. For the cohorts of men and women who represent our current ageing population, gender inequality in education and occupation was deeply entrenched.

Introduction

Following organized feminist pressure for gender equality in the 1970s, referred to as second-wave feminism, gender differences in opportunities for achievement have decreased fairly steadily, at least in certain domains. Educational attainment among young women now equals or exceeds that of young men in Great Britain (Corti, Laurie, & Dex, 1995). Great Britain, like many countries in Europe and North America, has seen dramatic changes in normative gender divisions between work and family over the past 40 years. Participation in paid work is now a fact of life for the majority of women, including those with family responsibilities, and fathers are more involved in childcare. While there is still a long way to go before equality is achieved, both between genders (EHRC, 2010; Schober, 2009) and among women in divergent socioeconomic circumstances, there is some evidence that shifting gender norms and women's increasing educational attainment and economic independence, along with decreasing rates of marriage and childbearing, have worked to decrease the gender differential in socioeconomic attainment, at least for some women (Dex, Ward, & Joshi, 2008; Duffield, 2002; Joshi & Paci, 1998). However, these social changes are relatively recent. We are regularly reminded that ours is an ageing society, and the current generation of people in their "Third or Fourth Age" (Laslett, 1996) established their careers and families prior to the height of second-wave feminism in the 1970s and the changes in women's education, maternity legislation, and family-friendly policies that followed. Knowledge of the predictors and impacts of gender differences in attainment for men and women born in the first half of the twentieth century is interesting in its own right; moreover, an illustration of gender relations in this period can provide a form of social baseline against which the extent of social change in subsequent generations can be compared.

The English Longitudinal Study of Ageing (ELSA) provides a unique opportunity to compare a variety of indicators of attainment over time for generations of English men and women born in the first half of the twentieth century. There are no other national longitudinal datasets that study such a variety of aspects of people's lives across all cohorts born over this time. ELSA is a large, national study of ageing that has followed people who were aged 50+ since 2002 (born before 1952), with follow-up information collected every 2 years. For this study, we use wave 3 of ELSA, collected in 2006, because it included a separate life history interview to collect past information on employment, partners, children, and residences across participants' lives from birth. Including original ELSA participants, and a new sample of people who were aged 50–55 in 2006 (born 1953–1956), we have a sample of 3,878 men and 4,783 women for our analysis. For much of our analysis, we have grouped respondents into the decade in which they were born in order to create quasi-birth cohorts.

In addition to life history information on work and family, ELSA provides detailed information across a variety of indicators of psychosocial attainment, such as paid work, socioeconomic position, family formation, health, and subjective wellbeing. This chapter examines the extent to which men and women differ in their attainment across these various life domains and whether any disparities between men and women have diminished across the generations born over the first half of the twentieth century in England.

Gender differences in socioeconomic attainment over time

We begin by looking at differences in various types of socioeconomic attainment. What we find are examples of changing gender differences embedded within strong continuities of inequality. Starting with a socioeconomic indicator from early adulthood, we examine gender differences in those who had attained a university degree or attended some higher education. We know that for current generations girls often do better than boys on educational outcomes,

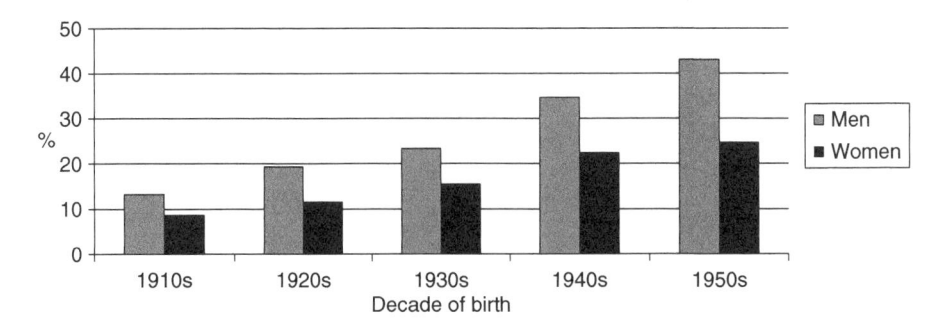

Figure 19.1 *Gender differences in having a university degree or some higher education by decade of birth*

but for older generations this was not the case. For the men and women in our study, the proportion accessing higher education increased rapidly across successive birth cohorts, but this increase was slightly greater for men than for women (Figure 19.1). The result is that gender differences in educational attainment remained fairly constant for those born in the first part of the century, with men at least 50% more likely than women to have attended higher education, and then increased slightly for those born in the middle of the century. Men born in the 1950s are 75% more likely to have attended at least some higher education than their female contemporaries.

Patterns at the other end of the educational distribution mirrored those seen for high educational attainment. For every decade of birth, women were significantly more likely than men to have no educational qualifications. The lack of a narrowing in the gender difference in educational attainment for these generations of men and women reminds us of the entrenched backdrop of gender inequality against which the subsequent elimination of gender differences in educational attainment was dramatically obtained (Corti et al., 1995).

While differences in educational attainment persisted for these generations of men and women, changes in labor market participation were much more dramatic. The difference between men and women in the average number of years they spent in paid work (up to 2006) decreased steadily for each subsequent decade of birth. Table 19.1 shows that, among those born in the 1910s, men were in paid work for at least 23 years longer than women on average, while for those born in the 1950s, men had been in paid work an average of 7.5 years longer than women of the same age by 2006. Men were also significantly more likely than women to be unemployed for a year or more, and the prevalence of being unemployed for a year or more increased significantly for each subsequent decade of birth, ranging from 2% for men born in the 1910s to 7% for those born in the 1950s (not shown). The equivalent proportions for women were 1% to 4%, with few remaining unemployed for much longer than a year. These levels of unemployment are relatively low compared with subsequent cohorts, although the ways in which people define and report unemployment are likely to have changed over time. In the 1930s, unemployment among women is likely to have been made less visible by the prevailing attitudes and policies, which identified employment as desirable only for unmarried women. For example, the 1931 Anomalies Act excluded married women from eligibility for claiming unemployment benefit, and marriage bars (which excluded married women from certain occupations) remained in place for some organizations until the 1960s (Rowbotham, 1997; TUC, 1944). There were virtually no men who spent a year or more as a full-time homemaker. While the number of years that women spent in paid work seems to have increased fairly steadily for women in this study, the proportion of women who identified themselves as full-time homemakers did not decrease steadily. The proportion of full-time homemakers was actually lowest for women born in the 1910s and 1920s (at around a third), a generation likely to have been drawn into the labor market during World War II when employment rates were temporarily high for women. Full-time homemaking was most common among women born in the 1930s (at 40%), the generation of women who reached adulthood during the traditional post-war period. Women born in the 1950s, many of whom reached adulthood at the peak of second-wave feminism, became less likely to identify as full-time homemakers, at a little more than a third (not shown).

We have seen that English women born over the first half of the twentieth century increased the number of years they spent in paid work, relative to men, but did the types of occupations they held also become closer to those held by men? Table 19.1 shows women's likelihood of being (or having been) in a managerial or professional occupation compared with that of men. Women were significantly less likely than men to have been in a professional or managerial occupation for each birth cohort. Women were less than half as likely as men to be or have been in a professional or managerial occupation among those born in the 1910s and 1920s. The gender difference decreased for those born in the 1930s and was at its smallest for those born in the 1940s. It then widened again for those born in the 1950s. This may partly reflect the changing composition of the female workforce in the 1950s when mothers of young children began to enter the labor market in larger numbers, often taking up low-paid, part-time jobs to fit in around family responsibilities (Rowbotham, 1997). In addition, women from working-class families may have had more opportunity to opt out of paid work in the 1950s, which saw the rise of full employment and the "family wage." This enabled working-class women to adopt the normative role of full-time homemaker that had previously been the domain of the middle classes.

So, the picture of gender differences in socioeconomic attainment for those in England born in the first half of the twentieth century is one of both continuity and change. While gender differentials in labor market participation decreased, those in educational attainment and occupational class did not. The oldest of the cohorts included here "came of age" in the 1930s when the demands for gender equality seen at the start of the century with the suffragette movement were in retreat in the face of widespread unemployment (Rowbotham, 1997), and

Table 19.1. *Gender differences in socioeconomic attainment by decade of birth*[a]

Decade of birth

	1910s		1920s		1930s		1940s		1950s	
	β	95% CI	β	95% CI	β	95% CI	β	95% CI	β	95% CI
Years worked[b]										
Men	0		0		0		0		0	
Women	−23.28	−27.67 to −18.90	−17.92	−19.41 to −16.43	−14.52	−15.57 to −13.47	−11.16	−11.95 to −10.36	−7.51	−8.41 to −6.61
	OR	95% CI	OR	95% CI	OR	95% CI	OR	95% CI	OR	95% CI
Likelihood of being in a professional or managerial occupation										
Men	1.00		1.00		1.00		1.00		1.00	
Women	0.40	0.25 – 0.62	0.36	0.29 – 0.45	0.57	0.48 – 0.68	0.69	0.60 – 0.80	0.42	0.32 – 0.57

[a] Both models adjusted for year of birth and a quadratic measure of age.
[b] Number of years spent in paid work up to age 50, women compared with men.

women generally left the paid labor market upon marriage, if financial resources allowed (Purvis, 1997). The mobilization of the war effort in the 1940s required all women aged between 19 and 40 to register at employment exchanges in order to be recruited for essential work (Rowbotham, 1997). Then, while the post-war decade has come to epitomize convention, we have seen that women continued to increase the amount of time they spent in the labor market so that by 1961 women made up a third of the labor force, and more than half of these women were married. During the 1960s British women became increasingly likely to remain in paid work until the birth of their first child, and by the 1970s, when the youngest of the ELSA participants were leaving full-time education, the women's liberation movement was in full swing. The Employment Protection Act of 1975 made paid maternity leave a statutory right, the Equal Opportunities Commission was created, and the Equal Pay Act of 1970 came into force in 1976 (although its impact was restricted) (Rowbotham, 1997). However, we have seen that the women in this study who were young enough to potentially benefit from these changes in the 1970s still spent, on average, over 7 years less in paid work than men and were much less likely to work in a managerial or professional occupation than their male counterparts. In terms of education, we have seen that gender inequality did not improve for those born in the first half of the last century. It was not until the 1980s, when the youngest women in our study were in their 30s, that gender equality in educational attainment was achieved in Britain (Corti et al., 1995; Crompton & Sanderson, 1986; Dale & Egerton, 1995).

Gender differences in the impact of family on socioeconomic attainment

We have seen that women of all ages in ELSA were less likely than their male counterparts to have access to higher education and high-quality occupations, and spent less of their lives in paid work, although gender differences in the latter decreased markedly for more recent generations. Traditional norms regarding gender divisions in responsibility for rearing children mean that parental status is likely to explain at least some of the gender differences in socioeconomic attainment for these generations of men and women. In this section we examine associations between parenthood and partnership on the one hand, and gender differences in socioeconomic attainment on the other.

Partnership

For our analysis of partnership we have combined marriages with unmarried cohabiting partnerships. Unmarried cohabiting partnerships became more common with each subsequent cohort. Overall, unmarried cohabitations rose from 2.5% for those born in the 1910s to nearly a fifth of those born in the 1950s (not shown). Figure 19.2 shows the number of partnerships (married or

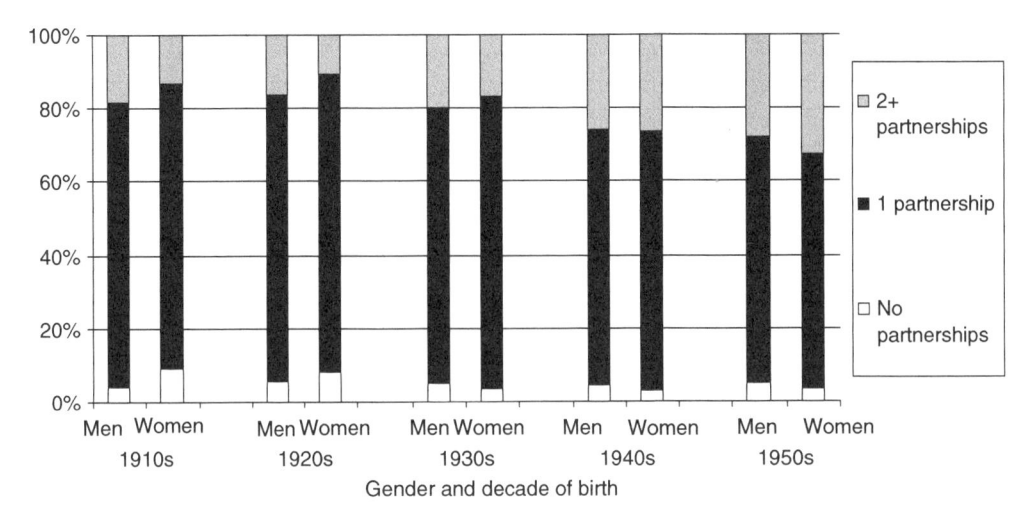

Figure 19.2 *Gender differences in lifetime number of cohabiting partnerships or marriages (as of 2006) by decade of birth*

unmarried) that men and women had up to 2006 by their decade of birth. Overall, while living with only one spouse or partner over the life course was the most predominant situation for men and women born in every decade, the proportion having lived with more than one spouse or partner was higher for those born in the 1940s and 1950s. Gender differences in the number of partnerships were small.

Older women (aged 75 and over) were significantly less likely than older men to be currently living with a spouse or partner (not shown). Experiencing a divorce or separation became more common with each subsequent cohort. Just under 10% of those born in the 1910s experienced a divorce or separation, rising to nearly 40% for those born in the 1950s (by the year 2006). There were no consistent gender differences in the prevalence of divorce or separation (not shown).

Parenthood

In terms of parenthood, the average age at which ELSA participants had their children decreased steadily so that those born in the 1950s had their first child about 5 years younger (at about 25 for men and 23 for women) than those born in the 1910s. The average age at which women had their first child was consistently 2 to 3 years younger than the age at which men had their first child (not shown). In terms of family size, it was those born in the 1930s that had the largest families, with over a third having three or more children (Figure 19.3). Gender differences were small.

So, we see that the considerable social changes in family formation seen in the latter half of the twentieth century are hardly apparent for those born in the

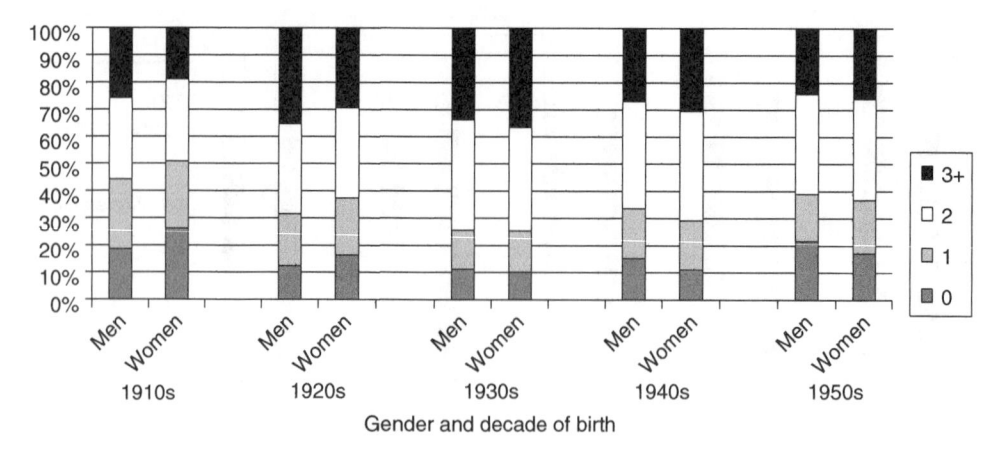

Figure 19.3 *Number of children by gender and decade of birth*

first half. There is some increase in the prevalence of divorce and unmarried cohabitation, but, predominantly, men and women across the sample lived with one spouse or partner over their life course. Age at first birth declined over the ELSA cohorts, highlighting, again, the highly traditional backdrop against which the rapid social changes in delayed fertility and increased childlessness in the latter part of the twentieth century occurred. Given the traditional family forms seen among participants in this study, we may equally expect to see traditional gender divisions of labor among these generations of British men and women. If so, we might hypothesize marriage and parenthood to have been more disruptive to forms of socioeconomic attainment, such as education and employment, for women than for men. The next section investigates relationships between family forms and gender differences in access to higher education in ELSA.

Family formation and higher education

Table 19.2 shows multivariate logistic regression models to assess the relationship between indicators of family formation and having a university degree or some higher education for men and women separately, adjusted for each of the family forms shown simultaneously and age. There were clear gender differences in the relationship between the number of marriages or cohabiting partnerships people had had over their life course and accessing higher education. Men who had never lived with a spouse or partner were significantly less likely than other men to have a university degree or some higher education, while women who had never lived with a spouse or partner were significantly more likely than other women to have had a university degree or some higher education. Perhaps having a degree, and, therefore, greater access to higher-paying occupations, made men in these generations more attractive as potential partners in their gendered role as providers. Women who forwent family roles may have

Table 19.2. *Odds ratios for having access to higher education by indicators of family formation in men and women*

		Degree or higher education*			
		Men		Women	
Family indicators		OR	95% CI	OR	95% CI
Currently cohabiting	No	1		1	
	Yes	2.23	1.74 – 2.85	1.40	1.15 – 1.72
Number of cohabitations	0	0.50	0.32 – 0.76	1.88	1.28 – 2.77
	1	1	–	1	–
	2 or more	0.90	0.74 – 1.10	0.75	0.61 – 0.93
Total duration of cohabitations (year)		1.01	1.01 – 1.02	1.00	1.00 – 1.00
Ever divorced/ separated	No	1		1	
	Yes	0.75	0.62 – 0.91	0.82	0.67 – 1.00
Age at birth of first child		1.06	1.05 – 1.08	1.10	1.08 – 1.12
Number of children	0	1	–	1	–
	1	1.15	0.85 – 1.55	0.67	0.50 – 0.90
	2	1.39	1.07 – 1.81	0.68	0.52 – 0.88
	3 or more	1.14	0.87 – 1.50	0.59	0.45 – 0.77

* Mutually adjusted for all indicators of family formation and for linear and quadratic age terms.

been more likely to have the freedom to pursue higher education, which in turn would have increased the opportunity cost of giving up work. There was no significant difference in the likelihood of having had some higher education by the number of partnerships men had had over the life course, while women who had had multiple partnerships were less likely than women in one partnership to have a university degree or some higher education.

The older men and women had been when they had their first child, the more likely they were to have attended higher education, but family size was much more strongly associated with attending higher education for women than for men. The likelihood of having attended higher education decreased dramatically by the number of children women had while men who had two children were significantly more likely to have attended higher education than childless men, suggesting potential gender inequity in the impact of parenthood on access to education. It is important to note, however, that these models do not suggest a direction of causality. Family formation for the generations of people in ELSA often occurred during the years that one might normally attend higher education. Decisions to form a family may have led women to decide not to carry on with pursuing their education, while women who did not have children, and men regardless of whether they had children or not, were freer to do so. These different clusters of education and family forms for men and women may have sent them down differing "attainment" tracks in terms of socioeconomic position and health or wellbeing. In subsequent sections we will examine whether educational attainment and family size attenuate gender differences in the number of years men and women spent in paid work, or being or having been in a professional or managerial occupation.

Family formation and number of years in paid work

When we examine gender differences in the relationships between family indicators and the number of years spent in paid work we see very different stories for men and women in these generations (Table 19.3). For men, both partnerships (i.e., marriage or cohabitation) and fatherhood were associated with a greater attachment to the labor market. Currently living with a spouse or partner and having had children were both associated with an increased number of years in paid work for men (2 to 3 on average), with increasing duration of partnership significantly associated with increasing duration of participation in paid work. Men who had never partnered had spent significantly fewer years in paid work (4 fewer on average) than partnered men.

Relationships between family and paid work ran in the opposite direction for women. Women who had been in one continuous partnership (marriage or cohabitation) had spent significantly fewer years in the labor market than both never partnered women and women who had experienced multiple partnerships, and increasing duration of partnership was significantly associated with decreasing years spent in paid work. Delaying childbearing was associated with increasing attachment to the labor market – the later women had their first child, the longer they spent in paid work – and the average number of years women spent in paid work decreased dramatically with each child that they had. Women who had three or more children spent more than 8.5 fewer years in paid employment than women who did not have any children. However, when we included family size in a multivariate model, it did not appear to attenuate gender differences in the number of years spent in paid work (not shown), suggesting that gender differences in labor market participation were due to more than the differential impacts of motherhood and fatherhood.

So, we see a picture of traditional gendered roles among English men and women in these generations. Results suggest that family roles dramatically curtailed women's labor market attachment, while for men they seem to signify the traditional male role as family provider, reinforcing attachment to the labor market. However, even among those with strong labor market attachment there were differences in occupational attainment. We have seen that women in this study were consistently less likely than men to be working in a professional or

Table 19.3. *Regression coefficients for number of years in paid work by indicators of family formation among men and women*

Family indicators		Number of years in paid work*			
		Men		Women	
		β	95% CI	β	95% CI
Currently cohabiting	No	0		0	
	Yes	2.20	1.33 – 3.08	0.20	−0.79 – 1.18
Number of cohabitations	0	−4.20	−5.93 – −2.47	7.17	4.78 – 9.56
	1	0		0	
	2 or more	−0.40	−1.12 – 0.33	1.50	0.50 – 2.49
Total duration of cohabitations (year)		0.09	0.06 – 0.12	−0.11	−0.14 – −0.07
Ever divorced/ separated	No	0		0	
	Yes	−0.59	−1.32 – 0.14	1.56	0.61 – 2.51
Age at birth of first child		−0.05	−0.13 – 0.02	0.17	0.07 – 0.28
Number of children	0	0		0	
	1	2.50	1.44 – 3.56	−3.61	−5.10 – −2.11
	2	2.74	1.79 – 3.69	−6.34	−7.64 – −5.04
	3 or more	2.05	1.00 – 3.10	−8.60	−9.97 – −7.23

* Mutually adjusted for all indicators of family formation and for linear and quadratic age terms.

managerial occupation. Next we examine the extent to which this gender difference is related to the differential impact of family roles on the occupational attainment of men and women.

Family formation and occupational attainment

We have seen that family forms had very different relationships with education and employment for men and women in this study. Similarly, there were strong gender differences in relationships between partnership, parenthood, and the likelihood of being in a professional or managerial occupation (Table 19.4). Partnership was associated with an increased likelihood of being in a professional or managerial occupation for men and a decreased likelihood of the same for women. Men who were currently living with a spouse or partner were significantly more likely than single men to be or have been in a professional or managerial occupation, and the longer a man had lived with a spouse or partner the more likely he was to be or have been in a professional or managerial

Table 19.4. *Odds ratios of being in a managerial or professional occupation by indicators of family formation among men and women*

		Managerial or professional occupation*			
		Men		Women	
Family indicators		OR	95% CI	OR	95% CI
Currently cohabiting	No	1		1	
	Yes	1.99	1.59 – 2.49	1.19	0.98 – 1.43
Number of cohabitations	0	0.50	0.33 – 0.75	2.62	1.82 – 3.77
	1	1		1	
	2 +	0.89	0.73 – 1.09	0.84	0.69 – 1.03
Total duration of cohabitations (years)		1.01	1.01 – 1.02	1.00	0.99 – 1.00
Ever divorced/separated	No	1		1	
	Yes	0.76	0.62 – 0.92	0.85	0.71 – 1.03
Age at birth of first child		1.04	1.03 – 1.06	1.06	1.04 – 1.08
Number of children	0	1		1	
	1	1.02	0.77 – 1.36	0.56	0.42 – 0.76
	2	1.21	0.94 – 1.56	0.51	0.40 – 0.66
	3 +	0.98	0.76 – 1.28	0.40	0.31 – 0.52

* Mutually adjusted for all indicators of family formation and for linear and quadratic age term.

occupation. For women, having remained single was significantly associated with an increased likelihood of being in, or having been in, a professional or managerial occupation, independent of parenthood. Perhaps partnership signified different activities for men and women in these generations regardless of whether they had children. For men, a partner may have signified an additional resource to free them from domestic labor, allowing them further time and energy to focus on their careers. In addition, men who occupied managerial or professional occupations may have been perceived as more attractive partners, and, therefore, were more likely to cohabit. The finding that single women were more likely to be in professional or managerial occupations is in line with other studies of women in these generations. A study of civil servants born 1930–1955 found that single women were more likely than married or cohabiting women to be in "high grade" occupations (Bartley, Martikainen, Shipley, & Marmot, 2004). The differences in occupation by partnership status that we find among women may partly reflect the "occupational downgrading" after childbirth that was a stable feature of the labor market for a large minority of mothers at least through the 1980s (Dex, 1987).

For both men and women, delaying parenthood seems to have been associated with occupational rewards as the likelihood of being in a professional or managerial occupation rose with the increasing age that participants had their first child. As with accessing higher education and years in paid work, family size was significantly associated with a decreasing likelihood of having been in a professional or managerial occupation for women only. The same was not true for men. However, as with labor market participation, including family size into a multivariate model did not attenuate gender differences in the likelihood of being in or having been in a professional or managerial occupation. Unlike labor market participation, educational qualifications did explain nearly 30% of women's reduced likelihood of having been in a professional or managerial occupation, but the gender difference remained strong and significant (Table 19.5). As we might expect, gender differences in attainment had greater consequences for differences in the quality of jobs that men and women occupied than for gender differences in labor market participation per se.

Gender differences in social mobility

We have been looking at gender differences in attainment in adulthood for English men and women born in the first half of the twentieth century. We also have some information about the social conditions of the early lives of ELSA participants that was collected retrospectively when they were aged 50 or older. Using these indicators, we can investigate whether there were gender differences in whether men and women were able to "improve their lot" from a socioeconomic perspective.

Participants were asked if they had ever experienced severe financial hardship, and, if so, at what age. Those who reported experiencing severe financial hardship have been divided based on whether they first experienced this hardship before or after age 26. There was no significant gender difference in the relationship between early hardship and educational attainment, but there was for occupational class. Figure 19.4 shows that the absolute gender difference in the proportion in a professional or managerial occupation was greatest for those who did not experience any financial hardship (with men much more likely than women to be in a professional or managerial occupation), but non-existent for those who reported experiencing severe financial hardship before age 26.

We find a similar phenomenon when we use another indicator of early life socioeconomic circumstances: father's occupation when participants were age 14. Paternal occupations were grouped into the following categories for purposes of this analysis:

- professional, managerial, technical occupations, and business owners;
- administrative, clerical, caring, leisure, service, and sales occupations;
- skilled tradesmen, plant, or machine operators;
- other casual employment;
- unemployed, sick, or retired.

Table 19.5. Gender differences in having been in a managerial or professional occupation

		Age-adjusted			Adjusted for age + educational attainment			Adjusted for age + family size			Fully adjusted		
		OR	95% CI		OR	95% CI		OR	95% CI		OR	95% CI	
Gender	Men	1			1			1			1		
	Women	0.55	0.50	0.62	0.71	0.63	0.81	0.55	0.49	0.62	0.71	0.62	0.81
Year of birth		1.02	1.01	1.03	0.98	0.97	0.99	1.01	1.01	1.02	0.98	0.97	0.99
Year of birth squared		1.00	1.00	1.00	1.00	1.00	1.00	1.00	1.00	1.00	1.00	1.00	1.00
Educational qualifications	Degree/higher education				1						1		
	A Level				0.29	0.23	0.36				0.28	0.22	0.36
	GCSE level				0.20	0.17	0.24				0.20	0.17	0.24
	Lower				0.08	0.06	0.12				0.09	0.06	0.12
	Foreign/other				0.11	0.09	0.14				0.12	0.09	0.15
	None				0.04	0.03	0.05				0.05	0.04	0.05
Children	None							1			1		
	1							0.82	0.67	1.00	0.82	0.65	1.04
	2							0.84	0.70	1.01	0.78	0.64	0.95
	3 or more							0.69	0.57	0.83	0.69	0.56	0.86

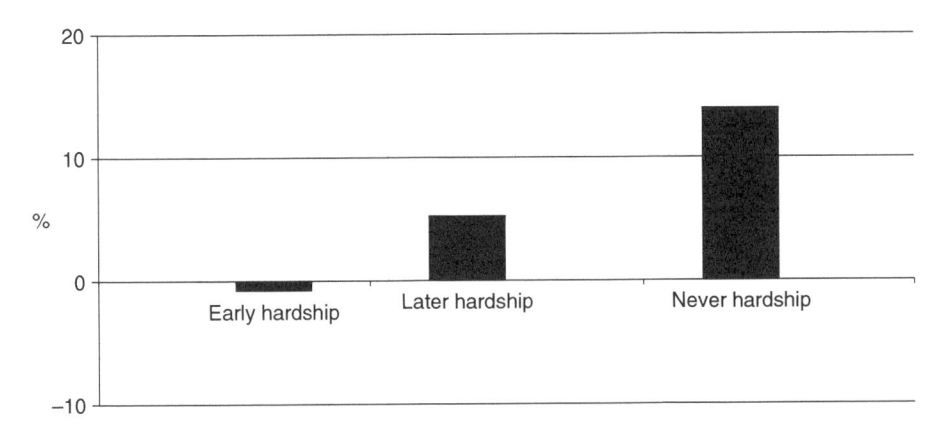

Figure 19.4 *Absolute gender gap in proportion in professional or managerial occupation by severe financial hardship*

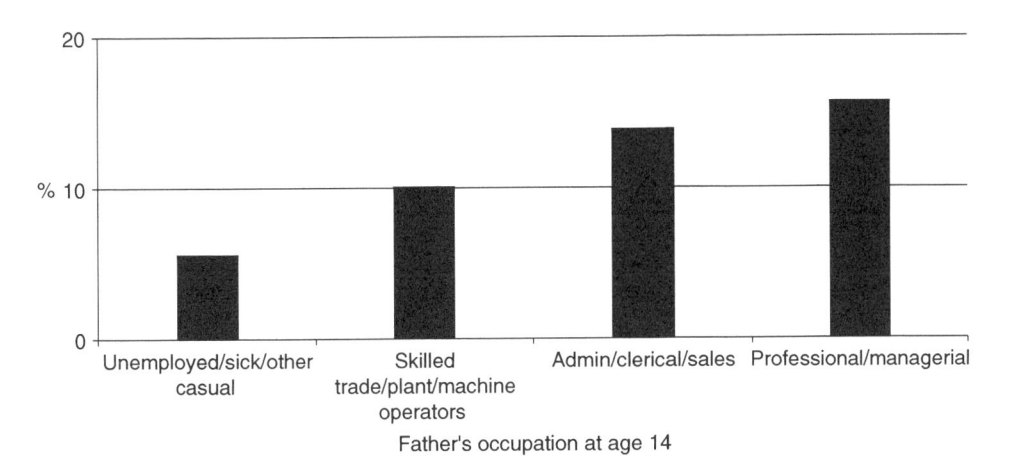

Figure 19.5 *Absolute gender gap in proportion in professional or managerial occupation by father's occupation at age 14: % male excess*

Figure 19.5 shows that the gender difference in being or having been in a professional or managerial occupation was greatest for those whose fathers had been in a professional or managerial occupation, and smallest for those whose fathers were unemployed or sick, or were casual laborers.

So, we find evidence to suggest that gender differences in occupational attainment were greatest for those from relatively advantaged backgrounds, and much weaker for those who experienced deprivation in early life. This may be the result of class differences in gender values in the first half of the twentieth century. The ideology of gendered spheres of public and private life was initially established among the middle classes and existed as an aspiration for working-class families for whom a single breadwinner was not an option (Davidoff & Hall, 1987;

Roberts, 1995; Williams, 1991). Therefore, gendered divisions in labor can be seen from a Bourdieuian perspective as a distinctive lifestyle associated with middle-class status and privilege reproduced within class and gender structures (Bourdieu, 1984). There is some evidence to suggest that these class patterns in gender norms have subsequently shifted. In a nationally representative sample of adults in 2002, Crompton (2006) showed that working-class women reduced their employment to a greater extent than professional women when their children were young, and men and women from routine and manual occupations expressed more gender-stereotypical attitudes than those from professional or managerial occupations.

Gender differences in subjective wellbeing attainment

So far, we have been examining gender differences in socioeconomic attainment; however, it is increasingly recognized that financial affluence is not the only indicator of "success" (Bok, 2010; Helliwell, Layard, & Sachs, 2012; Kahneman, Krueger, Schkade, Schwartz, & Stone, 2006; Michaelson, Abdallah, Steuer, Thompson, & Marks, 2009; see also Abele, this volume). This chapter, therefore, defines attainment broadly to include physical functioning and subjective wellbeing as well as socioeconomic attainment. Attainment in subjective wellbeing was measured by three indicators: a measure of quality of life, depressive symptoms, and life satisfaction. The quality of life measure used, called the CASP-19, is a 19-item scale comprising four domains: control, autonomy, self-realization, and pleasure, which was specifically developed to measure quality of life at older ages (Hyde, Wiggins, Higgs, & Blane, 2003). Response categories, which ranged from "often" to "never," were assigned a score of 0–3 and summed to create a total score with higher scores indicating better quality of life. Life satisfaction was measured using the 5-item version of the Satisfaction with Life Scale (Diener, Emmons, Larsen, & Griffen, 1985), with scores ranging from 5 to 35 and higher scores reflecting more life satisfaction. Figure 19.6 shows that there were no substantial gender differences in mean quality of life or in mean life satisfaction score for any age group. Both indicators of wellbeing followed a similar age pattern for men and women with a slight decrease after age 75.

Depressive symptoms were measured using the 8-item version of the Center for Epidemiologic Studies–Depression Scale (CES-D) (Radloff, 1977). The CES-D asks the degree to which participants experienced depressive symptoms, such as restless sleep, being unhappy, and so on, over the past month and has been extensively used in a range of clinical and non-clinical settings and in different populations. Cut-offs of three, four, or five items have been suggested when using the 8-item CES-D (Steffick, 2000). In this study a dichotomous categorical measure of depression is used, defined by reporting three or more items on the CES-D. Figure 19.7 shows the well-documented gender differential in the prevalence of

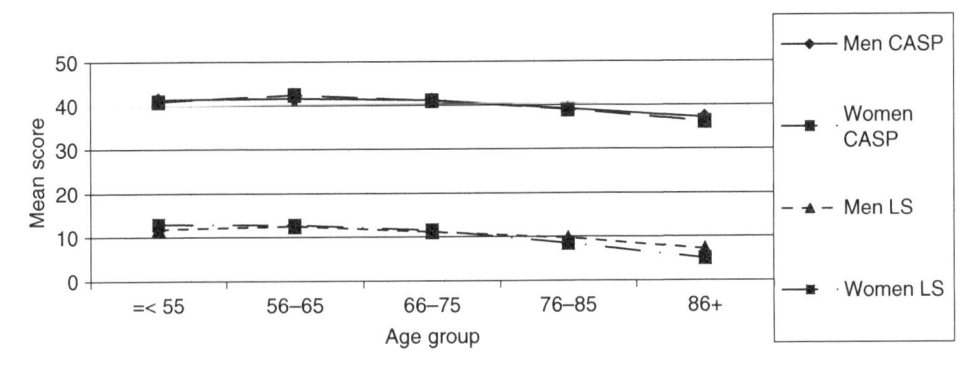

Figure 19.6 *Gender differences in mean quality of life score and mean life satisfaction score by age*

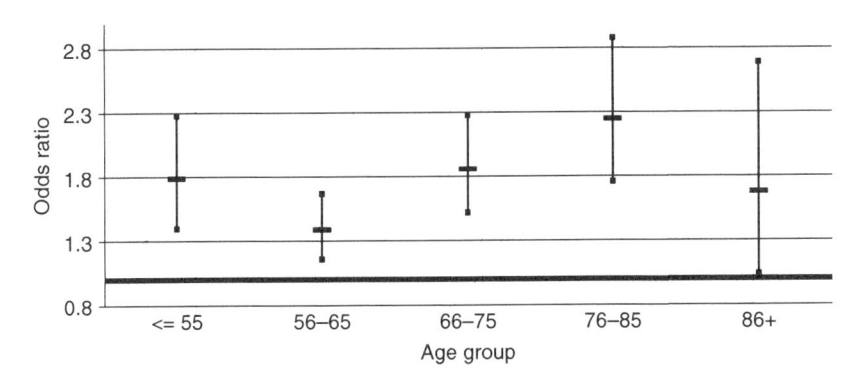

Figure 19.7 *Gender difference in likelihood of having depressive symptoms by age*

depressive symptoms (Bebbington, 1996). Women were consistently more likely than men to have three or more depressive symptoms. The gender difference was largest for those in their late 70s and early 80s, with women well over twice as likely as men to have three or more depressive symptoms, but the size of the gender difference did not vary significantly by age.

We next examine whether relationships between family indicators and wellbeing differ for men and women. Table 19.6 shows that cohabitation was generally associated with positive wellbeing for both men and women. Both current partnership and duration of partnership were positively associated with quality of life and associated with a lower likelihood of depressive symptoms for both men and women. Duration of partnership was also significantly associated with higher life satisfaction for both men and women. Current partnership was significantly associated with lower life satisfaction for women; however, this may be a statistical artifact as it is seen once duration is accounted for in the model. While divorce/separation and multiple partnerships were associated with reduced quality of life and increased likelihood of depressive symptoms, perhaps strangely, these factors were significantly associated with greater reported life satisfaction among

Table 19.6. *Wellbeing by indicators of family formation among men and women*

		Quality of life*			
Family indicators		Men		Women	
		β	95% CI	β	95% CI
Currently cohabiting	No	0		0	
	Yes	2.17	1.17 – 3.18	3.15	2.42 – 3.88
Number of cohabitations	0	−2.58	−4.23 – −0.92	−0.84	−2.38 – 0.70
	1	0		0	
	2+	−0.76	−1.60 – 0.08	−1.03	−1.80 – −0.26
Total duration of cohabitations (year)		0.06	0.04 – 0.08	0.05	0.03 – 0.07
Ever divorced/ separated	No	0		0	
	Yes	−1.22	−2.04 – −0.40	−2.01	−2.75 – −1.28
Age at birth of first child		0.02	−0.06 – 0.10	0.10	0.03 – 0.17
Number of children	0	0		0	
	1	0.24	−0.94 – 1.43	−0.32	−1.43 – 0.79
	2	0.92	−0.12 – 1.96	−0.20	−1.18 – 0.77
	3+	0.44	−0.66 – 1.53	−0.84	−1.86 – 0.18
		Life satisfaction*			
Family indicators		Men		Women	
		β	95% CI	β	95% CI
Currently cohabiting	No	0		0	
	Yes	−0.78	−1.96 – 0.40	−1.50	−2.38 – −0.62
Number of cohabitations	0	0.82	−1.42 – 3.05	−0.12	−2.39 – 2.15
	1	0		0	
	2+	0.57	−0.32 – 1.45	1.51	0.64 – 2.37
Total duration of cohabitations (year)		0.06	0.03 – 0.08	0.05	0.03 – 0.07
Ever divorced/ separated	No	0		0	
	Yes	0.68	−0.23 – 1.59	1.13	0.25 – 2.02
Age at birth of first child		0.01	−0.07 – 0.09	0.11	0.03 – 0.19
Number of children	0	0		1	
	1	−0.01	−1.52 – 1.49	0.84	−0.50 – 2.18
	2	0.35	−0.95 – 1.64	0.60	−0.62 – 1.82
	3+	−0.26	−1.60 – 1.08	−0.31	−1.61 – 0.99

		Quality of life*			
		Depressive symptoms*			
Family indicators		Men		Women	
		OR	95% CI	OR	95% CI
Currently cohabiting	No	1		1	
	Yes	0.30	0.24 – 0.38	0.40	0.33 – 0.47
Number of cohabitations	0	1.47	0.98 – 2.20	1.00	0.69 – 1.46
	1	1		1	
	2+	1.02	0.80 – 1.28	1.41	1.18 – 1.69
Total duration of cohabitations (year)		0.99	0.99 – 1.00	0.99	0.99 – 1.00
Ever divorced/ separated	No	1		1	
	Yes	1.33	1.07 – 1.66	1.50	1.27 – 1.78
Age at birth of first child		0.97	0.94 – 0.99	0.96	0.95 – 0.98
Number of children	0	1		1	
	1	0.84	0.61 – 1.16	1.06	0.81 – 1.39
	2	0.69	0.52 – 0.92	0.87	0.68 – 1.11
	3+	0.76	0.56 – 1.02	1.21	0.95 – 1.55

* Mutually adjusted for all indicators of family formation and for linear and quadratic age terms.

women. These somewhat contradictory relationships may reflect conceptual differences between an evaluative, summation of wellbeing, such as life satisfaction, and the measure of quality of life used here which is designed to reflect met and unmet needs (Schwarz & Strack, 1999). Perhaps higher levels of life satisfaction among previously partnered women reflect an evaluation of improved circumstances after leaving a negative relationship, or entering into a superior second relationship.

Having children later was associated with higher quality of life and higher life satisfaction for women and was protective against depressive symptoms for both men and women. Men who had two children were significantly less likely to have depressive symptoms than childless men, but otherwise family size was not associated with indicators of wellbeing.

We also examined the extent to which educational qualifications, partnership, or parenthood might explain the gender difference in depressive symptoms. While those with fewer educational qualifications were more at risk of suffering from depressive symptoms, the inclusion of educational qualifications reduced the gender difference in the prevalence of depressive symptoms by only 7%.

In the final model the gender difference in depressive symptoms was reduced by 19%, with nearly all of this reduction being due to the inclusion of current partnership; therefore, women's greater risk of depression was not explained by gender differences in education or family responsibilities in this study. There are many other factors, such as labor market experiences, which could be explored in future work.

Gender differences in physical functioning

Here we examine gender differences in physical functioning as measured by reporting a limiting long-standing illness or having difficulty with one or more activities of daily living (ADLs) at wave 3 of ELSA (2006). The activities of daily living included were: dressing, walking across a room, bathing or showering, eating, getting in and out of bed, and using the toilet. Figure 19.8 shows that, for each of the age groups, women were very slightly more likely than men to suffer from a limiting long-standing illness or to have difficulty with one or more ADLs. However, these gender differences were not statistically significant. The prevalence of both indicators of poor physical functioning increased steadily with age, although most dramatically for difficulty with ADLs.

Partnership was generally associated with better, and divorce/separation with worse, physical functioning for both men and women (Table 19.7). Those who were currently cohabiting were less likely to report a limiting long-standing illness or difficulty with an ADL. Those who had experienced a divorce or separation were significantly more likely both to report a limiting long-standing illness and to report difficulty with an ADL. Also, having been in multiple partnerships was associated with an increased likelihood of reporting a limiting long-standing illness, and with reporting difficulty with an ADL for women only. Single men and women differed in that women who had never married or lived with a partner were more likely than women in one continuous marriage/partnership to have difficulties with ADLs, although this was not the case for limiting long-standing

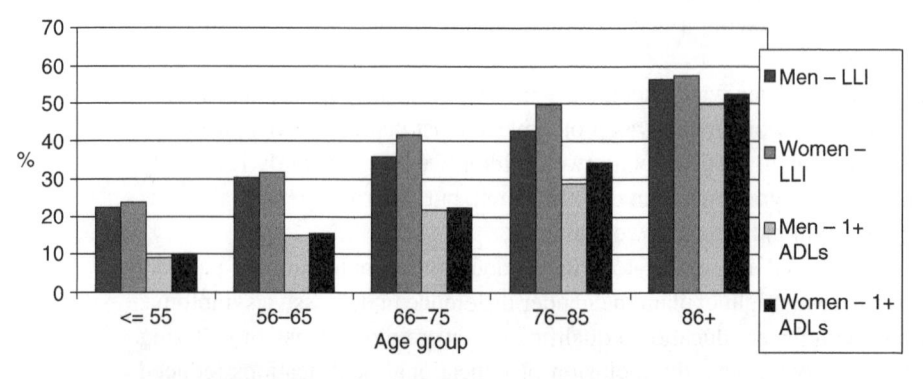

Figure 19.8 *Gender differences in the prevalence of limiting long-standing illnesses and difficulties with activities of daily living by age*

Table 19.7. *Limiting long-standing illness by indicators of family formation among men and women*

		Limiting long-standing illness							
		Men				Women			
		Age-adjusted*		+ adjusted for childhood health		Age-adjusted*		+ adjusted for childhood health	
Family indicators		OR	95% CI	OR	95% CI	OR	95% CI	OR	95% CI
Currently cohabiting	No	1.00		1.00		1.00		1.00	
	Yes	0.73	0.59 – 0.90	0.73	0.60 – 0.90	0.60	0.51 – 0.70	0.59	0.51 – 0.69
Number of cohabitations	0	1.18	0.82 – 1.70	1.17	0.82 – 1.68	1.51	1.07 – 2.14	1.52	1.08 – 2.15
	1	1.00		1.00		1.00		1.00	
	2 +	1.24	1.03 – 1.49	1.23	1.02 – 1.48	1.31	1.16 – 1.62	1.36	1.15 – 1.62
Total duration of cohabitations (year)		0.99	0.99 – 0.99	0.99	0.98 – 0.99	0.99	0.99 – 1.00	0.99	0.99 – 1.00
Ever divorced/separated	No	1.00		1.00		1.00		1.00	
	Yes	1.42	1.18 – 1.70	1.41	1.18 – 1.70	1.47	1.25 – 1.73	1.47	1.25 – 1.74
Age at birth of first child		0.99	0.97 – 1.01	0.99	0.96 – 0.99	0.96	0.95 – 0.98	0.96	0.95 – 0.98
Number of children	0	1.00		1.00		1.00		1.00	
	1	0.97	0.73 – 1.29	1.14	0.81 – 1.60	0.70	0.53 – 0.92	0.81	0.61 – 1.08
	2	0.91	0.71 – 1.16	0.86	0.65 – 1.12	0.73	0.58 – 0.93	0.73	0.58 – 0.93
	3 +	1.14	0.88 – 1.46	1.16	0.88 – 1.51	0.84	0.66 – 1.06	0.86	0.68 – 1.09

* Adjusted for linear and quadratic age terms.

illness. We thought cohabiters might be in better physical condition because those who were healthier earlier in their lives might be more likely to form partnerships in the first place (a health selection argument). However, accounting for childhood health did not change relationships between family forms and physical functioning much at all (Table 19.7).[1] Perhaps the salutary effects of partnership that have been shown elsewhere (Zhang, 2006; Zhang & Hayward, 2006) work their way through to improved physical functioning in later life as well. It could also be that the support of a spouse or partner reduces the impact of declines in functioning (Guralnik, Butterworth, Patel, Mishra, & Kuh, 2009).

Having had children was associated with better physical functioning for women, but not men. Mothers were less likely than women who did not have children to report a limiting long-standing illness or difficulties with ADLs (Tables 19.7 and 19.8). Perhaps the physical demands of parenting kept mothers more active, thereby maintaining functioning for longer, although there is not currently other empirical work to support this. In addition, it may be that women who were physically fitter in early adulthood were more likely to have children, particularly in these generations of women, who formed their families prior to the general availability of contraception that introduced more choice into becoming a mother.

Conclusion

This chapter has investigated gender differences in socioeconomic attainment, health, and wellbeing among English men and women born in the first half of the twentieth century, including change over time and the impact of family formation. We have seen that women's attainment was significantly and substantially lower than that of men. Women were much less likely than men to have attended higher education or to have worked in a professional or managerial occupation, and, in these older cohorts, there was no evidence of a decrease in these gender differences with each subsequent birth cohort. In fact, gender differences in accessing higher education were greater for those born in the 1950s than for men and women born earlier in the century. A steadily decreasing gender differential was seen in the number of years men and women spent in paid work, however. As of 2006, men born in the 1910s worked 23 years longer than women born in the same decade on average, and the equivalent figure for men and women born in the 1950s was 7 years.

Relationships between family forms and socioeconomic attainment ran in opposite directions for men and women. Non-normative family forms, such as

---

[1] ELSA respondents were considered to have been unhealthy in early life if they indicated experiencing any of the following: missed school for over a month due to health as a child, physical activities restricted for over 3 months by health as a child, confined to bed for over a month due to health as a child, in hospital for more than a month due to health as a child, had more than three inpatient stays in 1 year as a child.

Table 19.8. *Physical functioning by indicators of family formation among men and women*

<table>
<thead>
<tr><th rowspan="3">Family indicators</th><th colspan="8">Difficulties with 1+ activities of daily living</th></tr>
<tr><th colspan="4">Men</th><th colspan="4">Women</th></tr>
<tr><th colspan="2">Age-adjusted*</th><th colspan="2">+ childhood health</th><th colspan="2">Age-adjusted*</th><th colspan="2">+ childhood health</th></tr>
</thead>
<tbody>
<tr><td></td><td>OR</td><td>95% CI</td><td>OR</td><td>95% CI</td><td>OR</td><td>95% CI</td><td>OR</td><td>95% CI</td></tr>
<tr><td>Currently cohabiting</td><td colspan="8"></td></tr>
<tr><td>No</td><td>1.00</td><td></td><td>1.00</td><td></td><td>1.00</td><td></td><td>1.00</td><td></td></tr>
<tr><td>Yes</td><td>0.74</td><td>0.58 – 0.94</td><td>0.74</td><td>0.58–0.94</td><td>0.61</td><td>0.50 – 0.73</td><td>0.60</td><td>0.50 – 0.73</td></tr>
<tr><td>Number of cohabitations</td><td colspan="8"></td></tr>
<tr><td>0</td><td>1.03</td><td>0.67 – 1.60</td><td>1.03</td><td>0.67–1.59</td><td>1.47</td><td>1.01 – 2.15</td><td>1.48</td><td>1.01 – 2.16</td></tr>
<tr><td>1</td><td>1.00</td><td></td><td>1.00</td><td></td><td>1.00</td><td></td><td>1.00</td><td></td></tr>
<tr><td>2 +</td><td>1.11</td><td>0.88 – 1.40</td><td>1.10</td><td>0.87 – 1.40</td><td>1.31</td><td>1.06 – 1.61</td><td>1.30</td><td>1.08 – 1.60</td></tr>
<tr><td>Total duration of cohabitations (year)</td><td>0.99</td><td>0.98 – 0.99</td><td>0.99</td><td>0.98 – 0.99</td><td>0.99</td><td>0.99 – 1.00</td><td>0.99</td><td>0.99 – 1.00</td></tr>
<tr><td>Ever divorced/separated</td><td colspan="8"></td></tr>
<tr><td>No</td><td>1.00</td><td></td><td>1.00</td><td></td><td>1.00</td><td></td><td>1.00</td><td></td></tr>
<tr><td>Yes</td><td>1.32</td><td>1.05 – 1.65</td><td>1.32</td><td>1.05 – 1.65</td><td>1.34</td><td>1.09 – 1.63</td><td>1.33</td><td>1.09 – 1.63</td></tr>
<tr><td>Age at birth of first child</td><td>0.99</td><td>0.97 – 1.02</td><td>0.98</td><td>0.96 – 1.00</td><td>0.96</td><td>0.94 – 0.97</td><td>0.96</td><td>0.94 – 0.98</td></tr>
<tr><td>Number of children</td><td colspan="8"></td></tr>
<tr><td>0</td><td>1.00</td><td></td><td>1.00</td><td></td><td>1.00</td><td></td><td>1.00</td><td></td></tr>
<tr><td>1</td><td>0.64</td><td>0.44 – 0.93</td><td>0.82</td><td>0.53 – 1.28</td><td>0.81</td><td>0.59 – 1.10</td><td>0.94</td><td>0.68 – 1.30</td></tr>
<tr><td>2</td><td>0.90</td><td>0.67 – 1.22</td><td>0.98</td><td>0.70 – 1.38</td><td>0.67</td><td>0.51 – 0.89</td><td>0.66</td><td>0.50 – 0.88</td></tr>
<tr><td>3 +</td><td>1.10</td><td>0.81 – 1.49</td><td>1.24</td><td>0.88 – 1.73</td><td>0.86</td><td>0.65 – 1.12</td><td>0.89</td><td>0.68 – 1.17</td></tr>
</tbody>
</table>

* Adjusted for linear and quadratic age term.

never having lived with a spouse or partner or not having had children, were associated with higher socioeconomic attainment for women, but lower socioeconomic attainment for men. This was true for accessing higher education, labor market participation, and being in a professional or managerial occupation. In contrast, while non-normative family forms were associated with socioeconomic advantage for women, they were associated with worse physical health. Women who never lived with a spouse or partner, or experienced a divorce or separation, were more likely than those who lived with one spouse or partner throughout to have a limiting long-standing illness or difficulties with physical functioning, and these relationships were not explained by poor health in early life selecting people into non-normative family forms. Indeed, the generations of men and women in our study formed their careers and families prior to the individualization that characterizes contemporary, or "late modern," societies (Beck, 1992; Giddens, 1991), i.e., during an era when norms regarding the traditional male-breadwinner model were growing in strength. Previous analysis of a cohort of women born in 1946 has also shown that those who followed non-normative work and family life courses were less healthy in their 50s than those who did not (McMunn, Bartley, Hardy, & Kuh, 2006). We have also seen that gender differences in being in a professional or managerial occupation were greatest for people from more advantaged backgrounds and smallest – sometimes non-existent – for men and women from disadvantaged socioeconomic backgrounds.

Social changes in gendered roles and family forms are currently a topic of great interest to policy makers, service providers, and the wider public (Asher, 2012; Clegg, 2011; Hinsliff, 2012; Lexmund, Bazalgette, & Margo, 2011; Park, Clery, Curtice, Phillips, & Utting, 2012; Royal College of Midwives, 2011). However, this work reminds us how recent such changes are (to the extent that they have happened at all; McMunn, Lacey, Sacker, & Booker, 2012). Those currently in midlife or older lived through periods of fairly extreme gender differences in access to education and high-quality paid work, particularly for those who entered into cohabiting relationships and parenthood. Evidence of whether these gender differences have led to lower levels of wellbeing for one gender or the other is mixed, however. We did not see any gender differences in quality of life or life satisfaction, and parenthood was not significantly associated with wellbeing in later life for men or women. Living with a spouse or partner was associated with lower, while divorce was associated with higher, life satisfaction for women, perhaps suggesting that some women considered their lives to be improved by remaining or becoming single. Gender differences in depression are seen consistently and were not explained by gender differences in education, motherhood, or partnership. There are, however, many aspects of family and work life that have not been examined here. "Suburban neurosis" – the dissatisfaction of middle-class homemakers – received much attention over the middle decades of the twentieth century (Gavron, 1966; Oakley, 1974a, 1974b; Rowbotham, 1997), when the women in this study were raising their children and/or building their careers. It remains to be seen whether the large, consistent gender differences seen in rates of depression are maintained for the most recent generations that have been exposed to different social conditions.

Some limitations in this work should be considered. Differential mortality should always be kept in mind when interpreting the results shown in this chapter by age or decade of birth. Less healthy and less advantaged people born in the early part of the century are less likely to be alive in 2006 than their healthier and more advantaged peers. Also, relationships between family indicators and socioeconomic attainment shown here cannot disentangle the timing of events. It is not possible to say whether women left education or the labor market upon the birth of a child, for example. Despite this imprecision, results here suggest that the reductions seen in gender inequality have been not so much a gentle shift over the course of the century, but the result of relatively swift and dramatic social change. For the cohorts of men and women who represent our ageing population – those who are currently retired and equally those currently facing retirement – gender inequality in education and occupation were deeply entrenched. In addition to their generational specificity, this study is representative of England and may not reflect gender differences in attainment for historical cohorts elsewhere. For example, we know that currently Great Britain has higher levels of unmarried cohabitating partnerships and births outside marriage than the United States (Kiernan, 2003). Future work could examine the relationships seen here in studies of comparable generations elsewhere. A focus on the lives of those who have come before reminds us that advances in gender equality in the realms of education, occupation, and family following second-wave feminism are recent and potentially fragile.

References

Asher, R. (2012). *Shattered: Modern motherhood and the illusion of equality*. London: Vintage.

Bartley, M., Martikainen, P., Shipley, M., & Marmot, M. (2004). Gender differences in the relationship of partner's social class to behavioural risk factors and social support in the Whitehall II study. *Social Science & Medicine*, 59, 1925–1936.

Bebbington, P. (1996). The origins of sex differences in depressive disorder. *International Review of Psychiatry*, 8, 295–332.

Beck, U. (1992). *Risk society: Towards a new modernity* (M. Ritter, Trans.). London: Sage.

Bok, D. (2010). *The politics of happiness: What government can learn from the new research on well-being*. Princeton University Press.

Bourdieu, P. (1984). *Distinction*. Cambridge, MA: Harvard University Press.

Clegg, N. (2011). *The universal right to request flexible working*. Retrieved from www.dpm.cabinetoffice.gove.uk/news/parenting-speech.

Corti, L., Laurie, H., & Dex, S. (1995). *Highly qualified women* (Employment Department Research Series No. 50). London: Employment Department.

Crompton, R. (2006). Class and family. *The Sociological Review*, 54, 658–677. doi: 10.1111/j.1467-954X.2006.00665.x.

Crompton, R., & Sanderson, K. (1986). Credentials and careers: Some implications of the increase in professional qualifications amongst women. *Sociology*, 20, 2542.

Dale, A., & Egerton, M. (1995). *Highly educated women: Evidence from the National Child Development Study*. London: Employment Department.

Davidoff, L., & Hall, C. (1987). *Family fortunes*. London: Hutchinson.

Dex, S. (1987). *Women's occupational mobility: A lifetime perspective*. London: Macmillan.

Dex, S., Ward, K., & Joshi, H. (2008). Gender differences in occupational wage mobility in the 1958 cohort. *Work, Employment and Society*, 22, 263–280.

Diener, E., Emmons, R. A., Larsen, R. J., & Griffen, S. (1985). The satisfaction with life scale. *Journal of Personality Assessment*, 49, 71–75.

Duffield, M. (2002). Trends in female employment 2002. *Labour Market Trends*, 110, 605–616.

Equality & Human Rights Commission (EHRC). (2010). *Gender pay activity in large non-public sector organisations*. Retrieved from www.equalityhumanrights.com/uploaded_files/research/gender_pay_baseline_report.pdf.

Gavron, H. (1966). *The captive wife*. Harmondsworth: Penguin.

Giddens, A. (1991). *Modernity and self-identity: Self and society in the late modern age*. Stanford University Press.

Guralnik, J. M., Butterworth, S., Patel, K., Mishra, G., & Kuh, D. (2009). Reduced midlife physical functioning among never married and childless men: Evidence from the 1946 British birth cohort study. *Aging Clinical and Experimental Research*, 21, 174–181.

Helliwell, J., Layard, R., & Sachs, J. (2012). *World Happiness Report*. New York: The Earth Institute, Columbia University.

Hinsliff, G. (2012). *Half a wife*. London: Chatto & Windus.

Hyde, M., Wiggins, R. D., Higgs, P., & Blane, D. B. (2003). A measure of quality of life in early old age: The theory, development and properties of a needs satisfaction model (CASP-19). *Aging & Mental Health*, 7, 186–194.

Joshi, H., & Paci, P. (1998). *Unequal pay for women and men: Evidence from the British Birth Cohort Studies*. Cambridge, MA: MIT Press.

Kahneman, D., Krueger, A., Schkade, D., Schwartz, N., & Stone, A. (2006). Would you be happier if you were richer? A focusing illusion. *Science*, 312(5782), 1908–1910. doi: 10.1126/science.1129688.

Kiernan, K. E. (2003). *Cohabitation and divorce across nations and generations* (CASE paper 65). London: Centre for Analysis of Social Exclusion, London School of Economics.

Laslett, P. (1996). *A fresh map of modern life*. London: Macmillan.

Lexmund, J., Bazalgette, L., & Margo, J. (2011). *The home front*. London: Demos.

McMunn, A., Bartley, M., Hardy, R., & Kuh, D. (2006). Life course social roles and women's health in mid-life: Causation or selection? *Journal of Epidemiology and Community Health*, 60, 484–489.

McMunn, A., Lacey, R., Sacker, A., & Booker, C. (2012). *Cohort and gender differences on work–family patterns in the UK*. Paper presented at the Third Meeting of the Society for Longitudinal and Life Course Studies & European Cohort Studies Network, Paris, France, October 29–31.

Michaelson, J., Abdallah, S., Steuer, N., Thompson, S., & Marks, N. (2009). National accounts of wellbeing: Bringing real wealth into the balance sheet. *New Economics Foundation.* Retrieved from www.nationalaccountsofwellbeing.org.

Oakley, A. (1974a). *Housewife.* London: Allen Lane.

(1974b). *The sociology of housework.* London: Martin Robertson.

Park, A., Clery, E., Curtice, J., Phillips, M., & Utting, D. (Eds.). (2012). *British social attitudes: The 29th report.* London: National Centre for Social Research.

Purvis, J. (Ed.). (1997). *Women's history: Britain, 1850–1945 – An introduction.* London: UCL Press.

Radloff, L. S. (1977). The CES-D scale: A self-report depression scale for research in the general population. *Applied Psychological Measurement,* 1, 385–401.

Roberts, E. (1995). *Women and families: An oral history, 1940–1970.* Oxford: Blackwell.

Rowbotham, S. (1997). *A century of women: The history of women in Britain and the United States.* London: Penguin Books.

Royal College of Midwives. (2011). *Reaching out: Involving fathers in maternity care.* Retrieved from www.rcm.org.uk/college/policy-practice/government-policy/fathers-guide.

Schober, P. (2009). *The parenthood effect: What explains the increase in gender inequality when British couples become parents?* Paper presented at the ESRC Gender Equality Network Conference, "Gender Inequalities in the 21st Century," Queen's College, Cambridge, March 26–27. Retrieved from www.genet.ac.uk/Events/March2009/index.html#StreamA_sesssion2.

Schwarz, N., & Strack, F. (1999). Reports of subjective well-being: Judgemental processes and their methodological implications. In D. Kahneman, E. Diener, & N. Schwarz (Eds.), *Well-being: The foundations of hedonic psychology* (pp. 61–84). New York: Russell Sage.

Steffick, D. E. (2000). *Documentation of affective functioning measures in the Health and Retirement Study.* Ann Arbor, MI: HRS Health Working Group.

Trades Union Congress (TUC). (1944). *Marriage bar, red tape.* London: London Metropolitan University, TUC Library Collections.

Williams, J. C. (1991). Domesticity as the dangerous supplement of liberalism. *Journal of Women's History,* 2, 69–88.

Zhang, Z. (2006). Marital history and the burden of cardiovascular disease in midlife. *The Gerontologist,* 46, 266–270.

Zhang, Z., & Hayward, M. D. (2006). Gender, the marital life course, and cardiovascular disease in midlife. *Journal of Marriage and Family,* 68, 639–657.

20 Gender inequality by choice? The effects of aspirations on gender inequality in wages

Silke Aisenbrey and Hannah Brückner

Abstract
Focusing on the role of occupational choices in maintaining gender stratification, this chapter analyzes occupational aspirations and attainment among those born in the United States between 1942 and 1964. Although male and female life course patterns have strongly converged among younger cohorts, the gender wage gap is still significant. In scholarly and public debates, the differences in choices and characteristics of men and women are seen as one of the main driving forces in gendered wage inequalities. This chapter is structured around the question of whether gendered choices are the driving force for the gender wage gap. We start out with a longitudinal analysis, showing the development of the actual gender wage gap and what we refer to as the aspired gender wage gap. We then demonstrate that, for the youngest cohort, gender differences in human capital, family obligations, and work-life characteristics do not account for the gender wage gap. We also show that it is not – as assumed by human capital theorists – gendered aspirations and expectations that drive the gender wage gap. Our findings support structural demand-side theories that hypothesize that inequality in wages is mainly generated by the different evaluation of women and men in the labor market.

Introduction

Gender inequality in wages has been decreasing over the last century in most, if not all, industrialized countries. Looking only at full-time workers, in 1960, women in the United States (US) earned 60 cents for every dollar men earned, a relation that remained stable into the early 1980s. After this, women gained some ground between the early and late 1980s. In 1990, women earned 72 cents for every dollar men earned. This gain was followed by hardly any change in the gender wage gap during the 1990s and very little change in the first years of the new century. The process that seemed to be closing the gender wage gap, resulting in equal wages for men and women, thus came to an extreme slowdown. In 2010 women earned 76 cents for every dollar earned by men, just as they had in 2000. At the "current pace of progress, [the] wage gap for women [is] expected to close in 2057" (Institute for Women's Policy Research, 2013).

This development in the gender wage gap is only one factor in the bigger picture of gender inequalities. Looking at other economically relevant factors, women's status vis-à-vis men's continued to improve. Women born after the mid-1950s have obtained as much – or more – education and training as men. Women's labor force participation has become increasingly similar to that of men. Fewer and fewer housewives exclusively work at home and more and more women work in the labor force (Goldin, 1990). Thus, gender differences in educational attainment have virtually disappeared from the labor market in the last 20 years. According to human capital theory, gender differences in investment in education and labor force experience are the primary explanation for the gender wage gap: because women expected to interrupt their work lives and care for children, they invested less in the labor market and in education (Polachek, 1981). The recent stability of the gender gap in wages in the face of disappearing differences in education and labor force experience is the puzzle that motivates this chapter: inequality in wages between men and women has not decreased over the last decade, although educational attainment and labor market patterns have converged.

With women catching up in education and labor force participation, one growing academic – as well as commonsense – explanation for the persistence of the gender wage gap relies on the idea that men and women choose to be different. Gender socialization is seen to generate gendered occupational preferences beginning in childhood, where different activities are deemed appropriate for girls and boys (Marini, 1978). There is broad agreement that women have different preferences and choose to work in different and lower-paid occupations than men, which leads to different economic rewards (Marini, Fan, Finley, & Beutel, 1996; Polachek, 1981). To differentiate expectations about the kind of work activity from general expectations about work lives discussed above, we refer in the following to occupational aspirations.

This chapter reaches out to empirically include the concept of occupational aspirations in the research on the development of the gender wage gap. Do men and women end up in different economic positions because they have different aspirations? Would the gender wage gap look different if women behaved more like men? This chapter takes up these questions from a theoretical perspective and provides evidence of a gap in labor market rewards that is not driven by gendered choices, but gendered rewards.

The starting point of this analysis is a description of the gender wage gap over time that confirms previous research: (1) the gender wage gap has been decreasing over recent decades; (2) the decrease in the gender wage gap came to a halt in the 1990s; and (3) the gender wage gap is increasing over the life course (Goldin, 1990; Maume, 2004; Petersen & Morgan, 1995; Polachek & Siebert, 1993; Reskin, 2003). Based on these results, the focus turns to the role of gendered choices for economic rewards. We use an innovative method to measure aspirations, translating occupational aspirations into wage aspirations, which turn out to be more constant over the life course than occupational aspirations. Using this concept, we are able to demonstrate that if there were no gendered wages, gendered aspirations would not lead to a gap in wages. Taking the claim of human capital theory seriously, that aspirations are one driving force in the determination of wages, we also include educational aspirations and family expectations in our analysis.

This chapter attempts to evaluate predictions from different theoretical arguments by looking at the development of the gender wage gap over the last century in the context of women's and men's wage aspirations and expectations. Using this approach, we seek to make a contribution to recent efforts to disentangle the triangle of social forces composed of social structure, choices, and economic rewards. Or, as Brückner (2004, p.16), puts it: "The debate circles in a blind alley: how much gender inequality stems from differences, from choice, from structure?"

Supply- and demand-side theories

Research on the gender wage gap is shaped by the theoretical debate between supply- and demand-side theories (Reskin, 1993). Supply-side theories underscore the relevance of individual differences between workers. One focus of supply-side theories is on the effect of actual differences in women's and men's choices and occupations for the observed differences in wages. This behavior of men and women results in a segregated labor market that generates the gender wage gap. Another perspective on these issues can be derived from demand-side theories that focus on structural differences in the labor market, which male and female workers encounter. Arguing from the demand-side, equally qualified men and women are evaluated and/or treated differently in the labor market and therefore their economic rewards differ.

According to supply-side theories, women make lower investments in human capital – in their education and work experience – because they expect and aspire to be in and out of the labor market due to their family role in society. Explanations of the driving forces behind men's and women's different expectations and aspirations are twofold and range from gender differences created by society to biological differences. Mincer and Polachek stated in 1974 that these forces are not separable: "Of course, individual endowments are not merely genetic; they can be augmented by the process of investment in human capital and reduced by depreciation" (p. S77). Stemming from the inseparability of society vs. biology approaches, with two very different implications, supply-side theories can be divided into two main perspectives: the rational choice or human capital perspective and the socialization approach. According to human capital theorists, gender segregation is the outcome of choices men and women make and women's lower wages are due to lower productivity in these occupations. Because of the role of women in the family, they expect to be in and out of the labor market over their life cycle. They therefore aspire to lower training and invest less in training. The concentration of women working in occupations with lower wages is thus seen as a rational outcome of women's lower expectations and investments in training. In other words, since women expect to spend less time in the labor market, they invest less in human capital in order to start working sooner, therefore maximizing their economic rewards over the life cycle (Polachek, 2006).

The socialization approach, while also emphasizing supply-side factors, focuses on differences in the socialization of men and women. The assumption is that gendered socialization teaches men and women what is appropriate and desirable for each gender. Expectations and choices are an outcome of gendered socialization and this process places men and women in different occupations. From this perspective, choices are also shaped by gendered expectations, but these expectations are the result of a gendered socialization (Marini & Fan, 1997). Another perspective that is closer to the socialization approach argues that cultural beliefs about gender form career aspirations (Correll, 2004). The common ground of these "supply-side" theories is the emphasis on gendered expectations and choices.

On the other hand, demand-side theories emphasize the role that employers play in the labor market. Demand-side theories offer explanations for gendered wages that are driven by the different situation women and men face in the labor market, and by the different evaluation of the human capital that women and men bring to their jobs. The gender segregated labor market, from this structural point of view, is a by-product of gender discrimination (Brückner, 2004; Nelson & Bridges, 1999; Reskin, 2003).

Neither of these dominant theories is mutually exclusive. Still, for the purposes of disentangling mechanisms and to evaluate the predictions of the theories, we state the following hypothesis:

> Inequality in wages between men and women today is less due to women and men having different expectations and making different choices and more due to the different evaluation of men and women in the labor market.

By different evaluation, we refer not only to the different evaluation and devaluation (England, 1992) of men's and women's human capital and labor market performance, but also to their differing evaluations of expectations and aspirations.

We will evaluate this hypothesis by looking at the gender wage gap under different hypothetical scenarios: (a) if women made men's *choices*, (b) if women had men's *aspirations and expectations*, and (c) if women actually had men's *characteristics*.

One common way of testing these theories is to divide the gender wage gap into a proportion that can be explained by differences between men and women and an unexplained component. The residual (the unexplained component) is then used as an estimate for labor market discrimination. Because the causes and outcomes are highly entangled, one of the main challenges of using this approach lies in the attempt to strictly eliminate the gender wage gap from the explanatory side of the model.[1] We use a similar approach, but control for further

---

[1] Polachek and Siebert (1993) argue that the residual gender wage gap can be explained by men and women having different expectations. As Brückner (2004) points out, in their operationalization of expectations current wages are also included, which opens a back door for the gender wage gap into the explanatory side of the model and therefore it cannot be properly used to explain residuals.

effects that – following the human capital approach – drive the gender wage gap: *expectations* and *aspirations*. Very often these models are also criticized for being biased by unobserved gender differences (hereafter, unobserved heterogeneity). We argue that, by including aspirations and expectations, this bias can be significantly decreased. Before estimating the gender wage gap and the individual role of expectations and aspirations for economic rewards, we take a look at the long-term development of the gender wage gap and compare it with the hypothetical wage gap if everybody had the chance and desire to fulfill their occupational aspirations. Specifically, we ask: What would the gender wage gap look like if everybody at age 35 worked in the occupation they aspired to at the age of 20? Has this hypothetical gender wage gap changed over time?

Analysis, concepts, and indicators

The analysis we conduct is twofold: the first part focuses on a longitudinal descriptive analysis of the observed and aspired gender wage gap in the US for cohorts born between 1940 and 1964 at age 27 and 35. Following this analysis, we estimate an individual-level multivariate model to isolate the factors that produce the gender wage gap for the younger cohorts born between 1960 and 1964. Our analysis is based on data collected for the National Longitudinal Survey of Youth (NLSY) and the National Longitudinal Survey (NLS). On the aggregate level we use census data.

Table 20.1 summarizes all concepts and indicators used in the analysis. The explanatory variables include *expectations*, *aspirations* and *socialization* at the age of 20 – an age where first educational decisions are made and first family expectations have been formed.[2] Where possible, concepts are first measured as expectations and aspirations at age 20 and then as achieved at age 35. As shown in Table 20.1, participants are asked at age 20 what occupation they aspired to work in at age 35. Hakim (2000) suggests that the process of women's career choices is essentially completed by then. Thirty-five is also often used as a more mature labor market age (Mayer & Aisenbrey, 2007; Polachek, 2006). Concepts measured at age 35 include *human capital, family formation, occupation- and job-specific attributes*, and *economic rewards*. *Social background* is included as a time invariant concept.

There is an ongoing debate in the research on aspirations that questions the role of aspirations for subsequent behavior. Looking at occupations themselves, Jacobs (1989) finds too many changes in individual occupational preferences to use occupational aspirations of young adults as predictors for their later behavior. However, looking at occupational prestige or percentage of females in a given occupation, for example, demonstrates a close relationship between aspired and realized occupation (Okamoto & England, 1999; Shu & Marini, 1998).

---

[2] Doing the same analysis looking at age 18 showed no significant differences.

Table 20.1. *Concepts and indicators*

Concept	Indicator
Aspirations and expectations at age 20	
Economic rewards	Occupation-age-gender-specific wages for aspired occupation
	Male occupation-age-specific wages for aspired occupation
Human capital	Expected years of education
	Expected ability to achieve aspired occupation
Family formation	Expected number of children
Socialization at age 20	
	Women's place is at home (1–3/3 agree)
	Men and women should share housework (1–3/3 agree)
Realized characteristics at age 35	
Economic rewards	Hourly wages
Human capital	Years of education
	Work experience
	Weekly hours worked
	Work in aspired occupation
Family formation	With partner
	Number of children
Occupation spec. attributes	
	Mean percentage female
	Government sector
	Private sector
	Non-profit sector
	Industry (in 12 categories; see Table 20.3)
Age independent attributes	
Social background	Parents education in years
	Race (African American, other minorities, white)

In our research, we use an innovative method to estimate aspirations, specifically by using information on the occupation that respondents aspire to as an indicator for aspired wages. We use information on occupational aspirations and estimate the average occupation-age-cohort-gender-specific wage derived from census data and attach it to each individual's record as an aspired wage at the age of 35 (Aisenbrey & Brückner, 2008; Marini & Fan, 1997). Even though there might be differences in the occupations to which respondents aspire (Jacobs, 1989), using this estimate for economic aspirations, we did not find substantial differences between the wages aspired to at ages 20 and 22.

The first, longitudinal, part of the analysis explores differences in the aspired and the realized wage gap (*Aspired and Realized Wage Gap*). For comparability between the two indicators (aspired to and realized economic rewards) in this part of the analysis, we report estimated wages and not the wages reported by the respondents.[3] Wages are estimated the same way we estimated the aspired economic rewards. To analyze the development of the gender wage gap across cohort and over the life course, we also include an estimated wage at age 27 in the descriptive part of the analysis.

The second, multivariate analysis, proceeds in three steps: (a) a mean comparison, (b) a regression analysis using ordinary least square regression, and (c) a decomposition of the gender wage gap. The mean comparison demonstrates how different or similar men and women are in their expectations, aspirations, and characteristics (*Gender Differences in Expectations, Aspirations, and Characteristics*). The regression model shows the different effects of these indicators on individual wages (*Gendered Effects of Expectations, Aspirations, and Characteristics*). Finally, taking these two together, we decompose and recompose the regression model to put the results from the regression model in the context of the initial research question (*Differences and Effects of Hypothetical Gender Equality*): How would the gender wage gap change if men and women had the same aspirations, expectations, and characteristics? How much of the gender wage gap is due to men's and women's differing evaluations in the labor market? In other words, we use the results from the mean comparison and the regression results and try to imagine a world from two different perspectives:

1. What would the gender wage gap look like if women shared the same external characteristics as men? For this analysis, women are assigned men's distribution from the mean comparison.
2. What would the gender wage gap look like if women's characteristics had the same effect on wages or were evaluated in the same way as men's? Here women are assigned men's slopes from the regression model.

For the multivariate regression model *expectations*, *aspirations*, and *achievements* are measured in three different spheres that are relevant in the literature on aspirations and the gender wage gap: family formation, human capital, and economic rewards.

Expectations and aspirations are measured at the age of 20: the expected number of children is used as an indicator of family formation expectations and the expected number of years spent in educational institutions indicates expectations for education. To control for expectation of economic rewards, we include an item asking participants at age 20 if they expect to work in their aspired jobs at age 35 and the estimated aspired economic rewards. As explained above, we

---

[3] Overall the estimated wages are very similar to the individually reported wages (Figure 20.1).

measure aspirations by calculating the age- and gender-specific wages for each occupation to which men and women aspired, using average wages for these occupations derived from census data. In contrast to the longitudinal analysis, in order to minimize (eliminate) the gender wage gap in the explanatory variables, the estimation of aspired wages is exclusively based on the male occupation-cohort-age-specific wages.

The same three spheres – family formation, human capital, and economic rewards – are also measured at age 35. *Family formation* is measured by number of children and a dummy variable measuring the presence of a partner. *Human capital* is accounted for by educational attainment (years of education at age 35) and work experience (weeks worked until age 35). To test for the effect of work availability on wages as part of the human capital concept, weekly hours worked are also included in the model. We also include a variable that measures whether or not individuals at age 35 worked in the occupation they had aspired to earlier in their lives. *Economic rewards* are included as the dependent variable, measured in hourly wages at age 35.

To estimate the effects of a gendered *socialization* toward the labor market, two items are included in the model. Both items, agreement with the statement that women's place is in the home and that men and women should share housework, indicate attachment to a traditional division of labor between men and women at age 20. For *social background*, we include parents' education as well as race.[4]

Criticisms of this approach to estimating the gender wage gap often focus on the unobserved heterogeneity biasing regression models that estimate wages (Kim & Polachek, 1994). Including expectations and aspirations in the analysis accounts for a great deal of unobserved heterogeneity. To further reduce the unobserved effects, we also include *occupation- and job-specific attributes*. These latter factors are included because we lack sufficient measures of employer behavior (demand-side factors) that lead to inequalities (Fields & Wolff, 1995; Maume, 2004; Tomaskovic-Devey, 1993), including the devaluation of women's work (England, 1992). More specifically, we include the sector (private for-profit, governmental, and non-profit), the industry, and the percentage of women employed in the respondent's occupation, derived from age- and cohort-specific census data.[5] It bears saying that we are not eliminating unobserved heterogeneity completely. Still, the inclusion of expectations and aspirations in the estimate and the exclusion of the gender wage gap from the explanatory side of the model significantly decrease the bias of the model due to unobserved heterogeneity.

---

[4] We use the mean education of both parents; if information about only one parent is available we use this instead. Measuring education with an indicator that only captures vertical education could be problematic since research shows that a lot of gender differences in wages get generated on the horizontal level. The same criticism applies for using an occupational scale that does not differentiate between a surgeon and a pediatrician. Given that we hardly find gender differences in the effects that educational expectations and wage aspirations have on wages, the vertical indicator seems sufficient.

[5] Self-employed are excluded since we have no reliable census data to properly estimate wages.

Data

We explore this issue by merging data files with longitudinal information on workers. The NLSY (and the earlier NLS) is sponsored and directed by the US Bureau of Labor Statistics and conducted by the Center for Human Resource Research at Ohio State University. Interviews are conducted by the National Opinion Research Center at the University of Chicago (for a detailed description of the NLSY and the NLS data, see Bureau of Labor Statistics: www.bls.gov/nls).

For the aggregate level of occupation-cohort-age-gender-specific economic rewards, we merge the NLS and the NLSY with census data. Operationalizing the aspired wage at age 35 on the basis of the respondents' occupational aspirations for age 35 at age 20 requires occupational scales that are identical over these two markers in a life course. The occupational scale also has to be identical for the entire observation window that includes cohorts born between 1944 and 1964, turning 35 between 1964 and 1999. For this purpose, we use the translation variable for occupational classification from 1950, which is used by the Minnesota Population Center in the Integrated Public Use Microdata Series (IPUMS). The IPUMS translates all occupational scales into the occupational scale used by the census in 1950. We translated occupational scales used in the NLS and the NLSY into the 1950 scale, allowing us to match occupation-specific data from all appropriate censuses to the individual-level data. The downsides to this approach include the loss of information due to using the older, not improved, scales and fewer occupational categories. We explored the limitations and the possibility of using different data (Current Population Survey) and scales (Standard Occupational Classification) for some birth cohorts, and the differences turned out to be marginal.

Results

The first part of the analysis explores how choice matters and how this changes over time. One focus in this section is on the comparison of aspired and achieved wages over time as an indicator of the role of gendered choices.

Aspired and realized wage gap

Figure 20.1 shows the estimated average occupation-specific wages and the hypothetical wages achieved if everybody at age 35 worked in the occupations they aspired to age 20 (referred to as the *aspired wage*). The aspired wages for men and women at age 35 for cohorts born between 1943 and 1964 are higher than the wages in the occupations that men and women actually work in (referred to as achieved wages).

This gap between aspired and achieved wages increases for the more recent cohorts, more so for men than for women. It is noteworthy that the difference

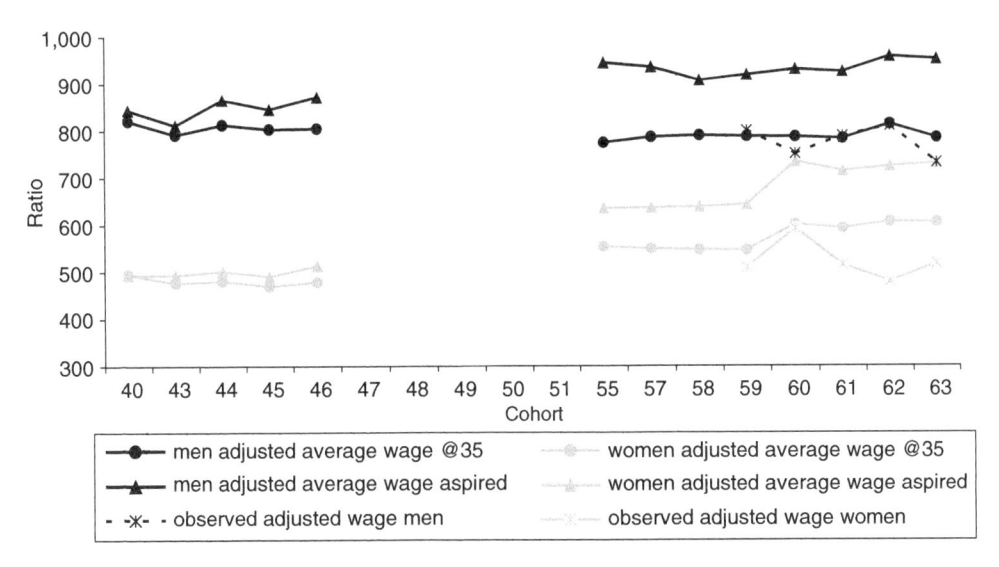

Figure 20.1 *Estimated aspired and achieved wages*
Wages adjusted for inflation, fixed at 2000 (US Department of Labor and Statistics, Bureau of Labor Statistics)

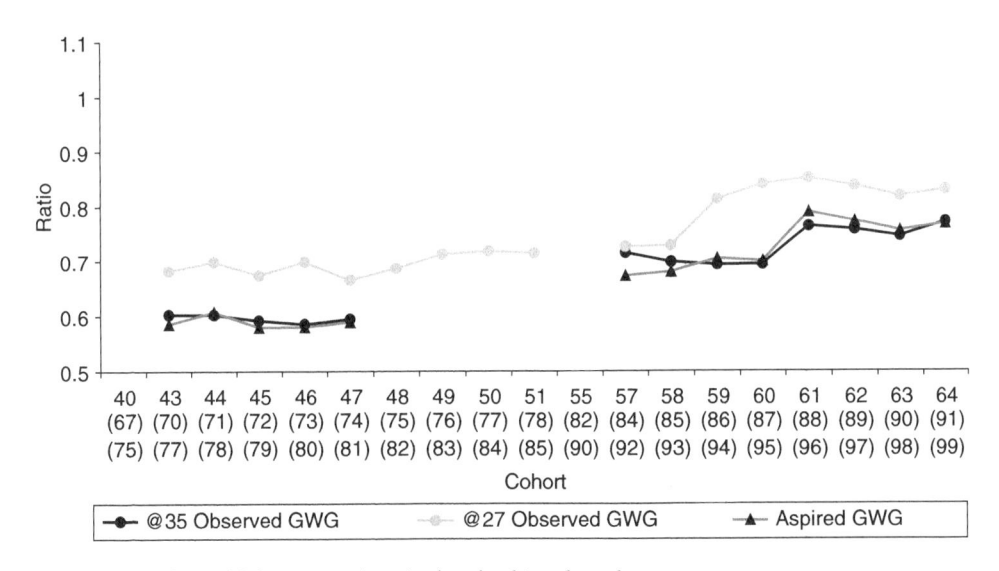

Figure 20.2 *Estimated aspired and achieved gender wage gap*

between the aspired and the achieved wage hardly matters in the context of the gender wage gap: for all cohorts, the aspired gender wage gap and the observed gender wage gap at age 35 are nearly identical (Figure 20.2).

Figure 20.2 also shows that the gender wage gap increases over the life course. For all cohorts, with the exception of the 1957 cohort, the wage gap is smaller at age 27 than at age 35.

Gender differences in expectations, aspirations, and characteristics

In this next stage of the analysis, we focus on mean comparisons between the younger cohorts born between 1960 and 1964, showing differences in aspirations, expectations, and attributes between men and women. We excluded from this analysis men and women who earned less than $1 per hour and more than $150 per hour or who worked less than 15 hours per week. Looking at the aspired gender-specific wage, however, women aspire to significantly lower weekly average wages than men (women $725; men $963). This picture changes dramatically if we assign women the average male wage for the occupation they aspired to when they were 20 years old (denoted as weekly wage aspired (male) in Table 20.2): matching women's aspired occupations with male wages, we find that women and men aspire to nearly the same wages (women $956; men $963). In other words, in a hypothetical world without a gender wage gap, men and women aspire to nearly the same economic rewards: the previously noted gender difference in aspirations stems not from the fact that women aspire to different occupations; it stems from within-occupation gender differences in wages.

At the age of 20, women and men also expect to have almost the same human capital. Women expect to spend 14.3 years in education, men 14.1 years; in addition, 76% of men and women expect to achieve their occupational aspirations at age 35. With respect to family formation, there are only minor gender differences. Women on average expect to have somewhat fewer children (1.9) than men (2.3).

In sum, men and women have very similar expectations and aspirations at the age of 20 on the dimensions of human capital and family formation. With respect to occupational aspirations, in terms of expected economic rewards, our analysis shows the importance of within-occupation wage differences. These findings qualify the assumptions of human capital theory that it is, in part, these aspirations and expectations that shape the gender wage gap.

In a further step, we examine the realized situations of these men and women at age 35. More women (12%) than men (8%) work in the occupations they aspired to. Men earn significantly more than women: women earn 82 cents for every dollar men earn.[6] Looking at realized human capital, women spend slightly more time in education than men (on the average 13.7 years vs. 13.3); they have significantly less work experience than men (510 weeks vs. 546), and work fewer hours per week than men (39 hours vs. 45). Men and women have, on average, the same number of children at age 35 (1.5), but men more often live with a partner than do women (70% vs. 64%).

---

[6] This is a somewhat smaller gap than estimated in the descriptive analysis, due to the exclusion criteria used for this analysis.

Table 20.2. *Cohorts 1960–1964: means and percentages, standard deviation in parenthesis*

	Men		Women	
		SD		SD
Aspirations and expectations (@ age 20)				
Economic rewards				
Weekly wage aspired (gendered)	963.1	(404.1)	725.4	(327.1)
Weekly wage aspired (male)	963.1	(404.1)	956.5	(389.4)
Human capital				
Expected years of education	14.1	(2.3)	14.3	(2.1)
Expect ability to achieve aspired occupation	0.76	(0.42)	0.76	(0.42)
Family formation				
Expected number of children	2.3	(0.6)	1.9	(1.2)
Realized (@ age 35)				
Percentage work in aspired occupation	8		12	
Economic rewards				
Hourly wage	16.6	(10.7)	13.7	(8.5)
Human capital				
Years of education	13.3	(2.6)	13.7	(2.4)
Work experience (weeks worked in thousands)	546.5	(147.5)	510.2	(173)
Weekly hours worked	45.0	(9.5)	39.2	(8.9)
Socialization/gender attitudes				
Women's place is at home (1–3, 3 agree)	2.0	(0.6)	1.5	(0.6)
Men and women should share housework (1–3)	2.0	(0.6)	2.4	(0.6)
Family formation				
Number of children	1.4	(1.2)	1.5	(1.2)
Percentage with partner	70		64	
Occupation-specific attributes				
Mean percentage female	28		58	
Percentage government sector	15		18	
Percentage private/for-profit sector	80		72	
Percentage non-profit sector	04		10	
Percentage in industry				
Agriculture, forestry, fisheries	03		01	
Mining	01		00	
Construction	11		01	
Manufacturing	25		14	

Table 20.2. (cont.)

	Men		Women	
Transport, communication, public utilities	10		05	
Wholesale and retail trade	15		16	
Finance, insurance, real estate	04		09	
Business, repair services	09		06	
Personal services	02		04	
Entertainment, recreation services	01		01	
Professional and related services	12		36	
Public administration	08		07	
Age-independent attributes				
Social background				
Parents' education (years)	11.2	(3.2)	11.0	(3.1)
Percentage African American*	30		30	
Percentage other minorities*	10		10	

Note: NLSY data here shown without sample weights. Using weights the percentage of African American is 14 and of other minorities 6.

Gendered effects of expectations, aspirations, and characteristics

In a multivariate regression analysis (Table 20.3), we estimate the wage at age 35, looking at the effects of these rather small differences presented in the mean comparison. In a model (not shown) including men, women, and interaction effects for the relevant variables, we also tested for significant differences between men and women. The aspired wage has a significant positive effect on wages that is somewhat stronger for men than for women. For women, the positive effect of expected education is marginally stronger than for men.

Our measure of the expected ability to work in the aspired occupation is only significant for women, as is the expected number of children. Both of these variables have a positive effect on women's wages. Overall, expectations and aspirations tend to play a larger role in determining women's wages than men's wages. We interpret this result as evidence for the view that the wage gap is less driven by gender differences in expectations and aspirations and more by the gendered effects that these have on wages.

Realizing one's aspired occupation has a significant and positive effect on wages for men and women, but for women the effect is stronger. The effect of achieved years of education is positive and the same for men and women. Work experience also has a significant positive effect on men's and women's wages, but the effect is significantly larger for men. Weekly hours worked is only significant for women.

Table 20.3. *Coefficients from regression of wages (logged)*

	Men		Women	
	Beta	Std. Err.[x]	Beta	Std. Err.[x]
Aspirations and expectations (@ age 20)				
Economic rewards				
Weekly wage aspired (male)	0.099*	0.043	0.085*	0.423
Human capital				
Expected years of education	0.017*	0.008	0.020*	0.008
Expect ability to achieve asp. occupation	0.045	0.029	0.048+	0.028
Family formation				
Expected number of children	0.012	0.009	0.016+	0.009
Realized (@ age 35)				
Human capital				
Work in aspired occupation	0.121**	0.042	0.196**	0.039
Years of education	0.060**	0.008	0.059**	0.008
Work experience (ln weeks worked in thousands)*	0.255**	0.028	0.190**	0.024
Weekly hours worked	0.001	0.002	0.003+	0.002
Socialization/gender attitudes				
Women's place is at home*	−0.058**	0.019	−0.014	0.021
Men and women should share housework	−0.026	0.021	0.019	0.020
Family formation				
Number of children	−0.001	0.010	−0.015	0.011
With partner**	0.161**	0.028	−0.002	0.026
Occupation-specific attributes				
Mean percentage female	0.000	0.001	−0.001*	0.001
Government sector (ref. cat.: non-profit)**	0.156**	0.068	−0.089+	0.052
Private sector (ref. cat.: non-profit)**	0.290**	0.068	0.053	0.045
Industry (professional and related services)				
Agriculture, forestry, fisheries	−0.199*	0.094	−0.064	0.121
Mining	0.072	0.313	−0.156	0.196
Construction	0.073	0.064	−0.071	0.116

Table 20.3. (cont.)

	Men		Women	
Manufacturing	0.027	0.058	0.041	0.042
Transport, communication, public utilities	0.167**	0.057	0.080	0.056
Wholesale and retail trade	−0.205**	0.062	−0.224**	0.041
Finance, insurance, real estate	0.046	0.070	0.132**	0.048
Business, repair services	−0.044	0.069	0.003	0.053
Personal services	−0.377**	0.097	−0.221**	0.057
Entertainment, recreation services	0.021	0.142	−0.108	0.086
Public administration	0.189**	0.053	0.252**	0.053
Age-independent attributes				
Social background				
Parents' education (years)	0.010*	0.005	0.011+	0.004
African American (ref. cat.: white)	−0.138**	0.028	−0.130**	0.027
Other minorities (ref. cat.: white)	−0.009	0.056	0.045	0.043
Constant	−1.925**	0.663	−1.425*	0.636
r-square		0.371		0.42
N		1,400		1,189

Robust standard errors; + significant at 10%; * significant at 5%; ** significant at 1%; if variables are marked as significant in the first column a full model with interaction effects for gender indicated significant gender effects.

Looking at gender attitudes or gendered socialization, it is striking that men seem to get punished in the labor market for having traditional gender attitudes when they were younger: men's wages are significantly lower the stronger their agreement is to the item that women's place is at home. Surprisingly, gendered attitudes have no significant effect on women's wages. This result questions the predicted strong influence of gendered socialization on wages.

The number of children has no significant effect on wages. The presence of a partner has a significantly different effect for men and women. We find a positive effect on men's wages, but no effect on women's wages (a result that is very common in wage estimations; Sørensen, 2004).

Differences and effects of hypothetical gender equality

Gender differences in earnings may stem both from different characteristics and from assets that men and women bring to the labor market (Table 20.2), and from the different effects of these characteristics (Table 20.3). In a final step of the analysis, we present a decomposition of the regression

Table 20.4. *Decomposition of the gender wage gap*

The observed gender wage gap	0.83	

	Characteristics (distribution)	Effects (slopes)
Percentage reduction of the GWG through inserted MALE		
Expectations/aspirations		
Wage aspirations	0.04%	
Expectation to realize occupational aspiration	0.03%	
Educational aspirations	−1.93%	
Family aspiration (no. children)	2.56%	
Human capital		
Education	−13.16%	1.53%
Work experience	11.45%	212.14%
Realization of aspired occupation	−3.54%	−4.72%
Socialization		
Gender-role attitudes	−7.16%	
Family formation		
No. children	1.00%	11.47%
Partner yes/no		56.69%

Note: GWG = gender wage gap.

model (Table 20.4) to show what would change if women looked like men (i.e., if women had the same characteristics as men) or if women were evaluated like men (i.e., if these characteristics had the same effect on women's wages than they have on men's wages).

If women had men's wage aspirations, the gender wage gap would barely be reduced (0.04%). If women had the same belief as men in being able to achieve their occupational aspirations, the gap would also basically stay the same (0.03%). Encouraging women to have the same educational aspirations as men would widen the gap by about 2%. Even assigning women men's expectations for the number of children would only reduce the gap by 2.5%. Overall, encouraging women to have the same aspirations as men would have little influence on the gender wage gap.

Focusing on the achieved situations, if women had men's attributes, women's wages would look significantly different. If women had men's education, the gender wage gap would be 13% larger. On the other hand, if women's education were evaluated by the labor market according to the standards for men, the gap would be 1.5% smaller. Men do have more work experience and the greater payoff is clear in our hypothetical world: assigning women men's work experience, the wage gap would be 11% smaller. However, assigning women the same economic rewards that men get for work experience, the gap would be reduced by *over 200%*, showing that women's work experience is worth significantly less on the labor market. These last results strongly support the predictions of structural and demand-side theories that claim that discrimination against women in the labor market explains a substantial part of the gender wage gap.

Turning to gendered socialization as a factor responsible for the gender wage gap (according to socialization theory), the data show that if women had men's gender attitudes, the wage gap would widen by 7%. This result should not be over-interpreted, but it can be taken as an indicator of the negligible power of socialization theory in accounting for the gender wage gap.

The last factor that we test is the gendered effects of family formation on the wage gap. The gap would be less than half if the presence of a partner had the same positive effect on women's wages as it does on men's wages. And, if the number of children had the same implications for women as for men, each child would reduce the gap by over 10%. These results regarding family formation are in line with other research that demonstrates that family responsibilities, even today, have mainly negative effects on women's careers and positive effects on men's.

In sum, encouraging women to have the same aspirations as men would not lead to much change in the gender wage gap. If women had men's wage aspirations, the gap would decrease less than half of a percent; if women had men's educational aspirations, this would widen the gender wage gap by about 2%; if women had men's family aspirations, this would decrease the gap by 2.5%. Women's choices cannot be held responsible for women's lower wages. If compared on relevant dimensions, men and women look fairly similar, but the accumulation of this "being fairly similar" turns out to be rewarded very differently in the labor market.

Conclusion

Although young US women today are at least as qualified as men, and male and female life course patterns have strongly converged across the cohorts studied in this chapter, men and women are still extremely segregated in the labor market and earn highly unequal wages. The gender gap in wages has thus changed more slowly than gender differences in all the other characteristics that are said to explain the wage gap, most prominently educational attainment and labor force experience, but also expectations, aspirations, and socialization.

Intuitively, occupational aspirations and choices are important in maintaining the gender wage gap at the level that we see, in spite of younger women's huge gains in human capital. Programs and public campaigns aimed at encouraging young women to aspire to higher education and choose male-dominated occupations are popular policy responses. These policies make sense if gender inequality in earnings is significantly driven by women being different than men with respect to aspiring to and having less human capital, and aspiring to and working in different occupations; these differences matter for the gender wage gap. We have been able to show that choices matter, but much less than expected and much less than the gendered evaluation of men and women on the labor market.

The results of this chapter should be seen in the context of taking human capital theory seriously and demonstrating that expectations and aspirations do not matter as much as predicted: men and women differ little with respect to educational attainment; women's preferences for family formation, as well as gender-role attitudes, explain very little of the gender gap in wages; most importantly, we show that differences in the kinds of occupations men and women aspire to do not explain the gender gap in wages either, once we eliminate within-occupation wage differentials. The results presented here demonstrate the similarity of men and women with respect to expectations and aspirations and the very small differences in the effects of these expectations and aspirations on wages. One major conclusion, therefore, is that it is not gendered aspirations and expectations that gender wages.

Since we include a broad range of aspirations in our models, unobserved heterogeneity should also be minor. On the other hand, our findings support structural demand-side theories that assume that a great deal of wage inequality is generated on the labor market as a result of discrimination against women. We have been able to show that women get fewer economic rewards than men for the same investments in their human capital.

As long as research mainly focuses on looking for, and finding evidence of, why choices matter and focuses less on what happens to these choices on the labor market, the reason for the gender wage gap will always be the "women's fault." Aspiring to a world with fewer gender inequalities doesn't only mean that we have to encourage women to be like men, but much more that our society has to aspire to treat men and women more equally.

References

Aisenbrey, S., & Brückner, H. (2008). Occupational aspirations and the gender gap in wages. *European Sociological Review*, 24(5), 633–649.

Brückner, H. (2004). *Gender inequality in the life course: Social change and stability in West Germany, 1975–1995*. Hawthorne, NY: Aldine de Gruyter.

Correll, S. J. (2004). Constraints into preferences: Gender, status, and emerging career aspirations. *American Sociological Review*, 69, 93–113.

England, P. (1992). *Comparable worth: Theories and evidence*. New York: Aldine de Gruyter.

Fields, J., & Wolff, E. N. (1995). Interindustry wage differentials and the gender wage gap. *Industrial and Labor Relations Review*, 49, 105–120.

Goldin, C. D. (1990). *Understanding the gender gap: An economic history of American women*. New York: Oxford University Press.

Hakim, C. (2000). *Work-lifestyle choices in the 21st century: Preference theory*. Oxford University Press.

Institute for Women's Policy Research. (2013). *At current pace of progress, wage gap for women expected to close in 2057*. Retrieved August 19, 2013, from www.iwpr.org/initiatives/iwpr-quick-figures.

Jacobs, J. A. (1989). *Revolving doors: Sex segregation and women's careers*. Stanford University Press.
Kim, M., & Polachek, S. W. (1994). Panel estimates of male-female earnings functions. *The Journal of Human Resources*, 29, 406–428.
Marini, M. M. (1978). Sex differences in the determination of adolescent aspirations: A review of the research. *Sex Roles*, 4, 723–753.
Marini, M. M., & Fan, P.-L. (1997). The gender gap in earnings at career entry. *American Sociological Review*, 62, 588–604.
Marini, M. M., Fan, P.-L., Finley, E., & Beutel, A. M. (1996). Gender and job values. *Sociology of Education*, 69, 49–65.
Maume, D. J. (2004). Wage discrimination over the life course: A comparison of explanations. *Social Problems*, 51, 505–527.
Mayer, K. U., & Aisenbrey, S. (2007). Variations on a theme: Trends in social mobility in (West) Germany for cohorts born between 1919 and 1971. In R. P. M. Gangl, G. Otte, & S. Scherer (Eds.), *Social stratification, education and the life course* (pp. 125–156). Frankfurt: Campus Verlag.
Mincer, J., & Polachek, S. (1974). Family investments in human capital: Earnings of women. *The Journal of Political Economy*, 82, S76–S108.
Nelson, R. L., & Bridges, W. P. (1999). *Legalizing gender inequality: Courts, markets, and unequal pay for women in America*. New York: Cambridge University Press.
Okamoto, D., & England, P. (1999). Is there a supply side to occupational sex segregation? *Sociological Perspectives*, 42, 557–582.
Petersen, T., & Morgan, L. A. (1995). Separate and unequal: Occupation-establishment sex segregation and the gender wage gap. *The American Journal of Sociology*, 101, 329–365.
Polachek, S. (1981). Occupational self selection: A human capital approach to sex differences in occupational structure. *Review of Economics and Statistics*, 58, 60–69.
(2006). How the life-cycle human capital model explains why the gender wage gap narrowed. In F. D. Blau, M. C. Brinton, & D. B. Grusky (Eds.), *The declining significance of gender?* (pp. 102–124). New York: Russell Sage Foundation.
Polachek, S., & Siebert, W. S. (1993). *The economics of earnings*. New York: Cambridge University Press.
Reskin, B. F. (1993). Sex segregation in the workplace. *Annual Review of Sociology*, 19, 241–270.
(2003). Including mechanisms in our models of ascriptive inequality. *American Sociological Review*, 68, 1–21.
Shu, X., & Marini, M. M. (1998). Gender-related change in occupational aspirations. *Sociology of Education*, 71, 43–67.
Sørensen, A. (2004). Economic relations between women and men: New realities and the re-interpretation of dependence. *Advances in Life Course Research*, 8, 281–297.
Tomaskovic-Devey, D. (1993). *Gender & racial inequality at work: The sources and consequences of job segregation*. Ithaca, NY: ILR Press.

21 Comparing young people's beliefs and perceptions of gender equality across 28 different countries

Bryony Hoskins and Jan Germen Janmaat[*]

Abstract

This chapter explores young people's perceptions of and beliefs in gender equality across 28 countries and the relationship between these two phenomena. The findings show that while the levels of young people's *beliefs* in gender equality follow patterns of economic development (GDP) and are associated with actual measures of gender equality (Gender Empowerment Measure), nevertheless, young peoples' *perceptions* of gender inequalities are found to be independent of beliefs in gender equality, actual levels of gender equality, and economic development. Sweden is found to be the only country where more than 50% of young people combine beliefs in equality with perceptions of inequality. In our analysis, we also find that the willingness to engage in political action is stronger among those young people who believe in gender equality and at the same time perceive reality not to be in accordance with this ideal. These findings suggest that political action is premised on the combination of not only believing in gender equality but also perceiving gender inequality.

Introduction

Beliefs in gender equality are said to be increasing along with economic development and modernization (Inglehart & Norris, 2003; Inglehart & Welzel, 2005). At the same time the existence of gender discrimination has been found to be frequently and continuously "denied, played down and ignored" in higher education and more broadly across advanced post-industrial states (Morrison, Bourke, & Kelley, 2005, p. 151). At first glance, these results appear to be inconsistent. However, both claims could be correct. A conviction that women *should* be treated equally need not necessarily be accompanied by a perception that they *are* treated unequally, even in situations where gender discrimination is overt. People may well underestimate structural processes of exclusion because of their inclination to see gender inequality as resulting from individual differences in effort, talent, and determination, and not as a result of institutional structures (Morrison et al., 2005; David & Robinson, 1991). Thus, the perception

---

[*] Both authors have contributed equally to this chapter. The preparation of this chapter was supported by the ESRC LLAKES Centre – grant reference RES-594-28-0001.

is that women who do not attain the same social positions as men are themselves to blame, not society at large.

It has been argued that people have a psychological need to believe that the world is just (Lerner, 1980). This conviction that society is fair might prevent people from seeing and recognizing gender discrimination. It is quite possible that people perceive society to be coherent with their beliefs in gender equality, even if society is treating women unequally and their perception is thus incorrect. Such a combination of perceptions and belief, we would posit, reduces the desire to act politically to improve the levels of gender equality. If we reformulate this argument in a positive direction we would expect that for people to engage in political action it is necessary that endorsement of the principle of gender equality needs to be accompanied by a perception of gender discrimination (in other words a perception that reality is not in accordance with the ideal).

These reflections lead us to formulate two hypotheses. First, although socioeconomic development may indeed generate a strong belief in the principle of gender equality as suggested by Inglehart and Norris (2003), we do not expect *perceptions* of gender equality to be strongly related to either real gender inequality or to a belief in gender equality. In other words, believing in gender equality need not lead to a heightened awareness of gender discrimination, and an awareness of gender discrimination may not reflect actual gender inequality. Second, we posit that believing in gender equality is not sufficient to create social change; for people to engage in political action it is necessary that they both believe in gender *equality* **and** perceive gender *inequality* to occur. We believe that by investigating these hypotheses we begin to unravel the mystery of persistent political passivity in contexts combining strong support for gender equality with continued actual gender inequality or discrimination. By addressing this major omission and enigma in gender research we hope to develop the field significantly further.

The chapter starts by discussing the theories informing the links between socioeconomic development, gender attitudes, and civic participation in greater detail. Subsequently it describes the data sources and indicators used to measure the concepts of interest. Next, descriptive statistics will be provided on participation, on beliefs in and perceptions of gender equality, and on socioeconomic development and actual gender inequality. Thereafter we correlate perceptions and beliefs with indicators of socioeconomic development and actual gender equality. Lastly we explore whether believing in gender equality and perceiving the actual inequalities that woman face increases positive attitudes toward participation in civic and political action.

Theories on people's beliefs in and perceptions of gender equality

Prominent political scientists have argued that beliefs in gender equality have been growing stronger across the world and are part of a modernization process associated with changes in improved social conditions (Inglehart & Norris, 2003; Inglehart & Welzel, 2005). They see such beliefs as a component of a more comprehensive set of values (so-called self-expression values) that have become more salient in the post-war decades. Proceeding from Maslow's (1943) "pyramid of needs" idea, they argue that self-expression values are developed by people who have had a secure and affluent childhood (i.e., values emphasizing self-fulfillment, freedom, autonomy, gender equality, tolerance). By contrast, people who have grown up under conditions of scarcity and insecurity will tend to develop survival values (i.e., values stressing economic and physical security), which underpin citizen identities particularly in poorer authoritarian states (Inglehart & Welzel, 2005). As new generations have grown up under ever more prosperous circumstances in the Western world from World War II onwards, young generations with self-expression values have steadily replaced older cohorts who still experienced scarcity in their childhood years and who therefore tended to endorse survival values. The result of this process of generation replacement has been a gradual cultural shift away from survival toward self-expression values, including the belief in gender equality.

Modernization theory further suggests that the change toward greater security and prosperity is combined with less physically demanding work, the move toward the knowledge-based economy, and greater education and employment opportunities for women, leading to higher levels of actual gender equality (Inglehart & Norris, 2003). This change of circumstance for women is also said to strengthen beliefs in gender equality among both women and men. Thus, according to modernization theory, socioeconomic development has not only produced higher levels of gender equality in reality but has also led to a stronger belief in the value of gender equality, both as a component of a wider process toward self-expression and as a side effect of enhanced opportunities for women.

Also drawing on the same principles of macro-economic modernization theory, Lundmark (1995) distinguishes between perceptions of and beliefs in gender equality. She examined data from the Eurobarometer survey to understand changes in "feminist values" (a belief in gender equality and a perception of gender inequalities) across the period 1975 to 1983. She tested the modernization hypothesis developed by Inglehart and Welzel (2005) and Inglehart and Norris (2003), suggesting that general improvements for the position of women in society will have changed people's attitudes toward gender equality. Although she found that beliefs in gender equality (as proxied by attitudes toward women's participation in politics) had indeed become more salient, she also found that perceptions of women not having the same chances as men had decreased significantly between 1975 and 1983. Her interpretation was that inequality was becoming more hidden and complex during this period, making people become less aware of existing inequalities. She also observed a link between perceptions of inequalities and actual inequalities cross-nationally, noting that countries with relatively high levels of actual gender inequality (Italy and Greece) showed a stronger awareness of inequalities. These findings can be said to be consistent with Sen's (2000) theory of social justice, which assumes that perceptions of inequality are an accurate reflection of objective inequalities.

However, we question if perceptions of gender equality really mirror or reflect reality. There is a significant body of nationally based feminist research suggesting that women and men are in denial of the continued forms of exclusion that exist (Figes, 1994; Morrison et al., 2005; Rhode, 1997). As noted earlier, this denial may well be related to the idea that inequalities are the result of individual failure (Morrison et al., 2005), which in turn could well reflect a belief in a just world (Lerner, 1980).

The Just World Theory, according to Lerner (1980), suggests that people have a need to believe that the world is fair and that people get what they deserve. In this process the individual constructs psychological mechanisms that prevent the individual from considering a situation to be unjust either for themselves or for others in order to reduce stress. Using the Just World Theory in the context of gender equality, we would expect that both men and women perceive that, for example, a woman's lack of success or failure to get equal pay has its roots in individual failings or lack of effort. This has been described by feminist research as the "denial of continued discrimination against women" (Morrison et al., 2005, p.151) or the holding of a "romantic vision of a meritocracy" (Titus, 2000, p. 27). This position has been described as some form of protection against the uncomfortable feeling that females should need to contest this situation against their male friends and colleagues (Morrison et al., 2005). At this point it is important to highlight that we see Inglehart's theory on value change and Lerner's Just World Theory as compatible. Self-expressionism, in fact, can be said to contain an element of Just World thinking as it has been argued that people with self-expression values also strongly believe in self-efficacy – i.e., the idea that individuals have the ability to shape their own life course (Janmaat & Braun, 2009). In other words, they tend to ignore or downplay the role of social and institutional factors in constraining the life chances of people in disadvantaged positions.

Lerner (1980) has tested the Just World Theory and has concluded that people are successfully convincing themselves that the more privileged groups justifiably enjoy their benefits. Rubin and Peplau (1975) take this argument one step further by arguing that believing in the just world reduces the feeling of need to engage in activities to change society or to alleviate the plight of social victims. This takes us to the second question of this chapter: the link between beliefs, perceptions, and action.

Lundmark (1995) found that women or men who held feminist positions (where beliefs in equality are matched by perceptions of inequality) were more interested in politics than those who did not believe or see inequalities. David and Robinson's (1991) study of gender attitudes in the UK, US, West Germany, and Austria also showed that it is the combination of believing in gender equality and being aware of unequal treatment that motivates people to take action. The idea that beliefs in social justice are not sufficient and need to be complemented by an awareness of social injustice for political mobilization to take place is well established in the literature (e.g., Giddens, 1973; Rhode, 1997).

The problem that we thus discern for achieving gender equality is that perceptions of gender equality may not reflect the reality, making it difficult to mobilize both women and men who believe in gender equality toward transformative action. In the following we thus examine our two hypotheses. First, *perceptions* of gender equality are not assumed to be strongly related to either real gender inequality or to a belief in gender equality. Second, believing in gender equality is not sufficient to create social change; for people to engage in political action it is necessary that they both believe in gender *equality* **and** perceive gender *inequality* to occur.

Data and indicators

In this chapter we use data from the 1999 Civic Education Study (CIVED), which measures the civic knowledge, skills, values, and behaviors of 14-year-olds. The data for this study were collected in April 1999 by means of a large-scale test and questionnaire survey among a sample of 90,000 Grade 8 students in 28 countries worldwide (Torney-Purta, Lehmann, Oswald, & Schulz, 2001). A major advantage of the CIVED study, in addition to the large national samples (3,000 students and more) and the low non-response rates, is the inclusion of ready-made composite scales in the database, which have been tested for conceptual equivalence cross-nationally (Schulz, 2004). This means that the items composing the scales have been understood in the same way across countries and that the data are thus comparable internationally. Given the nested character of the national samples, with all the students of one classroom per school being selected in each of the 150–200 sampled schools, the CIVED study further allows researchers to explore both contextual effects pertaining to classrooms and schools and individual-level factors.

Moreover, CIVED is the only existing international data source collected from nationally representative samples that measures both beliefs in and perceptions of gender inequality and includes attitudes toward civic participation.[1] As such, it offers a unique opportunity to investigate how groups of individuals with different perceptions of and beliefs in gender equality engage in active citizenship.

In terms of content, the survey focused on three domains: (a) democracy/citizenship, (b) national identity/international relations, and (c) social cohesion and identity. Within the three domains information was gathered on knowledge of the content, skills in interpretation and concepts, attitudes, and expected actions in the future. Knowledge of the content and skills in interpretation was tapped

---

[1] The International Civics and Citizenship Education Study (ICCS) conducted in 2009 is the formal successor of CIVED. Crucially, however, ICCS lacks items on perceptions of gender equality, which makes it unfit to use for this study.

with a test using items with one correct answer. Attitudes and future actions were measured with a questionnaire containing items with Likert-type answer scales (for more information on the test and the questionnaire, see Schulz, 2004; Torney-Purta et al., 2001) (for examples of these items, see Appendix 21.1). We used questionnaire items to measure our dependent variable and one of our explanatory variables. We furthermore used a construct based on test items as a control variable (see subsequent section).

In addition to the CIVED study we drew on data from the World Bank and the United Nations Development Programme (UNDP) to find measurements for socioeconomic development, the other variable of interest in this chapter.

Dependent variable: participation

The dependent variable in our analysis is positive attitudes toward civic and political participation. The assessment of these attitudes was based on one dimension of the Civic Competence Composite Indicator (CCCI) developed by Hoskins, Barber, Van Nijlen, and Villalba (2011): participatory attitudes (henceforth *participation*). The dimension *Participation* is a measure of participatory attitudes assessing self-efficacy as well as the disposition toward involvement in actions that can create change. It is formed as the linear combination of 5-Item Response Theory (IRT) scales:[2] internal political efficacy, expectation of social movement related participation, expected participation in political activities, self-confident participation in schools, and expectations associated with voting (see Appendix 21.1 for the items that these IRT scales comprise). *Participation* includes items mainly related to attitudes toward future participation in different contexts: community, politics, or school, as well as interests in participating in political discussion in a school context. It has a satisfactory internal consistency in view of the number of scales that it comprises; the Cronbach's alpha coefficient is 0.652. The scale was created by the CIVED methodological experts (see Husfeldt, Barber, & Torney-Purta, 2005; Schulz, 2004; Torney-Purta et al., 2001) and by researchers at the Centre for Research on Lifelong Learning (CRELL) at the Joint Research Centre of the European Commission. The dimension has the advantage of summarizing a complex phenomenon in a single number, ranging between 0 (minimum participation) and 100 (maximum participation), making its exploration easier.

Explanatory variables 1: perception and belief categories

In this section we define perceptions of and beliefs in gender equality as our key explanatory variables and then explain how we build our categories

---

[2] Item Response Theory (IRT) refers to the way the scales have been built modeling responses to the items, as opposed to classical test theory that models a whole test.

of respondents. The terminology in the field of inequalities is varied and inconsistent. David and Robinson (1991) use the word "consciousness" to refer to "first perceiving that inequality exists, and then decide that this inequality is sufficiently unfair that some corrective action is warranted" (p. 72). Gurin (1985) uses the terminology "gender consciousness" to refer to an individual's believing in the need for "collective action geared to change" (p. 146). Lundmark (1995), alternatively, uses the words "feminist orientation" to encompass the perception of gender inequality that she refers to as "feminist cognition," a "gender perspective" that highlights the belief in gender equality and finally a strategy toward creating social change (p. 255). Both Lundmark (1995) and David and Robinson (1991) state that a "feminist orientation" or "gender consciousness" can be a position held by both men and women. In this chapter, we also take the position that both girls and boys can hold similar perceptions and beliefs. However, the terminology we use is *perceptions* of inequalities rather than "feminist cognition" in order to highlight the fact that we are measuring subjective perceptions of reality, which may not be an accurate reflection of reality. Thus the notion of *perceptions of inequalities* refers to the individual's subjective observations/perceptions of everyday reality of inequalities. Perceptions are assumed to be based on own experiences and observing experiences of others in the immediate social context. Thus within everyday experience individuals build their own understanding of the social world based on their own reflection of social action and their own internalized beliefs.

In addition, we use the terminology of *values* or *beliefs* in gender equality referring this time to how individuals believe the world should actually be. A belief in gender equality is, in contrast to our understanding of perceptions, referring to an abstract and ideal situation. Our hypothesis is that both perceptions of inequality and beliefs in equality are needed to achieve political mobilization.

Following Bergman (2001) and Bergman and El-Khouri (2003) we used a person-centered approach for our analysis as this enabled us to explore how perceptions and beliefs combine within individuals. Key to this approach is the identification of four categories of respondents to capture the distinction between perceptions and beliefs and to make it possible to assess the effect of both on participation, our outcome. The four categories were formed by combining the individuals' responses to two items: "Women should have the same rights as men" and "Women have fewer chances than men." The first item captures beliefs in gender equality while the second item is a proxy for perceptions of inequality/unequal treatment. Both items were assessed with a Likert response scale ranging from 1 – "strongly disagree" to 4 – "strongly agree." The following categories identifying four gender-attitude groups were created for both girls and boys:

1. The *egalitarian-satisfied* group combining a belief in gender equality ("agree" and "strongly agree") with a perception that there is no unequal treatment ("disagree" and "strongly disagree").

```
                    Positive beliefs in
                    gender equality
                            ▲
                            │
              Egalitarian-  │  Egalitarian-
              dissatisfied  │  satisfied
                            │
Greater perceptions  ◄──────┼──────────────
of gender inequality        │
                            │
              Traditionalist-│ Traditionalist-
              satisfied     │  dissatisfied
                            │
                            │
```

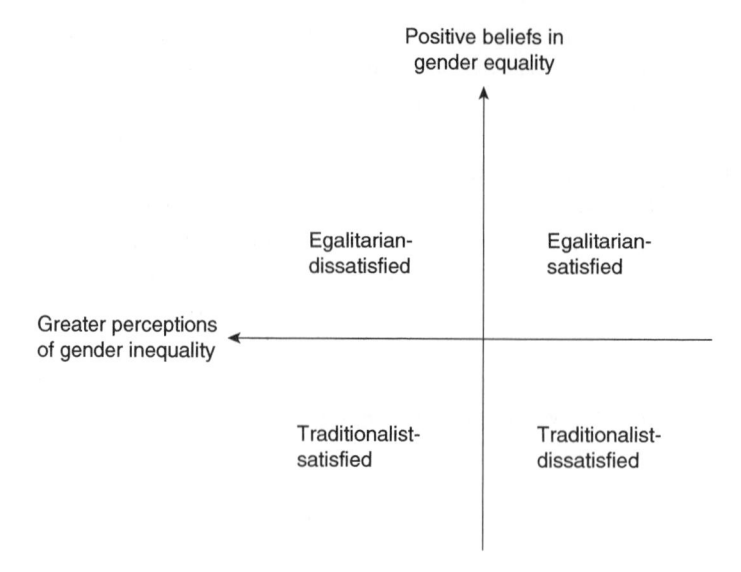

Figure 21.1 *The construction of the four measurement categories that combine responses to the two variables on beliefs in and perceptions of gender equality*

2.   The *egalitarian-dissatisfied* group combining a belief in gender equality ("agree" and "strongly agree") with a perception that there is unequal treatment ("agree" and "strongly agree").

3.   The *traditionalist-satisfied* group combining a belief in gender inequality ("disagree" and "strongly disagree") with a perception that there is unequal treatment ("agree" and "strongly agree").

4.   The *traditionalist-dissatisfied* group combining a belief in gender inequality ("disagree" and "strongly disagree") with a perception that there is no unequal treatment ("agree" and "strongly agree").

These groupings are visualized in Figure 21.1. Based on the Just World Theory discussed previously, our hypothesis is that people who believe in gender equality do not necessarily perceive much inequality. We thus expect more students in the egalitarian-satisfied category than in the egalitarian-dissatisfied category. In addition, we expect the egalitarian-dissatisfied group to be the most motivated to participate politically.

Explanatory variables 2: socioeconomic development and gender inequality

The first hypothesis introduced the concepts of socioeconomic development and gender equality. To tap into the former we used we used GDP per capita (purchasing power parity) following the assumption that more developed states are characterized by higher levels of prosperity. The GDP data that we used pertain to the year 1999 and are drawn from the *World Bank 2000–2001*

Development Report. Many scholars, including Inglehart and Welzel (2005) and Delhey and Newton (2005), have used GDP per capita as indicators of development and modernization more broadly.

There are furthermore two well-known indices available to assess actual gender equality, the Gender Development Index (GDI) and the Gender Empowerment Measure (GEM). We decided to select the latter. Unlike the GDI, which only measures the expansion of opportunities and rights, the GEM focuses on the degree to which women have actually been able to use these opportunities and rights (UNDP, 2012a; for the debate on the use of these and other indicators of gender equality, see Klasen, 2006; Klasen & Schuler, 2011). It thus provides a more precise picture of the positions that women have attained in a society. The GEM is a composite index comprising four indicators: (a) the percentage of seats in parliament held by women; (b) the percentage of legislators, senior officials, and managers who are women; (c) the percentage of professional and technical workers who are women; (d) the ratio of estimated female to male earned income (UNDP, 2012b). A high score on this index demonstrates a high level of equality. No country has a score of 100% indicating absolute gender parity. We selected the GEM data of 2001, as the data available for other years was not as complete or close to the CIVED data of 1999.

Control variables

We included a number of control variables in the models explaining participation (see the penultimate section). All of these variables, except GEM, were based on CIVED data. They concern *social background* (based on an item assessing the number of books at home[3]), *ethnicity* (identified through an item on language spoken at home), *academic achievement* (measured with TOTCGMLE, a ready-made composite index in the CIVED database representing performance on a civic knowledge and skills test), *educational motivation* (indicated by an item on expected further education), as well as *peer effect* (tapped with the classroom average of the number of books at home). The influence of all these variables on participatory intentions and on civic attitudes more broadly has been well documented in the literature (for the effects of social background and academic performance, see Campbell, 2006; Galston, 2001; Nie, Junn, & Stehlik-Barry, 1996; for that of ethnicity, see Janmaat, 2008; Rice & Feldman, 1997; for that of educational motivation, see Schulz, Ainly, Fraillon, Kerr, & Losito, 2010; Torney-Purta et al., 2001; for that of peer effects, see Janmaat, 2011; Van der Werfhorst, 2007).

---

[3] Measuring social background solely with number of books at home may seem a bit thin. However, the many missing values on parental education level, another well-known indicator of socioeconomic status, prevented us from developing a more encompassing construct of social background.

Descriptive statistics

In this section we provide basic descriptive statistics of the outcome of interest and the key explanatory variables. To begin with the former, we can see that there is a marked variation in participation both within and between countries (see Table 21.1, which ranks the countries on mean values). The country with the largest internal variation is the US with 68% of respondents having participation scores ranging between 37.30 and 69.30 (i.e., the mean value of 53.30 –/+ 1 *SD* of 16.00). All the remaining countries have slightly lower within-country variability (see the *SD*s, which range between 12.41 and 15.96). The between-country variation is also striking. While several Latin American and Southern European countries display relatively high mean levels of participation hovering around the value of 60 (Cyprus, Colombia, Greece, and Chile), many North-West European states trail the ranking order with scores lower than 50 (Finland, Germany, Switzerland, Sweden, England, Denmark, French Belgium, and Norway). Eastern European countries do not show a particular pattern as they can be found both among the top performers (Romania, Poland, and Slovakia) and among the countries trailing the league (Estonia, Czech Republic, Lithuania, Bulgaria). The good performance of Latin countries both in Europe and in the Americas could be an indication of strong norms of participation reflecting a republican tradition of nation- and statehood (Green & Janmaat, 2011; Lovett, 2010).

Turning now to the four gender-attitude groups, Table 21.2 shows that, as predicted, almost all of the young people believe in gender equality, as the two egalitarian groups constitute more than 85% of all respondents. Moreover, girls and boys appear to hold similar attitudes, with just slightly fewer boys who believe in gender equality than girls (Table 21.2). As expected, the results show that for both boys and girls more than 60% of respondents are in the egalitarian-satisfied group, suggesting that the belief in a just world without gender discrimination is indeed widespread. The second largest group is the egalitarian-dissatisfied group of boys and girls, comprising together a bit less than 30% of the respondents. These respondents may be said to represent critical feminists as they combine a strong belief in gender equality with a perception that reality does not live up to this standard. As noted before, we expect this group to show the strongest inclination to participate in political action. Only a very small number of girls and boys reject the principle of gender equality altogether, as shown by the small percentages in the traditionalist categories (4.4% of girls and 12.8% of boys). Among these traditionalists the dissatisfied groups are slightly larger than the satisfied groups for both boys and girls, indicating that among those who do not believe in gender equality there are more who perceive that women do actually have equal chances in reality than those who perceive that reality is in accordance with their beliefs.

In the next step, we examined the size of the four attitude groups across different countries (see Table 21.3, which ranks the countries on the percentage of egalitarian-dissatisfied for both boys and girls). We found that the patterns in the

Table 21.1. *Descriptive statistics for participation*

Country	Mean	SD	N
Cyprus (CYP)	61.44	12.91	2938
Colombia (COL)	59.89	13.68	4549
Greece (GRC)	57.18	12.86	3192
Chile (CHL)	56.91	14.79	5218
Romania (ROM)	55.68	13.40	2686
Poland (POL)	55.49	14.03	2997
Slovak Republic (SVK)	54.09	12.41	3174
Portugal (PRT)	53.99	12.61	2795
USA	53.30	16.00	2230
Italy (ITA)	51.14	13.28	3383
Hong Kong (HKG)	50.13	14.63	3901
Australia (AUS)	49.66	15.12	2640
Slovenia (SVN)	49.38	12.79	2640
Hungary (HUN)	49.29	12.50	3082
Norway (NOR)	49.26	14.95	2704
Latvia (LVA)	48.87	14.14	2180
Russia (RUS)	48.66	13.51	1949
Belgium (French) (BFR)	48.19	14.19	1744
Denmark (DNK)	47.37	14.31	2478
Bulgaria (BGR)	47.30	14.43	2232
Lithuania (LTU)	46.88	13.71	2775
Czech Republic (CZE)	46.61	12.85	3237
England (ENG)	46.38	15.37	2431
Sweden (SWE)	46.25	15.96	2421
Switzerland (CHE)	45.68	13.99	2645
Germany (DEU)	45.67	14.01	3220
Estonia (EST)	45.60	13.40	2884
Finland (FIN)	45.33	13.69	2285

Table 21.2. *Size of the four gender-attitude groups*

	Boys N	Boys %	Girls N	Girls %
Traditional-satisfied	2,085	5.2	666	1.5
Traditional-dissatisfied	3,043	7.6	1,263	2.9
Egalitarian-dissatisfied	10,262	25.6	13,042	30.1
Egalitarian-satisfied	24,680	61.6	28,412	65.5

Table 21.3. *Four gender-attitude groups by country and gender*

	Girls					Boys			
	Trad.-sat.	Trad.-dis.	Egal.-dis.	Egal.-sat.		Trad.-sat.	Trad.-dis.	Egal.-dis.	Egal.-sat.
SWE	1.1	1.1	64.3	33.5	SWE	4.1	5.5	47.5	42.9
HKG	2.7	2.3	41.5	53.6	HKG	6.3	5.3	32.9	55.5
FIN	0.5	0.6	37.2	61.8	CHL	3.6	4.2	30.8	61.4
CZE	0.7	2.0	36.5	60.9	LTU	6.1	9.6	29.7	54.5
DEU	0.6	1.7	36.0	61.7	POL	5.8	7.8	29.7	56.7
LTU	1.8	3.4	34.1	60.8	ROM	10.4	10.3	29.7	49.7
SVK	0.6	2.1	32.9	64.4	CYP	4.3	4.5	28.8	62.4
NOR	0.3	1.4	32.5	65.8	GRC	8.2	8.3	28.6	55.0
USA	2.1	2.2	30.7	64.9	BGR	8.6	14.3	27.7	49.5
CYP	0.5	1.0	30.3	68.2	PRT	4.0	7.0	27.0	61.9
POL	1.0	2.6	30.2	66.1	COL	2.7	4.4	26.0	66.9
CHL	0.6	1.2	29.2	69.0	FIN	2.7	4.2	25.2	68.0
DNK	0.8	2.0	29.0	68.2	DNK	6.5	7.3	25.1	61.2
PRT	1.9	5.7	29.0	63.4	DEU	5.9	6.3	25.0	62.8
ROM	4.6	5.5	28.8	61.0	NOR	5.1	5.5	24.7	64.7
ENG	1.2	2.1	28.6	68.0	USA	5.8	10.2	24.3	59.8
GRC	1.6	2.1	28.3	68.0	LVA	7.7	13.5	24.0	54.9
SVN	1.2	2.8	27.3	68.7	CZE	2.2	5.0	23.4	69.4
AUS	1.6	4.0	27.2	67.3	SVK	3.1	5.7	22.1	69.0
BGR	6.6	6.9	26.8	59.8	AUS	5.1	9.7	22.0	63.2
COL	1.2	3.2	25.4	70.1	ENG	5.3	8.4	21.7	64.6
CHE	1.4	2.1	25.1	71.3	CHE	4.3	7.1	21.3	67.3
EST	1.4	3.8	23.8	71.0	BFR	8.8	8.0	21.2	62.0
HUN	1.1	3.3	23.4	72.2	SVN	5.3	9.3	19.6	65.8
LVA	2.1	6.0	23.3	68.6	ITA	4.8	8.7	18.9	67.6
BFR	1.3	1.6	21.3	75.8	EST	4.9	9.2	18.4	67.5
ITA	1.6	3.4	18.5	76.5	RUS	5.4	13.5	17.0	64.1
RUS	3.3	9.3	16.8	70.5	HUN	3.9	11.4	15.6	69.2

pooled data were largely replicated in the individual countries, as the egalitarian-satisfied group constituted the largest and the egalitarian-dissatisfied group the second largest group everywhere. The notable exception to this pattern was Sweden where the egalitarian-dissatisfied group was the largest for both girls (64%) and boys (48%). Russia, on the other hand, had the fewest egalitarian-dissatisfied girls (17%) and Hungary the fewest egalitarian-dissatisfied boys (16%) of all countries.

It is tempting to read regional patterns in these findings, but a closer look at the data shows that the countries topping and trailing the ranking order are very diverse. Thus, former communist countries are both among the top group in terms of size of the egalitarian-dissatisfied group (Lithuania, Czech and Slovak Republics for

Table 21.4. *Levels of prosperity and gender equality across 25 countries*

Country	GDP per capita 1999	Country	GEM
CHE	38,350.00	NOR	83.60
NOR	32,880.00	SWE	80.90
DNK	32,030.00	FIN	78.30
USA	30,600.00	DEU	74.90
DEU	25,350.00	USA	73.80
SWE	25,040.00	AUS	73.80
BFR	24,510.00	DNK	70.50
FIN	23,780.00	CHE	69.60
ENG	22,640.00	BFR	69.20
AUS	20,050.00	ENG	67.10
ITA	19,710.00	PRT	62.90
GRC	11,770.00	SVN	57.40
PRT	10,600.00	EST	55.20
SVN	9,890.00	CZE	54.60
CZE	5,060.00	SVK	54.60
CHL	4,740.00	ITA	53.60
HUN	4,650.00	LVA	53.40
POL	3,960.00	POL	51.80
SVK	3,590.00	GRC	50.20
EST	3,480.00	HUN	49.30
LTU	2,620.00	LTU	47.40
LVA	2,470.00	ROM	44.90
RUS	2,270.00	CHL	44.50
ROM	1,520.00	RUS	43.40
BGR	1,380.00		

girls and Lithuania, Poland, and Romania for boys) and among the bottom group (Estonia, Hungary, Latvia, and Russia for girls and Slovenia, Estonia, Russia, and Hungary for boys). Similarly, Western European countries can be found both topping (Sweden, Finland, and Germany for girls and Sweden, Cyprus, and Greece for boys) and trailing the league table (Switzerland, French Belgium, Italy for both genders). Lastly, it can be seen that the countries with a relatively small group of egalitarian-dissatisfied individuals also have a relatively large group of egalitarian-satisfied, particularly for girls. Thus, small numbers of egalitarian-dissatisfied do not indicate lack of support for the principle of gender equality.

Our data on socioeconomic development and gender equality show that we have information on all but three countries (Colombia, Cyprus, and Hong Kong) that participated in CIVED (see Table 21.4, which ranks the countries on GDP per capita and GEM). We can see that a country's place in the ranking order on GDP per capita is a very good predictor of that country's position in the league

Table 21.5. *Correlations between GEM, GDP, and attitudes on gender equality*

	Perception: Women have fewer chances than men	N	Belief: Women should have the same rights as men	N
GEI	.23	24	.57**	24
GDP	−.04	25	.60**	25
Perception			.02	28

Notes: * p < .05, ** p < .01.

table on gender equality. In other words, the more prosperous a country is, the better its score on gender equality. These results confirm the claim of modernization theorists that the position of women in a society is closely linked to level of socioeconomic development. Indeed, a bivariate correlation between the data of Table 21.4 produces a strong positive relationship ($r = .86$; $p < .001$; N = 24). The data also reveal quite a variation across countries in gender equality. While some Scandinavian countries are not that far from total gender parity with scores of over 80% (Norway and Sweden), some countries in Latin America and in Southern and Eastern Europe have scores of 50% or less (Greece, Hungary, Lithuania, Romania, Chile, and Russia).

Results

Hypothesis 1

Having explored the background data, we now test the first hypothesis: Are perceptions of gender inequality indeed different from normative beliefs, i.e., are they not related to objective conditions, and are they not linked to beliefs in gender equality either? Table 21.5 shows correlations at the country level between GDP per capita and GEM, on the one hand, and aggregate data on gender attitudes on the other. There appears to be strong endorsement for the first hypothesis. While beliefs in gender equality grow stronger at higher levels of socioeconomic development and gender equality (see the strong positive relationships between GDP and GEM and between GDP and beliefs in gender equality), perceptions of gender inequality are not related to either the two indicators of objective conditions (GDP or GEM) or to beliefs in gender equality. In other words, the more prosperous and more gender-equal countries also show high levels of support for the principle of gender equality, but perceptions of gender inequalities are not necessarily more salient. Thus the thesis of socioeconomic development indeed applies for beliefs but not for perceptions. Perceptions appear to lead a life of their own in our analysis, which contrasts sharply with the findings of Lundmark (1995) and refutes Sen's (2000) aforementioned proposition that they are shaped by the actual degree of inequality in a country.

Hypothesis 2

Do the findings also support the second hypothesis? In other words, are people only inclined to participate in civic and political action if they both believe in gender equality and perceive reality not to concur with that ideal? We explored this question by analyzing the determinants of participation with multilevel analysis (MLA) on the pooled CIVED data (see Snijders & Bosker, 1999, for an extensive explanation of this method of analysis). The explanatory variables included in the MLA models are the four gender attitude groups (with the egalitarian-satisfied group being the reference category), the control variables mentioned before and the GEM index to capture potential environmental influences on our outcome of interest. MLA is necessary as the data that we use is nested (students in classrooms – in schools – in countries) and our model includes explanatory variables at various levels: five variables at the individual level, peer effect at the classroom level, and GEM at the country level. With MLA we can accurately assess the effects of these higher-level variables (Snijders & Bosker, 1999). Using OLS regression would overestimate their effects. The only difference between MLA and OLS regression is that the former splits up the variation in the dependent variable in several levels. We performed separate analyses for girls and boys. Variables were standardized to facilitate interpretation.

For both girls and boys we find a significant positive relationship between the egalitarian-dissatisfied groups and participatory attitudes in addition to and above the influence of the control variables (see Table 21.6). This association is slightly stronger for boys than girls. Compared to those in the egalitarian-satisfied group (the reference group), the egalitarian-dissatisfied girls have on average a .28 and the egalitarian-dissatisfied boys a .38 higher level of participatory attitudes on a scale ranging from −3.5 to 3.3 (that is a 4.1% and 5.6% higher level of participatory attitudes). In addition, there are significant negative associations between the traditionalist categories and participatory attitudes, again for both genders but most particularly for boys. By comparison to the reference group, these categories have between .24 and .61 lower scores on participatory attitudes.

Together these results lend support for our hypothesis that it is the combination of a strong belief in gender equality and a perception of inequality that really motivates people to engage in civic and political action. Nonetheless, the results for boys also show that those who believe in gender equality (whether they perceive inequality or not) have higher participatory intentions than those who reject it, which somewhat diminishes the argument that both conviction and awareness are needed for participation.

We also ran the analysis across three groups of countries differing in their positions on the GEM index (low; medium; high) to see if the position of women in society mattered for the relation between the gender attitude groups and participation. The results of this analysis turned out to be the same for each country grouping.[4] This indicates that the results found for the pooled data are robust.

---

[4] These results can be obtained from the authors upon request.

Table 21.6. *Determinants of participation*

	Girls		Boys	
	Estimate	t-value	Estimate	t-value
Egalitarian-satisfied (ref.)				
Egalitarian-dissatisfied	.28***	4.6	.38***	5.73
Traditional-satisfied	−.10	−1.63	−.30***	−4.9
Traditional-dissatisfied	−.24***	−4.38	−.61***	−10.1
Controls				
Educational motivation	1.80***	18.74	1.61***	16.31
Ethnicity	−.05	−.57	−.01	−.07
Social background	1.23***	12.63	1.32***	12.78
Academic achievement	2.89***	29.84	2.19***	22.21
Peer effect	−1.32***	−9.31	−1.38***	−9.0
GEM	−1.62*	−2.364	−2.1**	−3.48

Notes: * $p < .05$, ** $p < .01$, *** $p < .001$.

Control variables

As expected, the control variables are strongly related with attitudes toward participation both for the girls and boys. Academic performance for both girls and boys has the strongest association with positive participatory attitudes. Intended levels of education and social background both have strong positive associations with our dependent variable for boys and girls, suggesting that relatively privileged and academically motivated students are more in favor of civic participation. Ethnic background does not have a significant effect for either boys or girls. The effect of peers is rather unexpected as it shows a negative association with participation for both girls and boys. In other words, the higher the social status of your peers, the lower are your participatory attitudes. Finally, another unexpected finding is that the Gender Empowerment Measure (GEM) has a negative impact on participation, meaning that the higher the level of gender equality in a country, the lower the level of participatory attitudes.

Conclusion

This research confirms theories of gender equality and modernization, arguing that a belief in gender equality follows patterns of economic growth (Inglehart & Norris, 2003; Inglehart & Welzel, 2005). However, and as predicted, perceptions of gender inequality appear to be independent from beliefs in gender equality. In addition, they are neither associated with actual levels of gender equality nor with levels of economic development. We argue that this could be due to a psychological preference to believe that the world is fair (Lerner, 1980). Such a belief removes the anxiety that would be caused by having to challenge the privileged positions of male partners, friends, relatives, and colleagues (Morrison et al., 2005).

If we want to understand how awareness of gender equality is enhanced, it is useful to explore the case of Sweden. Sweden was the only country that has over 50% of young people in the egalitarian-dissatisfied group and combines this with the second highest score on the gender-equality index. Thus Sweden has achieved greater levels of gender equality and managed to raise awareness within young people about gender inequalities (as expressed as a high level of perceived inequality). Sweden has been a leading country in the world in terms gender-equality policy and practice, and "it has a history of 'social engineering', a form of social planning stemming from the 1930s that combines research, politics and an aesthetics of rationality in order to create 'the good society' (*det goda samhället*) and produce a particular kind of new, aware and socially desirable person or citizen (*den nya människan; den nya medborgaren*)" (Woodford-Berger, 2009, pp. 68–69). The gender equality policies and practices that stem from the social plans are still very present today in Swedish society and may account for the higher levels of awareness of gender inequality in Sweden. It would be worthy of further investigation to establish whether these policies can indeed explain why Sweden is more successful than its fellow Nordic countries in achieving not only high levels of equality but also greater perceptions of gender inequality.

In a final step, we found that participatory attitudes were highest among the egalitarian-dissatisfied group, for both boys and girls. This confirms our hypothesis that to enhance the motivation for political change it is necessary both to perceive gender inequality and believe in gender equality. This has implications for critical pedagogy as it highlights the need for young people not only to develop beliefs in gender equality, but in addition to learn to perceive real circumstances of inequalities. Without both of these qualities failure can be blamed on the individual rather than on systemic forms of exclusion and the motivation to engage in political action to bring about positive social change is reduced.

We have to note, however, that the positive effect of an awareness of gender inequality on the motivation to participate is not so powerful that these motivation levels are also highest in the countries where this awareness is strongest. Evidently there are many other, and more powerful, factors at work that influence this motivation.

References

Bergman, L. R. (2001). A person approach in research on adolescence: Some methodological challenges. *Journal of Adolescent Research*, 16, 28–53.

Bergman, L. R., & El-Khouri, B. M. (2003). A person-oriented approach: Methods for today and methods for tomorrow. *New Directions for Child and Adolescent Development*, 101, 25–38.

Campbell, D. (2006). What is education's impact on civic and social engagement? In R. Desjardins & T. Schuller (Eds.), *Measuring the effects of education on health and civic engagement: Proceedings of the Copenhagen symposium* (pp. 25–126). Paris: CERI, OECD.

David, N., & Robinson, R. (1991). Men's and women's consciousness of gender inequality: Austria, West Germany, Great Britain, and the United States. *American Sociological Review*, 56(1), 72–84.

Delhey, J., & Newton, K. (2005). Predicting cross-national levels of social trust: Global pattern or Nordic exceptionalism? *European Sociological Review*, 21, 311–327.

Figes, K. (1994). *Because of her sex: The myth of equality for women in Britain*. London: Macmillan.

Galston, W. (2001). Political knowledge, political engagement and civic education. *Annual Review of Political Science*, 4, 217–234.

Giddens, A. (1973). *The class structure of the advanced societies*. New York: Barnes and Noble.

Green, A., & Janmaat, J. G. (2011). *Regimes of social cohesion: Societies and the crisis of globalization*. Houndmills, Basingstoke: Palgrave Macmillan.

Gurin, P. (1985). Women's gender consciousness. *The Public Opinion Quarterly*, 49(2), 143–163.

Hoskins, B., Barber, C., Van Nijlen, D., & Villalba, E. (2011). Comparing civic competence among European youth: composite and domain-specific indicators using IEA civic education study data. *Comparative Education Review*, 55(1), 82–110.

Husfeldt, V., Barber, C., & Torney-Purta, J. (2005). *Students' social attitudes and expected political participation: New scales in the enhanced database of the IEA* (CEDARS Working Paper). Retrieved from http://terpconnect.umd.edu/~jtpurta/Original%20Documents/CEDARS%20new%20scales%20report.pdf.

Inglehart, R., & Norris, P. (2003). *Rising tide: Gender equality and cultural change around the world*. Cambridge University Press.

Inglehart, R., & Welzel, C. (2005). *Modernization, cultural change, and democracy: The human development sequence*. New York: Cambridge University Press.

Janmaat, J. G. (2008). The civic attitudes of ethnic minority youth and the impact of citizenship education, *Journal of Ethnic and Migration Studies*, 34(1), 27–54.

(2011). Ability grouping, segregation and civic competences among adolescents. *International Sociology*, 26(4), 455–482.

Janmaat, J. G., & Braun, R. (2009). Diversity and postmaterialism as rival perspectives in accounting for social solidarity: Evidence from international surveys. *International Journal of Comparative Sociology*, 50(1), 39–68.

Klasen, S. (2006). UNDP's gender-related measures: Some conceptual problems and possible solutions, *Journal of Human Development*, 7(2), 243–274.

Klasen, S., & Schuler, D. (2011). Reforming the gender-related development index and the gender empowerment measure: Implementing some specific proposals. *Feminist Economics*, 17(1), 1–30.

Lerner, M. L. (1980). *The belief in a just world: A fundamental delusion*. New York: Plenum Press.

Lovett, F. (2010). *A general theory of domination and justice*. Oxford University Press.

Lundmark, C. (1995). Feminist political orientations. In J. van Deth & E. Scarborough (Eds.), *The impact of values* (pp. 250–274). Oxford University Press.

Maslow, A. H. (1943). A theory of motivation. *Psychological Review*, 50(4), 370–396.

Morrison, Z., Bourke, M., & Kelley, C. (2005). Stop making it such a big issue: Perceptions and experiences of gender inequality by undergraduates at a British university. *Women's Studies International Forum*, 28, 150–162.

Nie, N., Junn, J., & Stehlik-Barry, K. (1996). *Education and democratic citizenship in America*. Chicago: Chicago University Press.
Rhode, D. (1997). *The denial of gender equality*. Cambridge, MA: Harvard University Press.
Rice, T. W., & Feldman, J. L. (1997). Civic culture and democracy from Europe to America. *The Journal of Politics*, 59(4), 1143–1172.
Rubin, Z., & Peplau, L. (1975). Who believes in a just world? *Journal of Social Issues*, 31(3), 65–89.
Schulz, W. (2004). Scaling procedures for Likert-type items on students' concepts, attitudes and actions. In W. Schulz & H. Sibberns (Eds.), *IEA Civic Education Study: Technical report* (pp. 93–126). Amsterdam: IEA.
Schulz, W., Ainly, J., Fraillon, J., Kerr, D., & Losito, B. (2010). *ICCS 2009 international report: The civic knowledge, attitudes and engagement among lower secondary school students in 38 countries*. Amsterdam: IEA.
Sen, A. (2000). Social justice and the distribution of income. In A. B. Atkinson & F. Bourguignon (Eds.), *Handbook of income distribution* (Vol. 1, pp. 59–85). Amsterdam: North-Holland.
Snijders, T., & Bosker, R. J. (1999). *Multilevel analysis: An introduction to basic and advanced multilevel modelling*. London: Sage Publications.
Titus, J. (2000). Engaging student resistance to feminism: How is this stuff going to make us better teachers? *Gender and Education*, 12(1), 21–37.
Torney-Purta, J., Lehmann, R., Oswald, H., & Schulz, W. (2001). *Citizenship and education in twenty-eight countries: Civic knowledge and engagement at age fourteen*. Amsterdam: IEA.
United Nations Development Program (UNDP). (2012a). *Measuring inequality: Gender-related Development Index (GDI) and Gender Empowerment Measure (GEM)*. Retrieved October 2, 2012, from http://hdr.undp.org/en/-statistics/indices/gdi_gem.
(2012b). *Gender Empowerment Measure*. Retrieved from http://hdr.undp.org/en/media/HDR_20072008_GEM.pdf.
Van der Werfhorst, H. (2007). *Vocational education and active citizenship behavior in cross-national perspective* (AIAS Working Paper Number 2007/62). Retrieved from www.uva-aias.net/files/aias/WP62.pdf.
Woodford-Berger, P. (2004). Gender mainstreaming: What is it (about) and should we continue doing it? *IDS Bulletin*, 35, 65–72. doi: 10.1111/j.1759-5436.2004.tb00157.x.

Appendix 21.1: The composition of the participation scale

Internal political efficacy

- I know more about politics than most people my age.
- When political issues or problems are being discussed, I usually have something to say.
- I am able to understand most political issues easily.
- I am interested in politics.

Categories: very bad, somewhat bad, somewhat good, very good for democracy, disagree, agree.

Expected social movement related participation

What do you expect that you will do over the next few years?

- Spray-paint protest slogans on walls.
- Block traffic as a form of protest.
- Occupy public buildings as a form of protest.

Categories: I will certainly not do this; I will probably not do this; I will probably do this; I will certainly do this.

Political activities

When you are an adult, what do you expect that you will do?

- Join a political party.
- Write letters to a newspaper about social or political concerns.
- Be a candidate for a local or city office.

Categories: I will certainly not do this; I will probably not do this; I will probably do this; I will certainly do this.

Self-confident participation at school

- I am interested in participating in discussions about school problems.
- When school problems are being discussed I usually have something to say.

Categories: strongly disagree, disagree, agree, strongly agree.

Expectations associated with voting

When you are an adult, what do you expect that you will do?

- Vote in national elections.
- Get information about candidates before voting in an election.

Categories: very bad, somewhat bad, somewhat good, very good for democracy.

Index

ability, 5, 6, 32, 56, 68, 81, 82, 96, 111, 127, 132, 155, 173, 207, 213, 225, 226, 227, 267, 269, 270, 271, 287, 392, 393, 395, 407, 478
   academic, 293, 299, 389
   beliefs, sex-typed, 59
   innate, 80, 81, 84, 85, 96, 269
   intellectual, 395, 396, 397, 399, 401, 402, 403, 405, 407
   math, 13, 176, 206, 225, 226, 269, 270, 276, 278, 300, 312
   math and reading, 170
   reading, 13, 16, 176, 178, 206, 217
   science, 15, 203, 205, 206, 208
   verbal, 269, 273, 275, 276, 278
ability self-concept, 13, 16, 58, 79, 80, 81, 83, 84, 86, 93, 94, 95, 161, 268, 270, 271, 278, 279, 395
   academic attainment, 13
   beginning of primary school, 83
   math, 88, 89, 92, 93, 242, 243, 267, 270, 271, 273, 276, 278, 393
   math and reading, 79, 80, 83, 84, 85, 86, 88, 94
   reading, 92, 94
academic attainment, 12, 13, 20, 161, 163, 164, 166, 178, 204, 366, 367, 374
achievement behavior, 346, 351, 353, 354
achievement goal theory, 351
achievement-related choices, 204, 225, 226, 228, 242, 243, 392
   see also Expectancy-Value Theory of Achievement-Related Choices (EVT)
ACT, *see* American College Testing
adolescence, 11, 14, 18, 20, 29, 30, 31, 33, 34, 101, 116, 126, 127, 128, 129, 131, 133, 146, 147, 148, 153, 154, 155, 156, 204, 260, 267, 271, 331, 333, 338, 339, 348, 389, 391, 393, 395, 399, 405, 406
   career transitions, 127, 129, 132
   development of gender identity, 101
   educational and career aspirations during, 162
   gender attitudes, 134
   life transitions, 140
   motivational competence, 126
   planning and decision-making, 126
   self-regulatory skills, 126

adolescent, 10, 29, 30, 34, 101, 103, 107, 110, 112, 125, 126, 127, 128, 129
   explicit motive, 135
   female, 18, 109, 114, 136, 138, 139
   goal clarity and aspirations, 134
   male, 115
   psychological needs of, 10
   psychology at school transition, 104
   self-conceptions, 133
adrenarche, 103
adulthood, 11, 31, 33, 34, 103, 127, 128, 131, 139, 150, 162, 166, 250, 347, 366, 393, 395, 396, 404, 432, 441
   emerging, 125
   middle, 19, 20, 389, 391, 393, 394, 398, 399, 403, 407
   young, 6, 146, 147, 154, 273, 326, 327, 333, 334, 338, 348, 394, 430, 450
affective attitudes, 42, 43
African American, 273, 285, 290, 312, 314, 315
age cohorts, 21, 161, 162, 166, 167, 175, 177
ageing population, 429, 453
agency, 4, 8, 10, 11, 18, 19, 20, 23, 149, 162, 323, 347, 348, 412, 414, 415, 416, 419, 421, 422
age-related norms and expectations, 7
American College Testing (ACT), 294
   see also United States
Anomalies Act, 432
   see also United Kingdom
apprenticeship, 186, 188, 189, 190, 191, 192, 195, 197
   see also United Kingdom: Young Apprentice program
aspirations
   academic, 29, 30, 34, 164
   career, 165, 167, 169, 171, 172, 174, 175, 177, 178, 184, 204, 224, 229, 230, 231, 232, 233, 236, 238, 240, 242, 268, 291, 321, 325, 459
   certainty in, 161, 172, 176
   educational, 12, 29, 30, 33, 35, 38, 44, 46, 60, 152, 161, 163, 165, 167, 171, 172, 173, 175, 176, 178, 224, 247, 248, 249, 250, 251, 256, 258, 259, 260, 365, 394, 406, 458, 471, 472

aspirations (*cont.*)
  occupational, 15, 16, 22, 30, 33, 166, 169, 173, 174, 212, 217, 271, 325, 333, 456, 457, 460, 464, 466, 471, 472
  uncertainty in, 165, 169, 170, 173, 177, 178
  see also adolescent; family; gender differences; physical sciences, mathematics and engineering (PME); Science, Engineering and Technology (SET)
attributional theory of motivation, 80
Australia, 114, 209
Austria, 212, 322

Belgium, French, 484, 487
BHPS, *see* British Household Panel Survey (BHPS)
British Cohort Study (BCS70), 162, 166, 169, 170, 172, 173, 174, 175, 176, 177, 178, 385
  see also United Kingdom
British Household Panel Survey (BHPS), 18, 165, 321, 325, 326, 327, 328, 334, 337, 338
  see also United Kingdom
British Youth Survey (BYS), 326
  see also United Kingdom
Bulgaria, 484

Canadian longitudinal study, 394
  see also Pathways on Life's Way Project
career
  advice, 164, 165, 166, 170, 177
  certainty, 15
  choice, 4, 11, 15, 16, 21, 29, 30, 101, 114, 139, 162, 183, 194, 195, 213, 218, 236, 249, 267, 268, 269, 270, 271, 273, 278, 323, 460
  decisions, 12, 279, 413
  development, 4, 12, 15, 21, 128, 132, 161, 162, 173, 178, 292, 413
  expectations, 162, 206
  mentorship, 178
  outcomes, 165, 239, 278, 338, 391, 413
  pathways, 128, 226, 270, 275, 279, 326
  patterns, 348, 413
  planning, 11, 14, 102, 131, 139
  satisfaction, 21, 131, 412, 413, 415, 416, 420, 421
  science, 213, 215, 260, 279
  STEM, 17, 204, 213, 266, 267, 268, 269, 272, 278, 288, 289
  success, 20, 131, 346, 347, 413, 414, 415, 416, 417, 419, 420, 421, 423
CASP-19, 444
CCCI, *see* Civic Competence Composite Indicator
census data, 460, 461, 463, 464
Center for Epidemiologic Studies–Depression Scale (CES-D), 444
  see also United States

Center for Human Resource Research, *see* United States
CES-D, *see* Center for Epidemiologic Studies–Depression Scale
childbearing, 380, 430, 438
childbirth, "occupational downgrading" after, 440
childcare, 20, 136, 139, 183, 188, 191, 413, 421
  facilities, 422
Childhood and Beyond (CAB) study, 13, 84
  see also United States
childhood, early, 6, 22, 23, 34, 132, 412
Chile, 484, 488
citizen identity, 477
citizenship, active, 479
CIVED, *see* Civic Education Study (CIVED)
Civic Competence Composite Indicator, 480
Civic Education Study (CIVED), 22, 479, 480, 483, 487, 489
civic knowledge, 479, 483
class, 323, 338, 381, 429, 432, 441, 443
  gender values, 443
  middle, 59, 60, 61, 71, 72, 84, 95, 273, 324, 432, 443, 444, 452
  patterns in gender norms, 444
  social, 5, 7, 12, 95, 174, 358, 366, 367, 369, 383
  specific, 12, 59, 60
  upper, 60, 70
  working, 59, 273, 443, 444
Classification of Educational/Occupational Field, 251
COCON, *see* Swiss Survey of Children and Youth
Coeducation, 19, 365, 366, 367, 369, 372, 373, 374, 376, 377, 378, 379, 382, 383, 384, 385, 386
cognitive ability, 57, 204, 205, 394
cognitive test scores, 367
College Board exams, 299
college entrance examinations, *see* test; American College Testing (ACT); College Board exams; Scholastic Achievement Test (SAT)
Commission of the European Communities, 184
  see also European Union (EU)
communist countries, former, 486
compensation, 126, 129, 140, 147, 148
competencies
  basic cognitive ability, 57
  cognitive, 12, 53, 62, 63, 67, 70
  curriculum-related cognitive, 57
  pre-academic, 57, 61
  productive, 57, 58, 62
  social, 57, 59, 62, 67
Connexions, 170, 177
  see also career advice; United Kingdom
context, socio-historical, 10, 11, 23, 162, 166, 175, 218
contraception, 450

co-regulation, 147, 148, 162, 163, 172
counselor, 289, 290, 291, 294, 313
  guidance, 307
cultural capital, 64, 68, 323
  family-related, 59
Current Population Survey, 464
  see also United States
Cyprus, 484, 487
Czech Republic, 209, 484, 486

DAA, see Differential Ability Analysis (DAA)
debt, 162
decision making, 7, 15
  individual, 10, 11
democracy/citizenship, 479
Denmark, 206, 322, 484
depression, 133, 378, 379, 444, 448, 452, 453
  see also Center for Epidemiologic Studies–Depression Scale
depressive symptoms, 146, 148, 152, 444, 445, 447
  see also gender differences
developmental-contextual approach, 6, 162
deviant groups and learning behaviors, 111
Differential Ability Analysis (DAA), 397
discrimination, 6, 15, 110, 194, 413, 459, 472, 473, 475, 476, 478
divorce/separation, 357, 379, 380, 385, 386, 435, 436, 445, 448, 452
domain-specific academic self-beliefs, 226, 227
dual-impact model of gender and career-related processes, 413

economic development, 475, 490
economic growth, 22, 163, 215, 217, 490
economic recession, 163, 176
economic rewards, 203, 457, 459, 460, 462, 463, 464, 466, 471, 473
economy, 186, 191, 215, 266, 322, 422
  knowledge-based, 218, 322, 477
education
  academic, 131, 398
  compulsory, 167, 391
  post-compulsory, 70, 155, 162
  postsecondary, 17, 18, 285, 287, 288, 290, 292, 293, 298, 315, 316
  secondary, 11, 14, 156, 287, 326, 368
  tertiary, 17, 70, 147, 203, 216, 217, 287, 390
  university, 389, 390, 391, 392, 398, 405
  upper secondary, 150, 391
  vocational, 70, 147, 182, 196, 260, 391, 397, 398, 407
Education Longitudinal Study (ELS), 292
  see also United States
elective selection, 128, 129, 131, 132
ELS, see Education Longitudinal Study (ELS)
ELSA, see English Longitudinal Study of Ageing (ELSA)

employers, 183, 191, 192, 195, 381, 459
employment, 9, 11, 136, 162, 165, 171, 176, 183, 184, 266, 323, 324, 339, 348, 354, 356, 381, 383, 414, 415, 416, 423, 430, 432, 434, 436, 438, 439, 441, 444, 477
employment, field of, 20, 417, 421
Employment Protection Act, see United States
Employment Rights, Institute of (IER), see United Kingdom
England, see United Kingdom
English Longitudinal Study of Ageing (ELSA), 21, 430, 434, 435, 436, 437, 441, 448
  see also United Kingdom
EOC, see Equal Opportunity Commission
Equality and Human Rights Commission's Triennial Review, 188
Equal Opportunity Commission (EOC), 188, 191
  see also United Kingdom
Equal Pay Act, see United States
EQUAL project, 15, 196
  Danish, 194
  German, 195
  Netherlands, 195
  Spanish, Barcelona, 194, 195
  see also European Union (EU)
  see also United Kingdom
Estonia, 484, 487
ethnicity, 4, 6, 7, 23, 174, 315, 483
Eurobarometer survey on Young People and Science, 477
  see also European Union (EU)
Europe, 132, 149, 156, 182, 196, 203, 326, 389, 408, 429, 484
  Eastern, 213, 484, 488
  Northern, 213, 484
  Southern, 213, 484, 488
  Western, 484, 487
European Union (EU), 183, 390
  Civic Competence Composite Indicator, 480
  Commission of the European Communities, 184
  EQUAL, 196
  Eurobarometer survey on Young People and Science, 323, 477
  European Union (EU) Labour Force Survey, 2005, 389
  Eurostat, 184
  Fifth Framework Project, 196
  Joint Research Centre of the European Commission, 390, 480
  Swedish 2005 EU Labour Force Survey, 390
European Union (EU) Labour Force Survey, 2005, see European Union (EU)
Eurostat, see European Union (EU)
evolution, 5, 103, 116, 315

EVT, *see* Expectancy-Value Theory of Achievement-Related Choices
expectancy effects, 13, 83, 94
expectancy-value model, 20, 204, 250, 259, 260, 392
    behavioral choice, 7, 247
    motivation, 20, 80, 81, 389, 392, 393, 405
Expectancy-Value Theory of Achievement-Related Choices (EVT), 16
expectations, 12, 20, 114, 163, 164, 166, 170, 172, 227, 239, 299, 389, 393, 395, 399, 402, 403, 405, 406, 407, 408
    educational, 287, 292, 312, 394, 406, 408

family
    aspirations, 321, 335, 339, 472
    background, 12, 19, 53, 54, 59, 213, 292, 321, 325, 367
    context, 62, 126
    demographics, 5
    disadvantaged, 108, 161, 163
    income, 391, 392, 394, 395, 397
    patterns, 321, 324, 326, 334
    role, 136, 140, 436, 438, 439, 458
    size, 435, 437, 438, 441, 447
    socioeconomic background, 323, 334
    socioeconomic status, 163, 399
    wealth, 395
family formation, 15, 21, 337, 367, 430, 435, 436, 437, 450, 460, 462, 463, 466, 472, 473
family forms, non-normative, 429, 450, 452
family-related social capital, 60
family socialization model, 392
femininity, 20, 107, 325, 414
feminism, second wave, 21, 429, 430, 453
feminist, 373, 429, 478
    values, 477
feminist cognition, 481
feminist orientation, 481
Fifth Framework Project, 196
    see also European Union (EU)
financial hardship, 441
FinEdu, *see* Finnish Educational Transition Studies
Finland, 146, 147, 149, 150, 156, 196, 208, 213, 215, 218, 258, 484, 487
    Finnish Educational Transition Studies (FinEdu), 150, 152, 250
    Ministry of Education and Culture of Finland, 251
France, 322

GCSE, *see* General Certificate of Secondary Education
gender
    attitudes, 45, 134, 135, 470, 472, 476, 478, 488
    bias, 79, 83, 93, 218

    categories, 132
    discrimination, 4, 5, 6, 22, 53, 459, 475, 476, 484
    disparities in engagement and interest, 33
    equality, 12, 21, 22, 185, 194, 195, 196, 197, 322, 339, 404, 408, 429, 432, 434, 453, 462, 470, 475, 476, 477, 478, 479, 480, 481, 482, 483, 484, 487, 488, 489, 490, 491
    expectations in early adolescence, 103
    group, 37, 55, 354
    historical and continued interaction, 104
    identity, 4, 22, 101, 104, 413
    imbalances, 182, 196
    inequality, 15, 21, 22, 23, 185, 195, 196, 285, 339, 346, 429, 431, 434, 453, 456, 458, 472, 475, 476, 477, 479, 481, 482, 488, 490, 491
    inside perspective, 20, 413, 414, 421, 423
    issues in management, 423
    outside perspective, 20, 413, 423
    schema, 102, 104
    self-construct, 104
    social construction of, 413
    socialization, 4, 240, 243, 278
gender-atypical, 373
gender awareness activities, 15, 193
Gender Development Index (GDI), 483
gender differences
    ability self-concept, 13
    academic achievement, 13, 16, 53, 54, 64, 72
    academic attainment, 3, 11, 16, 44, 164, 206, 366, 386
    academic-related self-beliefs, 41
    academic wellbeing, 146, 148, 152, 153, 154
    achievement behavior, 346, 354
    achievement goals, 31, 352
    across contexts, 162
    adaptation, 13
    adolescents' occupational aspirations, 101, 212, 326
    aspirations and attainment, 4, 10, 14, 23
    aspirations and choice, 29, 243
    attainment, 16, 21, 205, 430, 441, 453
    attitudes, 29, 32
    beliefs, 29
    career aspirations, 11, 15, 30, 204, 232, 242
    choices for economic rewards, 457
    depressive symptoms, 146, 148, 445, 447, 448
    emotional health at transition, 104
    essentialism, 5
    expectations in early adolescence, 103
    happiness pathways, 147
    household division of labor, 4
    human capital, 456, 457
    identities, 101, 103, 115

innate, 5, 56, 59, 72, 102, 269
lifestyle, 5, 272, 273, 278
math ability self-concept, 266, 267, 273
motivation, 29
occupational choice and attainment, 5, 438
opportunities for achievement, 429
peer relationships, 34, 104
physical functioning, 448, 450
play, 30, 38
quality of life, 444, 452
rewards, 457
school engagement, 13, 101, 152
school transition, 101, 116
science participation, 286
self-ascribed gender-related attributes, 134
sex-typed competence beliefs, 57
skills and interests, 38, 40
socialization, 56, 59, 68, 71, 133, 459, 463, 470, 472
social mobility, 383
social world, 6, 101
STEM, 17, 224, 249, 267
subjective task values (STVs), 16, 248, 249, 250, 258
subjective wellbeing attainment, 444
teachers' perceptions of ability and effort, 13, 79, 82, 83, 86, 87, 89, 95
test performance, 16, 176, 203, 206, 233
uncertainty, 15, 162
university majors, 224, 229
verbal ability, 266, 267, 273
gender differential in socioeconomic attainment, 430
gender divisions between work and family, 429
gender divisions of labor, traditional, 436
gender gap, 29, 30, 226
  career attainment, 347
  life satisfaction, 14
  math, 289, 346
  science, 324
  self-concept, 373
  self-confidence, 373
  SET occupations, 18, 321, 323, 337, 339, 340
  STEM fields, 31, 33, 203, 217, 272, 276, 287, 289, 291, 292, 307
  wages, 4, 21, 184, 191, 322, 339, 456, 457, 458, 459, 460, 462, 463, 465, 466, 470, 471, 472, 473
Gender stereotype
  beliefs, 133
Gender-Intensification Hypothesis, 103, 133
gender-organized relationships, 44
gender-related
  attitudes, 14, 42, 44, 102, 125, 126, 132, 135
  attributes, 126, 133, 134
  attributes in adolescence, 133
  behavior, 133, 137
  intergroup biases, 42
  motives, 133
gender-role
  attitudes, 136
  behavior, 133
  characteristics, 132
  children's academic achievement, 41
  children's educational interests, 33
  division at home, 136
  social change, 452
  stereotypic, 177
  traditional, 134, 135
gender segregation
  apprenticeship, 185, 188, 190, 191, 197
  children's, 41
  education, 19, 110, 367
  labor market, 4, 6, 15, 21, 22, 182, 185, 197, 382, 384, 432, 438, 441, 456, 458, 471, 472, 473
  occupational, 6, 367, 458
  tackling, 193
  VET, 182, 183, 193
gender-specific
  education, 67, 72
  occupational trends, 18, 414
  parental expectations, 12, 59
  socialization practices, 13, 53, 56, 61, 70, 71
gender stereotype, 177
  adolescence, 116, 140
  attitudes toward occupations, 192
  behavior, 43, 111, 133
  beliefs, 22, 103
  children's beliefs, 30, 33, 43, 291
  education, 41, 95, 377, 378
  imbalances, 182
  labor, 136
  parental, 406
  social context, 214, 267
  socialization, 6, 56, 104, 134
  teachers' ability perceptions, 13, 58, 61, 79, 93, 324
  vocational training, 15
  see also EQUAL project
gender-typed occupational choices, 184
General Certificate of Secondary Education (GCSE), 185, 366
  see also United Kingdom
Germany, 53, 59, 114, 196, 208, 212, 224, 230, 393, 422, 478, 484, 487
  Gymnasium, 230, 233
  Transformation of the Secondary School System and Academic Careers (TOSCA), 16, 230
  vocational training and labor market, 357
globalization, 161
global market, 161

goal
  achievement, 351, 352
  adjustment, 19, 125, 129, 132, 349, 350, 355, 356, 357, 358
  attainment, 129, 139
  behavior, 357
  development in adolescence, 126, 127, 130, 131, 132
  disengagement, 346, 347, 350, 356, 357, 358
  educational, 31, 32, 33, 34, 54, 128, 183
  engagement, 19, 347, 350, 356, 357, 358
  explicit, 19, 352, 353
  family-related, 14, 126, 129, 134
  implicit, 353
  long-term, 5, 9, 17, 127, 172, 273, 278, 279, 354
  mastery, 351, 352, 358
  motivation, 115
  multiple goal perspective, 351
  performance, 351, 358
  pursuit, 125, 126, 128, 129, 130, 135, 139, 355, 356
  relevant actions, 129
  selection, 4, 125, 126, 128, 129, 130, 133, 134, 135, 346, 349, 350, 355, 357
  self-perception, 4
  self-regulatory processes, 14
  short-term, 9
goal choice, optimized, 355, 356
gonadarche, 103
GPA, *see* Grade Point Average
Grade Point Average (GPA), 151, 251, 256, 258, 260, 294, 312, 416
Great Britain, *see* United Kingdom
Greece, 132, 196, 207, 208, 218, 477, 484, 487, 488
growth spurt, 103
Gymnasium, 230, 233, 390, 407
  see also Germany; Sweden

habitus, 55, 56, 57, 59, 67, 323
Holland's person–environment matching approach, 130
homemaker, 421
  full-time, 432
homosexuality, 365
housing prices, 162
human capital, 412, 459, 460, 462, 463, 466, 472, 473
  variables, 413
human capital theory, 456, 458, 466, 473
Hungary, 212, 213, 486, 487, 488

Iceland, 208, 218
ICT, *see* Information and Communications Technology (ICT)
IDA, *see* Sweden; Swedish Individual Development and Adaptation
identity construction, 218

ILO, *see* International Labour Organization (ILO)
individual's perception of the range of possible choices, 9
Information and Communications Technology (ICT), 328
Information Technology (IT), 328
Integrated Public Use Microdata Series (IPUMS), 464
intellectual aptitude, 266, 267, 268, 269, 273
internal/external frame of reference model, 224, 225, 227, 228, 229, 230, 231, 235, 236, 238, 240
International Labour Organization (ILO), 212
International Standard Classification of Occupations (ISCO), 212, 328
Internet, 194
intrinsic value, 247
  see also subjective task values (STVs)
ipsitive effect, 228
IRT, *see* Item Response Theory (IRT)
ISCO, *see* International Standard Classification of Occupations (ISCO)
ISCO-88 occupational coding scheme, 229, 231
IT, *see* Information Technology (IT)
Italy, 213, 215, 477, 487
Item Response Theory (IRT), 480

Japan, 212, 213, 270
Joint Research Centre of the European Commission, 480
  see also European Union (EU)
Just World Theory, 478, 482, 484

knife-edge behavior, 111
Korea, 322

labor force, 4, 22, 457
  experience, 457, 472
  highly skilled, 7
  STEM fields, 287
  women, 434
labor market, 4, 11, 15, 161, 162, 191, 194, 218, 292, 348, 357, 367, 391, 432, 438, 441, 448, 452, 457, 458, 459, 470
  changing, 7, 431
  female-dominated, 183
  patterns, 457
  rewards, 457, 472
  women, 3, 6, 183, 184, 185, 322, 339, 381, 382, 385, 432, 434, 438, 440, 453, 472
  youth, 165, 182, 183
  see also gender segregation
language play, 39, 40
  boys, 40
  girls, 39, 40
latent profile analysis (LPA), 252, 253
Latin America, 484, 488

INDEX

Latino, 285, 290, 299, 312, 314, 315
Latvia, 487
leaky pipe phenomenon, 326, 338
life course, 5, 6, 10, 12, 22, 23, 54, 126, 315, 327, 348, 435, 436, 437, 452, 457, 462, 464, 465, 478
　framework, 8
　patterns, male and female, 456, 472
　perspective, 7, 9, 11, 23, 54
Life-Course Developmental Theory, 22
life history information on work and family, 430
life satisfaction, 14, 15, 134, 150, 151, 353, 444, 445, 447, 452
life-span model of motivation, 146, 147, 149, 153
literacy, 31, 41, 94, 208, 209, 210, 218, 259, 322
Lithuania, 484, 486, 487, 488
Longitudinal Study of Young People in England (LSYPE), 162, 164, 165, 167, 169, 171, 172, 173, 175, 176, 177, 178
　see also United Kingdom
loss-based selection, 129, 132
LPA, *see* latent profile analysis (LPA)
LSYPE, *see* Longitudinal Study of Young People in England (LSYPE)
Luxemburg, 206

malaise inventory, 378
marriage, 114, 118, 162, 365, 367, 379, 430, 432, 434, 436, 438, 448, 453
masculinity, 20, 115, 324, 414
maternity legislation, 430
maturity status markers, 102
MBA programs, 354
mental rotation ability, 269
Michigan Study of Adolescent Life Transitions (MSALT), *see* United States
Milwaukee study, 104, 109, 114, 116
　see also United States
Minnesota Population Center, *see* United States
minority, ethnic, 170, 174, 177, 288, 368
modernization, 475, 483
modernization theory, 22, 476, 477, 488, 490
motivated behavior, model of, 9
motivation, 115, 324
　achievement, 55, 57, 60, 347, 353, 354
　beliefs, 17
　certainty, 172
　educational, 3, 33, 38, 79, 81, 94, 96, 115, 156, 161, 164, 170, 172, 176, 178, 270, 346, 347, 483
　individual differences in, 18, 19, 266, 267, 347, 350
　intrinsic, 54
　math and science, 267, 270, 339
　political, 491

　self-regulation, 19, 346, 347, 356, 357, 358
　STEM major, 266, 276, 279, 290
motivational theory of life-span development, 18, 347, 348
motive
　explicit, 135, 346, 352, 353
　explicit and implicit, 346, 352, 353
　implicit, 352, 353, 354
MSALT, *see* United States

National Child Development Study (NCDS), 367, 368, 369
　see also United Kingdom
National identity/international relations, 479
National Longitudinal Survey (NLS), 464
　see also United States
National Longitudinal Survey of Youth (NLSY), 394, 395, 464
　see also United States
National Pupil Database, 167
　see also United Kingdom
National Statistics Socio-economic Classification (NS-SEC), 169
　see also United Kingdom
NCDS, *see* National Child Development Study (NCDS)
NCES, *see* United States, US National Center for Educational Statistics (NCES)
NEET, *see* Not in Education, Employment or Training (NEET)
Netherlands, 185, 195, 206, 208
New Zealand, 322
NLS, *see* National Longitudinal Survey (NLS)
NLSY, *see* National Longitudinal Survey of Youth (NLSY)
North America, 324, 429
Northern Ireland, *see* United Kingdom
Norway, 213, 322, 484, 488
not in education, employment or training (NEET), 165, 166, 171, 172, 175, 178, 183
　see also United Kingdom

Observational Research and Classroom Learning Evaluation (ORACLE), 108, 110, 112, 113, 115
　ORACLE replication study, 112, 113, 116
　see also United Kingdom
OECD, *see* Organisation for Economic Co-operation and Development (OECD)
optimization, 126, 129, 131, 132, 140
ORACLE, *see* Observational Research and Classroom Learning Evaluation (ORACLE)
Organisation for Economic Co-operation and Development (OECD), 22, 203, 204, 205, 206, 208, 210, 215, 286, 287, 321
　Canberra Manual, 328
　Frascati Manual, 328

Parental education and occupation, 334
parental expectations
  in adolescence, 20, 395, 399, 405, 406
parenthood, 20, 162, 380, 412, 415, 416, 417, 419, 420, 421, 422, 434, 435, 436, 437, 439, 440, 447, 452
partnership, 162, 336, 379, 434, 435, 437, 438, 439, 440, 445, 447, 448, 450, 452
  unmarried cohabiting, 434, 436, 438, 453
peer group, 22, 32, 34, 101, 104
  norms about education, 34
  same-sex, 36, 37
  segregated, 35, 46
peers
  academic-related outcomes, 31
  associations between peer characteristics and academic outcomes, 34
  attitudes about, 41, 45
  behavioral avoidance of other-sex, 42
  children's development, 30, 33
  children's interpersonal experiences and attitudes, 41
  contexts, 38, 39, 40, 44
  enforcing social norms regarding the desirability of educational success, 34
  interactions, 7, 12, 30, 35, 36, 39, 41, 45, 70, 290
  long-term effects on behavior, 36
  modeling, 34, 37
  other-sex, 12, 36, 38, 39, 40, 41, 42, 43, 44, 45
  pressure, 128, 377
  providing information and help, 34
  relationships, 34, 38, 44, 45, 58
  role model, 156, 290, 292, 315
  same-sex, 12, 35, 36, 37, 38, 39, 40, 41, 42, 43, 44, 45, 46, 104
  selection effects, 34, 46
  socialization, 36, 37, 40
  subculture, 36
  young children's early school behaviors and adjustment, 34, 35
perceptions of ability, 56, 164, 166, 170, 172, 176, 289
  self, 178
  see also teachers' perceptions of ability and effort
person-centered approach, 16, 17, 248, 249, 250, 258, 259, 260, 481
  person-oriented approach, 146, 152, 153
person–environment-fit theory, 10
  motivation, 10
physical sciences, mathematics, engineering and technology (PME), 16, 226, 231, 238
  aspirations, 227, 239, 242
  college major, 227, 230, 235, 238, 240
  fields, 228, 232, 238, 242
  women, 16, 242

PISA, see Programme for International Student Assessment
PME, see physical sciences, mathematics, engineering and technology
Poland, 213, 322, 484, 487
political mobilization, 479, 481
political participation, 22, 480
  see also motivation
Portugal, 196, 210
Programme for International Student Assessment (PISA), 16, 204, 205, 206, 207, 208, 212, 213, 217, 233, 321, 322
puberty, 103, 104, 107, 109, 155
  see also transition
pyramid of needs idea, Maslow's, 477

qualifications, educational, 322, 348, 356, 367, 385, 431, 441, 447
quality of life, 444, 445, 447
  measure, 444, 447

race, 4, 314, 315, 463
reading performance, 85, 92, 94
role model, 133, 299, 300, 312, 315, 324
  adult, 195, 290, 307
  parent, 139, 324, 334, 338, 406
  peer, 156, 290, 292, 315
  professional, 114, 291, 292, 324, 325, 340
Romania, 484, 487, 488
Russia, 486, 487, 488
Rutter aggression and anxiety scales, 372

SAMSAD, see Secondary and Middle School Adolescent Development (SAMSAD) Study
SAT, see Scholastic Assessment Test
Satisfaction with Life Scale, 444
SCA, see ability self-concept
Scandinavian countries, 488
Scholastic Assessment Test (SAT), 269, 289, 294
  see also United States
school
  comprehensive, 146, 147, 148, 149, 150, 151, 154, 156, 365, 368, 369, 372, 379
  direct grant, 368
  elementary, 3, 10, 12, 29, 30, 31, 35, 53, 54, 55, 56, 57, 61, 64, 65, 67, 71, 79, 83, 84, 102, 103, 104, 113
  engagement, 101, 147, 150, 152, 155, 156
  grammar, 368, 369, 371, 372
  grammar and technical, 368
  high school, 14, 34, 113, 125, 126, 128, 129, 130, 131, 134, 135, 137, 139, 146, 147, 149, 152, 153, 154, 155, 184, 247, 248, 249, 250, 258, 259, 270, 271, 276, 278, 286, 287, 288
  junior high, 10, 104, 115, 149, 352
  kindergarten, 31, 32, 35, 55, 84, 147, 194, 269

middle school, 10, 34, 104, 149, 271
post-comprehensive, 150, 151
postsecondary, 17, 251, 286, 287, 291, 293, 298
preschool, 11, 29, 30, 31, 34, 36, 37, 38, 41, 45, 61, 136, 137, 138, 139
primary, 12, 13, 79, 80, 81, 83, 84, 94, 95, 103, 104, 194
private, 368, 369, 379, 383, 384
secondary, 3, 10, 12, 15, 17, 18, 19, 22, 34, 54, 101, 103, 104, 112, 149, 150, 194, 195, 204, 217, 224, 233, 250, 286, 287, 288, 290, 291, 292, 293, 294, 299, 365, 367, 384, 391, 398
single-sex, 19, 46, 365, 366, 367, 368, 369, 373, 374, 375, 376, 377, 378, 379, 380, 382, 383, 384, 385, 386
vocational, 154
school burnout, 14, 146, 147, 148, 150, 151, 152, 153, 154, 155, 156
School Burnout Inventory, 151
Science education, relevance of (ROSE) study, 323
Science, Engineering, and Technology (SET)
    aspirations, 18, 325, 328, 335, 337
    careers, 18, 321, 324, 325, 326, 333, 334, 335, 338, 339, 340
    definition, 328
    occupations, 22, 321, 326, 327, 328, 333, 340
    young people's interest in, 18, 326, 338
    see also gender gap
scientist, 18, 203, 205, 213, 324, 340
    female, 325, 340
    female role model, 291, 324, 325, 340
Scotland, see United Kingdom
scripts of life, 7
Secondary and Middle School Adolescent Development (SAMSAD) Study, 106, 107, 108, 109, 110, 111, 112, 113, 114, 116
    see also United Kingdom
sector
    government, 463
    non-profit, 463
    private, 19, 184, 414, 416, 417, 421, 463
    public, 183, 184, 414, 416, 417, 421
selection, optimization, and compensation (SOC), 125, 128
    predictors for career goal clarity, 131, 132
    self-regulatory, 14
    self-regulatory processes, 14, 126, 132
selective secondary control strategies, 356
self-affirmation, 218
self-blame, 356
self-concept, 235
    academic, 16, 17, 64, 106, 155, 174, 227, 233, 236, 241, 242, 243, 373
    agentic, 412, 415, 419
    dimensions, 422

femininity, 20, 414
gender, 419
masculinity, 20, 414
positive, 94, 110
reading, 89
social, 12, 53, 58, 60, 63, 67, 68, 70, 71
see also ability self-concept; gender gap
self-confidence, 194, 269, 300
    see also gender gap
self-esteem, 104, 106, 109, 110, 113, 115, 116, 133, 152, 356
self-expression values, 477, 478
self-perceptions, 4, 5, 23, 80, 82, 93, 96, 155, 226, 227, 242
self-protection, 346, 356, 357
self-schema, 9
SES, see socioeconomic status (SES)
SET, see Science, Engineering and Technology (SET)
significant others, 7, 11, 22, 162, 163, 172
Slovakia, 209, 484
SOC, see selection, optimization, and compensation; see Standard Occupational Classification (SOC)
social change, 7, 21, 22, 128, 429, 430, 435, 436, 452, 453, 476, 479, 481, 491
social cohesion and identity, 479
social context, 6, 8, 10, 14, 15, 21, 22, 55, 132, 154, 227, 290, 339, 340, 354, 481
    see also gender stereotype
socialization approach, 458, 459
socialization process, 55, 267
    social and learning habitus, 55, 57, 67
socialization theory, 472
social justice, 183, 478
    injustice, 479
    Sen's theory of, 478
social role theory, 136
social roles, 7, 9
socio-cultural capital, 395
socio-cultural expectancy-value model of motivated behavior, 8, 9, 10
socioeconomic development, 476, 477, 480, 482, 487, 488
socioeconomic status (SES), 397
Spain, 132, 213
Stage-Environment-Fit Theory, 10, 14, 55, 146, 147, 149, 150, 153
Standard Occupational Classification (SOC), 335, 464
STEM (science, engineering, technology and mathematics)
    college major, 17, 18, 224, 225, 285, 286, 289, 291, 292, 293, 294, 299, 307, 312, 315
    education, 17, 288, 292, 300
    fields, 17, 33, 224, 225, 260, 266, 287, 290, 307, 347

STEM (Science, Engineering, Technology and Mathematics) (cont.)
   gender differences in training and careers, 225, 316
   labor shortage, 215, 218, 260
   pathway, 218, 276, 278
   skills, 208, 210
   subjects, 209
   women, 17, 18, 118, 267, 271, 272, 287, 289, 292, 315, 346
STEM and non-STEM, 270
   pathways, 266
STEM Communication Campaign, 323
   see also United Kingdom
STEM pipeline, 293, 299
   boys, 314
   courses, 285
   ethnicity, 299
   girls, 285
   high school, 293, 298, 299
   postsecondary, 286, 287
   secondary, 285
   secondary school, 286, 292, 293, 298, 299
STEM-trained teachers, 290
stereotypical self-evaluations, 16, 226, 227, 228, 239, 242
structural discrimination, 5
STVs, see subjective task values
subjective task values (STVs), 247, 248, 249, 250, 251, 253, 256, 258, 259, 260
   intraindividual hierarchical patterns, 249, 250, 256, 258, 259, 260
   intraindividual hierarchies of task-values, 16
   see also gender differences
suffragette movement, 432
   see also United Kingdom
supply- and demand-side theories, 458
   demand-side theories, 458, 459, 472, 473
   supply-side theories, 458
survival values, 477
Sweden, 22, 185, 209, 213, 390, 391, 404, 406, 408, 475, 484, 486, 487, 488, 491
   Gymnasium, 407
   Swedish 2005 EU Labour Force Survey, 390
   Swedish Adoption/Twin Study on Aging, 394
   Swedish educational system, 391
   Swedish Individual Development and Adaptation (IDA), 390
   Swedish Individual Development and Adaptation (IDA), 390
Switzerland, 53, 54, 61, 72, 127, 206, 395, 484, 487
   Swiss elementary school system, 54
   Swiss Survey of Children and Youth (COCON), 55
synaptic pruning, 103

task-avoidant, 112, 115
task-oriented, 112
teachers' perceptions of ability and effort, 12, 13, 53, 58, 61, 79, 80, 81, 82, 83, 86, 88, 89, 92, 93, 94, 95
   math and reading, 86
   reading, 92
test
   achievement, 31, 34, 203, 206, 230, 233, 238, 395
   American College Testing (ACT), 288
   College Board exams, 299
   college entrance examinations, 288, 289, 294
   PISA, 16, 206, 213, 217
   Scholastic Assessment Test (SAT), 288, 289
   scores, 34, 45, 170, 176, 206, 270, 288, 289, 369, 373, 395
   standardized, 16, 45, 203, 268, 289, 395
   see also gender differences
Test of English as a Foreign Language (TOEFL), 231
Third International Mathematics and Science Study (TIMSS), 230
Third or Fourth Age, 430
TIMSS, see Third International Mathematics and Science Study
TOEFL, see Test of English as a Foreign Language
TOSCA, see Transformation of the Secondary School System and Academic Careers
traditional gender ideology, 134, 135
Transformation of the Secondary School System and Academic Careers (TOSCA), 16
transition
   adaptation, 116, 125, 126, 128, 132, 140, 146, 147
   adolescence, 126, 149
   adopting the institutionalized student role, 55
   adulthood, 150
   apprenticeship, 125, 127, 129, 191
   beginning school, 12, 53, 54, 55, 56, 58, 60, 61, 64, 67, 70, 71, 73
   boys' self-esteem, 109
   changing schools, 101, 104, 106, 107, 109, 115
   comprehensive school to academic or vocational track, 146, 149, 151, 153
   coping, 53, 54, 55, 56, 57, 73
   developmental strategies, 128
   early adolescence, 101, 149
   educational, 146, 147, 148, 153, 154, 155, 156
   elementary school, 61
   emerging adulthood, 125
   girls' self-esteem, 109, 116
   high school, 126, 132, 287

high school to college, 125, 126, 127, 128, 129, 130, 132, 133, 135, 139, 140
high school to workforce, 126, 127, 128, 129, 130, 132, 133, 135, 139, 140
junior high, 149
life, 109, 140, 148, 273
multiple, 101
post-comprehensive, 150
postsecondary, 286, 287
postsecondary to STEM, 298
post-transition, 106, 107, 108, 110, 111, 113, 116, 150
pre-transition, 113, 116
primary school, 54
primary to secondary education, 12, 13
puberty, 13, 101, 103, 114, 155
school, 54, 55, 57, 73, 101, 149
school to a career path, 229
secondary, 150
SOC strategies, 132
to adulthood, 250
uncertainty, 136
vocational school, 154
workforce, 196
transition quality to school, 54, 61, 65, 67, 70, 71
truant, 111, 372
Turkey, 207

US Bureau of Labor Statistics, *see* United States
UK, *see* United Kingdom
unemployment, 129, 139, 163, 266, 431, 432, 441
youth, 129, 132, 183
United Kingdom
　A-levels, 178, 322, 376, 385
　Anomalies Act, 432
　British Cohort Study (BCS70), 162, 166, 169, 170, 172, 173, 174, 176, 177, 178, 373, 385
　British Household Panel Survey (BHPS), 18, 165, 321, 325, 326, 327, 328, 334, 337, 338
　British Youth Survey (BYS), 18, 326
　Connexions, 164, 170, 177
　Direct Grant schools, 368
　Employment Rights, Institute of (IER), 328
　England, 21, 162, 163, 167, 182, 183, 186, 188, 189, 190, 191, 322, 323, 367, 374, 430, 432, 453, 484
　English Longitudinal Study of Ageing (ELSA), 21, 429, 430, 434, 435, 436, 437, 441, 448
　Equality and Human Rights Commission's Triennial Review, 188
　Equal Opportunities Commission (EOC), 4, 188, 191
　General Certificate of Secondary Education (GCSE), 185, 331, 366
　Grammar and Technical schools, 368
　Great Britain, 15, 386, 429, 453
　Longitudinal Study of Young People in England (LSYPE), 162, 164, 165, 166, 167, 169, 170, 171, 172, 173, 174, 175, 176, 177, 178
　National Child Development Study (NCDS), 367, 368, 369
　National Pupil Database, 167, 170
　National Statistics Socio-economic Classification (NS-SEC), 169, 381
　Northern Ireland, 322, 367
　Not in Education, Employment or Training (NEET), 161, 165, 166, 171, 172, 175, 178
　Observational Research and Classroom Learning Evaluation (ORACLE), 106, 108, 110, 112, 113, 115, 116
　O-level, 374
　Scotland, 188, 189, 190, 367, 369, 374, 377
　Secondary and Middle School Adolescent Development (SAMSAD) Study, 104, 106, 107, 108, 109, 110, 111, 112, 113, 114, 116
　STEM Communication Campaign, 323
　suffragette movement, 432
　UK Resource Centre for Women in Science, Engineering and Technology (UKRC), 324
　vocational education and training (VET), 182, 183, 185, 193
　Young Apprenticeship program, 186
United Nations Development Programme (UNDP), 480
United Nations Educational, Scientific and Cultural Organization (UNESCO), 328
United States
　American College Testing (ACT), 288, 294
　Center for Epidemiologic Studies–Depression Scale (CES-D), 444
　Center for Human Resource Research, 464
　Childhood and Beyond (CAB) Study, 13, 79, 84
　Current Population Survey, 464
　Education Longitudinal Study (ELS), 292
　Employment Protection Act, 434
　Equal Pay Act, 434
　Michigan Study of Adolescent Life Transitions (MSALT), 112, 273
　Milwaukee study, 104, 109, 114, 115, 116
　Minnesota Population Center, 464
　National Longitudinal Survey (NLS), 460, 464
　National Longitudinal Survey of Youth (NLSY), 394, 395, 460, 464
　Scholastic Assessment Test (SAT), 269, 288, 289, 294
　US Bureau of Labor Statistics, 464

United States (*cont.*)
   US National Center for Educational Statistics (NCES), 293
   Wisconsin model of educational and status attainment, 233
   Women's Movement, 354
University
   degree, 20, 54, 153, 336, 399, 415, 421, 430, 436, 437
   major, 16, 224, 225, 229, 230, 231, 232, 233, 234, 236, 238, 239, 240, 242, 243, 259, 290
   see also education; physical sciences, mathematics, engineering and technology (PME); STEM (science, technology, engineering, and mathematics)
urban disadvantaged schools, 290

value change, Inglehart's theory on, 478
variable-centered approach, 248, 249, 258
VET, *see* vocational education and training
vocational education and training (VET), 182, 183, 185, 193, 196, 197
   see also gender segregation; United Kingdom
volitional goal engagement, 356

wage gap, *see* gender gap
wellbeing
   academic, 146, 147, 148, 150, 152, 153, 154, 156
   positive, 445
   subjective, 21, 131, 135, 356, 357, 444
   see also gender differences, academic
women, single, 440
Women's Movement, 354
   see also United States
workload, 20, 149, 412, 414, 415, 419
   career continuity, 414
   career discontinuity, 412
   childcare reduction, 20, 415, 417, 421, 422
   see also career
World Bank, 480
   World Bank 2000–2001 Development Report, 482
World War II, 432, 477

Young Apprenticeship program,
   see apprenticeship; United Kingdom
youth training schemes, 164, 170
   see also apprenticeship